ISLAM AND POLITICS

This book is an accessible and comprehensive account of political Islam in the twenty-first century. Drawing on insights from comparative politics and Islamic studies, it explains the complex interaction between Islam, society, the state, and processes of globalization. The book demonstrates that political Islam, far from being a monolithic phenomenon, varies considerably from country to country depending on its position in relation to society, the state, and the broader political environment. The book provides a portrait of Islam and politics through a combination of detailed case studies and country over-views that span the globe from the Middle East to Central and South Asia, Southeast Asia, Europe, and North America—as well as a detailed account of the global jihadist movement. Engaging the debate on "post-Islamism" and the aftermath of the Arab Uprisings, the book also provides a roadmap of possible futures for Islam and politics. Subjects covered include:

- history of Islam and politics, and an overview of key concepts
- how political Islam interacts with the nation-state and the global economy
- a wide variety of global case studies
- profiles of key movements and individuals.

Fully illustrated throughout, featuring maps, a glossary, and suggestions for further reading, this is the ideal introduction to the crucial role of political Islam in the contemporary world.

Peter Mandaville is Professor of Government and Politics and Director of the Ali Vural Ak Center for Global Islamic Studies at George Mason University, USA. He is the author of *Transnational Muslim Politics: Reimagining the Umma* and has also co-edited several volumes of essays. His research interests include the impact of globalization in the Muslim world, global political development, and post-Western international relations.

ISLAM AND POLITICS

2nd Edition

Peter Mandaville

thinks no distinction between religion & politics

Routledge
Taylor & Francis Group

LONDON AND NEW YORK

First published 2014
by Routledge
2 Park Square, Milton Park, Abingdon, Oxon OX14 4RN

and by Routledge
711 Third Avenue, New York, NY 10017

Routledge is an imprint of the Taylor & Francis Group, an informa business

British Library Cataloguing in Publication Data
A catalogue record for this book is available from the British Library

Library of Congress Cataloging-in-Publication Data
Mandaville, Peter G., 1971–
  Islam and politics / Peter Mandaville. — Second edition.
     pages cm.
  Includes bibliographical references and index.
  1. Islam and politics.   I. Title.
  JC49.M259 2014
  320.55'7—dc23
  2013034332

ISBN: 978-0-415-78256-2 (hbk)
ISBN: 978-0-415-78257-9 (pbk)
ISBN: 978-1-315-81477-3 (ebk)

Typeset in Garamond
by Apex CoVantage, LLC

CONTENTS

List of illustrations   vi
A note on transliteration and style   ix
Preface to the second edition   x
Acknowledgments   xiii
Abbreviations   xv

1   Introduction: Thinking about Islam and politics in global perspective   1

2   Islam and politics: History and key concepts   28

3   State formation and the making of Islamism   64

4   Islam in the system: The evolution of Islamism as political strategy   121

5   Islam as the system: Islamic states and "Islamization" from above   203

6   Islam for lack of a system: Islamism in weak and failed states   270

7   Radical Islamism and *jihad* beyond the nation-state   328

8   Towards post-Islamism? Globalization and Muslim politics   369

9   Conclusion: The Arab Uprisings and beyond   400

Appendix: Key economic and political indicators for selected Muslim countries   419
Suggestions for further reading   420
Glossary   426
Index   429

ILLUSTRATIONS

FIGURES

1.1	Protests against the novel *The Satanic Verses* in the UK in 1988	22
2.1	Jamal al-Din al-Afghani, anti-colonial activist and Islamic reformist	61
3.1	One of Ataturk's signature reforms: Turkish in the Latin alphabet	71
3.2 and 3.3	Hassan al-Banna and Sayyid Abu'l-A'la Mawdudi, key twentieth-century Islamist thinkers	79
3.4	Sayyid Qutb, modern theorist of *jihad* and radical Muslim Brotherhood ideologue	98
3.5	Islamic Salvation Front leaders Ali Belhadj (left) and Abbasi Madani	117
4.1	Tahrir Square in Cairo during Egypt's 2011 revolution	151
4.2	A Salafi politician campaigning in Egypt's 2011 parliamentary election	154
4.3	Mohamed Morsi, Egypt's short-lived Muslim Brotherhood president	157
4.4	En-Nahda leader and Islamist thinker Rachid Ghannouchi	160
4.5	Turkish Prime Minister and AKP leader Recep Tayyip Erdoğan	171
4.6	Insignia of the PKS party in Indonesia	176
4.7	Leaders of the Islamic Action Front in Jordan	180
4.8	PJD logo in Arabic, French, and Tamazight (Berber)	184
4.9	Hopeful times: Egypt's first parliament after the 2011 revolution	196
5.1	Saudi Arabia has maintained a close relationship with the U.S.	215
5.2	Cover of the Jama'at-i Islami party constitution	236
5.3	Poster commemorating Khomeini, leader of Iran's Islamic Revolution	250
5.4	Governmental structure of Iran	255
5.5	Green Movement protestors in Iran's controversial 2009 election	263
5.6	Sudanese Islamist leader Hassan al-Turabi	267
6.1	Hamas organizational diagram	283
6.2	Street art supporting Hamas	287
6.3	Supporters of Jabhat al-Nusra in Syria	303
6.4	Taliban fighters in Afghanistan	313
7.1	Al-Qaeda leader Usama bin Laden	342
7.2	Al-Qaeda leader Ayman al-Zawahiri	348

8.1 Pakistani protesters rally against Denmark to show their anger against the reproduction of cartoons depicting the Prophet Muhammad in Danish newspapers, March 7, 2008, in Multan, Pakistan   379
8.2 Yusuf al-Qaradawi speaks on Al-Jazeera satellite television   381
8.3 Fetullah Gülen   385
8.4 Popular Egyptian television preacher Amr Khaled   394

MAPS

1.1 The global Muslim population   6
2.1 The early spread of Islam   35
2.2 The gunpowder empires   55
3.1 European colonies in the Muslim world, 1914   66

TABLES

1.1 Largest Muslim populations by country   8
1.2 Muslim views on religion and politics   20
4.1 Islamists in legislative elections (1990–2013) for selected countries   128
8.1 Internet penetration rates for select Muslim countries   390
A1 Key economic and political indicators for selected Muslim countries   419

BOXES

2.1 What is *shari'ah*?   41
2.2 The Sunni–Shi'i divide in Islam   51
3.1 Theories and debates in the study of Muslim politics   86
3.2 Algeria: Islamists *almost* in power   115
4.1 The new Salafi factor in Arab politics   153
4.2 Tunisia: Islamists and the legacy of secularism   159
4.3 Indonesia: A paradigmatic "Muslim democracy"?   174
4.4 Morocco: Islamism in the shadow of the palace   183
4.5 Why did the Islamists win big after the Arab Uprisings?   192
5.1 Women and political Islam   226
5.2 Religious minorities and political Islam   231
5.3 Malaysia: Islamization and national development   238
5.4 Hassan al-Turabi and Sudan's "Islamic Experiment"   266
6.1 Nigeria: *Shari'ah* law and the politics of federalism   272
6.2 Islamists and the Syria conflict   302
6.3 Iraq after Saddam: Sectarianism and Muslim politics   308

6.4 Boko Haram: The "Nigerian Taliban"?   317
6.5 Central Asia: "Official Islam" and its alternatives   321
8.1 The Danish cartoon affair   378
8.2 The Gülen "movement": A product of globalization?   385
9.1 Political Islam in Europe and North America: Islamists in
     Muslim-minority settings   409

A NOTE ON TRANSLITERATION AND STYLE

In order to make it accessible to a broad, non-specialist readership, this text has adopted a minimal scheme for the transliteration of Arabic, Urdu, Farsi, and Turkish terms. Very few diacritics have been used, and generally only the medial *hamza* or *ayn* of Arabic terms has been indicated.

In rendering Muslim names, effort has been made wherever possible to adopt the English spellings preferred by the individual in question or by the standard works on them.

All dates, unless otherwise specified, are common era (CE).

Preface to the second edition

This book is designed as a resource for broad audiences in the social sciences and humanities—as well as the advanced general reader—seeking to understand the emergence, evolution, and possible futures of what is commonly called political Islam. This second edition of the text has been thoroughly updated and revised, and in the process has acquired a new title. I felt that the more simple and straightforward *Islam and Politics* better captures the generalist and comparative thrusts of the book. The change in title also felt well advised since the book does not make any particular claims about the "global" nature of Islamism or posit any hard causal links with the processes we commonly term globalization. As is clear from the discussion in Chapter 1, I continue in any case to harbor considerable ambivalence towards the formulation "political Islam" and its embedded assumptions. Two other significant changes in the new edition warrant a mention here. First, the book now gives Hizbullah a full case study treatment (it received only textbox coverage in the first edition), with a primary emphasis on recent events in Lebanon and the region. Second, a couple of chapters—on transnational Islamic groups and debates about Islamic authority—have been dropped altogether. I felt they detracted from the flow of what was otherwise a straightforward, integrated, and coherent account of comparative Islamist politics. Where relevant, portions of these chapters that relate to the broad theme of post-Islamism have been incorporated into the newly expanded penultimate chapter.

In order to facilitate use of the book across multiple academic fields, disciplinary jargon has been kept to a minimum—even at the risk of rendering the text somewhat atheoretical. By providing a rich pool of case study information, however, it is hoped that readers and instructors alike will find the text a valuable empirical base from which they might examine various political and sociological theories of their choosing. An extensive textbox in this new edition of the book provides an overview and sampling of some of the main theories that have been advanced to explain the emergence, evolution, and transformation of political Islam without, however, firmly anchoring itself within any particular tradition of thought. That is not to say, however, that the text is wholly devoid of theoretical perspective (such a thing is, of course, impossible anyway). By seeking to appreciate Muslim politics "in global perspective," this book, particularly in its later chapters, hopes to draw the reader's attention to the crucial interplay between local and global forces as well as formal and informal spaces of the political in shaping Muslim politics as a lived reality in today's world. To this end, we cover not only those Muslim political actors whose discourses and practices are organized transnationally, but we also look closely at how global flows— of people, images, ideas, money—inflect the conduct of Muslim politics in local settings.

Initially commissioned in the aftermath of September 11, 2001 as an overview of global political Islam, this book took quite some time to come together. Part of this was a deliberate desire on my part to get some distance from, and perspective on, the geopolitical aftermath of those events so as to avoid producing a reactionary "post-9/11" book. It also became increasingly clear to me that, as many new observers of Muslim politics came to understand the nature of political Islam through the prism of 9/11, they were likely to bypass the complex history of mainstream (and mostly non-violent) Islamism that so transcends the relatively narrow moment of Al-Qaeda. For this reason, it seemed to me that a comparative overview of Islamism around the world was what was called for at this time. To those readers struck by the seemingly disproportionate amount of history in what is, after all, essentially a social science text, I would just say that this book first took shape in Washington, DC during a time when most conversations about Muslim politics tended to proceed in a worryingly dehistoricized manner. Subsequent years have seen little improvement in this regard.

This second edition appears in the wake of another set of tectonic events in the realm of Islam and politics: the Arab Uprisings that began in 2010 and that continue to reverberate today. Popular uprisings toppled long-standing incumbent governments in Tunisia, Egypt, and Libya, and produced a negotiated regime change in Yemen, crisis in Bahrain, and civil war in Syria. Even in countries relatively unaffected by popular revolt, such as Morocco, Jordan, and most of the Arab Gulf states, these events have fundamentally changed the political calculus of governments. Most relevant for our purposes is the fact that the political opening that followed in the aftermath of these momentous events permitted Islamist parties long excluded from politics openly to contest power. In Egypt and Tunisia, Islamists— both Muslim Brotherhood-affiliated parties and newly politicized Salafis— won decisive victories at the ballot box. The new edition of this book had originally been planned to go to press just as popular revolts in the Arab world were brewing. As it became clear that Islamists were likely to be among the greatest beneficiaries of these events, we decided to delay the second edition in order to be able to reflect on the performance of newly elected Islamists with some modicum of hindsight. While this new era of "Islamists in power" is still relatively young, some clear variations are already starting to emerge. In Egypt in 2013, for example, the failing presidency of Islamist Mohamed Morsi was cut short by a military coup plunging the country into violence and even greater political uncertainty. In Tunisia, by contrast, the more deliberative path followed by the Islamist En-Nahda party, combined with that country's more pluralistic political environment, seems to have enabled slow but solid progress towards a more sustainable form of democracy. *Islam and Politics* includes new and updated coverage of the relevant parties and movements, analysing their role in the Arab Uprisings and the various factors that have contributed to their successes and struggles in the aftermath of revolution.

Many of the countries and movements dealt with in this book (e.g. Egypt and the Muslim Brotherhood) continue to experience significant and rapid developments as it goes to press. By its very nature, this is material that dates rather quickly in terms of basic chronology. As much as possible, however, I have sought to frame my coverage of these events in terms of the larger and longer-term patterns and trends to be found within given countries and movements, and it is these elements that hopefully will come across most strongly to the reader.

Washington, DC
August 2013

Acknowledgments

A work of this sort inevitably leaves its author deeply indebted to many benefactors, and in this case so many have helped it along the way—both directly and indirectly. Conversations with numerous colleagues over the past ten years have had a significant impact on the shape and content of this book, and I would like to take this opportunity to thank: Bekim Agai, Steve Artner, Osman Bakar, Shaul Bakhash, Asma Barlas, Nathan Brown, Dan Brumberg, Dale Eickelman, Greg Fealy, Graham Fuller, Bassam Haddad, Yvonne Haddad, Mohammed Hafez, Sumaiya Hamdani, Shireen Hunter, Paul Lubeck, Marc Lynch, Eric McGlinchey, John Paden, Michael Peletz, Tariq Ramadan, Olivier Roy, Armando Salvatore, Meena Sharify-Funk, Steve Simon, Diane Singerman, Kathryn Spellman, John Voll, Carrie Rosefsky Wickham, Quintan Wiktorowicz, Hakan Yavuz, Muhammad Qasim Zaman, and Malika Zeghal. All of them influenced my thinking, made suggestions, or provided important sources as well as much appreciated support and encouragement. I also need to offer my gratitude to the many students and instructors who have used the first edition as a course text and offered such valuable feedback, much of which has been incorporated in the preparation of this new edition.

I am particularly grateful to several scholars who read and offered extremely valuable feedback on early draft chapters, notably Robert Hefner, Bruce Lawrence, and Vali Nasr. Todd Silverstein read the manuscript of the first edition in its entirety and offered very constructive editorial and substantive feedback throughout. The insights of all those mentioned above have been reflected in the text wherever possible, but I alone am responsible for any errors and shortcomings in the final product.

Valuable early research assistance was provided by Tanya Fraikin, Xander Meise, and Julia Whitelock, while Elizabeth Gramza and Eric Grynaviski helped to identify and update crucial source material. Christopher Anzalone drafted the glossary and also provided valuable input on early drafts of the main text. A special debt of gratitude is owed to Fatima Ayub and Tariq Mangru, both of whom have been involved in various aspects of the project. They provided key research assistance and offered important suggestions for the main text. For the second edition, special thanks are due to Ger Fitzgerald, Ayah Ibrahim, and Emily Smith, all of whom provided crucial help in preparing chapter updates and rethinking the overall shape and balance of the text. Ger was especially helpful in drafting some of the updates to the country case studies and the section on Hizbullah. Only their tireless work in the final phase of manuscript preparation made its completion possible.

At Routledge I would like to thank Nadia Seemungal, Natalja Mortensen, Nicola Parkin, and Peter Harris for their valuable editorial assistance. My biggest thanks, however, goes to Craig Fowlie, who first approached me with the idea of writing the book, and helped significantly to shape its content and scope. His patience and kindness of spirit at times when altogether different dispositions on his part would have been wholly warranted should be an inspiration to us all in these trying times.

Alicia Phillips Mandaville rallied and encouraged me when my faith in the project dwindled. Her advice and support added much to the book and sustained me through its conclusion. The interregnum between the book's initial publication and this new version has seen our family double in size. Our son Ike and daughter Eliza have been wonderful and wholly appropriate reasons for this second edition to be somewhat delayed in finding its way into print.

Some of the research contained in this book was carried out with the generous support of the Pew Charitable Trusts, the Faculty of Social Sciences at the University of Kent, and the Office of the Provost at George Mason University.

Portions of Chapter 7 are reprinted with the kind permission of Princeton University Press.

Abbreviations

ABIM	Angkatan Belia Islam Malaysia/Malaysian Islamic Youth Movement
AKP	Adalet ve Kalkınma Partisi/Justice and Development Party (Turkey)
Amal	Afwaj al-Muqawama al-Lubnaniyya (Lebanon)
AQAP	Al-Qaeda on the Arabian Peninsula
AQIM	Al-Qaeda in the Islamic Maghreb
ARAMCO	Arabian American Oil Company
CDLR	Committee for the Defense of Legitimate Rights (Saudi Arabia)
FIS	Front Islamique du Salut/Islamic Salvation Front (Algeria)
FJP	Freedom and Justice Party (Egypt)
FLN	Front de Libération Nationale (Algeria)
FSA	Free Syrian Army
GIA	Groupe Islamique Armé/Armed Islamic Group (Algeria)
GSPC	Groupe Salafiste pour la Prédication et le Combat/Salafist Group for Preaching and Combat (Algeria)
Hamas	Harakat al-Muqawama al-Islamiyya/Islamic Resistance Movement (Palestine)
HT	Hizb ut-Tahrir/Islamic Liberation Party
HW	Hizb al-Wasat/Party of the Center (Egypt)
IAF	Islamic Action Front (Jordan)
ICMI	Ikatan Cendekiawan Muslim Se-Indonesia (Association of Indonesian Muslim Intellectuals)

ICU	Islamic Courts Union
IDF	Israeli Defense Forces
IFE	Islamic Forum Europe
IRGC	Islamic Revolutionary Guards Corps
IRM	Islamic Renaissance Movement (Algeria)
JI	Jama'at-i Islami (Pakistan)
JUI	Jamaat Ulama-i-Islam/Assembly of Islamic Clergy (Pakistan)
MB	Muslim Brotherhood
MMA	Muttahhida Majlis-e-Amal/United Council of Action (Pakistan)
MSP	Movement for the Society of Peace (Algeria)
MTI	Mouvement de la Tendance Islamique/Islamic Tendency Movement (Tunisia)
NDP	National Democratic Party (Egypt)
NIF	National Islamic Front (Sudan)
NSM	New Social Movement
NSP	National Salvation Party (Turkey)
PA	Palestinian Authority
PAS	Parti Islam Se-Malaysia/Pan-Malaysian Islamic Party
PCP	Popular Congress Party (Sudan)
PDPA	People's Democratic Party of Afghanistan
PJD	Parti de la Justice et du Développement/Justice and Development Party (Morocco)
PK	Pakatan Rakyat/People's Alliance (Malaysia)
PKS	Partai Keadilan Sejahtera/Prosperous Justice Party (Indonesia)
PLC	Palestinian Legislative Council
PML	Pakistan Muslim League
PLO	Palestine Liberation Organization
PNA	Pakistan National Alliance
PPP	Partai Persatuan Pembangunan/United Development Party (Indonesia)
PPP	Pakistan People's Party
RPP	Republican People's Party (Turkey)
SAVAK	Sazeman-e Ettela'at va Amniyat-e Keshvar/Organization of Intelligence and National Security (Iran)
SCAF	Supreme Council of the Armed Forces (Egypt)
SCC	Supreme Constitutional Court (Egypt)
UAE	United Arab Emirates
UMNO	United Malays National Organization
UN	United Nations
UNRWA	United Nations Relief Works Agency
UNSCR	United Nations Security Council Resolution
UOIF	Union des Organisations Islamiques de France
USSR	Union of Soviet Socialist Republics
YMMA	Young Muslim Men's Association

CHAPTER 1

Introduction: Thinking about Islam and politics in global perspective

There is little doubt today as to the importance of Muslim politics in contemporary world affairs. From the emergence of transnational networks pursuing global militant agendas in the name of Islam, to the persistence and transformation of traditional Islamic political parties—several of which experienced dramatic political success in the wake of the Arab Uprisings that began in 2010—to the appearance of global media personalities claiming to speak as authoritative and authentic Islamic voices: Islam and politics seem today to be everywhere. But how well do we actually understand this phenomenon? Muslim politics are certainly much discussed today, but—arguably—little or poorly understood within most circles of debate and deliberation. How can we best make sense of this highly complex, diverse, and sometimes even contradictory world of religion and politics? How to understand the relative importance of the multiple manifestations of Muslim politics around the world and the many competing voices claiming to speak on behalf of Islam? What is the difference between those Islamist movements that emphasize *jihad* and those that pursue politics through nonviolent, even democratic, means—and how do they relate to each other? What possible futures might we predict for political Islam?

These are a few of the questions that this book addresses. In some cases possible answers to several of these puzzles will be offered, while in other instances the book aims to provide the reader with the background information and analytical tools necessary to reach his or her own conclusions. It should be clarified that this book, while certainly ambitious in scope, does not attempt to provide anything like a grand, unified theory of Islam and politics. While key cross-cutting themes are certainly identified, the primary emphasis throughout is on the inherent pluralism and diversity of Muslim politics— that is, on the *impossibility* of a single theory to account for political Islam. It is suggested, however, that there are better and worse explanations as to why Islamic social and political movements appear and assume the forms that they do under certain circumstances. As numerous analysts of political Islam have observed over the years, particular formulations of Islam and politics certainly do seem to suit specific social, political, and economic conditions. This text is offered, then, in the spirit of a comparative, synthetic overview: a guide to the wide-ranging global landscape of Islam and politics, an introduction to the broad ecology of thought and practice in contemporary Muslim politics, and a critical survey of some of the key ideas advanced by leading scholars in their efforts to explain the phenomenon of political Islam. In a modest way, this book also hopes to offer the rough contours of its own distinctive analytic— one that emphasizes the importance of the interplay between global and local contexts of Muslim politics in a time of unprecedented social interconnectedness and interdependence.

The structure of the book is roughly as follows. This introductory chapter orients the reader to some of the key themes and concepts surrounding the discussion of religion and politics more generally (e.g. the idea of religion and politics as separate domains; debates on secularism) and the specific challenges we face when dealing with this topic in the context of Islam. Readers are also asked to reconsider some of their assumptions about just what counts as politics, and how to recognize the presence of politics or religion in a given setting and social relationship. In other words, even though we may often be dealing with Muslim-majority countries, how do we know when Islam is actually a relevant factor in a given political situation—that is, how can we tell when Islam really has an influence? Because this book seeks to emphasize the wider global context of Islam, this first chapter also offers some suggestions about how to approach the interplay between local and global levels of analysis in a world of intense interconnectedness. While not a text on globalization *per se,* it is nevertheless important to evaluate whether and how some of the trends and transformations commonly associated with this term may inflect our analysis of Muslim politics in distinctive new ways.

The analysis offered in this book is firmly rooted in a belief that an understanding of the interplay between Muslim societies and various local, regional, and world political issues throughout history is absolutely crucial to achieving any kind of handle on contemporary Muslim politics. To this end, the next two chapters briefly explore key themes and concepts in the history of Islam and politics, while progressively introducing a new framework for understanding today's political Islam. Chapter 2 covers a broad swath of history from approximately the seventh century CE up to the late eighteenth century. It looks at Muslim politics in the time of the Prophet Muhammad and immediately after, explaining the emergence and consolidation of certain key institutions and norms in Muslim politics prior to the expansion and fragmentation of the early Muslim community. The various regional polities and Islamic empires that rose and fell over the subsequent ten centuries are briefly surveyed before acclimatizing the reader to the onset and implications of European colonialism in the Muslim world. The chapter then analyzes a variety of Islamic responses to Western imperialism before moving on to examine the process of modern state formation in the Muslim world in the post-colonial period. The chapter concludes with an overview of the interaction between world politics more broadly and Muslim politics in and across particular local and national settings. We look at how what seemed initially to be a crisis for Islam in the face of widespread support for the secular nation-state model in the early twentieth century quickly evolved into the precursors of what eventually became the political project of Islamism.

Chapter 3 provides a detailed overview of the emergence of modern Islamism through an examination of post-colonial state formation in the Muslim world. It looks at major Islamic political theorists in the twentieth century, and also the key activists and thinkers who gave birth to the Islamist project. The conventional model of state-based Islamism is then illustrated through a detailed study of the formation and evolution of the Muslim Brotherhood (MB) in Egypt—the prototypical modern Islamist movement, and the model for many subsequent groups around the Muslim world. We analyze the ideology and organization of the Brotherhood, and trace its development through three generations. The chapter concludes by surveying major developments in twentieth-century Islamism in a number of other key settings. An extensive textbox in this chapter provides an overview of key theories and debates in the study of political Islam so as to familiarize the reader with the major explanatory paradigms currently available for understanding Muslim politics.

Having identified the major animating forces behind Islam and politics today, the next section of the book seeks to provide the reader with a wealth of concrete empirical detail regarding how these trends are actually playing out in specific Muslim contexts. The next four chapters offer detailed case studies of Islam and politics across a range of national, regional, and transnational settings. The reader will find chapters that deal with topics such as Islamist participation in elections and normal political processes, the nature and evolution of Islamism in those countries that style themselves as "Islamic states," and the impact of conflict and war on Muslim politics. Key countries—such as Turkey, Iran, Pakistan, Egypt, and Saudi Arabia—are covered, but in an attempt to emphasize the global context of Muslim politics, this section moves away from the conventional country-by-country case study model to include dedicated sections on important transregional and transnational movements such as Al-Qaeda and the global jihadist movement.

The final chapter presents an argument that Muslim politics—through the intervening effects of globalization, and the emergence within certain Muslim communities of a political consciousness transcending national borders as well as conventional spaces of formal politics—is entering a phase in which the methods, goals, and vocabularies of Islamism are undergoing considerable transformation. It is suggested that "classic" Islamism, as a totalizing project seeking to capture state power, increasingly is forced to compete with Muslim political agendas above *and* below the state that seek, respectively, to establish transnational Islamic polities, or to open up spaces for the inclusion of religion in public life and greater recognition of Muslim identity claims within the context of broadly secular societies. The idea that the net effect of these developments is moving us towards a condition that some analysts have termed "post-Islamism" is considered through a discussion of several contemporary Islamic movements that operate outside the formal political realm, but whose activities nonetheless need to be seen as forms of Muslim politics. The book concludes with some reflections on how these disparate strategies and politics will likely play out in the coming years.

ISLAM IN THE WORLD: SOME BASIC FACTS

Before getting into substantive discussion, it will be helpful to orient the reader to the subject matter at hand: Muslims and the Muslim world. Comprising approximately 1.6 billion people across almost every continent, Islam constitutes one of the great world religions today—and certainly the fastest-growing.[1] Often thought of as a Middle Eastern phenomenon, it is worthwhile taking note of the fact that the four countries with the greatest number of Muslims are actually in Southeast Asia (Indonesia) and South Asia (Pakistan, Bangladesh, and India). The states of the former Soviet Union are home to large numbers of Muslims, and significant populations are to be found in West and East Africa. So it is important immediately to disabuse ourselves of the idea that the Middle East and the Muslim world—despite their common overlap in contemporary discourse—are coterminous. Today we also hear much about the idea of Islam and the West as two separate entities. As Chapter 2 demonstrates, it makes much more sense in historical perspective to emphasize overlap and exchange between these world cultures, rather than conflict and incompatibility. Furthermore, with sizeable Muslim populations in Western Europe and North America, Islam is an increasingly important religion today in many of the countries that we would think of as part of the West.

It almost goes without saying that, given this size and geographical breadth, Islam is a thoroughly diverse phenomenon—a fact that makes it difficult and even dangerous to try conclusively to define what Islam has to say about a given idea or situation, or what the "Islamic" view on something might be. Inevitably, this perspective will vary significantly from context to context. As explained in greater detail below, this book uses the term "Islam" to refer to a particular tradition of discourse and practice that is variously defined across multiple social and historical settings. There is therefore no connotation of normativity implied in our usage, for example, of the term "Islamic." Islam should always be considered in relation to how it is understood and experienced in specific contexts and circumstances. That does not mean that anything and everything counts as Islam. Embodied within the very idea of a tradition is the notion that this tradition has boundaries—but these, it should be emphasized, are always open to contestation and negotiation. Likewise, there is no attempt made here to define who or what counts as Muslim. For our purposes a Muslim is anyone who identifies him or herself, at least in part, with Islam—regardless of how the latter may be understood.

BROADENING OUR UNDERSTANDING OF POLITICS

It may strike the reader as slightly strange to begin with a discussion of the definition of politics, but this is necessary given the wide range of phenomena under consideration in this book, some of which we propose to treat as "political" although they would not generally be considered part of the commonplace world of politics. Conventional understandings of politics tend to equate it with particular sets of activities and institutions—more specifically, the processes through which actors pursue governmental power in the context of the modern nation-state. We generally have a sense of the kinds of activity that count as political (e.g. elections, *coups d'état,* lobbying) and the relevant sorts of actors and institutions (political parties, nation-states, militaries). To be sure, many of the Muslim countries and organizations covered in this volume correspond quite closely to this model. In Jordan and Kuwait, for example, Islamist political parties contest parliamentary elections in the hope of having a greater role in legislative processes. In the case of certain other social forces examined here, however, we need to recalibrate some of our assumptions in order to recognize them as properly political. For example, a few of the movements we look at reject the very model of the nation-state, and seek instead to establish forms of political community premised on very different norms and principles. It is still not difficult, however, to see such groups as political, since it is clear that they are seeking to challenge prevailing institutions through which social power is exercised. More challenging, however, are the cases of certain mystical orders or movements that emphasize personal piety—many of which ostensibly eschew politics altogether. The approach advanced by this book is one

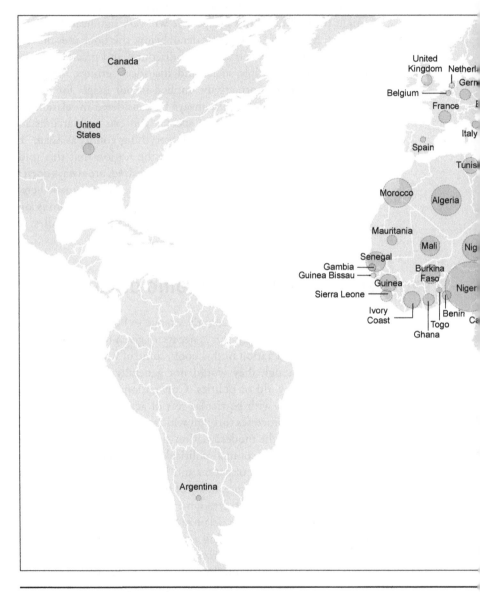

Map 1.1 The global Muslim population

Source: The Pew Forum, *The Future of the Global Muslim Population,* Washington, DC: Pew Research Center, 2011.

that would see any rejection of politics as a particular sort of political act. Usually what is being articulated in such claims is a challenge to a specific vision of public morality that understands social order and "the good" to accrue from the direct exercise of power via the institutional channels of government. By way of an alternative, these movements seek to emphasize

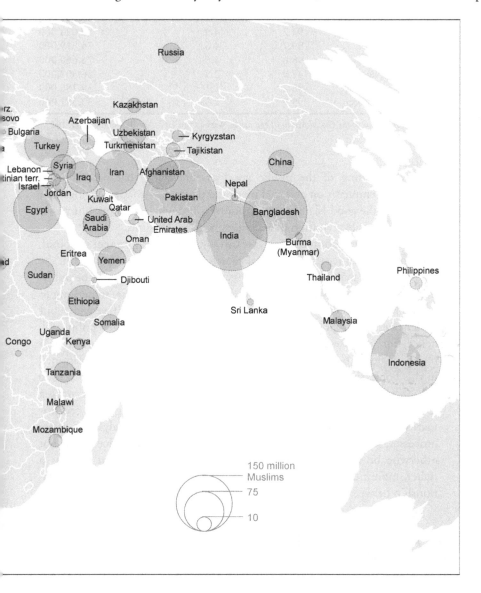

Table 1.1 Largest Muslim populations by country

Rank	Country	% Muslim	% global Muslim pop	Total Muslims
1	Indonesia	88.1	12.7	204,847,000
2	Pakistan	96.4	11.0	178,097,000
3	India	14.6	10.9	177,286,000
4	Bangladesh	90.4	9.2	148,607,000
5	Egypt	94.7	4.9	80,024,000
6	Iran	99.7	4.6	74,819,000
7	Turkey	98.6	4.6	74,660,000
8	Nigeria	47.9	2.9	46,302,000
9	Algeria	98.2	2.1	34,780,000
10	Morocco	99.9	2.0	32,381,000

Source: *The Future of the Global Muslim Population*, Washington DC: Pew Research Center, 2011.

an understanding of the public good as something that best emerges through an emphasis on personal piety and devotion—that is, the idea that one creates the good Islamic society not by top-down legislation, but rather through the collectivization of individually pious Muslims.

With this illustration in mind, we can say that, for our present purposes, it is important to regard as political all actors and activities involved in the establishment, maintenance or contestation of particular visions of public morality ("the good") and of social order. There is, of course, something to be said for the analytic utility of narrow definitions. Indeed, if we widen our understanding of politics too far, then everything becomes political—hence, for purposes of analysis, nothing is political. Well aware of this pitfall, it should be pointed out that, in the vast majority of cases examined in this book, the end point of Muslim politics involves challenges to state authority via methods and tactics easily recognizable as political according to standard criteria. A broader definition of politics is being proposed primarily to enable us to recognize, and include in our analyses of these processes, social actors and even ideas whose political relevance might not otherwise be immediately discernible. It is an approach that permits a richer, more nuanced, and more comprehensive appreciation of the relationship between Islam and politics.

RELIGION AND POLITICS IN EUROPE AND THE MUSLIM WORLD

Before we wade into the comparative analysis of Muslim politics that constitutes the central focus of this book, it would be worthwhile to dwell briefly on a number of more general issues surrounding the analysis of religion and politics in a globalizing world. The intersection of religion and politics is notoriously tricky terrain to navigate, and we would do well to examine some of the baggage we inevitably bring to the analytical table. This is not only because religion and politics are usually highly emotive and polarizing subjects unto themselves, touching on issues around which people frequently stake strong senses of identity, morality, and worldview. This is also because we often tend to hold particular views about the proper relationship between these two spheres, and feel varying levels of comfort when we encounter situations in which the two seem to be mixing. Different societies around the world inevitably have different histories, traditions, and norms relating not only to the intermingling of religion and politics, but to the very definition of the boundaries that delineate and—sometimes—separate these two domains. Of particular importance here, of course, is the vexed question of secularism. Secular norms are arguably part of the foundation of the modern sovereign state model that seems to have propagated around the world during the past century. There is, however, a very strong sense in which this understanding of secularism is a legacy of the very particular historical experience of political modernity that played out in Europe over several centuries. A closer examination reveals that the rise of secularism in the West was not simply a case of the modern state eradicating the church, but rather something more resembling a process of the state reorganizing, repositioning, and co-opting aspects of religious authority—a pattern we will see repeated in the Muslim world after the colonial period. As the sovereign nation-state system began to reproduce itself in parts of the world culturally and historically distinct from Europe—settings possessing their own understandings of how religion and politics do, or do not, fit together—it was inevitable that tensions would flare around the question of secularism. It is thus important to begin our undertaking by looking at some of the prevailing assumptions about secularism, and how the terms of this debate map onto and compare with similar discussions in the Muslim world.

Secularism in the West

Secularism, as it developed in the sociocultural bloc commonly known as "the West," can be understood primarily as the product of major shifts in two aspects of European society beginning in the fifteenth century and consolidating around a number of key historical events in the seventeenth. The first of these deals with the realm of philosophy. With the advent of the period known as the Renaissance, there began in Europe a transformation over how and where people sought knowledge about the world. Where Medieval Europe had been dominated by an understanding of knowledge as a means to salvation—and hence relying on holy scripture to the exclusion of worldly knowledge—the Renaissance, and eventually the Enlightenment, marked a rediscovery of classical learning from antiquity and a new empha-sis on the transformative capacity of human reason and rationality. No longer was worldly endeavor confined to a narrow confirmation of divine revelation, but emphasis came to be on the idea that people could, through the production of knowledge and, eventually, through science, control the world around them. People were again to be the agents or makers of history, rather than merely the passive components of divine schemas. Knowledge was increasingly to be based on observable, empirical facts rather than exclusively on faith, mysticism, and myth (which continued to have impor-tant roles for some time). It is important to note that this trend did not initially herald a decline in the social influence of religion—rather, people simply began to seek rational proofs for the existence of God and reason-based evidence for the truth of religious teaching.

The second shift tied to the emergence of secularism is concerned with responses to the increasingly prevalent role of the Catholic Church in Europe's political economy since at least the fourteenth century. Proton-ationalist princes found themselves at odds with efforts by Rome to protect and enforce, by increasingly political means, the universalist remit of papal authority. By the early sixteenth century, theologians and sovereigns alike had come to resent the pervasive influence of the Catholic Church. Dissident religious thinkers, such as Martin Luther—instigator of the Protestant Reformation in 1517—took issue with what he saw as the excessive com-modification of spirituality through practices such as the selling of indulgences. As the Reformation gathered force, the political landscape of Europe was reorganized along political and religious fault-lines with various imperial houses allying themselves with competing religious forces that in turn sought to supplant the authority of these same princes. From the mid-sixteenth to mid-seventeenth century, Europe was mired in a series of religious wars, culminating in the Peace of Westphalia in 1648 at the con-clusion of the bitter Thirty Years War, during which up to 20 percent of Germany's population was killed.

This date is conventionally cited as marking the start of the modern system of sovereign states in Western Europe. It is important to note that one of the primary aims of the treaty that finally brought an end to hostili-ties was to embed a principle of noninterference by the church in the affairs of sovereign princes. This was still not the idiom of secularism that eventu-ally came to define the liberal tradition (since kings, rather than individuals, were still able to determine the official religion of their political domains), but it did mark a watershed moment in the reorganization of the relation-ship between church and state as societal institutions. Over the next 200 years, the advent of political liberalism in Europe—with its emphasis on individual over collective rights, combined with increasing instances of religious persecution by sovereign authorities, led to a recasting of secular-ism within political systems such as the modern French Republic and the new United States of America. In the religious realm, the Protestant Reformation had served to "reworld" the church by reorienting the social meaning of doctrine such that it served to link the imperatives of everyday life (work, education, etc.) with one's fate in the hereafter. This was not an individualization of religion—pressures from the church to conform certainly continued—but Protestantism questioned the logic of exceptionalism that sealed the official Church from the advent of modernity. Even this "standard" form of secularism varies significantly between national contexts in the contemporary world. The *laïcisme* of France, which empties public life and discourse entirely of anything to do with religion, contrasts with the British tradition of secularism as religious pluralism and tolerance, and with the American version focused on the individual right to religious freedom.

In summary, then, the received tradition of Western secularism that constitutes the default lens through which many of us view questions of religion and politics can be understood as the cumulative outcome of several distinct but interrelated developments:

- a philosophical shift in early modern Europe whereby human reason, rationality, and empirical inquiry came to cast doubt on pure faith and the mystical aspects of religious experience as legitimate foundations for the production of knowledge
- the difficult and violent history whereby the institutions of church and state in Europe were decoupled
- the emergence and eventual normalization of a set of political values based on liberalism that emphasized the rights of individuals above all else—most particularly the state and the church.

In addition to this "formal" mode of secularism, it is also important for us to understand a more generic, largely sociological, dimension of the secular. As we will see, this is an understanding of secularism that figures particularly prominently in many debates regarding the compatibility of Islam with secular norms. What we are alluding to here is that sense in which the idea of secularism is often taken today to refer to a constellation of similar (but by no means identical) trends, found especially in Europe and North America from the late nineteenth century onward. This includes the privatization or compartmentalization of religion as a sphere of social activity ("once a week on Sundays"), lower levels of active participation in organized religion, and a general decline in the influence of religion in everyday life—in short, a turning away from religion in the West over the past century (if measured, say, according to levels of regular church attendance). Some caution is certainly merited when positing such a trend. This is not only because the prevalence of, and popular participation in religion, varies significantly across Western societies (with consistently higher levels, for example, in the United States than in Western Europe), but also because events of the past 15 years have suggested that many people, even in countries with longstanding secular norms, are once again turning to religion as a source of meaning, identity, and values—although not always in ways that register on conventional measures of religiosity. It is nonetheless important to make this point about the multiple meanings of secularism since, as we will see, part of the controversy in the Muslim world surrounding the idea of the West or of "being Western" is that a lack of religiosity, and even hostility towards religion, is widely understood to be one of its defining characteristics.

The religious and the political in Islam

The anthropologist of religion Talal Asad cautions us against the dangers of transplanting the very particular set of assumptions about religion and politics that derives from the preceding history of European secularism onto the history of other faith traditions.[2] Indeed, he goes so far as to argue that our commonplace understanding of the religious and the political as separate, clearly demarcated spheres of human activity is itself a product of our locatedness in the European tradition, rather than a "natural" analytic distinction. "[W]hile religion is integral to modern Western history," he argues, "there are dangers in employing it as a normalizing concept when translating Islamic traditions."[3] In short, we are being warned that, while it may seem obvious to Western liberals (although not all Westerners fit this bill—witness conservative Catholics, Evangelicals, Mormons, etc.) that religion and politics constitute two quite separate spaces, each with its own rules, norms, and logic, this may not be the case in other cultures and societies. It is important for the following discussions that we gain some comparative insight into how the boundaries and debates between "being religious" and "being political" have played out historically in the Muslim world.

Before looking closely at the interplay between these forces in Islamic history, it is worth making a few quick observations by way of direct comparison with what were identified above as the driving forces of secularism in the West. We are able, this way, immediately to throw into relief key points of similarity, but also sharp contrasts that help us to understand why these issues are particularly challenging in the Muslim context. First, within the realm of philosophy, it is important to note that the Muslim world witnessed its own version of a debate regarding the status of reason versus pure revelation as sources of knowledge some five centuries before this took place in the West. Without going into the details of this period (some of which are touched on in later chapters), suffice it to say that the net effect of these debates was to restructure the enterprise of knowledge production in the Muslim world such that an early tendency towards relatively open inquiry (inspired by Greek philosophy) gave way to a sharp distinction between knowledge concerning morality and law, seen as not amenable to reason or rational thought, and the realms of science and technology. The importance of this distinction will become clear later when we go on to examine the meaning and nature of the political in Muslim contexts.

As regards the competition between "church" and state in the Islamic world, the first and most obvious point to make is that, unlike the Christian tradition, Islam does not possess a formal church or hierarchy of religious authority—at least not in the Sunni tradition, to which 90 percent of the world's Muslims adhere. This certainly does not mean, however, that voices of, and claims to, religious authority have been absent from the machinations of worldly power in Islam. While not organized as a centralized, institutional authority, the Muslim world historically has seen the emergence of various classes of privileged interpreters and transmitters of religious knowledge. The *alim* (pl. *ulama;* "religious scholar"), *faqih* (pl. *fuqaha;* "legal specialist"), and *imam* ("prayer leader," but also a generic term for a person in a position of religious authority) are all terms and titles that invest their holders with the ability to speak with authority in the name of Islam to state and society alike. More important than this social class, however, is the cumulative tradition of method and knowledge that it has produced and, in turn, been produced by. This perhaps is the key distinction to be drawn with Christianity. Where "official" Christianity could be found in the formal institutional hierarchy of the Church, the closest thing to "official" Islam resides in a highly diverse yet remarkably cohesive tradition of theology and jurisprudence, developed and passed down through the centuries by an elite corps of specialists in the field of religious knowledge. These figures and the tradition they represent, as we will see, have at various times in Islamic history been allied with, co-opted by, and directly opposed to state power. The key point to grasp for now, though, is that the lack of formal church-like institutions in Islam renders direct comparison with Europe's early experience of secularism as a decoupling of church and state rather difficult. Likewise, when one begins to contemplate the idea of an "Islamic Reformation,"[4] we find that there exists no centralized religious authority either to lead such an effort or to serve as its target—no "church," in other words, to undertake reform or to be reformed.[5] Rather, the hegemony of particular understandings of religion exists, as Talal Asad shows us, within a discursive tradition rather than within any given institution.[6]

The final point of comparison to make at the outset relates to the relationship between secularism and liberalism in the European tradition. Where prevailing secular norms in Europe and North America tended to develop in parallel with the consolidation of the modern liberal state, the experience of state formation outside the West generally has not been marked by the same primary emphasis on liberal political values. In Europe, the norms of political liberalism, buttressed by the emergence of a market-based capitalism premised on concomitant economic values, came to be organically intertwined with the institutional forms of the sovereign nation-state over several turbulent centuries. When this particular model of the state spread beyond Europe and North America, mainly in the post-colonial period, it entered countries with very different kinds of social order and political history, very few of which were premised on liberal ideals. As we will see in later chapters, this inevitably has been a major source of tension as regards both the successful consolidation of modern nation-states outside the West, but also the question of religion's role in political societies not defined by liberalism.

Islam is often represented as a "comprehensive" way of life that pervades all sectors of human activity and experience among its adherents. The idea of the divine connectedness of all things, as invoked by the central precept of *tawhid* ("oneness"), is often taken to imply that in Islam it makes no sense to speak of the separateness of religion from any other domain of life. In the realm of politics, this idea is most commonly expressed through the maxim *al-islam din wa dawla* ("Islam is [both] religion and state")—a phrasing which, while recognizing the possibility of a conceptual distinction between these two spheres, refutes the practical possibility of their disjuncture in Islam. Where Christian scripture, in the notion of rendering unto Caesar that which is Caesar's, allows for a clear division between worldly and divine authority, Islamic sources tend to emphasize the totalizing sovereignty of God. Of greatest relevance for our purposes, however, is not the fact that the Qur'an and other key scriptural sources make a case for the all-encompassing nature of Islam, but rather the fact that they offer very little by way of detail regarding the proper forms and conduct of politics—except to state that these activities should occur in accordance with the moral system of Islam. Unsurprisingly, these ambiguities and silences—as we will see later—have given rise over the centuries to vociferous debate as to the relationship between Islam and politics. On one hand, some Muslim scholars have held that from the Qur'an and the traditions of the Prophet Muhammad can be derived a very specific and distinctively Islamic model of governance. On the other, there are those who maintain that *any* system of government is acceptable so long as it is compatible with the moral principles of Islamic teaching. This ongoing effort by—and, deliberatively, *between*—believers to discern the political implications of Islam is introduced below as a core component of what we will come to call Muslim politics. Modern Islamic political theory—as we will see in Chapter 3—gives us a sense of the wide range of perspectives within the Muslim world regarding the intersection of religion and politics. Theorists such as Rashid Rida, for example, argued that any political system must indeed be derived from the *shari'ah* of Islam, and in the absence of a caliphate Muslims should strive to create a distinctly Islamic form of the modern state. His contemporary Ali Abd al-Raziq took quite a different view, however, arguing that the separation of religion and politics was integral to

Islamic history and that the Qur'an did *not* seek to establish any particular political order.[7] Later thinkers, such as Abdolkarim Soroush, writing in the wake of Iran's Islamic Revolution, would argue a position that many saw as tantamount to secularism, but that reversed the logic of the Western model. For Soroush, it is not the case that the nonempirical reason of religion threatens the conduct of modern politics, but rather that the inherently corrupting dimensions of political power pose a danger to religion. So religion and politics should indeed be kept separate, but in the name of protecting the former from the latter.[8]

Aside from the theoretical relationship between Islam and politics as defined by scriptural sources, we also look to the historical record of Muslim societies to determine whether something like a distinction between religion and politics can be found. Our survey of early Islamic political history in Chapter 2 is particularly revealing in this regard, but the short answer is that Islamic history is replete with examples of Muslim sovereigns who seemed to operate with a very clear notion of religion and politics as quite distinct arenas, indeed with a highly developed sense of how manipulation of the former could prove useful in achieving political power in the name of all manner of tribal, ethnic, and imperial formations. While the institution of the caliphate (see Chapter 2) was in theory to serve as the worldly guardian of a divinely ordained moral system, fragmentation and factional competition in the rapidly expanding Muslim community meant that, within a century of the Prophet's death, the caliphate effectively had become beholden to dynastic politics. Over the centuries, politics came to be recognized in the Muslim world as a distinct discipline unto itself. In the eleventh century, for example, some 500 years before Machiavelli's *The Prince,* there appeared in several Muslim languages various kingship manuals—such as Nizam al-Mulk's *Siyasatnama* (*Book of Politics*)—describing techniques and tactics of governance easily recognizable to any practitioner of the modern political arts.

Despite this apparent differentiation between religious and political spheres in Islam, it is worth noting that, until relatively recently, there was no formal distinction drawn between religious and secular law in most of the Muslim world. Historically, rulers of Muslim peoples derived a large measure of their legitimacy from religion and from the enforcement of religious law—which, certainly by the Middle Ages, had itself become a diverse body of jurisprudence, overlapping in significant ways with the customary laws of the various cultures and societies that came to embrace Islam. Right up to the dissolution of the Ottoman Empire after World War I, the legitimacy of the Sultan-Caliph in Istanbul ultimately rested on his executive authority as the chief enforcer of the law. And although the Ottoman Empire recognized, through the *millet* system and the *qanun* courts, legal pluralism in relation to religious identity and customary practice, its Muslim subjects generally had little experience of court systems that were not ultimately *shari'ah*-based—at least symbolically, if not in substance. We should not forget, however, that in a number of other Muslim-majority settings, the advent of European colonialism tended to mean the introduction of dual legal systems featuring elements of both common law (regarding civil and criminal matters) and religious law (usually with respect to issues of personal status). In the post-colonial period, the legal systems of most Muslim-majority countries have been primarily based on secular common-law models (often derived from British and French cognates). In this regard, we can say that a strong measure of formal secularism has been present in Muslim countries for over a century.

What, then, are the implications for our comparison of secularism in the Western tradition and the relationship between religion and politics in Islam? Aside from the observations made at the outset regarding certain key institutional differences between these traditions (the lack of a formal religious hierarchy in Islam; the absence of liberalism in the political societies of the Muslim world), we might now consider the following additional points. First, while Islamic scripture and theology does not formally recognize a division between religion and politics, it remains sufficiently circumspect regarding the specifics of politics under Islam as to permit considerable latitude of thought and practice in this area. Moreover, and second, Islamic history is full of many examples of Muslim rulers co-opting religious authorities and using the mantle of religion as a means through which to pursue goals better understood in terms of dynastic or proto-national agendas. Third, while the subjects of Islamic empires up until the nineteenth century (and in the central provinces of the Ottoman Empire through World War I) lived under legal systems that made no formal division between religious and secular law, most citizens of Muslim-majority nation-states today (and before that as subjects of various European colonial powers) have considerable direct experience of secular law.

Up until this point, our discussion of secularism in Islam has been structured largely around issues of law. In the absence of a formal "church," the legal system has served as the best institutional manifestation of the tradition we have equated above with "official" Islam. The aspect of secularism least examined so far in the Muslim context relates to the sociological question of the extent to which religion endures as a source of social normativity. Have Muslim societies experienced an overall decline in religiosity comparable with that in the West? This is far too complex a question to answer here in meaningful sociological terms, given the problems associated with speculating as to the inner moral worlds and intentions of individuals. Two observations that we might make a little more safely, however, relate to the embeddedness of religion in wider social institutions, and the presence of religion in public consciousness. In many Muslim countries, particularly those where hereditary monarchy (such as Saudi Arabia) and the influence of tribal ties (such as Pakistan) remains strong, religion often plays a role in underpinning the legitimacy of these institutions. When it comes to the issue of everyday consciousness of religion, it might be useful to turn to some polling data. When we look at a selection of Muslim countries polled by the World Values Survey between 2000 and 2002, the average percentage of respondents indicating that God is very important in their lives is 91 percent. Compare this with 23 percent for a selection of Western countries on the same question, a figure that falls to 12 percent if we remove North America from the sample. We need to be very careful, however, in terms of what significance we impute to these figures. They tell us nothing about linkages between religious consciousness and social or political behaviors. As discussed below, it is not always so easy to tell when religion matters in a given situation. Indeed, there is a strong sense in which a question such as the importance of God—given the social embeddedness of religion alluded to above—functions as something like a "mom and apple pie" question in Muslim settings—that is, one that everyone rallies around, but which tells us very little about the extent to which religion actually figures in everyday decision-making. What we do get some sense of, however, is the large extent to which religion is present in the public vocabulary and is readily available as a discursive resource for social mobilization, a point that will become relevant later as we examine various examples of Muslim politics.

In summary, it becomes clear that Muslim traditions—and the relationship between religion and politics within them—cannot be fully understood when approached through an analytical lens defined primarily by the Western experience of institutional secularism. The histories have been distinctive, the institutional manifestations of religion quite disparate, and the social location and role of religion rather different. Furthermore, the prevailing sentiment regarding secularism in the Muslim world is negative, equating it primarily with a lack of religiosity or "Godlessness" rather than the formal legal separation of religion and politics. This does not mean, however, that Muslims do not in practice recognize—and, as we will see below, seemingly *desire*—some distance between religious authority and processes of modern state governance.

WHEN DOES ISLAM COUNT?

While we have now been able to say something about secularism in the West, and the comparative historical experience of religion and politics in the Muslim world, the more directly pertinent question of religion's influence on political behavior and decision-making has not yet been addressed. That is, we have not actually tackled the question of how, as analysts of Muslim politics, we are able to determine the role and relative importance played by religion in a given situation. The central purpose of this section is to sound a cautionary note regarding the danger of imputing too much significance to the role of Islam in Muslim settings. There are three main points to be made in this regard.

First, even to speak of the "Muslim world" is to engage our subject matter at a very high level of abstraction, one that gives us very little sense of the social reality of Islam as a lived experience. What is at stake in describing something as part of the "Muslim world"—or in speaking of "Muslim peoples?" We always need to ask ourselves what, analytically, we seek to accomplish by framing our subject in a particular way, and via specific terms or labels. To choose the Muslim world as a unit of social analysis suggests, at the very least, that we recognize all those contained within it to possess— at some level—a relationship to something called Islam. In and of itself, this is not problematic, although it is worth asking why we have chosen Islam as an organizing principle. Is it the most appropriate lens through which to view our subject matter, given what we are hoping to discern? When might other categories of analysis—such as the "post-colonial world" or "tribal-patrimonial societies"—sometimes be more helpful when trying to explain particular forms of politics? Just to provide a brief example: the societies of Europe and North America could be considered as part of something we might call the "Christian world." Yet, in contemporary commentary regarding society, politics, and economics in these countries, we rarely find them referred to in this way. Indeed, for most of us it would probably seem rather strange to do so, since it is not clear that Christianity has much to do with these issues. Compare this with today's discourse on Islam, where it seems to be quite commonplace and apparently not at all odd to find constant references to the "Muslim world." Why this discrepancy, and what lies behind it? Is it that we feel these societies to be best understood through reference to their "Muslimness?" Do we have an assumption, tacit or otherwise, that Islam is somehow the primary determinant of social outcomes in these settings? Thus where we absolutely need to be careful is where we begin to ascribe norms, behaviors, and sentiments to Islam—or to a particular people as Muslims—without a more nuanced appreciation of how and where those who constitute a given society understand the role of Islam (see third point below). As studies by numerous scholars have suggested, religion does not always constitute the primary political identity assumed by Muslims—sometimes national, tribal, or ethnic claims trump the religious.[9] In short, as analysts of Muslim politics, we need to avoid prematurely projecting Islam onto a given setting, or defining it in terms of its "Muslimness" without being very clear as to why we are choosing to do so. This point is offered in a spirit of self-reflexivity, given that the term "Muslim world" occurs throughout this text.

A second point, and one that serves only to re-emphasize the importance of what has just been said, relates to the vast size and diversity of the Muslim world: approximately 1.6 billion people encompassing hundreds of distinct ethnic, national, and linguistic groups across multiple continents spanning the globe. Religious thought and practice in the Muslim world mirror this enormous pluralism, with Islam often understood in very different ways from one society to another. Likewise, the social and political significance of the religion varies greatly from setting to setting. In this regard, we need to be very careful when evaluating statements that make claims about the Muslim world as a whole, or that purport to explain *the* Islamic position on a given issue. A keen appreciation of the pluralism intrinsic to the Muslim world is hence crucial to meaningful social analysis, as is an understanding of the idiosyncrasies of religion in particular Muslim settings. It is, however, also dangerous to go too far to the other extreme and assume that particular forms of Islam somehow arise *sui generis* in each distinct Muslim locale. As has been explained above, Islam refers to a religious tradition that has developed cumulatively over some 1,400 years. While it has certainly traveled far and wide over the years, picked up many local flavors, and been mediated by countless sociocultural and political contexts, Islam still endures as a distinct tradition of discourse recognizable across manifold societies and communities. It is also a dynamic tradition insofar as it is constantly and contextually interpreted and reinterpreted. The lived embodiment of Islam may vary from setting to setting; the terms and parameters of Islamic normative discourse will certainly differ; but there is also a core corpus of Islam that somehow connects all Muslims. Indeed, one of the great challenges of analyzing Islam and politics lies in achieving some understanding of how particular groups of Muslims, or even individual believers, engage this tradition and understand its relevance to the situations they face on a daily basis across the Muslim world.

To make these various points more tangible, and to illustrate this issue of the diversity of the Muslim world, let us look for a moment at some public opinion data from the Muslim world regarding religion and politics. When asked by the Pew Global Attitudes Project whether religion is a matter of personal faith that should be kept separate from government policy, majorities in all Muslim countries surveyed indicated that they mostly or completely agreed with this statement (ranging from highs of 90 percent and 88 percent in Lebanon and Turkey to a low of 53 percent for both Jordan and Pakistan).[10] However, when subsequently asked how much of a role Islam should play in the political life of their countries, the very same respondents indicated in large majorities (with the exception of Turkey) that religion should play a fairly or very large role in politics. On the face of it, these two responses might be seen as contradictory. One reasonable interpretation of this apparent discrepancy is that people draw a clear distinction between specific, substantive matters of policy being subject to the religious beliefs of policy-makers, and politics as a general sphere of activity requiring the moral guidance provided by religious teaching. As we will see in several of the case studies later in the book, this latter view correlates strongly with support for religiously based political parties that run on a strong anti-corruption platform.

If we turn to the question of the appropriate political role for religious leaders, the results become even more interesting and varied. Asked if religious leaders should play a role in politics, strong majorities (63–77 percent) in Jordan, Pakistan, and Bangladesh agreed; Indonesia was on the borderline with 51 percent agreement; and only 40 percent in Turkey agreed with the statement. In order to understand this variation across settings, it is necessary to examine the history of involvement in politics by religious leaders. We also need to ask questions about who is understood to count as a religious leader, and what people understand by "playing a role in politics." The strong Nigerian response, for example, does not indicate widespread desire amongst Muslims in that country for an Iranian-style theocracy, but rather indicates the important social role that religious leaders have recently played in ensuring regional identity and unity *vis-à-vis* other religious and political communities. In other words, it is a response that tells us more about domestic politics and the popular desire for law and order in Nigeria than it does about the political nature of Islam. When it comes to Indonesia, there is much less of a tradition of religious leaders playing a direct role in post-colonial politics; but simultaneously there is a keen sense that figures from some of the country's mass religious movements have played an important role in furthering the causes of political reform and democratization (see "Indonesia: A paradigmatic 'Muslim democracy'?" in Chapter 4). This is perhaps a counterintuitive interpretation of what is implied by religious leaders playing a larger role in politics, but one that we would be able to offer only after delving into Indonesia's recent political history. As we can see looking across these cases, and the many others examined throughout this book, a sensitivity to local histories, understandings, and experience of religion and politics emerges as the crucial factor in making meaningful sense of the various Muslim politics we encounter in the world.

Table 1.2 Muslim views on religion and politics

Statement: Religion is a matter of personal faith and should be kept separate from government policy.

	Jordan	Pakistan	Bangladesh	Egypt	Indonesia
Completely Agree	17	48	59	47	28
Mostly Agree	27	25	24	4	44
Mostly Disagree	30	10	10	26	20
Completely Disagree	23	9	6	23	8
Don't know/refused	3	9	2	0	1

Source: Pew Research Center (2007).

Which brings us to our third point: the fact that Muslims in different settings will often develop unique understandings (based on local history and experience) of how and where their religion relates to everyday life and practical politics. As we have just seen, this sometimes can render direct comparison between Muslim settings very tricky, but it does not mean that we should give up altogether. It may often be difficult for us to determine—and actually even dangerous, from a social analysis point of view, to speculate about—whether an individual has behaved in a particular way because of his or her religion, or because of some other factor altogether. While it is certainly inappropriate, as emphasized above, quickly to impute causality to religion, it is equally problematic to discount religion altogether, or to view it in exclusively instrumentalist terms. To provide a sense of these complexities, we might consider some examples of conflict from the past 20 years. In several cases of civil war since the end of the Cold War, most notably that in Bosnia, the conflicting parties seemed to be organized along religious lines. Much has been made, and with good cause, of the ways in which religious identity was used in this conflict to mobilize political actors and to sharpen antagonisms in a dispute that was really about political autonomy, territory, and uneven access to resources. Or take the example of Northern Ireland, another example of a conflict that broke down along religious lines, but which very few observers really understood to be driven by disagreements over theology. Or consider the case of the Rushdie affair in 1988, where thousands of disenfranchised South Asian immigrants in the UK marched in protest and burned copies of what they perceived as a blasphemous novel in Salman Rushdie's *The Satanic Verses*. Parallels can certainly be drawn between this case and the furore over the Danish newspaper cartoons of the Prophet Muhammad that erupted in early 2006. Finally, what about the case of Palestinian suicide bombers? Much is made by some of the religious motivations to be found in discourses of martyrdom and the promise of lavish rewards in the hereafter for those who die in the name of *jihad*. Other analysts, however, would interpret such an act as a relatively instrumentalist, albeit extreme, military tactic in the context of a political struggle for national liberation. After all, a number of suicide attacks have also been carried out by members of Fatah and other secular Palestinian factions. How can we understand where religion figures in all of these examples? While it may be true that better explanations of the wider contexts in each of these cases are to be found in notions such as ethno-nationalism, territorial dispute, unequal access to resources on the part of minority communities, and racial discrimination, we would be wrong to discount religion from our analysis altogether. For some actors in these various events, an understanding of religion may have been very important, or even decisive, in terms of how they behaved in given situations. In other cases, actors clearly appealed to religion to try and define group boundaries in particular ways and also to provoke certain responses. We might, as analysts, want to enquire as to the

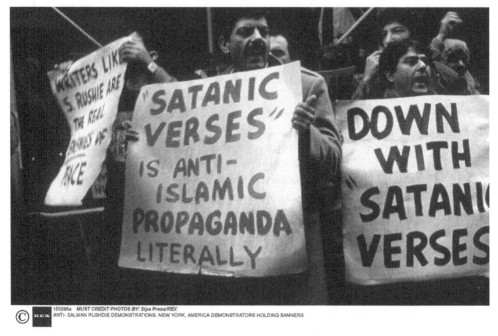

© Sipa Press/REX

Figure 1.1 Protests against the novel *The Satanic Verses* in the UK in 1988

circumstances under which such appeals succeeded or failed. In short, despite the challenges entailed in trying to identify the precise role of religion, there is clearly still much of interest to be learned by looking at how, and under what conditions, different understandings of religion become relevant and are invoked with regard to political questions.

ON MUSLIM POLITICS

Up to this point, we have been using the term "Muslim politics" as if its meaning were fairly self-evident. However, in this particular choice of terminology there is an important point about the distinctive analytical approach advanced in this book. Muslim politics, in our understanding, is not the same as "political Islam" or "Islamism," two terms the reader may regard as largely synonymous. Islamism, as clarified in more detail in Chapter 3, refers to a particular kind of Muslim politics—one that seeks to create a political order defined in terms of Islam (usually a *shari'ah*-based state). Political Islam, while certainly preferable to terms such as Islamic fundamentalism, is less useful for our purposes in two respects. First, in positing "political" as a qualifier for Islam, it ends up reinforcing some of the very boundaries between spheres of thought and practice that we are trying to challenge. To say that we are dealing with an instance of political Islam would be to suggest that there are times when Islam is not political (that it is sometimes "just" religious). The term Muslim politics is useful because it allows us to keep the diversity and pluralism of Islam front and center through an emphasis on Muslims as social actors. To focus on Muslims rather than Islam is to emphasize real people, in real settings, facing real issues. The more we stress Islam as a unit of analysis, the more we face the dangers of abstraction and unwarranted generalization. Islam keeps us mired in debates about normativity, where an emphasis on Muslims allows us to appreciate the dynamic nature of Islam as a lived experience. The use of the adjectives Muslim and Islamic is hence significant in what follows. When we speak of, for example, Muslim thinkers and Islamic intellectuals, we are referring to two quite different things. The first includes any Muslim engaged in intellectual effort, while the second points more specifically to Muslims whose intellectual projects are framed specifically in terms of Islamic normativity or claims to the same.

To study Muslim politics, then, is to look at the diverse ways in which people who identify themselves as Muslims in a variety of social locations—be they religious scholars, bureaucrats, intellectuals, merchants, scientists—understand, make use of, and mobilize the symbols and language of Islam around issues of social order, power, and authority. This approach tends to resist making claims about the nature and content of Islam, and instead concerns itself primarily with the various ways in which people engage and draw upon religious tradition as they construct and contest social orders. It helps us both to broaden our understanding of what counts as politics (as per the appeal made above) and to appreciate how certain issues, conventionally understood as limited in their political import, can be transformed into highly politicized public symbols. The emphasis on Muslim politics rather than "Islamism" is also a more inclusive formulation that allows us to examine political actors who define their motivations and goals, at least in part, as related to Islam, but who do not pursue anything like the establishment of formal Islamic political systems. In other words, Muslim politics allows us to focus on a broader range of, and the interplay between, actors engaged in all manner and means of Muslim politics, whether or not they have as their goal the establishment of an Islamic political order. So, then, political parties seeking to implement political systems based on *shari'ah* law, such as the Muslim Brotherhood, are certainly engaged in Muslim politics—as are the groups that in early 2006 mobilized around the publication of cartoons in a Danish newspaper perceived as insulting to the Prophet Muhammad. Appeals to, and mobilizations around, the language and symbols of Islam in the pursuit of normative agendas were common to both—hence our description of them both as forms of Muslim politics.

This book is certainly not the first to advocate a Muslim politics approach. As a new and distinct analytical trope, the phrase was probably first coined and systematically elaborated by Dale Eickelman and James Piscatori in their 1996 book of the same name.[11] The reader should refer to this title for the most substantive social scientific statement to date on Muslim politics. While subsequent edited volumes have also embraced the general approach, this book constitutes the first attempt to offer in monographic form a broad, comparative, and global overview of Muslim politics with integrated case studies.[12] Where the primary empirical emphasis in this book lies in explaining variation in those forms of Muslim politics that fit within the parameters of what we identified above as "Islamism," its final chapter uses the Muslim politics approach to convey the political import of several contemporary Muslim movements whose orientation seems to be in keeping with "post-Islamist" sensibilities and strategy.

LOCAL POLITICS IN A GLOBAL WORLD

The final set of introductory points that need to be made here concern this book's emphasis on the global nature of Muslim politics. Writers in academia and journalism tend to use the term "global" to mean several different things: to identify something as part and parcel of the wider phenomenon known as globalization; as a way of referring to international phenomena while de-emphasizing the nation-state; and to contrast—or emphasize the relationship between—broader transnational social contexts, and more local ones. It will hopefully not confuse the reader too much that this book proposes to use, variously, all three meanings.

More specifically as regards Muslim political contexts, our emphasis on the global hopes to serve the following four central purposes.

- To clarify the role played by globalization in animating and enabling new forms of Muslim politics (on which we have more to say below, and again in Chapter 4).
- To emphasize the relationship and interplay between local instances of Muslim politics and events, trends, and ideas to be found not only in the wider Muslim world, but also within the emergent spaces of transnational culture and politics (new media, global lifestyles, increasing awareness of "global" issues—and their concomitant political vocabularies—such as human rights and the environment). This perspective is particularly pronounced in Chapter 8. The central idea here is that, while all politics may indeed be local, there remain very few spaces of local politics that are not connected in some way to other global contexts.

- Through an emphasis on the global/local and transnational dimensions of Islam, to find a middle space for exploring comparative politics in the Muslim world that avoids, on the one hand, treating national contexts of Muslim politics as self-contained units of analysis largely sealed off from the wider world; and, on the other, positing the existence of a monolithic global Islam or "Muslim international." The emphasis here is on exploring the *relationality* of various Muslim political contexts, not on either staking claims to the utter uniqueness of each, or seeing each as part of an undifferentiated Islamic bloc.
- To bring into focus the fact that there now exist Muslim political actors and movements (moderates and radicals alike) that are organized and operating on a global scale, some of whose ambitions and goals are similar in scope. We can also point to various locally based actors making use of media and networks to build up global constituencies for their particular accounts of what it means to be a Muslim today. Chapters 7 and 8 both explore this point in some detail.

While this is not meant primarily to be a book about Islam and globalization, it will be suggested that aspects of globalization have been important in terms of enabling new forms of Muslim politics, permitting them to reach new audiences, and—in some cases—becoming an actual target of these politics. Globalization is a complex phenomenon that in its common usage has both analytical and normative connotations depending on context. It is most commonly associated with the rise of a world political economy and the ever-closer integration of markets and regions through, for example, lower barriers to trade and transnational finance. More broadly, it can be seen as the world propagation of neoliberal economic norms. The normative discourse on globalization, then, is one that understands this process to be a route to greater prosperity for the world's nations, and is most commonly identified with advocates of the so-called "Washington Consensus" such as the World Bank, the International Monetary Fund (IMF), and many of the world's leading economic powers and multinational corporations. There are also to be found in the literature definitions that try to achieve a more sociological understanding of globalization, and it is primarily from these authors that the idiom of globalization employed in this book is drawn. Stated in broad terms, these approaches emphasize the unprecedented levels of interconnectedness between societies and peoples that globalization enables. Some authors, such as David Harvey and Anthony Giddens, have spoken of this in terms of the compression of time and space.[13] Others, such as Jan Aart Scholte, emphasizing the notion of "supraterritoriality," connect globalization with a decline in the importance of territory in the establishment and maintenance of social relations.[14] The most commonly cited manifestations of globalization give credence to aspects of all these approaches. They include, to cite just a few examples, dramatic increases in the numbers of people traveling and moving around the world due to shifting labor markets and the relatively cheap availability of air travel; the rise of "global cities" such as London, New York, and Tokyo (not to mention Shanghai and Bangalore, India)—all of which have to some extent become disembedded from their national-territorial contexts and now serve as nodal points in the global economy referred to above; and the emergence of new breeds of information and communications technologies and new media such as the internet and satellite television, all of which have significantly reduced the barriers and costs associated with communicating across borders and getting messages in front of broad, worldwide audiences.

Indeed, it is tempting to speculate, as has Roland Robertson, one of the earliest sociological theorists of globalization, about the impact of these developments on people's understanding of the world as a social space. He has proposed the notion of "globality" in reference to a particular type of consciousness enabled by globalization, one that refers to the idea that people are now increasingly able to imagine the world as a single space and to have a clearer sense of the complex array of cross-cutting relationships at various levels that define their place in it.[15] Following quite naturally from this, other scholars have been led to speculate about the effects of globalization on how people understand their identities and social affiliations.[16] Taking these theoretical insights into the Muslim world, some writers have speculated about the extent to which globalization might give new credence—and social reality—to the notion of the *umma,* a term with long-standing universalist connotations referring to the world community of Islam.[17] The "people flows" alluded to above have involved large numbers of Muslims traveling regionally and globally as labor migrants, and new media forums have begun to create global public spheres for Muslim discourses of all sorts.[18] While claims about a new *umma* may be somewhat premature at this point, it is undoubtedly the case that Muslims today have a greater awareness of the lives and predicaments of their co-religionists across diverse national settings. As a number of our case studies demonstrate, this intensified sense of "Muslim globality" has major implications for the nature and forms of Muslim politics that we find in the world today.

NOTES

1 The Pew Forum, *The Future of the Global Muslim Population,* Washington, DC: Pew Research Center, 2011.
2 T. Asad, *Genealogies of Religion: Disciplines and Reasons of Power in Christianity and Islam,* Baltimore, MD: Johns Hopkins University Press, 1993.
3 Ibid., p. 1.

4 D. Eickelman, "Inside the Islamic Reformation," *Wilson Quarterly* 22, no. 1, 1998, pp. 80–89.

5 D. Brumberg, "Islam is Not the Solution (or the Problem)," *Washington Quarterly* 29, 2005, pp. 97–116.

6 Asad, op. cit., pp. 200–201.

7 J. Esposito, *Islam and Politics,* 4th edn, Syracuse, NY: Syracuse University Press, 1984, pp. 72–73.

8 A. Sadri, M. Sadri (eds), *Reason, Freedom, and Democracy in Islam: Essential Writings of Abdolkarim Soroush,* New York: Oxford University Press, 2000.

9 M. Fandy, "Tribe vs. Islam: The Post-colonial Arab State and the Democratic Imperative," *Middle East Policy* 3, 1994; Brumberg, op. cit., pp. 97–116.

10 See the Pew Research Center's Global Attitudes Project data archive at www.pewglobal.org/category/datasets/.

11 D. Eickelman, J. Piscatori, *Muslim Politics,* Princeton, NJ: Princeton University Press, 1996.

12 D. Eickelman, J. Anderson (eds), *New Media in the Muslim World: The Emerging Public Sphere,* Bloomington, IN: Indiana University Press, 2003; R. Hefner (ed.), *Remaking Muslim Politics: Pluralism, Contestation, Democratization,* Princeton, NJ: Princeton University Press, 2005.

13 D. Harvey, *The Conditions of Postmodernity: An Enquiry into the Order of Cultural Change,* Malden, MA: Blackwell, 1990; A. Giddens, *The Consequences of Modernity,* Stanford, CA: Stanford University Press, 1990.

14 J. A. Scholte, *Globalization: A Critical Introduction,* 2nd edn, Basingstoke: Palgrave, 2005.

15 R. Robertson, *Globalization: Social Theory and Global Change,* London: Sage, 1992.

16 A. Appadurai, *Modernity at Large: Cultural Dimensions of Globalization,* Minneapolis, MN: University of Minnesota Press, 1996; S. Croucher, *Globalization and Belonging: The Politics of Identity in a Changing World,* Lanham, MD: Rowman & Littlefield, 2003.

17 P. Mandaville, *Transnational Muslim Politics: Reimagining the Umma,* New York: Routledge, 2004.

18 Eickelman, Anderson, op. cit., passim.

CHAPTER 2

Islam and politics: History and key concepts

This book is concerned primarily with Muslim politics in the contemporary world. It is, however, impossible for the reader to understand the nature, form, and symbols of Islamic politics today without some appreciation of their evolution through history. This chapter offers a historical overview of politics in the Muslim world and, in the process, introduces the reader to key concepts and terms that will be necessary for understanding contemporary Muslim politics and political discourse. As is perhaps inevitable when one aspires to survey nearly 1,500 years of history over multiple continents in a single chapter, the coverage here is far more superficial than a proper historical inquiry would warrant. The aim is to allow the reader to discern the broad trajectory of Muslim politics over time, and to understand key patterns, as well as important moments of disjuncture and upheaval. In addition to covering major historical events, the narrative offered here also incorporates an overview of the development of Islamic political thought from the time of the Prophet Muhammad up to and including Muslim responses to the formation of modern nation-states and the advent of globalization in the Muslim world.[1]

THE ORIGINS OF ISLAM

An integral component of the great monotheistic tradition, the history of Islam is inextricably intertwined with that of Judaism and Christianity.

While Islamic history is conventionally dated from the time of the Prophet Muhammad in the early seventh century, Muslims, like all followers of the three great monotheistic faiths, believe the origins of their religion to lie in Adam and Eve. In Islam, particular importance is placed on the Prophet Ibrahim (the Arabic form of Abraham). Muslims believe that the *Ka'aba,* a structure in the center of Mecca's Grand Mosque and the holiest site in Islam, was built by Ibrahim and his son Ismail (Ishmael). For Muslims, the books and prophets of the Old Testament are considered sacred, and Muslims also assign a place of special significance and reverence to the figure of Jesus—who appears frequently in the Qur'an. Although differing in significant ways from the other two religions on certain matters of theology and law (as, of course, do Judaism and Christianity), Muslims nevertheless worship the same God as Jews and Christians and adhere to the teachings of the same moral universe.

For our purposes, it will be convenient to begin our account of Muslim political history with the emergence of the Prophet Muhammad in the Arabian peninsula in the seventh century, and the growth around him of a social movement. It is particularly important to understand accurately the significance of the Prophet Muhammad in the Islamic tradition. Muhammad is believed by Muslims to be the final prophet in the line of Abraham, specifically chosen by God to deliver his last revelation to humankind. Where Christians understand Jesus to be God, Muhammad is wholly human. Indeed, it would violate the basic monotheistic credal impulse of Islam to impute to him any kind of divine significance. Muhammad is primarily God's messenger, the medium through which the Holy Qur'an—the divine text of Islam—was revealed. Beyond his role as a human conduit for the delivery of the final revelation, however, Muhammad does have further significance for Muslims. Despite his exclusively human status, the Prophet is believed to be the living embodiment of Qur'anic teaching, an idea captured in the notion of Muhammad as *insan al-kamil* ("the perfect person"). It is for this reason that, in addition to the Qur'an, the living example of the Prophet is considered as a definitive source of Islamic authority—a concept we cover in greater detail below.

Let us familiarize ourselves with the social context of the Arabian peninsula at the time Muhammad's prophethood began. Arabia in the seventh century was populated primarily by various nomadic and seminomadic tribes. Western Arabia, the subregion with which we are most immediately concerned, constituted an important segment in a transnational trade route that connected Jerusalem and other cities of the Levant with Yemen and, via seafaring merchants, to points further east. The city of Mecca, about halfway up the Red Sea coast between Yemen and the Levant, was a particularly important nodal point in this trading system. Every caravan bound for the Levant passed through Mecca, and the city had grown rich on account of its strategic location and its key role in providing all manner of goods and services relating to mercantile activity. It was into a prominent Meccan clan, the Quraysh, that Muhammad was born in about 570. Orphaned early in his life, Muhammad was raised by his uncle and learned the family's trade, eventually taking up a role within the city's bustling commercial activity, and earning a reputation as a particularly upstanding and judicious provider of financial services.

Muhammad's religious role does not begin until about the age of 40. In order to escape from what he had come too see as the hectic, alienating, and overly materialistic commercial life of Mecca, he would sometimes hike out to an outcropping cave beyond the city walls to be by himself and to think. It was during one of these excursions in 610 that, according to Islamic tradition, the archangel Gabriel appeared to Muhammad and informed him of his prophetic calling. Having confessed to his wife of the time, Khadija—herself a prominent Meccan business figure—that he feared he was going insane, Muhammad was urged by her to embrace rather than turn away from his calling, and Khadija pledged to live by the revelation he brought. Ali—his young cousin (and eventual son-in-law)—followed suit, and the two of them are generally credited as being the first to adopt Islam.

At this point, it is useful to say something about the nature of religion in Arabia at this time so that the reader can understand how genuinely different—and, to some, dangerously revolutionary—the message brought by Muhammad was. Mecca in the seventh century was a thoroughly polytheistic society, worshipping a complex and seemingly endless array of gods and deities—often in the form of idols—at shrines and temples throughout the city. People appealed to different deities for different purposes—so, for example, one god to seek intercession regarding the fate of a particular caravan, and another to influence the weekly price of aromatic gums. Indigenous Arabian religion was not so much a source of moral guidance as it was a cosmology that offered resources for seeking control over the natural world for profit and personal gain. It is worth noting that Judaism and Christianity were not wholly foreign to this milieu, given the presence of Jewish and Christian communities in Arabia.

The message that Muhammad brought could not have been more at odds with prevailing religious norms. At its very core was the notion of God's essential oneness (*tawhid*) and omnipotence, a strict monotheism that expressly forbade the worship of anyone or anything other than the one God of the Abrahamaic tradition. Even representations of God were considered dangerous distractions that could lead the believer back to the path of *shirk* (idolatry). The relationship between humanity and the divine was to be direct and without intercession. Hence it is submission to the divine will of God that defines what it means to be a Muslim, in contrast to the instrumentalism characteristic of religious practice in Muhammad's Mecca.

Islam in Arabic refers to the notion of submission or surrender to God, and a *Muslim,* therefore, is "one who submits." More than just a metaphysics of divine oneness, however, there was also a complete moral system to be found in the revelation brought by Muhammad. Over the years, as we will see later, this became embodied and codified as an actual body of law. Suffice it for now to summarize those aspects of the religion that eventually came to be known as the "Five Pillars of Islam":

1. The *shahada* ("bearing witness") or profession of faith as to the unique and singular nature of God and the recognition of Muhammad as his messenger. Technically, the embrace of this simple creed is all that is required to become a Muslim.
2. The practice of *salat,* or prayer, to be performed five times daily by believing Muslims.
3. Fasting—*sawm*—from dawn to dusk during the holy month of Ramadan.
4. The payment of *zakat,* a kind of tithe, in the form of a percentage of income dedicated to charitable purposes.
5. The requirement that once during a lifetime, all able-bodied Muslims with sufficient means make a pilgrimage (*hajj*) to the holy city of Mecca.

It is worth noting that, although Islam represented a sharp theological rupture in terms of religion in Arabia, there are many elements of pre-Islamic tribal practice and customary law that came to be integrated into, or at least tolerated by, Islam as its influence and significance expanded. What this means in practice is that, from very early on, it has sometimes been difficult to discern definitively when a given norm or behavior is the result of religion, and when its origins lay in customary practices that have come to be articulated and justified in terms of religion. This is a point that will prove important later when we go on to examine some of the characteristics commonly associated with Muslim political societies.

At this point, we can also identify the two primary sources of authoritative knowledge and practice in Islam. The first of these is the Holy Qur'an itself, believed by Muslims to be the literal word of God as revealed to the Prophet. The chief supplement to the Qur'an is found in Muhammad's *sunna*—that is, Prophetic tradition. The model of thinking and behavior that Muhammad provided during his lifetime is considered by Muslims to be the best example of how the divine knowledge of the Qur'an was to be translated into lived practice. In this sense, Muhammad is regarded as the worldly embodiment of Qur'anic normativity. The *sunna* is hence pre-eminent among the various "secondary" (in the sense of not being intrinsically divine) sources of Islamic authority. The collection and categorization of reports about what the Prophet said and did in various situations—known as *hadith*—emerged as a distinctive scholarly discipline in the years following his passing. More detail about the nature and uses of the *sunna* is provided below.

■ THE *HIJRA* AND EARLY COMMUNITY IN MEDINA

Muhammad did not receive a sympathetic hearing from the notables of Mecca when he began to speak publicly about, and encourage others to accept, his new religion. This is not surprising, given that part and parcel of the message was a direct critique of the city's entire social order. Meccan life was castigated as ungodly and corrupt, and the prevailing religious practices denigrated as blasphemous. Muhammad and those who had accepted Islam soon found themselves the target of considerable persecution and hostility. After several difficult years, Muhammad decided that his position in Mecca was untenable. Thus in 622, when the Prophet received an invitation from the nearby city of Yathrib to move to that city along with his community of Muslims, he accepted. So important was this migration or *hijra* to Yathrib that it marks the beginning of, and gives its name to, the Islamic calendar. More than just the movement of a people from one setting to another, it had symbolic significance as a shift in the very basis of social affiliation and polity. Many of Muhammad's followers broke with their family in order to go with the Prophet, and in this sense the *hijra* represented a migration from a model of community premised on tribal and clan affiliations to a form of community based on a shared vision of divinely given social order.

Yathrib, soon renamed Medina (after *medinat al-nabi*—"City of the Prophet"), was a far less affluent and politically unstable city to the northeast of Mecca. Rife with sectarian and tribal factionalism, Muhammad had been hired by the Yathribi tribal authorities to act as an arbiter in public affairs. As part of the deal, his status as a Prophet was recognized and the security of his community guaranteed. Thus begins Muhammad's career as a politician, public official, and leader of a political community. After consolidating his position in Medina, the Prophet began forming alliances with local tribes and attracting more and more followers to Islam. With these new forces, he began to conduct highly successful raids against Meccan trade caravans, and this eventually brought him into direct conflict with his former home city. Over the next half decade Medina and Mecca fought a number of battles, and in 630 Muhammad's forces triumphed over Mecca and returned to a city now eager to accept the new faith. One after another, the tribal leaders of Arabia swore oaths of allegiance to Muhammad over the next two years. By the time of the Prophet's death in 632, he had managed to bring all of central Arabia under his effective control.

In terms of the theory and practice of Muslim politics, the death of Muhammad is significant in two regards. As the indisputable political leader of all Muslims during his lifetime, the Prophet's death marked the first time the Muslim community had to settle questions of political leadership and the conduct of public affairs. It was also significant in that it represented the disappearance of an immanent model of Islamic normativity. While Muhammad was alive, correct and "authentic" Islam was always immediately available, embodied in the Prophet's conduct. His death thus also marks the beginning of Muslim politics in the sense of debate and contestation between multiple interpretations of the religion.

Regarding the question of who should succeed the Prophet as the community's political leader, there was initially some debate between two distinct camps. One group believed that the leadership of the community should remain vested within Muhammad's family. They favored the candidacy of Ali, the Prophet's cousin and son-in-law, citing various occasions upon which the Prophet had publicly recognized Ali as a pre-eminent leader of the community. This group would eventually evolve into the *Shi'i* sect of Islam (from *shi'at Ali*, "partisans of Ali"). The other camp, disputing the idea that Muhammad had ever stated unequivocal views on his successor, preferred the idea of choosing a leader according to the consensus of the community's senior figures. This latter view prevailed, and Abu Bakr, one of the Prophet's oldest and closest friends, was quickly chosen as the first caliph (from *khalifa*, "successor"). Hence was born the political institution of the caliphate, a position and office that endured in some form for 1,300 years until its abolition in 1924 by Mustapha Kemal at the founding of the modern Turkish republic.

THE *RASHIDUN* CALIPHS

The first four successors to the Prophet (who ruled from 632 to 661) are known as the *rashidun* ("rightly guided") caliphs, and the events and personalities of this period have carried a special normative valence throughout Islamic history. This is widely regarded in Muslim tradition as a period when the affairs of the Muslim community were conducted in very close accordance with the Qur'an and the *sunna* of the Prophet. In short, things are perceived as having been done correctly under the *rashidun*. As we will see, later social and political movements, responding to what they perceived as diversions from the path of Islam, would often call for a conscious return to the model of the Prophet's early companions.

The *rashidun* period also marked a time of phenomenal growth in terms of both the geographical expanse of lands under Muslim control, and the diversity of the Muslim peoples. The first caliph, Abu Bakr (632–34), spent most of his short reign reintegrating a number of recalcitrant tribes who had rebelled in the wake of Muhammad's death—a process that later became known as the Wars of Apostasy. It was during the rule of the second caliph, Umar (634–44) that Islam's amazing territorial expansion began. Muslim forces were able to gain significant lands from both the Persian Sassanid Empire in the east and the Byzantines in the north—with the result that, within a decade, much of the Middle East from Egypt across to Palestine,

Syria, and even some areas of Persia and Armenia had been integrated into the Muslim state. Umar was also responsible for establishing most of the administrative and economic practices and policies of the new Muslim polity. Rather than directly occupying newly acquired territories, the Arabian Muslims would tend to dispatch governors and revenue officials to administer through a system of garrison towns.

Religious growth was also significant during this period, with mass conversions to Islam. While much of Islam's territorial expansion occurred via military conquest, coercion was not the primary means by which the religion acquired new followers.[2] Rather, people embraced Islam for a variety of reasons, including the favorable tax status associated with being a believer, or because a local notable or tribal leader had decided to convert. In other cases, people were genuinely impressed by the successes of the Muslims, or drawn to the religious message itself. Those who chose not to convert were generally left to practice their faith under Muslim rulers as protected religious minorities or *dhimmis*—which usually involved paying a higher rate of tax.[3]

The next caliph, Uthman (644–56), the first to be "elected" by a more formally constituted commission, continued many of his predecessor's policies and his general style of rule. Unlike Umar, however, Uthman tended to be more partial to members of his own family when making selections for senior regional governorships. As a member of one of the most prestigious clans of the Quraysh tribe, there is a sense in which Uthman's reign represented the beginning of a re-encroachment on Muslim politics of tribal influences. Under Uthman, more of North Africa and Persia came under Muslim rule. He also oversaw the collection of the first standardized edition of the Qur'an, with the chapters (*surat*) appearing in the order with which we are familiar today. That Uthman felt the need to do this was indicative, at least in part, of discomfort at the religio-political heart of the Muslim empire with certain localized approaches to Qur'anic recitation and interpretation. In other words, the emergence of religious pluralism in this regard was seen as a threat to the political authority of the center and the cohesiveness of the faith. Indeed, Uthman's rather heavy-handed attempts to centralize religious authority were at the root of the general discontent about his rule that began to emerge, particularly among those already alarmed at his tendency toward clan favoritism.

When, at the apex of this displeasure in 656, Uthman was assassinated, Ali finally ascended to the leadership of the Muslim community. His authority was immediately challenged, however, by several prominent figures, not least of all the governor of Syria, Mu'awiya, a kinsman of Uthman who accused Ali of making insufficient efforts to identify and punish his predecessor's assassins. While this pretext was certainly part of the issue, the challenge to Ali was the natural next phase in a growing search for decentralization among the most powerful regions of the Muslim empire—exacerbated

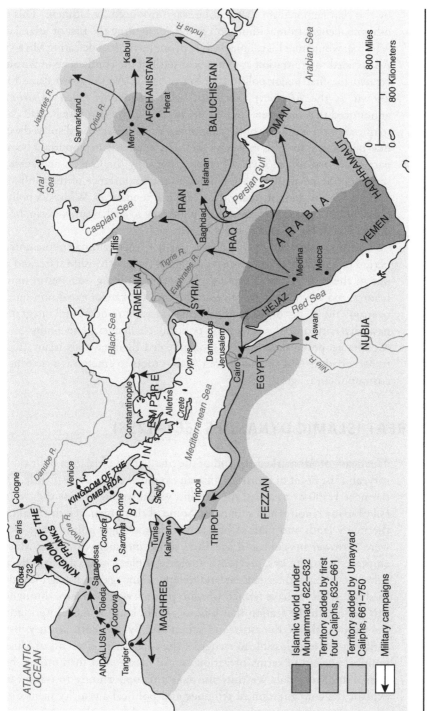

Map 2.1 The early spread of Islam

by the clan factionalism that had been reintroduced by Uthman. This and other challenges from within soon found Ali fighting the first of several civil wars that would mar his caliphate. When, on the verge of defeating Mu'awiya, Ali acceded to arbitration as a means of settling the conflict, he unwittingly created the first major political schism in Islam. A group that came to be known as the *Khawarij* ("seceders," also frequently called "*kharijites*") announced that they were loyal to neither Mu'awiya (because he had dared to question the authority of the caliph) nor Ali (since he had displayed weakness by not subduing his mutinous foe). The Khawarij are important because part of their platform involved recognizing only the Qur'an and *sunna* as sovereign. Some analysts have pointed to the importance of their influence on later Islamist movements with secessionist tendencies. With Ali's political position fatally compromised, he soon fell prey to a Khawarij assassin, bringing an end to the *rashidun* period in 661.

The three decades following the death of Muhammad represented a period of phenomenal activity on the part of the new Muslim state, and also one of the most impressive and rapid empire-building exercises in human history; too rapid perhaps, since, in the end, the rate of expansion quickly overtook the ability of the political center to accommodate and integrate its new diversity and the attendant political challenges. The limits of the Medina geopolitical worldview soon revealed themselves as Islam quickly transcended its Arabian—and even Arab—roots to emerge as a thoroughly cosmopolitan religion.

THE GREAT ISLAMIC DYNASTIES (661–1258)

The death of Ali marked the end of the first period of Islamic political history, and the point of transition into an extended era of dynastic rule. Over the next 1,300 or so years, the Muslim world would witness the rise and fall of many empires and sultanates. Some of them managed to encompass the many lands and nations of Islam within a single polity, while others were narrower in scope and coexisted simultaneously with other Muslim empires. In some cases, previously subject peoples rose up to seize effective rule from their former masters and defend Islam against foreign invaders. In short, what we have termed Muslim politics were pervasive throughout this period. In the section that follows, we look at the most important of the various Islamic dynasties and sultanates. By the tenth century, if not earlier, it was also possible to recognize the constituent elements of Muslim political society in terms of various social classes and institutions, both formal and informal. We thus also take this opportunity to outline and explain the configuration of religious and political authority in medieval Islam, a period that saw the emergence of social forces that remain important even today.

The Umayyad dynasty (661–750): The limits of Arabo-centric power

After Ali's demise, Mu'awiya was able to make a successful bid for the caliphate, and so was born the first of the great Islamic dynasties, with its capital now moved from Medina to Damascus. If the *rashidun* period had been defined by rapid territorial expansion, the Umayyad period could be described primarily as an attempt to consolidate and rationalize the Arab administration of foreign territories. Mu'awiya and his heirs—this was a dynasty after all, in contrast to the nonhereditary system of succession followed under the first four caliphs—went about establishing a complex administrative system and bureaucracy. The basic structures for these were often borrowed from the empires the Muslims had conquered. Much of the emphasis during this period was on fiscal policy, with the introduction of ever more complicated systems of taxation that maximized revenues from non-Muslims and, most importantly in terms of future political ramifications, non-Arab Muslims. Land revenues were also emphasized as more and more fertile territories came under Muslim control.

The Umayyad period also saw the emergence of a decisive sectarian schism with the emergence of Shi'i Islam. As has already been mentioned, the roots of Shi'ism trace back to a disagreement at the time of the Prophet's death over who should assume the political leadership of the community. This resentment festered among certain supporters of Ali ("Alids") even during the *rashidun* period, with some feeling that his role was consistently and deliberately marginalized—a situation that ripened into open hostility once he assumed the caliphate. Before Mu'awiya died, he named his son, Yazid, as his successor, destroying any hope on the part of those who continued to support Ali that one of his sons might come to power. Ali's younger son Husayn declined to accept Yazid's authority, and traveled from Medina to the Iraqi city of Kufa to join with a group of Alids in mounting a rebellion against the Damascus caliphate. They were pre-empted in this by the arrival of an Umayyad army and, during the ensuing Battle of Karbala (680 CE), Husayn and his family were all killed. The martyrdom of Husayn is commemorated by Shi'a each year on the anniversary of this battle, the tenth day ("*Ashura*") of the month of Muharram. This was a decisive moment in the emergence of Shi'ism as a separate sect in Islam. More details regarding the doctrinal and political differences between these two sects will be provided below.

Territorial gains under the Umayyads were significant. By the end of this first dynasty, Muslim rule extended from Spain in the West, down across all of North Africa and the Middle East and throughout Persia into parts of present day Pakistan. Despite the increased geographical and cultural diversity of the Muslim state, effective power came to be concentrated in the hands of a relatively small Arab aristocratic elite. Concern began to mount, amongst those who had taken it upon themselves to be the guardians and transmitters of religious knowledge, the *ulama* ("religious scholars"), that the Umayyad rulers had lost sight of the egalitarianism, austerity, and humility at the core of Islam and the *rashidun* period's model of "good governance." Although the caliph and his regional agents did create positions charged with the enforcement of religiously prescribed norms and arbitration of the same, these came to be perceived as just another extension of what looked increasingly like monarchic rule.

The final decade of Umayyad rule saw the emergence of opposition movements on a number of fronts. Resenting the decadence of the Umayyad rulers and their narrow circles of favoritism, Muslims—Arab and non-Arab alike—began to decry the failure of their rulers to properly implement an Islamic system of equitable governance. They were joined in this by other long-standing detractors, such as the Khawarij and the Shi'a. Religious scholars, many of them based at centers of learning in Iraq, had begun the process of codifying Islamic morality into a legal system, the *shari'ah*. They were prompted to do this, at least in part, by a desire to establish a standard of conduct that would throw the policies of the present rulers into stark contrast. After a series of revolts, the Umayyads fell in 750 to the Abbasids, a clan descended from al-Abbas, one of the Prophet's uncles.

The Abbasid dynasty (750–1258): Cosmopolitanism and fragmentation

Abbasid rule, which saw the capital move yet again from Damascus to Baghdad, technically lasted some 500 years, although the clan of al-Abbas lost effective power by the tenth century. Often regarded as Islam's "golden age," under the Abbasids the empire made its greatest achievements in the fields of science and philosophy. This period also saw the consolidation of the four schools of jurisprudence that would come to define the dominant Sunni ("orthodox") denomination—of which more below. Although we can wonder whether the Abbasid rulers were actually any more religious than their Umayyad forebears, it is certainly the case that they were great patrons of religion and religious learning. Many new mosques and associated centers of religious scholarship were established, and the Islamic legal sciences flourished. In the field of philosophy, the early ninth century saw the rise of the *Mu'tazili* school of thought, strongly influenced by Greek rationalism. The politicians even took an interest in these developments, adopting Mu'tazilism as the official doctrine of the empire under the caliph Ma'mun. This orientation remained dominant until challenged by the rival school of *Asharism*, which sought to uphold the superiority of revealed knowledge. The later Abbasid period also saw major contributions to philosophy (and the revisiting of certain aspects of this same debate) by figures such as al-Ghazali in Baghdad and Ibn Rushd in Cordoba.

In political terms, although the Abbasid caliphs based much of their authority on claims to greater religiosity and the "re-Islamization" of governance, they did little to alter the essentially imperial and monarchical structure of the Umayyad bureaucracy. Two areas in which important changes were made, however, related to the extensive use of non-Arab officials in various senior court positions; and the reintroduction of a taxation system based on the early Islamic distinction between Muslims and non-Muslims, meaning that non-Arab Muslims were no longer taxed at a higher rate. The Abbasid period was also characterized by considerable political fragmentation. Although the "official" caliphate rested with the Abbasids through 1258 (and then, in purely symbolic terms, even until 1517), the dynasty's capacity for centralized rule had been effectively eroded by the mid-tenth century. A number of regional kingdoms and sub-dynasties began to emerge, such as the Shi'i Fatimids in North Africa. Control of the Iraqi heartland fell into the hands of another Shi'i clan, the Buyids, and eventually to the Seljuq Turks. Meanwhile, the Umayyads had reappeared in Spain, making a separate claim to the caliphate from 929, and the growing autonomy of various local governors in nominally Abbasid territories saw them acquiring more and more real political power from the late tenth century. The dynasty formally ended in 1258 when Baghdad was sacked by the Mongols and the caliph killed—although by this time the Abbasid rulers were little more than figureheads.

THE RISE OF MUSLIM POLITICAL SOCIETY: KEY CONCEPTS, ACTORS AND MOVEMENTS

We find here a convenient spot at which to temporarily pause our historical narrative and look more closely at a number of key concepts and social roles that will emerge as relevant in our later analyses of contemporary Muslim politics. It was under the Abbasids that the various social classes and institutions that collectively compose what we might call "Muslim political society" emerged. By this term we are referring to the interwoven system of political and religious authority composed of the caliph (as Commander of the Faithful and chief enforcer of religious law), the religious scholars or *ulama* as repositories of religious learning who simultaneously provide a mediating layer between the state and society, and the institutions and traditions of religious law and jurisprudence. This latter subsystem, as we will see, is particularly complicated in terms of both its relationship with the state, and various developments in legal thought during the Abbasid period that rendered rather ambiguous the question of how far it was possible to supplement the law further once the parameters and central content of the four orthodox legal schools had consolidated. In this section we provide an overview of the major concepts, persons, and institutions that compose this political society.

In its broad sense, the term *"alim"* (pl. *ulama*) can be applied to individuals trained in any of the various branches of religious scholarship. The *ulama* hence comprise specialists in fields such as *tafsir* (Qur'anic interpretation), *sira* (biographical work on the Prophet), *kalam* (theology), and the collection and verification of *hadith*. In a more specific sense, the term *"ulama"* is also commonly used in reference to those invested with the capacity to engage matters of religious law. In this sense it also encompasses the more specific titles of *mufti, faqih,* and *qadi* detailed below.

While it was under the Abbasids that the *ulama* emerged as a fully developed social and professional class, it is certainly possible to identify persons engaged in aspects of religious scholarship from the *rashidun* period onward. Under the caliph Uthman, in particular, efforts were made to standardize the ordering of verses in the Qur'an and to begin the systematic preservation of reports (*hadith*) about the Prophet's life. *Hadith* science evolved into a complex discipline, involving the collection and categorization of thousands of narrative accounts relating to the Prophet Muhammad. Every person within the chain of transmission (*isnad*) of each *hadith,* all the way back to the individual who had actually witnessed what the Prophet had done or said, was subject to scrutiny in terms of their reputation and biography. Based partly on the strength of the *isnad* but also partly on the presence of corroborating reports, each *hadith* was assigned a grade indicating its reliability. Those with the strongest and most sound *isnad* received a grade of *sahih* ("genuine"), in contrast with those at the other end of the spectrum graded as *da'if* ("weak").[4] The early Abbasid period saw the publication of the two major authoritative collections of *sahih hadith,* those of Bukhari and Muslim.

The science of jurisprudence (*fiqh*) began to emerge during the late Umayyad period. One of the earliest and still most respected sources for legal methodology is the *Muwatta* (*The Trodden Path*) of Imam Malik, a Medinan scholar whose work joined that of three other scholars working between the early eighth and mid-ninth centuries (Abu Hanifa, al-Shafi'i, and Ibn Hanbal) to create four eponymous legal schools (*madhahib;* sing. *madhhab*) of Sunni Islam. By the late ninth century, Islamic jurisprudence had become a well-developed science and the *shari'ah* (literally, "the path") of the Qur'an codified as a living body of law. As *fiqh* became a discipline in its own right, a corps of theorists and technicians—the *fuqaha* ("jurists"; sing. *faqih*)—emerged as its chief architects. Working in tandem with other religious scholars, the jurisconsults created the *usul al-fiqh* (principles of jurisprudence), introducing important distinctions regarding various categories of law such as the division between matters of worship (*ibadat*) and issues of social normativity (*mu'amalat*).

▌ BOX 2.1 WHAT IS *SHARI'AH*?

Commonly translated as Islamic law, the term *shari'ah*—whose Arabic root refers to the idea of a "pathway"—refers in its broader sense to the moral and ethical system of the Islamic religion. There is no single, definitive account or source of *shari'ah*. Like all legal systems, its practice relies heavily on precedent. In the Sunni tradition, for example, there are four schools of legal thought, each of which approaches jurisprudential objectives and methodology slightly differently. What it means to apply or implement *shari'ah* in practical terms depends considerably on the matter at hand. With respect to certain issues—such as matters of family law (marriage, divorce, adoption, inheritance, etc.)—the Qur'an is very specific as to how these affairs are to be managed, and their codification into legal statutes is relatively straightforward, if not always uncontroversial. On other issues not directly addressed by revelation, Islamic scholars have had to rely on the traditions of the Prophet Muhammad when engaged in jurisprudence. Sometimes the Qur'an provides basic principles—such as the importance of deciding matters based on communal consensus (*ijma*)—and legal scholars are then left to divine how best to apply these precepts to actual situations and problems that arise.

The implementation and status of *shari'ah* law in contemporary Muslim societies and states is complex. While a few countries, such as Saudi Arabia and Iran, claim to have legal systems based entirely and exclusively on *shari'ah,* most other Muslim-majority countries that integrate aspects of religious law into their legal system do so through a division of competencies or parallel courts. In Malaysia, for example, there is a system of *shari'ah* courts whose jurisdiction is limited for the most part to matters of family law and personal status.

In Western societies, the idea of Islamic law frequently conjures up ideas of harsh punishments such as the stoning of adulterers and cutting off the hands of thieves. While there is body of statutes in the *shari'ah* focused on corporal punishment for certain kinds of criminal offense (known as the *hudud*), there are very few countries today where it is actually applied. Indeed, when Muslims are asked their understanding of *shari'ah* and which aspects of it they feel most comfortable with, there is an overwhelming tendency—as public opinion polling shows—to focus on family law (see the Pew Forum report listed below).

Further study

W. B. Hallaq, *An Introduction to Islamic Law*, Cambridge: Cambridge University Press, 2009.

R. W. Hefner (ed.), *Shari'a Politics: Islamic Law and Society in the Modern World*, Bloomington, IN: Indiana University Press, 2011.

M. H. Kamali, *Shari'ah Law: An Introduction*, Oxford: Oneworld, 2008.

Pew Forum, 'Beliefs About Sharia,' *The World's Muslims: Religion, Politics and Society*, Washington, DC: Pew Research Center, 2013, pp. 41–58.

With the completion of the great *hadith* collections and the legal treatises of the four great classical scholars, matters of jurisprudential deliberation came to be structured around four key sources of authority, as follows.

- *Qur'an*—as the literal word of God, the Qur'an was always the paramount source of authority. The discipline of Qur'anic exegesis (*tafsir*) emerged as particularly important in terms of debating the precise meaning of the Word and its implications for the daily lives of Muslims. Perhaps inevitably, there also ensued numerous debates regarding allegorical versus literal understandings of Qur'anic verse and the created versus eternal nature of the Qur'an.
- *Sunna*—second only to the Qur'an, the Prophet's tradition was regarded as a living model for the correct application of *shari'ah*. Certain of the *hadith* (the *hadith qudsi*) are assigned a status almost tantamount to that of the Qur'an insofar as they are regarded as the revelation-sourced knowledge that came to the Prophet in dreams, or which were rendered in his own words.
- *Ijma*—the "consensus" of the leading scholars of the age—is also considered a relatively safe grounding point for legal deliberation. The Qur'an exhorts Muslims to decide matters on the basis of the community's *ijma*—investing this notion with significant democratic potential. In practice, however, it came to refer only to the consensus of the learned jurisconsults.
- *Qiyas*—a term referring to the method of analogical deduction. When neither the Qur'an nor *sunna* is clear on a particular point of law, a legal scholar may deduce an opinion based on examples from an analogous situation involving similar core principles.

Another key concept in legal methodology, particularly prevalent during the years in which the critical mass of the *shari'ah* was assembled, was *ijtihad*—or the exercise of independent judgment and interpretation regarding legal matters. Confidence in *ijtihad* as a method more or less paralleled the fortunes of Mu'tazili philosophy, which relied in large measure on the power of reason. When Asharism began to question the dangers of rational knowledge, similar concern came to be raised about *ijtihad* as a basis for building the *shari'ah*. By the tenth century, a prevailing opinion emerged to the effect that *ijtihad* was no longer necessary and, moreover, was becoming increasingly dangerous by introducing various distortions (read: personal preferences) into the canon. This event became known as the closing of the gates to *ijtihad*. Numerous later scholars would debate the question of whether the gates were completely or permanently closed, and also the issue of who might hold the keys that could open them again.[5] For the time being, however, the law was now Law, and subsequent jurisprudential efforts were focused on the interpretation and application of existing *shari'ah* rather than on expanding its content.

As Islamic jurisprudence evolved, there emerged a clearer division of labor in terms of the various roles played by figures within the legal profession. In the early years of Islamic expansion, much in the way of legal interpretation and enforcement was left to the discretion of regional and local governors. As the bureaucracy expanded under the Umayyads, specialized positions were created to ensure that commerce was conducted in accordance with the *shari'ah* and also to enforce public virtue. The creation of an actual court system saw the appointment of the first *qadis* (judges). It is important to note that while the legal system was *shari'ah* based, religion was by no means the exclusive source of law. Considerable measures of customary law (*urf*) were incorporated into the statutes so long as they were compatible with the *shari'ah*. In addition to the aforementioned juristic class, it is also worth mentioning the role of the *mufti*. Literally this term refers to anyone possessing the credentials necessary for issuing *fatawa* (legal opinions). In many cases, however, the *mufti* became a quasi-official role and referred to the chief legal scholar of a given state.

Some clarification regarding the notion of the *fatwa* is also warranted, particularly given the confusion surrounding the meaning of this term that emerged at the time of the Rushdie Affair in the late 1980s, when it came to be understood in popular discourse as referring to a "death sentence." A *fatwa* (pl. *fatawa*) refers to a legal opinion as issued by a competent authority, usually an *alim* or *faqih*. Its content may be based on any of the four methodologies mentioned above, but a *fatwa* can also be the result of an act of *ijtihad*. Since a *fatwa* is nothing more than the opinion of a scholar, the strength of its influence is generally a function of the reputation of its promulgator and his skill in situating his reasoning within the mainstream of Islamic legal discourse. *Fatawa* are rarely binding and can usually be abrogated by subsequent acts of *ijtihad*. Religious scholars over the ages have frequently debated the question of just who is authorized to issue a *fatwa*. While most *muftis* generally possess a certain modicum of formal training in the legal sciences, there have been instances of individuals with little or no formal qualification issuing *fatawa* that entered into mainstream political discourse—such as Usama Bin Laden's 1998 "*fatwa*" declaring war on the United States. In this regard, *fatawa* and their ambiguous status have been the site and source of considerable Muslim political contention.

The social role and position of the *ulama* evolved alongside the increasingly expansive and complex Muslim state throughout the medieval period and into the Middle Ages. Under the early caliphs, the *ulama* were nothing more than a small cadre of specialists who had dedicated their lives to the collection and elucidation of religious knowledge. As a group of "learned men," they were consulted by the authorities on various matters, but did not yet constitute a discrete social milieu. It was the advent of jurisprudential science from the late Umayyad period onward that allowed the *ulama* to emerge as a distinctive professional class. In terms of the question of where the *ulama* fit within Muslim political society, it is worth remembering that part of the impulse behind the codification of the *shari'ah* was the perceived failings and irreligiosity of the Umayyad rulers. In this regard, the early *ulama* played a quasi-civil societal role in buttressing emerging forms of opposition politics. Subsequently, the Abbasids were careful to patronize religious scholarship and to keep certain *ulama* very close to them as something akin to official scholars of the state. When the caliph or his deputies required religious sanction for a particular policy decision, it was helpful to have jurists on hand who could articulate this justification in the language of *shari'ah*. Thus we can say that the relationship between the *ulama* and the state varied over time, witnessing both periods of official co-option, and also times when the *ulama* served as a mediating layer between the state and the concerns of popular society. Though generally hesitant directly to question the authority of the state for fear of prompting social disorder (*fitna*), many *ulama* did not hesitate to issue dissident *fatawa* when consulted by members of the public. Unsurprisingly, some of them found themselves out of favor with the authorities on occasion, and even spent periods of time in prison or entered exile abroad.

Muslim imperial bureaucracies produced, and soon came to rely on, their own self-sufficient legal systems. And what of the authority of the caliph himself? As we have already seen above, the Commander of the Faithful, while still vested with some religious authority as the chief enforcer of the *shari'ah*, evolved into more of a secular authority during the dynastic period. In some cases, the political sovereigns introduced their own parallel legal systems (the *mazalim* courts) that permitted the enforcement of royal ordinances and the prosecution of various matters outside the remit of personal status law, the one area where the jurisdiction of *shari'ah* went unquestioned. In summary, then, we can say that whereas early caliphs had direct experience of, and were hence better able to represent, Prophetic tradition, later holders of this office were alienated from the idea of the pious sovereign. The religious component of caliphal authority was certainly invoked when it was politically expedient to do so, but for the most part this was largely symbolic. It is hence safe to say that those present-day political movements in the Muslim world that seek to re-establish the caliphate have the *rashidun* rather than the late Abbasid model in mind.

Mystics and puritans: Sufis and Salafis in historical and contemporary perspective

Also central to the social fabric of Islam during the entire period under consideration were the various Sufi brotherhoods. Sufism, the mystical variant of Islam, has been in existence in organized form since shortly after the death of the Prophet. It emphasizes the emotive dimensions of religious experience, and the spiritual pursuit of divine love. Sufi religious practice involves a number of distinct forms of worship, the most common collective form of which is known as *dhikr* ("remembrance"), during which the attributes of God or short sections of Qur'an and *hadith* are meditatively intoned. In terms of its social organization, Sufism is composed of a vast array of brotherhoods (*tariqat,* "paths"), and it is generally through joining a *tariqa* that one embraces the Sufi path. There are often various levels of brotherhood affiliation available, but the standard model involves a disciple (*murid*) placing himself under the spiritual tutelage of a master (*sheikh*). By the twelfth century, the social significance of the Sufi brotherhoods had become undeniable. Many of the *tariqat*—such as the Naqshbandiyya and Qadiriyya—became thoroughly transnational, with branch lodges (*zawiyas*) in all major cities.

It is important to note that Sufism does not represent a sect or legal school. Rather, it constitutes a complementary mode of seeking religious knowledge and experience that is not, in and of itself, opposed to or incompatible with the *shari'ah* and other aspects of Islamic orthopraxis. Indeed, many of the early religious scholars admired the spiritual vitality of Sufis, and a great many of Islam's pre-eminent philosophers and orthodox jurists, such as al-Ghazali, were supporters—if not practitioners themselves—of Sufism. As we will see in the next chapter, major figures associated with modern Islamist movements have also been heavily influenced by Sufi thought and practice. Of further sociological significance is the fact that, in many settings, Sufism attracted mass followings among Muslims in search of spirituality but less inclined to inculcate themselves in the more formal normativity of the *shari'ah*. Certain manifestations of Sufi populism, such as the celebration of saintly birthdays and the visitation of graves, eventually attracted the ire of more conservative jurists, particularly modernist

exponents of the Hanbali school of jurisprudence, who regarded these practices as quasi-idolatrous. And yet figures such as Ibn Taymiyyah, an early
fourteenth-century Hanbali jurist much admired by today's Salafis (see
below) and other conservative scholars, was himself a member of at least
two *tariqat*—a fact that exemplifies the extent to which Sufism was embedded within the Islamic social order and thoroughly intertwined with
orthodox normativity. Sufi networks remain politically influential to this
day, and many have used the infrastructures and technologies of globalization to expand their capacity and effective reach.

It is common to contrast Sufism with another theological orientation in
Islam, namely Salafism. Salafis and Salafism—which represents an effort to
purify Islam of external and cultural influences and return to the model of
the Prophet and his earliest companions—are the subject of much discussion and debate today because many contemporary jihadists (see Chapter 7)
consider themselves to be Salafis, and also because Salafi political parties
rose to unexpected prominence in the aftermath of the 2011 Arab
Uprisings.

The term "Salafi" refers to the *salaf al-salih*, or "pious ancestors"—a designation for the companions of the Prophet Muhammad (the *sahaba*) and
the first three generations of Muslim scholars. In one sense, this is a generic
term, while in quite another it describes a more specific approach to jurisprudence and the core tenants of faith. So one may well encounter Muslims
who express their admiration for, and a desire to emulate, the model of the
salaf, without actually themselves being "Salafis." Salafis proper, or practitioners of "Salafism," are defined by their exclusive reliance on sources and
evidence from this earliest period of Islam. Later generations of Muslims
and Islamic scholars are believed to have introduced various innovations
that diverge from, and dilute, the purity of Islam. While there have always
been theological movements in Islam arguing for greater purity and fidelity
to the religion's earliest sources, Salafism as a distinct current of thought is
actually a relatively modern phenomenon. While there are certainly key
figures in the medieval period whom contemporary Salafis regard as major
points of reference—such as Ibn Taymiyya—Salafism did not come into its
own as a movement until the early twentieth century.

Strictly speaking, Salafism is a *manhaj*, or method, that describes a particular way of relating textual sources and religious knowledge to one's life.
Following, but also supplementing, Quintan Wiktorowicz's scheme, we can
identify six key features of the Salafi approach.[6]

- An emphasis on *tawhid* (divine oneness, monotheism) as the core and
  defining doctrine of Islam; *tawhid* should be reflected in every aspect
  of a Muslim's thought and practice—and most crucially with regard to
  worship. Even to give the appearance of worshipping anything or anyone other than God is tantamount to *shirk* (idolatry), and is a grave sin.

- A strict reliance on Qur'an and, with regard to *sunna,* on those *hadiths* whose authenticity is unquestioned. The various *sahih* (authentic) collections of *hadith* are the preferred source, and particularly those reports whose chain of transmission (*isnad*) are the strongest.
- Rejection of sectarianism and jurisprudential pluralism. For Salafis there is no such thing as different groups of Muslims or different interpretations of the religion. One either is, or is not, a true Muslim based on one's adherence to the Salafi path. Likewise, there is only Islam, and from it flows a single, true method. Therefore, the idea of the various schools of jurisprudence (*madhhabs*) in Sunni Islam is also rejected. In practice, however, much Salafi jurisprudence looks similar to the highly literalist Hanbali school.
- Following closely from this, a rejection of the jurisprudential practice of *taqlid*—or blind emulation of legal precedents. For a religious scholar simply to follow, in an unexamined manner, the lead of an earlier jurist is to avoid the obligation of making sure that a given ruling is in accordance with evidence and has been arrived at through the proper methodology. Salafi legal methodology can therefore be described as a form of constant *ijtihad* (independent judgment), but not in the sense of permitting individual or subjective interpretation. Rather, this sense of *ijtihad* refers to the scholar's obligation to perform due diligence by going directly to the sources.
- Rejection of *bid'a,* or "innovations" that distort the purity of the message and the method. Salafis believe that after the *salaf* generations, subsequent Muslims and Islamic scholars have adopted various forms of *bid'a* that caused them to stray from the proper path. Examples would include various Sufi rituals such as the visitation of graves or veneration of saint—both practices that Salafis would see as contravening the regulations of worship (*ibadat*) that stipulate God as the only object of worship. For scholars to engage in *taqlid* (see above) is seen as dangerous because it may lead them to reproduce some *bid'a* from an earlier precedent—hence the need to go directly to the sources.
- With regard to religious epistemology, Salafis reject forms of philosophy, practiced by those such as the Mutazilites and Asharites (see above), that permit the exercise of reason in determining the outward meaning of religion. Rather, one must rely exclusively on a strict and literal reading of direct revelation (Qur'an) and the direct example of the Prophet (*sunna*). To permit individual reason to enter the picture, Salafis believe, would be to introduce unconscious desires into one's understanding of Islam. Matters of *aqeeda* (creed or core tenants of faith) are therefore of great importance to Salafis.

Despite the strong aversion to emulation, contemporary Salafis hold a number of scholars in particularly high regard in terms of their contribution to the development of the Salafi method. These include figures such as the early fourteenth-century jurist Ibn Taymiyya, who they laud for his contributions in terms of reorienting Islamic legal practice towards the earliest sources and for his efforts to expunge from Islam various forms of *bid'a*—particularly practices associated with Sufism. Today one will also often see the terms "Salafi" and "Wahhabi" used interchangeably. While this is understandable since the two approaches share much in common, there are also important reasons to differentiate them. Wahhabism—which can be considered a variant of Salafism—takes its name from the eighteenth-century Arabian religious revivalist Muhammad Ibn Abdul Wahhab. Much influenced by the ideas of Ibn Taymiyya, Wahhab's main concerns related to the centrality of *tawhid* and the dangers posed to Islam by *bid'a*. His political alliance with the Saud family, and the fact that the Saudi religious establishment is founded on his teachings, have led Wahhabism to be strongly identified with the Saudi practice (and projection) of Islam. While sharing, as we have noted, much of the same doctrinal orientation as Salafis, Wahhabis have tended to emphasize and prioritize certain dimensions (*tawhid* and *bid'a*) over others. The public and social implications of Salafism have also been interpreted in very particular ways by Wahhabis. The social structure of Arabia, for example, led Wahhabi scholars to lay great emphasis on differentiating true believers from infidels in the name of justifying political expansion and the use of violence against other Muslims. This has led to an emphasis among Wahhabis on the practice of *takfir*—that is, declaring someone to be an infidel or an apostate from Islam. As we will see in Chapter 7, the concept of *takfir* has also been central to contemporary debates about *jihad*.

The Salafi/Wahhabi distinction is further confused by the fact that many of the most prominent Salafi scholars known and followed around the world are figures who spent part of most of their career within the Wahhabi religious establishment of Saudi Arabia. These include *ulama* such as the Albanian-Syrian scholar Muhammad Nasiruddin al-Albani (d. 1999), Muhammad ibn al-Uthaymeen (d. 2001), and Rabee' al-Madkhali (b. 1931). Some dissident Saudi figures such as Salman al-Audah (b. 1956) also have a global following in Salafi circles.

Another common source of confusion regarding Salafism, particularly when it comes to social and political movements, is the fact that the line of nineteenth-century religious reformers beginning with Jamal ad-Din al-Afghani, and which includes figures such as Muhammad Abduh and Rashid Rida—all of whom we will discuss below—are often described as the progenitors of the modern Salafi movement. If one looks at their ideas, particularly those of Abduh, who was the first to refer to his movement as Salafiyya, they seem anything but highly conservative and literalist—indeed, in many respects they appear relatively progressive. Abduh's idiom of Salafism, however, was rather different from that of those who we today call

Salafis. For him, the *salaf* symbolized the individual's effort to understand and practice Islam according to a living, active model and without resorting to the cloistered and arcane teachings of religious scholars. It was an injunction to bypass centuries of crusty tradition in the name of discerning religion's direct relevance to modern issues and predicaments. The *salaf,* for Abduh, were more of a metaphor for the idea that Muslims should have confidence in taking religion into their own hands—in much the same way as the Prophet's early companions were forced to do. A genealogy of today's Salafism does indeed lead back to Muhammad Abduh's movement, but only via several mediating figures who reoriented its trajectory in crucial ways. Rashid Rida (see Chapter 3), an Islamic political theorist and discipline of Abduh, is generally credited with outlining the idea of the modern Islamic state after the abolition of the caliphate in 1924—initially, interestingly, emphasizing the compatibility of the *shari'ah* with modern political norms. As he watched the growing and, to his mind, morally corrosive influence of secular nationalism take hold across Arab society, however, Rida sought refuge in the security of a highly conservative and literalist understanding of religion—adjusting the meaning and thrust of the Salafiyya movement accordingly. His ideas were taken up, developed, and further disseminated by figures such as Abu Ala Mawdudi and—most importantly—Sayyid Qutb. The latter, in particular, played a signal role in making the final conversion of Salafism into a doctrine of political activism and violent struggle.

It is important to note that Salafi religious doctrine does not, in and of itself, lead to political activism or radicalism. In fact, most Salafis today eschew politics altogether and deem it wholly inappropriate for religious scholars to become involved in activism, much less *jihad.* Thus, while all Salafis are intensely conservative and strict literalists in terms of their understanding of religion, they do not all espouse the active pursuit of Islamic political orders or encourage violence. Rather, Salafism represents a spectrum of thought and practice, with several distinctly identifiable positions within it. With regard to issues of social and political activism, we might postulate the existence of three forms of Salafism.

- *Salafi quietists*—emphasize the importance of individual adherence to proper thought, practice, and *shari'ah,* but reject the idea of actively pursuing an Islamic political order as a distinct religious duty (or even Islamically permissible) unto itself; to do so, in their mind, would lead one to emphasize the pursuit of worldly power at the expense of piety and religious obligation. The correct Islamic society will emerge when, through *tarbiya* (education), Muslims have collectively adopted the correct method. Most Salafis today fall into this category, and it is a tendency whose influence is growing in many Muslim settings, particularly those, such as in the West, where Muslims feel their religious identity to be under threat.

- *Salafi Islamists*—believe in the active pursuit of an Islamic political order defined in terms of the Salafi method. Violence may be a necessary part of this, but only under very specific conditions. This approach to Salafism developed in Saudi Arabia from the 1960s, when a number of intellectuals and scholars associated with the Muslim Brotherhood in Egypt (mostly followers of Sayyid Qutb) came to Saudi Arabia and began to teach in Saudi universities. It might therefore be regarded as a fusion of Wahhabi theology and the activist method of the MB. It became influential among a small but dedicated group of scholars and future activists who studied in the Kingdom. This was in stark contrast to the Saudi religious establishment, most of whose members were firmly in the quietist camp. More recently, we have seen a rebirth of Salafi Islamism in the form of Salafi groups participating in elections and mainstream politics. This phenomenon appeared first in countries such as Kuwait in the 1990s, and then a little later in places such as Yemen and Lebanon. The new Salafi Islamist trend was most clearly and dramatically visible in the wake of Egypt's 2011 revolution. A number of Salafi political parties—such as Hizb al-Nour, Hizb Al-Asala, Hizb al-Watan, and Hizb al-Benaa w'al Tanmia (the latter comprised of former jihadis)—become prominent players in Egypt's political transitional by winning over a quarter of the seats in the country's first post-Mubarak parliament.
- *Salafi jihadis*—combine the political imperatives of the Salafi Islamists with a conviction that contemporary circumstances make violent struggle an individual duty incumbent upon all Muslims (see section below on *jihad*). Quietism and the pursuit of societal transformation via political participation are both regarded as illegitimate—the former because it ignores what Salafi jihadis and Islamists see as a Qur'anic requirement for Muslims to actively and immediately implement the *shari'ah* by whatever means possible, and the latter because the willingness of Islamists to work within political systems defined and controlled by infidels is tantamount to recognizing the legitimacy of those regimes.

Much of the current focus on Salafi Islam has actually centered on the activities of a narrow group of Salafi jihadis and, to a lesser extent, Salafi Islamists. Thus it becomes important to differentiate between what we might see as mainstream Salafi religious doctrine—conservative and literalist in its religious orientation but not particularly active politically—and a thoroughly "political Salafism" wherein the doctrinal dimensions of the Salafi *manhaj* become vested with an activist impulse that seeks, through violence or otherwise, to replace infidel political orders with *shari'ah*-based models.

Some scholars have pointed to what appears to be a global resurgence in interest in Salafism today, particularly among young people. This phenomenon appears to be driven by two major factors: first, a perception that

Islam faces external threats from globalization and Western—particularly U.S.—culture, coupled with the idea that adherence to conservative Islam in the form of Salafism serves as a bulwark against such forces; and second, a sense that the fragmentation of religious authority in the Muslim world (itself a byproduct of globalization) has created considerable uncertainty about the locus of reliable, grounded religious knowledge. This trend does not appear to be limited to any particular region of the Muslim world— part of its potential significance lies precisely in the fact that it seems to be occurring in multiple and highly varied Muslim settings worldwide. Indeed, some observers today question whether Salafism might represent a "new global movement" in the Muslim world in ways that resonate with the debate on post-Islamism that we address in Chapter 8.[7]

We have spent some time outlining and clarifying these various aspects of Muslim political society, religious authority, and key theological movements in Islam, but not because they have come down to us unaltered since the Middle Ages. Rather, it is important for the reader to understand the genesis and evolution of religious authority in Islam—and its relationship to the state—in order to better appreciate the various elements of transformation and continuity that we see today. The caliphate may no longer exist, but we do find today a number of political authorities that stake their legitimacy on religious foundations (the Saudi royal family and the Islamic Republic of Iran). The *ulama* certainly continue to function as important intermediaries between the state and Muslim society. In the age of satellite TV, as we will see, their constituencies are potentially global. Sufi brotherhoods are thriving in the era of globalization, and debates regarding the role of *shari'ah* and the permissibility of *ijtihad* continue to be part of contemporary Muslim discourse. The politics may be different today, as may the structure of the political systems in which they play out, but many of the actors and key reference points remain the same.

BOX 2.2 THE SUNNI–SHI'I DIVIDE IN ISLAM

While the roots of the schism between Sunnis and Shi'a go back to the death of the Prophet Muhammad, the emergence of a fully formed political identity among Shi'a ("partisans" of Ali and the Prophet's family) is more accurately associated with the early Umayyad period. The martyrdom of Ali's son Hussain at the Battle of Kerbala in 680, an event commemorated by Shi'a each year on the Day of Ashura (the tenth of Muharram), is generally recognized as the event that crystallized a sense of dispossession among those whose political loyalties lay with the Prophet's family. What is generally called Sunni Islam also did not emerge until later. Sunni ("orthodox") Islam refers to followers of the consensus that developed among the early, great legal scholars—meaning that one could meaningfully speak of such a thing as Sunni Islam only after the middle of the ninth century.

Over the decades and centuries following the rise of dynastic politics in Islam, Shi'i theology and jurisprudence took on certain unique characteristics, while continuing to share a great deal with the Sunni core (including the Qur'an and many of the most important collections of *hadith*). The Ja'fari legal school, for example, emerged in the eighth century as the central jurisprudential reference point for the Shi'i tradition, and a strong Sufi ("mystical") path also developed within Shi'ism. Members of the community, however, found themselves viewed with increasing suspicion and tended to live apart from Sunnis, or to hide their religious identities (*taqiya*) in order to avoid being persecuted for holding "heterodox" views. Certain Shi'i political groups did eventually enjoy better fortunes, going on to found a number of important regional empires such as the *Fatimids* in Egypt (910–1171) and the *Safavids* in Persia (1501–1736), the precursor to modern Iran.

The Shi'i tradition operates with a conception of religious authority that differs significantly from the Sunni variant—and this can be seen to have important political implications. In terms of the overall leadership of the community, Shi'a do not recognize the institution of the caliphate. For them, the *imamate,* a line of spiritual leaders that traces back through Ali, serves an analogous but distinct function. This reflects a Shi'a belief that the qualities of spiritual leadership are vested in the descendants of the Prophet. Where Sunnis tend to regard authority as residing within a canonical textual tradition (hence the emphasis on legal orthodoxy), Shi'a have tended to emphasize the embodied authority of a living spiritual guide. Hence the presence in Shi'i Islam of something more closely resembling a formal clergy, and the tendency for many observant Shi'a to choose and follow the jurisprudential practice of a particular living cleric.

Within Shi'i Islam, one finds multiple subdivisions. The vast majority (approximately 80 percent) of the world's Shi'a belong to the "Twelver" branch, so-called because they recognize twelve *imams.* The twelfth or "Hidden Imam" is believed to be in a state of spiritual occultation, destined to return one day in the form of the Mahdi—a redeemer figure. Other important branches are the "Seveners" or Ismailis and the "Fiver" Zaidis. The Druze and Alawis, religious communities found in Syria and

Lebanon, regard themselves as rooted in Shi'ism, but some followers of mainstream Shi'i branches dispute this.

Shi'a today constitute approximately 10 to 15 percent of the world's Muslim population, or 130 to 195 million. Over half are to be found in two countries, Iran (90 percent of the population) and Iraq (around 60 percent of the population), with other significant communities to be found in Lebanon, India, Pakistan, Bangladesh, Afghanistan, Azerbaijan, and many of the Arab Gulf Sheikhdoms (Bahrain, Saudi Arabia, Kuwait, Qatar, and the United Arab Emirates, UAE). Significant pockets also exist throughout the Central Asian states of the former Soviet Union, Turkey, and Yemen.

While Sunni–Shi'i tensions have been part of the politics of state formation in the Middle East for many decades now (see, for example, the case of Saudi Arabia in Chapter 5), the upsurge in sectarian tensions in Iraq in the aftermath of the U.S.-led war to topple Saddam Hussein has led some to speculate about the possibility of a widespread "Shi'a revival" throughout the region.[8]

More recently, some observers have called attention to an apparent rise in sectarianism following in the wake of the Arab Uprisings of 2011. In this analysis, the combination of regime changes and direct challenges to the legitimacy of longstanding incumbents in a number of countries throughout the Arab world have removed an "authoritarian overlay" that permits sub-national groups—such as sectarian identities—to rise to the fore. The core dynamic here resembles the "Balkanization" process that occurred in Southeastern Europe with the dissolution of Yugoslavia. This effect is particularly pronounced in those contexts, such as Bahrain and Iraq in aftermath of Saddam, where a Sunni minority has ruled over a Shi'i majority. In the case of Syria, the equation is reversed, with Alawis—representing about 11 percent of the country's population and led by the Assad regime—ruling over a Sunni majority. Amidst ongoing volatility in a number of countries, Iran has sought to stoke sectarian tensions to its own advantage.

THE GUNPOWDER EMPIRES AND EUROPE'S RISE

While one might be tempted to consider Islam down for the count with the fall of the Abbasid empire in 1258, to do so would be to ignore the extent to which the Islamic world had by then far exceeded the political boundaries of any sovereign entity. This can be nicely illustrated by shifting our lens southward for a moment. While the weak central state was being plundered by foreign invaders, the Indian Ocean was emerging as a vibrant space of commercial and intellectual exchange. Although not all of the countries and ports involved were part of a centralized Islamic empire, Muslim traders and itinerant scholars were the animating force behind a cosmopolitan system stretching from East Africa to Southern Arabia and then across to India, China, and the Malay peninsula. The next three centuries would see the rise of new Muslim empires in Persia, India, and—via South Asian and Yemeni traders—the spread of Islam and the creation of Muslim kingdoms throughout the archipelagos of Southeast Asia. From the early fourteenth century, Islam also began to find new lands in sub-Saharan Africa, reaching into Mali and down into modern-day Nigeria. Centralized political control may have vanished, but the *umma,* the "community of believers," had never been more expansive.

Three dynasties from this period are of particular significance. Commonly referred to as the Islamic "gunpowder empires" due to the role military technology played in ensuring their pre-eminence, these are the polities via which the Muslim world eventually encountered political modernity in the form of European imperialism.[9] These are the Safavid Empire (1501–1736), roughly coterminous with—and an important precursor to—modern Iran; the Mughal Empire in the Indian subcontinent (1526–1857); and one that we consider in some detail, the Ottoman Empire (1300–1922), which, at the height of its power ruled Asia Minor, Southeastern Europe from the Balkans across to the Caucuses, the North African coast, Iraq and the Levant, and the western coast of Arabia.

A case study, for the most part, in the successful integration and administration of a highly diverse population, the Ottoman Empire had rather humble beginnings. Born from several Anatolian tribal cantons sandwiched between the Seljuqs and Mongols, the ethnically Turkic Ottomans (named for the dynasty's founder, Osman—a Turkic rendering of the Arabic name Uthman) proved themselves highly adept at managing rapid expansion through the creation of a governmental system capable of matching pace with the empire's growth. In 1453 the Ottomans under Mehmet II conquered Constantinople from the Byzantines, renamed it Istanbul, and made it their capital for almost the next half millennium. Making extensive use of foreign and non-Muslim administrative expertise, the Ottomans created a bureaucracy unlike any other the Muslim world had ever seen. As a military state, the empire relied heavily on Janissaries and the *devshirmeh,* a slave-soldier institution reminiscent of the Mamluks under the Abbasids, whose ranks tended to be recruited from non-Muslim lands, particularly Southeastern Europe.

From 1517, Ottoman sultans began to claim for themselves the title of caliph, and by the time the empire reached its zenith in the late seventeenth

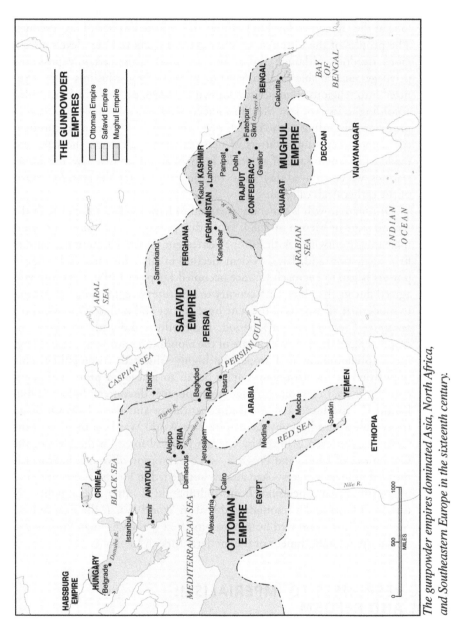

The gunpowder empires dominated Asia, North Africa, and Southeastern Europe in the sixteenth century.

Map 2.2 The gunpowder empires

century, Istanbul's sovereign had generally come to be recognized as the pre-eminent political authority in the Muslim world. Using a form of subsidiary governance, the Ottomans relied on a system of provincial governors to rule their territories. These local vassals were granted significant autonomy so long as they remained loyal to Istanbul and remitted sufficient tax revenues. The peoples of the Ottoman empires generally enjoyed high levels of religious freedom, although those who accepted Islam certainly possessed privileges unavailable to non-Muslim subjects. Non-Muslims were organized into religious communities known as *millets,* each of which was ruled according to its own law. Muslim subjects were generally subject to *shari'ah* provisions according to the Hanafi rite—the official Ottoman jurisprudential school—regarding matters of personal status, although the state also made wide-ranging use of a parallel body of administrative law, the *qanun* statutes, which enjoyed their own court institutions (cf. the *mazalim* courts of the earlier Arab caliphs).

Ottoman growth is generally regarded to have reached its apex with the second siege of Vienna in 1683. From that point onward, the empire grew increasingly entwined with Europe's emergent imperial ambitions. Sensing first stagnation and, later, evident decline in their fortunes as European powers began to encroach (France occupied Egypt in 1798), the Ottomans agreed during the nineteenth century to institute sweeping political reforms to modernize all aspects of the state bureaucracy and military. Known as the *tanzimat* ("reorganization") period, these efforts did little to check the empire's rapid decline. Well aware of the republican sentiments now emerging as predominant in Europe, the highly educated, cosmopolitan core population of the Ottoman empire began to take on a proto-nationalist consciousness. In response to widespread popular discontent, Sultan Abdulhamid II introduced a short-lived constitution and Basic Law. Ottoman treaty obligations brought the empire into World War I on the side of the Germans, but even before this, internal political forces in the form of the Committee of Union and Progress—an organization of young, nationalist-minded military officers—had already succeeded in forcing a second round of constitutional concessions from Abdulhamid II. After several politically turbulent years and a resounding defeat in World War I, the final Sultan, Mehmet VI, was removed from power in 1922 as the Ottoman Empire dissolved upon establishment of the modern Turkish Republic.

ISLAMIC RESPONSES TO IMPERIALISM: REVIVAL AND REFORM

The Ottomans were not the only world power on the rise from the sixteenth century. Europe, now fully emerged from the cocoon of Medievalism, was rapidly gaining in political, economic, and technological strength. The year

1492 marked both the date of Columbus' landing in the New World, and the Spanish crown's reconquest of the Iberian peninsula with the fall of the last Muslim rulers in Granada. Over the next 300 years, the Spanish would be joined by the Portuguese, the Dutch, the French, and the British as seafaring powers in search of new lands for crown and market. Britain developed extensive interests in the New World from as early as the fifteenth century, but did not undertake significant colonial expansion in the Muslim world until representatives of the British East India Company tangled with Mughal rulers in the mid-1700s on their way to establishing British imperial suzerainty over the entire subcontinent. A brief and ultimately unsuccessful foray by the French into Egypt at the end of that century marked the beginning of French interest in the Muslim heartland, culminating in French rule in Algeria, and significant colonies and commercial interests in both West Africa and the Levant. The British occupied Egypt from 1882, and by the time her overseas holdings reached their zenith, fully one-quarter of the world's population lived under British colonial rule.

How did Muslim thinkers and activists respond to the growing encroachment on their lands by foreign powers? In order to understand the Muslim response to Europe's rise, we need to gain an understanding of two central currents prevalent in Islamic thought from the second half of the eighteenth century: the movements commonly known as *revivalism* and *reformism*. While it is fair to say that the first of these was inwardly focused and the latter more oriented toward external challenges, they can be read collectively as an evolving Muslim response to Islam's perceived decline and the rise of Europe.

Islamic revivalism

Manifestations of what came to be known as the revivalist or renewalist (*tajdidi*) trend were visible from the mid-eighteenth century in settings as diverse as India, Nigeria, Sudan, and central Arabia. We focus here on revivalism in the latter context, as the figure with whom it is most commonly identified continues to animate Islamist thought and Muslim politics today. Muhammad Ibn Abdul Wahhab (1703–92) was a pious religious reformer active in the central heartland of the Arabian peninsula in the middle of the eighteenth century. While it would be a stretch to describe Ibn Abdul Wahhab as a cosmopolitan in terms of the breadth of his engagement with the world beyond central Arabia, he was certainly keenly aware of the predicament facing Muslims throughout the *umma,* and also had some very clear ideas about what was to be done about it. He developed a reputation for preaching a fairly austere Islam premised on the need to return to the model and practices of the Prophet Muhammad and the immediate generations that followed him. This emphasis on the early pious companions, the *salaf al-salih,* has led later movements modeled on this aspect of Ibn Abdul Wahhab's teachings to be labeled *Salafi*—the standard orientation of much of the religious establishment in present-day Saudi Arabia.

Such prescriptions were hence reflective of how Ibn Abdul Wahhab viewed the ills of Islam. To his thinking, the Muslim world had fallen into decline because Muslims had strayed away from the core teachings and practices of the faith. Ibn Abdul Wahhab had particular concern about the prevalence of what he saw as deviant practices associated with Sufi mysticism. Labeling these activities, such as the worshiping of saints, as dangerous forms of *bid'a* ("innovation"), Ibn Abdul Wahhab sought to purify Islam and return it to its original essence through an intense and often very literal engagement with the original sources and the early companions of the Prophet. It is this approach that later came to be called Islamic Revivalism, a trend that represents an important precursor of what eventually in the twentieth century evolved into the Salafi movement (see above).

The central concept in his teaching was that of *tawhid,* referring to monotheism or the oneness of God, a theme elaborated in his key work *Kitab al-Tawhid* (*The Book of Divine Unity*). To Ibn Abdul Wahhab, praying for saintly intercession and visiting graves seemed too close to idolatry, and these actions represented everything that was wrong with Islam. The rejuvenation of Islam was to be achieved through a return to the universal core teachings, free from the distorting influences of sociocultural innovation. We know that Ibn Abdul Wahhab spent some time in Basra in present-day Iraq, where he encountered and debated with other leading religious scholars. It is here that translation of his ideas into a political program began in earnest. Returning to Arabia, he formed an alliance with Muhammad Ibn Saud (the direct forebear of Saudi Arabia's present kings), and with the military support of the latter undertook a campaign to spread the message of pious reform across the Arabian peninsula. Although Ibn Abdul Wahhab's teachings did not initially find widespread purchase beyond the frontiers of Arabia, his ideas have formed an important reference point for successive generations of the Islamist political project—not least among contemporary advocates of Islamic radicalism such as Usama Bin Laden and Ayman al-Zawahiri.

Islamic reformism

In contrast to Ibn Abdul Wahhab, Jamal al-Din al-Afghani (1839–97) was thoroughly in tune with the latest trends emanating from a wide variety of intellectual milieu. Where the former's worldview was shaped somewhat in the abstract in the relatively isolated setting of central Arabia (an area not under Ottoman or any other kind of foreign rule), Afghani theorized the Muslim condition through a direct engagement with the reality of colonial occupation. His biography is particularly telling in this regard. Afghani was born in Persia and lived at various points throughout his life in India, Egypt, Turkey, and even Europe. An itinerant scholar-activist *par excellence,* Afghani moved from setting to setting, seeking each time to identify and rally a new generation of socially mobile Muslims around the cause of religious reform. In order to understand how the notion of Islamic reform figured in Afghani's analysis, it is necessary to look first at how he viewed the current state of the Muslim world *vis-à-vis* the West. The most concise statement of his thinking in this regard is contained in a famous essay entitled "An Islamic Response to Imperialism."

Afghani begins by seeking to decouple the direct agents of foreign occupation (e.g. Britain, France) from that which he understands to be the enabling force behind imperial power, namely superior military technology. He refutes the notion that any given country or culture can meaningfully lay exclusive claim to scientific capacity. Afghani implies instead that at different historical junctures, the center of world scientific production has varied, noting that science "is continually changing capitals." For him, the Muslim world in the tenth to twelfth centuries constituted the hub of global scientific innovation. This setting, for him, has simply changed with time, and with it, the locus of geopolitical hegemony. He is not, however, a technological determinist. Science and technology are only so good as the *philosophy* that underpins them, for "community without the spirit of philosophy [can]not deduce conclusions from ... sciences." Indeed, for Afghani, philosophy must precede and lead to science in order for the significance of the latter to be properly understood and responsibly deployed:

> The first Muslims had no science, but, thanks to the Islamic religion, a philosophic spirit arose among them, and owing to that philosophic spirit they began to discuss the general affairs of the world and human necessities. This was why they acquired in a short time all the sciences with particular subjects that they translated from the Syriac, Persian, and Greek into the Arabic language ...[10]

He goes on to decry the present state of intellectual output in the Muslim world, and herein lies the crux of his internal critique of Islam. Afghani is concerned that the early philosophical spirit of Islam had been abandoned over the centuries as the moral principles of the religion became codified as rigidly dogmatic jurisprudence. Present-day scholars of Islam, in his view, had become intellectually stagnant through their unreflective and uncritical use of medieval models and frameworks of moral philosophy. He elaborates:

> The science of principles consists of the philosophy of the *Shari'a,* or *philosophy of law.* In it are explained the truth regarding right and

wrong, benefit and loss, and the cause for the promulgation of laws. Certainly, a person who studies this science should be capable of establishing laws and enforcing civilization. However, we see that those who study this science among the Muslims are deprived of understanding of the benefits of laws, the rules of civilization, and the reform of the world.[11]

It is here that Afghani reveals himself to be most sharply at odds with Ibn Abdul Wahhab. Where the latter seeks to rescue Islam from its doldrums by emphasizing a literalist reading of a specific and narrow range of religious sources, Afghani equates civilizational strength with having a dynamic orientation towards knowledge. We should note, however, that his prescription is not simply one that exhorts Muslims to expend more energy studying science and technology. He notes in the essay, for example, that while the Khedive (the Ottoman governor) of Egypt had undertaken considerable educational reform and placed an emphasis on the empirical sciences, the lack of philosophical inquiry within the educational system had rendered pointless the mere acquisition of technical knowledge. Afghani's goal then is to reform Islamic thought and scholarship so as to reinfuse it with what he sees as an originary spirit of philosophical inquiry. According to Afghani, it is not the case that Muslims were engaged in deviant behaviors that distracted from the core teachings of their religion (as per Ibn Abdul Wahhab), but rather that they had lost the will and capacity to engage in original inquiry and critical thinking.

Also crucial to bear in mind is that, for Afghani, this project of Islamic intellectual reinvigoration possessed a distinctly political valence insofar as it was understood to constitute a path out of colonial rule. The political program to which it was attached went under the mantle of "pan-Islam" and deliberately invoked notions such as the *umma* rather than narrower, nationalist sentiments. Through appeals to Muslim unity, Afghani hoped to mobilize the best and brightest of his day around a vision of Islamic emancipation—but emancipation both from foreign rule and from internal religious stagnation. Afghani's political activities took him to all of the major Muslim metropoles, and he was perhaps the first modern Islamic activist to use Europe as a base for publishing and distributing propaganda materials. Indeed, it was the increased literacy rates in Muslim lands from the early nineteenth century that had, in part, made Afghani's mode of activism and social mobilization even possible. His tenure in several settings was short as, more often than not, he quickly fell out of favor with local rulers who tended to perceive his ideas as potentially threatening to their authority. This happened in Egypt, Iran, and eventually within the court of the Ottoman sultan himself.

Figure 2.1 Jamal al-Din al-Afghani, anti-colonial activist and Islamic reformist

During his time in Egypt, Afghani exerted considerable influence on the intellectual formation and social consciousness of several figures who would later figure prominently in reformist circles. Perhaps the most important of these was Muhammad Abduh (1849–1905), one of the founders of the modernist movement in Islam. His was a varied career that included political activism, journalism, educational reform, and jurisprudence—eventually rising to the rank of Egypt's Grand Mufti. Abduh is strongly associated with social innovations such as the introduction of universal education for all Egyptians irrespective of gender. As a religious intellectual, he argued for the contemporary relevance of *ijtihad* (Afghani's influence was clear here) and the importance of returning to the spirit of the *salaf,* the Prophet's earliest companions. Abduh was actually the founder of the modern Salafiyya movement, but his understanding of what this entailed differed considerably from the approaches both of Ibn Abdul Wahhab a century and a half before him, and of later exponents of Salafism from Hassan al-Banna onward. For Abduh, the *salaf* provided a model for how to make Qur'anic normativity—to which the pious companions had had direct access, unadulterated by centuries of distortion and corruption—relevant to contemporary social challenges through the creative and judicious exercise of reason and human ingenuity. It was an approach that would also inspire later proponents of reformist thought, such as the Pakistani scholar Fazlur Rahman, who drew a sharp distinction between the purity of "normative Islam" and the miscegenation of "historical Islam."[12]

Despite his wide-reaching influence, Afghani's pan-Islamic vision never came to fruition. The parallel and competing project of nationalism captured the popular imagination far more effectively. The emergent middle classes of Alexandria and Cairo, for example, found it far easier to rally around the banner of Egyptian national self-determination than to define their political identities in concert with distant co-religionists in India, West Africa, and Southeast Asia: a politically independent Egypt was a tangible goal, the *umma* less so. Although the United States president had not intended it for the colonized world, the climate of post-World War I Wilsonian international liberalism—and the notion of national self-determination in particular—drifted over to the Middle East and India. It animated anticolonial movements that now began increasingly to define themselves in nationalist terms: Sa'ad Zaghlul and the Wafd Party in Egypt, for example, or the Indian National Congress (and, later, Muhammad Ali Jinnah's All India Muslim League)—and, of course, the Young Turks at the very core of the Ottoman Empire.

Aspirations for a pan-ethnic state in the Arab territories of the Ottoman Empire dissipated when it became clear after World War I that Britain and France continued to harbor designs in the central Middle East. The British put nominally independent rulers on the thrones of Egypt and Iraq, but in effective terms their political control in these countries continued through World War II, and similarly in the mandate territories (established by the new League of Nations) of Palestine and Transjordan alongside renewed French influence in Syria and Lebanon. The one entirely new polity to appear in the Middle East at this time—aside from the new Turkish Republic—was Saudi Arabia (see Chapter 5), founded in 1932 by the Nejdi (central Arabian) prince Abdul Aziz Ibn Saud, who managed to unify disparate tribal provinces into a minimally cohesive kingdom. With the abolition of the caliphate in 1924, Islamic political thought was plunged into a crisis. This period represented the first time since the Prophet's death that the Muslim world was without a symbolic religio-political figurehead. The crisis of the caliphate prompted considerable debate among Muslim intellectuals (see Chapter 3). Some argued for the necessity of this institution, whereas others found it largely superfluous to the modern world.

Although various forms of pro-caliphate activism occurred during the inter-war years—such as the emergence of the Khilafa Movement in India and the various Islamic Congresses sponsored by Egypt—it never gathered sufficient political momentum against the rising tide of nationalism.

In the next chapter we examine the process of state formation in the Muslim world, and the emergence of Islamism as a political project in the context of the modern system of nation-states. Of particular interest are the interplay between societal forces, political elites and ideologies, and the question of wider geopolitical impacts on contemporary Muslim politics.

NOTES

1 Unless otherwise specified, the general treatment of Islamic political history contained in this chapter is based on a synthesis of the following standard sources: M. Hodgson, *The Venture of Islam: Conscience and History in a World Civilization,* vols 1–3, Chicago, IL: University of Chicago Press, 1974; I. Lapidus, *A History of Islamic Societies,* 2nd edn, Cambridge: Cambridge University Press, 2002; A. Hourani, *A History of the Arab Peoples,* New York: Warner Books, 1991.

2 J. Berkey, *The Formation of Islam: Religion and Society in the Near East, 600–1800,* Cambridge: Cambridge University Press, 2003.

3 Lapidus, op. cit., p. 36; W. Mandelung, *The Succession to Muhammad: A Study of the Early Caliphate,* Cambridge: Cambridge University Press, 1997.

4 M. Siddiqi, *Hadith Literature: Its Origins, Development & Special Features,* Cambridge: Islamic Texts Society, 1996, p. 109.

5 W. Hallaq, "Was the Gate of Ijtihad Closed?," *International Journal of Middle Eastern Studies 16,* no. 1, 1984, pp. 3–41.

6 Q. Wiktorowicz, "The Salafi Movement: Violence and Fragmentation of Community," in M. Cooke, B. Lawrence (eds), *Muslim Networks from Hajj to Hip Hop,* Chapel Hill, NC: University of North Carolina Press, 2005, pp. 211–213.

7 R. Meijer (ed.), *Global Salafism: Islam's New Religious Movement,* New York: Columbia University Press, 2009.

8 V. Nasr, *The Shi'a Revival: How Conflicts Within Islam Will Shape the Future,* New York: Norton, 2006.

9 Hodgson, op. cit.

10 S. Afghani, "An Islamic Response to Imperialism," in J. Donahue, J. Esposito (eds), *Islam in Transition: Muslim Perspectives,* New York: Oxford University Press, 1982, p. 18.

11 Ibid.

12 F. Rahman, *Islam & Modernity: The Transformation of an Intellectual Tradition,* Chicago, IL: University of Chicago Press, 1984.

CHAPTER 3

State formation and the making of Islamism

With the collapse of the Ottoman Empire, and a rising tide of anti-colonial sentiment throughout most Muslim-majority lands under European control (see Map 3.1), the stage was set for a debate between two (seemingly) distinct and incompatible approaches to Muslim political independence: a system of Islamic political universalism, represented by a renewed caliphate; or the nationalist option, which held language, territory, and shared history as the proper foundations of a political order. Various leading scholars and activists debated the merits of these two options, and some also proposed models that sought to combine elements of each. Read together, the ideas of these thinkers—figures such as Rashid Rida, Ali Abd al-Raziq, Abu'l-A'la Mawdudi, and Hassan al-Banna—provide us with a clear sense of how Islamic response to the Western liberal order evolved over the first half of the twentieth century. Understanding the complex interplay of Islam and secular nationalism in three core Muslim states, Turkey, Egypt, and Pakistan, also helps to set the stage for explaining later instances of Islamic revivalism. This is the period that saw the establishment of the prototypical modern Islamist movement in the form of the Muslim Brotherhood in Egypt. Highly influential in terms of later developments, its formation, evolution, ideology, and political role are worth considering in some detail before sketching out the general course of Islamism over the remainder of the twentieth century.

MODERN STATES IN THE MUSLIM WORLD

The shape of the international order changed significantly in the half-century following World War I. With European empires dissolving into constituent nation-states and new states forming in previously colonized territories, the international system of sovereign states expanded considerably—particularly once the process of decolonization gathered pace after World War II. In the early twentieth century, there were only 50 or so sovereign states in the world. By the end of decolonization, that number had more than tripled. The formation of modern states in the Muslim world must be understood as part and parcel of this transformation. In the first instance, this shift represented a phenomenal rise in popular support for the doctrine of nationalism, a project that was soon co-opted by political elites in much of what came to be known as the Third World or the developing world.

The debate over nationalism took on various forms in different parts of the Muslim world, reflecting the diverse political conditions, histories, and power arrangements under which Muslim communities were living at the time. In the Turkish Republic, the successor state to the Ottoman Empire, Mustapha Kemal Ataturk instituted a veritable cultural revolution, seeking as much as possible to distance the new republic from its Ottoman heritage through an emphasis on rapid modernization and intensely secular norms. In the Arab Middle East, however, this shift played out initially as an exchange between advocates of political futures based on Islam, and those advocating the primacy of nationalist arrangements. As nation-states consolidated in the Arab world, this evolved into a debate between political forces seeking to establish an Islamic version of the nation-state, and those—mainly social and political elites—who grounded their legitimacy in discourses of Arab nationalism. In the Indian subcontinent, which at the time was the most populous Muslim country in the world—initial concerns about the un-Islamic character of nationalism gave way to more pressing worries about the community's future in a Hindu-dominated India. This resulted in calls for the establishment of a separate homeland for Muslims, with Islam itself transformed into a form of nationalism.

Theorists of the post-caliphate order: Rashid Rida and Ali Abd al-Raziq

The Arab response to the abolition of the caliphate is best illustrated through the contrasting approaches of Rashid Rida and Ali Abd al-Raziq, two leading intellectuals working in Egypt during the interwar years. These two offer an interesting comparison because they also represent

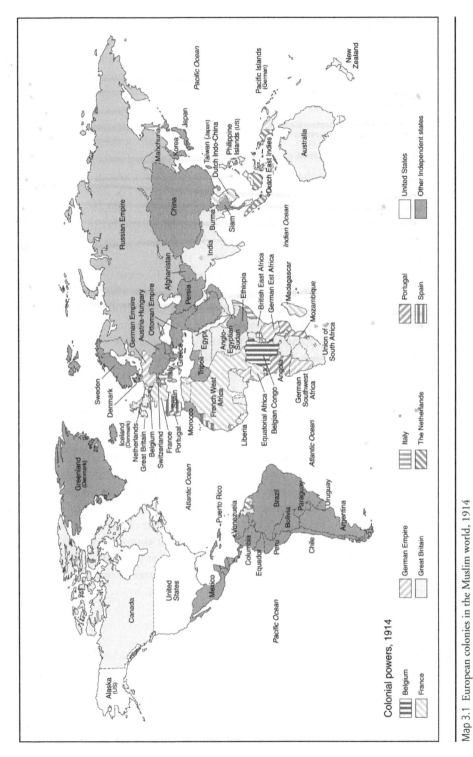

Map 3.1 European colonies in the Muslim world, 1914

Source: Peter Mandaville, *Global Political Islam*, London: Routledge, 2007 (p. 50) figures whose early thinking was strongly influenced by Jamal al-Din al-Afghani and the Salafiyya movement of Muhammad Abduh. As we will see, however, each of them took this project in rather different directions as regards Islam's political priorities. Hailing originally from Tripoli in modern-day Lebanon, Rashid Rida (1865–1935) was strongly influenced by Muhammad Abduh's reformist ideas, to which he was exposed while studying a combination of modern subjects alongside the traditional course of Islamic sciences. He later moved to Cairo and worked with Abduh to begin publishing what would become the Salafiyya movement's primary print forum, *Al-Manar* (*The Beacon*). Rida is best known for a major work of political theory, *The Caliphate, or the Supreme Imamate* (1923), published just before the crisis prompted by the abolition of the caliphate by Mustapha Kemal in 1924. After making a case for the necessity of the caliphate through his reading of the classical sources, Rida goes on in his text to outline the role of this institution throughout Islamic history. While *The Caliphate* is framed as an argument for the desirability, in theory, of a renewed caliphate, it ultimately proves itself to be a work of political realism by recognizing that prevailing conditions simply did not permit its rejuvenation. Instead, Rida reconciled himself to the notion of an Islamic order within the framework of the nation-state.[1] Rida remained convinced, however, of the importance of a strong relationship between the *ulama*—as keepers of the tradition and the law—and the political authorities. As the forces of secular modernism became more firmly entrenched amongst Egyptian political elites between the wars, Rashid Rida became increasingly conservative and literalist in terms of his understanding of the central impulse behind the Salafiyya movement. Where Abduh had advocated a general spirit of intellectual rejuvenation inspired by the model of the Prophet's early companions, Rida veered in his later life towards a more constrained normativity based exclusively on the Qur'an and the traditions of the Prophet and his companions. In this regard, his eventual orientation is closer to the approach espoused by contemporary groups that go under the mantle of Salafism (see Chapter 2).

The stance taken by Ali Abd al-Raziq in this debate could not have been more different from that of Rashid Rida, despite the fact that they both considered themselves followers of Afghani and Abduh. Abd al-Raziq, interestingly enough, had undergone an even more traditional religious education than Rida. As a graduate of Cairo's Al-Azhar, the pre-eminent institution of Sunni learning in the Arab world and a bastion of the traditional *ulama,* his formal credentials as a scholar of Islamic law and tradition were unquestionable. Imagine, then, the sensation created by the publication of his 1925 text *Al-Islam wa usul al-hukm* (*Islam and the Principles of Governance*)—partly a response to Rashid Rida—whose core point was to deny not only the necessity, but even the authorization for a caliphate in the canonical sources of Islam. Abd al-Raziq's case was built on two key points—first, that nowhere in the Qur'an or *hadith* is anything like an institutionalized caliphate mentioned; second, that throughout history the caliphate, more often than not, was maintained and legitimized primarily through force and by threat of discord should it fall, rather than in terms of its intrinsic good. So unconventional a view, which flew in the face of centuries of scholarly consensus, would already have been enough to ensure Abd al-Raziq's notoriety within the religious establishment. He might have denied the need for a caliph but then gone on to argue for the necessity of a national state organized according to Islamic law. Instead, he went even further and suggested that, while a government of some sort is indeed necessary, there is nothing in Islamic sources that requires the state to conform to any particular model. For Abd al-Raziq, any form of government that did not violate the core principles of Islam was acceptable.[2] There was for him no intrinsic relationship between religion and state. In the eyes of many, with this latter position Abd al-Raziq had placed himself firmly within the realm of the secular, and in that regard had strayed into territory where even the most reform-minded religious scholars could not follow. Indeed, in the wake of *Al-Islam wa usul al-hukm*, Ali Abd al-Raziq was removed from his position as a judge. It is clear that for him the reformist impulse behind the Salafiyya movement was iconoclastic in nature. It made possible calling into question even some of the most taken-for-granted elements of Islamic political thought and history. If one is tempted to wonder who, Rida or Abd al-Raziq, was closer to the ideals of the Salafiyya as originally promulgated by Muhammad Abduh, it is probably safe to say that both ended up espousing extremes with which the movement's founder would likely have been uncomfortable. For Abduh, the model of the *salaf* was meant to provide a set of ideational resources and inspiration rather than, as Rida ended up arguing, the sole correct source of social morality. On the other hand, Abduh was not a revolutionary in terms of his political theory, and Abd al-Raziq's denial of the caliphate would likely have struck his mentor as a step too far in this direction.

The intellectual foment in the wake of the abolished caliphate also saw some analogous political organization in the form of a number of Muslim Congresses that were convened between 1924 and 1931.[3] Ostensibly attempts by senior Muslim scholars and leaders from across the *umma* to discuss Islamic issues and determine a solution to the predicament of Muslim leadership, these meetings were mostly opportunities for political aspirants to jockey for position. After Kemal abolished the caliphate in 1924, the Hashemite emir of western Arabia, Sharif Hussein Ibn Ali, had proclaimed himself caliph—a claim that was never widely recognized. On the Indian subcontinent a Caliphate Movement and

Indian Caliphate Committee were formed as responses to perceived threats to Islam by Western powers, but both proved short-lived. By the outbreak of World War II, little intellectual or political activity around the caliphate remained.

Nationalist thought and state formation

Despite the intensity of deliberations within the religious camp, the audience for these various arguments remained relatively small. For most Muslims, the public—or political—dimensions of their religion did not seem to be of paramount importance. The primary goal in this arena was the achievement of independence from European colonial rule, and nationalism was certainly proving itself a far more attractive prospect in this regard. In the Middle East, a parallel cadre of intellectuals arose within the nationalist camp, arguing that post-colonial political futures should be built around an Arab identity that mined a rich heritage of language, culture, and history tracing back to well before the founding of Islam.[4] Some of the key figures in the intellectual formation of Arab nationalism included the Egyptians Lutfi al-Sayyid and Taha Hussein, Shakib Arslan from Lebanon, and the Iraqi lawyer Abd al-Rahman al-Bazzaz. While certainly aligned with a contrasting set of sociopolitical sentiments, it is worth noting that many of these writers actually had extensive contact, and were even friends, with central figures in the Salafiyya movement. Rather, their worldviews and cultural compasses were calibrated differently. For figures such as Sati al-Husri (1880–1967), the modern German and Italian nationalist experiences were inspirational. For him, nationalism was a perfect space for the formation of enduring political identities, providing as it did an ideal middle ground between local communalist tendencies and the excessive abstraction of religious universalism.[5] Husri, from a family of Syrian origin, traveled extensively throughout his career. In many regards the Pan-Arabist counterpart to Afghani's itinerant pan-Islamism, Husri spent time in Yemen, the Balkans, Syria, and Egypt before emerging as a central figure in the formation of modern Iraqi nationalism and eventually retiring as a senior figure within, fittingly, the League of Arab States. One of the political currents with which Husri had come into contact early in his life (in Macedonia, interestingly enough) would go on to emerge as the driving force behind the formation of the modern Turkish Republic. The Committee of Union and Progress, an organized manifestation of the Young Turk movement comprising Ottoman military officers of a modernizing disposition, was the group that eventually managed to force major political concessions from Abdulhamid II, the last significant Ottoman Sultan. It is via the Committee of Union and Progress that a certain Mustapha Kemal (later known by the honorific Ataturk, "father of the Turks") began his rise to prominence. Following a record of distinguished military service and a rapid rise through the ranks during World War I, Mustapha Kemal emerged as one of the leaders of the Turkish Independence movements following the war. Consolidating his position in Ankara, in the heart of Anatolia, Kemal in 1920 was proclaimed president by the National Assembly of a new Turkish Republic.

The state ideology of the Republic, commonly known as Kemalism, represents a paradigmatic form of modern nationalism in the Muslim world. Over the next ten years, Ataturk instituted a sweeping set of cultural, bureaucratic, economic, and military reforms that sought fundamentally to reorient the social basis and worldview of modern Turkey. Almost no sector of life was left untouched by these reforms. In the realm of language, a new system for rendering Turkish in Latin (rather than Arabic) script was introduced and enforced. Elements of "oriental" and Islamic dress, such as the fez, were banned and the wearing of Western clothes encouraged. In terms of history, Turkey's Ottoman and Islamic past was de-emphasized in favor of a new emphasis on the glories of Anatolia's pre-Islamic civilizations. Schoolbooks, based on an exclusively modernist curriculum, sought to inculcate a particular self-image on the part of a new generation of Turks. The children depicted in these texts, distinctly Caucasian in complexion and dress, demonstrated a mastery of Ataturk's modernist program and encouraged their readers to do the same. As part and parcel of a conscious process of Europeanization, Turkey under Ataturk also looked to the West for new models of military and bureaucratic organization, and also sought to lay the groundwork of a new industrially based economy.

And what of religion in the new Turkish Republic? Perhaps not surprisingly, Ataturk viewed Islam as a vestige of the Ottoman past he was seeking to eradicate. Islam for him was backwards, anti-modernist, and an obstacle to the Westernizing future he dreamed of for Turkey. While he knew it would be impossible to eradicate the influences of religion altogether (Sufism was also particularly strong in Turkey), he sought as much as possible to bring it under the control of the state and to deploy it in the service of his modernist project. The Kemalist variant of secularism, which emerged over several decades, eventually evolved into a degree of alienation between religion and state that is almost unprecedented in the modern world. For example, the wearing of "Islamic" clothing—such as women's headscarves—came to be legally proscribed in all public (i.e. state-run) spaces such as government ministries, state universities, and the National Assembly. Furthermore, the government established a directorate of religious affairs (the *Diyanet Isleri Baskanligi,* or "Diyanet") to organize and oversee all institutions—such as mosques and Qur'anic schools—providing religious services in Turkey. It established a network

Figure 3.1 One of Ataturk's signature reforms: Turkish in the Latin alphabet

Source: Ataturk-September 20, 1928

of religious educational facilities, the *Imam-hatip* schools, through which all state-licensed *imams* were required to pass. The curriculum in these schools was designed to emphasize the essentially private nature of religion and focused exclusively on matters of individual piety and worship (*ibadat*)—which nicely expressed the Republic's definition of the boundaries of Islam. All mosques were to be registered with the Diyanet, and on each Friday this central directorate would also provide the text for a common sermon (*khutba*) to be delivered during *juma'a* (Friday) prayer at all Turkish mosques. A social role for religion, much less any political aspiration, was out of the question. The intensity of this secularizing trend, combined with a quarter-century of one-party rule, certainly had implications for later manifestations of Muslim politics in Turkey (see Chapter 4). It undoubtedly represents the most extreme form of secular nationalism to appear in the Muslim world during the early period of modern state formation.

The case of Egypt provides a model of nationalist politics that parallels aspects of the Turkish example while also diverging from it in significant ways. Although it had been under nominal Ottoman control since 1517, Egypt—since the mid-nineteenth century, and after a dangerous challenge to Istanbul from the modernizing pasha Muhammad Ali—had operated with a great deal of political autonomy. In 1882, the British were led to occupy Egypt directly in order to protect their interests in the Suez Canal, and at that point all Ottoman suzerainty effectively ended. British rule, which in theory was exercised jointly with an Egyptian monarch, continued even after formal independence in 1922. Ongoing British involvement in the run-up to, and during, World War II ensured that Egypt's early experiment with democratic nationalism did not consolidate. The country's true political independence had to wait until the emergence of the Free Officers Movement, a group of secular-nationalist-minded military officers who instigated a *coup d'état* in 1952 to depose the ineffectual and unpopular monarch Farouk I, a last vestige of Egypt's Ottoman-affiliated dynasties. Out of this revolution arose perhaps the paramount figure of Arab nationalism—and a major world leader—Gamal Abdel Nasser. A key figure not only in the Pan-Arabist movement which bore his name ("Nasserism"—which fused elements of nationalism, socialism, and nonalignment in Cold War geopolitics), Nasser was also at the center of various geopolitical intrigues during his 16-year tenure, including the nationalization of the Suez Canal in 1956 and the formation of the Nonaligned Movement in 1961. A highly adept statesman, Nasser managed to play both sides of the Cold War to Egypt's advantage—a feat that only increased his stature as a symbol of relative Arab independence in what was experienced by many countries in the developing world as a new era of bipolar imperialism.

Nasser's leadership during the Suez Crisis, from which he emerged as the Arab hero who had thwarted a direct threat from Britain, France, and Israel, helped to consolidate his stature as the paradigmatic figurehead of Pan-Arabism—an ideology that traced back to the World War I machinations of Sharif Hussein, the Hashemite emir of the Hijaz in Arabia, and which would later figure in the program of the Ba'ath Party in Syria and Iraq. The zenith of Pan-Arabism in symbolic terms was undoubtedly the ambitious and ultimately short-lived political union of Egypt and Syria into a single country, the United Arab Republic, from 1958 to 1961. Although not nearly as aggressively secularizing as Kemalism, Pan-Arabism—particularly in its Ba'athist variant—eschewed Islam in favor of ethnolinguistic nationalism. Nasser certainly respected, but downplayed, the importance of religion. After initially seeking alliances with religious forces such as the MB, he turned against them when it became clear that they could not be brought into the fold to buttress and lend religious legitimacy to Egypt's post-1952 secular nationalist order.

Moving over to Pakistan, we find Muslims facing a rather different set of political circumstances and, consequently, engaging the Islam/nationalism debate in a unique way. Muslim Mughals had been in power in India until the Mutiny of 1857, at which point Britain imposed direct rule and deposed them. Despite the concerns of some traditional religious scholars, who either stayed completely apart from politics or advocated more extreme responses such as departing India or enjoining *jihad*, most Muslims in India developed an anti-colonial, pro-independence stance alongside Hindus. This sentiment found political expression in 1906 with the founding of the Muslim League, an organization that in its early years worked very closely with the broader Indian National Congress towards a common goal of political independence from Britain. A series of events over the next 20 years—including British threats to Muslim property, rising intercommunal violence between Muslims and Hindus, and increased Hindu control of the Indian National Congress—prompted a reassessment by Muslims of their prospects in India. From the 1930s, momentum began to gather around a new Muslim League orientation in favor of the establishment of a separate Muslim homeland on the subcontinent. While earlier Muslim intellectuals, such as Abul Kalam Azad, held fast to the idea of a multi-religious Indian nationalism, other prominent Muslim figures, such as the celebrated philosopher-poet Muhammad Iqbal, had become increasingly skeptical about the desirability or viability of such arrangements. Muhammad Ali Jinnah, the political architect of Indian partition, provided the clearest articulation of this new stance in his "Two Nations Theory." According to this thesis, Islam and Hinduism represent two separate moral and social orders that, while they may manage some minimal coexistence, will never successfully integrate. Jinnah's manifesto was in effect a statement on religious nationalism. Its inevitable conclusion was to argue that Muslims and Hindus should pursue separate political futures. Most of India's senior *ulama*, however, were not initially on board with this position, arguing that nationalism represented an ideology foreign to, and incompatible with, Islam. Nevertheless, in 1940 the Muslim League formally resolved to seek the creation of a separate homeland for Indian Muslims (the "Lahore Resolution"), and within two years of World War II Indian partition occurred and the new state of Pakistan was born. Explicitly styled as an "Islamic state," the precise implications of this were a matter of some controversy and confusion during the early years of Pakistan's political history. Was it primarily a homeland for Muslims with some nominal recognition of Islam as the primary source of public morality, or was it an Islamic state in the sense of a political system based on religious law? As we will see, this question has been central to various debates about Pakistani identity and politics.

THE EMERGENCE OF ISLAMISM

It is at this point, in the aftermath of the establishment of nation-states in the Muslim world, that we can begin to speak of the emergence of *Islamism* as a distinctive form of Muslim politics. The term "Islamism" throughout this book refers to forms of political theory and practice that have as their goal the establishment of an Islamic political order in the sense of a state whose governmental principles, institutions, and legal system derive directly from the *shari'ah*. In the eyes of those who advocate Islamist solutions, religion is generally viewed as a holistic, totalizing system whose prescriptions permeate every aspect of daily life. Islamists, as we will see, often differ in their methods and priorities. Some advocate gradualist approaches while others are more revolutionary. Certain Islamist parties pursue the "*shari'ah*-ization" of only limited areas of law, whereas others insist on a completely Islamized system. Despite these differences, they share a common commitment to the idea that Islam and public life—and politics more particularly—are not independent domains, but rather are inextricably intertwined. While earlier advocates of caliphate systems might accurately be seen as Islamists of a sort, our usage of the term here refers specifically to the pursuit of Islamic public normativity within the context of modern nation-states. There is, however, another vitally important qualifier to be made before we look more closely at Islamism. This is to remind the reader that not all political actors who articulate their motivations or goals in terms of Islam, or who make use of religious symbols, qualify as Islamists. As we will see throughout this book, many of the actors involved in Muslim politics have little interest in pursuing totalizing political orders that conform to *shari'ah*. Many have very different attitudes about the relationship between Islam, society, and politics. Indeed, some avowedly reject the Islamist approach, while still defining their own visions as authentic expressions of Islam.

It is commonplace, particularly in Western analysis, to associate the emergence of Islamism with an "Islamic revival" that began to gather force in the 1970s, reaching its zenith with the 1979 Islamic Revolution in Iran. While it is certainly the case that we can identify a significant upsurge in the number and prominence of Islamist groups during this period, to identify Islamism primarily with a period of supposed Islamic revival would be to neglect important continuities. Islamism, it can be argued, has been a feature of Muslim politics since shortly after nation-states began to take root in Muslim lands. Its political fortunes have ebbed and flowed over the past century, but Islamism in one form or another has been a consistent feature of Muslim politics. How and under what conditions did Islamism first emerge, and what forms did it take in different contexts?

Early Islamist activists and intellectuals: Hassan al-Banna and Sayyid Abu'l-A'la Mawdudi

To understand the genesis of Islamism in thought and practice, it will be useful to examine the ideas of two figures generally identified as the progenitors of modern Islamism. Hassan al-Banna (1906–49), founder of the MB in Egypt, and Sayyid Abu'l-A'la Mawdudi (1903–79), creator in Pakistan of the Jama'at-i Islami (JI) party, are widely regarded—along with Sayyid Qutb, whose ideas we will examine in a subsequent section—as having provided important initial formulations of the meaning and nature of Islamist politics. Each played a crucial role not only in the national contexts in which they worked, but also as key reference points for later generations of Islamists across the Muslim world.

Hassan al-Banna was born into a religious family in a village in the Nile Delta north of Cairo.[6] A number of events and factors affected his religious and political consciousness while growing up. These included early contact with, and experience of, the anti-colonial movement, his affiliation from a relatively young age with a Sufi order, and a keen awareness, no doubt amplified by his father, a local *imam,* of the declining religiosity associated with modernization in Egypt. Eventually choosing to train as a teacher in Cairo, he accepted a position at a government school in Isma'iliyya, a town in the Suez Canal Zone. Banna's interest in teaching as a vocation had developed as something considerably more than a desire to impart knowledge in a narrow sense. For him, education implied something closer to the religiously inflected notion of *tarbiya,* suggesting a more holistic sense of human growth and development that accrues through knowledge of religion. The religious knowledge Banna sought to emphasize, however, was not the formal and often abstract methods of jurisprudence and theology. He had no credentials, nor did he seek to act, as an *alim.* Banna's initial efforts were more oriented towards helping adults and children in Egypt to exercise greater consciousness and awareness of religion in their daily lives. If anything, Banna had become rather skeptical of the apparent social and political apathy displayed by the formal religious establishment. In this he followed Muhammad Abduh and Rashid Rida. Although his father had inculcated in him a deeply seated respect for religious learning, Banna found the scholars of Al-Azhar insufficiently concerned about the creeping secularization of Egyptian society.

Banna's early efforts took the form of lectures and classes taught in his spare time at local mosques, meeting halls, and coffee houses. As his reputation as a public speaker grew, he found himself invited into private homes to address small groups. His message combined elements of anti-colonialism and rejection of Western influence with *da'wa* ("calling" to Islam) and appeals for greater religiosity. It was a platform that resonated particularly well in Isma'iliyya, where outward signs of foreign influence were particularly visible. As it became clear that there was a demand for the approach he advocated, Banna decided to create an organization to carry the mission forward. In 1928 he founded the Muslim Brotherhood as a social movement dedicated to religious education and advocating a greater role for Islam in public life. Given its central importance within contemporary Islamism, we examine the development of the MB in much greater detail in a subsequent section.

In one sense, we might view Banna's efforts as an attempt to embody in daily life the ethos of the Salafiyya movement, with its emphasis on "true" Islam and the model of the Prophet's early companions. Moving to Cairo in 1932, Banna significantly expanded the Brotherhood's bureaucratic framework over the next few years, establishing a central secretariat in addition to numerous local branches throughout the country. Many commentators have emphasized the influence of Sufism's teacher–disciple model on how Banna chose to organize the MB in its early days. He prescribed a daily regimen of worshipful activities designed to maximize religious consciousness, including in this the practice of *dhikr* (the Sufi ritual of "remembrance"). It should be pointed out that the Sufi order with which Banna had been affiliated, the Hasafiya, was relatively orthodox in terms of its emphasis on living in accordance with *shari'ah*. In addition to his emphasis on ritual observance, Hassan al-Banna encouraged members of the MB to adopt certain attitudes and demeanors he regarded as enjoined by Islam. These included everything from personal hygiene and exercise to the importance of a strong work ethic and professional growth. Banna wanted to emphasize the possibility of "being modern" while remaining true to Islam. The adoption of Western ways, he taught, was not the only path to social mobility and personal growth.

While the MB had been founded initially as a social movement, its phenomenal growth through the 1930s and 1940s, combined with its founder's holistic approach, tended to ensure that it would take on a more political demeanor. Hassan al-Banna was not primarily a public intellectual, and certainly was not a political theorist. In this regard, his views on issues such as the Islamic state were not articulated as systematically or thoroughly as those of some of his contemporaries (such as Mawdudi, see below). Banna emphasized the practical side of lived Islamism, and in this regard is much better viewed as an instigator, organizer, and activist rather than as a theorist-intellectual. Through his description of the Brotherhood as "a Salafi movement, an orthodox way, a Sufi reality, a political body, an athletic group, a scientific and cultural society, an economic company and a social idea,"[7] we can see that Banna envisaged membership in the MB as an all-encompassing experience. But what were his views regarding the proper Islamic political system and the role of the Brotherhood within it?

It should be said at the outset that Hassan al-Banna's primary emphasis was never on the establishment of an Islamic state, nor did he view the government as the primary agent of Islamization—although later MB thinkers certainly would go this route. Rather, Banna sought to reform the existing state through an emphasis on what we might term "social Islam." His focus was on creating a properly Islamic society, and this for him was something that would come about primarily through individual Muslims embracing truly Islamic ways. There is certainly a utopian dimension to his thinking insofar as, according to Banna, the properly constituted Islamic society would have no need for political parties or labor unions since all sources of social tension and cleavage would be eliminated. On the issue of the caliphate, Banna's position was that ultimately such an institution was desirable, although he was perfectly comfortable with the idea of pursuing an Islamic social order within the framework of the nationalist state. Banna's stance towards nationalism was rather ambivalent. On one hand, he agreed with many traditional religious thinkers of the day that, in essence, the idea of national ties as the primary basis of social affiliation was in conflict with Islamic teachings. At the same time, however, he admired the anti-colonial potential within nationalism and the social mobilizing power of patriotism. Thus, knowing that nationalism was the popular flavor of the day, Banna would often incorporate elements of nationalist rhetoric within his own political discourse—emphasizing, for example, love for one's country as a Muslim duty (so long, of course, as it didn't interfere with one's primary commitment to Islam).

On the more specific issue of the state, we should reiterate that Banna's initial position was one that sought to reform that state from the outside. He was not particularly sanguine about the idea of the Brotherhood, in its early iterations, acting as a political party or taking any active role in government. His main hope was to influence the existing state and help lead it towards proper Islamic conduct. While he certainly did see a role for the state in terms of encouraging public morality (e.g. enforcing bans on certain kinds of social behavior and "un-Islamic" ceremonies), Banna's preferred mode of Islamizing the state in the early days focused on encouraging the state to integrate greater attention to religion and spirituality across all sectors of public life, to hire more graduates of religious schools, and to encourage greater religiosity on the part of the populace. Much of his early political discourse focused on issues of socioeconomic inequality, and Banna certainly saw a role for the state in pursuing social justice via the redistribution of resources accruing from *zakat* (Islam's obligatory income-based tithe). Certainly one of Banna's major complaints with the Egyptian state during the post-independence constitutional period (1922–36) was its emulation of Western liberalism, and he was highly vocal in condemning the state's adoption of un-Islamic models. Indeed, Banna was keenly aware that, during this important period of political transition, his Islamic model was competing within a market of ideologies, many of which were of foreign origin. He sought to position Islam as an approach that embodied the best features of all other options while avoiding their contradictions and negative aspects. To understand his populist characterization of competing political ideologies and the Islamic alternative, it is worth quoting Banna at some length.

> In a whimsical moment, I happened to say to my audience at a meeting—which, thanks to God, was a complete success—that this Islamic prayer which we perform five times a day is nothing but a daily training in practical social organization uniting the features of the Communist regime with those of the dictatorial and democratic regimes. Astonished, my questioners demanded an explanation. "The Greatest value of the Communist regime," I said, "is the reinforcement of the notion of equality, the condemnation of class distinction, and the struggle against the claim to property, source of these differences." Now this lesson is present in the mind of the Muslim; he is perfectly conscious of it and his spirit is filled with it the moment he enters the mosque; yes, the moment he enters, he realizes that the mosque belongs to God and not any one of his creatures; he knows himself to be the equal of all those who are there, whoever they may be; here there are no great, no small, no high, no low, no more groups or classes. And when the muezzin calls, "Now is the hour of prayer," they form an equal mass, a compact block, behind the imam. None bows unless the imam bows, none prostrates himself unless the imam prostrates himself, none moves or remains motionless unless following the imam's example. That is the principal merit of the dictatorial regime: unity and order in the will under the appearance of equality. The imam himself is in any case limited by the teachings and rules of the prayer, and if he stumbles or makes a mistake in his reading or in his actions, all those behind him—young boys, old men, or women at prayer—have the imperative duty to tell him of his error in order to put him back on the right road during the prayer, and the

imam himself is bound absolutely to accept this good advice and, forsaking his error, return to reason and truth. That is what is most appealing in democracy. How, therefore, can these regimes be superior to Islam, which astonishingly unites all their merits and avoids all their sins?[8]

Despite Banna's convictions regarding the self-evident superiority of the Islamic system, this does not mean that in his mind there was no role for the MB in terms of more direct political engagement. As the 1930s wore on into the 1940s, MB activism took on a more overly political tenor. Within a few years of founding the Brotherhood, Banna had established a special wing within the movement whose members were trained in the use of coercive and even violent tactics. For his own part, Banna began in the late 1930s to issue open and direct calls to the palace to initiate Islamizing reforms. Tensions between the MB and various hostile political factions within Egypt intensified, culminating in the assassination of the Prime Minister in 1948 by a member of the Brotherhood. A year later, Hassan al-Banna himself was on the receiving end of the government's successful reprisal.

© Getty Images

Figures 3.2 and 3.3 Hassan al-Banna and Sayyid Abu'l-A'la Mawdudi, key twentieth-century Islamist thinkers

A second figure whose ideas were of central importance to the making of modern Islamism was Sayyid Abu'l-A'la Mawdudi, a contemporary of Hassan al-Banna who worked primarily in the South Asian context. Although Mawdudi's political activities are most closely associated with Pakistan and the JI party—which he founded and presided over for 30 years—many of his writings on Islamic political theory are cast in universalist terms and have been highly influential across the Muslim world. An avowed intellectual, his ideas were generally far more systematic, more consistent, and better elaborated than those of Hassan al-Banna. It is for this reason that Mawdudi is generally considered to be one of the leading ideologues, rather than primarily a practitioner, of modern Islamism.

Born and raised in southern India, Mawdudi was from a family of Muslim notables with a long record of service to the Mughal emperors and with strong Sufi ties.[9] The family had left Delhi after the Mughal reign came to an end, but Mawdudi's father sought to remind his children of their lineage by steeping them in the classics of Islamic civilization. While studying Arabic and Persian at home, Mawdudi also acquired familiarity with modern subjects, such as science, from the local school he attended. While his formal education was quite short, Mawdudi was an avid and disciplined autodidact, and he read widely throughout his life in a variety of languages including English. Given the controversial nature of many of his religious views, there has been some debate as to his level of training in religious scholarship. While many observers of Mawdudi—and certainly his religious detractors—have portrayed him as wholly self-taught in matters of Islam, at least two biographers report that, while living in Delhi in the 1920s, Mawdudi completed the curriculum at a Deobandi seminary and received certification as an *alim*.[10] One thing that is certain, however, is that Mawdudi did not publicly acknowledge his status as a religious scholar or use it to endow his ideas with greater authority. Like many of the Islamic modernists, such as Afghani, Rida, and Banna, Mawdudi was critical of most *ulama*, seeing them as disengaged from society and lacking in political consciousness at a time of crisis. He may therefore have wanted to avoid being associated with their ranks or perceived in any way as a product of their system, as opposed to the Islamist alternative his life's work would offer.

Working initially as a journalist, Mawdudi became associated with a wide range of pro-nationalist, anti-colonialist movements and publications. His early output was not communalist in orientation, and he was generally very supportive of the Congress movement and many of the key Hindu nationalist figures such as Gandhi. A distinctly Muslim political consciousness began to form in the young Mawdudi when he became associated with the Society of Indian Ulama. With the collapse of the Caliphate Movement, with which he had been associated, Mawdudi found himself reconsidering his position on nationalism, and also at odds with the religious establishment. Whereas most *ulama* in India tended to back the Congress party's nationalist agenda,

Mawdudi was becoming increasingly skeptical about nationalism's compatibility with Islam and its implications for Muslim interests in India. Over the next decade and a half, Mawdudi—with a renewed and highly politicized religious consciousness—devoted himself to the cause of reinvigorating the heritage and status of India's Muslims. He authored a number of texts that offered, for the South Asian context, a variant of Afghani's diagnosis regarding Islam's decline. Muslims had strayed from the true path of Islam and allowed local distortions, innovations, and undue reliance on stagnant scholarship to corrupt their faith. His prescription, like that of the Arab Salafiyya, was for a return to "true" Islam—although it should be said that he emphasized the path of revival more than the model of the *salaf*. By the late 1930s, he was squarely in the center of the political debates regarding the future of Muslims in India. On one hand, he rejected the Congress Party as a route to further Muslim marginalization in a Hindu-dominated independent India. At the same time, he also spurned the Muslim League's agitation for a separate national homeland for Muslims. With regard to the latter, he could not countenance nationalist ideology within his Islamic framework, and also harbored suspicions regarding the secularist tendencies of the League's leadership, in particular Muhammad Ali Jinnah.

When, in 1940, the Muslim League adopted the cause of Pakistan as the core of its platform, Mawdudi was prompted to establish a rival entity through which his alternative political vision could be pursued. In 1941 he set up the JI as an advocacy organization and political party seeking Muslim autonomy and rights within India, as well as the propagation of Mawdudi's message of Islamic revivalism. Mawdudi's pragmatic streak was evident when, at the time of partition in 1947, he elected to remain in the part of India that had become Pakistan, moving the Jama'at's headquarters to Lahore. His new cause would be the proper Islamization of Pakistan, and working to ensure that the new country's status as an Islamic state was reflected in the adoption of a properly Islamic system and political order, rather than in a more mundane sense of Muslim nationalism. He remained a controversial figure in Pakistani political life for the next three decades, until his death in 1979, finding himself at odds with the authorities and imprisoned on more than one occasion. Indeed, one reason Mawdudi was admired by so many Islamists living under hostile regimes is because he remained so steadfast in his convictions, even when he knew they were likely to land him in hot water with subsequent secular and military-dominated governments. Mawdudi's status as a major intellectual figure in the eyes of Islamists the world over—he was one of the few non-Arab Islamist thinkers whose works were translated into Arabic—was confirmed during this period, and he spent considerable time traveling and speaking internationally.

What about the content of Mawdudi's political thinking? As we have already seen, his intellectual formation took place within the crucible of anti-colonial sentiment. While a great supporter of Indian independence from Britain, he was certainly no fan of nationalism. Not only was this ideology, in Mawdudi's view, contrary to the universalist ethos of Islam, but it also enabled ethnic chauvinism and served as a handmaiden to aggressive colonialism, arguing that "[even] if [a nationalist] upholds any world ideology, that ideology would necessarily take the form of imperialism or world domination."[11] From quite early in his career, then, Mawdudi's primary task came to be the elaboration of the political theory of Islam. Authoring several full-length books on the subject, Mawdudi's conceptualizations in this area were clearly far more extensive and systematic than those of Hassan al-Banna. While their methods may have differed, Banna and Mawdudi occupied essentially the same ideological terrain. Both understood Islam as a totalizing way of life, and the *shari'ah* as more than just a legal corpus. Rather, the *shari'ah* was better regarded as a moral system than as a provider for an entire social order. No political authority could possibly stand apart from this order, and therefore the state must work to install and enforce the Islamic system within society.

The fundamental building block of Mawdudi's political theory is the idea that sovereignty belongs exclusively to God. No worldly political power, therefore, can be truly sovereign. The nature and purpose of human political agency, it then follows, is to bring about a social order reflective of divine ordinance. Mawdudi argued that this representation—or vice-regency—of God's will on Earth is the responsibility of all people, or as he termed it, a "democratic caliphate." Although the particular arrangements of a given social setting may invest certain individuals (kings, sultans, presidents) with political authority, they are never sovereign over the people. The responsibility for maintaining God's vice-regency always falls to society:

> The position of a man who is selected to conduct the affairs of the state is no more than this; that all Muslims (or, technically speaking, all caliphs of God) delegate their caliphate to him for administrative purposes. *He is answerable to God on the one hand and on the other to his fellow "caliphs" who have delegated their authority to him.*[12]

It is within the context of this notion of collective vice-regency that Mawdudi understood the role of the caliphate, and through which he sought to emphasize the essentially democratic nature of the Islamic system—although, as we will see, his understanding of democracy is rather different from the Western liberal variant. He spoke of the importance of ongoing consultation (*shura*) between state and society, but did not place excessive importance on ideas such as power sharing between parties, or on processes that produce turnover in terms of who holds the reins of governments (e.g. elections). So long as a society was properly Islamic and *shura* was ongoing, Mawdudi argued, the sorts of societal tension that lead people to demand new rulers would not be a major concern:

If I were permitted to coin a new term, I would describe this system of government as a "theo-democracy," that is to say a divine democratic government, because under it the Muslims have been given a limited popular sovereignty under the suzerainty of God. The executive under this system of government is constituted by the general will of the Muslims who have also the right to depose it.[13]

Thus Mawdudi's conception of democracy is premised not on notions of individual liberty and political pluralism, but rather on the notion of a body politic as the repository of divine vice-regency. For him, democracy properly achieved also seems, at least in part, to involve a sense of solidarity and an absence of social divisions and tension. We should note that, for Mawdudi, the desired absence of social division was understood to fall primarily along the horizontal rather than the vertical axis of society. In other words, it was not a call for egalitarianism. Inequalities between people, he posited, were part of the natural order of things. People have equal rights and should expect to be treated as such, but the Islamic system was not one that sought primarily to place everyone on an equal footing in terms of their material resources or position within social hierarchies. It was, however, incumbent upon the state to make sure that these naturally occurring inequalities were not exploited in ways that violated Islamic normativity. Hence, for example, the Islamic proscription against usury (excessive interest charged on loans).

As we can see in the final passage of the quote above, Mawdudi's theo-democracy also permitted Muslims to depose any political authority that abuses or fails to carry out their duties as deputized caliphs. It is in this area that we encounter some of Mawdudi's more controversial reinterpretations of core Islamic jurisprudential concepts—or, at least, choices of terminology. Mawdudi describes the method according to which individual Muslims are to assess the policies of the state as a form of *ijtihad*—that is, independent legal reasoning. As we will recall from the previous chapter, most orthodox jurists hold that *ijtihad* effectively ceased to constitute a viable legal methodology in the tenth century—and, moreover, that even if it were permissible, it could be carried out only by properly trained jurists. Mawdudi states his case as follows:

All administrative matters and all questions about which no explicit injunction is to be found in the Shari'ah are settled by the consensus of opinion among the Muslims. Every Muslim who is capable and qualified to give a sound opinion on matters of Islamic law, is entitled to interpret the law of God when such interpretation becomes necessary.[14]

The point turns perhaps on what one understands by "capable and qualified." This could be interpreted to mean that only formally trained experts in *shari'ah* (i.e. *ulama*) are permitted to carry out *ijtihad* with regard to administrative matters, or it might mean that any well-educated Muslim

within the "democratic caliphate" has the right to exercise this kind of judgment. Regardless of how we interpret this ambiguity, it is certainly the case
that Mawdudi courted controversy here simply by framing his implementation of Islamic democracy in terms of *ijtihad.*

In terms of political practice, Mawdudi is, in essence, a theorist of Islamic
revolution. In his schema, however—and in contrast with later theorists of
revolution such as Iran's Khomeini (see Chapter 5)—this does not necessarily involve a fundamental change in the political order. Mawdudi's preference
was to reform the existing political order such that the state could become
a central agent for the Islamization of society. Here we also find a point of
contrast with Banna. The latter had not envisaged a principal role for the
state in Islamizing the people, emphasizing instead a primarily societal locus
for the desired transformation. Mawdudi, on the other hand, realizing the
state's enormous capacity and resource base, hoped to see the government
initiate large-scale Islamizing reforms, but only once it comes under the
stewardship of those who are appropriately educated:

> The state is an instrument of reform and must act likewise. It is a dictate
> of this very nature of the Islamic state that such a state should be run
> only by those who believe in the ideology on which it is based and in the
> Divine Law which it is assigned to administer. The administrators of
> the Islamic state must be those whose whole life is devoted to the obser-
> vance and enforcement of this Law, who not only agree with its
> reformatory programme and fully believe in it but thoroughly compre-
> hend its spirit and are acquainted with its details.[15]

Mawdudi's revolution was certainly not an exclusively top-down affair,
however. He comes back towards Banna in his thinking when expressing a
preference for the Islamization of society before the Islamization of the
state. In this view the political order is subsidiary to, rather than constitutive of, the social order. An Islamic state that seeks to enforce *shari'ah* upon
a society that has itself not yet sufficiently internalized Islamic normativity
is bound to resort to coercive and authoritarian methods. A sustainable
Islamic order will arise when there is a natural symbiosis of purpose between
society and state. Mawdudi's revolution was hence processual in nature.
Reflecting this view in his political activism, Mawdudi did not form the
Jama'at with a view to acquiring state power. Although the party did contest
political elections at various points, most of its career under Mawdudi was
spent in more of a watchdog and advocacy role, rather than aspiring to
govern. In Mawdudi's view, the state essentially reflects the character of its
population, and therefore societal progress towards true Islam was of paramount importance in achieving a lasting revolution. In this, as some
commentators have noted, we can see a certain idealism in Mawdudi's
thinking—a point that crystallizes when we examine his views on issues

such as the *hudud,* the *shari'ah's* code of punishment for serious crimes. Mawdudi's position maintained the veracity and the necessity of the *hudud,* but argued that it could be implemented only in a properly Islamized society, one in which the normative parameters it enforces have already been internalized. Under such conditions, Mawdudi reasoned, there would in practice be no need actually to apply this penal code, as the behaviors that invoke it would not occur.

Given that he was read and cited appreciatively by a number of later Islamists (including Sayyid Qutb, see below) who advocated a more militant path toward Islamic revolution, Mawdudi's views on *jihad* have been of particular interest and also a matter of some debate amongst contemporary analysts. The text that ostensibly constitutes Mawdudi's major statement on the theme, *Jihad in Islam,* was written while he was very young and also as a reaction (some have said as an apologetic) in the wake of a media controversy that was critical of Islam's supposedly violent nature. The major thrust of the book is towards decoupling the notion of *jihad* from an exclusively martial connotation and refiguring it as a more generic sense of "struggle" towards the realization of the Islamic way. Mawdudi does indicate that it may sometimes be necessary, and is permissible, to use violence as part of this process, although he gets caught up over the issue of defensive versus offensive *jihad.* He makes it clear, however, that education or *tarbiya* is his preferred method for achieving social change and Islamization, and in this sense it would not be accurate to label him a jihadi in today's sense of the term (see Chapter 7).

Looking at Mawdudi's complete body of work, one is certainly struck by the intellectual consistency and fierceness of logic that runs through it. His ideas are simultaneously conservative—in terms of the social values they espouse, including a very limited social role for women—and revolutionary, both in the sense of seeking fundamental social change, and in terms of how he interprets and deploys central concepts of Islamic sociopolitical thought to this end. Hassan al-Banna and Abu'l-A'la Mawdudi both regarded Islam as a total system encompassing all aspects of life—and, furthermore, one from which the state cannot possibly be separated. To realize this system, an Islamic revival was required at the level of society, particularly in the face of what both figures saw in their day as the advancing threat of secularism. Through a return to "true" Islam and the achievement of the social order it prescribes, Banna and Mawdudi aspired to be the harbingers, in L. Carl Brown's assessment, of something like an Islamic "End of History"—that is, a human order in which all existing contradictions and tensions are resolved through the realization of a universal normativity.[16] While they diverged in terms of certain priorities, methods, and choice of personal vocation (one essentially a social activist, the other a public intellectual), the formulations of Mawdudi and Banna went on to inspire the theory and practice of Islamism across several generations and a wide variety of settings.

BOX 3.1 THEORIES AND DEBATES IN THE STUDY OF MUSLIM POLITICS

There is an extensive academic literature focused on explaining the factors that cause Islamism, accounting for changes in strategy on the part of Islamist actors, distinguishing between different types of Islamist movements, and even trying to provide basic definitions for concepts such as "political Islam" and "Islamism."

Explaining political Islam

Following author Salwa Ismail, we can distinguish between two broad schools of thought that represent very different basic assumptions about what drives the emergence of political Islam.[17] Some scholars place primary emphasis on cultural factors. They adopt an ascriptive approach that sees political Islam as a natural manifestation of Muslim beliefs and history. Bernard Lewis, author of *The Political Language of Islam* and *What Went Wrong? The Clash Between Islam and Modernity in the Middle East,* is among the best known representatives of this approach. Critics of the culturalist school worry that it essentializes Islam, reduces the motivations and behavior of Muslims to their religious beliefs, and pays insufficient attention to context and the historical dynamism of Islamic thought.[18] In contrast, structural approaches to explaining political Islam emphasize the importance of material conditions, socioeconomics, and political institutional factors in explaining the emergence of Islamic activism. Its exponents include Nikki Keddie, Saad Eddine Ibrahim, and Michael Fischer.[19] Their critics charge that they do not pay sufficient attention to ideational factors or social agency, and that they reduce political Islam to an analysis of social class.[20]

In his book *A Fundamental Fear,* Bobby Sayyid provides a useful overview of the main explanations offered by observers from both camps as to the specific causes of Islamism. These include seeing Islamism as a response to the failure of national-secular elites to deliver on the promise of modernization; a reaction to political disenfranchisement and exclusion from democracy; uneven economic development the Muslim world; and cultural erosion in the face of pressures to adopt Western ways of life.[21]

Understanding varieties of Islamism

Other scholars have sought to develop typologies of different kinds of Islamist groups and movements. Their various schemas—which tend to rely on "ideal type" analysis—identify different ways of thinking about which aspects of these movements best help to differentiate them. Hakan Yavuz, for example, uses a bi-axial analysis of the goals (society-oriented versus state-oriented) and methods (legitimate versus illegitimate) adopted by Islamist groups to identify four major types of group: reformist, societal, revolutionary, and spiritual.[22] Amr Hamzawy comes up with a similar roster comprised of missionaries, moderates, and militants.[23] For Syres Rudy, the significant distinctions are those between personal, communitarian, and militant Islamism.[24] As with all analytical frameworks that rely on ideal types, none of these frameworks—by their authors' own admission—corresponds directly to social reality. They do, however, represent useful tools to begin identifying and framing the complex world of Muslim politics.

Definitional quandaries

Some scholars have asked more fundamental questions about political Islam and Islamism as concepts. In his article "What is Political Islam?," Charles Hirschkind points out that a focus on political Islam reinforces that idea that, in the Middle East and elsewhere, religion is improperly inserting itself into the political realm. He would rather we ask questions about the nature of authoritarianism and efforts by the state to totalize its control of society.[25] Two prominent commentators on the Islamic world, Donald Emmerson and Daniel Varisco, recently debated the utility of "Islamism" as a concept in the social sciences. Varisco fears that the term has turned into a politicized lightning rod in the aftermath of the 9/11 attacks, and that its usage obscures rather than elucidates anything that falls under the label. Emmerson, in contrast, defends the usage of Islamism in the social sciences when employed carefully and consistently.[26] Adopting something of a meta-theoretical approach, Frederic Volpi, in *Political Islam Observed*, provides a cross-disciplinary critical analysis of efforts to study Islamism, showing that the origins, assumptions, and priorities of particular academic disciplines lead them to approach the issue of political Islam in very different ways.[27]

Trends and debates in the study of Islamism

Over the past decade, the academic literature on political Islam has seen a number of debates that bear in important ways on the question of whether and how Islamist activism resembles other forms of social mobilization; how best to explain recent shifts in the strategy and identity of

Islamist groups and political parties; and whether the primary locus of Muslim politics is still to be found in the movements we conventionally term Islamist.

Islamism and social movement theory

Scholars such as Ziad Munson, Quintan Wiktorowicz, Charles Kurzman, and Carrie Wickham have argued that the body of theory developed for explaining social mobilization more broadly, such as social movement theory, holds explanatory value when used as a lens for understanding Islamic activism.[28] Their work argues that key social movement theory concepts, such as resource mobilization, changing political opportunity structures, and framing dynamics, allow us to engage in comparative analysis between political Islam and broader instances of social mobilization.

The "new" Islamists? Inclusion and moderation (see Chapter 4)

Many scholars have noted the trend among contemporary Islamists to opt for political participation over confrontation with the state. They have coined a wide range of terms, such as "Muslim democracy," "liberal Islamism," and "civil Islam" to describe this phenomenon.[29] One of the more systematic efforts to provide a social scientific account of this apparent shift is Jillian Schwedler's work on the "inclusion–moderation" thesis.[30] Her research in Jordan and Yemen tests the hypothesis—with inconclusive results—that participating in democratic politics will have a moderating impact on groups previously driven by ideology. The idea here is that when a political party becomes accountable to voters for governance outcomes, and finds itself needing to cooperate with other political groups who do not share its ideology in order to achieve common interests, it is far more likely to adopt a pragmatic orientation.

Are we in the age of post-Islamism? (see Chapter 8)

Some authors have asked whether conventional Islamist movements such as the Muslim Brotherhood represent the center of gravity for Muslim politics today. They contend that we have entered the age of "post-Islamism," and argue that—particularly among young people today—the agenda and priorities of political Islam as an ideological project have largely lost legitimacy. Some proponents of the post-Islamism thesis, such as Asef Bayat, argue that grassroots politics in the Muslim world today are concerned less with the establishment of *shari'ah* law and more with fundamental struggles for dignity, governmental accountability, and livelihood.[31] Another variant of thinking on post-Islamism is found in the work of Olivier Roy, who argues that the current upsurge in religiosity in the Muslim world is focused primarily on individuals and an emphasis on personal piety rather than collective mobilization to Islamize the state.[32]

"ISLAM IS THE SOLUTION": THE EVOLUTION AND EXPANSION OF THE MUSLIM BROTHERHOOD

As the original and, arguably, most influential Islamist movement of the twentieth century, the MB merits closer examination. We learned something of the circumstances surrounding its founding while discussing Hassan al-Banna above; given its rapid growth and the central role it came to play not only in Egyptian politics but in a number of countries throughout the Muslim world, it is worth looking more closely at how it evolved and expanded as an organization both during and after Banna's tenure as leader. In this section we survey the development of the MB in Egypt, looking particularly at its transformation from a social and educational movement into an avowedly political, and eventually even militant, group. Sayyid Qutb, chief ideologue of the MB during the height of its militancy in the 1960s, went on to become one of the most influential Islamist thinkers across the Muslim world, affecting many of the groups and movements we examine in later chapters, so we will want to gain some understanding of his thinking on Islam and politics. Examining developments with the MB since the 1970s, particularly in terms of its changing relationship with the Egyptian government, will help to lay the groundwork for our analysis of Islam in state and society relations in later chapters. As branches of the MB were established in other Arab countries (and later even beyond the Middle East)—each of them adjusting the model and methodology to suit local circumstances and priorities—it became possible to identify a distinction between the MB as an organizational entity (particularly the original Egyptian group) and something like "Muslim Brotherhoodness" or *Ikhwanism*—which describes a broad tendency within contemporary Islamism, the core tenets and methods of which are shared by all manner of group and movements regardless of whether they have any affiliation with the official MB. Drawing this distinction between the MB as a formal group and as a broad ideological current will help us to appreciate the complex nature of the MB today. A brief look at the diverse paths followed by some of its various branches outside Egypt will also allow us to understand how local conditions and political imperatives can serve to inflect models originally developed elsewhere.

The MB founded by Hassan al-Banna in 1928 sought primarily to offset the corrosive effects of Westernization and secularism by educating Egyptian society about the importance of religion in public life and by advocating a return to "true" Islam. An important precursor to the Brotherhood can be found in the Young Men's Muslim Association (YMMA), founded the year before Banna's organization. Its similarity to the well-known Christian group of the same name is certainly no coincidence. The Young Men's Christian Association (YMCA) had been present in Egypt since around the turn of the century, and those within Banna's circle perceived it as an aggressive missionary force whose influence needed to be countered. Many of the YMMA's teachings regarding proper Islamic lifestyle, and even some of its more public and political positions, were later incorporated into the platform of the MB.

During the first few years of its existence, the Brotherhood worked primarily to consolidate a committed membership in Isma'iliyya and the immediate environs of the Suez. Funds were secured to build a mosque, to which were also attached schools for both boys and girls. It is interesting to note that, even during these earliest days, Banna attracted attention and suspicion from Cairo, where the palace was unsure what to make of him—communist, nationalist, disgruntled royalist, petty racketeer?[33] "Islamist" was not on the radar yet as a form of opposition politics. It was with the MB's move to Cairo in 1932 that the establishment of the Brotherhood's institutional infrastructure began in earnest. After quickly merging with or assimilating a number of other Islamic groups in the capital, the MB began a period of growth which, over the next decade, would see its base grow to some half million active members across 2,000 branches. More impressive than the size of its following, perhaps, was the fact that the Brotherhood had succeeded in finding supporters across a considerable range of social milieu and professional sectors. Its potential political influence hence also increased over this period, with Banna having a more direct influence in politics from the mid-1930s. Much of this activity was focused on anti-missionary, anti-colonial, and anti-Zionist efforts. Banna also wrote a number of letters to the king in which he related concerns regarding the socially divisive political climate in the country as well as the importance of establishing an Islamic order. By this time, there had already emerged within the Brotherhood itself certain tensions between the gradualist approach to social change espoused by Banna and a small faction of Brothers—the "hasty and the anxious," as the leader labeled them—seeking to adopt more directly confrontational methods.[34] This particular division within the movement is one that would repeat itself on several occasions later in the Brotherhood's history, and one that also shows up in a number of other Islamist groups.

There are a number of interesting observations to make about the nature of MB ideology and its reflection in the movement's social organization. First, although religious in nature, the Brotherhood needs to be seen as a thoroughly *modern* entity. This can be seen in terms of its systematic organization, its methods and locations of recruitment, its division into cadres of professional classes, and its appreciation of the nature of bureaucratic politics. In its rhetoric we find an acknowledgment of modern domains of thought (e.g. sciences versus humanities), categories of social division (e.g. social classes and the interplay of various forms of social authority), and a distinction between fields such as culture, politics, economics, and society. All these reflect Banna's modern education and the appreciation he gained from studying recent forms of mass social mobilization. While he was certainly at odds with the fascists of Italy and Nazi Germany—both on moral grounds and because of their exclusively nationalist focus—he certainly admired the mobilizing potential, totalizing politics, and intense discipline that these movements represented. Another area in which the MB shows its modernist colors relates to issues of theology and jurisprudence. Rather than adopting an official school of jurisprudential thought (one of the four Sunni *madhahib*), Banna and the MB instead disavowed these as unnecessary obstacles to the singularity of true Islam. This stance, often identified with the Salafiyya movement, is generally recognized as "modernist" in its rejection of the "traditional" practice of *taqlid*—that is, the emulation of precedent within a particular school of juristic practice. That said, it is also possible to identify certain traces of traditional practice in the MB—holdovers, perhaps, from Banna's extended affiliation with the Hasaniya Sufi brotherhood. This is most clearly present in the emphasis he placed on the student–teacher relationship within the MB, and the crucial importance of obedience to the movement's leader. Combining these various elements, some observers have seen in Banna and the MB a "reconstruction of modernity according to Islamic models and motifs."[35]

What of the Brotherhood's organizational structure? This is worth covering to some extent so that we can see how the Brotherhood ethos came to be reflected internally through the various divisions and structures that Banna created. In addition to the executive organs of the MB (the General Guide, the Consultative Assembly, and the Guidance Council) and administrative units such as the General Secretariat, Banna created a number of distinct institutions amongst the rank-and-file membership whose purposes were primarily related to indoctrination, communication, and the protection of the MB.

- **Family system** (*nizam al-usra*)—formally established in the early 1940s, the family system became the fundamental building block of MB organization. Brotherhood "families" were composed of five to ten active members, each of which had an elected senior member charged with representing the family to, and disbursing the authority of, the local MB branch. Initially founded as an instrument for *tarbiya* (education or indoctrination), the family system, according to Mitchell, was "in fact the real basis of the Power of the Society of Muslim Brothers; permitting, as it did, authority to express itself through a well-recognized, clearly-defined, and tightly knit chain of command . . . "[36] It is the central role of the family system that has led some observers to regard the MB as organized through "cells."

- **Rover battalions** (*jawwala*)—established in an early form while Banna was still in Isma'iliyya, the rovers were initially the athletic and orienteering division of the MB. Reorganized and eventually folded into the national scout movement once the MB moved to Cairo, the rovers came to serve three purposes during the height of their activity from 1935 to 1953: a locus for the acquisition of traditional scouting skills and athletic training; the conduit for the Brotherhood's social service and public welfare projects; and, on occasion, a readily mobilized cadre that could be used for maintaining public order or protecting the Brotherhood's interests and property. It is interesting to note that, during the 1940s, the rover battalions received some training and aid from retired military personnel within the MB, at times with the blessing and even encouragement of figures within the nascent Free Officers Movement. It was also the rovers who provided the basis for the MB's controversial activities in Palestine in 1948.

- **Secret Apparatus** (*al-jihaz al-sirri*)—the existence and operations of the Secret Apparatus provided the basis for the government's crackdown on the Brotherhood in 1954. The Apparatus was composed of a relatively small number of Brothers (estimates ranged from 400 to 3,000 in the early 1950s) who received special training in weapons, espionage, and tactics, and then took a special oath of allegiance and a vow of secrecy. Widely regarded as the militant wing of the Brotherhood, the organization's second general guide, Hassan al-Hudaybi, tried to shut down the Apparatus upon assuming leadership of the MB in 1951, only for it to be created anew without his knowledge.

Through these various sub-organs, Banna was able to create a large, affluent network of branches—growing from four in 1929 to some 2,000 by 1949—and an effective system for the accumulation of what modern sociologists would term "social capital"—that is, the influence and mobilizing potential that accrues through building cross-cutting horizontal ties of trust and common interest.[37] By the late 1940s, the Brotherhood could reasonably claim a following of one million, divided evenly between active members and "lay participants" or sympathizers—certainly a mass movement by the standard of the day.

Perhaps not surprisingly, the Brotherhood's support for Britain in the immediate run-up to, and during, World War II was minimal at best. The movement's anti-colonial activities continued, and it lobbied the Egyptian government against playing a more prominent pro-Allied role in the hostilities. By the early 1940s, after the British had replaced the government with an administration more amenable to its requirements, the Brotherhood found itself at odds with the authorities and experienced some measure of suppression at its hands, including the brief imprisonment of its leader. Twice during the 1940s Banna was on the verge of holding elected office, but on both occasions this was denied him—in the first instance after withdrawing his candidacy at the request of the government; in the second after losing the election in the aftermath of suspected government manipulation of the polling process. Over the next several years, the MB became increasingly active in leading a number of uprisings and protests against government policies and continued British interference in Egypt. With the United Nations (UN) partition of Palestine in 1947 and the first Arab–Israeli war a year later, the MB adopted a new cause. The Brotherhood sent a battalion of fighters to undertake *jihad* in Palestine and this move, coupled with a number of local attacks in which Banna's movement became suspect, led to a government decree dissolving the Brotherhood. With the arrest and scattering of many key members in the MB's "Secret Apparatus" (see below), Banna effectively lost control over the organization's militant wing. In late 1948, a member of the Brotherhood assassinated the Prime Minister, and the following year Hassan al-Banna himself was killed by the government's secret police.

Before looking at the next post-Banna phase of the MB's development, it would be helpful to consider for a moment several aspects of society and economy in Egypt during the 1930s to help us understand why, and to whom, the message of the Brotherhood was appealing. The case of the MB draws our attention to the importance of political economy and to various socioeconomic factors in terms of how we explain the social bases of support for modern Islamism. Most important among these, perhaps, is the emergence in the Middle East, from the early twentieth century onward, of a new middle class—the *effendiyya,* as they were commonly known in Egypt—and their growing political importance. A combination of merchants, landowners, and a new professional class of teachers, lawyers, and bureaucrats, the *effendiyya* came to be regarded as a vital constituency by all three components of the Egyptian power triangle of the time: the palace, the nationalists, and the British. This middle class, and its political consciousness, came to be formed around a distinct set of perceived stakeholding interests in Egypt's political future. They became central interlocutors with successive governments from the 1920s forward and, at times, among their most vociferous critics. Although not part of the milieu of the political elite *per se,* the *effendiyya* came to occupy an important mediating layer between the government and broader national sentiment. The Egyptian economy in the early twentieth century was most heavily dependent on cotton exports. A decline in world commodity prices from the 1920s, associated with the global depression, spelled significant hardship for Egypt's agricultural sector, and put the new constitutional government under considerable pressure. However, widespread discontent regarding the socioeconomic effects of the policies pursued by political elites and their allies are insufficient to explain why Islamism emerges as a viable alternative political discourse. In order to understand this, we need to understand how the politics of state formation in the Arab world, or, in this case, in Egypt, became simultaneously enmeshed within a broader set of cultural debates about modernity, values, and social authority.

The modernizing state, with its emphasis on economic and bureaucratic rationalization, came to be identified with a shift away from Arab-Islamic heritage. As it came to identify "traditionalist" institutions such as the pious foundations (*awqaf*, sing. *waqf*) and *shari'ah* courts, increasingly, as obstacles in the path of modernization, the question of the cultural authenticity of this approach became a feature of political discourse. As Mansoor Moaddel observes:

> To a disinterested observer, the Egyptian version of liberal nationalism would not have appeared to be simply a discourse to resolve the problem of politics in a constitutional direction. It would rather have appeared to be an all-encompassing and comprehensive ideology, dictating a worldview that ranged from a philosophy of history to a style of dress. To a Muslim observer, in particular, the feature of this ideology was defined less in terms of the necessity of liberating Egypt from the vestiges of foreign domination than in terms of opposition to an Islam that was, in the nationalist perception, deleterious to the construction of modern Egypt.[38]

The path chosen by the MB proved uniquely powerful in this context. The MB was not a "nativist" organization, advocating a return to a traditional Arab-Islamic utopia in which modernity in all its forms was rejected. Indeed, as we will see in greater detail below, the MB, like most other subsequent Islamist organizations, was wholly modern in its organization and outlook. By combining an appreciation of modern education, science, and technology with a rejection of blind emulation of the West (initially framed in anti-colonial, but then increasingly geoculturalist, terms), the Brotherhood was able to tap into a vein of growing concern across numerous sectors of Egyptian society: how does one partake in modernity's potential for social mobility and national development while avoiding becoming (or continuing to be) beholden to both its culturally and morally eroding effects, and the pervasive influence of its foreign agents? As Moaddel argues, "changes in class relations and the dynamics of inter-elite political rivalries undeniably shaped the resources and opportunity structures from which the MB drew in its contention for political power and cultural supremacy."[39]

As successive waves of political elites—particularly those, such as the Wafdists, whose early legitimacy was based on an agenda of popular emancipation—came to pursue policies that served their narrow interests and even to allow their own co-option by the British, widespread suspicions towards the dominant political tendencies grew—as did support for the MB "alternative." That this wasn't a political alternative in the conventional sense of a fully developed political party is significant here. By sitting back from the political order of the day and building a broad base of social support, Hassan al-Banna ensured that his group's support was widely courted, at various points, by more or less every significant political party and institution in Egypt, while managing to remain untainted—at least up until the post-World War II period—by direct involvement in the machinations of the day. Neither did the MB become a "client" for any particular political faction. Even though Banna, by the late 1940s, appeared to be accelerating his plan for the direct politicization of MB activity in light of contemporary events, we can say that the legitimacy of the Brotherhood during this first phase lay in its capacity to serve as a repository of spiritual and cultural authenticity in a time of great turbulence.

The Brotherhood's main priority in the years following Banna's death was to rehabilitate its reputation in the eyes of the government so that it could once again operate openly. The decision was hence made to choose a successor to Banna, not from the existing ranks of deputies and senior leaders—many of whom were tainted in the eyes of the authorities—but by looking outside the ranks of the Brothers to appoint a new "general guide" (as the head of the movement had been known since 1945). After two years of interim leadership by Salih Ashmawi, who had been Banna's deputy, the decision was made to appoint Hasan al-Hudaybi, a well-respected judge, as the MB's new general guide. Hudaybi was not formally a member of the Brotherhood, merely a sympathetic figure of some official standing who had developed tremendous admiration for Hassan al-Banna and his ideas. In the eyes of the MB's senior deputies, Hudaybi's appointment was intended as a temporary measure to help cleanse the organization's reputation after the violence and unrest of 1946–49. Almost immediately, tensions emerged between Hudaybi and certain former lieutenants of Banna. The latter had expected Hudaybi to be little more than a rubber-stamp figurehead, a public persona whose reputation was beyond official reproach. Hudaybi, however, was intent on affecting a genuine transformation in the movement, seeking to return it more clearly to the status of a religious organization, and to get away from politics. One of his first acts, in addition to appointing a new cadre of loyal deputies, was to abolish the MB's Secret Apparatus. When it soon became clear that the militant wing continued to operate under a leadership pillar outside Hudaybi's control, he threatened to resign.

This internal dispute temporarily played second fiddle to seismic events happening on the national political landscape, more specifically the Free Officers Revolution of 1952, which led to the king's deposal and also sounded the real end to British control of Egypt. While the MB played no direct role in these events, close contact and coordination between the Brothers and the Free Officers Movement is well documented. Indeed, the military conspirators envisaged important roles for the MB in terms of preserving order on the streets at the time of the *coup d'état*, and also within their contingency planning, should things not have proceeded according to plan.[40] Although the Free Officers were diametrically opposed to the MB in terms of ideology, a fact that would be made all too clear very shortly, there was a history of contact between them dating back to the time of Hassan al-Banna. What brought the two together, it seemed, was a shared sense of dissatisfaction about the state of politics in Egypt and a common conviction that none of the existing parties could successfully rid the nation of its endemic corruption. Clearly, each of these two groups hoped to make tactical and strategic use of the other: for the Free Officers, the MB represented a potential source of widespread popular legitimacy and "spiritual" endorsement of the otherwise highly secular revolution they were plotting. Indeed, the precursors to the Free Officers in the 1940s had even entrusted to the Brotherhood the keeping of several stores of armaments in case they might be needed in the struggle to come. To the MB, on the other hand, the Free Officers represented a possible vehicle upon which, in the context of genuine political revolution, an Islamic system could be institutionalized at the level of the state. In the immediate aftermath of the revolution in the summer of 1962, the Brotherhood was generally supportive, but the relationship between the new government, first under Muhammad Naguib and then later under the iconic Gamal Abdel Nasser, and the MB quickly soured.

The Free Officers, now institutionalized as the Revolutionary Command Council, banned in 1953 all political parties except the Brotherhood, which it labeled—for tactical reasons, rather than through ignorance—a social welfare group. Once it became apparent to the MB that the government was not going to heed its calls for instituting an Islamic order, or to allow the Brotherhood any significant public influence, their support quickly disappeared and animosity between the two began to grow. It is here that the emerging schism within the movement came to take on increased importance. As tensions grew between Hudaybi's vision of the Brotherhood's mission and those who supported the existence of the Secret Apparatus and a more confrontational approach, the Revolutionary Command Council exploited the rift to discredit Hudaybi's leadership. After an attempt on Nasser's life in 1954, the government banned the organization for seditious activity, and imprisoned or put to death a number of its key leaders. Since this time the MB, while certainly very active in Egypt over the next 50 years, did not operate openly as a political organization until it founded the Freedom and Justice Party

(FJP) in the wake of the 2011 popular uprising that toppled the regime of Hosni Mubarak. In the late 1950s and early 1960s, the Brotherhood—now firmly controlled by the militants, and more convinced than ever of the necessity of direct, armed confrontation in the wake of the government's crackdown—continued to operate as an underground opposition movement. While many of its leaders had been imprisoned or killed, or had gone into exile abroad, a new generation of ideologues emerged during this more militant phase of the movement's existence. Of these, none was more important than Sayyid Qutb. Qutb, who did not even join the Brothers as an active member until 1952, provided the theoretical basis for the evolution of Hassan al-Banna's mission of social transformation into an approach to Islamic politics whose only possible course of action under the prevailing order was armed struggle, or *jihad*. Qutb served as the chief ideologue of the Brothers during the underground period, and was imprisoned during much of it. Finally hanged in 1966 in connection with a plot to overthrow the government, Qutb garnered a reputation around the Muslim world as a major theorist of Islamism and *jihad*. Like Mawdudi, his importance transcends the immediate national context of his efforts. Indeed, in the case of Qutb we can say, arguably, that no other modern Islamist thinker has had quite the same influence in terms of giving voice to the revolutionary and jihadi worldview within modern Islamism. His thinking will be apparent in the formulations of several groups we examine later in this book (see Chapter 7), and so Qutb—the last individual Islamist thinker we address in this chapter—is worth looking at in some greater detail.

Sayyid Qutb: *hakimiyyah, jahiliyya,* and *jihad*

Sayyid Qutb (1906–66) was born and raised in Upper Egypt (the south of the country), and like Hassan al-Banna before him eventually traveled to Cairo to attend teaching college.[41] Unlike Banna, however, his early work did not reflect immediate Islamist convictions. In Cairo he fell primarily into literary rather than social activist circles, and many of his writings during this period—when they did involve religion—were concerned with the aesthetics (rather than the sociopolitical imperatives) of the Qur'an. He also seemed to be searching for a worldview at this early point, uncertain as to the pre-eminence of the Egyptian, Arab, or Islamic frames of identity. The hierarchy of moral obligation was also a concern for the young Qutb, and his work from the 1940s shows him working through some of the central predicaments in modern normative theory, such as the balance of obligation between individual rights and those of the community—a theme to which he would return in his later "Islamic" writing. Eventually taking a job as a teacher, and then later as an inspector and official within the Ministry of Education, Qutb did not show any early interest in transforming the

Figure 3.4 Sayyid Qutb, modern theorist of *jihad* and radical Muslim Brotherhood ideologue
Source: Sayyid Qutb, 1965

social order of his day, although he certainly participated in the key debates and, like most public intellectuals of the time, held broadly anti-colonial views. It was not until the late 1940s that his intellectual output came to settle within a predominantly Islamic frame. His first major work in this vein was *Social Justice in Islam* (1948), a text that seeks to work through questions of social obligation and to establish the superiority of the Islamic paradigm of equity and justice in the face of both liberal individualism and socialist egalitarianism—the two competing models of the day.

From 1949 to 1950, Qutb was dispatched to the United States by the Ministry of Education to study American educational administration methods. His stay there seems to have had a major impact on his worldview and the development of his thinking with regard to Islam. While certainly impressed with the material achievements of American society, he felt that these had been obtained at an unacceptable cost. His account of American culture focused on what he saw as the devastating erosion by capitalist individualism of that society's moral character. This experience appears to have shifted his understanding of the threat from the West such that it came to be about much more than just colonial occupation. Rather, the West represented a pervasive system of values and beliefs that would undermine any society that chose its path. For Qutb, as Charles Tripp argues, "British Imperialism was characterized merely as one aspect of a more wide-ranging and sinister form of collective enmity—that of the secular, materialist, individualist and capitalist West."[42] Qutb was perhaps much more interested in the United States because it was a relatively young nation, having been formed when the British Empire was already ascendant. In this regard it represented for him a case study in what happens when a primarily agricultural nation rapidly industrializes and embraces secular modernity—trends that were dominant in Egypt at his time. If America were Egypt's future, he reasoned, then the crisis at hand was perhaps more severe than he had originally imagined, and required urgent redress.

Upon Qutb's return to Egypt, it is therefore not surprising that he began to take a greater interest in those groups which, beyond writing about the need for social reform, were actually trying to enact it in practice. Quite naturally, he was led towards the MB in this regard, although it does not seem that he actually joined the group until around 1952. Upon becoming an active member, Qutb was immediately placed in charge of the MB's public outreach section. Like many of his Brotherhood contemporaries, Qutb had high hopes for Egypt when the Free Officers Revolution of 1952 occurred. Indeed, reports suggest that he worked quite closely and enthusiastically with the new regime in an effort to integrate a stronger dimension of Islamization into their reform agenda. As Nasser rose to prominence within the Revolutionary Command Council and consolidated his power base, however, it became clear that an Islamic social order was nowhere on the agenda, and Qutb soon found himself among the ranks of disillusioned Brothers. Imprisoned briefly during the first round-up of MB activists in 1953, Qutb's more concerted confrontation with the regime began in 1954, when he was sentenced to 15 years in jail for his role in encouraging subversive activities. Writing and publishing from prison (a privilege afforded him seemingly due to his early support for the Free Officers), the next decade was the most prolific in Qutb's career. During this time he produced *Fi Zilal al-Qur'an* (*In the Shade of the Qur'an*), a major *tafsir* work that he had actually started in 1952, and that would not be completed until 1965, shortly before his death; and, most importantly for our purposes, the seminal *Ma'alim fi al-Tariq* (*Signposts on the Road*; hereafter *Signposts*). The latter text represents his most strident and polemical statement regarding the need to eliminate, by force if necessary, the infidel order that currently dominated Egypt. It is also a text whose core ideas have continued to animate the discourse of Islamist thinkers and activists, particularly those of a more jihadi persuasion, up to today. Initially cleared for publication, *Signposts* was soon banned by the state when it became clear that it was circulating widely as an inspirational text for MB followers meeting clandestinely. In 1964, Qutb was released from prison and immediately approached by the Brotherhood's underground leadership to serve as their spiritual guide. It appears that Qutb agreed to take on this role, with the strident, activist tenor of his recent writings clearly representing a dominant trend within the MB. The following year, Qutb was arrested along with several other MB activists and accused of reconstituting the Secret Apparatus with the aim of overthrowing the Egyptian government and killing the president. All involved were given the death penalty and these sentences, including Qutb's, were carried out in 1966.

Sayyid Qutb's social and political thought reflected a wide range of influences over the course of its development. We can find elements of both mysticism and rationalism. Where one might think that his eventual focus on pure *shari'ah* would lead Qutb to eschew Sufi thought entirely, there is also a sense in which the all-encompassing nature of Sufi devotion comes very close to the Qutbian ideal. Indeed, some of the aesthetic and almost emotive dimensions of direct, individual access to the divine present in his early thinking transferred over into his later thoughts, albeit with a rather different set of worldly priorities. As someone who engaged most key debates of the day during the period of his own intellectual formation, it is perhaps inevitable that the path towards Qutb's Islamism occurs in stages. During the first phase in which he begins to combine social and religious thinking, in the late 1940s, Qutb is seeking primarily to situate his understanding of Islam amongst competing ideologies of the day. Charles Tripp has observed that, at this point, Qutb seems to be trying to reconcile and balance within Islam aspects of liberalism, such as the emphasis on individual rights, with the requirements of the community.[43] An illustrative quote from *Social Justice in Islam* reflects these efforts:

> So the [Islamic] regulations lay down the rights of the community over the powers and abilities of the individual; they also establish limiting boundaries to the freedom, the desires, and the wants of the individual, but they must also be ever mindful of the rights of the individual, to give him freedom in his desires and inclinations; and over all there must be the limits which the community must not overstep, and which the individual on his side must not transgress.[44]

By the time he produced *Signposts* in the mid-1960s, as we will see, any interest and concern about the rights of the individual had been wholly subjugated to the higher necessity of the Islamic order.

Qutb's return from the United States in 1950 marks the beginning of the next clear phase in his intellectual development. This begins with his newfound conviction that Islam was far more than just a matter of personal spirituality, piety, or moralism, but rather that it prescribed and necessitated the active pursuit of an entire social order. It was this shift that prompted his interest in the activities of the MB and the programmatic ideas of the recently deceased Hassan al-Banna. Qutb began to emphasize the value of organized movements in the pursuit of social change as a vital counterpart to preaching. As he would later write in *Signposts*:

> If "preaching" sets right the beliefs and concepts, "movement" removes from the path other material obstacles, foremost of which is the political power that it established on intricate and complex but interrelated ideological, racial, class, social, and economic foundations. And these two—preaching and movements—jointly collaborate in influencing the established system from all four directions, and are conducive to bringing about the new system . . .[45]

It was also around this time that Qutb's long-held suspicions regarding the social irrelevance of the *ulama* and traditional religious orthodoxy seem to have been consolidated. Qutb had been critical in earlier writings about the apparent apathy of the religious establishment, represented by institutions such as Al-Azhar, towards the downtrodden masses of Egyptian society. Qutb's writing now began increasingly to emphasize the importance of direct engagement by individual believers with the truth of the *shari'ah*, bypassing the mediating influence of the established canon as transmitted by religious authorities—a mode of religious knowledge production which Qutb understood to have been tainted by centuries of un-Islamic innovation (*bid'a*). As Tripp observes, Qutb appeared to be calling for no less than the creation of a new "Qur'anic generation," modeled on the example of the Prophet's companions, who were forced to rely on their direct experience and first-hand knowledge of revelation rather than on blind *taqlid* (emulation) of figures claiming religious authority.[46] It is in this sense that we can also regard Qutb's thinking as yet another discrepant take on the Salafiyya project instigated by Muhammad Abduh half a century before.

Qutb was also influenced by other emerging currents in Islamist thought during this time. We know, for instance, that from the early 1950s he read and quoted the works of Abu'l-A'la Mawdudi, which by that time had been translated into Arabic. Like Mawdudi, and in contrast with Banna, Qutb was primarily an intellectual and theorist. He would have appreciated the comprehensive and systematic reasoning to be found in the work of the former, and it is clear that he drew from Mawdudi in developing his own exposition of Islamic politics. It is perhaps to Mawdudi that we can attribute Qutb's initial discussions of the notion of *jahiliyya*, a concept that would later develop into a central foundation in Qutb's religio-political worldview. *Jahiliyya* is a term that, in its most common usage, refers to the period of "ignorance" prior to the coming of Islam. Mawdudi's modernist interpretation began to equate *jahiliyya* with contemporary social orders that fail to institute the Islamic system—in other words, that proceed as if they were ignorant of Islam's truth. In Sayyid Qutb's thought, *jahiliyya* comes to represent his fundamental diagnosis of the malaise—cultural, moral, political—gripping his society. More than just a metaphor for slack morals, *jahiliyya* in the Qutbian context came to figure as one half of a thoroughly Manichean worldview. For Qutb there were only two possible routes. One could embrace true Islam and its *shari'ah* as a total way of life, or one could live in *jahiliyya*. His later thinking allowed no middle ground, no "almost" or "mostly" Islamic way of life; it was one or the other. *Jahiliyya*, he reasoned, named the order of the day in Egypt and in other Muslim countries run by secular regimes or corrupt, "pseudo-religious" monarchs. *Jahiliyya* was also the catch-all term that allowed him to thematize all those Western values (secularism, materialism, individualism, capitalism) that threatened to colonize anew—even worse, to colonize the hearts and minds—of Muslims.

But for Qutb *jahiliyya* was more than just a moral category. In his later work it became an integral component of his theorization of the necessity of *jihad*. Several observers have noted that Qutb's analysis of what was implied by the condition of *jahiliyya*, or in this case the presence of unjust Muslim rulers, was a major departure from conventional Islamic political thought. The general consensus up to that point had been that, when faced with a Muslim ruler who did not properly enforce the *shari'ah*, Muslims should make the ruler aware of his shortcomings, but should not actively seek to resist or overthrow the political authorities for fear of bringing about social disorder and strife (*fitna*). That is to say, it is not the responsibility of the believer to sit in judgment of a ruler's conduct *vis-à-vis* the *shari'ah*. This is a moral account that the ruler would eventually settle directly with God.[47] In stark contrast to this norm, Qutb argued—working off precedents in the thought of the fourteenth-century jurist Ibn Taymiyya—that it is incumbent upon the believer who knows his Muslim ruler to be delinquent in upholding *shari'ah* actively to resist that regime, and to take action to bring about the proper Islamic order. In effect, this meant that it became the responsibility of Muslims to decide whether those around them were infidels (*kaffirun;* sing. *kafir*), or if they were true Muslims upholding the *shari'ah*. This emphasis on *takfir* ("excommunication," or declaring someone to be a *kafir*) and its prominence within the discourse of many jihadi Islamists today is seen by some as evidence of Qutb's direct influence. This is particularly evident in the emphasis today, in the discourse of certain Islamists, on what they see as fighting the "near enemy" (see Chapter 7).

Qutb's decade of imprisonment and reported torture at the hands of Nasser's regime seems to have crystallized his conviction that it was no longer possible to pursue the reform of *jahiliyya* social orders through methods of dialogue and persuasion: *tarbiya* (education) and *da'wa* (calling to true Islam) were, for him, insufficient in the face of so totalizing a threat. At this point, direct resistance and *jihad* were the only possible—indeed, the obligatory—methods. *Signposts* represented Qutb's manifesto for the pursuit of this goal, and is the best textual embodiment of the final phase of his thinking. Most observers have tended to read *Signposts* as a text intended for an audience already most of the way there in terms of embracing Qutb's worldview—in this case, Brotherhood members severely suppressed by the regime and gathering in secret. Rather than being a gentle introduction for the lay reader, designed to persuade one of a political role for Islam, *Signposts* assumes an activist stance and then proceeds to elaborate an account of what is required of those who have already embarked "on the path of God" (*fi sabil Allah*). Those who argue against this course of action, even from a position of religious authority (e.g. *ulama*), are themselves complicit in the *jahiliyya* order. As Tripp has observed, Qutb urged his followers to have confidence in their "direct, non-philosophical apprehension of the truth," arguing that as the activist harbingers of a divinely sanctioned order, their interpretation and understanding of *shari'ah* was intrinsically superior.[48]

This brings us to the issue of *jihad* and how this concept figured in Sayyid Qutb's thought. That it was present and quite central to his later writing is undeniable. Where commentators have differed, however, is in their analysis of how important violent *jihad* was to the Qutbian project. Some, such as Sayyid's brother Muhammad Qutb, have argued that invocations of this term in the work of the former should be understood to be referring primarily to the overall struggle to achieve the Islamic order in the literal sense of *jihad* as "struggle." On the other extreme, there are those who see Qutb's significance to lay exclusively in his theorization and advocacy of violent *jihad*.[49] As is usually the case with such issues, the truth probably lies somewhere in between. Qutb, certainly in his early and middle periods, would have generally eschewed violence in favor of reform via persuasive and deliberative methods. That said, he also recognized that there were more material dimensions to the struggle that may at times call for militant tactics. Even in his very late writings, however, Qutb is not operating exclusively within the framework of violent *jihad*. To quote from *Signposts*:

> This movement does not confine itself to mere preaching and persuasion while confronting the physical power, nor does it deem it proper to utilize force and coercion for converting the ideas and thoughts of the common man. Both of these principles are of equal importance in the application of the method of this religion. The very purpose of this movement is to set human beings free from the yoke of human enslavement and make them serve the One and Only God.[50]

His focus here on the "common man" as an inappropriate target for coercive *jihad* is significant in that Qutb wants to make clear that he holds those political regimes which bring about and sustain *jahili* orders as most culpable in sin and therefore the proper object of active resistance.

Looking at Qutb's later writings, those in which the discourse of *jihad* is most prevalent, it is possible to identify two distinct trajectories for this concept, and it seems that each of the two camps seeking to interpret the jihadist import of Qutb's thought has simply chosen to emphasize one over the other. The section of *Signposts* in which Qutb elaborates his understanding of *jihad* begins with an emphasis on the more holistic sense of that term. Qutb argues that the struggle called for by Islam "is a practical [*jihad*], which progresses stage by stage and at every stage provides parallel and proper resources according to its practical needs and requirements." It is therefore not inherently violent, but, depending on contingencies, it certainly may need to take on this character. The goal of the *jihad* is to achieve a total Islamic order, and coercion may or may not be required to get there. Qutb's discussion also takes issue with the prevailing attitude of the *ulama* of his day towards *jihad*. For them, generally, the only legitimate *jihad* was one that sought to defend Muslim lands against direct threats from outside. Qutb denies this territorial conception of Islam ("a creation of the modern age")[51] and seeks to replace it with an understanding of Islam as a moral system whose manifestation in social order must be sought through active struggle:

> From the Islamic point of view, the real justification for declaring Jihad is the defense of the Islamic faith, or the defense of that way of life that presents the practical exposition of faith or the defense of that society in which that way of life is operative. As regards the soil of the country, it is itself of no significance in the eyes of Islam nor does it hold any weight. If anything can impart the respectability and greatness to the soil of the country under the Islamic concept, it is exclusively the establishment of God's rule there and the implementation of the way of life required by God.[52]

Qutb's writing does not lay great emphasis on the need for a caliphate. His concern lies primarily with achieving the proper Islamic order. In this view, any specific political system or form of government that conforms to the normativity of the *shari'ah* would therefore be acceptable.

Much has certainly been made of the influence of Sayyid Qutb's thinking on subsequent generations of jihadi-oriented Islamists. Some of these have been labeled "Qutbists," indicating the centrality of his prescriptions in their thought and practice. While many of these groups—such as Gemaa Islamiyya or Islamic Jihad in Egypt (see below), or the transnational Al-Qaeda network (Chapter 7)—do indeed embrace the use of violence, it may be a misinterpretation to identify this as Qutb's primary legacy to them. Of equal, if not greater, importance is the dualistic worldview (Islam versus *jahiliyya*) according to which Qutb and many of these latter-day movements organize their understanding of particular nations and societies.

While "Qutbism"—if such a thing really exists—potentially would represent a highly militant form of Islamism, its distinctiveness obtains primarily in its mapping and categorization of sociopolitical normativity and the obligations concomitant on Muslims seeking to follow the path of God.

The Muslim Brotherhood revitalized: Sadat and beyond

There was something of a revival in the MB's public fortunes and reputation under Gamal Abdel Nasser's successor, Anwar al-Sadat, who assumed the presidency upon the former's death in 1970. While Nasser had certainly never hesitated to make rhetorical use of religion when it seemed politically expedient to do so, Sadat, the self-styled "believer-president," systematically integrated religion into his public discourse, and went much further than his predecessor in terms of reaching out to the religious sector. Sadat built thousands of new mosques and reinvigorated the government's relationship with Al-Azhar University. Numerous Muslim Brothers, imprisoned since the mid-1960s, were released, and significant latitude was granted to the organization in terms of resuming its publications and some of its social welfare activities. We should note, however, that the Brotherhood still was not legally recognized as a political party. The re-emergent MB was cautious in its efforts, a pale shadow of the Qutbian zeal that defined the early 1960s. While it did not hesitate to criticize the government when it disagreed with policies— such as Sadat's move to liberalize certain aspects of Muslim family law—the MB of the 1970s resembled its 1930s incarnation far more than it did the group's confrontational manifestation of the 1950s and 1960s.

It is fair to say that, by the late 1970s, Sadat's Islamization efforts had begun to backfire. It became clear to the religious organizations that had gained a new lease of life during his early tenure that Sadat was not ready to push for meaningful Islamic reform as they understood it in the sense of more *shari'ah* across multiple sectors of Egyptian society. Furthermore, a number of his foreign policy initiatives had made him progressively unpopular with important segments of Egypt's population. From the *infitah* ("open door") economic policy, a liberalizing gesture that brought significant instability to Egypt's economy, to his condemnation of the Islamic revolution in Iran, Sadat appeared more and more to be aligning Egypt with the West. The final straw here was undoubtedly his signing of a peace agreement with Israel in 1979, the Camp David Accords. In 1981, Sadat was assassinated by associates of Islamic Jihad, one of a number of militant organizations that had emerged in Egypt over the course of the 1970s. Islamic Jihad, along with groups such as Takfir w'al-Hijra and Muhammad's Youth, emerged from the early 1970s as hardline Islamist alternatives for those drawn to the jihadist impulse of Sayyid Qutb but disillusioned with the moderate stance of the MB. Both Takfir and

Muhammad's Youth were involved in various attacks and kidnappings during Sadat's period in power, drawing a strong response from the government, and leading to both groups having large numbers of their followers imprisoned or killed. That these were very small extremist groups is certainly not in doubt, but there was a sense in which they represented the fringe of a broader re-Islamization of Egyptian public consciousness. While the methods of Islamic Jihad in killing Sadat were extreme, the nature of their critique of his government—whom they depicted as a despotic "Pharaoh"—was not isolated from certain more mainstream sentiments.

Under Sadat's successor, Hosni Mubarak, the government's cat-and-mouse game with the Islamists has continued. While the extremist groups that formed in the 1970s have been mostly shut down or exiled, new challenges to the Egyptian government have cropped up on both the militant and moderate fronts. From the mid-1980s, a group known as Gemaa Islamiyya emerged as an umbrella organization to coordinate the efforts of a number of small but highly militant groups operating across Egypt. Composed primarily of extremist student activists from the 1970s, these groups carried out a number of attacks on foreign tourists and other targets that symbolize Western culture. Some have viewed Gemaa Islamiyya as another example of "Qutbism" in action.[53] The Egyptian government's response to these operations has been very aggressive, making full use of the special powers permitted under the special "state of emergency" regulations that were put into effect at the time of Sadat's assassination and then never rescinded. Two developments of note regarding mainstream Islamist movements in Egypt under Mubarak will be looked at in considerable detail in the following chapter. The first of these relates to a noticeable shift in the MB's sociopolitical strategy. This has involved a greater emphasis on seeking social influence via the attainment of leadership roles in the increasingly important professional associations or "syndicates" to be found in major Egyptian cities. The Brotherhood, while still formally banned as a political party until 2011, sought political office by running candidates with no formal party affiliations—including women and Christians—and seeking alliances with former political foes including the new Wafd party. Second, as a byproduct of increased factionalism within the MB, a breakaway group attempted in 1996 to establish a new religiously based Party of the Center (HW—Hizb al-Wasat). This group, which was unable to obtain official recognition from the Mubarak government (and barely registered at the ballot box after the same regime fell in 2011), embraced the moral guidance of religion as a path to good governance and a solution to corruption, but did not include as part of its platform an emphasis on *shari'ah* or the pursuit of an Islamic state—a hallmark of the "new Islamist" tendency discussed in Chapter 4.

But the Brotherhood's political fortunes are not to be traced exclusively within the Egyptian context. Less than a decade after its founding, the movement was already branching out, establishing chapters in Syria and Palestine. Over the next few decades, MB parties would become political actors of central importance in countries such as Tunisia, Sudan, and Jordan. Hamas in Palestine today began life as an offshoot of the Brotherhood. In numerous other countries outside the Arab World, such as Turkey, Pakistan, and Malaysia, groups and parties sharing the Brotherhood's core values and basic operational method would emerge. While it is possible at some level to talk about MB transnationalism, it is more helpful to reiterate the point made above about the distinction to be drawn between the MB as an organizational entity (particularly in Egypt, but also throughout the Arab world) and the MB "way" as representing a broad tendency within contemporary Islamism that refers to a basic worldview and a general mode of political organization. As we will see, the specific methods and political priorities adopted by MB national chapters and MB-inspired groups vary considerably depending on local circumstances (there is, arguably, little to nothing by way of centralized control within the movement globally).[54] Nonetheless, insofar as the MB represented the first sustained and successful articulation of a modern Islamist method, all of these groups owe a debt to the project Hassan al-Banna initiated in 1928.

The Muslim Brotherhood as a proto-typical Islamist movement

Our analysis of the MB has permitted us to gain some understanding of how and why Islamism—as an intellectual and political project—emerged in the context of secular nationalist state formation in certain parts of the Muslim world. We have seen the discursive and mobilization strategies employed by Hassan al-Banna in order to reach out to wary and increasingly disenfranchised segments of Egyptian society. Likewise, an analysis of Sayyid Qutb's theorization of Islamic social order and *jihad* permitted us to track the intellectual evolution of the Islamist project through a particularly turbulent militant phase and to improve our understanding of some of the antecedents of ideas and approaches employed by contemporary Islamists.

In summary, there are three key points to take away from our analysis of the MB—one of which is particular to this movement, the other two pertaining to Islamism more generally.

- *Islamism as a thoroughly **modern phenomenon**,* the establishment and growth of which depended on the existence of ideas and social structures typical of modernizing society. Its organizational structure and methods of recruitment and indoctrination likewise represented this orientation. Those drawn to Islamist movements generally have little interest in the "traditional" bastions of Islamic knowledge such as Al-Azhar and the ranks of the *ulama*. Theirs is rather a direct, active, and living engagement with religious knowledge that speaks to the political imperatives of the day. It is worth quoting Sami Zubaida at length in his characterization of the typical Islamist social profile:

[W]e are talking about urban populations in the major cities . . . plus layers of rural or provincial migrants who arrived at various stages, mostly over the last few decades, first into the old quarters then further out into the sprawling suburbs and shanty towns . . .

. . . The most active, as we have seen, are the new intelligentsia, the products of modern educational systems facing grim prospects of employment in a society and state which cannot absorb the mass of intellectual proletariat which they produce and where the prizes go to those who have access . . .[55]

- *Material and ideational factors are both crucial to understanding the emergence of modern Islamism.* It is insufficient to focus exclusively on socioeconomic disenfranchisement as the basis of Islamist mobilization, but neither is the phenomenon of Islamism explained solely by reference to concerns regarding the rise of political systems premised on secular-national values and Western cultural hegemony.
- The *distinction between the MB as an organizational entity and the MB "tendency"* as a more generic current within contemporary Islamic thought and social activism. Even groups not formally affiliated with the Brotherhood have been strongly influenced by its analysis and solution for social reform. Likewise, official branches of the Brotherhood outside Egypt are almost wholly autonomous and pursue political agendas based on the specific conditions of their national settings.

ISLAM AND POLITICS THROUGHOUT THE TWENTIETH CENTURY

While the MB is certainly the original and still paradigmatic case of modern Islamism, it represents only a single instance of one particular form of Muslim politics. Over the course of the twentieth century, and particularly in its second half, the world witnessed all manner of Muslim politics, Islamist and otherwise. In some cases these were state-led efforts to establish governmental systems based on Islam, or to co-opt Islam in the name of the state's national development agenda, or to provide religious legitimacy for ruling monarchies. In other cases we find groups defining themselves in religious terms, emerging in the context of war, civil conflict, or failed states to defend either the nation or a Muslim subgroup within it in the name of Islam, or to provide social services in situations where a vanquished or absent state lacks that capacity. Others are manifestations of Islamism similar, although by no means identical, to the circumstances that produced the MB. These for the most part are cases where political parties based on Islam have sought to challenge the legitimacy and effectiveness of (usually) secular national regimes. In some instances we have seen the formation of social movements or religious groups—organized around a particular understanding of Islam—which are not, on the face of it, particularly political in nature. Some of the Muslim mass movements or student groups in Southeast Asia come to mind, as do predominantly quietistic *da'wa* groups such as the Tablighi Jamaat or the Sufi brotherhoods of West Africa. Through their use of Islamic symbols and the nature and location of their social mobilization, however, it can be argued that groups of this sort are actually key participants in what we have termed Muslim politics. The late twentieth century saw the emergence of various new forms of Muslim transnationalism in the form of diasporic and migrant communities, worldwide internet forums, and, of course, radical networks—such as Al-Qaeda—pursuing global *jihad* and a new caliphate. In subsequent chapters, this book looks in greater detail at many of these cases and more. For now, we round off our survey of state formation and Islam by looking briefly at several other key countries where Islam and politics were particularly important in the second half of the twentieth century. These cases—some of which are examined more closely in later chapters—allow us to track some of the other major trajectories of Muslim politics in the modern era.

Saudi Arabia and Pakistan: The new Islamic states

Founded as "Islamic states" prior to or just after World War II, Saudi Arabia and Pakistan represent two countries whose geopolitical significance increased enormously over the subsequent decades—the former because of its enormous oil reserves, the latter because of its strategic location in South-Central Asia. Saudi Arabia was consolidated as a state in 1932, when Abdul Aziz al-Saud secured the allegiance of all major tribes in the Arabian Peninsula and proclaimed a kingdom in his family's name. As in the case of his eighteenth-century ancestor, an alliance with religious forces was crucial to Saud's political aspirations, and much of the new state's legitimacy lay in the claims of its namesake family to conduct themselves as righteous Islamic rulers. In declaring the Qur'an to be the law of his land, Saud set his country on a path that would distinguish it from many of the secular national regimes soon to appear alongside it in the Arab world. The conservative religious ideology at the foundation of this new state would also, at times, place Saudi Arabia seemingly at odds with emergent global normative agendas such as human rights and women's rights. For example, when the Universal Declaration of Human Rights came before the UN in 1948, Saudi Arabia was one of the few countries to abstain in the vote for its adoption. It did so in protest of the provision in the Declaration (Article 18) that guaranteed an individual the right to change his or her religion. According to the Saudi interpretation of Islam, individuals do not enjoy the freedom to enter and exit religion at will. The Kingdom developed close relations with the West over the next decades as the United States, in particular, cultivated—both geologically and politically—the Saudi potential to ensure America's energy needs during the Cold War and beyond. Relations between the royal family, the Saudi bureaucracy, and the religious establishment would ebb and flow, but have remained a key dynamic in terms of the country's internal division of power. Long regarded as the home of a particularly austere and hardcore brand of Islam—commonly known as Wahhabism—Saudi Arabia actually contains considerable religious diversity. From the late 1970s onwards, but gathering strong momentum after the 1991 Gulf War, groups of dissident *ulama* and political activists have mounted a series of challenges to the Saudi regime, questioning its Islamic legitimacy (see Chapter 5). Saudi Arabia has also been one of the chief sponsors of various Islamic causes abroad, at times deploying its considerable material assets and distributive capacity towards the cause of propagating its own variant of Islam. In recent years, a gradual and still tentative process of political and religious reform has begun, and is certain to prove vitally important in terms of determining the future course—indeed, the viability—of the Saudi nation.

Pakistan represents another Islamic state founded in the first half of the twentieth century, but under circumstances very different from those of the Saudi kingdom. As we will recall, Pakistan emerged out of the partition of India in 1947 as a homeland for the Muslims of the subcontinent. The early years of Pakistani politics and political discourse were characterized by debates about what it meant to be an "Islamic state"—the two basic positions being on one hand, a relatively secular understanding of the Islamic state in Pakistan as representing the nationalist claims of Indian Muslims for their political independence; and on the other hand, a firm belief in the need to organize the political system in Pakistan according to the requirements of Islam. Over the next several decades, political regimes of various sorts—both military and civilian—would exploit this ambiguity by appealing to, and seeking to appropriate, Islamic symbols and institutions in the pursuit of their particular visions of Pakistan's "Islamic state." Waves of Islamization, such as that pursued from 1977 by Zia ul-Haq, would prompt numerous debates regarding the proper role of *shari'ah* in Pakistani society. Pakistan's security services would also become embroiled in various regional conflicts through their sponsorship of Islamic causes in neighboring countries, while simultaneously seeking to protect the Pakistani state from internal forms of Islamism that they found distasteful.

The new "Islamic revival"

Most analyses of Islamic politics in the later twentieth century are couched in terms of an "Islamic revival" that supposedly began in the wake of the 1967 Arab–Israeli war. The immediate impetus for this movement is generally understood to be the disillusionment of former Arab nationalists after the resounding defeat of Arab armies during the Six Day War. With Nasserism well on the decline, question marks had begun to appear over the Pan-Arabist project and the secular-nationalist political order at its foundation. Over the next 10–15 years, culminating in the Islamic Revolution in Iran in 1979 and the 1981 assassination of Anwar Sadat by followers of Islamic Jihad, analysts point to an upswing in popular support for Islamist causes throughout much of the Muslim world. The appropriateness of the term "revival" to describe this phenomenon has been much debated. It is certainly the case that segments of Middle Eastern and other Muslim-majority societies not previously interested in religious alternatives to the secular national state did indeed begin gathering behind Islamist causes during this period. However, it would be wrong to regard this rejuvenation of Muslim politics as *sui generis*. Neither was it indicative of an end to Islamist dormancy. Its advocates and their approaches consciously drew on the thought and practice of earlier Islamists and, indeed, in many cases represented the continuation and recatalyzation of those very same movements once the political field had opened up somewhat. In other words, there was nothing wholly new about the Muslim politics that defined the Islamic revival. Some of the groups involved, such as Takfir w'al-Hijra and Muhammad's Youth in Egypt, were composed of former Muslim Brothers seeking new forms of confrontational activism. One movement within this broader revival, however, did represent some thing significantly new. Iran's Islamic Revolution, the significance and implications of which we will look at more closely in Chapter 5, marked the first time that a nominally Islamic political order had been achieved by means of a popular Islamic revolution.

Iran's Islamic revolution

Becoming the third significant Islamic state after Saudi Arabia and Pakistan, the revolution that created the Islamic Republic of Iran in 1979 makes for a fascinating case study of both modern social mobilization and the revisionist interpretation of classical Islamic political theory. Although the *ulama* had been frequent participants in Iranian political debate since the first constitutional agitations late in the nineteenth century, Khomeini's doctrine of *vilayat-e faqih*—establishing the obligation of religious scholars to govern the country—represented a major departure from the traditional social role assigned to the *ulama*. Shi'i political theory in particular (Shi'a make up

90 percent of Iran's population) historically had been associated with a tendency toward political quietism. Riding a wave of popular discontent aimed squarely at the pro-Western Pahlavi dynasty—successors to the Qajar dynasty, which itself took over from the Safavid empire—Khomeini leveraged political forces of all persuasions (including communists and liberals) to depose the Shah's ruling regime. While regular elections have been held in Iran since the revolution (and their results generally respected), the preponderance of power held by the country's Supreme Leader has meant that the religious establishment maintains strict control of the country's security services and all forms of media—rendering serious political dissent all but impossible. Iran's population has grown increasingly frustrated at the restrictions enforced by the clerical authorities, but reformist politicians, even when occupying the highest levels of executive power, have been unable to find sufficient latitude to enact meaningful change. Iran has also been active abroad, sponsoring various Shi'i organizations, such as Hizbullah in Lebanon (see Chapter 6 and, briefly, below), and competing with Saudi Arabia for leadership in the Muslim world. It is also worthwhile noting that Iran's Islamic revolution had important implications beyond the world of Islam, occurring as it did in the midst of the Cold War. In some parts of the developing world, Iran's transformation was viewed as a victorious form of "Third Worldism" in which the popular voices had risen up to get rid of a pro-Western, neo-imperialist regime in the name of an alternative "indigenous" system.

Islam and politics beyond the Cold War

This latter point about the broader reception of Iran's Islamic revolution points to the importance of considering the wider geopolitical context in which various forms of Muslim politics occur. While all politics may indeed be local (a formulation which today is not at all at odds with a declaration that all politics are simultaneously global), the nature of political power in an interconnected and interdependent world has meant that for some time now—and certainly in the wake of decolonization after World War II—the political orders to be found within many countries in the Muslim world have been strongly affected by the prevailing geopolitical order. In most cases this has meant a shift in the source or location, but not the general nature, of the threat identified by Islamists. Where the late colonial and early decolonization periods were about Islamism as an alternative to direct colonial rule and then later the Westernizing erosion of the secular-national order, the onset of the Cold War meant that nationalist regimes were engaged from within, based in part on how they positioned themselves *vis-à-vis* the two global hegemons— the United States and the Soviet Union. In time, liberal nationalism and socialism both came to be defined as foreign ideologies, particularly when their adoption by ruling regimes seemed to have little or no positive impact on the daily lives of the masses. From the 1960s, the rhetoric of Pan-Arabism, often with strong socialist overtones, rang hollow, particularly in the wake of 1967 and the Arab defeat at the hands of Israel. For many it was the blind adoption of, or even co-option by, Western methods and politics by these governments that was understood to be the source of their inefficacy and rising internal socioeconomic disparities. It is in this context that we have to understand how inspirational Iran's Islamic revolution might have first appeared to many in the developing world. It appeared to represent a success story of a country "opting out" of the geopolitics of superpower patronage in the name of a wholly different and non-Western order.

Other instances of Islamism, however, were directly implicated in these Cold War machinations. The Soviet invasion of Afghanistan in late 1979 led to the emergence of an Islamic resistance in the form of the Afghan Mujahideen, which was enthusiastically supported by the United States. Tribally organized resistance fighters, mobilizing under the banner of Islam, fought an eight-year war of attrition with the far better-armed and -equipped military superpower that was the Union of Soviet Socialist Republics (USSR), and seemingly emerged victorious when Moscow withdrew its troops in 1989. This set the stage, however, for a civil war between regional warlords in Afghanistan (see Chapter 6) and the emergence of a newly confident form of transnational jihadism that took as its goal the elimination of infidel powers worldwide (see Chapter 7). The end of the Cold War, in turn, prompted the emergence of Muslim politics in areas where Islam had been strongly suppressed for generations. In the new Muslim-majority states of the former Soviet Union, for example, Islam was suddenly available as a political vocabulary, and various social forces—governments, oppositions, and regional militias alike—sought to mobilize in its name (see Box 6.5, "Central Asia: 'Official Islam' and its alternatives"). Likewise, Muslim countries outside the immediate region, but also some close Muslims neighbors (ethnically and geographically), sought to exert new influence in Central Asia, in part through religion.

Other forms of Islamism during this period had more to do with regional politics, civil wars, and territorial conflicts. The emergence of groups such as Hizbullah and Amal in the 1980s in the context of the Lebanese Civil War is a good case in point, as is the establishment of Hamas at the outset of the first *intifada* ("uprising") in the Palestinian territories in 1987. Both are examples of groups that emerged during times of conflict to combat the presence of foreign armies through militant means, while simultaneously mobilizing popular support and providing social services to disenfranchised populations (the Shi'a of Lebanon, and Palestinians in the Occupied Territories, respectively). As we will see, both have also since gone on to play an active role in their country's political process and even to form governments (see Chapter 6). In other contexts, the rise of Islamism has been strongly linked to internal ethno-religious cleavages and regionalism. This is how we can best understand Sudan's self-designation as an Islamic state since 1989 (see Box 5.4, "Hassan al-Turabi and Sudan's 'Islamic experiment'") and also the declaration of Islamic law in certain states of Nigeria in 2000 (see Box 6.1, "Nigeria: *Shari'ah* law and the politics of federalism").

Perhaps most interesting to observe, however, have been those cases where Islamist movements have entered the political process and sought to contest elections as political parties. The participation of Islamists in elections has been one of the lynchpin issues within the debate over Islam and politics. Some, claiming that Islamists represent a "one man, one vote, one time" approach, argue that any Islamist party elected to power would seek to eradicate the democratic system through which they came into office so as to ensure that they cannot be voted out. Others argue that Islamist parties will see it as serving their long-term interests to adhere to the norms of pluralistic, participatory politics, citing various instances where Islamist parties have entered and exited legislative bodies as the results of elections demand.[56] There is also an ongoing debate, as we will see in the next chapter, as to the very nature of contemporary Islamist movements and their political goals. Part of the problem, of course, is that there is a very scarce evidence trail that allows us to know what happens when an Islamist party comes to power through the ballot box under relatively normal circumstances, as this had never happened until Tunisia and Egypt in 2011–12. In the case of the Refah Party in Turkey (see Chapter 4)—which was briefly in power as part of a coalition government—extra-political forces (in this case the military and the Kemalist courts) severely circumscribed their latitude of action. The 2006 election of Hamas to lead the Palestinian Authority (PA) is a difficult case to assess, given that it occurred in the context of ongoing political occupation and conflict, and without the existence of a meaningful state. Turkey has been ruled by the Justice and Development Party (AKP—Adalet ve Kalkınma Partisi), a party rooted in Refah but which refuses to be characterized as "Islamist," since 2002, and Tunisia and Egypt have both seen Islamists elected to executive power with varying degrees of success since 2012.

Prior to the victory of Tunisian and Egyptian Islamists, the closest we had come to an Islamist party achieving state power through legitimate means and under relatively normal political conditions was in Algeria in late 1991, when the Islamic Salvation Front (FIS—Front Islamique du Salut) contested and won the national elections. With the FIS poised to set up a new government, the Algerian military stepped in to annul the results of the elections, impose martial law, and ban the FIS from further political activity—setting off an eight-year period of near-civil war and untold loss of life (see Box 3.2, "Algeria: Islamists *almost* in power"). While the Algerian test case of Islamism in power never came to pass, it prompted an important debate about the implications of Islamist groups entering the political process. Some have pointed to this example as evidence in support of the "repression leads to radicalization" thesis—with some asking similar questions about the future tenor of Islamist politics in Egypt after elected Islamists were removed from power by the military in 2013. It is clear that the Algerian example points ahead to a key issue that we will engage in considerable detail in Chapter 4: the question of where and how Islamist groups have sought to enter the political process, and the implications and effects of their doing so on the orientation, agendas, and modes of political activism employed by the movements. Indeed, there is considerable debate today about the impact of political participation on these movements and the broader project of Islamism.

BOX 3.2 ALGERIA: ISLAMISTS *ALMOST* IN POWER

Algeria is crucially important to the study of Muslim politics and Islamism in several respects. First, the Algerian national elections of late 1991 represented the first time an Islamist party had ever been on the verge of being brought into government through a popular ballot. Had the Islamic Salvation Front (FIS) been allowed to come to power, it would have provided us with a unique opportunity to see what government by Islamists looks like in practice—something that was not possible until the Islamist victories in Tunisia and Egypt in 2011–12. Second, the Algerian Islamic movement in the form of the FIS was itself a study in the diversity of Islamism and Islamist agendas. Under the Front's umbrella were to be found at least two quite distinct factions, one whose socio-political vision was broadly in line with that of the Egyptian Muslim Brotherhood during the time it sought to work within the framework of the Egyptian system, and another with strongly militant tendencies that questioned the legitimacy of the existing Algerian political order. Finally, the violence and instability that engulfed Algeria in the 1990s provided several catalyzing forces—in the form of movements, ideologues, and experiential knowledge—that would later become crucially important to the global jihadist movement (see Chapter 7).

Algeria gained its independence in 1962 after a long war that gradually wore down the political will of its former colonial power, France. Religion figured as a marker of national identity during this conflict through, for example, the use by pro-independence forces of the slogan *"Algérie musulmane"* ("Algeria for the Muslims") rather than an ethnolinguistic referent. Behind this rhetoric, however, lay a cultural rift that soon emerged as a defining feature of Algerian politics once the country gained its independence. In broad terms, this cleavage took the form of tensions that emerged between a French-speaking political and economic urban elite and the rural masses, generally oriented towards identity formations emphasizing Arab linguistic, cultural, and religious heritage. Aside from the obvious socioeconomic divide represented by this bifurcation, there was a further ideological aspect to bear in mind here, in that Algeria's French speakers had a greater tendency to gravitate towards forms of leftist, that is, secular, thought.

Economic tensions in the late 1980s (tied to a sharp decline in oil prices) led to widespread protests against unemployment, government corruption, and shortages of housing and foodstuffs. It is this context that gave rise to the FIS as a political movement. An FIS precursor can be found in the Al-Qiyam Society, a cultural heritage organization founded in the late 1960s by a group of highly educated Algerians seeking to preserve Arabo-Islamic heritage in the face of what they perceived as an increasingly dominant Francophone trend. The early FIS drew from this movement, and built up its influence via voluntary associations, mosque networks, schools, and factory floors. While the Francophone–Arabophone divide was certainly one factor driving the formation of the Islamist movement, membership in the latter did not split so easily along such simplistic cultural lines. The failure of the political left in Algeria to provide socialist solutions to encroaching impoverishment further emboldened the Islamists and swelled their ranks. While the ruling Front de la Liberation National (FLN) sought to introduce liberalizing reforms as an emergency measure, this gesture turned out to be much too little, far too late.

Rather than a single, unified political party, the FIS designation actually referred to something that was more of an "umbrella" organization under which were to be found two quite distinctive factions. The first of these, led by Abbasi Madani (b. 1931), was strongly influenced by the basic model of the MB. It opposed the secularizing trend and sought to establish a basis in public life and law for Islamic norms and legal codes. The second faction, around the younger Ali Belhadj (b. 1956), represented a more confrontational and even militant tendency, seeking to reshape the Algerian political order fundamentally along Islamic lines. The latter group drew energy from the support of Algerian veterans of the Afghan war against the Soviet occupation (see Chapter 7). While these two groups within the FIS were clearly at odds in terms of their core agenda and methods, the advantages of working together during the early years of the Islamist opposition were sufficient to achieve minimal cohesion within the movement.

The FIS had its first electoral venture in the summer of 1990, when it participated in municipal elections just a year after being formed. Its sweeping victory prompted the government, led by the secular-nationalist

© Getty Images

Figure 3.5 Islamic Salvation Front leaders Ali Belhadj (left) and Abbasi Madani

FLN, to crack down on the movement, arresting key figures, cutting off its funding, redrawing electoral districts to the disadvantage of the Islamists, and postponing parliamentary elections in the face of what was perceived as a popular tide of Islamist support. Despite these blocking maneuvers, the FIS still fared relatively well once national elections finally took place in late 1991. With the Islamists poised to win a parliamentary majority in the second round of voting scheduled for early 1992, the Algerian military intervened in January of that year to annul the elections, impose martial law, and ban the FIS as a political party.

Once it was declared illegal and driven underground, the FIS "coalition" splintered into its constituent pieces. With Madani and Belhadj both in prison, followers of the latter took the opportunity of the military intervention to argue that it was impossible to pursue their aims via the political process. This faction split from the main movement to form the Armed Islamic Group (GIA—Groupe Islamique Armé), which soon subdivided further along class lines, and proceeded to commence a militant campaign against the Algerian state and even certain civilian targets (journalists, etc.) who it regarded as agents of the secular order. During much of the 1990s, Algeria was in a state of virtual civil war, with casualty levels topping 100,000. Most of the violence in this conflict can be attributed to the GIA and other, sometimes even more militant offshoots. Some of the killing, however, was also linked to groups of paramilitary special forces commonly known as the *eradicateurs,* accused of carrying out attacks on various population centers and then trying to pass them off as the work of the radical Islamists.

Some semblance of order began to return to Algeria from the time of the 1997 elections and a simultaneous ceasefire agreement. The shift towards reconciliation served further to marginalize the radical Islamist factions, who refused to participate in this process. The most extreme among these, the Salafist Group for Preaching and Combat (GSPC— Groupe Salafiste pour la Prédication et le Combat) began to form connections with the global jihadist movement (see Chapter 7), while the capacity of the GIA to wage armed conflict quickly began to dwindle after the turn of the millennium. Under the leadership of Abdelaziz Bouteflika, a veteran politician with roots in the FLN, Algeria worked toward the nearly unanimous popular adoption of a Charter for National Peace and Reconciliation, whose provisions became law in 2006. 2011 finally saw the lifting of the State of Emergency that had been in place since 1992.

Parliamentary elections in 2007 and 2012 saw national secular forces predominating, although a coalition of Islamist parties (the Green Algeria Alliance) led by the Movement of Society for Peace—moderate Islamists who had shown a willingness to cooperate with the military and the FLN—met with some success, and has now become a regular fixture in the legislature. From 2007, the Islamists even served in an FLN-led coalition government, but withdrew in 2012, emboldened in part by the recent political success of Islamists elsewhere in the region. Algeria remained largely untouched by the political upheaval that swept much of the rest of the Arab world in 2010–11, perhaps because its recent history has led most political groups to shy away from confrontational and polarizing politics. Some observers, however, have pointed out that the same socioeconomic conditions that proved to be important drivers of the Arab Uprisings elsewhere also exist—and seem to be getting worse—in Algeria.[57]

NOTES

1 H. Enayat, *Modern Islamic Political Thought,* Hong Kong: Macmillan Press, 1982.
2 Enayat, op. cit., pp. 62–68; A. Raziq, "The Problem of the Caliphate," in M. Moaddel, K. Talattof (eds), *Modernist and Fundamentalist Debate,* New York: Palgrave Macmillan, 2000, pp. 95–100.

3 M. Kramer, *Islam Assembled,* New York: Columbia University Press, 1985.
4 R. Khalidi, *The Origins of Arab Nationalism,* New York: Columbia University Press, 1991; A. Dawisha, *Arab Nationalism in the Twentieth Century: From Triumph to Despair,* Princeton, NJ: Princeton University Press, 2003.
5 W. Cleveland, *The Making of an Arab Nationalist: Ottomanism and Arabism in the Life and Thought of Sati al-Husri,* Princeton, NJ: Princeton University Press, 1972.
6 D. Commins, "Hasan al-Banna (1906–49)," in A. Rahnema (ed.), *Pioneers of Islamic Revival,* London: Zed Books, 1994; L. C. Brown, *Religion and State: The Muslim Approach to Politics,* New York: Columbia University Press, 2000, pp. 143–148.
7 Brown, op. cit., p. 146.
8 J. Donahue, J. Esposito (eds), *Islam in Transition: Muslim Perspectives,* New York: Oxford University Press, 1982, pp. 81–82.
9 S. V. R. Nasr, "Mawdudi and the Jama'at-I Islami: The Origins, Theory and Practice of Islamic Revivalism," in Rahnema (ed.), op. cit.; Brown, op. cit., pp. 148–153.
10 Ibid.
11 J. Donahue, J. Esposito (eds), op. cit., p. 95.
12 J. Donahue, J. Esposito (eds), op. cit., p. 259. Emphasis in original.
13 J. Donahue, J. Esposito (eds), op. cit., p. 254.
14 Ibid.
15 J. Donahue, J. Esposito (eds), op. cit., p. 257.
16 L. C. Brown, op. cit., pp. 146, 153.
17 S. Ismail, *Rethinking Islamist Politics: Culture, the State, and Islamism,* London: I.B. Tauris, 2003, pp. 4–19.
18 F. Halliday, *Islam and the Myth of Confrontation,* revised edn, London: I.B. Tauris, 2002, ch. 7.
19 N. Keddie, *Roots of Revolution: An Interpretive History of Modern Iran,* New Haven, CT: Yale University Press, 1981; Saad Eddin Ibrahim, "Anatomy of Egypt's Militant Islamic Groups: Methodological Note and Preliminary Findings," *International Journal of Middle East Studies* 12, 1980, pp. 423–453; M. M. J. Fischer, "Islam and the Revolt of the Petit Bourgeoisie," *Daedalus* 111, 1982, pp. 101–125.
20 Charles Hirschkind, "What is Political Islam?' *Middle East Report* Oct–Dec 1997, pp. 12–14.
21 S. Sayyid, *A Fundamental Fear: Eurocentrism and the Emergence of Islamism,* revised edn, London: Zed Books, 2004.
22 H. Yavuz, *Islamic Political Identity in Turkey,* Oxford: Oxford University Press, 2003, pp. 15–36.
23 A. Hamzawy, "The Key to Arab Reform: Moderate Islamists," *Policy Brief* 40, Washington, DC: Carnegie Endowment for International Peace, 2005.
24 S. S. Rudy, "Subjectivity, Political Evaluation, and Islamist Trajectories," in B. Schaebler, L. Stenberg (eds), *Globalization and the Muslim World: Culture, Religion, and Modernity,* Syracuse, NY: Syracuse University Press, 2004, pp. 39–79.
25 Hirschkind, op. cit.
26 R. Martin, A. Barzegar (eds), *Islamism: Contested Perspectives on Political Islam,* Palo Alto, CA: Stanford University Press, 2009, pp. 17–50.
27 F. Volpi, *Political Islam Observed,* London: Hurst, 2010.

28 Q. Wiktorowicz (ed.), *Islamic Activism: A Social Movement Theory Approach,* Bloomington, IN: Indiana University Press, 2004.

29 R. Hefner, *Civil Islam: Muslims and Democratization in Indonesia,* Princeton, NJ: Princeton University Press, 2000; V. Nasr, "The Rise of Muslim Democracy", *Journal of Democracy* 16, 2005, pp. 13–27; A. R. Norton, "Thwarted Politics: The Case of Egypt's Hizb al-Wasat," in R. Hefner (ed.), *Remaking Muslim Politics: Pluralism, Contestation, Democratization,* Princeton, NJ: Princeton University Press, 2004, pp. 133–161.

30 J. Schwedler, *Faith in Moderation: Islamist Parties in Jordan and Yemen,* New York: Cambridge University Press, 2006.

31 A. Bayat, *Making Islam Democratic: Social Movements and the Post-Islamist Turn,* Palo Alto, CA: Stanford University Press, 2007.

32 O. Roy, *Globalized Islam: The Search for a New Ummah,* New York: Columbia University Press, 2004.

33 R. Mitchell, *The Society of Muslim Brothers,* New York: Oxford University Press, 1993, p. 9.

34 Mitchell, op. cit., p. 18.

35 S. Zubaida, *Islam, the People and the State: Political Ideas and Movements in the Middle East,* London: I.B. Tauris & Co, 1993, p. 157.

36 Mitchell, op. cit., p. 198.

37 P. Bourdieu, "Forms of capital," in J. C. Richards (ed.), *Handbook of Theory and Research for the Sociology of Education,* New York: Greenwood Press, 1983; J. Coleman, *Foundations of Social Theory,* Cambridge, MA: Harvard University Press, 1990.

38 M. Moaddel, *Islamic Modernism, Nationalism, and Fundamentalism: Episode and Discourse,* Chicago, IL: University of Chicago Press, 2005, p. 211.

39 Moaddel, op. cit., p. 198.

40 Mitchell, op. cit., pp. 103–104.

41 C. Tripp, "Sayyid Qutb: The Political Vision," in Rahnema (ed.), op. cit.; Brown, op. cit., pp. 153–159.

42 Tripp, op. cit., p. 158.

43 Tripp, op. cit., p. 157.

44 Donahue, Esposito, op. cit., p. 126.

45 S. Qutb, "War, Peace, and Islamic Jihad," in Moaddel, Talattof (eds), op. cit., p. 229.

46 Tripp, op. cit., p. 179.

47 Brown, op. cit., p. 158.

48 Tripp, op. cit., p. 173.

49 P. Bergen, *The Osama bin Laden I Know: An Oral History of Al-Qaeda's Leader,* New York: Simon & Schuster, 2006, pp. 18–20.

50 Qutb, op. cit., pp. 225–226

51 Ibid.

52 Qutb, op. cit., p. 241.

53 Qutb, op. cit., p. 178.

54 A. Pargeter, *The Muslim Brotherhood: The Burden of Tradition,* London: Saqi Books, 2010, ch. 3.

55 Zubaida, op. cit., p. 159.

56 Schwedler, op. cit.

57 D. Ottaway, "Algeria: Bloody Past and Fractious Factions," in R. Wright (ed.), *The Islamists Are Coming: Who They Really Are,* Washington, DC: Woodrow Wilson International Center for Scholars, 2012, pp. 57–70.

CHAPTER 4

Islam in the system: The evolution of Islamism as political strategy

In Chapter 3 we examined the process of state formation in the Muslim world, and the emergence of Islamism as an intellectual and political movement in response to the perceived Westernization of modern regimes and their failure to deliver on the promises of modernization. Through the ideas and work of figures such as Hassan al-Banna, Abu'l-A'la Mawdudi, and Sayyid Qutb, we came to understand how Islamism also represented a new approach to the creation of a "living Islam," as lay activists and intellectuals rather than classically trained *ulama* emerged as the vanguard class of public religiosity understood as the pursuit of a modern, systematic Islamic social and political order. National-secular regimes were perceived as overly secular and concerned primarily with furthering the interests of existing political elites. Likewise, the religious scholars had either been co-opted by the state, or had their heads buried in medieval texts—rendering them, in both cases, ineffectual in terms of pursuing meaningful social transformation along Islamic lines.

This chapter looks more closely at the evolution of Islamism as a political strategy from, roughly, the 1960s up to the present day. Our main focus is on the question of how the shifting terrain of internal politics and external geopolitics has affected how groups pursue social and political activity in the name of Islam. In particular, we pick up a theme first mentioned in Chapter 1—that of modern globalization—and try to come to some better understanding of how this disparate set of macro-level forces has reconfigured the nature of Islamism over several decades. As will quickly become clear, it is impossible to read Islamism as an atavistic response to modernization that seeks a wholesale return to pre-modern Islamic society. Islamism as a political strategy, we argue, is thoroughly modern in terms of its ideology and organization; embraces many of the core precepts of modernity; and, in strategic terms, makes sense only as an approach to politics under conditions of political modernity. In other words, modernity constitutes the very preconditions for the emergence of Islamism as a distinct political strategy. As globalization—as a particular stage in the evolution of the modern political economy—has systematically reached into Muslim societies and restructured social life, so has Islamism itself changed with the times.

This chapter begins by providing a more thorough analysis of the political sociology of classic Islamism as represented by groups such as the Muslim Brotherhood. We look in greater detail at their bases of social support, and try to connect the social location of Islamism with prevailing political economies within certain key states in the Muslim world. Next, we examine the emergence of a new generation of pragmatic Islamists, sometimes referred to as "New Islamists" or moderate Islamists, who have sought to pursue religiously oriented political change through participation in elections, and by entering into broad coalitions with non-Islamist groups and parties similarly committed to overthrowing authoritarian regimes. We then look briefly at an emerging trend identified by several observers that sometimes goes by the name of "Muslim democracy." This refers to groups that do not seek directly to institute a political order defined by religion (e.g. through the introduction of *shari'ah* laws), but which instead work towards secular and pluralistic goals in cooperation with a wide variety of political groups, while taking their general moral cues from religious norms. The chapter then goes on to illustrate how these different strategies have evolved in different settings by presenting a series of case studies. First, we look at how Egypt's MB, formally banned as a political party for decades, has changed its strategy in recent years in response to generational changes within the movement itself, as well as the opportunities and radically altered political environment presented by the downfall of Egypt's longstanding authoritarian regime in 2011. We then move on to the case of Turkey to examine the shift from classic Islamism, as defined by parties such as Necmettin Erbakan's Refah (Welfare) Party, to the apparent "Muslim democracy" approach of the current ruling AKP—all of this within the context of a political order defined by the highly secular ideology of Kemalism as enforced by a strong military. In Jordan, finally, we look at the case of an MB-affiliated party, the Islamic Action Front (IAF), participating in national elections and pursuing a diverse and pragmatic political platform defined partly in response to a rapidly changing regional political climate. Jordan also provides us with an opportunity to understand better what Islamist politics look like in monarchical systems where rulers sometimes invoke some measure of religious warrant to back their political legitimacy.

■ THE SHIFTING SOCIAL PROFILE OF ISLAMISM

We begin with a point made several times in the previous chapter about the social profile of those drawn to Islamist movements such as the MB. We noted that Islamism was not primarily a rural phenomenon, nor were its main activists and advocates to be found among the uneducated poor. Those active within the Brotherhood traditionally have been urban-based, educated in secular institutions, and often employed within modern professional fields such as medicine, engineering, or government bureaucracy. But why should this social group be drawn to a political movement defined in religious terms? In order to understand this seeming incongruence, we need to delve somewhat deeper into the nature of the political economy in the Arab world during the 1960s and 1970s, and its interaction with shifting conceptions of Arab and Muslim identity.

The political sociology of classic Islamism

Within a generation of the emergence of modern states in much of the Muslim world, particularly in the Middle East, it had become clear that the promises of secular nationalism (independence, prosperity, and a proud national or even Pan-Arab identity) were unlikely to be fulfilled. While no longer directly occupied by foreign colonizing powers, it appeared to most Arabs that much of their fate was still decided by the machinations of superpower geopolitics and the intricacies of the Cold War. The failure of Egypt's experimental union with Syria between 1958 and 1962, the defeat of Arab armies by Israel in 1967, and the opening up of the Egyptian economy to world markets during the "Open Door" policy under Sadat all provided Arabs with a sense of growing inefficacy over their political fate. In terms of local politics, it also became clear quite quickly that behind the façade of modern republican states lay a political system still governed by all manner of patronage ties, clan and tribal allegiances, and an alliance between political and economic elites intent on maintaining their grip on power at any costs.

The various programs and schemes through which the government initially sought to provide some form of participation for the newly educated masses very quickly came to be out of synch with the pace of societal development. So, for example, while universities were churning out thousands of graduates in modern fields such as engineering, chemistry, and medicine, there were not enough job opportunities to employ this aspiring middle class. For many, the government bureaucracy became the standard fallback when no other job was available, but even the ranks of the technocrats were soon swollen to a point where the government could no longer take on any new employees. The few coveted positions available within the private sector tended to be reserved for those elites whose patronage propped up the state. Far from opening up new paths for participation and social mobility, the new system seemed to have done no more than re-entrench existing patterns of social influence behind a new "modern" façade. In many cases, the gap between rich and poor actually widened, with meaningful political enfranchisement completely nonexistent outside the few perks offered to members of pro-regime parties, cadres, and inner circles. What we witnessed during this period was a classic case of "relative deprivation" caused by rapidly rising economic and political expectations that were not being met by material conditions.[1] While relatively well off compared with those living in the abject poverty of rural areas, the members of this aspiring middle class had come to calibrate its social identity in relation to those of the political elite. By moving to the city and seeking out education, they had expected to benefit from the modernizing economy. Alienated from its affluence and unable to gain real access to positions of power, this modernizing generation soon began to explore other vectors and discourses of social action. A number of political sociologists have shown how this kind of volatile environment can be prone to various forms of "contentious politics" and the rise of oppositional social movements.[2]

We have already noted, but it is worth saying a few more words about, the primarily urban nature of modern Islamism. Olivier Roy has written on the importance of the reconfiguration of urban space for the organization and mobilization of Islamist sentiment.[3] As rural families flocked to rapidly expanding cities in the 1950s and 1960s, the very landscape of urban space in the Middle East was transformed. Sprawling suburbs and peri-urban zones sprang up around the traditional centers of cities— spaces the state found increasingly difficult to control, and where other modern forms of social organization (workers' groups, trade unions) also found little purchase due to the absence of regular employment.[4] The population of these new urban areas was composed of a mixture of the semi-enfranchised (such as low-level bureaucrats who would commute to government offices while also holding down part-time jobs at night) and a new, younger generation of the wholly disenfranchised. This is the generation who were born in the city and who, unlike their parents, were unable to gain entrance to university, or saw it as pointless to do so given the lack of job prospects afterwards. The advent of Sadat's Open Door (*infitah*) policies of the 1970s disproportionately subjected the lower-middle classes to the disruptive effects of exposure to free markets and neoliberal reform—further exacerbating among this group the alienating effects of modernization described above.

It was these spaces and this generation that the Islamists made their own from the late 1960s. With Arab socialism revealed as a chimera, and the advent of an identity crisis prompted by events such as the massive Arab defeat and loss of huge territories including Jerusalem during the Arab–Israeli war of 1967, the situation was ripe for a new ideological basis for sociopolitical mobilization to emerge. This space was increasingly filled by the Islamists when support for Pan-Arabism and Marxism began to decline sharply. The attraction of Islamism as an ideology can be understood in roughly the following terms: modernity—in the form of techno-scientific knowledge, industrialization, and urbanization—is a positive force that should be embraced. Political and economic elites—old and new—had, however, become so thoroughly corrupted and seduced by the excesses of Westernization that they could no longer be trusted to pursue the interests of the nation as a whole. The pervasive spread of Western modes of consumption and the "worship" of status symbols (jeans, automobiles, girlfriends/boyfriends) was akin to a new form of *shirk* ("idolatry"). The alternative, then, was to turn away from Western modernity and internalize instead the idea that "Islam is the solution"—a standard slogan of the MB during its decades in political wilderness. According to this approach, the technical trappings of modernity should be maintained (e.g. science, industry, techniques of management, and social organization) but within an identity and normative framework that took Islam as the exclusive source of all morality. As Roy saw it, this was about turning to the values of Islam and refiguring them not as symbols of backwardness, but rather as a new source of dignity.[5] The West may have science and capitalism, but Islam possesses the far more important and powerful force of morality. Groups did different things with, and mobilized around, this vision in different ways. The MB's "Islam is the solution," combining modernity and piety, represented the most pervasive form of mainstream Islamism. Others took the logic to a more radical extreme. Radical groups such as Takfir w'al-Hijra sought to separate from what they saw as a society irreparably corrupted and—taking a cue from Sayyid Qutb—mired in un-Islamic ignorance (*jahiliyya*) so as to work for the eradication of the prevailing order, through *jihad* if necessary.

The urban masses in cities such as Cairo developed new forms of social organization that, for the greater part, escaped most attempts at state regulation. Informal networks of voluntary associations and neighborhood groups became the new norm. If the state and the "modern economy" could not provide, then neighborhoods and urban quarters would become largely self-sufficient, constructing their own informal sector economies to trade goods and services, and creating alternative "avenues of participation," to use Diane Singerman's language.[6] The MB proved masterful at socializing these new spaces, building strong relationships with various local associations, and defining their normative essence in terms of an Islamic framework. Piety and mutual welfare became wholly intertwined. In sociological terms, we can understand the networks and conduits of Islamist activism as crucial sites for the production of what scholars such as Pierre Bourdieu have called "social capital."[7] Variously defined in the literature, the notion of social capital here refers to the value gained (in terms of enhanced personal capacity, pluralized opportunity structures, and so forth) from membership and participation in social networks characterized by mutual trust, reciprocity, and a shared normative framework. Urban clubs, reading rooms, and night classes became spaces in which one could pursue self-betterment, but the Brotherhood, through its neighborhood cell structure (the so-called "family" system), also made sure these were also spaces of *da'wa* and *tarbiya*—that is, religious education and the propagation of sacred consciousness. Social mobility and piety were constructed as mutually constitutive. One naturally flowed from the other. And with the state almost wholly absent from these spaces, the Islamists had no meaningful competitors.

What were the political implications of this trend? We will remember that in the paradigmatic case of popular Islamist mobilization, that of the MB in Egypt, the group remained formally banned as a political party from the mid-1950s until the second decade of the twenty-first century. While the Brotherhood enjoyed a brief upswing in its fortunes under Sadat (see Chapter 3), it was still not able to contest elections openly and independently until 2011. As we will see, these political constraints led the Brotherhood in Egypt to shift its political strategy considerably over the past two decades, exploring a wide range of alternative routes to political influence and also new alliances—resembling, in many ways, the "new Islamism" or second-generation Islamism described below. The unprecedented opportunity presented by Egypt's popular revolution in 2011 posed yet another dilemma for the Brotherhood. Suddenly free to contest elections, should it immediately seek to maximize its formal political power through state structures, or should it continue to work at the level of society as Egypt passes through a difficult and turbulent transition?

Prior to the Egyptian MB's phenomenal political rise after 2011, the best case we had to look at in terms of understanding Islamism as a political strategy was that of Algeria (see Box 3.2, "Algeria: Islamists *almost* in power"). The Front Islamique du Salut (FIS; "Islamic Salvation Front"), responding to a growing sense of disenfranchisement among Algeria's Arab-oriented masses (urban- and rural-based), leveraged their support within local neighborhoods and associations into sweeping electoral success at the municipal level. When poised to win national elections in 1991 and form the region's first Islamist government, however, the military stepped in to prevent this from happening. When their counterparts in neighboring Tunisia, the Mouvement de la Tendance Islamique (MTI—Islamic Tendency Movement)—which changed its name in the early 1990s to Al-Nahda ("Renaissance") to avoid direct reference to Islam—sought to enter politics directly, the highly secular regime of Zein Abedine Ben Ali outlawed the party, and its leadership went into exile abroad. Ben Ali's ouster in 2011 handed Al-Nahda an opportunity—much like the Egyptian MB—openly to vie for political power as Tunisia embarked on a difficult transition to democracy (see Box 4.2, "Tunisia: Islamists and the legacy of secularism").

The standard complaint leveled against Islamist parties by incumbent regimes and external stakeholders is that their participation in democratic processes is purely instrumental. It is often said that their ostensible embrace of individual political rights—the "one citizen, one vote" principle—should actually be understood, in the words of a former U.S. government official, as "one citizen, one vote, one time"—implying that once in power, they would work quickly to eradicate democracy and political pluralism, institute shari'ah, and structure the political process such that they could never be removed from office by a popular plebiscite. In other words, those wary of political participation by Islamists seek to characterize Islamism as inherently autocratic and anti-democratic. Despite assurances by most Islamists that they would govern according to constitutional norms and leave government if and when they were voted out, the Muslim world has little experience of elected Islamists in power. The short MB presidency in Egypt (2012–13) was certainly inept, but was removed through military intervention rather than through the ballot box. How, then, do we assess claims and counterclaims about whether Islamists are willing to respect the procedural aspects of democracy? To what extent is anti-Islamist alarmism simply a strategy by various regimes—many highly authoritarian in their own right—or military-backed "deep states" to raise suspicions about a social force by which they feel threatened? On the other hand, to what extent is it possible to embrace the democratic rhetoric of Islamist movements when the specifics and practical implications of their stated intention to introduce shari'ah remain vague and the limits of their political pluralism (regarding women, non-Muslims, and secular parties) are equally ambiguous?[8]

The next generation of "new Islamists" and "Muslim democrats"

The persistent persecution of conventional Islamist parties, along with certain demographic changes within the Islamists' traditional bases of social support, have led some Islamist groups from the mid-1990s onwards to pursue new political strategies. Observers have variously described this group as "new Islamists"[9] or "moderate Islamists,"[10] but the analysis of their emergence is essentially the same. Throughout the 1980s and 1990s, several regimes in the Muslim world had developed into what Daniel Brumberg calls "liberalized autocracies."[11] Such governments hold regular elections, tend to allow some semblance of multiparty pluralism, profess support for global human rights norms, and enthusiastically embrace foreign-funded anti-corruption and democracy capacity-building programs. All the while, however, these processes are carefully stage-managed in a "theater of democratization" to give the impression of far more power-sharing and pluralism than actually exists.[12] While various parties may be able to gain access to state-controlled legislative bodies and to express their views through relatively open media, the regime makes sure that they are never actually able to become meaningful political threats.[13]

Table 4.1 Islamists in legislative elections (1990–2013) for selected countries

Country	Election year	Party/movement	Results		Total seats in assembly
			Seats won	Percentage of seats won	
Algeria	2012	Green Algeria Alliance (MSP/IRM/El Islah)[a]	47	10%	462
		Front for Justice and Development (FJD)	7	2%	
		Front for Change (FC)	4	1%	
	2007	Movement for the Society of Peace (MSP)	52	13%	389
		Islamic Renaissance Movement (IRM)	5	1%	
	2002	Movement for the Society of Peace (MSP)	38	10%	389
		El Islah	43	11%	
	1997	Movement for the Society of Peace (MSP)	69	18%	380
		Islamic Renaissance Movement (IRM)	35	9%	
	1991	Movement for the Society of Peace (MSP)	0		430
		Islamic Renaissance Movement (IRM)	0		
		Front Islamique du Salut (FIS)	188[b]	44%	
Egypt	2011	Freedom and Justice Party[c]	232	47%	498
		Al-Nour Party	121	24%	
		Hizb Al-Wasat (HW)	10	2%	
	2005	Muslim Brotherhood[d]	88	20%	444
	2000	Muslim Brotherhood[d]	17	4%	444
	1995[e]	Muslim Brotherhood[d]	1	< 1%	444
	1990[f]		—		—
Indonesia	2009	Prosperous Justice Party (PKS)	59	11%	560
		United Development Party (PPP)	39	7%	
	2004	Prosperous Justice Party (PKS)	45	8%	550
		United Development Party (PPP)	58	11%	
	1999	United Development Party (PPP)	58	13%	462
	1997[g]	United Development Party (PPP)	89	21%	425
	1992	United Development Party (PPP)	62	12%	500
Jordan	2013[h]		—		—
	2007	Islamic Action Front (IAF)	6	5%	110
	2003	Islamic Action Front (IAF)	17	15%	110
	1997[h]		—	—	—
	1993	Islamic Action Front (IAF)	16	20%	80
Kuwait	2012	Islamic Bloc (Sunni)	3	6%	50
		Shi'ite Parties	17	34%	
	2009	Islamic Bloc (Sunni)	3	6%	50
		Shi'ite Parties	9	18%	
	2006	Islamic Bloc (Sunni)	18	36%	50
		Shi'ite Parties	4	8%	
	2003	Islamic Bloc (Sunni)	23	46%	50
		Shi'ite Parties	4	8%	
	1999				50
	1996	Islamic Bloc (Sunni)	20	40%	50
	1992	Islamic Bloc (Sunni)	16	32%	50
		Shi'ite Parties	8	16%	
	1990				50
Lebanon	2009	Hizbullah	10	8%	128
		AMAL (Afwaj al-Muqawama al-Lubnaniyya)	12	9%	
	2005	Hizbullah	14	11%	128
		AMAL (Afwaj al-Muqawama al-Lubnaniyya)	15	12%	

	2000	Hizbullah	8	6%	128
		AMAL (Afwaj al-Muqawama al-Lubnaniyya)	19	15%	
	1996	Hizbullah	9	7%	128
		AMAL (Afwaj al-Muqawama al-Lubnaniyya)	13	10%	
	1992	Hizbullah	12	9%	128
		AMAL (Afwaj al-Muqawama al-Lubnaniyya)	15	12%	
Libya	2012	Justice and Construction Party (JCP)	17	9%	200
Malaysia	2013		21	9%	222
	2008	Parti Islam Se-Malaysia (PAS)/PMIP	23	10%	222
	2004		7	3%	219
	1999		27	12%	219
	1995		7	3%	219
	1990		7	3%	219
Morocco	2011		107	27%	396
	2007	Justice and Development Party (PJD)	46	14%	325
	2002		42	13%	325
	1997	Constitutional and Democratic Popular Movement (MPCD)[i]	9	3%	325
	1993	—	—	—	333
Pakistan	2013	Jamiat Ulema-e-Islam (JUI) (both factions)	14	5%	272
	2008	Muttahhida Majlis-e-Amal (MMA)	6	2%	272
	2002	Muttahhida Majlis-e-Amal (MMA)	53	19%	272
	1997	Jamiat Ulema-e-Islam (JUI)[j]	2	1%	237
	1993	Jama'at-i Islami (JI)	3[k]	1%	237
	1990	Jamiat Ulema-e-Islam (JUI) (both factions)	9	4%	207
Palestine	2006	HAMAS (Harakat al-Muqawama al-Islamiyya)	74	56%	132
	1996	Independent Islamists	4	5%	88
Tunisia	2011	Renaissance Party	89	41%	217
Turkey	2011	Justice and Development Party (AKP)[l]	326	59%	550
	2007	Justice and Development Party (AKP)	341	62%	550
	2002	Justice and Development Party (AKP)	363	66%	550
	1999	Fazilet[m]	111	20%	550
	1995	Refah	158[n]	29%	550
	1991	Refah	62	11%	550
Yemen	2003	Tajammu' al-Yamani li'l-Islah (Yemeni Association for Reform)	46	15%	299
	1997		53	18%	301
	1993		62	21%	301

Notes:

a. Green Algeria Alliance is a coalition of Movement for the Society of Peace (MSP), Renaissance, and the El Islah movement.
b. Algerian military annulled election results.
c. Freedom and Justice Party (FJP) is the political party formed by the Muslim Brotherhood after the 2011 uprising.
d. The Muslim Brotherhood is banned as a political party in Egypt. Islamist candidates run as independents, although their affiliations are widely known.
e. Muslim Brotherhood candidates faced mass arrests and intimidation in the run-up to the 1995 election.
f. Muslim Brotherhood boycotted the 1990 elections.
g. Before 1999 the Indonesian government severely limited contestation.
h. The Islamic Action Front boycotted the 2013 and 1997 elections.
i. MPCD was the previous name for Freedom and Justice Party until 1998.
j. JI boycotted the 1997 elections; shown instead are the election results for the JUI, a longtime political ally of the Jamaat.
k. In 1993, JI participated in an alliance with the socialist PPP.
l. AKP is not a conventional Islamist party, but much of its leadership and membership base is drawn from Fazilet and Refah.
m. Fazilet is the reconstituted Refah party (see Note i.)
n. Refah formed a coalition government but was forced out by the military in 1997.

The "new Islamists" are essentially those groups that have chosen to participate in this system in the hope of one day bringing about meaningful change—"new" functioning here as a shorthand to denote those Islamists who have accepted the legitimacy of procedural democracy (even if, as we shall see, their commitment to a fuller conception of democracy remains in doubt). While some of these groups have their origins in, and in some cases are still closely affiliated with, classic, "old" Islamist parties as described above, the shakers and movers behind this new ethos of active participation tend to be of the younger generation. A generation that grew up during the height of the ban on Islamist political participation, and with a climate of relatively authoritarian decision-making within Islamist movements themselves, these younger Islamists grew impatient at their elders' skepticism about open political participation and began to pursue new strategies. Not only did they express a new willingness to compete as regular political parties on the same terms as other political groups, but they also expressed a preference for more participatory deliberations within the movement as a whole—in contrast to the intensely hierarchical model that characterized first-generation Islamist movements.[14] While their ultimate aims are still defined in terms of classic Islamism, their "goal horizons"—and certainly their political methodology—have shifted somewhat. First, we might say that this shift represents a new embrace of political gradualism over rapid political reform. Where first-generation Islamists sought political power to reform the social order along Islamic lines, the new Islamists hold out a longer-term vision for reform. They are more content to contest elections, take up whatever seats or offices they may win, and use their period of incumbency gradually to introduce elements of the Islamist platform—only to leave power when voted out and prepare to campaign again. The hope is that, through this approach, they will be able to introduce piecemeal reforms and gradually build up support, enabling the party to enjoy longer and more frequent tenures in legislatures and governments.

The adoption of the "new Islamist" participatory approach also has meant a shift in political platforms and electoral strategy. Most of these groups now emphasize the importance of concepts such as democracy, human rights, and rule of law far more than their first-generation forebears.[15] It has also, at times, meant entering into alliances and coalitions with non-Islamist parties similarly committed to democratic reform. Where first-generation Islamists would have seen such cooperation as politically impossible, the new Islamists have embraced a pragmatic approach that understands it as more important to be actively shaping the campaign for reform, rather than sitting on the sidelines. So although it may, at times, require certain compromises, the new Islamists have actively sought partnerships not only with other religiously based groups, but even with secular and leftist alliances. They tend to place less emphasis on, or even to drop altogether, the rhetoric of *shari'ah*. Sometimes they will emphasize the values they see accruing from *shari'ah* (social justice, individual rights) rather than the goal of *shari'ah* itself. Even though much of their platform seems to be compatible with, or even to lead towards, a largely secular order, they still realize that this is a lightning-rod term, and prefer to speak in terms of supporting a civil state.[16]

So who are these new Islamists, and how do they relate to other conventional Islamist parties? Several of them, such as Egypt's Hizb al-Wasat, are profiled in greater detail below. The Wasat party broke away from the MB in order to pursue a less narrowly defined and rigid form of Islamism. Their centrist approach (*wasat* meaning "center" in Arabic) reaches out to non-Muslim groups and emphasizes the socially mobile and economically modernist dimension of Islam over literal adherence to the *shari'ah*. In some regards, the Wasat party actually straddles the spectrum between new Islamism and the "Muslim democrat" approach outlined below. The Wasat, which did not manage to gain a political party license until shortly after Egypt's 2011 revolution, has previously counted a number of Coptic Christians within its executive council, and emphasized the importance of cross-sectarian values and interests. The MB, with its overtly religious identity, has found itself far more constrained in terms of being able to reach out to non-Muslims, even when trying to be as inclusive as possible when establishing its Freedom and Justice Party (FJP) in 2011. This does not mean, however, that the central Brotherhood movement has been untouched by this second generation. As we see below, during the 1990s and 2000s it was possible to detect clear signs of a generational split, even within the core of the MB structure. The opportunity to compete for political power since 2011, however, seems to have brought these differences within the Brotherhood to a head. Sharp disagreements over the movement's priorities and proper strategy led key reformist figures, and many of its youth leaders, to abandon the MB altogether and start up their own political parties. Like Hizb al-Wasat after 2011, however, these have been mostly fringe affairs that have failed to pull a critical mass of members and voters away from the organizational juggernaut that is the MB.

Where some new Islamist groups have encountered difficulties, others have enjoyed considerable electoral success. Morocco's Justice and Development Party (PJD—Parti de la Justice et du Développement), which in some respects also resembles the Muslim democracy approach detailed below, rapidly increased its representation in parliament over the course of the 2000s and now represents the largest party in the legislature. In the wake of the constitutional reforms that King Muhammad V hastily pushed through to stave off popular pressures in the face of the Arab Uprisings, the PJD today even finds itself holding the country's prime ministership—even if real political power continues to reside with the palace (see Box 4.4, "Morocco: Islamism in the shadow of the palace"). In 2003, the IAF— more clearly identifiable with the MB tendency—won nearly a quarter of all seats in parliament. That same year, the Yemeni Reformist Union won a quarter of the popular vote and a sixth of the legislative positions. In both cases, however, subsequent years have found these parties increasingly at odds with incumbent powers. Jordan's IAF boycotted parliamentary elections in both 2010 and 2013, complaining that the palace was manipulating the country's electoral law to favor its preferred candidates.

The mixed record and political fortunes of these parties mean that assessments of the significance of the new Islamist movement vary considerably. Some see it as an approach that will force Islamists to "normalize" their political platforms and bring them closer in tune with emerging pluralist norms in order to gain a seat at the electoral table. They emphasize the generational split between old and new Islamists as something genuine and substantive, seeing in the younger generation a tendency to interpret Islamism in a more inclusive manner. Others continue to harbor fears about instrumentalism, fearing that the Islamists' apparent new-found willingness to cooperate with non-Islamists is nothing other than a convenient route to power. So far there is little evidence to support the latter view, but it will take some time for the full political implications of this shift to become manifest.

Another current that some authors have identified in the Muslim world is one that commonly goes under the rubric of "Muslim Democracy."[17] Muslim democrats are commonly compared with the "Christian democratic" parties that emerged in Europe from the late nineteenth century. Described by one prominent theorist as "Islamic-oriented (but not Islamist),"[18] the Muslim democracy movement is typified by several parties whose social base tends to be religiously conservative and who derive their political values from religion, but without seeking to reform the political order in terms of Islam. Turkey's Justice and Development Party (AKP) has been cited as perhaps the clearest example of a Muslim democratic party, but we also find similar groups in countries such as Indonesia and Pakistan. Vali Nasr characterizes the approach thus:

> Muslim democrats view political life with a pragmatic eye. They reject or at least discount the classic Islamist claim that Islam commands the pursuit of a shari'ah state, and their main goal tends to be the more mundane one of crafting viable electoral platforms and stable governing coalitions to serve individual and collective interests—Islamic as well as secular— within a democratic arena whose bounds they respect, win or lose.[19]

It may seem difficult, based on this description, to differentiate Muslim democrats from some of the new Islamist groups described above. Indeed, there are sometimes significant areas of overlap between the two. Likewise, and looking towards the more secular side of the spectrum, it is difficult to differentiate Muslim democrats from wholly secular political parties that happen to represent somewhat rightist or conservative values. In the first instance, perhaps the best way of telling Muslim democrats apart from Islamists relates to the relative importance of *shari'ah* in the political platform and rhetoric of the two groups. Even second-generation Islamists who do not make much of religious law in their public profile will still frame their overall platform in terms of closer adherence to the *shari'ah*. "Muslim Democrats, by contrast," writes Nasr, "do not seek to enshrine Islam in politics."[20] As regards the differentiation of Muslim democrats from other parties of the right, perhaps the best way to do this is to look to the social bases of membership, recruitment, and mobilization. The AKP in Turkey, for example, has a number of active members who joined the group from the remnants of the more conventionally Islamist Refah party, and also draws heavily on the Sufi-oriented Nurçu movement in Turkey.

Nasr draws our attention to several distinct features of the Muslim Democracy approach. First of all, he notes that, unlike classic Islamism, which has a rich intellectual tradition, Muslim democracy looks more like an electoral strategy than an ideology. This speaks to the pragmatic nature of the approach, and the fact that its fortunes are subject to the exigencies of interest-group politics rather than theoretical prescriptions. While certainly leveraging the increase in public religiosity or religious consciousness found today in many parts of the Muslim world, Muslim Democracy seeks to channel this energy into support for a political platform that emphasizes prosperity and economic growth. It is not then surprising, as Nasr notes, that these movements tend to be stronger in contexts characterized by a strong and economically significantly private sector. A pluralistic political field is also seen as likely to push religiously oriented groups towards centrist politics, a fact noted by both Brumberg and Nasr. The latter also emphasizes the important role of the military in pushing together Islamists and non-Islamists who share common concerns about the army's threat to democracy—something we can see in both Turkey and Pakistan, in each of which the military has intervened on more than one occasion in the name of securing the state against forces that threaten public order.

In assessing the prospects of Muslim Democrats, Daniel Brumberg points out that the political conditions in those countries where they have seen some success, such as Turkey and Indonesia, are quite unique and difficult to replicate in the wider Muslim—and particularly Arab—world. Picking up on Nasr's point regarding the importance of both a vibrant private sector business class and a relatively pluralistic political field, he suggests that Morocco might be the one country in the Middle East in which Muslim Democrats could succeed.[21] We have already noted the resemblance between the PJD in that country and Turkey's Justice and Development Party—not only in name, but also in terms of their electoral strategy and the core constituency targeted in their platforms. An Egypt that manages to address short-term economic crises and move beyond its post-2011 political impasse and polarization might also resemble the kind of environment that could potentially foster a Muslim Democracy movement—perhaps composed of disaffected former MB pragmatists who manage to find a critical mass of supporters in society.

In summarizing the Muslim Democracy approach, let us turn again to Vali Nasr:

> The rise of Muslim Democracy suggests that the values of Muslims— which are not to be confused with the demands of Islamists—can interact with practical election strategies to play the main role in shaping political ideas and driving voter behavior. In the end, Muslim Democracy represents the triumph of practice over theory, and perhaps of the political over the Islamic. The future of Muslim politics is likely to belong to those who can speak to Muslim values and ethics, but within the framework of political platforms fit to thrive in democratic settings.[22]

Another analytical value-added that hence accrues from an emphasis on Muslim Democracy is the way it leads us to pay attention to actors in Muslim contexts whose preferences, values, and political behavior derive at least in part from their religion, but who do not view Islamist parties as the only ballot choice permitting the expression of that worldview.

Perhaps the best way to understand the complicated contrasts, points of convergence, and interrelationship between the various approaches to religious politics outlined above—classic Islamism, the new Islamism, and Muslim Democracy—would be to examine their evolution and staging in several country-specific settings. So we will move on now to case studies of Egypt, Jordan, and Turkey in order to more fully explore and contextualize these various shifts in Islamist political strategy. An accompanying textbox analysis of Indonesia provides us with some points of comparison from a large and important Muslim country outside the Middle East.

EGYPT: CHANGING FORTUNES OF THE MUSLIM BROTHERHOOD

The MB in Egypt is synonymous with the modern Islamist movement. Since its founding in 1928, the Brotherhood has provided both the intellectual foundations and the core methodology for many similar groups across the Muslim world. As we saw in Chapter 3, the MB has gone through several phases, each characterized by varying levels of social, political, and even militant activism—and often as a function of its continually changing relationship with the Egyptian state during a turbulent period in that country's history. After several decades underground, the Brotherhood gradually re-entered public life from the mid-1970s, and even electoral politics. Banned from forming a political party from 1954–2011, the MB instead occupied a whole host of civil and associational spaces at the level of society. Having socialized a well-educated and socially mobile generation of Egyptians in the ways of the Islamist current (*al-tayar al-islami*), the coming of age of this generation within the movement has led it to begin developing its own distinct political vision and, moreover, one that resonates with wider intellectual currents also circulating in Islamic circles. In this section we trace the emergence of the Wasatiyya (Centrist) trend in Islamic thought and its political manifestation in the form of the Hizb al-Wasat party to illustrate the development of generational cleavages within the MB. We will begin by describing how, from the 1970s onwards, the MB progressively socialized almost every available voluntary and associational space in Egypt, creating significant networks of social influence that granted considerable power despite the limitations placed on them in the formal political sphere. We will then review the relationship between the Islamist movement and the Egyptian state under Hosni Mubarak up until the mid-1990s, focusing on the shift from a policy of limited engagement on the part of the state in the 1980s, to an all-out offensive against the Islamists in the following decade. It is at this point that we will take up the theme of the generational divide, internal factionalism, and the emergence of the Wasatiyya movement, both intellectually and politically. We conclude by assessing the Brotherhood's phenomenal political rise—and equally dramatic fall—in the aftermath of Egypt's 2011 revolution and the formation of the MB's Freedom and Justice Party.

Our coverage of Egypt in Chapter 3 briefly touched on the Sadat and Mubarak presidencies. We will recall that Anwar al-Sadat inherited the presidency from the iconic Gamal Abdel Nasser upon the latter's death in 1970. Rather than simply emulating the policies of his predecessor, Sadat undertook a broad realignment of Egypt's international and domestic posture. More specifically, the Open Door (*infitah*) policies sought to pursue a course of greater economic liberalization and to open Egypt up to world markets. Domestically, Sadat allowed space for a "rehabilitated" MB—banned since the 1950s—to come back into Egyptian life. After formally renouncing violence in the 1970s, many regard the Brotherhood as having been co-opted by Sadat's regime. This led to factionalization within the Islamist movement when several radical splinter groups, rejecting what they saw as the MB's accommodationist stance, emerged to pursue more militant forms of activism. This culminated in the assassination of Anwar al-Sadat in 1981 after he signed a peace agreement with Israel. Sadat was succeeded by his vice president, Hosni Mubarak, who has continued to rule without appointing a vice president, or rescinding the "state of emergency" declared at the time of Sadat's death that, under the constitution, grants him extended executive powers. Mubarak's party political instrument, the National Democratic Party (NDP), is a nonideological group whose sole purpose is to retain power. In this regard the NDP has generally had to rely on co-opting various social forces and ideas in order to lend it vision and legitimacy.

The Islamization of the social sphere

The growth of the Islamist presence within civil society and associational life needs to be understood against the backdrop of the economic reform process that began in Egypt under Sadat in the 1970s, and continued apace once Mubarak was in office. Its chief goal was to dismantle the Nasserist welfare state, where the public sector had been the sole provider of all basic services and the major source of employment. Through various job-guarantee programs, for example, university graduates could count on government employment once they had completed university. The state provided free medical care to all citizens. The reform process that started under Sadat initially aimed at building up the private sector after years of flirting with socialism under Nasser. Once the international community became involved, and particularly the IMF after 1987, the economic reforms took on the flavor of a fully fledged structural adjustment process. Egypt was put under pressure to downsize its enormous public sector by, for example, privatizing a number of government-owned companies. The ranks of its bloated bureaucracy were also regarded as being in need of trimming. Loans and external debt reduction became tied to reductions in import duties and the reduction of subsidies on basic goods. Egyptians hence saw the price of bread and electricity increase substantially during the late 1980s and early 1990s. As is commonly the case with this kind of systemic economic "shock therapy," the initial effects on society did not feel good. The ending of government job guarantees led to massive unemployment; affordable housing became difficult to find; young couples delayed marriage because they and their families could not bear the expense; and many—including civil servants and doctors—found themselves having to work a second job to make ends meet.[23] University completion rates soon far outgrew job creation in both the public and private sectors, forcing highly skilled and professional graduates who had viewed higher education as a path to prosperity to live on small service wages or even agricultural labor. In overall terms, the disparities between Egypt's upper and upper-middle classes and the lower-middle and lower classes increased substantially during this period. Bribery and corruption was rife.

This "retreat of the state" opened up substantial space for other social forces to flourish within neighborhood and civil society spaces, and the MB soon proved itself most adept at leveraging these opportunities. Realizing the potential to create an "Islamic sector" for the provision of basic welfare and charity services, the Brotherhood decided from the late 1970s to make Egyptian society—rather than state political institutions—the target of its reform and mobilization efforts. Soon Islamic social organizations were springing up everywhere: charities, hospitals, schools, mosque organizations—all providing a combination of basic services and a source of new jobs that were not forthcoming from either the state or the private sector. Mosques, the vast majority of which were privately run and financially independent of the state, once under Brotherhood control set themselves up as purveyors of redistributive social justice. Some of the more entrepreneurial beneficiaries of economic liberalization established a system of "Islamic investment companies" during the 1980s. Wholly unregulated, and bypassing official banks, these local and supposedly more "authentic" institutions promised investors enormous rates of return (often double that available in the formal banking sector) alongside a commitment—tapping into the upsurge of popular religiosity—that all funds were handled according to *shari'ah* requirements.[24] The Islamic investment companies also contributed substantially to Brotherhood political candidates and other MB causes, until a financial meltdown led the sector to be investigated and shut down by the government at the end of the decade. Opponents claimed the companies were at best little more than elaborate pyramid schemes or, worse, that they were profiting from criminal activities—in either case, hardly "Islamic." Advocates of the practice cited their strong local character ("investment in Egypt by Egyptians") and claimed that the government intervened because it feared the strength of a vibrant economic sector outside its control—particularly one contributing substantial sums to opposition causes.[25] This was not the only segment of the "Islamic sector" that had been enjoying success at the expense of the government, however. Islamic charities had become pervasive and highly efficient by the end of the 1980s. So much so, in fact, that when Cairo suffered a devastating earthquake in 1992, the Islamic relief services were on the scene and dispensing aid hours before the state was able to mobilize its own emergency services—prompting one government official to voice concerns that the Islamists had created a "state within a state."[26] All in all, Islamic social organizations increased from representing a quarter of the voluntary sector in the early 1970s to more than 75 percent by the end of the 1980s.

In addition to the "Islamic sector" composed of service organizations owned or operated by the Brotherhood, Islamists also became a major force in other key civil society spaces throughout the 1980s. From the mid-1970s, the MB began to establish themselves on student councils and unions in all Egyptian universities, particularly in science and engineering faculties. They quickly became the dominant voice on nearly every campus, completing a rout of secular and leftist rivals. Soon the Brotherhood also began to contest elections within the influential professional syndicates. From the mid-1980s, the Brotherhood progressively took over the engineering, pharmaceutical, and medical associations, culminating with a 1992 victory in the Egyptian Bar Association, long regarded as the last bastion of secularism within the professional classes.[27] Although less successful in the workers' unions, which were still heavily influenced by leftist thought, even here the Islamists saw an upswing in their fortunes during the 1980s.[28] The Brotherhood's socialization of associational space in Egypt is highly significant, not only because it allowed them to build enormous social capital in some of the most influential and upwardly mobile segments of the country's population, but also because it permitted them to use civil society groups for oppositional politics by proxy. With the MB banned as a political organization, and political party culture generally weak in Egypt, the Brotherhood's enormous footprint in society allowed them to wield considerable clout without becoming directly involved in political processes.[29] Indeed, one could even argue that, far from being a form of protest against its exclusion from the political sphere, the Brotherhood actually preferred to operate this way—foreshadowing a debate that would take place within the movement once the 2011 revolution made actual political power a viable option for the MB. By exercising their normative discipline at the level of society, the Islamists could enjoy considerable influence, but without having to be formally accountable (or targetable) within the political system. As Esposito and Voll put it:

> The fact that Islamists are specific in their indictment of the government but general in terms of their own programs tends to work in their favor. They are able to criticize the failings of the government, from employment and housing to corruption and maldistribution of wealth, without having to offer their own specific solutions to seemingly intractable problems. They employ Islamic rhetoric and symbols, call for an Islamic solution and the implementation of the Sharia, but do not delineate precisely what these would mean in terms of specific policies. Moreover, although at the macro level, they often only offer general prescriptions and promises, the source of their credibility and success is that at the micro level. Their educational and social programs demonstrate to ordinary people the concrete, tangible meaning and impact of an Islamic order.[30]

The Brotherhood's strategy also had two other significant dimensions. The first of these is related to their deliberate targeting of youth spaces—not only through universities, as mentioned above, but also via religious outreach (*da'wa*) to young people active in mosque organizations. This revealed the MB to have a long-term sociopolitical vision based on instilling in the younger generation the idea that societal reform along religiously prescribed lines is an obligation that should be pursued through civic activism.[31] The Brotherhood was, in effect, "staging" young people towards the Islamist movement, and seeking to calibrate their horizons of public normativity in terms of religion. "You raise Muslim Brother students in the university," one observer put it, "then five years later you have an electoral base for the professional associations. It's like planting seeds on a farm."[32] The second dimension concerns the Brotherhood's ability to capture and harness the upsurge in religiosity that emerged in Egypt from the 1970s. By tapping into veins of popular piety, the Islamists were able to channel this force towards their social organizations and causes in ways that leftists, nationalists—and certainly not the "empty shell" of the NDP or the secularists—simply could not. By framing its various social welfare activities in terms of "being a better Muslim," the Brotherhood leveraged this swelling religiosity into a privileged role as society's normative arbiter.[33] As Azzam puts it:

> They have been able to foster and direct this [religious] current through their organizational ability and dedication, and there is no rival opposition group to match them. The stress on devotional practice and cultural purification from all that is "un-Islamic" . . . provides a framework of action for their followers and has contributed to the Islamization process. . . . This emphasis has borne fruit, insofar as the basic belief and practice of Islam have been reasserted and spread among a new generation and throughout a cross-section of society.[34]

The Islamists and the Egyptian state (1981–95)

But Islamist activity was not confined exclusively to the social sphere during this period. Although banned from forming a political party for six decades (1954–2011), the MB has contested elections in Egypt since 1984 either by running independent candidates or through alliances with other political parties. Although constrained by a state as pervasively present in the political sphere as the Brotherhood was in society, their relative electoral success and subsequent pressure on the regime prompted a crackdown on their activities from the early 1990s and significant public scrutiny of the Islamist trend as a whole. When Mubarak came to power in the wake of the trauma of Sadat's assassination, he immediately pursued a course of limited social and political liberalization in the name of national unity. This was manifested in greater press freedoms; an expansion of civil, associational, and political party rights; and an invitation to all political currents (Islamists, secularists, leftists, and so forth) to participate in the public sphere.[35] Certainly not unaware of the upsurge in popular religiosity mentioned above, Mubarak initially hoped to co-opt this energy by emphasizing those aspects of religion that were in tune with his ongoing efforts at economic liberalization. This naturally led him to pursue a policy of limited engagement with the social force most clearly identified with this trend, the MB. For its own part, the MB decided to use this opportunity to re-enter politics. In 1984 they formed an unlikely alliance with the Wafd party, whose own political fortunes had been in severe decline. Both parties were victims of the post-1952 Nasserist order, and both saw tactical value in the partnership. Egypt's election law required a party to receive more than 8 percent of the popular vote in order to take parliamentary seats, and by running under the Wafd banner, the Brotherhood permitted them to cross this threshold. This marriage of convenience fell apart rather quickly, however, and the Islamists were forced to look elsewhere. In 1987, the MB entered into a partnership with the Liberal and Labor parties—where key figures had been leaning towards a form of "Islamic socialism"—and formed the "Islamic Alliance." Although it enjoyed some political success in both cases, gaining a number of seats in parliament, it was near impossible for the Brotherhood to pursue its reform agenda via political means as the overwhelming control of parliament by the government party, the NDP, blocked them at every juncture. From its inception through 2011, the NDP held more than a two-thirds majority in every parliament, allowing all "presidential legislation" to pass easily, and even permitting the party to change the constitution.

Despite its stranglehold over the political system, the regime became increasingly wary of the Islamists from the late 1980s. The MB was using the parliament as a public forum to pressure the government to bring all Egyptian laws into accordance with the *shari'ah* as specified in article two of the constitution. More alarming from the government's point of view, however, was an upsurge in violence associated with several of the radical groups—such as Gemaa Islamiyya and Islamic Jihad—that had emerged during and just after the Sadat years. From the late 1980s, Egypt experienced a spate of attacks by militant groups who were no longer targeting only instruments of the state. The geographical scope of their activities also broadened beyond Cairo to include various towns in Upper Egypt (the southern part of the country). Foreign tourists, police officers, and even members of Egypt's Coptic Christian community were killed by the radicals. The Copts, representing about 10 percent of the country, became the target of widespread discontent on the part of disenfranchised Muslims who resented their relative prosperity in comparison with the wider population. This was hence also a period of heightened interfaith tension. In addition to the violence, radical groups also sought to coercively enforce "public virtue" in various towns and villages by forcing women to wear veils and by carrying out Islamic punishments (*hudud*) as self-appointed judiciaries. The government's response was swift and strong, with key radical Islamists imprisoned or killed—leading to a tit-for-tat cycle of violence between the regime and the radicals during the early 1990s.

But the radicals were not the only Islamists targeted by the regime. Wary of the MB's enormous influence within the social sphere, and dissatisfied by their unwillingness unequivocally to condemn the radical violence, the government began moving against the MB in the late 1980s. They sought to forge a link in the public's mind between the MB as an Islamist organization and the radical Islamism of the militant groups. Many of those in the radical groups had, at one time or another, been members of the MB, but had left the movement after it rejected violence in the mid-1970s. They found the Brotherhood's unwillingness to engage in direct *jihad* to be un-Islamic and a betrayal of the movement's activist forebears (e.g. figures such as Sayyid Qutb). So, in the eyes of the regime, the MB was guilty of providing the intellectual foundations and religious justifications for the violence of the radicals. The government's initial efforts were geared towards rolling back the Brotherhood's influence within civil society organizations. Their actions amounted to a "securitization" of various social sectors, such as education and mosques. Suspected Islamists were purged from schools, and new regulations were introduced whereby the deans of university faculties were to be appointed by the institution's rectors rather than elected by faculty.[36] Efforts were also made to bring private mosques—regarded as recruiting and mobilizing grounds for radicalism—under government control. Given that over 80 percent of Egypt's approximately 200,000 mosques were privately controlled, however, it soon became clear that this would be logistically and financially impossible. Plans to have all Friday sermons (*khutba*) vetted by the Ministry of Religious Affairs were soon shelved. The government moved against the Islamist presence in professional and student associations as well, blocking the election of MB candidates to student union councils. In 1993 they also changed the regulations governing elections in professional syndicates. These were now subject to strict quota requirements that demanded the presence of a large percentage of the organization's membership for any election to be valid. If these were not met, then the leaderships of the professional associations were to be appointed directly by the government.[37] What these actions amounted to was an attempt by the regime to shut down or tightly control any space in society where popular elections occurred. In the eyes of the government, unregulated social space came to be viewed as dangerous since the Islamists always seemed to win.

Finally, from 1994 to 1995, the government moved against the MB directly. Scores of Brotherhood activists were arrested and accused of illegal political activities, providing the regime with an opportunity to make a dramatic case against, and attempt to undermine the legitimacy of, the Islamist movement. Many members were put on trial, convicted, and sentenced to jail terms of varying lengths. Most significantly from the point of view of the government's attempts to curb MB influence, those convicted of even relatively light crimes were subsequently disbarred from standing as candidates in associational elections (according to syndicate regulations, no-one with a criminal record is permitted to stand).[38] Some have subsequently interpreted these actions as a tactic to keep the Brotherhood out of civil society by legally disbarring their participation, since other attempts to sideline them had failed. Such efforts even extended to the realm of foreign policy, where the Mubarak regime asked its close ally the United States to cease all contacts with representatives of the MB. Under this comprehensive and withering pressure from the state, the MB retreated from the social and political spheres, keeping a very low profile through the rest of the 1990s.[39]

Islamic intellectual centrism: The Wasatiyya movement

Before moving on to look at the Egyptian MB amidst its rapidly changing political fortunes in the twenty-first century, we should spend some time examining an intellectual trend that emerged out of the Islamist current from the 1980s, and which has been influential in terms of subsequent developments within the Brotherhood mainstream. To say that this trend developed "out" of the Islamist mainstream is significant insofar as the relevant thinkers and activists, while many of them have been influenced by, and even affiliated with, the MB at one time, should be considered neither part of the Brotherhood nor under its control. The emergence of this group can be linked to the distinction made above between "classic Islamism" and "new Islamism." One writer, Ray Baker, has used the term "new Islamists" to describe this particular group of intellectuals.[40] For our purposes, however, the "new Islamists" will connote a broader generational and strategic shift identifiable in Muslim movements across several settings today. We will refer to the intellectual trend more descriptively as the Wasatiyya (Centrist) movement—as do, it should be noted, several members of the group itself, in addition to other observers.[41]

Identifiable for Baker more in terms of tendencies and "family resemblances" rather than a clearly delineated ideology or program, Wasatiyya thinkers nevertheless share a common set of general intellectual trajectories. This is also a relatively heterogeneous group in terms of its professional composition. Journalists, social activists, academics, and religious scholars can all be counted among its numbers. Baker identifies three core groups from which Wasatiyya members are drawn: 1. former leftists who adopted a more Islamist orientation from the 1980s, including figures around the opposition (and at times quite radical) newspaper *al-Shaab*, such as Adel Hussain and Ibrahim Shukry; 2. figures whose social consciousness was formed through participation in civic and charitable associations run by the MB, but who chose not to become affiliated with the MB; and 3. a group of religious scholars emphasizing the relevance of traditional Islamic knowledge to contemporary issues and problems, and seeking to provide nonauthoritarian guidance for their solution.[42] Many proponents of the Wasatiyya current—such as historian Tariq al-Bishri and the well-known religious scholar Yusuf al-Qaradawi (see Chapter 9)—are, and were already, quite famous in their own right before becoming associated with this movement. Indeed, the "manifesto" of the Wasatiyya trend, *Towards a Contemporary Islamic Vision,* should be regarded as an aggregate text composed of ideas contributed by a wide range of thinkers over a decade. First sketched out by Kamal Abul Magd in the early 1980s, it was finally published for the public in 1992 after circulating and evolving for a decade within various Islamic circles. Variants of Wasatiyya thinking have been visible in the Egyptian public sphere for well over a decade now, including a famous debate on "secularism versus Islam" between Farag Foda (who was assassinated by Islamic Jihad shortly afterward) and one of the key figures in the Wasatiyya movement, Sheikh Muhammad al-Ghazzali. A separate but related effort to establish a political party inspired by elements of Wasatiyya thought emerged from 1996 in the form of Hizb al-Wasat ("Party of the Center"—see below).

What is the nature and character of Wasatiyya thinking? We might summarize its core values in terms of holism, inclusivity, and dialogue. These are all clearly "progressive"-sounding terms, a fact that has led many observers, particularly in the West, to take an interest in the movement. But what is meant by them, particularly in the context of Egypt? First and foremost, the Wasatiyya needs to be regarded as an intellectual movement with a social consciousness, and moreover one that seeks reform and social transformation. Its thinkers express considerable concern about the plight and poverty of Egypt—materially and culturally—but they diagnose this in terms of both internal and external causes. The movement takes its inspiration from the notion of social justice found in Islam, and seeks to achieve a social order that embraces the spirit of the *shari'ah*. There would be some variation within the group as to what exactly this latter part means. Some would want to understand the Qur'an as the source of general principles for good society whereas others would tend towards actually legislating based on the *shari'ah*. While the roots of the Wasatiyya are clearly in the Islamist current, their holism lies in how they depart from the common Brotherhood slogan "Islam is the solution." For them, religion is just one part of the solution, and needs to be regarded in conjunction with national interests, economic realities, and cultural traditions. In this sense, we can begin to view the Wasatiyya approach as essentially pragmatic rather than ideological. While embracing religiously inspired reform, Muslims are not seen by the Wasatiyya as the sole agents of that process—another contrast with the Brotherhood. This is where the element of inclusivity comes in. Viewing Egyptian reform as a national project, the Wasatiyya emphasize the need to include those embracing disparate political tendencies and also non-Muslims as equal partners. Active participation by women in processes of social change is seen as particularly important by many within the movement. Finally, the Wasatiyya trend highlights the importance of dialogue and collective deliberation—rather than coercion or violence—as the only possible way to achieve sustainable social reform.

Looking at these principles, some observers, such as Baker, have been led to draw parallels between the Wasatiyya and what are commonly known as "new social movements" or NSMs.[43] While this is correct in terms of the social location of NSMs (the middle class), it could give the impression that the values of the Wasatiyya are closely in tune with the kinds of progressive cause generally associated with new social movements, such as the environmental agenda and global feminism. Some figures within the Wasatiyya current, such as Sheikh Yusuf al-Qaradawi, while relatively centrist and modern for a religious scholar, nevertheless still hold views regarding, for example, the status of women and the permissibility of suicide bombing that many progressives would find difficult to accept. The "progressivist" label is a little more on target when we consider Baker's characterization of the Wasatiyya as a form of "Islam without fear." By this he means that those within the movement are not using Islam as part of a defensive discourse, or as a form of "cultural coercion"—such as by making sweeping statements to the effect that "Islam is under attack" or "as Muslims you must defend your religion" that achieve little other than to tarnish Islam and instill fear in believers and non-Muslims alike. Rather, they seek to figure Islam as a discourse of positive change in tune with emerging norms of pluralism, freedom, and human rights.[44] In other words, one asserts one's "Muslimness" not because it is vulnerable and under attack, but rather as a call to improve society. In this dimension of the Wasatiyya phenomenon we can see several common NSM traits, such as an emphasis on post-material concerns and the attempt to challenge dominant cultural codes.[45] Some observers have noticed that, as an intellectual trend, this approach is not unprecedented in the Muslim world. In the reformist thought of Muhammad Abduh (see Chapter 2), for example, one can identify clear precursors of Wasatiyya ideas.[46] Indeed, in some regards it might be seen as an approach seeking to recover the heritage of Muhammad Abduh and to take the Islamist movement in a direction less obsessed with the achievement of the correct "Islamic political order" and more focused on the common (and not necessarily exclusively Muslim or Islamic) public good. It is, in other words, Islam as civilizational potential rather than religious difference.[47]

Muslim Brotherhood generations and the emergence of "centrist" Islamism

The "re-entrenchment" of the MB in the mid- to late 1990s corresponded to the emergence within its ranks of a clear generational divide. This pitted an "old guard," many of whom had joined the group while Hassan al-Banna (1906–49) was still alive, against a "middle generation" that had joined the movement from the late 1970s. The younger generation, many of whom had been socialized into the movement via various student and professional associations, were interested in exploring new avenues of political participation for the Brotherhood. They resented what they saw as the authoritarian control of a small group of septa- and octogenarians largely out of touch with modern society.[48] For the middle generation, the priorities of the Islamist movement should be understood in pragmatic terms and as adaptable to changing social realities, rather than simply being judged on how faithfully they followed the classic program and method of the Brotherhood. Their influence had already been felt somewhat in 1995 when the MB declared its support for the principle of multiparty politics, a significant departure from the teachings of Hassan al-Banna, who had always maintained that in a truly Islamic society political parties would not only be unnecessary but were inherently divisive.[49] In short, this younger group was looking for a more inclusive Islamic politics outside the exclusive confines of the Brotherhood. By refusing to cooperate and form alliances with other political trends, the leaders of the middle generation argued, the Brotherhood would remain marginal in terms of its political influence.[50] Carrie Wickham points out, importantly, that these differences of vision did not break down solely along generational lines, but that the leaders of the modernist, pragmatist trend were clearly to be found within the middle generation.[51]

Out of this divide there emerged in 1996 an attempt by several key figures within the younger generation, led by Abou Elela Mady, to set up a Party of the Center (HW—Hizb al-Wasat). Several of the founding figures were quickly arrested and charged with seeking to form an illegal political organization. It eventually became clear to the government that HW was not simply an attempt by the MB surreptitiously to establish a political party. Indeed, the Wasat founders were widely condemned for having betrayed the Islamist cause. HW applied twice, in 1996 and 1998, for a license to operate as a legal political party, and was twice denied, with subsequent appeals also failing. The MB itself registered formal opposition to the formation of HW during the application process.[52] Several dozen Brotherhood members who had joined the Wasat founders quickly returned to the MB once the new party began to experience difficulties—a fact cited by the Brotherhood leadership as evidence that many early Wasat followers realized the new party would hurt the Islamist cause, and by the government as evidence that Wasat was simply the MB under a different name.[53] We should also note that the formation of Wasat did not in any way represent an exodus from the MB by the middle generation. Several of the most prominent figures within this wing remained behind, and since have risen to senior positions within the Brotherhood. Some have suggested that they share the same overall vision as those who left to form Wasat, but did not agree with the decision to break with the mother group, while others cite this as evidence for a potential reconciliation between the two groups—a point subsequently borne out by certain communications from the MB leadership.[54] The fact that Abou Elela Mady obtained a political party license for Hizb al-Wasat within ten days of Mubarak's ouster in 2011, however, demonstrates that the MB never fully succeeded in reincorporating these dissenting voices.

Despite the shared emphasis on "centrism," HW and its membership is by no means identical with that of the broader Wasatiyya intellectual movement—although lines of communication and cooperation certainly did exist, with many in the latter group expressing support for the upstart politicians. In HW's subsequent legal battles with the state, one of the central Wasatiyya figures, lawyer Muhammad Selim al-'Awwa, did work on behalf of the political group. Furthermore, several Wasat figures and Wasatiyya intellectuals collaborated successfully in 2000 to petition for a license to establish, along with a number of prominent secular figures, a Center for Culture and Dialogue. In the absence of both Wasatiyya institutions, and a legal space for the discussion and further refinement of the Wasat platform, this association has served as a proxy.

The HW's early political platform, which was issued in several iterations from 1996 to 1998, emphasized democratic reform, government accountability, human rights and—more significantly—support for participation by non-Muslims, secular activists, and women in its activities. Several Coptic Christians were included as members, and a Protestant served on the party's executive council and also played a lead role in authoring one version of the party platform. This is in sharp contrast to the MB which, while generally allowing for the idea that Christian citizens should participate in the political process, would not accept Christians as members of the movement. In another significant break from the MB, the Wasat platform sees sovereignty as vested in the citizens rather than the standard Islamist formulation to the effect that sovereignty belongs to God alone.[55] Some have observed that, while mentioning the important role of women in social transformation, the parameters of their activity are still seen in largely traditional terms, with women assigned primarily to the domestic sphere.[56] While *shari'ah* is conceptualized as an inclusive and participatory process, there still remain certain ambiguities as to its place within the Wasat program.[57]

In the 2000 parliamentary elections the MB fared relatively well, taking advantage of new rules that required independent judicial oversight of all polling activities. They took 17 seats in parliament and also regained control of the law syndicate. More significantly, in 2005, Egypt had its first presidential election featuring more than one candidate. Although Hosni Mubarak won by a wide margin, the precedent was important. In the face of considerable external pressure, particularly from the United States, to make greater efforts towards democracy, Egypt also permitted a longer and more liberal campaigning period in the run-up to the legislative elections that same year. 2005 also saw the emergence of Kifaya ("Enough"), a popular movement demanding political reform that held large demonstrations in the spring and that, with hindsight, can be seen as a harbinger of the street movement that would overthrow Mubarak in 2011. Although the Islamists were not a large part of the Kifaya contingent (some have even suggested that the MB struck a deal with the state to boycott the protests), some in the Wasatiyya movement expressed general sympathy with their aims. Most importantly, however, the MB in 2005 achieved its best ever electoral showing in the parliament despite an intimidation campaign by the government as voting began. In total, Brotherhood-affiliated candidates won 88 out of 454 seats, creating an opposition bloc composed of 20 percent of the parliament—the largest ever seen in the assembly. While the NDP still commanded a two-thirds majority, it was forced to be considerably more vigilant than in the past in terms of how it handles parliamentary procedure, given the disciplined presence of a large Islamist bloc.[58] Some prominent figures within the Brotherhood subsequently started to talk about the division of the movement into two distinct organizations, one a political party and the other a religious organization—holding out the possibility of either accommodation (i.e. an "official" split) or direct competition with the Wasat group.[59]

Within the past two decades, the Brotherhood has seen significant changes in terms of its internal composition and cohesion as well as the strategies it has adopted to deal with both the political environment around it and a rapidly evolving marketplace of religious ideas.

It is testament to how rapidly the MB was evolving as a movement that when in 2007—a decade after the initial HW split—it leaked a draft political party platform statement, many of its positions on key issues (e.g. pluralism, democracy, inclusivity, *shari'ah*) appeared virtually identical to Hizb al-Wasat's earlier rhetoric. The MB's leadership was clearly cognizant of the fact that there were a multiplicity of voices within the movement, some of whom had their own audiences and constituencies in wider society. Khalil al-'Anani's analysis of generational differences within the contemporary Brotherhood describes what he terms the "technological generation."[60] This subset of Brotherhood members tends to be younger, tech- and media-savvy, and generally pragmatic when it comes to political issues. This cohort favors political participation, and its conception of an Islamic political order is generally less rigid. More likely to speak in terms of an "Islamic reference" or "Islamic framework" than to emphasize the direct and literal application of *shari'ah,* Brotherhood followers in this generation are also more predisposed to critically—albeit respectfully—interrogate the intellectual tradition of the movement. This cadre undoubtedly has its stars, many of who attract considerable attention in U.S. government and media circles due to their moderate and relatively pro-Western orientation. The first wave of "technological generation" stars, including figures such as Ibrahim El-Houdeiby, whose grandfather and great-grandfather both held the Brotherhood's top job, are certainly relatively liberal and pro-Western. For this reason they were frequently found on the Washington DC think-tank circuit in the mid-2000s. But, as Marc Lynch and others note, it is simply not possible to draw a direct correlation between being young and being liberal when it comes to the Brotherhood.[61] Furthermore, as another observer notes, this younger generation is all but absent from even mid-level leadership positions in the movement—not to mention the Brotherhood's highest governing body, the central Guidance Bureau. If anything, and as indicated by the results of recent Guidance Bureau and General Guide elections, among the septuagenarians clinging tightly to executive power, conservative forces seem resurgent of late.

So how, in the end, to assess the significance of the "new Islamist" trend in Egypt—particularly in light of subsequent political developments post-2011? Given that exponents of this approach, such as Abou Elela Mady's Hizb al-Wasat party and the ex-MB reformist figure Abdul-Munim Abou al-Fattouh, fared poorly in the 2012 parliamentary and presidential elections, it might be tempting to dismiss the Wasat as a fringe splinter group from the MB that happens to have swung to the left rather than to the right, as did the radical groups of the 1970s.[62] Even greater skeptics might insist that, at the end of the day, the Wasat represent nothing more than a new variant of old-school Islamism, employing pluralistic rhetoric instrumentally to forge alliances of political convenience. Viewed, sociologically, however, the Wasatiyya trend emerges as something potentially far more significant. While the extent of their popular influence is currently nothing like that of the MB, the fact remains that the Wasat emerged out of spaces initially socialized by the MB. This suggests that within that younger generation there is likely a critical mass of support for a more inclusive form of moderate Islamism. Likewise, the broader Wasatiyya current was first forged by non-MB intellectuals and activists, and this perhaps indicates a wider basis of social support for a trend outside the conventional Islamist movement.

In net terms, then, the potential would seem to exist for an explosion of popular support for "new Islamism" in the next decade—particularly after the "old guard" of the MB, as represented by figures such as deposed President Mohammed Morsi, appears to have failed dismally at practical governance. This does not mean, however, that "traditional" Islamist movements will cease to matter. As Egypt's recent politics have made clear, as political organizations conventional Islamists enjoy unique competitive advantages in the realm of social and political mobilization. As will be seen in our subsequent discussion of Islamist politics in the aftermath of the 2011 revolution, it is important to emphasize the increased pluralization in Egypt's religio-political sphere in order to understand the evolution of Islamist political strategy. While the MB undoubtedly remains the most important player, the remarkable rise of politicized Salafism (see Box 4.1, "The new Salafi factor in Arab politics")—alongside a large number of new political parties that claim some relationship to Islam—means that the MB's monopoly over Islamic politics in Egypt is at an end. Going forward, it will have to vie with a much broader range of actors claiming to represent Islam in the political sphere. Having staked its reputation on early post-revolutionary political power, and failed, there are necessarily question marks hanging over the MB's long-term fate.

Islamist politics after the 2011 revolution

While in the early 2000s the emergence of centrist Islamism as represented by Hizb al-Wasat might have seemed to represent the future of political Islam, developments in the later part of that decade paved the way for far more dramatic developments with respect to Islam and politics in Egypt. Almost as soon as the MB achieved its remarkable 2005 electoral feat, the regime began a new effort to marginalize the Brotherhood. Even as Mubarak announced new constitutional and democratic reforms, he simultaneously started arresting key MB figures (such as Khairat al-Shater, widely seen as the movement's main strategist) and closing down their offices and media outlets. In 2007, a still-confident Brotherhood leaked a draft political party platform statement—a document that explained the values and policies that any hypothetical MB-affiliated political party would stand for. The text was remarkable for what it revealed about the extent to which MB leaders were willing to emulate many of the ideals associated with the Wasatiyya movement, even while remaining studiously vague on many key issues relating to the status of minorities, women, and the question of *shari'ah* law. At least one aspect of the platform statement, a proposal to create a council of religious scholars that would vet all legislation to ensure conformity with Islamic law, created a good measure of controversy—prompting the MB to issue assurances that this was merely an "exploratory" document.

The increased assertiveness of the MB in political space led the Egyptian regime to intensify its crackdown, taking steps, for example, to exclude Islamist-affiliated candidates from municipal elections in 2009. These tactics certainly emboldened conservatives within the MB who were skeptical of the movement's ability to achieve its goals through formal politics. In late 2009, they swept a new round of elections to the MB's Guidance Bureau, with popular reformist figures such as Abdul-Munim Abou El-Fattouh losing his seat. 2010 proved to be a fateful year. Mohammed Badie—a stalwart conservative who had been in the movement since the days of Sayyid Qutb—was elected as the movement's new Supreme Guide, consolidating a leadership circle wholly devoid of centrist or reform-oriented figures. At the same time, the Mubarak regime found itself having to contend with the emergence of Mohamed ElBaradei, former chief of the International Atomic Energy Agency, as something of a figurehead in secular-liberal opposition circles. This followed in the wake of widespread protests in 2008 focused on labor conditions and led by an emergency secular activist network known as the April 6 movement. Under increasing pressure, the regime devoted considerable effort to interdicting the participation—and performance—of Islamists in the 2010 round of national parliamentary elections. Perhaps as evidence of their overreach, the ballot returned no Islamists to Egypt's legislature—despite the fact that they had won 20 percent of the seats in the previous election. With its gross manipulation of the electoral process more starkly on display than ever before, Mubarak's legitimacy seemed to be at an all-time low.

Egypt's leader was not alone in his predicament. In December 2010, the death of Muhammad Bouazizi, a fruit-stand vendor in Tunisia who took his own life by self-immolation in protest at the government's mistreatment of citizens, lit a spark that over the next six months would generate popular uprisings in six Arab countries and bring about the downfall of four long-standing leaders. The first to go in January 2011, following mass protests in the streets of Bouazizi's home town of Sidi Bouzid and the capital Tunis, was Tunisia's own Zin El Abidine Ben Ali (see Box 4.2, "Tunisia: Islamists and the legacy of secularism"). Inspired by the unlikely success of a popular revolution, opposition activists in Egypt began mobilizing in the hope of creating a similar effect. This movement, which comprised figures from the earlier Kifaya and April 6 movements as well as a grassroots network built around a social media page dedicated to Muhammad Said (a figure who functioned symbolically much like Bouazizi in Tunisia), was initially modest in scale. Taking to the streets of Cairo and other Egyptian cities on January 25 (chosen for its patriotism as the day is dedicated to honouring the country's police force), this popular movement grew rapidly and maintained a constant presence in key locales such as Cairo's Tahrir Square. Once it became clear that the Egyptian military, deployed to the streets as a precaution, was not going to open fire on the peaceful protests, the crowds swelled exponentially. After a tense, 18-day standoff, which saw scuffles and open fighting between protestors and violent mobs deployed by the regime, Hosni Mubarak resigned from his presidency at the behest of the military after 30 years in power. The country's leading military body, the Supreme Council of the Armed Forces (SCAF), announced that it would temporarily run the country to oversee a transition to democracy, parliamentary and presidential elections, and the writing of a new constitution. Egyptians from all walks of life hailed what became known as the "January 25 Revolution."

Before looking at Egypt's complex post-revolutionary politics, it is worth pausing to look briefly at the role played by the MB during the uprising itself. When popular protests first began to materialize on January 25, the MB's leadership initially ordered its followers to stay off the streets. The group feared that the protests would likely be crushed by the state and, if the MB was found to be involved, that the regime would use that as a pretext to pursue an even heavier-handed crackdown on the Islamists. After three days, and with many of the MB's younger contingent openly flouting the directive not to participate, the MB's Guidance Bureau released its members into the growing tide of protestors. Many protestors, including non-Islamists, credit the MB with playing a key role in keeping the protests organized, disciplined, and nonviolent, and with providing much-needed basic services (e.g. water, medical care) to those in the streets.

© mohamedguardian_sl

Figure 4.1 Tahrir Square in Cairo during Egypt's 2011 revolution

That said, one particularly noteworthy facet of the January 25 Revolution was its nonideological character. Egyptians came together to demand an end to a government they regarded as ineffective (particularly in the socioeconomic realm), corrupt, unaccountable, and disrespectful of them as citizens. They did not, however, share any common vision of a particular way forward politically. This was not in any sense an Islamist revolution. Indeed, if anything, the revolutionary credentials of the MB were initially somewhat suspect. They were late to join the protests, and among the first to indicate a willingness to compromise and negotiate with Mubarak when, in the dying days of his tenure, he desperately tried to hold on to power by any means.

After a short-lived debate within the MB about whether the movement should enter politics immediately, or sit out what was seen as likely to be a difficult and turbulent transition period, the formation of the Freedom and Justice Party (FJP) was announced in April 2013. This followed in the wake of a national referendum on constitutional amendments proposed by the SCAF that would place parliamentary and presidential elections ahead of a new constitution. The Islamists strongly supported the amendments, having calculated that they enjoyed a strong comparative advantage against other, relatively underdeveloped political forces in the country, and were therefore likely to do well at the polls. Many leaders of the revolution, however, were wary of the amendments, afraid that early elections would give Islamists overwhelming control over the process of writing a new constitution. In the end, the proposed amendments gained support from a large majority (77 percent) of the electorate.

With the formation of the FJP, the MB became, overnight, the most formidable force in Egyptian politics. Aware that many in society feared Islamist domination of the political sphere, the MB made various declarations and promises tailored to mitigate such concerns—most of which it eventually ended up backing away from. For example, the group announced that it would deliberately avoid seeking a majority in parliament (a tactic previously employed by the Islamist PJD in Morocco—see Box 4.4, "Morocco: Islamism in the shadow of the palace") and would not run a presidential candidate. It also began making regular use of the slogan "Participation not Domination" to describe its objectives. At the same time, however, the MB began moving to enforce political behavior within the movement, announcing that Brotherhood members were not allowed to join any political parties other than the FJP. When MB reformist leader Abdul Munim Abou Al-Fattouh announced that he was setting up his own political party, he was expelled from the MB. By this time, many leaders of the Brotherhood's youth wing had also left the fold. The consolidation of an old-guard, conservative cadre at the top of the movement, combined with the Brotherhood's initial hesitation when the revolution began, left many younger members feeling they had more in common with the activist networks that had served as the vanguard of January. By the summer of 2011, many of the more liberal-minded youth members of the MB had left the movement to form their own parties (such as Egyptian Current) or to join Al-Fattouh's.

These splits within the MB were minor insofar as they did not involve large numbers of personnel, although they did further alter the character of the MB as a movement—leaving it even more firmly in the hands of conservatives with an aversion to pluralism. At the same time, however, the landscape of Islamic politics in Egypt was expanding and diversifying. Alongside MB defectors and discontents, at least three other Islamic trends could be found—one of which would prove to be highly significant in political terms. These were the moderate, centrist Islamists as represented by Hizb al-Wasat (which finally gained a political party license only days after Mubarak's ouster), several ex-jihadi groups such as Al-Gamaa al-Islamiyya (see above and Chapter 7) that decided to form political parties, and—most notably—a number of new Salafi parties. While Salafis had been part of Egyptian religious life since at least the 1920s, and represented since the 2000s an ever larger segment of the public sphere through a number of dedicated satellite television stations, they were generally thought of as a quietist force that tended to emphasize personal piety rather than participation in formal politics (see Box 4.1, "The new Salafi factor in Arab politics").

2012 saw Egypt's first ever free and fair elections. Parliamentary balloting early in the year saw the MB-led coalition win a strong plurality of the vote (38 percent), with a very strong and surprise second-place showing by the Salafis (28 percent). This means that, between them, Islamic political parties controlled more than two-thirds of all parliamentary seats. Other than the nationalist Wafd party and the "social liberal" Egyptian Bloc, none of the other 13 parties in parliament won more than ten seats. The parliament sat for only a few months before Egypt's Supreme Constitutional Court (SCC) declared it invalid on the basis that the legislation that governed its election was unconstitutional. At around the same time, a presidential election saw an initially diverse range of candidates narrowed to a runoff between the FJP's Mohammed Morsi (previously head of the MB's bloc in the 2005 parliament) and Ahmed Shafiq, a former military officer and minister in Mubarak's government. Morsi won a narrow (52 percent) victory.

BOX 4.1 THE NEW SALAFI FACTOR IN ARAB POLITICS

The strong showing by Salafi parties at Egypt's ballot box in 2011–12 surprised many observers. Because Salafi groups had only recently entered politics, they were assumed to suffer from many of the same organizational disadvantages—lack of experience, lack of resources, lack of a mobilized social base—that other, non-MB parties faced. When the counting was finished, however, the Salafi 'Islamist Bloc' had won a quarter of the popular vote and the second largest bloc of seats in Egypt's National Assembly. Who are Egypt's Salafis, what is their agenda, and what explains their phenomenal political success? How do they compare with Salafis elsewhere in the Arab world?

While most Salafis are quietists—eschewing politics in favor of a focus on personal piety and purity of religious practice—there has been a politicized strain of Salafism present since at least the 1970s (see Chapter 2). In Egypt, where Salafis have been active since the 1920s, this activity was centered on Alexandria. By the 1990s, the Mubarak regime was deliberately opening up space for Salafis to become more assertive in the hope that they would draw support away from the MB. The past decade has also seen the establishment of a number of Salafi-oriented satellite television channels, giving rise to an expanding Salafi "public sphere" and ensuring that the Salafi political parties founded after Mubarak's ouster already had a ready base of support in society.

© Amr Dalsh / Reuters

Figure 4.2 A Salafi politician campaigning in Egypt's 2011 parliamentary election

Egypt's main Salafi political parties—Hizb al-Nour, Hizb al-Asala, Hizb al-Fadhila, and Hizb al-Watan—have a complex relationship with the MB. On one hand, there is a shared Islamic orientation and agenda focused on integrating religion into public life and law. But the MB and the Salafis are also political competitors. Furthermore, they do not always see eye to eye in terms of Islamic priorities and approaches. Salafis often view the MB and its followers as engaged in a project that instrumentalizes religion for the purposes of gaining political power—an orientation that does not sit well with the Salafi emphasis on religious purity. While the Salafis in Egypt's Constituent Assembly were certainly keen to make references to Islam in Egypt's new constitution as precise and predominant as possible, their political agenda has otherwise focused on issues relating to education, social issues, and efforts to protect Egypt from what they see as immoral cultural influences. In terms of the sources of their popular support, Salafis likely benefited from the fact that many Egyptians—while wanting to vote "Islamic"—regarded the MB as a movement that had shown itself to be too willing to accommodate the previous regime, or as a large, centralized, and rigid organization that was not conducive to bringing change.

It is also important to emphasize that the importance of Salafi influences in Egyptian society extends well beyond the political realm. The Salafi movement continues to be most prevalent at the local and communal levels, and those who express fears about its rising influence—such as Egypt's minority Christian population—are often more concerned with potential tensions arising from the actions of local Salafi groups (e.g. harassment of converts, attacks on churches, etc.) rather than the national Salafi political parties.

While the Salafi factor has been most prevalent in Egypt, there are also Salafi groups active in other post-Uprising settings in the Arab world, such as Tunisia, Morocco, and Libya. While not yet a major political factor in these other countries, Salafis have taken advantage of the openness provided by popular revolutions to press their issues and influence public debates. In Tunisia, Salafists have been linked to a number of controversies surrounding media programming and the role of women in society. They have also been linked to the assassination of prominent liberal politicians and attacks on foreign embassies. Tunisia's Salafis did not start to form political parties until somewhat later than their Egyptian counterparts.

Although the SCAF initially had laid out a more limited range of powers for the new president, Morsi moved quickly to consolidate his position. By the late summer, Morsi had ordered the resignation of the SCAF leaders and rescinded their earlier decree limiting his powers. Portrayed by Morsi's supporters and the FJP as evidence that the new president would not permit the military to prevail over the political sphere, others believed the apparent rebuff of the SCAF was a far more complex affair, that had been arranged in cooperation with the army itself in return for Morsi guaranteeing certain privileges for the military going forward (such as budgetary autonomy and limitations on civilian oversight). The SCAF had, in any case, never been comfortable wielding executive power, and welcomed the opportunity to return to barracks.

With sporadic protests and spates of street violence ongoing, the latter half of 2012 was occupied by progressively growing tensions around Morsi's presidency and the process to draft and approve a new constitution. The latter effort was guided by a Constitutional Assembly initially elected by the parliament (before the latter was dissolved) but immediately challenged on the grounds of being overly dominated by Islamists and insufficiently representative of Egyptian society. Despite various compromises over its composition, the Assembly's work was marred by persistent controversy and the potential threat of dissolution at the hands of the Supreme Constitutional Court. Morsi found himself increasingly at odds with the Court—and the country's judiciary more broadly—over the course of the year. While the courts claimed to be acting in the interests of preserving the rule of law and the integrity of constitutional process, Morsi accused the judiciary of being a sanctuary for remnants of the Mubarak regime seeking to undermine his leadership. In November 2012, Morsi issued a decree exempting his actions from judicial review and setting a short-fuse deadline for a national referendum on the draft constitution. Morsi insisted that the rapid timetable for constitutional approval was necessary to stave off efforts by the SCC to annul the Constituent Assembly and force it to start from scratch with new members. Over the protests of opposition figures, who decried what they perceived as Morsi's efforts to rush through a constitution whose substance reflected Islamist interests, a popular referendum approved the draft constitution in December 2012, albeit with very low turnout (estimated at 25–30 percent of the electorate).

The constitution in question does not, on the face of it, seem to reflect a strongly Islamist agenda. The primary reference to the relationship between religion and lawmaking indicates that the Islamic *shari'ah* are the main source of legislation (Article 2), the exact same formulation as was present in the 1971 version of the constitution. Unlike the 1971 text, however, the new constitution goes on in Article 219 to provide a more precise definition of "principles of *shari'ah*," although the practical implications of so doing are left vague and largely unintelligible to readers unfamiliar with the technical language of Islamic jurisprudence.[63] Article 4 specifies that Al-Azhar University, the country's premier institution of Islamic learning, is to be consulted in matters of Islamic law. The inclusion of this clause politicizes Al-Azhar even as the venerable university seeks to assert greater independence following decades under the thumb of the state. Building a role of Al-Azhar into the legislative process also means that the ongoing debate about governance within that institution takes on a new pale, with some observers already indicating that there are signs that the MB is trying to exert greater influences in Azhari circles.[64] Opponents of the constitution have also objected to the inclusion of passages that guarantee full freedom of religion only to members of the three Abrahamic faiths, require gender equality in conformity with the "provisions of *shari'ah*," and give the state a role in protecting ethics and morals.

With Egypt at a political impasse, Morsi's challenges multiplied over the first half of 2012. Efforts to arrest and intimidate media figures critical of his presidency, combined with a new draft NGO law that severely circumscribed civil society, led many opposition figures to decry Morsi's increasingly authoritarian style. The SCC postponed parliamentary elections scheduled for the spring on the grounds that the invalid electoral law that led them to annul the first post-revolutionary parliament still had not been sufficiently revised. This prolonged Egypt's political limbo, with an ever-worsening economic crisis looming. By the summer, Morsi's approval ratings were rock bottom and a movement calling itself Tamarod ("Rebellion") organized a grassroots effort to call for Morsi's resignation. Tamarod called for mass demonstrations on June 30, 2013 and succeeded in bringing at least 15 million opponents of the president into city squares across Egypt. At this point the army intervened, indicating that if the presidency and the opposition could not resolve their differences within a matter of days, then the army would present its own "roadmap" for Egypt's political future. This spelled the end of Morsi's presidency. On July 3, the army chief announced that President Morsi had been removed from power and an interim civilian president sworn in. In subsequent days the acting president, former chief judge Adly Mansour, announced a new nine-month transitional plan involving a half-year process to amend the constitution followed by new parliamentary and presidential elections in 2014—in effect decreeing the

Figure 4.3 Mohamed Morsi, Egypt's short-lived Muslim Brotherhood president

© Getty Images

"constitution first" approach that most secular forces had preferred in the immediate aftermath of Mubarak's ouster in 2011.

The army's actions were tantamount to a military coup against a democratically elected president, and Muslim Brotherhood supporters were predictably outraged. In addition to removing Morsi from office, the military also moved quickly to arrest key MB leaders, seize certain assets of the movements, and close their media channels and offices. For its part, the MB demanded the reinstatement of Morsi, and refused to participate in, or even recognize, the legitimacy of the newly appointed interim government (composed of a combination of technocrats and opposition figures). Salafi parties, which had been increasingly critical of Morsi, emerged as a particularly influential force after the coup. By not siding entirely with Morsi (while still decrying certain actions of the military) and holding out the possibility of cooperation with the interim government, they sought to capitalize politically on the moment by serving as something of a broker between the military-backed careholder regime and Islamist forces in Egyptian society. The extent and depth of the military's crackdown on the Brotherhood will have a major impact on the MB's future, as will whatever decision the Brotherhood's leadership makes about whether and how to engage this new phase of Egyptian politics. By legally proscribing, in September 2013, the activities of the Brotherhood and all entities linked to them, the military-led state seemed committed to comprehensively dismantling the MB as a social and political force.

How to assess Egypt's initial short-term experiment with Islamist rule? Arguably the Islamists were in power for too short a period—and one of highly volatile, turbulent transitional politics at that—to be able to say much that is definitive. Indeed, much of Morsi's and the FJP's behaviour while in government (2012–13) can be explained as a function of Egypt's broken political system without having to make reference to the party's underlying ideology. So, while we certainly saw evidence of authoritarian inclinations on the part of Egypt's current government, it is not entirely clear that (a) it is qualitatively different from the authoritarianism that dominated Egypt for decades prior; or (b) it has a primarily ideological—and more specifically an Islamist—basis. That said, it would be a mistake entirely to divorce the character of Morsi's governance from its underlying roots in a long-banned political movement. The MB experience was plainly reflected in Morsi's leadership, although not necessarily in the issues and policies that Morsi and the FJP have championed. Although we pointed above to some "Islamist" dimensions of Egypt's 2012 constitution, it is in fact hard to point to any explicitly Islamic initiative that Morsi's government pursued while in government. So, if their policies are not "Islamic," wherein lay the 2012–13 Egyptian government's Islamism? Arguably, the legacy of the MB was most apparent in the paranoid, exclusivist, and insular political style that Morsi and his FJP colleagues adopted. After decades of being banned from politics and persistently persecuted by the Mubarak regime, Egypt's Islamists—well versed in oppositional politics, but relative neophytes when it comes to actually governing—were not naturally inclined to cooperate and build trusting, functional relationships with other political actors. Furthermore, many of the Brotherhood's more pragmatic leaders had either been marginalized within the movement or decamped altogether, leaving the group in the hands of highly conservative leaders deeply suspicious of politics and the very state institutions that had fallen into their hands.

BOX 4.2 TUNISIA: ISLAMISTS AND THE LEGACY OF SECULARISM

The Arab Uprisings began in Tunisia in 2010, and that country's Islamists were the first to taste electoral victory as part of a broader regional trend whereby previously oppressed Islamist movements and parties found new opportunities to vie for political power. While Tunisia's efforts to transition to democracy after the ouster of Zin El Abidine Ben Ali in 2011 have faced considerable challenges, the situation there has been markedly different from the Egyptian experience. Who are Tunisia's Islamists, and why have they seemingly pursued a different strategy than their counterparts in Egypt?

Tunisia's main Islamist party, En-Nahda ("Renaissance"), was established in 1989 as the successor to the Islamic Tendency Movement (MTI—Mouvement de la Tendance Islamique). Tunisia had been an intensely secular republic since its independence from France in 1956, with the governments of founding prime minister Habib Bourguiba and his successor Zin El Abidine Ben Ali enforcing strict government regulation of religion, and a firm separation of mosque and state as per the French system of *laicité*. Tunisia's Islamist movement, which has been around in one form or another since the 1970s, has persistently found itself at odds with the state. Various waves of government crackdowns have meant that Tunisia's Islamists were a marginal political force at best until being banned outright in the early 1990s. While they gained some parliamentary presence in the late 1980s by running as independents, this direct involvement in the political sphere laid the groundwork for a comprehensive government campaign against En-Nahda. From the early 1990s, its leaders—such as Rachid Ghannouchi and Hamadi Jebali (the latter the editor of En-Nahda's newspaper *Al-Fajr*)—found themselves exiled or jailed, and En-Nahda itself was formally proscribed after an alleged plot to take over the state. The next decade represented the wilderness years for Tunisia's Islamists, with the movement completely absent from Tunisian politics.

While Islamism was dormant in Tunisia for nearly two decades, En-Nahda's chief ideologue, Rachid Ghannouchi, working from the safety of exile in Europe, grew in stature as a global Islamist thinker. He continued to be active in the transnational circuits of the MB tradition (in which En-Nahda has its roots), and by the 2000s had arguably become the most influential living Islamist thinker. Much of his work during this period was focused on resolving the apparent tensions between Islamic belief and modern democracy, and some credit him with developing a moderate approach to Islamism that could be compatible with political pluralism.[65]

When Ghannouchi returned to Tunisia following Ben Ali's fall from power in 2011, he was met by thousands of cheering supporters at the airport. While he has not assumed any formal political office, he continues to serve as the leader of the En-Nahda movement. Ghannouchi remains an active speaker on the international circuit, emphasizing the compatibility of Islam and democracy and extolling the moderate approach that En-Nahda has taken to stewarding Tunisia through its transition and constitutional process. As is common with political

© Zoubeir Souissi / Reuters

Figure 4.4 En-Nahda leader and Islamist thinker Rachid Ghannouchi groups subject to foreign exile, rifts inevitably emerge between leaders living abroad and movement members who have stayed behind, often under very harsh conditions (see e.g. Hamas' similar experience in Chapter 6). When combined with the same generational issues that many Islamist groups are facing today, it is legitimate to raise questions about the extent to which Ghannouchi's ideas represent the rank-and-file of En-Nahda as a movement and political party.

While the early years of Tunisia's post-2011 transition certainly involved a number of serious challenges, it managed to avoid the utter impasse and subsequent crisis faced by the MB in Egypt. En-Nahda emerged as the dominant political force in the country after elections to create a constituent assembly. En-Nahda has also led the country's transitional government. The party's leadership has argued that Tunisia's relatively functional politics—as compared with Egypt—is a function of the more pragmatic approach it has taken to the process of writing a new constitution. It is certainly the case that En-Nahda has compromised over issues such as including references to Islam in the draft constitution, and the addition of clauses relating to blasphemy crimes. Ghannouchi and others have cited this as evidence of En-Nahda's moderate character, but it is also the case that Tunisia's Islamists are operating in a more pluralistic political climate. Unlike Egypt, where secular-liberal forces lack unity, focus, and resources, Tunisia has a sophisticated and well-entrenched segment of secular parties in its system. Because of this, En-Nahda was forced even from the outset to enter the political process with a more accommodating stance. To its credit, the Tunisian constitutional process has been slower and more deliberative—a distinct contrast to the hectic and highly polarizing effort to fast-track Egypt's new constitution in late 2012. But secular-Islamist tensions have continued to simmer. Women's groups have expressed concerns about the rising influence of Salafi forces in Tunisian society. Assassinations of prominent secular politicians in 2013—presumably at the hands of Salafis or other more extremist Islamists—put pressure on En-Nahda since they are widely perceived as contributing to a political climate that keeps the country polarized. Like Egypt's Islamists, En-Nahda's leadership is also keenly aware that many Tunisians are looking to them first and foremost to address the country's dire socioeconomic problems. With social tensions mounting, En-Nahda agreed in principle, in autumn 2013, to resign in favor of a technocratic government that would see the nation through to new legislative elections—but negotiations towards this end repeatedly stalled.

TURKEY: RELIGION, SECULAR NATIONALIST IDEOLOGY, AND THE RISE OF "MUSLIM DEMOCRACY"

We turn now to a country whose recent political history has been viewed by many as a potential model for how other countries—and particularly Arab countries undergoing transition after 2011—might go about successfully fusing Islam and democracy. Turkey provides us with another, and in some regards even more extreme, case of Islamists vying for influence in a politically hostile environment. In Egypt, the MB was kept out of politics altogether by an NDP determined to stay in power by sidelining any potential rival. In the case of Turkey, however, Islamism has been viewed by the dominant forces of the military and judiciary as a rival not so much to any particular political party, but to the highly secular official state ideology of Kemalism. Unlike in Egypt, Turkish Islamist parties have been permitted to contest elections and to serve in coalition governments. In 2002, a political party with strong Islamist roots swept a full two-thirds of the Turkish parliament, and went on to gain even larger shares of the popular vote at two subsequent elections. As the self-appointed guardians of the secular order, however, the Turkish army has always lurked just behind the political stage. On four occasions, in 1960, 1971, 1980, and 1997, the army has intervened to suspend or alter the course of popular politics in the name of protecting the Republic. In this section our goal is to understand the evolution of the Turkish Islamic movement in the context of an ideologically rigid state. As we will see, the recent history of Islamism in Turkey has never been a simple case of religion versus nationalism. Rather, Islamist parties have always had a complex and multifaceted relationship with Turkish nationalism and the Kemalist legacy. Some of the most successful and deeply rooted manifestations of Muslim politics in Turkey also have strong nationalist leanings. In recent years, we have also seen the emergence of a new kind of "pietistic politics" with strong roots in the widespread popularity of Sufi movements in Turkey, and with strong nationalist undertones.[66] Some have also associated this with a shift or evolution in the nature of Turkish Islamism, citing the recent political success of the AKP as evidence. Analysts such as Vali Nasr see in the AKP the harbinger of a new form of "Muslim Democracy."[67] We might also be tempted to draw certain parallels here with the divisions that emerged in the Egyptian MB in the mid-1990s and that went on to produce the Hizb al-Wasat as a political alternative to a self-marginalized and rigid Islamism.

We begin by briefly reviewing the political legacy of Mustafa Kemal and the concomitant ideology that forms the foundation of the modern Turkish Republic. We then trace the emergence and evolution of Turkey's Islamist movement from the introduction of multiparty politics in 1956, but with primary emphasis on the period following the Refah Party's strong electoral success in 1994. In order to understand the complex nature of Turkish Islam in terms of its social roots, we also touch on several of the most important Sufi-based movements whose followers had an increasingly important role in shaping the nature of Islamist politics from the 1990s. After explaining the crackdown on the Refah Party and its various successors, we analyze the split within the Islamic movement that led to formation of the AKP in 2001 and its almost immediate electoral triumph the following year. The AKP's decade in power is assessed, with particular attention to the question of whether and how it is possible to regard the party as an "Islamist" actor in light of subsequent developments. Finally, the question of the AKP as a form of "new Islamism" or Muslim Democracy is considered.

As we will recall from Chapter 3, the modern Turkish Republic was founded by Mustapha Kemal Ataturk in 1922 out of the embers of the Ottoman Empire. He immediately set in motion a comprehensive program of modernization and secularization, seeking to eradicate all vestiges of Ottoman and Islamic "traditionalism" in the name of a Europeanized future. For Kemal, Islam was one of the greatest obstacles to the achievement of this vision, and he undertook to comprehensively remove its influence from public life. In 1924 the caliphate was abolished. All court *ulama* and *qadis* were removed from their posts. Pious endowments (*awqaf*) were seized by the state. A government agency, the Diyanet, was charged with the strict regulation of all religious activity in the country, and all mosques came under its jurisdiction. Religion, in the Kemalist view, needed to be molded and disciplined so as to become not only compatible with, but also a conduit for, the process of modernization. The state thus claimed for itself the authority to define religion and also the boundaries of the sacred.

Kemal's Republican People's Party (RPP) effectively ran the country as a single-party state until the early 1950s. The "Young Turk" movement that gave birth to the republican movement had its base within the military, and the army of the Turkish Republic quickly established itself—alongside the powerful Constitutional Court—as the chief guardian of the Kemalist legacy. As mentioned above, it has not hesitated on several occasions to intervene directly in politics when the Kemalist order is perceived to be under threat—and in two cases it has even suspended democracy for short periods of martial rule. Intense secularism has been a hallmark characteristic of the state ideology, and in Turkey it has been taken to levels almost unparalleled in other countries. For example, the wearing of headscarves is strictly banned in any government space and in many universities, and all religious institutions are closely and comprehensively regulated by the state. While some see this as a dangerous limitation on religious freedom, others consider it to be an essential component of social stability, fearing potentially destabilizing effects if too much religion were to merge into public life.

Ninety-nine percent of Turkey's population is nominally Muslim—the vast majority of them Sunni (but with some ethnic variation within that sectarian group), and also a considerable *Alevi* minority (a Shi'i offshoot regarded by many Sunnis as heterodox and subject to persistent persecution) and even some Shi'a. We should also note up front the pervasive and highly influential presence of Sufism in Turkish Islam. As we will see later, Sufi movements have played a major role in the evolution of contemporary ideas about the role of religion in society and politics. Despite the intense secularization program introduced by Kemal, clearly Turks were not simply going to put religion aside. The influence of religion, particularly in provincial and rural areas, remained strong at the societal level even as people accommodated themselves to the absence of religion in public life and "official" space. It is therefore not surprising that, once the political system was finally opened up to meaningful multiparty politics in 1950, a party perceived as allowing more space for religion, the Demokrat Party, defeated the RPP and ruled the country until 1960, when they were removed by the military. When first faced with the Demokrat Party threat, one of the RPP's responses was to try to appear more "religion-friendly" itself. From the late 1940s, for example, they began a process of upgrading the system of *Imam-hatip* (religious training) schools.[68]

As in Egypt, it is important for understanding Muslim politics in Turkey to get a sense of what Islam looks like at the societal level—but for a different reason. In the case of the Egyptian MB, we saw the systematic socialization of civil societal spaces by an Islamist movement pursuing the establishment of a *shari'ah*-based social and political order. This has not been the pattern of social Islam in Turkey, and nor does one find a similar influence of "neo-corporatist" politics on the state. In the case of Turkey, the most important manifestations of Islam at the societal level are to be found in various Sufi and modern reformist groups. The strongest Sufi order in Turkey is the Naqshbandiyya, a relatively orthodox, or "sober" *tariqa* founded in the fourteenth century, known for its emphasis on piety and discipline. The other important figure here is the early twentieth-century reformer and activist Said Nursi (1876–1960). Nursi, whose intellectual trajectory can be understood in parallel to that of other Islamic Reformists of the day, such as Muhammad Abduh, sought in his work to emphasize the compatibility of religion and modernity. Strongly influenced by both Naqshbandi Sufism and modern ideologies of national liberation, Nursi's major publication, the *Risale-i Nur* (*Epistle of Light*), is read widely by a large variety of grassroots religious groups in Turkey to this day. The direct inheritors of his thinking are within the Nurçu movement. Nurçu followers are to be found throughout Turkey, and are often associated with a wide variety of social organizations (charities, schools, clubs, etc.)—but, unlike the MB activists inhabiting the same spaces in Egypt, theirs is not primarily a political impulse. One of the best-known and most common Nurçu social formations is the *dershane,* or reading group. These "textual communities," as Hakan Yavuz calls them, are usually organized at the neighborhood level and involve meetings in apartment buildings or dormitories where readings from the *Risale-i Nur* are discussed and prayers said, followed by socializing.[69] The Nurçu meetings are, in effect, spaces for the building of like-minded social capital. Direct political influence has generally been difficult to discern, although, as we will see later, their support for the recently established AKP seems to provide an important base for that party in society. As Serif Mardin has put it:

> The influence of the Nurçu sect is ... a diffuse one: while the sect's newspaper disseminates the correct stand to take on current political, social, and economic issues, the effectiveness of the Nurçu is that of a freemasonry, of persons who establish social linkages and personal ties with each other, who support and promote people who think like themselves. But this diffuseness ... is an element to reckon with in the intellectual climate of contemporary Turkey.[70]

The *dershane* meetings hence represent a combination of Rotary Club-style social capital infused with Sufi piety and self-discipline. Yavuz sees in them a form of "counterpublic" in which new forms of Muslim subjectivity are created in relation to state policies and market practices.[71]

Another key Naqshbandi influence can be seen in the circle around Mehmed Zahid Kotku (sometimes called "Zahid Efendi"), the leader or *sheikh* of the *tariqa* in Turkey from the early 1950s until his death in 1980. Kotku pursued a multifaceted strategy as regards religion and politics, and clearly sought a more direct and active religious influence. He established circles across the country, set up publications, and even invested in manufacturing. Subsequent analysis of his writings reveals him to have had clear Islamist inclinations, but via an approach that combined elements of religious activism with a nationalist identity.[72] He also played a role in encouraging the formation of the first Islamist political party in Turkey, and in choosing its leader.[73] In Serif Mardin's analysis, the power of the various Sufi-influenced movements lay in their ability to provide a sense of meaning and a normative framework at the level of everyday life. Kemalism, as the state ideology, was a rather abstract body of enforced public norms sitting on an official and closely guarded pedestal. The Sufi way, on the other hand, allowed followers to understand personal piety as part of a much broader experience that invested everyday practice with spiritual meaning and significance. As its influence grew within Turkey's provincial middle classes, and eventually among intellectuals and urban populations, the broad Nurçu movement emerged as a significant repository of upwardly mobile social capital waiting to be channeled into a political project.

A more recent Nurçu-related group that has attracted considerable attention of late is the movement associated with Fethullah Gülen (see Chapter 8), a religious teacher whose work emphasizes an "Islamic ethic of education."[74] Gülen has established a network of schools whose curriculum is wholly modern and secular, but whose teachers are all members of the religious movement. Through dormitory *dershanes* and supplemental classes, they seek to create parallel spaces for religious education to occur alongside high-quality secular study. Some have interpreted Gülen as providing a form of religiously inflected nationalism that allows him to operate safely within the Kemalist framework. His schools, which also exist in the Balkans and Central Asia, can be seen as institutions seeking to provide the credentials required for participation in modern life (as engineers, lawyers, etc.) while also inculcating a sense of religious consciousness. The idea is hence to create a generation of Turkish elites who will be more comfortable with the idea of leaving greater space for religion in public life.

These, then, are some of the groups that collectively compose the Islamic movement in Turkey. By contrast, it does not become possible to talk about the formation of a discernible Islamist (that is, overtly political) movement until the emergence in the late 1960s of the National Outlook Movement, Milli Gorus. In part a product of the rapidly changing economic environment of the time, this group's primary concerns related to both the decline of morality associated with the rapid modernization and industrialization of Turkish society; and the threat posed to Turkey's independence by its growing ties to the European Community and the wider global economy. Out of this broad movement, Turkey's first Islamist political party, the National Order Party (soon renamed the National Salvation Party, NSP) was founded in 1970 under the leadership of Necmettin Erbakan. The NSP established itself as the party of the urban poor and the provincial middle class, becoming a permanent, although by no means dominant, fixture within the parliament during the 1970s.[75] Caught up in the military coup of 1980, the NSP found itself accused by the military of using religion for political purposes. Some observers have noted that, alongside the NSP's parliamentary efforts, a less organized and socially based Islamic movement had arisen in parallel. Operating through associational channels in much the same way as the MB in Egypt, many within these groups held to more radical views that had no place in the parliamentary discourse of the NSP. This is a development of which the military would no doubt have been aware.[76] The flexibility of the Islamist discourse is demonstrated by the course pursued by the Refah Party, NSP's successor, during the course of the 1980s. Moving away from the "defensive" Islamism of the 1970s (anti-global capitalism), Refah sought now to emphasize the idea of Turkey's integration into the world economy through leveraging its own resources. Refah, still under Erbakan, used religion partly as a tool to discredit the Turkish Left, arguing that religious leaders and local associations needed to be integrated into the program of national development.[77] This allowed the Islamists to buy into the so-called "Turkish–Islamic Synthesis" favored by the military as a way to marginalize the socialists. Fethullah Gülen's movement also found favor in this same climate.[78] The 1980s can hence be thought of as a period where the Islamists sought to realign their base. Many NSP conservatives, in any case, had departed for Turgut Ozal's conservative Motherland party once the NSP fell on hard times around the time of the coup. Ozal had been a disciple of Kotku, and was generally more open to religion. It was even rumored that he was receiving political advice from the Sufis, leading some to label members of the party as "crypto-Naqshbandis."

The 1990s marked a significant upswing in the electoral fortunes of the Refah Party. Growing popular religiosity, combined with the ill effects of economic liberalization reforms (compare with Egypt during roughly the same period), created a climate ripe for Erbakan's Islamist discourse. First in municipal elections during 1994, then in parliamentary polls the following year, Refah scored big—emerging as the single largest party in the assembly. Its bloc was not large enough to enable it to form a government alone, so Refah was forced into an awkward coalition with Tansu Ciller's "True Path" party and Mesut Yilmaz of Motherland, the premiership rotating between all three of them. Turkish politics soon descended into a mud-slinging match, with Yilmaz and Ciller trying to undermine each other, convinced that the Kemalists would keep Refah in check. Within Refah itself, tensions began to emerge between the conservative faction led by Erbakan and a "reformist" bloc that wanted to remake the party in the image of Europe's Christian Democratic parties—a divide that would become highly significant around the time of AKP's formation. The former group wanted to pursue issues such as lifting the ban on veils, and the realignment of Turkey's foreign policy with other leading Muslim countries—both of which, of course, greatly disturbed the Kemalist establishment. Matters came to a head in early 1997, when a pro-Hizbullah speech by the Iranian ambassador that had been sponsored by the Refah mayor of a provincial town snowballed into a national event after the military sent tanks into the town and arrested the mayor. The Refah government's subsequent show of support for their party member prompted the government to reprioritize politicized religion as the country's number one security threat, and to issue a set of secularizing demands to Refah for immediate implementation. When this was not forthcoming, the military—in what has been described as a "postmodern coup"—compelled the government to resign.[79]

Within a year, the Constitutional Court also forced the Refah Party to disband. After a few weeks, however, it had been reconstituted as the Virtue Party, with much the same membership and Erbakan still in control from behind the scenes. Over the next four years, the military and judiciary hounded several iterations of the Islamist party. Virtue soon found itself out of favor when, after the 1999 elections, one of their female members of parliament tried to take the oath of allegiance wearing a headscarf. By 2000 the courts deemed Virtue beyond the pale and shut it down as well.

This latest legal setback was the final straw for some within the Islamist party. In a move that, in some ways, bears strong family resemblances to the process through which Hizb al-Wasat emerged from the MB in Egypt, the reformist bloc within the now-banned Virtue Party broke with Erbakan's conservatives to form a new party called Justice and Development (AKP— Adalet ve Kalkinma Partisi). The conservatives also reconstituted themselves, this time as the Saadet ("Felicity") Party. Two points of comparison with the Egyptian case are particularly relevant here. First, one of the major concerns voiced by the reformist bloc—who also tended to be of the younger generation—was that Erbakan's tight circle of loyalists had been running the party in a highly authoritarian manner. Governance was seen as out of step with a rapidly growing provincial middle-class base that wanted to expand the party's platform beyond the more conventional Islamist agenda that Erbakan had been pursuing since the early 1970s. Second, the reformists were fed up with what they perceived as Erbakan's obsession with lightning-rod issues such as veiling. Where the reformists wanted to pursue a mainstream national development agenda, Erbakan kept wandering into territory certain to bring the party into disrepute with the Kemalist establishment. In much the same way as the Wasat group in Egypt resented the MB old guard's unwillingness to pursue a mainstream platform that would allow for sustained political participation, so the founders of the AKP sought a centrist synthesis that would allow them more access across the sociopolitical spectrum—and, likewise, to become more accessible to the masses. The reformist wing had "concluded that Turkey's military would never allow an overtly Islamist party back into power, and—still more importantly—that the ban on Islamic parties was helping other right-of-center parties . . ."[80] The AKP was founded in 2001 and one year later, in the November 2002 national elections, the party shocked the world with a landslide victory, gaining two-thirds of all seats in parliament and over 34 percent of the popular vote.

Who were these voters? How and why did the AKP receive such a strong mandate for so relatively immature a party and political vision? A wide variety of factors deserve mention here. For those whose sense of public normativity was derived from religion, but who had little interest in the idea of an Islamic political order, it made great sense to desert Erbakan's "old school" Islamism for the more moderate and inclusive shores of the new party. The AKP victory, then, represented "a clear mandate to redefine the political center in terms of societal values" under a political party that was "promising to create a space within which Muslim values can express themselves, but [without] pushing an Islamist legislative agenda."[81] The social conduits of this victory had been in the making for some time, with the aforementioned Nurçu networks and groups such as the Fethullah Gülen movement playing key roles. Gülen, for example, had sponsored a series of annual seminars since 1998 known as the "Abant meetings," where elites and intellectuals from both Islamic and secular backgrounds would gather to discuss—and usually find themselves in agreement on—issues of mutual concern.[82] A number of prominent Naqshbandi intellectuals were also integral members of the new party.[83] But this was not purely about an opportunity for more religion in public life. In explaining and understanding the formation of a social base for the AKP's political discourse, it is crucial to understand how notions of everyday "popular" piety interacted with the Turkish political economy during the 1980s and 1990s. For many, the AKP represented the possibility of reconciling economic liberalism with the traditional values of provincial populations who had been drifting into cities as urbanization and economic liberalization proceeded apace—a normative framework that had been evolving gradually within the upwardly mobile context of Nurçu networks over a decade or more. As Hakan Yavuz puts it:

> In the transformation of the Islamic movement in general, and the electoral victory of the AKP in particular, a "new" urban class, consisting of horizontally connected solidarity-based groups with rural origins and shared Islamic ethos, played an important role. This "new" urban class has been excluded culturally and economically by the Kemalist elite. The excluded segment of the population utilized Islamic idioms and networks to overcome their exclusion. Thus Islamic networks both facilitated this group's integration into modern opportunity spaces and offered it a hope for social mobilization.[84]

Hence the tremendous speed of the AKP's electoral success. It was not necessary for the party to socialize a constituency into its political framework—rather, a primed collective of communities or networks more or less "mobilized themselves" when they finally saw in the AKP the centrist synthesis they had been waiting for.[85] In other words, the AKP represented the party political vehicle for a socially mobile, non- and newly-urbanized, conservative-leaning and previously disenfranchised social class in Turkey. Also, in a climate of intense corruption and fiscal mismanagement, such as was to be found in Turkey in 1999–2002, *not* voting for the incumbent parties was very easy, even for many whose background did not correspond to the AKP's natural social base.

Also important is the fact that the AKP possessed built-in credibility in the form of its leadership. The party chief, Recep Tayyip Erdoğan, was an immensely popular former mayor of Istanbul whose tenure was remembered for the efficient provision of services and also for its fiscal responsibility. In terms of personal style, the contrast with Erbakan could not have been greater. Erbakan was the paternalistic, authoritarian overlord who informed the party faithful what needed to be done. Erdoğan, on the other hand, came across as someone who dwelled among the people—the neighbor, "the guy next door."[86] His was an emphasis on horizontal ties of solidarity rather than vertical ties of obligation. Erdoğan had also clearly been a victim of the Kemalist order. In the 1990s, he was arrested and jailed for several months for having read a poem with religious metaphors at a public rally. Since his criminal record barred him from standing as a candidate for parliament in 2002, he was initially unable to take up the premiership until a constitutional amendment made this possible in 2003. Erdoğan also consciously tapped into a nostalgia for Turgut Özal's brand of 1980s centrist conservatism. "In many ways," Vali Nasr has argued, "the AKP is less an extension of Welfare and Virtue than a reconstruction of the center-right, economically liberal Motherland Party . . ."[87]

Finally, there is also a sense in which the phenomenal rise of the AKP can be interpreted not simply as an endorsement of its specific platform, but as a symbolic renegotiation of the Turkish social contract. By voting in overwhelming numbers for a party certain not to be to the liking of the Kemalist establishment, the Turkish electorate—and particularly a newly educated and enfranchised generation of provincial or formerly provincial voters—sent a message to the effect that they, not the military or the Kemalists, were in control of the country's political future. This might be regarded as a direct retort to the "postmodern coup" of 1997.[88]

In the AKP's early days, it was sometimes difficult to identify it with a clear vision and policy program. The party was, as Vali Nasr put it, more of "an electoral strategy in search of a governing agenda."[89] There was a tendency for the AKP to try to be everything to everyone under the rubric of what Erdoğan called "conservative democracy"—an attempt to reconcile Islamic values with the legacy of Kemalism.[90] As Yavuz points out, the AKP tried to be "simultaneously Turkish, Muslim, and Western."[91] Indeed, during its first years heading the Turkish government, the AKP went to some lengths to flaunt its modernist credentials. It emphasized the importance of democracy and human rights, embraced neoliberal economics, and—contrary to fears that it would seek primarily to consolidate Turkey's ties with Muslim majority countries—the AKP came out more strongly in favor of Turkish membership in the European Union than any other political force in the country.

After something of a "honeymoon" period and several years focused on economic issues, the consolidation of political control at the municipal level, and the EU accession process (which formally began in 2005), a shift towards domestic politics quickly brought Erdoğan's government into conflict with Turkey's still formidable Kemalist institutions. This took the form of a dispute with the country's judiciary, which initially in 2006 saw Erdoğan at odds with the court over his right to appoint judges. In 2007 this blossomed into a full-scale conflict over AKP's proposal to run foreign

Figure 4.5 Turkish Prime Minister and AKP leader Recep Tayyip Erdoğan

© Umit Bektas / Reuters

minister Abdullah Gül as a presidential candidate after Erdoğan decided not to run himself. The dispute centered on Gül's Islamist past (he had been a Refah party stalwart) as well as more symbolic issues such as his wife's headscarf. In the face of significant opposition mobilization in parliament that threatened to deadlock the process, Gül initially withdrew his candidacy. In response to this challenge, Erdoğan decided to call a snap general election in July to demonstrate popular support for his party and to serve as a referendum on the direction it was charting for the country. This time, the AKP increased its share of the popular vote to almost 47 percent—although the party lost almost two dozen seats in parliament due to a strong showing by the Nationalist Movement Party and independent candidates. A month later, Gül's candidacy was proposed anew and he was duly elected president of the Turkish Republic. Turkish foreign policy was flourishing by this point, with key alliances (such as the United States) in good shape, and a broadening portfolio of global investments and diplomatic initiatives. Thought leaders in AKP circles talked of a "neo-Ottoman" orientation in Turkey's foreign policy—envisaged as a return to a time when Turkey was a major geopolitical player, particularly in its immediate region.

The following year, a proposal by AKP for a legislative amendment that would permit the wearing of headscarves at Turkish universities generated a substantial backlash from secular opposition groups and prompted widespread protests. Although the AKP was able to get the bill through parliament, its implementation was short-lived as the country's Constitutional Court annulled the law within months of its passage, on the grounds that it violated the laicist character of the state enshrined in the Republic's constitution. This, in turn, prompted an effort by the same court later in 2008 to have the AKP banned on the grounds that its activities amounted to a violation of constitutional secularism. The initiative did not succeed, but served to highlight the ongoing and increasingly entrenched conflict between the ruling party and Kemalist forces. Soon the centre of gravity of this conflict turned to the military. In late 2008, the government initiated an investigation into a shadowy organization known as Ergenekon—a supposedly ultra-nationalist, fervently secular movement with ties to the country's military and intelligence services. Although Ergenekon's existence had been quietly discussed for years, Erdoğan and the AKP's choice to open a formal inquiry into the group coincided with increased fears in the party that Turkey's "deep state" was working to undermine their power and legitimacy. The "deep state" concept refers to the idea of a set of informal organizations, networks, and relationships between power holders and brokers behind the scenes, who work to determine political outcomes beyond the scope of public accountability and outside the reach of formal state institutions. As we saw in the Egypt case above, the existence of a "deep state" comprised of former NDP supporters and their allies in the security services was a source of paranoia for the MB in the wake of 2011.

The AKP's dispute with the military reached new heights in early 2010, when it was announced that a secret plot—known as "Operation Sledgehammer"—to carry out a military coup against the ruling party had been discovered. Several waves of arrests targeting Turkish military personnel—active service and retired—would continue throughout the year in connection with the alleged plot. At the same time, the AKP succeeded in passing, via national referendum, a set of constitutional amendments designed, in part, to bring the military more fully under political control. While the ruling party insisted—with some measure of support from certain liberal groups—that these moves were needed to better consolidate democracy in Turkey and bring the country into line with civil-military norms in Europe, opponents saw the initiative as further evidence that the AKP was working to progressively undermine the state's Kemalist institutions. Turkey also assumed a more forceful regional posture in 2010. An Israeli raid on a Turkish flotilla bound for the blockaded Gaza strip and sailing in international waters left nine Turkish activists dead, prompting a crisis with Tel Aviv.

2011 and 2012 saw ongoing strain between Erdoğan, the AKP, and the military. The indictments and trials connected with the alleged Sledgehammer coup plot eventually resulted in several hundred prison sentences being handed down to past and present military officers, including a number of senior-ranking officers. The ongoing Ergenekon investigation eventually even touched a recent former Chief of the General Staff, the country's highest-ranking military position. Some saw in this accusation, which even Erdoğan seemed to regard as a step too far, evidence that Fethullah Gülen's movement had risen to prominence within Turkey's national police and were looking to exact revenge against the military. 2011 was also marked by what some saw as the AKP's growing intolerance of public criticism. Internet censorship and press laws were tightened, and a number of journalists critical of the government found themselves in jail. Nevertheless, the general election that year saw the AKP returned with over 50 percent of the popular vote. The government did not, however, receive the two-thirds majority of parliamentary seats required to be able to rewrite the country's constitution on its own terms.

In 2012 and 2013, perhaps buoyed by the strong fortunes of Islamist parties after the Arab Uprisings, the AKP embarked on a series of initiatives that seemed to have a more overtly religious focus—their first attempt do so since the failed repeal of the university headscarf ban in 2007. These included the introduction of optional classes on the Qur'an and life the Prophet Muhammad as part of the national secondary school curriculum, efforts to ban late-night alcohol sales in certain parts of the country and altogether on many domestic flights, and a proposal to change the uniform of Turkish Airways flight attendants to be more conservative. These initiatives, and the debate they prompted, were all part of the climate that produced, in the summer of 2013, the most serious domestic crisis of Erdoğan's tenure. What was initially a small-scale demonstration to protest plans to transform Gezi Park, near Taksim Square in Istanbul, into a shopping mall escalated due to heavy-handed treatment of those staging the sit-in, attracting national media attention and prompting large-scale demonstrations against police tactics and against the seeming indifference of the government. The Prime Minister's highly confrontational response—in which he boasted about how many supporters he could turn out in response to the demonstrations—inflamed the situation further. The protests grew, and spread to other cities throughout Turkey, prompting comparisons with the Occupy movement and also the popular uprisings in the Arab world of 2010–11. The original impetus for the demonstration was soon lost amidst a much broader expression of discontent about what many saw as the increasingly authoritarian and Islamic tendencies of Turkey's ruling party.

So how should AKP be thought of in relation to the question of Islamism or Islam and politics? Some will see in the party a new form of "Muslim democracy" that understands religion as a source of morality that can be brought to bear in the conduct of public administration, but that does not entail the pursuit of a *shari'ah*-based legislative agenda. Others harbor fear that the AKP is full of "crypto-Islamists" waiting to pounce once the populace has been lulled into complacency. As the 2013 events in Taksim Square and elsewhere in Turkey demonstrate, many citizens fear that Erdoğan's government was coming close to crossing certain lines with respect to the question of Turkish secularism. In a desire to emphasize its break with Refah and also to avoid undue scrutiny from the courts and military, AKP's leaders have always refused to accept the "Islamist" label—preferring instead to be regarded as conservative democrats. It is hard to characterize the party's agenda while in power—with a few notable exceptions—as being highly

Islamist in character. They have pursued pro-business, neoliberal reforms and a foreign policy that has balanced strong alignment with Europe, the U.S., and NATO with a growing role in the Middle East, Africa, and Central Asia. They have sought, with mixed results, to reach out to minority communities in Turkey (such as the Kurds), and introduced democratic reforms that have brought Turkey's law into conformity with much of the rest of Western Europe. It speaks to the complexity of Turkey's political culture that opponents of the AKP have perceived many of these same policies and initiatives as evidence of the party's Islamist nature.

It is difficult to reduce Turkey's current politics to a straightforward division between Islamists and secularists. For his part, Erdoğan has consistently extolled the virtues of secularism, including before a skeptical audience of hardened Islamists in Egypt after that country's 2011 revolution. At the same time, the AKP's conduct in recent years suggests that it harbors at least some degree of the same paranoia that, arguably, proved to be the Egyptian MB's downfall after its short tenure in power. Broader sociological factors, however, would suggest that in practical terms, a sharp Islamist/secular divide is today present more at the extremes of Turkey's political spectrum than at its core. Below the level of Kemalist and corporate elites, the secular-nationalist and provincial-religious currents of Turkish society have been inching towards each other for over a generation, and it makes sense that they should find their political synthesis in the AKP.

What can perhaps be said with somewhat more certainty is that Turkey is, with the AKP, entering into a "post-Kemalist" era. This does not necessarily entail a decline in the appeal of Kemalist principles such as modernism and secularism, but rather a dislocation of the political hegemony that previously monopolized the state in their name. While Turkey seems today to be the archetype of a "Muslim Democracy" *à la* Vali Nasr, it is not yet entirely clear whether this is a development unique to that country, or whether it represents a model which can develop in other countries that feature similarly configured social, political, and economic factors. As our next and final case study in this chapter, Jordan, will show, Muslim Democracy *per se* may not be a universal trend within the modern Islamist movement, but generational evolution in Islamist strategy in the context of shifting political economies certainly seems to be.

BOX 4.3 INDONESIA: A PARADIGMATIC "MUSLIM DEMOCRACY"?

Although it is the largest Muslim country in the world in terms of population (247 million, some 88 percent of whom profess Islam), conventional Islamism has not been a standard feature of Indonesian politics.

At the same time, it is fair to say that Indonesia has more "Islamic" or Muslim-oriented political parties than any country in the Muslim world today. How to explain this apparent enigma? Part of the answer lies in the nature of Indonesian Islam, but we also need to look at the role played by the official national ideology, *Pancasila* ("The Five Principles"), and its use by the state as a political tool over several decades.

Indonesian Islam is noteworthy for its generally tolerant and pluralistic character. As Islam settled alongside existing Hindu and Buddhist culture from the fifteenth century, Indonesian Muslims internalized norms of religious pluralism. While several waves of orthodox modernism from the early twentieth century certainly created a constituency for a more conventionally Islamist approach, Islamist parties in the early post-independence period (best represented by the Masyumi) were not particularly strong. Rather, a central government under Sukarno, and later Suharto, was already pushing the state ideology as the key organizing principle for Indonesian politics. While a strong endorsement of monotheism is central to the *Pancasila,* it is not specified in terms of Islam, nor is Islam declared to be the official religion of state. For many Indonesians, participation in social Islam took the form of membership in one of the country's two mass Islamic movements, Nahdlatul Ulama or Muhammadiyah, each of which claims over 30 million members.

In 1973, President Suharto's New Order regime "rationalized" the Islamic party political structure in Indonesia, forcing all of the religious parties under a single umbrella, the United Development Party (PPP— Partai Persatuan Pembangunan), and insisting that it adopt *Pancasila* as the basis of its political platform. In the 1990s, as support for his regime dwindled in the face of widespread nepotism, Suharto sought to buttress his religious credentials by creating a new association for Muslim intellectuals and technocrats, the Ikatan Cendekiawan Muslim Se-Indonesia (ICMI). Certain key religious figures, sensing another attempt by the state to co-opt Islam, stayed away. Among them was Abdurrahman Wahid, who emerged in 1999 as the compromise candidate for president in the wake of Suharto's fall from power. A former head of Nahdlatul Ulama, Wahid focused on questions of democratic reform and intercommunal tolerance rather than *shari'ah* or the creation of an Islamic state. He was found wanting as a head of state, however, and his tenure in government was short-lived. As Robert Hefner has argued in *Civil Islam* (Princeton: Princeton University Press, 2000), Islamic parties in Indonesia provided much of the core energy driving the movement for political reform in the 1990s.

Indonesia did experience a period of limited radical Islamist upheaval in the early years of the new millennium, with groups such as Laskar Jihad appointing themselves as purveyors of public morality à la the *mutawwa* of Saudi Arabia (see Chapter 5). Other groups sought to stoke intercommunal fires, leading to renewed Muslim–Christian violence in outlying islands. Even a Salafi–jihadi strain was to be found in the form of the Jemaah Islamiyah and its leader Abu Bakar Ba'syir. Most notoriously, this group perpetrated the October 2002 Bali bombing, killing over 200. But such activities and tendencies remained in the distinct minority when looking at the broad picture of Muslim politics in Indonesia. In recent years, groups such as the radical Islamist movement Hizb ut-Tahrir (see Chapter 7) and the conservative Salafis (see Chapter 2) have gained a foothold in Indonesia, although their discourse and agenda have been tailored to suit local religious sensibilities.

© Prosperous Justice Party

Figure 4.6 Insignia of the PKS party in Indonesia

Today, a handful of parties can be regarded as open or responsive to Muslim concerns. These groups do not espouse an Islamic state or a literal application of *shari'ah*. Rather, they tend to pursue agendas and policies guided by the principles of *shari'ah*—another example, perhaps, of what Vali Nasr calls the "Muslim Democracy" approach. This leads to an emphasis on accountability in public life rather than direct application of Qur'anic rule. According to the Pew Forum's 2013 global poll of Muslim attitudes about religion, society, and politics, a clear majority of Indonesians favor making *shari'ah* the official law of the land, even as they register some of the most unequivocal rejection of certain practices—such as the death penalty for adulterers of either sex—associated with Islamic law.[92] Indonesia's largest Islamist party is the Prosperous Justice Party (PKS—Partai Keadilan Sejahtera), a group with ideological roots in the Muslim Brotherhood, but which has sought in recent years to model itself after the AKP in Turkey. While the PKS agenda has focused primarily on anti-corruption and good governance issues, its religious orientation has led the party also to campaign for a ban on pornography sales and the local implementation of *shari'ah*-based statutes. Its share of the parliamentary vote in both 2004 and 2009 failed to pass the 8 percent mark, suggesting that PKS was struggling to broaden its appeal in the face of continuing dominance by entrenched mass parties and the popularity of president Susilo Bambang Yudhoyono's Partai Demokrat.

JORDAN: ISLAMISM AS LOYAL OPPOSITION IN AN EMERGING LIBERAL AUTOCRACY?

After studying the evolution of Islamist strategy in the cases of two republics (Egypt and Turkey), we turn now to examine Islamism in the context of monarchy. The case of the Royal Hashemite Kingdom of Jordan presents us with yet another mode of Islamist participation in the political system. Unlike the Egyptian MB which, as we have seen, went so far during certain phases of its activism as to openly challenge the legitimacy of the state order, the Jordanian branch of the Brotherhood has, for the greater part of its existence, enjoyed a considerably more cooperative and mutually supportive relationship with the regime. Since the inception of a gradual and, at times, wavering process of political liberalization in 1989, the Brotherhood's direct involvement in politics has placed certain strains on this relationship, and also led to considerable soul-searching within the Jordanian Islamist movement more broadly. In this section we survey the involvement of the MB in Jordanian politics from 1989—and in the guise of the Islamic Action Front (IAF) after 1993—with the aim of understanding how Jordan's shifting political environment has impacted Islamist strategies and self-understandings. As we will see, the case of Jordan does not allow us to view the evolution of Islamism as a "staging" process, with classic Islamism giving way to the pragmatism of a new Islamism or Muslim Democracy (as in the cases of Egypt and Turkey, above). Rather, mainstream Jordanian Islamism in some ways works in exactly the reverse direction, with an older generation of generally pro-regime pragmatists challenged by a younger generation of hardline activists harboring strong grievances towards key government policies.

The Jordanian branch of the MB was established in 1945, and the presence of King Abdullah I at its opening set the tone for the generally close and cooperative rapport between the palace and the Islamists that would endure for nearly half a century. While this relationship certainly experienced its share of turbulence over the years—such as when the regime appeared to lean too pro-Western, or to pay insufficient attention to Palestinian causes—the persistence of a critical mass of common interests tended to see it through these rough spots. Islamist support for King Hussein's 1970 violent crackdown on Palestinian groups operating out of Jordan (commonly known as "Black September"), for example, constituted a key moment in the alliance. In terms of the domestic political field, the regime and the Islamists generally found that they had a vested interest in working together to marginalize the influence of nationalist and leftist movements—ideological forces that both of them found distasteful and potentially threatening. Thus, until entering politics in 1989, the MB worked primarily at the social level as a charitable and *da'wa* organization. It advocated greater religious awareness and practice, but in a framework that did not at all challenge, and even lent support to, the royal regime. Even in 1957, when a royal decree banned all political activity, the Brotherhood was considered exempt due to its special status. In this regard, it is difficult to view the MB as wholly "owned" or co-opted by the state—their symbiosis does not necessarily mean the two sides always saw eye to eye. Rather, the palace left the Brotherhood to get on with its work so long as it did not interfere with regime policies.

King Hussein embarked on a program of political reform and liberalization in 1989 for several reasons. The kingdom had recently experienced a period of social unrest and protests connected with the harsh effects of IMF-mandated austerity that were part of efforts to introduce greater economic liberalization. Popular discontent about increasing levels of government corruption was also an important factor. The cautious political liberalization process initiated by the king can certainly be understood as an attempt to rebuild national morale and support for the regime. But we can also observe, as has Beverley Milton-Edwards, that King Hussein was well aware of the political support the MB had garnered over the years, and felt that it might be safer to bring the Brotherhood into a political system whose rules were dictated by the palace rather than to have it potentially working against the regime at the level of society.[93] Given their popularity, it was therefore not surprising that, in 1989, the Islamists did particularly well in Jordan's first parliamentary poll for nearly a quarter-century. Since the electoral system at this time did not permit the formation of actual political parties, the Islamists were all technically running as individual, independent candidates. Still, their affiliations were widely known and it was possible for some modicum of a party platform to come through during the short period of campaigning. All in all, MB-affiliated candidates won 20 out of the 80 seats in the assembly, with truly independent Islamists gaining another dozen spots. This made the "Islamist bloc" the single largest political faction within the new parliament.

It became clear very quickly that the direct involvement of the MB in politics would produce new strains on the Islamists' relationship with the regime. Although several of the MB politicians were brought directly into the government, the king's ability to rule by decree and bypass—not to mention dissolve—parliament at will meant that it was difficult for the Islamic bloc to accomplish very much that was meaningful in the way of Islamic reform. Although the regime and the Islamists saw more or less eye to eye on the issue of the 1991 Gulf War (with both supporting Saddam Hussein in the face of what they perceived as anti-Arab and anti-Islamic aggression by the United States), this "temporary alliance" quickly gave way to new conflicts.[94] For example, the government repeatedly struck down Islamist-led attempts to introduce an education bill mandating the segregation of schools by gender, and one of the most well-known and charismatic independent Islamists in parliament, Laith al-Shubailat, undertook an investigation into alleged corruption on the part of a former prime minister.[95] The Islamic bloc was uniformly critical of the regime for its support of the U.S.-sponsored Madrid peace process in late 1991, which they took as evidence of Jordan reaching out to Israel in the vein of Anwar Sadat in the 1970s—not to mention the fact that the king postponed the third session of parliament until after the Madrid talks had concluded in order to deny the Islamists an oppositional forum on the topic.

Late 1991 and 1992 saw a series of trials in which radical Islamist elements were accused of activities against the state. The government sought to link groups such as Muhammad's Army (Jaysh Muhammad), composed of Arabs who had joined the mujahideen in Afghanistan during the 1980s (see Chapters 6 and 7), with Islamism in the popular imagination, prompting accusations by mainstream Islamists that the government was out to slander them. The government even tried and convicted the aforementioned Laith al-Shubailat in connection with membership in a seditious movement. When this brought widespread condemnation from all sides of the political spectrum, the regime backed down, with the king rapidly granting clemency to many of those imprisoned. The government, however, continued in its efforts to sideline Islamist influence. In the run-up to the 1993 parliamentary poll, for example, they suddenly changed the election law, replacing a bloc or slate system of voting with a "one-person, one-vote scheme." Previously, voters had been able to cast as many votes as their districts held seats in parliament. This permitted them to distribute their political patronage among both local tribal leaders and Islamist groups—a system that favored a strong showing by the Islamists. In response to a new Political Party Law, the MB reorganized itself for the 1993 elections. In order to avoid being subject to provisions of the new law that required all parties to publicly disclose their financial sources and which disallowed parties with ties to any political groups abroad (the Brotherhood in Jordan could still be seen as loosely affiliated with the central party in Egypt), the MB decided not to register as a political party. Instead, it formed a new "umbrella party," the IAF, in which it played a leading—and in the eyes of some partners, a disproportionately powerful—role alongside several other Islamist groups and independents.

Immediately perceiving the new one-person, one-vote system as a deliberate attempt to decrease their parliamentary representation (as did most other political observers and parties), the IAF considered, but quickly dropped, the idea of boycotting the elections. As predicted, voters cast their

© Alex Abu Ata

Figure 4.7 Leaders of the Islamic Action Front in Jordan

choices primarily along tribal lines in 1993, with the result that the size of the Islamist bloc in the assembly was cut in half. The IAF immediately voiced calls for the election law to be changed. Their opposition to the government reached a fever pitch in 1995 with the signing of a peace agreement between Jordan and Israel. The following year, in response to new protests following the reduction of food subsidies (again stemming from an IMF economic recovery plan that the Islamists had opposed in 1992), the government undertook several initiatives widely regarded as a rollback of the political liberalization that had been introduced in 1989. A new restrictive press law was introduced that required higher capital outlays on the part of media outlets, and that made criticism of certain regime-friendly figures illegal. Furthermore, despite consistent and increasingly vociferous calls by the IAF to change the electoral system, the law was left untouched. This prompted the Islamists to organize a boycott of the 1997 elections, stating their opposition to the government's renewed authoritarianism and to the peace deal with Israel. This proved to be a miscalculation on their part, since they had hoped this appeal to populist sentiment would pay off in terms of support in the polls. Instead, it produced a parliament composed almost exclusively of pro-regime elements. The Islamists were effectively closed out of the political system from 1997.

We might wonder what had led the regime, which had previously enjoyed such strong relations with the MB, to turn against it so strongly in the mid-1990s. In considering this question, Glenn Robinson has offered an explanation focusing on three key factors. First, with leftists and secular-nationalists now sidelined in the political system, there was no longer any "common enemy" to unite the Islamists and the regime. Second, the climate of relative political openness after 1989 had encouraged the MB to go further than the government would have liked in terms of criticism—in short, the Islamists had become too difficult to control, and the regime needed to send a signal that they, rather than the opposition, would decide the timing and extent of political reform. And third, certain demographic shifts (which we will look at in greater detail below) were afoot within the Islamic bloc.[96] More specifically, the "old guard" of the MB, who had tended to be residents of the East Bank or of the former Transjordan, and largely pro-regime in orientation, were beginning to be replaced by a younger generation that was more adamantly pro-Palestinian and more likely to push the regime on this question.[97] In summary, a series of developments, both internal and exogenous to the Islamist movement in Jordan, had at least temporarily strained the symbiotic relationship with the regime beyond the point of continued mutual benefit, and the government was now actively looking to restrain the political influence of the MB.

After nearly half a century on the throne of Jordan, King Hussein passed away in 1999 and was succeeded by his son Abdullah. The new king's consolidation of power also coincided with the outbreak of the second *intifada* in the Palestinian territories in 2000, resulting in considerable tensions within Jordan. Citing the unavailability of new magnetic voting cards, but more likely driven by regional security concerns, the king in the summer of 2001 exercised his power to postpone that year's scheduled parliamentary elections after having earlier dissolved parliament. Over the next two years the palace ran the country by decree, issuing over 200 temporary laws that would not be subject to public review until the parliament was reconstituted. At the same time as he postponed elections, Abdullah also promulgated a new election law. This increased the number of seats in parliament, initially up to 104, and later by six more when it was decided to reserve a bloc for women candidates. Most of the new seats came about as a result of redistricting efforts that sought to increase the representation of particular areas, but most of these went to districts likely to return pro-regime representatives.

Despite expressing considerable regret at what they perceived as a complete reversal of the process of democratization and ongoing reservations about the electoral system, the IAF did contest the postponed parliamentary elections when they were finally held in the summer of 2003. While over half the seats were won by pro-regime candidates, the Islamists did manage to take 17 places in the assembly and, more importantly, to regain a presence within the political system. Interestingly, on a number of key issues, the Islamists now found themselves allied with leftist and secular parties also disgruntled with the heavy-handedness of the government during and after the pro-regime parliament.[98] While the new assembly did overturn several of the temporary laws passed by the king, there was no immediate standoff with the regime while the new multiparty assembly settled into place. Continuing to exert pressure to reform the electoral law, and emboldened by Islamist electoral successes in Egypt and Palestine, the IAF looked forward to what they hoped would be a sustained period of significant political influence in Jordan.

Within two years, and after growing tension with the parliament, the palace dissolved the legislature in 2009 and called for a new ballot. Protesting what they saw as election laws designed to minimize the influence of opposition political parties and maximize the prospects of pro-regime independent and tribal candidates, the IAF decided to boycott the subsequent parliamentary election in 2010. Ongoing wrangling over the election law—as well as the palace's refusal to allow the parliament to appoint a prime minister—characterized the IAF's dialogue with the regime over the next two years. Despite some modest changes in the legislation that would permit more seats for political parties, the IAF again boycotted the 2013 elections. In their absence, Jordan's Hizb al-Wasat was able to garner some of the vote that might have otherwise gone to the IAF. With growing impatience over the pace of democratic reform, socioeconomic tensions, complex decentralization processes, and an influx of refugees from the Syrian crisis, the IAF seems confident that, in time, the palace will need to extend an olive branch in order to garner Islamist support for its increasingly embattled position. The rising prominence of Islamists elsewhere in the Arab world no doubt gave the IAF greater confidence to raise the stakes in their complex and difficult relationship with the palace.

BOX 4.4 MOROCCO: ISLAMISM IN THE SHADOW OF THE PALACE

An assessment of Islamism—or any form of political opposition, for that matter—in Morocco must take into consideration the overwhelming power of the monarch. While King Mohamed VI has continued the modest reform process undertaken by his father, Hassan II, this has focused primarily on issues such as human rights, reforming marriage and divorce law, and greater openness about and discussion of corruption. The current king did little to address fundamental political rights until the events of the 2010–11 Arab Uprisings in nearby Tunisia and Egypt forced him to act to stave off growing protests at home. Following the ouster of Hosni Mubarak in Egypt, Morocco saw its own version of street politics emerge in the form of the February 20 movement. Mohamed VI was quick to promise new reforms, and over the next few months oversaw a process to significantly rewrite the country's constitution—culminating in a hastily arranged national referendum where the new document was approved. The new 2011 constitution is more explicit in establishing democratic guidelines for governance, and grants greater recognition and local autonomy to ethno-linguistic minorities. However, its critics point out that it does not in any way fundamentally alter the balance of power in Morocco, with the king retaining all of his executive privileges.[99]

Political participation by Islamists in Morocco is a relatively recent phenomenon, with the first organized electoral effort by a religious opposition movement coming only in 1997. In that year, the Justice and Development Party (PJD—Parti de la Justice et du Développement) gained nine parliamentary seats. Five years later, they more than quadrupled their representation, sending 42 deputies to the 2002 assembly. 2007 saw support for the PJD holding more or less steady, but that was to change significantly at the next poll. 2011's parliamentary elections, which took place in the wake of the Arab Uprisings and the aforementioned constitutional reforms, saw the PJD gain dozens of seats to become the largest party in the assembly. The PJD's 2011 victory was indicative of a broader trend sweeping the region at that time, whereby Islamist parties previously banned, oppressed, or discouraged from

Figure 4.8 PJD logo in Arabic, French, and Tamazight (Berber)

competing for real power found they were able to parlay popular discontent with incumbent regimes into huge political gains.

Several aspects of Morocco's political environment are important to bear in mind when considering the role of Islamism, and when comparing it with other countries we have examined in this chapter. First, while the other large parties in Morocco—such as Istiqlal, the National Rally, and the Socialist Union of Popular Force—are "secular" in nature, this term has a rather different connotation in the Moroccan context. Many of these groups would emphasize the importance of religion. What distinguishes the Islamists, then, is their emphasis on the idea that legislation and policy-making in Morocco should proceed with reference to an Islamic framework.

While Moroccan Islamists certainly do not face the same challenges as similar parties in the highly secular Kemalist order of Turkey (indeed, the Moroccan king claims religious leadership credentials via the title of *Amir al-Muiminin,* Commander of the Faithful), they do have to tread carefully in terms of not directly questioning the legitimacy of the crown. And at the end of the day, the king ultimately has power over parliament.

Who are the Islamists in Morocco? There are two main groups today: one a conventional party that participates in the political and legislative processes; the other a more hardline movement that questions the legitimacy of the monarchy.

- **PJD (Hizb al-Adala w'al-Tanmiya)**—formed in 1996 out of the religious movement Unity and Reform (*Al-Tawhid w'al-Islah*). Socially conservative, and strongly identified with an anti-corruption platform, PJD seeks reform within an "Islamic framework" rather than the establishment of a *shari'ah*-based state. Their support for the monarchy is crucial to ensuring an ongoing political role, although they try to keep a critical distance from the palace. The PJD initially campaigned against the liberalization of Moroccan family law, but eventually accepted passage of the new legislation.

- **Justice and Charity (Al-Adl w'al-Ihsan)**—an anti-regime religious movement founded in 1974 and strongly identified with its late mystical leader, Abdesslam Yassine (d. 2012). The latter has been a vocal critic of the royal family and questions the legitimacy of Morocco's monarchy. In and out of jail in recent decades, Al-Adl's leader consistently refused to take part in what he regarded as the kingdom's corrupt and un-Islamic political system. With strong roots in the Sufi orders, Al-Adl's revolutionary mysticism has prompted frequent run-ins with Morocco's security forces. The group's existence is generally tolerated by the palace through an understanding that it will not engage directly in politics—something Al-Adl has been reluctant to do for fear that its participation would grant legitimacy to a political system it rejects. The group is led today by Mohammed Abbadi, who was elected secretary-general after Yassine's death.

The palace has watched the rise of the PJD warily, and, for their part, the Islamists have been somewhat wary of their own success. Both have the experience of Algeria's FIS in mind (see "Algeria: Islamists *almost in power*" in Chapter 3), where the rapid rise of an Islamist tide led to a strong backlash from the state and a dissolution of the political and internal security order. Where the palace has at times moved to block the influence of the Islamists, the PJD seems to have voluntarily chosen a gradualist approach. For example, in the 2002 elections they deliberately did not field candidates in as many districts as they might have, so as to avoid setting off alarm bells. Much of their potential success will depend on avoiding the perception that their willingness to cooperate with the prevailing order is not tantamount to having been co-opted by it. Much of what is noteworthy about the PJD lies in its democratic management of internal party governance and its emphasis on transparency and integrity—leading the electorate to identify it as a force for anti-corruption. In this regard it seem to be modeling itself—like so many other Islamist parties of late—after Turkey's AKP.

One tangible 2011 reform that has benefited the PJD is the Moroccan King agreeing to name as prime minister the leader of whichever party has the largest share of parliamentary seats. Accordingly, in November 2011, PJD leader Abdelillah Benkirane became Morocco's Prime Minister—the first Islamist to serve in that capacity. Conscious of ongoing scrutiny, and governing as part of a coalition that included non-Islamist parties, the PJD in power has been cautious not to ruffle any feathers. It has emphasized relations with the European Union, announced ambitious targets for inclusive economic growth, and sought to shore up relations with Gulf countries that viewed regional change with alarm.

To better understand the development of Islamist political strategy in Jordan over the past quarter-century (1989–2014), we need to look more closely at how and where Islamists are located across Jordanian society, and to better appreciate the roles played by informal associations and networks in Islamic "public life." To begin with, we know that the demographic profile of MB/IAF members in Jordan parallels that of Islamist parties in other parts of the Muslim world—namely, that middle-class and professional occupations represent the bulk of the group's membership.[100] Most importantly, we need to take account of the rich web of sociality that links the "political" MB in the form of the IAF to the wider activities of the "social" MB as a charitable and *da'wa* organization. In short, the Islamists were able to operate as a formal political organization while simultaneously staying active in the social realm.[101] While both spaces are subject to considerable state regulation, enterprising Islamic groups are able to "socialize" nonreligious spaces (such as professional associations and hospitals) and also use informal social groups and connections to wield normative influence less easily regulated by the state. As Quintan Wiktorowicz puts it:

> In Jordan, formal organization is more a mechanism of state control than an instrument of collective empowerment. Despite political liberalization, the Jordanian state utilizes an array of administrative techniques to limit the scope and content of civil society organizations. While the most overt forms of pressure have been removed, authoritarian tendencies are embedded in bureaucratic processes, procedures, and regulations, which are used to shape the content of social interactions in civil society . . . To escape this form of state control, Islamic groups that challenge the regime retreat to personal networks based upon individuals with shared beliefs and do not rely upon organizations to achieve goals.[102]

While he makes this point primarily with regard to informal networks of Salafi-oriented groups not strongly tied to the mainstream MB, Wiktorowicz's insight holds true when referring to the social and political capital that can accrue from the socialization by Islamists of spaces not conventionally associated with religion (e.g. service providers), and not subject to the heaviest state regulation (see Egypt, above, for comparison). "Seemingly apolitical activities such as education and health care provision become political," write Wiktorowicz and Taji Farouki, "when they challenge other cultural codes and institutions."[103] The vast array of nongovernmental organizations and social service networks operated by the MB emerges as a crucial component of the movement's efforts to define public normativity— as well as a second terrain of struggle with the regime. But it is also a space in which the cooperative compact between the regime and the Islamists becomes relevant insofar as the MB aids the government at the level of the social by providing alternatives to more radical strains of Islamism.

How can we best understand the evolution of Islamist strategy in Jordan, and its interaction with the wider reform process in that country? To begin with, it is important to note that the IAF, the MB, and Jordan's wider Islamist movement are not monolithic entities. In addition to the state–society dynamic as a force shaping the course of Islamist political participation, this relationship was also modulated by considerable and ongoing internal politics within the movement. While the decision by the MB to contest the 1989 elections reflected, perhaps, an emerging consensus among that generation of the Brotherhood about the desirability of Islamists participating in democratic elections, there certainly were voices within the movement who did not want to get involved in politics. Some cited concerns that entering the political field would distract from the movement's focus on Islamic reform by forcing members to worry about campaigning and building alliances—in short, doing democratic politics.[104] Some Islamists were reluctant about being forced to debate and compromise on issues which—as derived from God and His *shari'ah*—were simply not open for discussion, as was likely to happen when Islamists worked alongside leftists and secular parties as co-legislators.[105] It was evident, however, that the vast majority of the Brotherhood's members did want to enter the political fray. Ishaq Farhan, a senior Brotherhood figure and eventual Secretary-General of the IAF, expressed the group's general approach to politics in the following way:

> We believe that Islam offers general guidelines on how political decisions are to be made. It instructs Muslims to consult with each other. But the form or mechanism of consultation has not been specified in the Quran. It is left to the believers to design such a form within its proper historical context. We believe that democracy is the proper form, and Islam is wholly compatible with parliamentary democracy. For sure the Quran and Sunna are sacred to us. We make laws according to social context and exigencies. Fatwas are not obligatory. We make decisions not based on this or that fatwa, but based on the consensus of our *shura*. This consensus should be respected. A general consensus such as that in the parliament is more important than the views of the ulama. I hesitate to consider those who disagree with us as being out of the bounds of Islam.[106]

The core dividing issue, then, was perhaps not so much one of whether or not to participate, but rather how to think about political participation in relation to the movement's ultimate goals. The party's statement following the successful 1989 elections emphasized its commitment to democracy, pluralism, and constitutionalism while simultaneously stating an intention to bring Jordanian law into conformity with the *shari'ah*. Likewise, the economic content of their electoral platform had also been a mixed bag of fiscal conservatism and support for private property alongside calls for elements of protectionism and a non-interest-based banking sector.[107] Islamists worked alongside fellow parliamentarians of very different political persuasion in, for example, drafting a new National Charter outlining political rights and freedoms—and in the process of doing so they signed off on certain provisions regarding the status of *shari'ah* (as being one among several sources of legitimacy and legislation) whose wording was probably not ideal in the eyes of the Brotherhood.[108]

This certainly does not mean, however, that once they entered the parliament, internal dissent within the MB disappeared completely. Particularly after tensions with the regime emerged in the early 1990s, the presence of factions within the Islamist camp became evident—but, as Clark and Schwedler have argued, the alignment of these factions was not fixed, and often changed based on the issue at hand.[109] This was evident, for example, in 1995 when some within the IAF considered joining the government, a move that to others in the coalition would have been anathema at a time when the regime was actively pursuing a peace agreement with Israel.[110] At other times, Islamist independents under the IAF umbrella complained of MB hegemony within the movement, and some even resigned over this. If pressed to identify somewhat more persistent groupings within the Jordanian Islamist movement, we might perhaps turn to Glenn Robinson's distinction between "cultural" and "political" Islamists. The former camp, composed primarily of East Bank Jordanians, has tended to be more reliably pro-Hashemite over the years, and understands Islamism as a political project primarily in relation to social issues such as education, gender segregation, and public virtue. The "political" Islamists, on the other hand, will often be of Palestinian background (West Bankers), and more concerned with issues relating to social justice and political imposition by external powers—the United States, Israel, the IMF—than with matters of cultural practice.[111] Indeed, the importance of the Palestinian issue within the Jordanian Islamist movement is difficult to overestimate. In many ways, the IAF has served as a proxy party for Palestinian interests due to its staunch and vocal opposition to the peace process. It also provides a space for Jordanians of Palestinian background to participate *en masse* without having to form a separate "Palestinian" party and risk condemnation as an ethnic faction seeking to undermine national unity.[112]

It is also possible to identify a distinct evolution in the Brotherhood's public discourse and internal deliberations after entering the political process. Jillian Schwedler, for example, points out that by 1993, the issue of whether participation in democracy was Islamically permissible had completely disappeared, with the discussion within the Islamist movement commonly structured around the more political question of whether it was worth continuing to contest elections, given the regime's attempt to sideline its influence.[113] Others note a marked shift in the nature of IAF discourse from *shari'ah*-based explanations to a form of public reason grounded in the pragmatics of national interest.[114] From stating general principles in 1989, the Islamists' tangling with other parties and ideologies in the public sphere led them by 1993 to articulate their concerns with far greater specificity. They began, for instance, to advocate a more publicly prominent role for women (albeit still within an Islamically prescribed framework) in order to stave off attempts by other parties—notably leftists and secular liberals—to monopolize this issue.[115] When their parliamentary fortunes declined from 1993, the IAF reached out to non-Islamist parties to pursue those aspects of their program shared by other parties, and also sought to leverage their strong presence in various social and professional organizations (e.g. student associations, trade unions—see above) as alternative venues for politics.[116] In evaluating the development of Islamist political platforms and practices in the years following their incorporation into participatory politics, several analysts have come to the conclusion that their embrace of democratic principles—even if initially strategic and instrumental—has led to the internalization of values that have shifted the Islamists' normative horizons.[117] As Schwedler puts it:

> This does not necessarily mean that the group had evolved to such an extent that it could no longer be considered Islamist, or that Islam was no longer central to the group's diagnosis of the problems faced by contemporary Jordanian society and the group's prognosis for solutions. But gradually . . . the Muslim Brotherhood and later the IAF came to explore and accept practices that seemed unthinkable just a few years earlier. Strategies that once triggered considerable debate no longer required any justification at all . . . [T]he continued participation of the party illustrated more than an accommodation of democratic practices for strategic reasons. Rather, the internal party debates and particularly its practices illustrate that the group had seriously incorporated elements of a democracy narrative that effectively redrew the boundaries of what practices and strategies the group could justify.[118]

We might want to see in this evidence of the phenomenon that Carrie Wickham has referred to as Islamist "auto-reform," referring to the tendency of various Islamist movements (cf. Egypt and Turkey above) not only to modify their political tactics, but also to recalibrate their strategies and public reasoning in response to changing political realities and the internalization of new normative frameworks.[119] In the case of the Jordanian Islamist movement, we see evidence of this not only in the aforementioned evolution of the IAF discourse, but also in the emergence on the political scene of new groups such as the Islamic Center Party (Hizb al-Wasat al-Islami), modeled on the similarly named Egyptian movement.

The case of Jordan thus presents us with the opportunity to gain an understanding of how a reformist rather than revolutionary breed of mainstream Islamism has responded to the onset of a gradual liberalization process that soon began to display many of the characteristics that Daniel Brumberg associates with "liberal autocracy."[120] We would want to stress the essentially symbiotic nature between the Islamists and the regime that has allowed their relationship, despite its ups and downs, to remain within the boundaries of normal politics. As Quintan Wiktorowicz summarizes it:

> Though the [Islamists] may disagree with policies or articulate opposition, [they] continue to act through the institutions of the political system without challenging the raison d'être of state or Hashemite power. The regime and the MB share an interest in maintaining the system since both benefit from its continuance. The regime benefits from the MB because the movement checks other more confrontational social movements and channels Islamic activism into a nonviolent agenda. The MB, on its part, has benefited from organizational opportunities produced by

the incumbent regime. State support has allowed the movement to extend its reach in society and had enabled the Brotherhood to more effectively deliver its religious message.[121]

Despite the general persistence of this accommodation over the years, there are those who see the potential for greater tensions between the Islamists and the state in the years to come. This is concern not so much that the core of the Islamist movement will become radicalized, but rather that a younger generation of activists—many of them Palestinian, many of them carefully watching wider regional trends—will break with the moderate Islamist center and turn towards more confrontational tactics. There was considerable outcry in 2006, for example, when several Islamist members of parliament went to pay their respects to the family of the Jordanian leader of Al-Qaeda in Iraq, Abu Musab Zarqawi, after he had been killed by U.S. forces. For others, the concern lies with formerly "cultural" Islamists deciding to more aggressively politicize their public virtue agenda should the process of liberalization in Jordan appear to tend towards the adoption of Western values and greater secularism. Jordan's mainstream Islamists, however, have felt sufficiently emboldened in recent years to sit out two rounds of parliamentary elections in protest at what they see as an electoral law designed to minimize their political influence. As they watch Islamists growing in prominence elsewhere in the region after 2011, and as the Jordanian state—and the palace in particular—contends with a range of domestic and international pressures—they feel that time is on their side. In this equation there is little need to force a high-stakes and potentially dangerous confrontation with the palace when trends suggest that the monarchy will sooner or later have to make accommodations for the Islamists in order to shore up their popular legitimacy.

THE FUTURE OF ISLAMIST PARTICIPATION: ISSUES AND CHALLENGES

This chapter highlights several key issues and challenges relating to the question of Islamist participation in political systems. As our case studies make clear, until 2011 Islamists often represented the only politically organized alternative to discredited authoritarian regimes. Furthermore, much of their influence was found within the social sphere, and it operated through a wide variety of associational spaces including civil society groups, informal neighborhood associations, and solidarity networks. We have noted a marked tendency within some Islamist movements, particularly among the middle and young generations, toward finding new avenues of mainstream political participation. In some cases this has also occurred alongside the emergence of new intellectual and social currents that emphasize Islam's compatibility with the norms of political pluralism and inclusivity.

It is clear that in Egypt and Jordan (although markedly less so in Turkey), the Islamists represented the sole form of political opposition with any kind of organized presence in society. By default, oppositional energy is channeled their way because they are the only political force with the wherewithal to effectively capture and deploy it. Their success at the polls therefore tells us just as much about how skilled they are at mobilizing this base and tapping into veins of discontent as it does about the extent to which people actually embrace their normative vision.

BOX 4.5 WHY DID THE ISLAMISTS WIN BIG AFTER THE ARAB UPRISINGS?

Islamists scored impressive political victories in Tunisia and Egypt after the Arab Uprisings. How can we explain their extremely strong showing at the ballot box in these elections? The sources of their success were varied.

- At the level of **political organization** they enjoyed an enormous comparative advantage over almost all of the competition by virtue of the fact that the Freedom and Justice Party was able to tap into the vast organizational networks that the MB had established over the past quarter-century at virtually every level of Egyptian society. Other political groups—with the exception of the nationalist Wafd party—were essentially starting from scratch.

- In the realm of **popular perception,** the Islamists went into the electoral game with the strongest track record of standing up to the previous regime (and paying the price for doing so in terms of regular crackdowns and jailings). Other perceptual factors were at work too. Some saw the Islamists as less prone to corruption because of their religious beliefs, or more able to deliver on basic needs due to the vast networks of charity and social services they had established. Others regarded them as less likely to serve Western interests, as had the regimes of Hosni Mubarak, Zine El-Abidine Ben Ali, and Ali Abdullah Saleh.

- But there was also an important **symbolic dimension** to Islamism after the Uprisings. Given the highly secular nature of the regimes that had fallen, and their pro-Western orientation, there is a sense in which Islam—and by extension Islamism—functioned as a generic symbol of difference, as something more locally authentic and expressive of a will to genuine sovereignty. At some level, in other words, Islamism functioned as the symbolic opposite of the previous, hated political order and, for many citizens, the hope of something different. The slow pace of change under Islamist-led government subsequently led many—particularly in Egypt—to reconsider their earlier support.

See also Box 4.1, "The new Salafi factor in Arab politics."

This same pattern is to be found in a number of other settings, particularly in the Arab world, such as Yemen and Kuwait—and in both of those countries we have also seen the same shift towards a more participatory posture of late. Islamist or pro-Islamic parties also constitute the largest oppositional bloc in Malaysia. It is also evident that, in all of the contexts we examined, the ability of Islamists to gain access to, socialize, and build social capital in various civil society and associational spaces has been crucial to their success. This phenomenon came about as a result of Islamists learning very quickly that many regimes would either heavily regulate or try to co-opt their political activities, or go to great lengths to keep them out of the political sphere altogether. Under these conditions, social spaces and voluntary, often informal networks emerge as important *politicized* spaces for the contestation of policy, morality, and the social order. Islamist activity within the social sphere, as we have seen, is something far more complicated than just proselytizing and persuasion. Rather, these movements seek to redefine peoples' understanding of everyday practices—work, study, shopping, leisure, neighborly chatting—such that they are understood within an Islamic framework. "By providing goods and services," Wiktorowicz and Taji Farouki argue, "Islamists hope to expand networks of shared meaning so that individuals will organize their lives in accordance with Islamic precepts, rather than Western values and norms."[122] But are these precepts inherently incompatible with Western values and norms? This is a vital question to consider when it comes to the issue of the nature and goals of Islamist participation in democratic politics.

In noting the recent inclination toward political participation, we can see that Islamists have understood that if societal reform and transformation are the goals, then confining one's activism to the social sphere only gets you so far. They are well aware that the financial and legal resources associated with the policy-making arena are often the best way to effect large-scale change, and that this space constitutes a vital complement to the work they are doing in terms of recalibrating normative horizons at the grassroots level. But this raised crucial questions about the nature and ends of Islamist political participation. What are their goals? What impact does democratic activity have on how they think about the meaning and nature of participatory politics? First, there are those who continue to express concerns that Islamist willingness to enter democratic politics is primarily instrumental. They fear that, once in office, the Islamists would implement a highly undemocratic legislative agenda and seek to alter the political system so as to make their future removal from power impossible. Others cite concerns that Islamists who suffer political defeat or repression at the hands of the state could potentially turn radical. The example of Algeria, where the banning of the FIS in 1991 became the precursor to years of militancy and bloodshed, is often held up as evidence here. Or there is the possibility that even if an Islamist party, or some faction within it, was willing to play by democratic rules, a radical splinter group could emerge to ruin the show. Likewise, could not the vast network of social organizations these groups have cultivated not also be easily turned toward violent ends?

The relatively short period of Islamism in government in Tunisia and Egypt has not afforded the opportunity to answer these questions with any certainty. Indeed, in the case of Egypt, the forced removal of the MB from the presidency would in some ways simply seem to confirm Islamist fears that even when they play by the rules—however ineptly and ungenerously—they will not be permitted to hold political power.

But some scholars have offered analytical frameworks that help us to think about some of the structural factors that bear on Islamist political participation. For example, there are those who have argued that becoming subject to institutional constraints and being forced to interact with, listen to, and consider a plurality of views can actually have a moderating effect on the ideology and conduct of political movements. This is the argument that participation leads to moderation.[123] As groups discover that genuine cooperation (and occasional compromise) often allows them to have a greater impact, they come to see this kind of pluralistic politics to be in their interest. In a recent study, Carrie Wickham goes even further, suggesting that we can see at work today something that she terms "Islamist auto-reform."[124] By this she is referring to various learning processes that occur over time as political groups come to internalize the norms of pluralistic politics and then to change their own internal norms, political party culture, and political behaviors. Citing some of the same movements we have looked at above, Wickham draws attention to the fact that this "auto-reform" seems to be occurring primarily among the middle and younger generations who do not share the classic Islamist vision wherein party politics compromises Islam. In their understanding, Islamic norms are wholly compatible with, and even encourage, deliberation and discussion between a multiplicity of views. In many ways, the issue comes down—as Daniel Brumberg points out—to whether Islamists are willing to share power. As he puts it:

> [T]he challenge is not to figure out whether Islamism is "essentially" democratic versus autocratic, or liberal versus illiberal. Instead it is to see whether this or that Islamist group is acting within a hegemonic political

arena where the game is to shut out alternative approaches, or else within a competitive—let's call it *dissonant*—arena where Islamists, like other players, find themselves pushed to accommodate the logic of power sharing.[125]

Egypt's MB certainly did not fare well in this regard during its brief tenure in power, although its supporters would likely contend that all manner of nefarious remnants and "sore loser" opposition elements were conspiring to ensure its failure. It is also the case, as Brumberg points out, that the "political dissonance" referred to above is most likely to be present in those settings where Islamists contest elections and public debates alongside several other political viewpoints, and not just in strict opposition to an authoritarian state. In this view, "Muslim democracy" becomes democratic only when there are other actors present making it difficult for one to play politics exclusively in a populist mode. This point bodes well in terms of the consolidation of Muslim democracy in, say, Pakistan, Turkey, or Indonesia—but perhaps less so in many countries in the Arab world where other, non-Islamic viewpoints lack an organized social base and/or are kept out of the political realm by autocratic regimes (or newly enfranchised but political paranoid Islamists). This would lead us to speculate that one needs to take into consideration not only the question of whether Islamist movements are evolving towards pro-democracy stances, but also whether other political tendencies are seeking to become better organized, and regimes are allowing more space for "dissonance."

In the end, perhaps it comes down to a question of what Islamists will do with the social capital they have accumulated. Political sociologists have drawn a distinction between "bonding" social capital and "bridging" social capital.[126] The first seeks to create forms of solidarity and trust premised on a shared exclusionary identity. The second, "bridging" kind of social capital, on the other hand, is characterized by its ability to establish and sustain connections across disparate frameworks of norm and identity. Perhaps we might see the evolution from the classic mode of modern Islamism to new Islamism as, in part, a shift from movements defined primarily in terms of their ability to create and deploy bonding social capital to an approach that emphasizes the primacy—or at least the complementarity—of the bridging mode. But Islamists face distinct challenges when it comes to making this shift, as we witnessed in Egypt with the MB in 2011–13. How, for example, does one refigure the commitment to a *shari'ah*-based order—the very thing that often defines one as Islamist—in ways that allow for partnerships and political investment on the part of non-Islamist, and certainly non-Muslim, groups? Many of the "new Islamists" emphasize the necessity of a new *ijtihad,* but without specifying the content or boundaries of that activity.[127] Who gets to develop these approaches? Is it possible to have democratic deliberation regarding points of *shari'ah?* Views on this question differ considerably across the Muslim world. The very idea of Western liberal

© Asmaa Waguih

Figure 4.9 Hopeful times: Egypt's first parliament after the 2011 revolution

secularism is still a nonstarter for many Muslims, but this does not, in and of itself, mean that pluralism and power sharing are impossible—just distinct challenges that require creative thinking.[128]

THE ARAB UPRISINGS AND THE FUTURE OF ISLAMIST POLITICAL STRATEGY

The aftermath of the Arab Uprisings has provided an opportunity to begin answering some of these questions by gathering evidence from actual test cases of Islamists in power. Some assumptions, such as the idea that Islamists represented the only organized political opposition force in many countries, proved true. In post-revolutionary Tunisia and Egypt, Islamist parties were able to capitalize early on their comparative advantage in terms of political organization, their ability to successfully represent themselves as consistent (and often oppressed) critics of the previous *status quo,* and their claim— by virtue of proximity to religious values—to be free of corruption and unethical politics. However, in subsequent months and years, they found themselves faced with enormous challenges relating to building consensus across partisan lines, accumulating "bridging" social capital (see above), and making the hard and risky decisions associated with steering these countries through bold experiments with democracy. In Egypt, the MB's unwillingness towards—or fear of—accommodating a wider range of voices in the political and constitutional processes led rapidly to their downfall. In Tunisia, however, where En-Nahda had to contend with a political environment in which a wider range of political actors was able to mobilize resources and supporters, the democratic experiment has proceeded more smoothly.

But there are also shifts afoot in the broader religio-political landscape that all Islamists seeking to participate in the system will have to contend with, going forward. Chief among these is the intense pluralization of Islamic space that has occurred in recent years. Political Islam's traditional "incumbents," such as the MB, have lost a monopoly on the claim to represent the sole articulators of a social and political project premised on Islam. Aside from obvious competitors such as the Salafis, and breakaway groups with a foot in Islamic politics such as Hizb al-Wasat and Egyptian Current, the "Islamists" will have to contend with the fact that a much wider range of ideological groups are making some reference (at least symbolically) to Islam in their political discourse. This observation speaks to the ongoing relevance of one particular school of thought in the study of contemporary Muslim politics—namely, the post-Islamism thesis discussed in Chapter 8. On the face of it, the idea that we have somehow moved beyond the political relevance of Islamism seems oddly out of tune with developments on the ground. This approach, however, does not argue that Islamist parties *per se* will disappear, but rather that political Islam as an ideological project will become increasingly diffuse in the face of forces pushing these groups to the political center, and the arrival of rival claimants to religious virtue across a range of sectors beyond the realm of formal politics (including, potentially, the renewed political relevance of traditional religious institutions such as Al-Azhar University in Egypt). In short, if it turns out that there is nothing ideologically distinctive about governance by political parties supposedly based in Islam, then the proponents of the post-Islamism thesis may find that their argument holds up—even in an age of unprecedented Islamist success.

Second, given pressures related to structural factors such as the economy and unemployment, political actors will be judged primarily by the outcomes of their actions and policies, not by the symbols and rhetoric they embrace. Will seasoned oppositionists, used to relying on relatively vague slogans and amorphous formulations ("Islam is the solution"; "civil state with an Islamic reference"), be able to reinvent themselves as problem-solvers and purveyors of effective governance? And in the face of a political environment in which non-Islamic political forces represent perhaps only a small minority in key institutions, who will they be able to blame if and when their solutions do not deliver?

It is clear that conventional, mainstream Islamist movements are facing an unprecedented opportunity to demonstrate that they can deliver in terms of solving practical problems. By virtue of their affiliation with religion, they may also be somewhat more immune to wholesale popular defection if they falter initially. But, at the end of the day, they will have to work with non-Islamic parties and social forces to address the deep-seated problems that plague the region, and it is likely that, over time, it will become increasingly clear that there is nothing uniquely "Islamic" about the solutions that work. So their political fate will begin to depend more on the claim that their proximity to Islam makes them harder-working and more ethical—all of which will be more difficult to sustain over time as other political forces close the gap with the current comparative advantage of the Islamists. So, going forward, the question may become one of asking whether there is still even a sufficiently distinct object called "political Islam" for us to analyze. At the very least, we will need to treat Islamists such as the MB as part of a wider Islamic ecology of actors, movements, and voices—at the same time as their own agenda and objectives become a function of their fortunes *vis-à-vis*, and relations with, other actors in the formal political realm. We must also consider the question of what effect the dramatic and comprehensive offensive mounted against the MB in Egypt after the July 3, 2013 military coup will have on the political calculations of other Islamist parties. If Islamists come to believe that they will not be permitted to retain power even after "playing by the rules," might they reconsider altogether the strategic value of formal political participation?

It is also clear—as the case studies in this chapter show—that the meaning and nature of Islamist participation in political systems has been evolving over the past generation. There are real signs afoot that younger activists and supporters of these movements are drifting towards the political center in terms of both ideology and method. Furthermore, sociological analysis of their popular bases of support suggests that there is something far more complicated here than mere political instrumentalism. That said, it is also clear that manifestations of centrist Islam are still very young and few in number. Far more research is required to gauge the level of popular support for this approach, and also to better understand the circumstances that both promote and discourage its wider adoption. It is clearly impossible to view Islamism in monolithic terms; likewise, we must not isolate it, or assume that it will remain unaffected by ambient social, economic, and political transformations. Islamism has always sought to be an active, lived manifestation of Islam. As worldviews and modes of living evolve, therefore, so must Islamism as well.

▌ NOTES

1 T. Gurr, *Why Men Rebel,* Princeton, NJ: Princeton University Press, 1969.
2 C. Tilly, S. Tarrow, *Contentious Politics,* Boulder, CO: Paradigm Publishers, 2006.
3 O. Roy, *The Failure of Political Islam,* London: I.B. Tauris, 1994.
4 Ibid.

5   Ibid.
6   D. Singerman, *Avenues of Participation: Family, Politics, and Networks in Urban Quarters of Cairo,* Princeton, NJ: Princeton University Press, 1995.
7   P. Bourdieu, "Forms of capital," in J.C. Richards (ed.), *Handbook of Theory and Research for the Sociology of Education,* New York: Greenwood Press, 1983.
8   N. Brown, A. Hamzawy, M. Ottaway, "Islamist Movements and the Democratic Process in the Arab World," *Carnegie Endowment for International Peace Policy Brief* 67, 2006.
9   R. Baker, *Islam Without Fear: Egypt and the New Islamists,* Cambridge, MA: Harvard University Press, 2003.
10 A. Hamzawy, "The Key to Arab Reform: Moderate Islamists," *Carnegie Endowment for International Peace Policy Brief* 40, 2005.
11 D. Brumberg, "The Trap of Liberalized Autocracy," *Journal of Democracy* 13, 2002, pp. 56–68.
12 Hamzawy, op. cit., p. 4
13 Brumberg, op. cit., pp. 56–68.
14 Brown, Hamzawy, Ottaway, op. cit., pp. 3–19.
15 Hamzawy, op. cit., p. 2.
16 Ibid.
17 V. Nasr, The Rise of "Muslim Democracy," *Journal of Democracy* 16, 2005, pp. 13–27.
18 Nasr, op. cit., p. 13.
19 Ibid.
20 Nasr, op. cit., pp. 13–14.
21 D. Brumberg, "Islam is Not the Solution (or the Problem)," *Washington Quarterly* 29, 2005, p. 110.
22 Nasr, op. cit., p. 20.
23 M. Hammoud, "Causes for Fundamentalist Popularity in Egypt," in A. Moussalli (ed.), *Islamic Fundamentalism: Myths & Realities,* Reading: Ithaca Press, 1998, p. 308.
24 Ibid, pp. 310–12; M. Azzam, "Egypt: The Islamists and the State Under Mubarak," in A.S. Sidahmed, A. Ehteshami (eds), *Islamic Fundamentalism,* Boulder, CO: Westview Press, 1996; S. Zubaida, "Religion, the State, and Democracy: Contrasting Conceptions of Society in Egypt," in J. Beinin, J. Stork (eds), *Political Islam: Essays From Middle East Report,* New York: I.B. Tauris, 1997, pp. 51–63.
25 Zubaida, op. cit., pp. 51–63.
26 C. Wickham, "Islamic Mobilization and Political Change: The Islamist Trend in Egypt's Professional Associations," in J. Beinin, J. Stork (eds), *op. cit.,* p. 130.
27 Wickham, op. cit., pp. 126–130.
28 H. Mustafa, "The Islamist Movements under Mubarak," in L. Guazzone (ed.), *The Islamist Dilemma: The Political Role of Islamist Movements in the Contemporary Arab World,* Reading: Ithaca Press, 1995, p. 167.
29 Mustafa, op. cit., p. 171.
30 J. Esposito, J. Voll, *Islam and Democracy,* New York: Oxford University Press, 1996, p. 190.
31 Wickham, op. cit., p. 124.
32 Wickham, op. cit., p.125.
33 Azzam, op. cit., p. 119.
34 Ibid.
35 Mustafa, op. cit., p. 166.

36 Esposito, Voll, op. cit., p. 187.
37 Esposito, Voll, op. cit., p. 185.
38 C. Wickham, *Mobilizing Islam: Religion, Activism, and Political Change in Egypt,* New York: Columbia University Press, 2002, pp. 214–216.
39 Wickham, op. cit., p. 217.
40 Baker, op. cit., p. 1.
41 M.L. Browers, *Political Ideology in the Arab World: Accommodation and Transformation,* Cambridge: Cambridge University Press, 2009.
42 Ibid.
43 J. Habermas, "New Social Movements," *Telos* 49, 1981, pp. 33–37.
44 Baker, op. cit., p. 241.
45 Q. Wiktorowicz, "The Salafi Movement: Violence and the Fragmentation of Community," in M. Cooke, B. Lawrence (eds), *Muslim Networks from Hajj to Hip Hop,* Chapel Hill, NC: University of North Carolina Press, 2005, p. 211.
46 A.R. Norton, "Thwarted Politics: The Case of Egypt's Hizb al-Wasat," in R. Hefner (ed.), *Remaking Muslim Politics: Pluralism, Contestation, Democratization,* Princeton, NJ: Princeton University Press, 2005, pp. 133–161.
47 Baker, op. cit., p. 193.
48 Wickham, op. cit., p. 218.
49 Norton, op. cit., p. 140.
50 Wickham, op. cit., p. 217.
51 Ibid.
52 Norton, op. cit., p. 142.
53 Ibid.; J. Stacher, "Post-Islamist Rumblings in Egypt: The Emergence of the Wasat Party," *Middle East Journal* 56, 2002, p. 422.
54 Stacher, op. cit., pp. 419–420; Wickham, op. cit., p. 222; S. Otterman, "Muslim Brotherhood and Egypt's Parliamentary Elections," *Council on Foreign Relations,* 2005, pp. 1–3.
55 Stacher, op. cit., p. 424.
56 Stacher, op. cit., p. 429.
57 Stacher, op. cit., p. 426.
58 D. Williams, "Egypt's Muslim Brotherhood May Be Model for Islam's Political Adaptation," *Washington Post,* February 3, 2006, A14.
59 Otterman, op. cit., pp. 1–3.
60 K. al-Anani, "Young Brothers in Search of a New Path," *Current Trends in Islamist Ideology* 9, Washington DC: Hudson Institute, 2009, pp. 96–109.
61 M. Lynch, "Young Brothers in Cyberspace," *MERIP* 245, 2007; J. Martini et al., *The Muslim Brotherhood, Its Youth, and Implications for U.S. Engagement,* Washington DC: RAND Corporation, 2012.
62 Stacher, op. cit., p. 430.
63 C. Lombardi. N.J. Brown, "Islam in Egypt's new constitution," foreignpolicy.com, December 13, 2012, http://mideast.foreignpolicy.com/posts/2012/12/13/islam_in_egypts_new_constitution
64 N.J. Brown, "Post-Revolutionary Al-Azhar," *Carnegie Papers,* Washington DC: Carnegie Endowment for International Peace, 2011.
65 A. Tamimi, *Rachid Ghannouchi: A Democrat within Islamism,* Oxford: Oxford University Press, 2001.
66 J. White, *Muslim Nationalism and the New Turks,* Princeton: Princeton University Press, 2012.

67 Nasr, op. cit., p. 14.
68 M. H. Yavuz, *Islamic Political Identity in Turkey,* Oxford: Oxford University Press, 2003, p. 60.
69 S. Mardin, "The Nakshibendi Order of Turkey," in M. Marty, R. S. Appleby (eds), *Fundamentalisms and the State: Remaking Polities, Economies, and Militance,* Chicago, IL: University of Chicago Press, 1993, p. 220.
70 Ibid.
71 M. H. Yavuz, "Islam in the Public Sphere: The Case of the Nur Movement," in M. H. Yavuz, J. Esposito (eds), *Turkish Islam and the Secular State: The Gülen Movement,* Syracuse, NY: Syracuse University Press, 2003, p. 14.
72 Mardin, op. cit., p. 222.
73 Ibid.
74 B. Agai, "The Gülen Movement's Islamic Ethic of Education," *Critique* 11, 2002, pp. 27–47.
75 R. Margulies, E. Yildizoğlu, "The Resurgence of Islam and the Welfare Party in Turkey," in J. Beinin, J. Stork (eds), *Political Islam: Essays from Middle East Report,* New York: I.B. Tauris, 1997, p. 148.
76 Ibid.
77 M. H. Yavuz, *Islamic Political Identity in Turkey,* Oxford: Oxford University Press, 2003.
78 J. White, "The End of Islamism? Turkey's Muslimhood Model," in Hefner (ed.), op. cit., p. 93.
79 D. Wakin, "Turkey Military 'in Charge'," *Associated Press,* June 21, 1997.
80 Nasr, op. cit., p. 23.
81 Yavuz, op. cit., p. 256; Nasr, op. cit., p. 24.
82 White, op. cit., p. 91.
83 Yavuz, op. cit., p. 250.
84 Yavuz, op. cit., p. 257.
85 Ibid.
86 J. White, *Islamist Mobilization in Turkey,* Seattle, WA: University of Washington Press, 2002, p. 138.
87 Nasr, op. cit., p. 23.
88 Yavuz, op. cit., p. 263.
89 Nasr, op. cit., p. 23.
90 S. Tepe, "Turkey's AKP: A Model 'Muslim Democratic' Party?," *Journal of Democracy* 16, 2005, p. 76.
91 Yavuz, op. cit., p. 263.
92 Pew Forum, *The World's Muslims: Religion, Politics, and Society,* Washington, DC: Pew Research Center, 2013, p. 46.
93 B. Milton-Edwards, "Climate of Change in Jordan's Islamist Movement," in A. S. Sidahmed, A. Ehteshami (eds), *Islamic Fundamentalism,* Boulder, CO: Westview Press, 1996, p. 124.
94 B. Milton-Edwards, "A Temporary Alliance with the Crown: The Islamic Response in Jordan," in J. Piscatori (ed.), *Islamic Fundamentalisms and the Gulf Crisis,* Chicago, IL: The Fundamentalism Project of the American Academy of Arts and Science, 1991, pp. 88–108.
95 G. Robinson, "Islamists under Liberalization in Jordan," in Moussalli (ed.), op. cit., pp. 169–196.
96 B. Milton-Edwards, op. cit., p. 134.

97 Robinson, op. cit., pp. 169–196.

98 R. Ryan, J. Schwedler, "Return to Democratization or New Hybrid Regime? The 2003 Elections in Jordan," *Middle East Policy* 2004, pp. 138–151.

99 P. Silverstein, "Weighing Morocco's New Constitution," *MERIP* Online, July 5, 2011, www.merip.org/mero/mero070511

100 M. Moaddel, *Islamic Modernism, Nationalism, and Fundamentalism: Episode and Discourse,* Chicago, IL: University of Chicago Press, 2005, p. 307.

101 J. Schwedler, *Faith in Moderation: Islamist Parties in Jordan and Yemen,* New York: Cambridge University Press, 2006, p. 169.

102 Q. Wiktorowicz, *The Management of Islamic Activism: Salafis, the Muslim Brotherhood, and State Power in Jordan,* Albany, NY: State University of New York Press, 2001, pp. 3–4.

103 Q. Wiktorowicz, S. T. Farouki, "Islamic NGOs and Muslim Politics: a Case from Jordan," *Third World Quarterly* 2000, p. 686.

104 Schwedler, op. cit., p. 158.

105 Schwedler, op. cit., p. 162.

106 M. Moaddel, "Islamic Action Front Party: Interview with Dr. Ishaq A. Farhan," in M. Moaddel, K. Talattof (eds), *Modernist and Fundamentalist Debates in Islam,* New York: Palgrave Macmillan, 2000.

107 Robinson, op. cit., p. 176.

108 Robinson, op. cit., p. 174; Schwedler, op. cit., p. 162.

109 J. Clark, J. Schwedler, "Who Opened the Window? Women's Struggle for Voice within Islamist Political Parties," *Comparative Politics* 35, 2003, pp. 293–313.

110 Robinson, op. cit., p. 188.

111 Robinson, op. cit., p. 189.

112 Robinson, op. cit., p. 191.

113 Schwedler, op. cit., p. 166.

114 M. Moaddel, *Islamic Modernism, Nationalism, and Fundamentalism,* op. cit., p. 313.

115 Schwedler, op. cit., pp. 164–165; Robinson, op. cit., p. 179.

116 Schwedler, op. cit., p. 167.

117 Schwedler, op. cit., p. 172; Robinson, op. cit., p. 178.

118 Schwedler, op. cit., pp. 169, 172.

119 C. Wickham, "The Causes and Dynamics of Islamist Auto-Reform," *ICIS International* 6, 2006, pp. 6–7.

120 D. Brumberg, "The Trap of Liberalized Autocracy," *Journal of Democracy* 13, 2002, pp. 56–68.

121 Wiktorowicz, op. cit., p. 95.

122 Wiktorowicz, Farouki, op. cit., p. 688.

123 Schwedler, op. cit., p. 172.

124 Wickham, op. cit., pp. 6–7.

125 D. Brumberg, "Islamists and the Politics of Consensus," *Journal of Democracy* 13, 2002, p. 112.

126 R. Hefner, "Introduction: Modernity and the Remaking of Muslim Politics," in R. Hefner (ed.), op. cit., p. 17; R. Hefner, *Making Democracy Work: Civic Traditions in Modern Italy,* Princeton, NJ: Princeton University Press, 1993.

127 Brown, Hamzawy, Ottaway, op. cit., pp. 9–10.

128 A. Tamimi (ed.), *Power Sharing Islam?* London: Liberty, 1993.

CHAPTER 5

Islam as the system: Islamic states and "Islamization" from above

In Chapter 4, we looked comparatively at some of the ways Islamist movements have sought to enter the political process in a variety of countries; how these strategies have evolved over time; and how Islamism itself may be undergoing certain transformations today. Our analytic perspective was predominantly "bottom-up" in the sense that we focused on how political parties and movements within society sought to challenge and compete with the authority of national-secular states, and varying governmental responses to the attempts by Islamists to enter the political field. The present chapter reverses the analytic lens to focus instead on those states that have sought to define themselves in terms of Islam, or to pursue strategies of Islamization as a form of political development, or as a means for assuming and retaining power. While the governments in some of the countries we looked at in the previous chapter have certainly sought at times to co-opt Islamists (such as Egypt in the 1970s under Sadat), or to appropriate Islamic symbols when politically expedient (such as Nasser's claims that Pan-Arabism represented a form of "Islamic socialism" or Saddam Hussein's description of the 1991 Gulf War as a *jihad*), our primary interest in the present chapter is in those nations that have actually declared themselves to be Islamic states, or where broad, pervasive, and systematic "Islamization" programs have been implemented. In this sense, our focus here is on the politics of "Islam from above."

But this distinction should not lead us to assume the existence of a real and meaningful dichotomy between "Islam from above" and "Islam from below." We would never suggest that, in the examples covered in this chapter, the state is the sole agent of Islamization, or possesses exclusive authority to define Islam. As will quickly become evident, there are many nonstate actors involved in the religious politics of so-called Islamic states. By calling this chapter "Islam as the system," we are rather pointing out that, when operating within a political environment characterized as "officially" Islamic, or where there is understood to be a privileged relationship between Islam and the state, Muslim politics at all levels play out differently. The opportunity structures encountered by Islamist actors, not to mention their choice of religious symbols, the likely impact of these symbols, and the state's response to them will vary considerably when the political system is defined in religious terms. This is the primary dynamic we are seeking to capture when focusing on the idea of Islam as the system.

But no Islamic state is a monolith, either in the sense of there being only a single path or course by which a country becomes one, or in the sense of an Islamic government being capable of excluding other forms of politics—Muslim or otherwise—and challenges to its authority. Each of the countries on which we focus in this chapter represents a different model and experience of state-led Islamization. Some, such as Saudi Arabia and Pakistan, were established as Islamic states, although this has meant rather different things in practice in each of their cases. In the case of Iran, an Islamic political order came about through a form of popular revolution, although the political system that has since evolved from it is based on a unique (and not necessarily very popular) interpretation of Islam's role in government. In the case of Sudan (see Box 5.4, "Hassan al-Turabi and Sudan's 'Islamic Experiment'"), Islamization was an "experiment" associated with a change in regime, while the Malaysian state's embrace of Islam was part of a national development strategy (see Box 5.3, "Malaysia: Islamization and national development"). Even in a country such as Pakistan, established as an Islamic state, successive regimes have related to and used Islam in very different ways, and we can hence point to something more like a series of Islamizing waves over the course of that country's political history.

The various cases we examine below will provide us with an understanding of the diverse range of approaches to, and experiences of, "official" Islamization in the Muslim world. We will come to appreciate that the theory and practice of the Islamic state has meant very different things in different settings, and that we can therefore assume very little about the likely behavior of a given state simply because it has declared itself to be "Islamic." Likewise, we will also examine the circumstances that might lead a particular state to pursue Islamization as a strategy and, again, the diverse range of goals they hope to achieve by doing so. As we will see, most Islamic states face various forms of internal challenge to their legitimacy, mostly by actors who question whether the government's embrace of Islam is genuine, or the correctness and authenticity of the Islamic order represented by the state. That is to say that, even within Islamic states, it is not uncommon to find Islamist opposition groups. The state's monopolization of Islamic normativity is never complete. So, while this chapter concentrates mainly on state-led Islamization efforts, it will be important to also give some attention to the counter-responses of various groups and parties—Islamic and otherwise—in order to appreciate the full political impact of Islamization from above.

DEFINING THE ISLAMIC STATE IN THEORY AND PRACTICE

Just what is an Islamic state and wherein lies its "Islamic-ness"? Let us begin by clarifying certain definitional confusions that often and easily arise when talking about Islamic states. The term "Islamic state" is sometimes mistakenly used to refer to any country with a predominantly Muslim population. While more than two dozen countries in the world fit this description, very few of them can be described as Islamic states according to the more specific sense in which we are using the term. They would more accurately be termed Muslim-majority countries or Muslim nations—two terms we use frequently throughout this book. In many cases the governments in question are highly secular in nature, and many of them actively seek to suppress the political ambitions of Islamically based groups and parties (as we saw in Chapter 4).

When we talk about "Islamic states," we are talking about a rather different situation, one in which the nature of the state and the political order is defined in Islamic terms. Again, there is room here for confusion. While the constitutions of a number of countries (among them Egypt and Tunisia) mention Islam as the religion of state or as the official religion, this does not in and of itself qualify these nations as having an Islamic state. Those very few countries that do style themselves as Islamic states tend to include further stipulations to the effect that the Qur'an or *shari'ah* is the primary (or exclusive) source of all legislation in the country, and that the nature and form of the governmental system is derived from Islam. So which are these countries and what, in theory, qualifies them as Islamic states? In order of their founding or transition to Islamic status, they are:

- **The Kingdom of Saudi Arabia** (founded 1932)—whose Basic Law (adopted in 1992) stipulates the Qur'an as the constitution of the country, the authority of the ruling regime as derived from the Qur'an, and the legal system to be based on *shari'ah*.

- *The Islamic Republic of Pakistan* (founded 1947)—established as a homeland for the Muslims of India, Pakistan's initial draft constitution spoke more of the state's responsibility to promote Islamic teaching and foster conditions that would allow its Muslim citizens to pursue their lives in accordance with the Qur'an and *sunna*; later versions included clauses stipulating that all laws should be "brought into conformity with the injunctions of Islam as laid down by the Qur'an and Sunna."
- *Iran*, known as the *Islamic Republic of Iran* (since 1979)—the constitution of which requires that all laws and policies be in accordance with Islam; mandates a political leadership role for the religious jurist (*faqih*); and derives most of the document's General Principles directly from Qur'anic sources.

These are the three major Islamic states examined in greater detail below. Two other countries, representing rather different approaches to the Islamic state—Sudan and Malaysia—are covered in accompanying textboxes. We should note that in addition to these *shari'ah*-based states, there are a number of other countries that maintain parallel court systems in which certain issues—usually limited to matters of personal status and inheritance—are dealt with according to Islamic regulations, but they have not been included here since the role of *shari'ah* is carefully controlled by what are in other regards often very secular states. Afghanistan under the rule of the Taliban (1996–2001) would also certainly have counted as an Islamic state, but this case will be dealt with in Chapter 6, which looks at the role of Islam in weak states and post-conflict settings.

We should also bear in mind that the Islamic state in theory and the Islamic state in practice will often mean quite different things. Beyond the constitutional stipulations and titular trappings that allow the states above to lay claim to Islamic status, the role of Islam in day-to-day governance and in the shaping of things such as political institutions, legislative processes, and foreign policy is very difficult to identify with any certainty. In some cases, for example when we see *hudud* criminal punishments being carried out in Saudi Arabia, or an institutionalized role for the clergy in Iran's government, it is easier to recognize the presence of norms and social roles explicitly associated with Islam. In other situations, this will be more difficult. We should remember that our main challenge as analysts is not to pronounce upon whether Sudan is "really" an Islamic state or whether Iran's revolution was "genuinely" Islamic. Rather, what we should be focusing on are the ways in which actors in a variety of social and political situations have sought to mobilize peoples and legitimize institutions on the basis of appeals to Islamic norms and symbols. In the present chapter, we are most concerned with the question of how those actors associated with the structural capacities and institutional legitimacy of the state have included Islam in their politics—but also with the ways in which other political actors in society have responded to the state's claims regarding religious authority. Our inquiries about the state and Islam are hence framed primarily in terms of "why" and "how" questions, rather than in terms of trying to gauge the veracity or authenticity of the state's claims *vis-à-vis* Islam.

Given that we are dealing with Islamic states, our discussions in this chapter will inevitably call to mind some of the deliberations in earlier chapters—most notably Chapter 3—regarding the correct nature and form of the Islamic political order. As we may recall, various Islamic thinkers working during the period when modern states were being established in the Muslim world put forward widely differing views regarding the question of whether Islam was compatible with the modern nation-state. Even amongst those who stated a preference for an Islamic model of the state, we find quite different opinions as to what, exactly, this meant. For some, any form of government was permissible so long as it did not contravene Qur'anic requirements. Others preferred a more active and explicit application of *shari'ah* to legislative processes and outcomes. As we will see, the practice of Islamic statehood and Islamization has not led to a resolution of these issues, but rather provides us with a rich space in which to explore how these theoretical questions have played out in various efforts by state authorities to implement Islam in politics and policy.

SAUDI ARABIA: RELIGIOUS LEGITIMACY CUTS BOTH WAYS

For many people, the Kingdom of Saudi Arabia represents the Islamic state *par excellence*. Home to Islam's two holiest cities, Saudi Arabia for many evokes images of strict adherence to Islamic law, deeply conservative social values, oppressive attitudes towards women, and hostility to non-Muslims—all of which are generally taken to be characteristic of Wahhabism, the form of Islam most associated with the Kingdom. Islam lies at the very foundation of the Saudi state, and the legitimacy of the country's royal family has long rested on its claims to uphold the *shari'ah* and to rule according to the precepts of the Qur'an. But one would be very wrong to think that after claiming this status for themselves at the time of the Kingdom's founding, the religious legitimacy of the Saud family's rule has been taken for granted. The relationship between the royal family and the religious establishment whose support enabled the former to justify its political ambitions in Islamic terms has always been complex. Indeed, the evolving and, at times, highly ambivalent relationship between the palace and the *ulama* has long been a key factor in determining the course of Saudi politics. As we will see, the very same claims used by the Saud to legitimize their rule have also opened them to considerable criticism, from the religious establishment certainly, but also from political elements within society. This has led in recent years to the emergence of various forms of Islamism, even within this most conservative of Islamic states.

Our analysis of Saudi Arabia will begin by briefly discussing the historical circumstances surrounding the establishment of three waves of Saudi state-building over 200 years, beginning in the mid-eighteenth century and culminating in the modern Kingdom of Saudi Arabia in 1932. The evolving historical relationship between, as one author has put it, the "political ambition" of the Saud family and the "spiritual vision" of their allies among the religious scholars is the key to understanding the complex and multifaceted relationship that obtains between the crown and the religious establishment in the Kingdom today.[1] We will then move on to look at the formation of the modern Saudi state, again paying particular attention to questions relating to the division of competences and powers between the royal family, the government bureaucracy, and religious scholars. The question of how Islam has figured in the foreign policy of the Kingdom will be taken up, and we will also give some consideration here to the much-discussed issue of Saudi Arabia's role in propagating and supporting Wahhabism beyond its borders. Some further details regarding the nature of Saudi society in terms of religious demographics and socioeconomic composition will then be provided, and with this background in place, we will be prepared to look more closely at the development of religious opposition to the Saudi royal family in the Kingdom today. Beginning with the takeover of the Grand Mosque in Mecca in 1979, we will track the development of several distinctive undercurrents of Islamism within Saudi Arabia, focusing particularly on the period following the Gulf War of 1991. This context will also draw our attention to the question of where Saudi Arabia fits into the growth and development of transnational radical Islam of the sort represented by Al-Qaeda (see Chapter 7). The various reform initiatives introduced by the palace during this same period—such as the establishment in 1992 of the Consultative Council—will also be considered in light of various emergent social tensions and ongoing pressures from dissident religious elements. Finally, we will conclude by offering some reflections on recent political developments such as limited experiments with local elections, efforts by the state to rein in radicalism and to bring the religious police under more direct control, and Saudi responses to the Arab Uprisings of 2011.

But before we delve into this account of modern religious politics in Saudi Arabia, it would be worthwhile to spend a few moments discussing and coming to some better understanding of what is meant by Wahhabism—particularly since Saudi Islam is generally understood to be coterminous with this concept. This eponymous current of Islamic theology and jurisprudence derives from the thinking of the eighteenth-century religious reformer Muhammad Ibn Abd al-Wahhab (whose ideas we examined briefly in Chapter 2). As we may recall, Ibn Abd al-Wahhab's discourse of religious purification sought to cleanse Islam of the many forms of "innovation" (*bid'a*) that had been introduced over the centuries, diverting the religion from its true practice as embodied in the traditions of the Prophet and the example offered by those companions who were his contemporaries or near-contemporaries by a couple of generations—known as the *salaf*, or pious ancestors. In this regard, we can say that Wahhabism is a subset of, but not synonymous with, Salafism—an approach to Islam we look at more closely in Chapter 7.

The foundational concept from which all Wahhabi thought derives is that of *tawhid*, a term that refers to the "oneness" and uniqueness of God, and also the unicity of all things within the divine. It is the emphasis on *tawhid*—often and variously translated as "monotheism" or "unitarianism"—that led Ibn Abd al-Wahhab to repudiate any and all religious practices that involved even a semblance of worshipping anything other than God. This included various Sufi practices such as the visitation of graves associated with mystical saints, or the celebration of their birthdays. In his major work, the *Kitab al-Tawhid* (*The Book of Divine Unity*), Ibn Abd al-Wahhab cites favorably the ideas of the early fourteenth-century jurist Ibn Taymiyya, a proponent of the *salaf* and an ardent foe of what was taken to be Sufi heresy regarding matters of worship. Ibn Taymiyya is also regarded as one of the greatest legal minds within the Hanbali school of Sunni jurisprudence, an approach also closely identified with Wahhabism and the Saudi religious establishment. While the substance of Hanbali views on many issues is deeply conservative and often quite literalist, it is important to note that this particular legal school is, in a certain sense, rather less conservative when it comes to matters of legal methodology. Unlike other schools that place considerable emphasis on respecting the opinions and precedents of other jurists, Hanbalism prefers direct reliance on Qur'an and *hadith,* and encourages scholars to exercise *ijtihad* (independent judgment) based on these sources. This legal approach matched well Ibn Abd al-Wahhab's desire to achieve a pure Islam that reflected as closely as possible the model of normativity found in the Qur'an and *sunna*.

Aside from the emphasis on *tawhid,* the ideals of the *salaf,* and the importance of Hanbali jurisprudence, there is one further aspect of Wahhabism that deserves particular mention. This concerns certain aspects of Wahhabi normative discourse that evolved as a function of how the doctrine was put into practice in political terms. As we will explore more fully below, Ibn Abd al-Wahhab entered into an alliance with a powerful Arabian tribal family, the Saud, in the hope that this partnership would allow the theory of *tawhid* to be achieved in practice through a political order. This political movement advanced by conquering and gaining oaths of allegiance from various tribes across the Arabian peninsula—often at the point of the sword. In order to legitimize attacks against other clans who were also Muslim, Ibn Abd al-Wahhab had to be able to make the case that the non-Islamic practices followed by these groups had effectively placed them outside the remit of the religion—in other words, that by their incorrect religious practice they had made themselves into infidels (in which case the strictures against Muslims using violence on fellow Muslims no longer applied). Because of this early history of needing to differentiate between true Muslims and religious "others"—one that would be repeated at the time of the founding of the modern Saudi state—Wahhabi discourse today is often characterized by a tendency to establish and legislate moral categories that strongly differentiate various groups of people, and usually in very stark terms (e.g. believers versus infidels). It is this feature of Wahhabism that has gained it a reputation for intolerance, particularly as regards other religious groups and sects within Islam. Thus the considerable religious pluralism to be found in modern Saudi Arabia (e.g. Shi'a, Sufis, followers of other Sunni legal schools) has very little public profile due to the hostility of the religious establishment. Indeed, an overtly anti-Shi'i stance has long been an integral part of the Saudi state's self conception. It was not until 2009 that all four "orthodox" schools of Sunni jurisprudence came to be represented on the Kingdom's Council of Senior Scholars. One final but important point concerns use of the term "Wahhabi" itself. Generally speaking, those who hold these views will never refer to themselves as Wahhabi. Rather, with the exception of certain moments in the early history of the modern Kingdom, the terms "Wahhabi" or "Wahhabism" have been used (and usually in a derogatory manner) only by Muslims of other persuasions, or by non-Muslims. Those who do follow this tendency have historically been more likely to refer to themselves as *muwahhidun* ("monotheists" or "unitarians"), *ahl al-tawhid* ("people of oneness"), or sometimes just as Salafis. In summary then, Wahhabism is a variety of Salafi thought that evolved historically via the social and political experience of state formation and consolidation in Saudi Arabia. Its defining traits are an overwhelming emphasis on the doctrinal essence of *tawhid*, a marked but not exclusive reliance on Hanbali jurisprudence, and a tendency to draw strong normative distinctions between different categories of peoples.

Religion, the royal family, and the Saudi state

The original antecedent for the modern Kingdom of Saudi Arabia can be traced to an alliance made in 1744 between Muhammad Ibn Saud, a tribal prince in the Nejd region of central Arabia, and the religious reformer Muhammad Ibn Abdul Wahhab. The former saw in Ibn Abd al-Wahhab's purifying zeal the inspirational ideology and religious justification that would permit him to fulfill his political ambition of uniting the various tribes of Arabia, while Ibn Abd al-Wahhab saw Ibn Saud's tribal base as a formidable political vehicle that would permit the message of *tawhid* to be reflected in a living social order. While it would be wrong to assume that the two saw each other only in instrumentalist terms, both undoubtedly appreciated the great potential of the symbiosis. Ibn Saud implemented this state-building project by establishing a coalition of tribal units loyal to him that could act as the movement's army. Emphasizing their brotherhood in religion, Ibn Saud and Ibn Abd al-Wahhab called them the Ikhwan ("brotherhood"), and over the next 50 years these forces were able to secure more and more territory for the nascent Saudi polity, their numbers growing with each success. The resemblance between Ibn Saud's methods and the early community-building efforts associated with the Prophet Muhammad was certainly not lost on anyone and, indeed, there was a conscious effort to cultivate these kinds of parallels in the minds of potential supporters. The effort reached its symbolic zenith in 1802 when Ibn Saud conquered Mecca and Medina, bringing the two holiest cities of Islam under his control. It was at this point that Ibn Saud attracted the attention and concern of the Ottoman sultan, who otherwise tended to have little interest in the tribal intrigues of inner Arabia. With Ottoman control of the holy cities and the pilgrimage now under threat, Istanbul mobilized its Egyptian army—commanded by Muhammad Ali—to expel the Ikhwan from the Hijaz and crush the Saudi state. In 1819, Ibn Saud's capital near Riyadh was sacked, sending both the Saud and the al-Sheikh (the family of Ibn Abd al-Wahhab) into exile. The former managed to re-establish themselves near Riyadh by 1824 and preside over a "second" Saudi state—far more limited and less ambitious in scope—until the end of the nineteenth century. At this point, ongoing pressure from the Ottomans, increased British interest in Arabia, and challenges from other major tribes led the Saud once again to abandon their capital and flee, this time into Kuwait—a favor that would be returned exactly 100 years later in 1991, when that country's ruling family would take refuge in Saudi Arabia from Saddam Hussein's invading armies.

The establishment of the modern Kingdom of Saudi Arabia began with the efforts of Abdul Aziz Ibn Saud to reclaim his family's territories in the first decade of the twentieth century. In a sequence of events that closely mirrored the efforts of his family's forebear just a little over a century earlier, Abdul Aziz progressively reconquered all of the same territories that Muhammad Ibn Saud had held, and more beyond. His methods were also similar, and involved reconstituting the Ikhwan and animating them with the same religious fervor. The organization of the Ikhwan "v2.0" again echoed the early period of Islam, with Abdul Aziz establishing separate communities for his religio-political armies that evoked the Prophet's *hijra* from the *jahiliyya* of Mecca into true Islam. In 1926, after taking the Hijaz from the Hashemite dynasty of Sharif Hussein, Abdul Aziz's forces defeated the Rashid dynasty occupying Riyadh and declared this the capital of his new state. His efforts had attracted the patronage of Britain by this time, and he had frequent dealings with both the British military and London's political representative for the region. These foreign dealings—but also the enthusiasm with which he adopted Western technologies and entertained business propositions from abroad—soon brought Abdul Aziz into conflict with the Ikhwan, however. It is important to remember that, just as in the case of his ancestor, Abdul Aziz's legitimacy in the eyes of the Ikhwan was based on his credentials as an agent of piety and the advancement of Islam. Once it began to seem to them that Abdul Aziz was facilitating foreign interests in Arabia, and particularly when he started to prevent the Ikhwan from raiding certain tribes outside the Saudi confederation, they mounted a revolt against him. Abdul Aziz spent the next few years quelling this rebellion, and once this had been accomplished, he sought and obtained oaths of allegiance from the peninsula's remaining holdout tribes. This enabled him in 1932 to proclaim the birth of the new Kingdom of Saudi Arabia in the form in which we know it today.

Abdul Aziz's quest for foreign economic partnerships was evidence of a deep pragmatic streak in his leadership style. He suddenly found himself ruling over an enormous, peninsula-wide state whose only meaningful source of public income were the modest revenues associated with custodianship of the *hajj* pilgrimage. From the early 1930s, Abdul Aziz had received expressions of interest from a number of British and American companies interested in pursuing the possibility that there might be significant and commercially exploitable hydrocarbon resources under the Saudi soil. He granted an exclusive concession to Standard Oil of California (the forerunner to Exxon). In 1938, Dammam Well #7 in the Eastern Province, immediately adjacent to the Gulf coast, struck oil in commercial quantities. The emergence of Saudi Arabia as a world energy giant, and moreover one closely allied with U.S. commercial and later political interests, had now begun. The Saudi government gradually acquired greater ownership of the resulting oil company—the Arabian American Oil Company (ARAMCO)—from its American partners until 1980, when it became a wholly state-owned entity. In 1988, the company's name was changed to Saudi Aramco to reflect this and to reflect ongoing attempts to "Saudi-ize" the country's skilled workforce instead of relying so heavily on imported expertise—an issue that would prove sensitive later in terms of religious politics.

Let us make a few observations regarding the establishment of the Saudi state and the triangle of linkages that define the relationship between the royal family, the religious establishment, and wider Saudi society. The legitimacy of the Saudi state, as mentioned above, rests on the twin pillars of the royal family and the support they receive from the *ulama*. We can thus speak of the existence of something like a "contract" between the palace and *ulama* whereby the latter provides for the legitimacy of the former so long as the royal family upholds the *shari'ah,* while the crown ensures a privileged institutional role for the religious scholars. Also relevant is a second covenant or tacit "social contract" between the royal family and wider Saudi society, in which the Saud provide for the protection and welfare of the people in return for their allegiance and political quiescence. Both of these structures of legitimacy and authority are important to understand, and to bear in mind later when we move on to examine the emergence of Islamist opposition in Saudi Arabia and various popular voices seeking reform and greater political openness. Institutionally separate from the royal family and the religious establishment (but subject in various ways from the authority of both) is the Saudi government itself and its associated bureaucracy. Initially only a minor player in the governance of the Kingdom, the government bureaucracy came into its own once the influx of significant oil revenues necessitated the creation of ever more ministries and administrative capacities to oversee the rapidly growing and modernizing Saudi state.

The Islamic character of the Saudi state is to be found in several aspects. First among these is the idea of the Qur'an as the highest law of the land, and the Saudi dynasty as the guardian and enforcer of Qur'anic law within the Kingdom. All laws in Saudi Arabia are made in accordance with the *shari'ah,* and all legal processes, overseen by a Ministry of Justice, must conform to its requirements. While Saudi Arabia has no formal constitution, the Basic Law, promulgated in 1992, identifies the Qur'an as the basis for all public affairs. The second defining element of the Saudi model of the Islamic state is to be found in the special status granted to the religious establishment. Overseen by the Higher Council of Ulama, religious scholars have played a major role in buttressing the authority of the royal family by providing *fatawa* endorsing their policies. It would be inaccurate, however, to view the "official" *ulama* as rubber-stampers for the Saud. On numerous occasions throughout the history of modern Saudi Arabia, the *ulama* have not seen eye to eye with the royal family, and the latter has taken steps to circumvent their authority. The third component of the religious state is the *mutawwa* or religious police, a semi-autonomous institution with some connection to (but also at times operating quite independently of) the religious establishment. Charged with the maintenance of public virtue, it is the *mutawwa* who are responsible for what many in the West perceive as the excesses of Saudi religiosity, such as the harassment of women deemed to be in violation of religiously mandated dress codes. Their pervasive presence throughout the Kingdom is also designed to enforce requirements related to the closing of businesses during appointed prayer times, and they have reserved to themselves the right to administer justice "on the spot" in the form of canings and other types of punishment. Although a quasi-official corps, *mutawwa* activities have often been at odds with the policies and desires of the royal family, government ministries, and even the religious establishment. In 2002, for example, there were widespread calls from all quarters of Saudi society to rein in their influence when they prevented the evacuation of a girls' school during a fire because the students were not sufficiently covered. Fifteen primary school-age girls lost their lives in that incident, and 50 more were injured. More recently, and in response to popular perceptions that the religious police were overstepping their boundaries, there have been efforts to curtail some of their more excessive activities. In both 2009 and 2012, for example, the king replaced the head of the *mutawwa* in moves widely perceived as indicative of royal displeasure at the institution's intrusiveness. Some citizens have also been able to bring civil cases against the *mutawwa*.

How has the relationship between the Saud, the government, and the religious establishment evolved over the years? Granted broad jurisdiction by the royal family in terms of overseeing functions such as religious education and the annual pilgrimage, the *ulama* in Saudi Arabia have certainly played a more pervasive role than the "official" religious establishments found in several other Muslim countries. As we have already noted, they have also tended to play a prominent role in lending legitimacy to a wide range of political actions undertaken by the government and the ruling house. For example, the second monarch of Saudi Arabia, Abdul Aziz's son Saud, was widely viewed as incompetent by his own family, and the religious establishment played a key role in providing the Islamic justification behind the family's decision to remove him from the throne in 1964 in favor of his brother Faisal. But the influence of the religious scholars has by no means been absolute, witnessing considerable ebb and flow depending on which monarch has been on the Saudi throne and his vision of national priorities. Under King Faisal, for example, certain differences arose between the modernizing tendencies of the palace and the religious establishment, which made for a period during which the influence of the *ulama* was somewhat curtailed. In the wake of Faisal's assassination and the ensuing period of political and economic instability, however, the religious establishment was able to reassert itself under the new king in return for its support in maintaining social order.

The royal family has also employed certain measures and created institutions that have allowed them to exercise some degree of autonomy from the *ulama* in terms of introducing new laws. A number of legal regimes relating to labor and insurance were introduced in the early 1970s, for example, and the exercise of "administrative discretion"—a version of the *qanun* courts for customary law used by the Abbasids and the Ottomans—has also featured heavily. The *ulama* staff and perform a wide range of functions within the country's *shari'ah* court system, but they do so within the highly bureaucratic environment of the Ministry of Justice (rather than via a separate religious judiciary attached to the Councils of Ulama). The court system itself has also been amended on various occasions, adding layers of appeal beyond the *qadi,* and also establishing a special Board of Grievances that permits Saudi citizens some course of potential remedy in situations where they believe themselves to have suffered an injustice at the hands of the bureaucracy.

It is important to bear in mind that the negotiation and evolution of these relationships took place against a backdrop of tremendous and rapid modernization in terms of the Saudi economy, industry, infrastructure, military, and bureaucracy. Once serious oil revenues came on stream from the mid-1950s, the pace of change was frenetic. Inevitably, the rapid modernization of a society just one generation removed from a very traditional and conservative nomadic lifestyle would prove to be the source of considerable social tension—not only in terms of the compact between palace and *ulama,* but also in terms of the relationship between the royal family and a newly emerging, well-educated professional middle class. Of particular importance to the course of this development process were Saudi Arabia's relationships with the outside world, not least the United States. The idea of a "special relationship" between the Kingdom and Washington DC is best captured in the images of the iconic meeting between King Abdul Aziz and President Franklin Roosevelt in 1945. It was during this summit that the United States exchanged guaranteed access to Saudi oil for promises by the new global superpower to protect the sovereignty of the Kingdom and its royal family. While this covenant would represent the crux of the broad arc of U.S.–Saudi relations for the next half century and more, it was not always a smooth road. The Saudis raised objections in the mid-1950s, for

© Larry Downing / Reuters

Figure 5.1 Saudi Arabia has maintained a close relationship with the U.S.

example, to the extent of U.S. military support to Israel. The Palestine issue would rear its head again in the wake of the 1973 Arab–Israeli war, when Washington's crucial airlift of military supplies to Israel prompted a backlash from a number of Arab and Muslim oil-producing countries who realized that their influence over world oil prices could be used as a foreign policy weapon (not to mention an easy route to huge cash windfalls). Saudi oil revenues more than quadrupled over the single year from 1973 ($4.3 billion) to 1974 ($22.6 billion) and continued to climb precipitously to a high in 1980 of $102 billion.[2]

The role of Islam in Saudi foreign policy has also varied over the years. Although general support for Muslim causes abroad was a pillar of the Kingdom's foreign relations from very early on, Islam became a political issue in Saudi diplomacy only once the power balance in the Middle East region began to shift decisively in the mid- to late 1950s. The rise of Gamal Abdel Nasser in Egypt and his socialism-inflected brand of Pan-Arabism emerged as the dominant political current in the Arab world, and Cairo sought to exert influence over other countries in the region. Riyadh's response was to offer an alternative model of pan-Islamic solidarity, leveraging its symbolic power as the home of the two holy cities to challenge Egypt's efforts at establishing regional hegemony. The Kingdom would respond similarly to other instances of what it saw as imported Western ideology, such as Ba'athism in Syria and Iraq, and various experiments with Marxist thought throughout the region. Saudi–Egyptian rivalry continued for several years, nearly resulting in war when Egyptian troops entered Saudi Arabia's southern neighbor Yemen in 1962 to back the newly established republican government that was facing a strong challenge from Saudi-backed royalist forces. Also during this period, several of the more hardline activist leaders in the Egyptian Muslim Brotherhood—facing considerable persecution at the hands of Nasser's government—took refuge within the Saudi religious establishment. This would prove to be a significant development, as we will see, for the later development of Islamist opposition groups within the Kingdom. From the 1960s onwards, and particularly under King Faisal, Saudi Arabia played an instrumental role in establishing, funding, and providing leadership (both officially and unofficially) within a wide range of intergovernmental and nongovernmental Islamic organizations. It was the driving force, for example, behind the establishment of the Organization of the Islamic Conference, and also set up organizations such as the Muslim World League and the World Assembly of Muslim Youth as organs through which to express its pre-eminence within the Muslim world and to export aspects of Saudi-style Islam. Following the defeat of the Arab forces by Israel and the loss of Jerusalem during the Six Day War in 1967, Saudi Arabia saw an opportunity to package this to the rest of the Muslim world as the culmination of Nasser's failed secular nationalist project. In the wake of 1967, Riyadh became increasingly active in pro-Palestinian causes, and began for the first time directly to support the Palestine Liberation Organization (PLO). Saudi Arabia would also, at various times, provide support to Islamist parties abroad such as the MB in both Syria and Egypt, and also the Jama'at-i Islami (JI) in Pakistan. Riyadh also cultivated strong relationships with other prominent Sunni Muslim countries—with Pakistan, during the Islamization years of Zia ul-Haq, emerging as a particularly important ally in Riyadh's efforts to check Iran's growing influence in the Muslim world in the wake of that country's Islamic revolution.

The making of Islamist dissent in Saudi Arabia

Beginning with a major incident in 1979, but gathering significant and sustained force in the wake of the Gulf War of 1991, the Saudi establishment has faced various forms of internal political opposition. Most of this has been articulated in terms of questioning the religious credentials of the royal family, and has manifested itself as Islamism in various guises. In this section we chronicle the emergence and evolution of Islamism in the Kingdom, and situate this within the wider context of ongoing Saudi political development and world affairs.

It is certainly not the case that political opposition to the Saudi royal family was wholly absent until the late 1970s. Rather, the regime had proven itself particularly adept at co-opting dissent and maintaining the *status quo* in an already very conservative society. In order to better contextualize the emergence of overt discord during this period, we need to relate it to lingering tribal resentments dating back to the period when the first king, Abdul Aziz, turned against various elements within the Ikhwan forces that had enabled him to seize power. The religious establishment—and certainly the affected tribes—had long felt a sense of unease with the way Abdul Aziz had handled the Ikhwan revolt. Their suspicions increased when, in the years following the discovery of oil, more and more foreign workers and non-Muslims poured into the Kingdom to develop its industrial infrastructure. Abdul Aziz was even challenged by the *ulama* on the latter point. Sheikh Bin Baz, who would later rise to the rank of chief *mufti* within the official establishment, issued a *fatwa* in 1940s based on a *hadith* of the Prophet indicating that it was illegal to employ non-Muslims servants in Arabia. Bin Baz eventually backed down with reluctance but the incident identified him as autonomous-minded thinker, and over the years these credentials enabled him to play an important intermediary role between the royal family and the most hardline of scholars—even King Faisal once appointed him to head up the *ulama* establishment. One figure influenced and impressed by Bin Baz's early stance toward the regime was a young student at the University of Medina in the early 1970s named Juhayman al-Utaibi, who also happened to hail from the tribal areas connected with Abdul Aziz's crackdown on the Ikhwan. It seems to have been during his time at Medina—the institutional bedrock of Wahhabi thought—that Juhayman came to be convinced of the illegitimate nature of the Saud's rule. His complaints, however, were not just based on lingering soreness over Abdul Aziz's mistreatment of the Ikhwan. In the years following the latter's reign, and particular under the second king, Saud, the royal family had earned itself a considerable reputation for decadence and profligacy, even within the highest echelons of senior princes. Stories of immoral behavior by senior members of the royal family while vacationing abroad were rife, as were accounts of their lavish and excessive lifestyle. With some estimates claiming that 5 percent of all oil revenues went immediately into the private coffers of the Saud even before reaching the public treasury, it became clear how the family was able to sustain the enormous allowances paid to hundreds (if not thousands) of princes. Even the king at the time, Faisal, who did not have the same reputation for excess as his brothers, came in for suspicion due to his perceived Westernizing tendencies.

Certain that the Saud had abandoned all responsibility as proper Islamic leaders, Juhayman—who had served in the National Guard before entering university—moved onto an activist footing and spent several years constituting a small force modeled on the original Ikhwan. In November 1979, during the *hajj* season, Juhayman's forces dramatically seized control of the Grand Mosque in Mecca and held it for two weeks. His chief accomplice in this was Muhammad al-Qahtani, who claimed for himself the status of *Mahdi*—Islam's messianic figure. The regime secured a *fatwa* from the *ulama* to permit the use of force to expel the rebels, but Saudi Arabia's own national guard was unable to do this. Their initial failed attempt led to the death of over 100, and it is reported that some of them even decided to join Juhayman's forces. The siege ended after a fortnight when French and Pakistani special forces were finally brought in to subdue the rebels. Juhayman and his conspirators were jailed and most them eventually were executed. In addition to the public spectacle of the dissent itself, the regime's botched handling of the incident served only to confirm its inefficacy in the eyes of many.

The years following the Grand Mosque siege witnessed a relative upswing in the political fortunes of the *ulama*. Faisal's rather weak and short-lived successor, Khaled, did not undertake any meaningful reform in response to the events of 1979, but instead funneled ever more money to the religious establishment in return for their assistance in maintaining stability and the *status quo*. Saudi society had been shaken not only by the Mecca debacle, but by waves of riots that had broken out at the very same time within the Kingdom's Shi'a community (approximately 10 percent of the total population, concentrated in the oil-rich Eastern Province), newly emboldened by the recent success of their co-religionists' Islamic revolution in Iran. The *ulama* used their new-found influence to pressure the royal family and government on issues such as tightly enforced dress codes and various other measures relating to public virtue and proper religious observance. This climate also gave latitude to, and encouraged, the growth of a tendency that had been developing within the ranks of the religious scholars since the late 1960s. Commonly referred to as the Sahwa ("awakening") movement, this current can be described as a hybrid combination of Wahhabi theology with the political activism of the MB. Various influential thinkers from the more revolutionary wing of the MB had left Egypt for Saudi Arabia in the early 1970s. Among them, for example, was Muhammad Qutb, the brother of Sayyid Qutb (see Chapter 3), who eventually held various teaching positions within the Kingdom's religious university system. This ideological fusion led to the rise of a trend that might be thought of as a form of "activist Wahhabism" in contrast to the pietistic moralism traditionally associated with Saudi Salafism. As Gilles Kepel puts it, "Muhammad Qutb's reputation and his family's famous name attracted young readers who sought a confrontation between Islam and *jahiliyya* and yearned for invigorating, modern ideas for their battle against secularism, socialism, and the West."[3] It is worth noting here that, in the eyes of these young would-be activists, attraction to modern ideas and dislike of the West were not understood to be contradictory. This was a generation that had watched with a combination of wonder and ambivalence as their society was rapidly transformed. Their disillusion at what they saw as the culturally eroding effects of Western modernization led them to engage much more enthusiastically with approaches to political modernity developed by Islamic thinkers such as Hassan al-Banna and Sayyid Qutb. They were similarly disappointed by the religious establishment, which they viewed as too well co-opted by the Saudi regime ever to become an agent of meaningful Islamist reform.

During this same period, a major decline in world oil prices led to significant revenue shortfalls. From a high in 1980 of $102 billion, inflows dropped by some 80 percent over the next six years, putting a tight squeeze on the public budget, and forcing the government to begin reducing or abolishing outright a number of social welfare programs. Food and petrol subsidies declined, and the government was also forced to curb certain customary practices such as the promise of a job within the bureaucracy for every (male) Saudi who successfully completed university. The ranks of government positions by this point had swollen to such a point of redundancy that it was unable to sustain salaries, much less take in thousands of new employees each year.

This combination of factors made for a particularly volatile societal climate within the Kingdom in the late 1980s and 1990s. With the royal family's severe financial mismanagement more obvious than ever, the Gulf War of 1991 proved the major catalyzing event for the development of a concerted and sustained Islamist opposition. This was the case in several regards. First, although the Saudi government had spent an average of nearly $20 billion per year over the previous two decades to purchase from the United States and other Western countries the latest and most advanced weaponry systems (such as F-15 and Tornado jets), it became clear within days of Saddam Hussein's invasion of Kuwait that the Kingdom felt ill-prepared to defend itself against any Iraqi aggression. Instead, Riyadh was advised to accept U.S. military support, and within weeks the first of an eventual 500,000 foreign troops arrived in Saudi Arabia. Apart from the political disaster surrounding the Kingdom's inability to defend itself after so much military expenditure and foreign training, there was also the crisis associated with bringing hundreds of thousands of non-Muslim soldiers onto Saudi soil. If there had already been religious sensitivities surrounding the presence of purely civilian technical experts in the oil industry, it is easy to imagine the Wahhabi establishment's reaction to the stationing of a full scale "infidel" army in the land of the two Holy Cities. Anti-Saud sentiment increased considerably, particularly among nonestablishment *ulama* associated with the Sahwa movement. The final cost of the war was so high as to actually push the public budget temporarily into deficit, necessitating further austerity measures. In November 1990, in the midst of the uncertainty surrounding possible war with Iraq and the arrival of thousands of Western troops in Saudi Arabia, several dozen women drove into downtown Riyadh to stage a protest against the Saudi ban on women driving. While symbolically important in terms of the struggle for women's rights in the Kingdom, it is likely that this action at that time served mainly to embolden the religious sector. "This incident," Madawi al-Rasheed writes, "confirmed the fears of the Islamists, who thought that Saudi Arabia, its tradition and morality were now under greater threat than ever before."[4]

It was in this climate that Saudi Arabia saw the emergence in the 1990s of several political opposition movements. While various forms of Islamism certainly constituted the bulk of this activity, we should note that other political tendencies were present as well. One noteworthy instance of this was to be found in the petition presented to the king in early 1991. Signed by a group of commercial figures, writers, academic and former bureaucrats, this document requested the king to undertake a number of liberalizing reforms and to bring about a modicum of popular political participation through the establishment of a Consultative Council—something that almost every Saudi king had announced as an intention (particularly during times of popular discontent) but without ever following through on the commitment. Tighter restrictions on the power of the religious police were also suggested. It is worth noting that these early requests were not framed in terms of overt criticism of the Saud or their religious legitimacy; in fact, the tone is highly respectful and the signatories clearly emphasized their loyalty to the royal family. This document was followed several months later by a second petition, this one featuring the names of more than 50 religious scholars, with the Sahwa tendency particularly strongly represented. In stark contrast to the first petition, this text sought increased "Islamization" in all aspects of Saudi public life—with a particular emphasis on the conduct of government ministries—and a wider role for the *ulama* and *mutawwa*.

Two dissident *ulama* associated with the Sahwa movement emerged during the next few years as the figureheads of Saudi Arabia's new Islamism. The first of these, Safar al-Hawali, who hailed from the western Arabian town of Hawla, had been a former student of Muhammad Qutb. The second and slightly younger of the two, Salman al-Awdah, was from the town of Buraida in the Nejdi heartland of both the Saud and Wahhabism. In the late summer of 1992, these two figures were the masterminds behind a much more expansive protest document known the "Memorandum of Advice." The use of the term "advice" (*nasiha*) is significant insofar as various classical Islamic sources cite the offering of advice by Muslim citizens to their rulers as an obligation. The title was hence a political claim in its own right, testifying that not only was this action permissible under the *shari'ah,* but actually was *required.* This document was far more accusatory in tone, suggesting that the government and royal family had failed in their duty to uphold the *shari'ah,* and detailing a wide range of reforms to be carried out in nearly every sector of society. As "unofficial" *ulama* who had developed something of a reputation as dissidents, the public lectures of Hawali and Awdah had already been subject to restriction. The *nasiha* document attracted increased scrutiny of their activities, and both were subsequently arrested over the next two years as part of a large government crackdown on anti-establishment preachers. Significantly, the royal family looked to the official religious sector to condemn the document, but were left wanting in the response they received. While Bin Baz did offer a *fatwa* that warned against the threat of *fitna* (civil disorder) stemming from publishing the *nasiha* in such a public way, he did not pass judgment on any of its content.[5] Over the next two years, several protests calling for the release of Hawali and Awdah and the enactment of the *nasiha* demands took place in areas such as the Nejd—particularly in and around the latter's stronghold in Buraida—necessitating further arrests and governmental restrictions. More militant tendencies were also at work in the Kingdom, and both 1995 and 1996 saw bomb attacks on U.S. military facilities. It became clear that, in addition to the conventional Islamism of the Sahwa, there were elements of Usama Bin Laden's jihadist networks at work on the peninsula in the guise of the so-called Advice and Reform Committee.[6] Usama Bin Laden, son of one of the Kingdom's great industrial and commercial families, had gone to Afghanistan to fight alongside that country's mujahideen against the Soviets in the 1980s. Here he linked up with militant Islamists of varying national origins and began to assemble the network that would eventually become Al-Qaeda (see Chapter 7). Repulsed by a royal family that he perceived as having sold out to the West, he developed strong anti-regime views and was eventually stripped of his Saudi citizenship in the early 1990s. Strong condemnation of the Saud's rule and associated policies such as the continued presence of foreign troops in Arabia have been mainstays of the Bin Laden worldview for over a decade.

In the face of such unprecedented activist pressure, the king announced in 1992 the establishment of a national-scale *Majlis al-Shura* (Consultative Council) in addition to the promulgation of a new Basic Law—the closest Saudi Arabia had ever come to having a constitution. The Majlis, it should be noted, is not a legislative institution, but rather a representative body charged with the task of providing guidance to the king on various matters of state and public interest. Its religious legitimacy derives from the Qur'anic injunction to the effect that all matters of concern to the community should be decided through consultation (*shura*) amongst stakeholders. King Abdul Aziz set up a consultative body of sorts in the 1920s, but it never became more than a small and marginal presence. The new body set up in 1992, while hardly a potent institution in terms of its political power, was significant in a number of respects. Initially composed of 60 members, the size of the Majlis was later expanded to 150. All are appointed by the king, and charged with the review of laws and other matters brought before it, or issues of concern adopted by the Council itself. Although it possesses little in the way of formal power (legislative or executive oversight), the Majlis al-Shura has evolved into an important component of the Saudi political system. While the king is not in any way required to act on its guidance, he cannot simply ignore the view of the Majlis. The professional composition of its membership is also significant in that, unlike many other political bodies in the Kingdom that pronounce on matters of public good, the members of the Council are not primarily religious scholars. Instead they are mainly former bureaucrats and ministers, prominent commercial figures, and intellectuals. In this regard it can be argued that the Majlis provides some modicum of check against the monopoly of the *ulama* in public life. Particularly in recent years, as the imperatives for genuine reform have become clearer, the Council's growing influence as an institutionalized voice of managed change has consolidated somewhat. For example, from 2013 it was announced that 20 percent of the seats in the Majlis would be reserved for women. This was regarded as a response from the palace to increased public attention in recent years to the role of women in Saudi society.

The next phase of Islamist opposition, from late 1994, saw several of the key activist figures relocating to the relative safety of countries outside the Kingdom. The most important of these groups, the Committee for the Defense of Legitimate Rights (CDLR), set up shop in London and managed to garner considerable media attention for itself. A partnership between two scientists with Sahwa sympathies, Muhammad al-Mass'ari and Sa'ad al-Faqih, the CDLR waged a public relations campaign with the Saudi regime by distributing literature and sending thousands of faxes each day to government offices in the Kingdom. When Riyadh raised concerns with the British government about their activities and requested that they be shut down (with the tacit threat of jeopardizing future Saudi arms purchases), Al-Mass'ari won an injunction in the high court granting him indefinite leave to remain in the UK. This served only to draw more attention to the group, and they were at the height of their notoriety when a dispute between the movement's leaders led to a split and a significant loss of reputation within the Kingdom itself. Mass'ari, who kept the name CDLR, insinuated that Faqih may have been co-opted by the regime, while Faqih criticized Mass'ari—a highly flamboyant public personality—for allying the CDLR with globally oriented Islamist movements such as Omar Bakri Muhammad, Hizb ut-Tahrir, and al-Muhajiroun (see Chapter 7). Faqih, wanting to maintain a strict Saudi focus to their work, initiated a successor group, the Movement for Islamic Reform in Arabia, but never managed to regain quite the momentum CDLR had in its early days. The Movement for Islamic Reform has continued to publish materials and publicize otherwise unreported events in the Kingdom.

Within Saudi Arabia itself, the regime successfully weathered the difficult period of the early and mid-1990s and managed to reassert itself by the end of the decade. King Fahd's failing health after a stroke in 1995 led to a frenzy of speculation amongst Saudi watchers as to the regime's stability. The Crown Prince, Abdullah, as a half-brother to the other senior princes (the so-called "Sudeiri Seven"), was considered to be in a weak position, with the possibility that another of Abdul Aziz's sons might claim the throne on Fahd's death—or even that the succession might skip a generation. Abdullah was also known to be highly religious, and in the past had made remarks critical of certain aspects of the Kingdom's relations with the United States—and this had led some to conclude that he might have been significantly less pro-Western, or might once again use oil as a geopolitical tool. By the late 1990s, it became clear that the family had rallied around Abdullah, who was now effectively in day-to-day control of the Kingdom. Most of the dissident activists had been co-opted or imprisoned, and even figures such as Safar al-Hawali and Salman al-Awdah had been released from prison. Al-Awdah has regained public prominence within and beyond the Kingdom—initially by dropping his anti-establishment rhetoric—starting a website (www.islamtoday.net) and even a television program. Today he has become one of the most widely followed Salafi scholars on social media globally. Inevitably, there was considerable speculation in the wake of his "rehabilitation" as to whether he had been co-opted by the establishment, or had decided that toning down the activism in favor of gradualism is more likely to produce meaningful pro-Islamic reform. Of course, these two views are not necessarily mutually exclusive. In the aftermath of the Arab Uprisings of 2011, for example, Al-Awdah began directly to criticize the

Saudi authorities. Some of the former Sahwa *ulama* appear to have moderated their discourse more thoroughly, however, advocating an unlikely fusion of Islamism and liberalism.[7]

The most recent phase of Saudi Islamism can be dated to the aftermath of the 9/11 attacks on the United States. Fifteen of the 19 hijackers who flew planes into American targets that day were Saudi citizens, placing new strain on U.S.–Saudi relations amidst calls for Riyadh to crack down on militant currents within the Kingdom. During 2002, and several times again in 2003 after the U.S. invasion of Iraq (which occurred with more Saudi support than was publicly acknowledged by either side), various targets in Saudi Arabia were struck by militants claiming affiliation with Usama Bin Laden. In 2005 and 2006, officials became even more alarmed when attacks moved into the strategic Eastern Province—including an attempted bombing at Abqaiq, one of the nerve centers of the Kingdom's oil industry. Over the next few years, Saudi authorities would announce the arrest of hundreds of suspected militants in the Kingdom, many of whom had developed links and collaborations with jihadi networks in Iraq. With the perception that Islamic militancy based within Saudi Arabia itself was a growing problem, the Saudi Ministry of the Interior introduced a well-funded and much-vaunted "deradicalization" program in the mid-2000s—eventually claiming to have steered thousands away from *jihad*. Most analysts acknowledge that the Saudi approach, which combined both ideological training and the promise of extensive material benefits (jobs, homes, marriage partners), had been generally effective, although not necessarily on the scale claimed in official figures and not without problems relating to recidivism.[8]

The confusing landscape of Islamist opposition in Saudi Arabia can thus be said to consist today of three main strands, which function together as an ecosystem of sorts. The first of these is the Sahwa movement, representing the fusion of Wahhabi thought with MB-style activism. The vanguard of the opposition in the early 1990s, this group has now apparently moved towards a more gradualist orientation, with some members almost holding "quasi-official" status. With greater pressure for liberalizing reform in the wake of 9/11, the Sahwa seeks to reject this path in favor of Islamizing reform, but from an avowedly moderate and—by Saudi standards—relatively centrist stance. The second, and as yet still rather nascent, current is the one represented by the new Islamic liberals. Many of the relevant figures here, such as Mansur al-Nuqaidan and Hasan al-Maliki, formerly were associated with the Sahwa movement or even more radical groups. Having become disillusioned with Wahhabism, but still eager to maintain their Islamic credentials, they have sought to offer a religious critique of the Salafi–jihadi tendency and to keep the focus of their efforts on reform at the societal rather than political level. Their argument is essentially that Saudi society is not yet ready to deal with political openness, and to bring this now would only entrench the Wahhabi establishment further since this is the only normative discourse that most Saudis can recognize at this point.[9] The final Islamist tendency is to be found in the umbrella group Al-Qaeda on the Arabian Peninsula (AQAP—see chapter 7), the inheritors of the legacy of the Bin Laden-oriented Advice and Reform Committee, and a direct off-shoot of his early efforts in Afghanistan. Most of the regime's anti-Islamist efforts in recent years have been aimed primarily at identifying cells and affiliates of this group, since it is generally viewed as representing the greatest threat of violence in the short term. In the late 2000s, Saudi Arabia provided close counter-terrorism to the United States in combined efforts to target AQAP's leaders based in Yemen. AQAP ideologues such as the Yemeni–American Anwar al-Awlaki, widely regarded as the founder of Al-Qaeda's English-language magazine *Inspire,* had become a particular focus of U.S. efforts after his name cropped up in connection with a number of efforts to mount attacks in the United States. Saudi Arabia also regarded AQAP—whose position within the global jihadist movement we discuss further in Chapter 7—as a potential source of instability along its southern frontier, as well as a source of Islamic militancy elsewhere in the Kingdom.

How is Saudi Islamism likely to evolve in the coming years? This will most likely turn out to be a function of how the regime balances competing social, political, and religious forces during this very sensitive and volatile period of reform and transition. While the royal family seems now to have understood that undertaking genuine reform is necessary in order to permit the Kingdom in its present form to last into the next century, the challenge will be to make this happen quickly enough to stave off rapidly escalating social tensions, but not so quickly as to bring about instability and the collapse of social cohesion. Since the death of Fahd in 2005, the new king, Abdullah, has shown himself above all to be a pragmatist. The path to reform may also turn out to be something of a personal race for Abdullah since, like most of the other princes in direct line to the throne, he is nearly an octogenarian. Soon the royal succession will have to move down a generation, and for the most part this bodes well since the Western-educated grandchildren of Abdul Aziz tend to be more sensitive to the need for reform and to the exigencies of a global world than their fathers have been. There have been a few signs that the Kingdom is moving slowly in this direction. In 2005, in the Kingdom's first-ever national-scale elections, Saudi (male) citizens voted to choose the members of new municipal councils. While the role and powers of these councils are still unclear, and the winners tended to be those candidates who had received a nod of approval from the religious establishment, many observers have suggested that, in a society as closed as Saudi Arabia's, any participatory process of this sort is a salutary step. The regime had promised that for the next round of elections in 2011, women would also be allowed to vote, but in the run-up to balloting in that year it was announced that women would be excluded until the subsequent election in 2015. At around the same time, a group of women in the capital mounted a protest against the ban on women driving, initiating a new period of debate about the role of women in Saudi society. The admission of women to the Majlis al-Shura, announced in 2013, was widely perceived as an effort by the palace to appear responsive to these debates.

BOX 5.1 WOMEN AND POLITICAL ISLAM

Many observers of Islamist groups and countries that style themselves as "Islamic states" have expressed concern about the status and role of women in these societies. Islamist movements vary considerably in terms of their views on women, although it is safe to say that, for the most part, they advance a relatively conservative understanding of the position of women in society and public life. In some of the more extreme cases, such as Saudi Arabia, women are effectively invisible in the public sphere and live an entirely segregated existence. Under the strict interpretation of Islamic law enforced in the Kingdom, women are unable to drive and are expected to be accompanied by a male family member when out in public. In the Islamic Republic of Iran, women have more latitude to work and contribute to civil society and public life, albeit in the face of certain restrictions relating to modest dress.

Most modern Islamist movements, such as the MB, are comfortable speaking in terms of the equality of women in terms of faith, but then argue that Islam teaches that women have a different role in society—one focused primarily on the domestic realm and family care. Feminists in the Muslim world—of whom there are many—fear that under Islamist rule women could find themselves subject to various forms of restrictions or exclusion. A literal application of Islamic law could also severely disadvantage women involved in legal proceedings due to the disproportionate weight granted to evidence presented by men and the burden of evidence required to be presented by women bringing various claims before a *shari'ah* court.

But the issue of women and political Islam is a complex one. Major Islamist movements such as the MB, Hamas, and Hizbullah count many women among their members—although, it should be noted, they usually participate through separate, segregated women's branches, and are all but absent from the ruling bodies of these movements.

Over the past two decades there has been a bourgeoning academic literature on the role of women in relation to modern Islamist movements, as well as efforts to develop an Islamic approach to feminism.

Further study

L. Ahmed, *Women and Gender in Islam: Historical Roots of a Modern Debate*, New Haven, CT: Yale University Press, 1992.

L. Ahmed, *A Quiet Revolution: The Veil's Resurgence, from the Middle East to America,* New Haven, CT: Yale University Press, 2012.

L. Deeb, *An Enchanted Modern: Gender and Public Piety in Shi'i Lebanon,* Princeton, NJ: Princeton University Press, 2006.

D. Kandiyoti (ed.), *Women, Islam and the State,* Philadelphia, PA: Temple University Press, 1991.

S. Mahmood, *Politics of Piety: The Islamic Revival and the Feminist Subject,* Princeton, NJ: Princeton University Press, 2005.

Z. Mir-Hosseini et al., *Gender and Equality in Muslim Family Law: Justice and Ethics in the Islamic Legal Process,* London: I.B. Tauris, 2013.

Abdullah's credentials to steward such a reform process are relatively strong. He is not tainted by the penchant for decadence and excess that is associated with his siblings. His religious credentials and personal piety are beyond reproach, and he has always maintained strong relations with the tribally organized national guard—which means that his power base is relatively secure. Fears in the West about an anti-American bias have so far proved unfounded, with pragmatism tending to guide his foreign relations and energy policy. In the wake of 9/11 and the Iraq War, surging oil prices have brought Saudi revenues back up to levels not seen since the late 1970s. But the successful management of this much-needed transition will still depend on Abdullah—and his successors—carrying the center-right bulk of Saudi society along with him. The challenges are many, and Abdullah, whose time on the throne is limited given his age, will likely have difficulty managing the pace and extent of reforms in the context of a complex and conservative Saudi society that seeks reforms even as it harbors skepticism about broad-based change. The events of 2011 elsewhere in the Arab world demonstrated that considerable wellsprings of tension and volatility simmer just below the surface in much of the region. Abdullah has managed to introduce a number of gradual reforms, some of which have been covered above. Several others are particularly noteworthy because they bear directly on the nature of the relationship between the Saudi state, the religious establishment, and the country's legal system. In 2007, for example, Abdullah introduced judicial reforms designed to generate greater consistency in the application of *shari'ah* law and to allow some categories of cases to be heard in independent tribunals. In 2010, with many alarmed at some of the more extreme pronouncements coming from clerics affiliated in various ways with the Saudi religious establishment, it was announced that only scholars from the Senior Council of Ulama would be permitted to issue *fatawa*. From 2009, Abdullah announced a new initiative focused on interreligious dialogue, including a major summit in Spain and plans for a new center for promoting religious pluralism based in Vienna.

The Saudi response to the 2011 popular revolutions in Tunisia and Egypt was indicative of the many challenges faced by the Kingdom going forward. Beyond relatively small-scale demonstrations in the country's Eastern Province and mostly abortive attempts to organize protests in other cities, Saudi Arabia managed to avoid widespread impact from the Arab Uprisings. This is not because the Kingdom is immune to the pressures that brought millions out onto the streets of Tunisia, Egypt, Yemen, Syria, Libya, and Bahrain. Indeed, in the case of the latter country, where Shi'a-led demonstrations were brutally quelled by the state, Riyadh acted quickly to contain problems in its neighbors by sending Saudi forces (nominally under a GCC umbrella and technically at the invitation of the Bahraini authorities) to contain any elements that might seek to mobilize Shi'a in the Kingdom's Eastern Province. In fact, Saudi Arabia suffers from its own version of the very same problems—educated but unemployed youth, growing socioeconomic inequality—that were at the root of uprisings elsewhere. Where Saudi Arabia differs, however, is in its capacity to respond to such problems. In 2011, following the outbreak of mass protests across the region, King Abdullah announced a $130 billion program of salary increases for government workers, job-creation schemes, and subsidy increases—all specifically designed to immunize Saudi Arabia against what appeared to be a regional contagion. Later, as the MB gained political prominence and power in Egypt and Tunisia, Saudi Arabia was among those countries—such as the UAE—that sought to counter their influence for fear that it would inspire an increase in Islamically-based political opposition closer to home. The Saudis were widely suspected of providing support to the rapidly growing Salafi influence in countries like Egypt and Tunisia in the hope that it might serve as a counterbalance to the MB.

While it seems that the Kingdom succeeded in using its massive oil revenues to prevent immediate social instability, it is questionable how long this strategy can work in the face of the complex generational changes currently underway in the country. The deaths of two crown princes in close succession (Princes Sultan and Nayef), in 2011 and 2012, throw into relief the problems that Saudi Arabia faces in consolidating stable leadership under the current system. The considerable cultural, economic—and, increasingly, political—tensions present in the Kingdom today will not easily be assuaged, nor will the influence of the Wahhabi religious establishment (either at home or abroad) be easily contained. Most Saudis, as we have seen, still define their social and political identities in religious terms, and public discourse will continue for some time to be animated primarily by Islamic idioms and symbols.

PAKISTAN: POLITICS AND RELIGION IN AN AMBIGUOUSLY ISLAMIC STATE

Created as a homeland for Muslims of the subcontinent at the time of India's independence and partition in 1947, Pakistan's subsequent political history has reflected the fact that, in this particular context, the question of just what it means to be an Islamic state has never been definitively settled. Secularizing and Islamizing paths have been pursued by military and civilian regimes alike, with different actors advancing a wide range of claims about the meaning and nature of religion in Pakistani public life. This section first briefly reviews the circumstances surrounding Pakistan's foundation, then moves on to examine the changing course of the debate about Islam and the state through a short survey of the country's political and constitutional history. Next we consider the place of Islam in the contemporary political landscape of Pakistan, looking at former President Musharraf's attempts to co-opt certain forms of Islamism while keeping other currents of politicized religion at bay, and the subsequent collapse of the main Islamist coalition amidst rapidly evolving power dynamics in Pakistan. We then go on to look more closely at the main groups within Pakistani society agitating for a greater political role for Islam, focusing specifically on the JI and its evolving relationship with the state. We also examine some of the dynamics surrounding the apparent growth in recent years of religious intolerance and sectarianism. The section concludes by drawing out several key analytical themes that will help us to compare and contrast Pakistan not only with the Saudi case surveyed above, but also with the subsequent and final example of the Islamic state to be included in this chapter—that of Iran.

As we will recall, the idea of Pakistan was first advanced as a political cause by the Muslim League of India and Muhammad Ali Jinnah when Muslims came to be increasingly concerned about their fate in a Hindu-dominated India in the run-up to that country's independence after World War II. Jinnah's famous "Two Nations Theory" advanced the claim that, due to their religious differences, India's Muslims and Hindus were effectively two different national peoples, with their own unique histories and cultures. According to his logic, separate national homelands for each was the only possible political solution. To the highly Westernized and secular Jinnah, there did not appear to be any tension between this form of nationalist discourse and Islam. For those of a more religious, and particularly Islamist, persuasion, however, nationalism was anathema to Islam, leading them to reject the cause of a separate Pakistan. The leading voice in this camp was undoubtedly Abu'l-A'la Mawdudi, whose general approach to Islamism we have looked at in some detail in Chapter 3. The traditional religious scholars, such as those associated with major seminaries such as Deoband near Delhi, did not intervene directly in these debates and tended to default to a position that would have kept Muslims as part of India—perhaps with some measure of communal autonomy as regards the application of personal status law. In the wake of widespread violence between Muslims and Hindus from 1946, the Indian Congress Party consented to the idea of partition, and Pakistan was founded in August 1947 with Jinnah as its first Governor-General and effective head of government. The new country was composed of two distinct regions separated by over 1,000 miles of Indian territory. "West Pakistan" was composed primarily of the Punjab, Sindh, and Balochistan. "East Pakistan," which would become Bangladesh in 1971, consisted of most of the former Indian province of Bengal. The mountainous northern region of Kashmir has been claimed by both India and Pakistan, and has been the subject of several wars between the two since as far back as 1948.

The first years of Pakistan's existence were occupied primarily with the settlement of ongoing violence and the establishment of basic state institutions. Given the immediate territorial dispute and subsequent war with India over Kashmir, the military quickly became one of the most important prominent and influential institutions within Pakistani politics—the importance of which will become clear below. Mawdudi and the JI elected to remain in Pakistan and set themselves up as the leading voices advocating for a thoroughly Islamic political order in the new Muslim state. As regards the role of religion and politics, these early years were characterized by considerable debate between the secularizing tendencies of Jinnah (who died very shortly after the country's founding) and his followers, and the Islamism of Mawdudi and the JI. For the former group, Pakistan's status as an Islamic state was not meant to imply much more beyond the idea of a national homeland for Muslims. For Mawdudi and his JI followers, however, the creation of an Islamic social and political order was incumbent upon the new country's rulers. The impasse that arose between these two distinctive visions is illustrated by the fact that it took almost ten years to negotiate the country's first constitution. In the meantime, a temporary "Objectives Resolution" (1949) offered a minimal sense of state legitimacy. It opened with a statement to the effect that sovereignty belongs to God alone, and stated a desire for Muslims in Pakistan to be "enabled" to live their lives according to the prescriptions of the Qur'an and *sunna*.

Two further events that occurred during Pakistan's first decade also help to illustrate the tensions between these two approaches to the Islamic state. During the process of negotiations leading up to the first constitution, those from the religious sector (mainly Islamists and *ulama*) requested that the government declare members of the *Ahmadiyya* sect to be non-Muslims. The Ahmadis are named after Mirza Ghulam Ahmad, a religious reformer from the late nineteenth century. They are controversial because one subset of the movement regards Mirza Ghulam Ahmad as a prophet, raising the ire of orthodox Muslims—such as those represented by the Deoband establishment in Pakistan—who recognize no prophets after Muhammad. These views have made Pakistan's Ahmadi community the target of consistent persecution and violence since the country's founding. In the early 1950s, the Islamists—Mawdudi among them—argued that followers of the Ahmadiyya movement could not hold prominent government positions since they did not qualify as "true" Muslims. The ensuing public debate led to widespread rioting and violence against Ahmadis in the Punjab. In the wake of the investigation that followed, Mawdudi himself was convicted of inciting religious hatred and violence, jailed, and eventually even condemned to death—a sentence that was later abrogated. The Ahmadiyya controversy is important because it forced the Pakistani state for the first time to confront certain basic questions regarding who counted as a Muslim and how an Islamic state should behave towards Muslims and non-Muslims alike.[10] The second notable event was the adoption in 1956 of the country's first constitution. This document, for the most part, seemed to represent a vindication of the Muhammad Ali Jinnah vision. The bulk of it was devoted to outlining a modern parliamentary republic and to spelling out the division of competences between various institutions of state. Several components of this first constitution also mentioned religion, but in many cases these were largely symbolic, or left considerable room for interpretation: the name of the country was specified as the "Islamic Republic of Pakistan"; the state was based on "Islamic principles" (without explaining what these might be); the head of state was to be a Muslim; and a research institution was to be created, charged with drawing up guidelines relating to the Islamization of society. Finally, this first constitution also contained the so-called "Repugnancy Clause," which specified that no law could be adopted in contradiction to Islam.

BOX 5.2 RELIGIOUS MINORITIES AND POLITICAL ISLAM

Many Muslim-majority countries across the Middle East, South Asia, and Southeast Asia also have significant religious minority communities—including Christians, Jews, Hindus, and Baha'i, as well as some groups who consider themselves to be Muslims but whose status as such is denied by the state or prevailing religious authorities (such as the Ahmadiyya, Alevis, and some Shi'i communities). While Christians and Jews are given a privileged status in Islam as fellow "people of the book" (ahl al-kitab), many members of these communities fear that under Islamist rule they would—and in some cases do—live as second-class citizens. Hence, for example, the skepticism expressed by many Coptic Christians in Egypt regarding Hosni Mubarak's ouster in 2011. While Egypt's Christians did not hesitate to criticize Mubarak's regime for its authoritarianism and inability to solve the country's many problems, they were also aware that the secular state enforced by that government provided them with a certain measure of protection. With the rising influence of Salafism in Egypt after 2011, and despite assurances from Islamists such as the MB that Islamic law could only ever be applied to Muslims, religious minorities in the Middle East have continued to express anxiety amidst the ongoing turbulence and uncertainty that has followed the Arab Uprisings.

Elsewhere in the Middle East, minority religious groups such as Baha'i in Iran and Shi'a in Saudi Arabia and Bahrain have continued to face persecution and exclusion from society and politics—in some cases prompting the insertion of a new sectarian element into regional politics. Pakistan has also seen renewed tensions and violence around non-Muslim or heterodox Muslim communities in recent years, and in Southeast Asia Indonesia has seen various waves of anti-Christian, anti-Hindu, and anti-Chinese sentiment. While many of the constitutions of these countries—including Arab nations—contain language expressly guaranteeing religious freedom, such statutes are enforced only selectively. Emotions in society often run very high around issues of religious identity, and governments frequently hesitate to defend groups that find themselves on the receiving end of persecution or hate crimes.

The years between 1958 and 1977 represented a relative decline in the influence of the religious sector in Pakistan, but certainly not the disappearance of Islam from political discourse. Following the imposition of martial law and Muhammad Ayub Khan's coup in 1958, the government began to pursue a new course of Islamic modernization. Ayub Khan sought to implement an intensely secularizing approach to national development, looking to models such as modern Turkey under Mustapha Kemal. Westernization and rapid economic development were his core goals, and he sought to reform and tame the religious establishment so as to bring it in line with this project. Part of this involved revising the constitution in 1962, but Ayub Khan's attempts to remove many of the Islamic provisions of the 1956 document were soon rebuffed by a subsequent amendment. The 1962 version included a new section on "Islamic Institutions," which called for the creation of an Islamic Council to offer advice regarding the Islamic character of legislation. This body had relatively little real power, however, due to its advisory nature. Unlike, for example, the Guardianship Council in Iran, which is required to scrutinize every law adopted by parliament, legislators in Pakistan were free to bypass or ignore the Islamic Council. To head up the Islamic research council mandated by both versions of the constitution, Ayub Khan appointed Fazlur Rahman, a Western-trained intellectual, and charged him with assisting the government to promulgate a modernist interpretation of Islam compatible with the regime's national priorities. So not only did Ayub Khan pursue a secular path, but he also began to stake a claim by the state to speak on behalf of and to define the meaning of Islam for society. Perhaps unsurprisingly, this brought him into direct confrontation with the religious establishment, particularly when he sought to reform family law—an area the *ulama* regarded as their core turf—along modernist lines. The differing arguments presented by the modernist and *ulama* members of the Commission on Marriage and Family Laws also serve to illustrate once again the clear divide over the two approaches to Pakistan as an Islamic state, alluded to above. The modernists, for their part, advanced the claim that, because it would be impossible for the classic Islamic sources to imagine comprehensively the full range of circumstances and issues that would face humanity in the course of its development, it was necessary to leave considerable space for independent and innovative interpretation of religion within the "broad framework" of the Qur'an and *sunna*. The religious establishment, incensed by what it perceived as a frontal assault on its authority, accused the Commission of ignoring centuries of settled jurisprudential precedent, and questioned their authority to make any pronouncements regarding matters of religion.[11]

The next phase of the evolving dance between the state and Islam is associated with Zulfikar Ali Bhutto's tenure as President and Prime Minister (1971–77). In the late 1960s, East Pakistan's sense of marginalization within the republic had grown to a point where its population elected advocates of political separatism to almost all of East Pakistan's parliamentary seats in the 1970 elections. Widespread violence broke out when Yahya Khan (Ayub's successor) arrested the leader of this movement and sent the military into the East to suppress Bengali opposition. The leaders of East Pakistan declared independence as the new state of Bangladesh and a full-blown war developed over the ensuing months—ending quickly and decisively in favor of Bangladesh soon after India entered the conflict against Pakistan. The collapse of Yahya Khan's regime in the wake of this loss brought Bhutto to power. His party, the Pakistan People's Party (PPP), represented a largely socialist orientation and drew its support primarily from rural areas and the urban poor. Economic nationalism and agrarian reform were his initial priorities, as was to be expected, but Bhutto soon found himself having to adopt more and more religious rhetoric and symbolism in his policy-making, particularly in the face of rising government corruption and the failure of his economic initiatives. The religious establishment had been suspicious as to whether a committed socialist could ever be a Muslim, and were almost immediately hostile to his government. Bhutto sought to paint an Islamic face on much of his political platform, describing his policies as the pursuit of Qur'anic social justice in the name of, for example, Musawat-i-Muhammadi ("Muhammad's egalitarianism"). A new constitution in 1973 redistributed the balance of power between Pakistan's constituent provinces and its two senior government positions, in addition to enshrining Islam as the religion of state. In order to placate the *ulama,* he also compromised in terms of several issues long on their agenda. The weekly holiday was changed from Sunday to Friday, the Muslim holy day, and in 1974 he settled the Ahmadiyya issue by amending the oath of office taken by Pakistan's leaders to include a statement recognizing the final prophethood of Muhammad.[12] In terms of international relations, after the loss of Bangladesh Bhutto sought to emphasize Pakistan's affinities with the Arab world, securing new development funding for the country in the name of Islamic solidarity, and establishing a prominent role for Pakistan in the emerging bloc of Islamic nations whose geopolitical role had been enhanced in the wake of the oil shock of 1973.

The religious sector remained unconvinced, however, and in the run-up to the 1977 elections they formed a political umbrella called the Pakistan National Alliance (PNA) to challenge Bhutto's PPP. This coalition was driven by the JI, but also contained other religious parties and groups, including those representing the traditional *ulama.* Their basic complaint related to the intense corruption associated with Bhutto's regime, and they held out "true Islamization" as the antidote. Demographically, it is significant to note that their base of support was to be found primarily among the middle and lower-middle classes, as opposed to the PPP, which depended on the seeming unlikely combination of hardcore support among the political elite and the rural poor. Although Bhutto handily won the elections in 1977, the PNA refused to end its campaign against him, alleging poll fraud and undertaking a widespread national effort to discredit his leadership. It was the ongoing conflict between these two forces—the state and the religious sector—that was used by army chief Zia ul-Haq in July 1977 to undertake a *coup d'état* and declare martial law in the name of both Islam and national unity.

Zia's 11-year rule (1977–88) is particularly interesting for our purposes, given the centrality of Islamization to his endeavors. To begin with, his coup had been justified as necessary for the establishment in Pakistan of the "System of the Prophet." Zia immediately reached out to the PNA alliance, and particularly the JI, to be his partners in this project. They responded enthusiastically, hearing Zia's proposals—such as the introduction of an Islamic criminal code (*hudud*) and an interest-free economy—the closest any regime had come to the comprehensive Islamization of society that they had been seeking since Pakistan's founding. Not only were members of the JI appointed to cabinet positions (marking the first time they had ever served in government), but the Islamic Council created by the 1962 constitution was revamped to act as a direct advisory body to the executive. Significantly, however, Zia maintained martial law for eight years (after promising elections within 90 days of taking power) and also suspended certain democratic provisions in the constitution so that, he claimed, they could be reviewed to ensure their compatibility with the *shari'ah*.

Much of the Islamist enthusiasm for Zia's Islamization program was due to the fact that it was enacted across a wide range of social sectors. He created a system of Shari'ah Courts charged with ensuring that all laws in Pakistan were in accordance with Islam (although the martial law provisions and national taxation practices were exempt) and also legalized state enforcement of public virtue (e.g. no public consumption of food or drink during daylight hours in Ramadan). Other areas of social practice derived from religion that had previously been informally or privately regulated were also brought within the purview of the state. So, for example, with regard to the *zakat* system of alms (one of the five pillars of the religion) the government instituted a system whereby a 2.5 percent tax was levied annually on all bank accounts. This produced considerable discontent among both the country's Shi'a population, whose traditions handle the payment of *zakat* differently, and some segments of the urban populations who, as the only holders of bank accounts, felt unfairly targeted by this system of enforced direct tithing. Islamic studies became mandatory at all levels of education, and a new International Islamic University was established in Islamabad. The diplomas issued by the country's *madrasas* (religious schools) were also deemed to be the equivalent of secular university degrees, meaning the *madrasa* graduates would be eligible for positions in the government bureaucracy.[13] Under Zia and with the resounding approval of the conservative *ulama,* a number of measures that particularly affected women were undertaken—most notably a provision to create universities separated by sex, and to revise the Law of Evidence Act to reflect the view that evidence presented by a woman is worth only half that presented by a man.[14]

Although much of this would clearly be to the liking of the *ulama* and the Islamists, it was not long before they began to have concerns about Zia's regime. It became clear to them after several years that there were distinct limitations on how much political influence he would allow the Islamists to have. So long as their interests and input were confined to matters of religion, Zia was happy to listen. Once the Islamists began to pursue a wider political role for themselves in the wake of their first taste of real power, they suddenly found doors closing in their faces. As Husain Haqqani puts it, Zia "realized that he had overestimated the Jama'at-i Islami's ability to run a modern Islamic state."[15] Consequently he widened the breadth of his consultation on Islamic issues such that the Jama'at became one of many voices—from Pakistan and from abroad—contributing to Zia's Islamization project, including traditionally apolitical groups such as the Tablighi Jama'at. Zia cultivated close ties with Muslim allies such as Saudi Arabia, where remittances from thousands of Pakistani migrant laborers provided an economic boost. As Pakistan's strategic importance to United States Cold War interests in the region grew, financial support from Washington

© Jama'at-I Islami party constitution

Figure 5.2 Cover of the Jama'at-i Islami party constitution

for Zia's regime increased nearly threefold to $4.2 billion in combined development and military aid.[16] Much of this was linked to Pakistan's strong support for anti-Soviet forces across the border in Afghanistan, and contributed to the development and consolidation in northern parts of the country of a militant strain of Islamism (see Chapters 6 and 7).

As its discontent with Zia increased, the JI found itself in the predicament of trying to direct credible criticism toward a regime whose legitimacy they had done so much to build in its early years.[17] Initially this dispute led to some seemingly contradictory policies on the part of the Jama'at. For example, it began publicly to criticize the regime for continuing martial law and refusing to hold elections, but did not join the Movement for the Restoration of Democracy—a coalition of various social and political forces advocating a return to civilian rule. At the same time, it became an avid fan of Zia's new support for Islamic forces in neighboring Afghanistan, the mujahideen, who were fighting a Soviet invasion.[18] However, as the marginalization of Islamists—who, as Zia by now realized, constituted only a narrow segment of Pakistani society—continued during the mid-1980s, the Jama'at even began reaching out to nonreligious parties.[19] When martial law did eventually end in 1985, Zia took measures to ensure his position until the end of the decade through a referendum tying approval of Islamization to his continued rule.[20] The culmination of the broad project was cut short in 1988, when Zia was killed in a suspicious plane crash.

How to assess the motivations and meaning behind Zia's Islamization? At first glance it might be tempting to dismiss it as a very sophisticated form of religious co-option by the government—or, more accurately, the military. One might also suggest that Zia stepped in as he did in 1977 not so much to create space for Islam, but rather to "recontain" it after Bhutto had lost control of the religious sector.[21] Something considerably more complex was afoot here, though. Zia had long held a reputation for religiosity and personal piety, often making special provisions within the battalions under his command for religious observance.[22] Indeed, some have speculated that Bhutto put him in charge of the army specifically because he expected a pious military officer to harbor little in the way of political ambition.[23] It is likely, then, that much of his Islamization program was genuine in terms of intent, but overambitious in terms of the political role he initially envisaged for the Islamists and the *ulama*. Finding them lacking as public administrators, he began to include a wider range of voices in his policy-making deliberations. Once in power, he also likely discovered that the challenges of running a complex and fragile state—particularly one that became a frontline nation in the Cold War after Iran's revolution and the Soviet invasion of Afghanistan, not to mention ongoing tension with India—meant that Islamic idealism would have to give way to certain political realities.

BOX 5.3 MALAYSIA: ISLAMIZATION AND NATIONAL DEVELOPMENT

Malaysia provides an interesting example of state-led Islamization as an integral component of national economic development policy. While a small majority of Malaysia's population is ethnically Malay (or *bumiputra*—"sons of the soil"), much of the country's wealth historically has been concentrated in the hands of its minority communities: ethnic Indians, and particularly the Chinese. From the 1970s, with the announcement of the National Economic Policy, the government introduced a number of measures to effect a transfer of wealth into the hands of the ethnic Malays. At the same time, however, the ruling United Malays National Organization (UMNO) sought a unifying identity discourse that would stimulate Malay participation in the national development process and ensure a key economic role for the country's indigenous population. In choosing Islam to play this role, the state was able to accomplish two tasks simultaneously. By seizing for itself the banner of Islamization, UMNO was able to marginalize radical Islamists for whom dissent expressed in religious terms was a way to challenge the prevailing political order. Second, by introducing a sweeping Islamization program—with particular emphasis on public morality, work ethic, and Islamic finance—the state was able to use religion to socialize Malays into its vision for national development.

During the 1980s and 1990s, the two key players here were Prime Minister Mahathir Mohamed and his deputy and protégé Anwar Ibrahim. Anwar had previously been the leader of an Islamist youth movement, ABIM (Angkatan Belia Islam Malaysia—the Malaysian Islamic Youth Movement), that had played a key role in instigating the Islamization trend at the grassroots level in the 1970s. Mahathir calculated that by bringing the charismatic and skilled Anwar into the UMNO fold, he would be able to harness the energy of the Islamic movement in the name of state policy. Anwar, having been officially anointed from on high, rose quickly through the UMNO ranks, eventually attaining the rank of Deputy Prime Minister in the mid-1990s. Mahathir realized by the end of the decade that Anwar's popularity and ambition were likely a threat to his own political fortunes, and in 1998 Anwar was fired and jailed on charges of sexual deviance.

Shortly afterward, Mahathir and the UMNO faced a temporary challenge from another source of Islamism, the Parti Islam Se-Malaysia (PAS). This political party, developed in the mold of the Muslim Brotherhood, had been around since the time of Malaysian independence from Britain in the mid-1950s and had even served as part of a coalition government in the 1970s. Despite Mahathir's 2001 declaration that Malaysia was an Islamic state, the PAS platform was based on the complete *shari'ah*-ization of the Malaysian system—including *hudud* penalties. Although the PAS traditionally had enjoyed electoral support in a few of Malaysia's northern conservative states, in 1999 the party was able to take advantage of a wave of popular discontent over the mistreatment of Anwar Ibrahim. In the parliamentary elections that year, the PAS won control of a second state, Terrenganu, alongside Kelantan, and a total of 27 seats in the assembly. Their fortunes proved to be short-lived, however, when five years later the ruling UMNO party—now under the leadership of the new Prime Minister Abdullah Badawi—increased its majority. The PAS saw the loss of most of its parliamentary seats and only managed to maintain control of one state.

Anwar Ibrahim was released from prison in 2004 and, after a ban on his political participation expired, he returned to Malaysia in 2008 to head a new party, Keadilan ("Justice"), that had been founded by his wife during his imprisonment. Anwar, while no longer styling himself as an Islamist, became the natural leader of the opposition and went on to preside over a new coalition, the People's Alliance (PK—Pakatan Rakyat), that included PAS as well as the Democratic Action Party (which appeals primarily to Chinese voters and other ethnic minorities). In the 2013 parliamentary elections—amidst accusations of campaign and voting irregularities—Anwar's PK was defeated by the UMNO-led Barisan Nasional coalition despite a popular vote victory by the opposition.

For its own part, participation in Anwar's PK has led to a partial revival in PAS fortunes. It regained many of the parliamentary seats it lost in 2004 as well as full control of one state government and joint control of several others. But the PAS has also suffered from internal tensions, some of which—such as the so-called "Kalimah Allah" affair, which split the party over the permissibility of using the word Allah to describe the God of the Bible—had observers wondering where its priorities lie.

The years from 1988 to 1999 were turbulent ones in Pakistani politics. While arguably more democratic once elections resumed, this decade was marked by considerable instability, with governments changing every two to three years, reflecting power struggles between the leaders of various parties, and massive corruption being a mainstay of Pakistani politics, regardless of who happened to be in power. The two major figures in Pakistani politics throughout the 1990s were Benazir Bhutto, the daughter of Zulfikar, who had inherited the PPP mantle upon her return from abroad; and Nawaz Sharif, leader of the Pakistan Muslim League within the Islamic Democratic Alliance, a coalition of mostly religious parties that sought to claim Zia's legacy. The two exchanged the prime ministership twice over ten years, with Bhutto's tenure marking the first ever for a woman in the Muslim world. Even Nawaz Sharif's support for a Shariah Bill that would subjugate all Pakistani civil law to religion did not placate his JI partners as corruption grew and the latter increasingly were squeezed out of any meaningful policy-making role. Their relationship soon revealed itself for what it was: an alliance of convenience based on shared animosity toward Benazir Bhutto's PPP, and the Jama'at then broke with Nawaz in 1993 in order to contest elections directly. Despite the PPP's victory, the success of Nawaz's Pakistan Muslim League (PML) in drawing pro-religious votes away from the Islamists is cited by Vali Nasr as an early indication of the political potential inherent in the "Muslim Democracy" approach, examined in the Chapter 4.[24] Nawaz Sharif's second tenure as prime minister in the 1990s was characterized by an attempt to appropriate Islamic symbols in the course of pursuing rapid economic development *à la* Mahathir Mohamed in Malaysia and populist nationalism—the height of which was Pakistan's first official nuclear test in 1998, in response to a similar move by India.[25] Nawaz's increasingly autocratic rule and dismal economic record during the final years of his tenure led to tensions with the army, and he was replaced in a 1999 military *coup d'état* by General Pervez Musharraf.

Initial indications suggested that Musharraf was likely to go the secular and modernizing route espoused by Ayub Khan in the 1960s. The September 11, 2001 attacks on the United States proved to be a turning point in his tenure, however. Faced with choosing between active support for the United States and a more passive stance that risked American hostility towards his regime, Musharraf—who in the summer of 2001 had appointed himself Pakistan's president—took the former course. Unable to form a meaningful alliance with the grassroots of the PPP, Musharraf came to depend instead on a flank of the PML to serve as a "president's party"—but also on an unlikely alliance with the new Islamist bloc. The United Council of Action (MMA—Mutahida Majlis Amal), led by the JI, was ostensibly formed in opposition to Musharraf ruling as a military officer and also his willingness to promote American strategic interests in the region. In fact, he was able to strike a deal with them whereby greater Islamist participation in parliament, achieved via electoral redistricting, was exchanged for support by the latter in Musharraf's efforts to amend the constitution so that his period of rule could be extended. As part of this, he also promised to resign from the military two years after the elections of 2002. The Islamists did indeed see electoral gains, although they only polled 12 percent of the popular vote—a figure that provides a sense of how correct Zia had been to regard the Islamists as a niche force, politically. When Musharraf apparently reneged on his promise to put the army behind him, he lost—perhaps irrevocably—any willingness to work with him on the part of the Jamaat. Musharraf is aware that the real political threat, particularly if he is pressured to ease back the political chokehold, would come from the PPP, the party that actually won the greatest number of votes in the 2002 elections. By 2006, it was clear that the MMA had lost much of its clout within the parliamentary system when, against their efforts at a blocking maneuver, a coalition of secular parties managed to pass legislation moderating the country's strict *hudood* statues that dated from the time of Zia.

From 2007, there were also clear signs that the two largest parties were starting to feel confident as Musharraf's position appeared increasingly tenuous. Dogged by persistent efforts to question the constitutionality of Musharraf holding the presidency while wearing a military uniform, the general suspended the Chief Justice of the country's Supreme Court and sought to indict him on corruption charges. This put the president at odds with lawyers throughout the country, who accused Musharraf of seeking to undermine the independence of the judiciary. Backed into a corner, the president was forced to make political compromises to survive, including promising to permit the return of exiled PPP leader Benazir Bhutto. In a tumultuous year for opposition politics, both Bhutto and Sharif found their way back to Pakistan over the course of 2007, laying the groundwork for what would eventually prove to be Musharraf's political downfall. Benazir Bhutto was assassinated in the final days of 2007 (most likely by a Pakistani faction of the Taliban allied with Al-Qaeda), and in the election that followed soon thereafter her PPP won a resounding victory. The MMA lost most of its seats, falling to 2 percent of the popular vote. With the PPP and PML(N)—Pakistan Muslim League (Nawaz)—now dominating the parliament, the two parties joined forces to arrange for Musharraf's impeachment. In August 2008, the president resigned rather than face being removed by the legislature.

The country's security situation had also deteriorated during the latter stages of Musharraf's presidency. In 2007 Pakistan's security forces engaged in an intense confrontation on the grounds of the Lal Masjid (Red Mosque) complex in Islamabad, after the mosque's leadership came into conflict with the local municipal government over efforts to enforce strict *shari'ah* law in surrounding neighborhoods. The heavy-handed response by Pakistani special forces resulted in the deaths of some 150 mosque protestors and militants. Blaming Musharraf for the incident, allies of the Lal Masjid leadership in Waziristan began targeting army facilities, leading to renewed hostilities in the frontier provinces. Later that same year, Pakistan's military also found itself fighting Pakistani elements of the Taliban in the Swat Valley. Although the country's military and intelligence services previously had provided sanctuary to the Pakistani Taliban, the latter was perceived to be overstepping its boundaries by exerting influences in sub-regions outside the zones where it had been given license to operate. After a winter truce, in 2009 the Pakistani military began an aggressive campaign to remove the Taliban from the Swat Valley, signalling a broader effort on the part of Pakistani security forces to destroy militant elements linked to a variety of terrorist attacks throughout the country. At the same time, however, Pakistan's powerful intelligence services continued to provide sanctuary to Afghan Taliban leaders as part of a broader conception of regional security based on confrontation with India (see Chapter 7).

After 2008, the new PPP-led government found itself mired in charges of corruption and incompetence almost immediately. The country was wracked by ongoing instability, including widespread incidents of urban violence in Karachi. Chronic power shortages made life difficult and further threatened already dismal economic performance. As in Pakistan's past, many eyes turned to the military—seemingly the country's only function-ing institution—wondering whether it would once again step in to restore order. Civilian rule continued, but with the government increasingly unable to keep extremist forces in check. 2011 saw the assassination of two promi-nent figures espousing pluralism and tolerance: Punjab governor Salman Taseer and federal Minorities Minister Shabaz Bhatti. The fact that Taseer's killer—an affiliate of one of the country's largest Barelwi (Sufi) networks—was treated as a hero in some circles indicated how frayed Pakistani society had become. 2012 also saw increased sectarian tensions with multiple instances of anti-Shi'a violence.

Given the PPP's dismal performance, it was not surprising that it suf-fered a major defeat in the 2013 election. Nawaz Sharif emerged victorious, fending off a strong challenge from Imran Khan whose Tehreek-i-Insaf (Justice Movement) party was widely regarded as an independent force outside the corrupt realm of big party politics—especially by younger vot-ers. The same election also saw the dissolution of the MMA Islamist alliance, with the JI and Jamaat Ulama-i-Islam (JUI) contesting seats independently and gaining 2 and 3 percent of the popular vote, respec-tively. While Pakistan's ills seemed deeply entrenched and with extremism on the rise, the election was noteworthy insofar as it represented the first time in Pakistan history that one democratically elected government had peacefully handed power over to another civilian government chosen by the ballot box.

As we have seen from the preceding account, the role of Islam in Pakistani politics is a complex and multifaceted affair. With religion such an intrinsic and yet ambiguous part of public life in Pakistan, it becomes difficult to identify any single or main source of religio-political dis-course. The traditional *ulama,* particularly those alumni of the Deoband tradition, have a significant role to play—not least through the thousands of *madrasas* they have founded across the country (estimates range from 10,000 to 40,000). These are particularly important in the rural, mountainous, and isolated Northwest Frontier Province, where for many *madrasas* remain the only feasible source of education of any sort. The much-discussed links between the *madrasas* and militant extremism are discussed in Chapters 6 and 7, but they have played little direct role in mainstream Islamist politics except to provide a base for certain of the parties within the religious blocs—most particularly the *ulama* party, the JUI. Musharraf has sought, with considerable pressure from the West, to curb the influence of the more radical Kashmiri-based Islamist groups such as the Lashkar-i-Taiba, but he has been far more circumspect when dealing with associated humanitarian groups such as Lashkar's Jamaat-ud-Dawa.[26]

Without any doubt, the most significant force in Pakistan in terms of conventional Islamism has been the JI, although its role has evolved considerably over the years. Founded initially as more of an advocacy group seeking to ensure that an Islamic social order would be implemented in Pakistan, it developed into a voice for direct political dissent, and then finally into a *bona fide* political party, pursuing power like any other. It also demonstrates many of the hallmark features we have come to associate with conventional Islamism through our coverage in Chapters 3 and 4. The Jama'at's social base, for example, is not to be found in *madrasas* or mosques, but rather in modern associations and professional organizations.[27] Its student affiliate, the Islami Jamiat-i-Talaba, has been a major resource in terms of mass mobilization when necessary.[28] While it has certainly cooperated with traditional *ulama* by forming religious coalitions (e.g. the PNA and MMA) to challenge "un-Islamic" rulers, at other times the JI has sought to keep its distance from religious scholars, who they often view as insufficiently interested in comprehensive and active sociopolitical reform—an approach comparable with that of the MB in Egypt (see Chapter 3). While its electoral appeal has never been enormous, Jama'at supporters are to be found in some of the most socially mobile and influential segments of Pakistani society, ensuring a political influence disproportionate to their relatively small active membership and polling base. While persistently unable to break through at the national level, the JI has had some success in using local and provincial platforms to pursue its agenda, or to play the role of "kingmaker" by courting the support of larger parties in need of a broker to help reach more conservative and religiously inclined regions and population segments.

In summary, we can make the following broad points relating to Islam and politics in Pakistan. It becomes clear when looking at the country's political history that the initial ambiguity surrounding Pakistan's status as an Islamic state established the question of religion's public role as a primary political currency. As Vali Nasr puts it:

> [A] state built in the name of Islam and as a Muslim homeland, confronted with insurmountable ethnic, linguistic, and class conflicts, quickly succumbed to the temptation of mobilizing Islamic symbols in the service of state formation. This tendency has only been reinforced over the years as the state has failed to address fundamental socioeconomic issues, carry out meaningful land reform, and consolidate power in the center. This has opened the door for Islamic parties to enter the fray. The incremental sacralization of the national political discourse has clearly favored a political role for those who claimed to speak for Islam and who advocate Islamization. Their activism, in turn, strengthened the impetus for Islamization.[29]

We have seen, in both successive regimes and the multiple iterations of Pakistan's constitution, the ongoing efforts of different political actors to define the parameters of the state–religion relationship. This brings us to the second point, which deals with the question of who gets to speak on behalf of, or to define, Islam for Pakistani society. We will recall that Ayub Khan initially found himself in trouble with the religious sector (both the *ulama* and the Jama'at) due to his attempts to claim for the state the right to make authoritative claims about religion—and a particularly liberal modernist vision of Islam at that. This approach, also favored by Zulfikar Bhutto, involved the state mobilizing Islamic symbols in the name of its preferred policies while simultaneously marginalizing the *ulama* and Islamists. Zia ul-Haq's alternative model, which initially fared rather better, ceded the space of Islam to the religious specialists and brought them into a limited position of direct public authority while still carefully controlling their access to meaningful political power. We can recall the argument about Zia's seizure of power representing not only a desire for Islamic reform, but also an outflanking maneuver to ensure the Islamists did not become too powerful *vis-à-vis* the state once Zulfikar Bhutto had lost the ability to assert meaningful authority over them. Finally, the case of Pakistan leads us to reassess certain assumptions we might have about how the militaries within Muslim-majority states view Islam. While the case of Turkey and the Kemalists might lead us to assume that the secular-nationalist and bureaucratic tendencies of modern militaries predispose them to reject Islamism, the Pakistani example refocuses our analysis of the military's priorities more on social and political *order*. The army of Pakistan—which certainly does have Islamists within it—has not pursued a straightforward policy of seeking to marginalize and reduce the societal influence of religion. Rather, its main concern has been the preservation of public order, state authority, and the general course of national development. When striking up alliances with Islamists—as Zia ul-Haq did in the late 1970s, or like Pervez Musharraf after 2001—has proven useful in pursuing these goals, the army has not hesitated to do so.

IRAN: REVOLUTIONARY ISLAM AND THE CLERICAL STATE

The third and final model of the contemporary Islamic state that we will examine in some detail is that of Iran. Iran is significant for several reasons. It is the one example of an Islamic state that has come about through popular revolution, rather than being declared as such at the time of its founding (e.g. Saudi Arabia, Pakistan), or through a regime change in the wake of sustained internal conflict (Sudan, Afghanistan). The Islamic Revolution of 1979, for many observers, represented the zenith of modern Islamic revival, and a source for propagating revolutionary Islam to other national settings. For others it provided a test case of what Islam in power would look like. Subsequently, the example of Iran has been pointed to by those wary of Islamists participating in politics. As we will see, however, the doctrinal bases of the Islamic Republic of Iran are unique (many would argue wholly innovative), and certainly quite distinct from mainstream Islamist thinking as represented by the MB. There are parallels to be drawn, however, with the socioeconomic and political conditions that prompted popular mobilization toward Iran's revolution and the circumstances that have led to growing support for Islamists in other countries.

In this section we briefly review Iran's modern political history, focusing on the role of the *ulama* in politics under the late Qajar shahs and the Pahlavi dynasty through the 1970s. Next we examine the ideological basis for Islamic revolution in the thought of Ayatollah Khomeini, and more specifically in his doctrine of *vilayat-e faqih*. The contributions of other notable intellectuals, particularly those such as Ali Shariati, who reached a mass audience, are also assessed. We examine the course and events of the 1979 revolution itself, then offer an account of politics within the Islamic Republic and the implementation of the clerical state. The rise and fall of the reform movement under president Mohammad Khatami (1997–2005) is analyzed, as are the socioeconomic circumstances leading to popular support for electing a relative hardliner, Mahmoud Ahmadinejad, as his successor. We look at the development of growing tensions between the president and the Supreme Leader over the course of Ahmadinejad's tenure, and the question of increased factionalism within clerical circles. The section concludes by drawing out the major analytic themes that emerge from Iran's particular experience of the Islamic state.

As we will recall from Chapter 2, the modern Iranian state evolved via the Shi'i nationalism of the Safavid dynasty (1501–1736) and their successors, the Qajars (1781–1925). During the late Qajar period, where our account begins, the *ulama* of Iran enjoyed a prominent role within society and widespread legitimacy as deputies of the occulted twelfth *imam,* and as guardians of the spiritual legacy of the Prophet's family. While not directly involved in statist politics, they could claim pervasive social influence, and also played an important advisory role in certain matters of official policy. The rising autocracy that characterized late Qajar rule, however, led the *ulama* to adopt a more defensive stance *vis-à-vis* the regime, and they soon found their interests largely in line with those of the nascent nationalist movement that had arisen in response to both Qajar arrogance and creeping Western influence in the country's affairs. Two events in particular during this period help to illustrate the political role of the *ulama* and allow us to understand why it is that many Iranians understood the religious scholars to be a key player in popular agitations for social change—a point that will become important later, when we look at the sociology of the 1979 Islamic Revolution.

During the Tobacco Protest of 1891, leading *ulama* openly opposed Nasser al-Din Shah's granting of a concession for the sale and export of tobacco to a British commercialist. Their *fatwa* led to a widespread boycott of tobacco products in Iran, and their allies in the merchant class shut down major bazaars throughout the country, prompting the palace eventually to back off. These same ties with Iran's merchants, in addition to the mobilizing potential inherent in the country's mosque networks, also allowed the religious scholars to play a key role during the country's first Constitutional Revolution in 1906. As the palace began in the early twentieth century to cede more and more access to Iranian territory to Western powers and commercial interests, popular demand grew for curbs on their authority and the introduction of the rule of law. Widespread protests organized by religious scholars and merchants led to a five-year period of significant internal unrest as a constitution and parliament were repeatedly established and then abolished in the wake of direct interventions by Britain and Russia. After the country was occupied during World War I, a *coup d'état* by the head of a provincial military family, Reza Shah, brought an end to Qajar rule.

Essentially secular modernizers, the new ruling family sought to define and legitimize themselves in terms of Iran's ancient heritage, taking the name "Pahlavi," a language spoken in pre-Islamic Persia. Both Islam and Zoroastrianism were made the religions of state, and royal pageantry relied heavily on symbols from Iran's pre-Islamic past. If Reza Shah had a model, it was probably Mustapha Kemal Ataturk, who we will recall also deemphasized the modern Turkish Republic's links with Ottoman Islam in the name of a broader Turkish civilization. Unlike their Turkish cognate, however, the Pahlavis did not seek fundamentally and pervasively to restructure Iranian culture and society. The religious establishment, for example, was left intact, but was brought under state control—particularly when

Muhammad Reza took over from his father in 1941.[30] With the advent of the Cold War, Western powers courted the Pahlavi Shah for privileged access to Iranian oil, and he was only too happy to oblige. This pro-Western stance gave rise to considerable political opposition, exemplified by Mohammed Mosaddeq's National Front movement. The National Front, which enjoyed the support of the usual merchant-*ulama* coalition, initially supported Mosaddeq's nationalization of Iranian oil upon assuming the prime ministership in 1951. As he proceeded to introduce a number of liberalizing reforms—such as political rights for women—he quickly lost the support of the clergy. Fleeing the country after a popular revolt in the wake of his efforts to dismiss the Prime Minister, Muhammad Reza quickly returned to the throne when a CIA-orchestrated coup unseated Mosaddeq in 1953. Some scholars have speculated that, had Mosaddeq still had the support of the *ulama* and their mobilizing capacity, the coup may not have succeeded.[31] Having perhaps come to the same conclusion, and realizing the importance of *ulama* support for his political legitimacy, Muhammad Reza reached out to the religious sector with enhanced funding for their seminaries and various other causes. This period of relative *détente* was shattered in 1959, however, with the Shah's efforts to pass a new Land Reform Bill. The provisions in this legislation would have redistributed large quantities of land controlled by the *ulama* in the form of *awqaf*, the pious endowments from which much of their income—and hence their independence from the state—depended. While this particular dispute ended in an impasse (the bill was passed but never implemented), it was the harbinger of considerable tensions soon to arise.

Muhammad Reza's suspension of the parliament in 1961 prompted protests by a coalition of both secular and religious social forces, which eventually turned violent. The Shah's deepening dependence on the West led to increasingly vociferous public critique of his policies, and no figure was more ardent in this than Ruhollah Khomeini, a cleric from the seminary city of Qom. Despite being arrested and then released by way of warning, Khomeini did not tone down his rhetoric, and his success in mobilizing popular opposition sentiment led the government violently to suppress anti-government forces in a 1963 action that killed, by many estimates, several thousand. Khomeini himself was expelled from the country, going first to Turkey and eventually settling in the Iraqi Shi'i university city of Najaf. Throughout the rest of the 1960s and 1970s, the Shah turned Iran into a police state, relying heavily on the climate of fear instilled by his secret security service (SAVAK—Sazeman-e Ettela'at va Amniyat-e Keshvar) to maintain order and quell opposition. Half-hearted attempts at reform in the 1970s produced nothing but a growing sense of socioeconomic disparity between political elites and the masses, and endemic hatred of the Shah by the latter.

Before moving on to look at the events of Iran's Islamic revolution, it may be helpful to spend some time considering the evolution of Ayatollah

Khomeini's political thought. This will enable us to understand better the doctrinal and ideological foundations of 1979's political earthquake. Khomeini's religious education, which saw him studying under several of Iran's leading *ulama,* introduced him to a wide range of religious disciplines. He developed a particularly keen interest in philosophy and mystical thought, continuing to study and teach these subjects in private after coming under pressure from traditional scholars to remove them from his public lectures. Some have even speculated that Khomeini's intense engagement with mystical thought may have given him an early sense of being predestined to play a special role in public affairs.[32] Khomeini's first sustained reflections on politics are to be found in the 1942 text *Kashf al-Asrar* (*The Unveiling of Secrets*). Primarily a critique of "comprador" *ulama* unable to gain any critical distance from the Shah, the *Kashf* also reserves a few choice barbs for the Pahlavis themselves. Regarding matters of government, Khomeini is not yet at a point where he argues for the state to be led by religious scholars. Rather, he points out that since all law comes from God, any legitimate government must implement the *shari'ah* and remove any laws incompatible with it. No particular form of government is un-Islamic in and of itself, but if a monarchical model was to be followed, then it would be best for the king to be appointed by the leading religious leaders in order to ensure the "government of God."[33] He did hold out the possibility, however, that *ulama* might serve as members of parliament or have a privileged advisory role to the monarch.[34]

Khomeini's major statement on Islamic political theory is contained in *Hukumat-i Islami* (*Islamic Government*), first delivered as a set of lectures in Najaf during 1969–70, and later collected and published in book form. It is in this text that Khomeini provides the fullest explanation and justification of the doctrine of *vilayat-e faqih* ("guardianship of the jurist"). As a principle arguing that political authority should be vested in religious scholars, *vilayat-e faqih* is the basis for Khomeini's distinctive model of the Islamic state. *Hukumat* unfolds methodically, beginning with a lengthy proof of the necessity for government based on Qur'anic, Prophetic, and Shi'i tradition. Even in this first section of the book, it becomes clear that Khomeini has not only a theoretical purpose, but also a political intent. It is not just that an Islamic government is required, he argues, but that true Muslims also have the obligation to remove from power those forces that actively seek to prevent the establishment of such a government:

> Both law and reason require that we do not permit governments to retain this non-Islamic or anti-Islamic character . . . In order to assure the unity of the Islamic umma, in order to liberate the Islamic homeland from occupation and penetration by the imperialists and their puppet governments, it is imperative that we establish a government. In order to attain the unity and freedom of the Muslim peoples, we must overthrow the

oppressive governments installed by the imperialists and bring into existence an Islamic government of justice that will be in the service of the
people.[35]

Beyond the establishment of an Islamic government, Khomeini is clearly
starting to lay the groundwork for an activist orientation toward political
change. His criticism of obscurantist *ulama* disconnected from contemporary political challenges continued in his public lectures during this time,
and he urged his students to prepare for the obligations of establishing (and
running) a true Islamic order.[36]

The next section of *Hukumat-i Islami* is the most innovative, for it is
here that Khomeini seeks to make a case for the direct political authority of
religious scholars—to say, in effect, that the state should be in the hands of
the *ulama*. The groundwork for the argument is based on the idea of the
ulama as the trustees of the authority of the *imams,* themselves the vice-
regents of God. While Khomeini was by no means the first Shi'i scholar to
put forward a version of this argument, his was certainly the most comprehensive treatment of the subject in the context of the modern nation-state.
Until this time, the most direct exposition of the subject was to be found in
the work of the early nineteenth-century scholar Mulla Ahmad Naraqi, who
had argued for a unique and privileged governmental role for the *ulama* in
the absence of the Imam.[37] Khomeini opens this section of his work by
making a case for the unique nature of the political order he has in mind:

> Islamic government does not correspond to any of the existing forms of
> government . . . Islamic government is neither tyrannical nor absolute,
> but constitutional. It is not constitutional in the current sense of the
> word, i.e., based on the approval of laws in accordance with the opinion
> of the majority. It is constitutional in the sense that the rulers are subject
> to a certain set of conditions that are set forth in the Noble Qur'an and
> the Sunna of the Most Noble Messenger.[38]

Since the capacity to legislate is vested exclusively in God, Khomeini
reasoned, it would be necessary for anyone charged with implementing and
enforcing God's law to be an expert in the *shari'ah*. "Since Islamic government is a government of law," he argued, "knowledge of the law is necessary
for the ruler, as has been laid down in tradition. Indeed, such knowledge is
necessary not only for the ruler, but also for anyone holding a post or exercising some government function."[39] Khomeini reaches the culmination of
his argument by arguing that if a ruler does not know the *shari'ah* (i.e. if he
is a secular monarch) then he will have to rely on the guidance of those who
do and his authority will be undermined; and yet, if he does not accept such
counsel from the experts then it is impossible for him to rule justly. The
natural conclusion of this line of argument is to remove the mediating layer

of the nonjurist sovereign, and replace him with religious scholars. Hence Khomeini's assertion that " . . . the true rulers are the fuqaha themselves, and rulership ought officially to be theirs, to apply to them, not to those who are obliged to follow the guidance of the fuqaha on account of their own ignorance of the law."[40] In the most straightforward terms, *vilayat-e faqih* as a doctrine argues that in an Islamic state, the highest authority should be vested in those who have the greatest knowledge of the divine law upon which the political order is based. It therefore follows that the state should be in the hands of the religious scholars.

We should note that the lectures comprising *Hukumat-i Islami* were formulated for, and delivered to religious scholars in, a seminary setting. Its method of argumentation and evidence reflect the very particular discourse of the *ulama* and hence would not be persuasive to those outside this tradition. If Khomeini wanted to lay the basis for a popular revolution, he would need to find a mediator who could frame his ideas and imperatives for a wider audience. Two such figures played this role in Iran during the years of his absence—one of them as something of an official surrogate and the other as an independent public intellectual whose transformational worldview made it possible for an entire generation to see their aspirations reflected in Khomeini's project. As a Khomeini student of longstanding,

Figure 5.3 Poster commemorating Khomeini, leader of Iran's Islamic Revolution

Source: 'Khomeini' by Hasan Isma'ilzadeh; Iran, 1979

Murtaza Mutahhari became the Ayatollah's proxy during his years in exile. Unlike his teacher, however, he had studied contemporary Western ideology and philosophy and was conversant in the Marxism that so many young Iranians found attractive. While drawn to aspects of the anti-capitalism present in socialist thought, he found Marxism's lack of attention to spiritualism and morality to be a fundamental flaw. He was hence able to engage such ideas, but then to provide a comprehensive Islamic critique, aimed squarely at religiously inclined members of the educated, lower-middle class.

His lay counterpart, and eventual competitor, was a young intellectual named Ali Shariati. Shariati had studied in Paris for several years, eagerly imbibing all the latest currents in Western philosophy and social critique. Through Frantz Fanon he developed a sense of Third World consciousness, and via Ché Guevara the impetus to do something about it.[41] While skeptical about the material reductionism to be found in Marxism, he was enthralled by the emancipatory dimensions of socialist thought. He argued that Islam—and Shi'i Islam in particular—possessed the same critical edge and capacity to liberate the oppressed. What else was Shi'i history, he argued, if not an account of righteous struggle in the face of hegemony? "To Shariati," argues Vanessa Martin, "the imperialists and capitalists were enemies, and the Marxists were competitors. To Mutahhari, all were enemies."[42] We can see, in his claims that Islam already contained all the best that was to be found in various Western ideologies, echoes of other modern Islamist activist-intellectuals such as Hassan al-Banna. We also find here traces of figures such as Jamal ad-Din al-Afghani, and a foreshadowing of Fazlur Rahman in his distinction between "Alid" and "Safavid" Shi'ism—the conceptual device through which Shariati served up his own critique of the *ulama*. The "Alid" formulation referred to the core doctrine and experience of the Prophet's family, while "Safavidism" came to be a symbol for the corruption and undermining of this living tradition by the *ulama*. Where Mutahhari had first cooperated with Shariati because he thought the latter might be helpful in building support for the *ulama* among the educated middle classes, he soon began to see Shariati's immense popularity and anti-clerical stance as major threats. Far more than any figures within the clerical establishment, Shariati, who died in London in 1977 under suspicious circumstances, had found a tenor that successfully married religious discourse with the political aspirations of Iran's young, educated middle class. In this regard he played a major role in priming society so that they could comfortably get behind the major political transformation that was shortly to follow. It is therefore not surprising that, as the Islamic Revolution later unfolded, it was Shariati's formulations that worked their way into Khomeini's rhetoric and populism.

With the Shah's regime increasingly beholden to the United States, popular discontent with his rule became endemic. The accusation of *gharbzadegi*

("Westoxification"), coined by the intellectual Jalal al-Ahmad in the 1960s, seemed perfectly to capture the popular perception that the regime had by now wholly subordinated Iran to Western interests. Emboldened by the new U.S. president Jimmy Carter's emphasis on human rights, a group of secular intellectuals called for the Pahlavis to institute greater democracy and constitutionally guaranteed freedoms. Under Washington's wary eye, the Shah did not seek to suppress the movement, and this emboldened student groups who subsequently took to the streets. When in early 1978 these protests were joined by the *ulama* and bazaar merchants, however, the government cracked down, killing several dozen people. This set in motion a cycle that would continue over much of the rest of the year: mourning rituals would turn into political protests, police would arrive, violence would ensue, protestors would be killed, and the cycle would restart.[43] In September 1978 the Shah declared martial law, and on the following day—known as "Black Friday"—at least several hundred people were killed in Tehran's Jaleh Square. The sheer shock of this massacre prompted certain groups that until now had refrained from joining the protests, such as the secular-national middle class and many blue-collar workers, to get involved. Worried about Khomeini's growing symbolic influence, the Shah petitioned Iraq to kick the cleric out of the country, and in October 1978 he set up new headquarters in Neauphle-le-Château outside Paris, France. Ironically, this enabled his voice in Iran to grow even louder as he now had free rein to say whatever he wanted, whereas his public discourse in Iraq had been circumscribed. Not only did the Persian service of the foreign media broadcast his statements into Iran, but thousands of cassette recordings of his speeches were smuggled into the country and circulated widely, prompting some to regard Iran as the first "media revolution."[44] As Henry Munson puts it, "the technology and political freedom of the West brought Khomeini closer to Iran in France than he had been in Iraq."[45]

The brewing revolution reached its climax when a crowd of over 2 million—Islamists, *ulama,* communists, secular modernists, students, workers, professionals, and *bazaari* alike—all turned out for protests on the Shi'i holiday of Ashura in December 1978. The following month, the Shah fled the country and on February 1, 1979, the Ayatollah Khomeini made a triumphant return to Tehran. Over the next few months, revolutionary forces attacked various hold-outs from the Shah's regime and soon all remaining army and police units either had been defeated or had switched their loyalty to the clergy-led forces. Khomeini appointed Mehdi Bazargan, a scientist with strong but moderate Islamist credentials, to head up a new cabinet. The real power, as it quickly transpired however, lay with Khomeini's Islamic Revolutionary Council. When a group of militant students stormed the U.S. Embassy, holding several dozen American hostages for over a year, Bazargan found himself powerless to intervene due to the clergy's tacit support for the students. He and his cabinet resigned after only nine months in office, leaving the political field wide open for Khomeini's supporters. Over the previous months, the coalition of diverse political forces united in their opposition to the Shah fell apart as their disparate interests took over. The Tudeh (communist) party, the secular nationalists, and the Khomeinist clerics—all intrinsic components of the revolutionary forces—discovered very quickly that they had mutually incompatible visions of the post-Shah constitutional order. Those outside the Khomeini camp were surprised at the vehemence with which the cleric pushed his revolutionary Islamic agenda. It was not the outcome that most of the nonreligious groups who participated in the revolution had expected, and there were several reasons for this. The first point to make relates to historical precedent. The population at large would not have found it at all strange to see the *ulama* at the forefront of a popular reform movement, given their role in similar efforts throughout Iranian history such as the Tobacco Protest of 1891, the first Constitutional Revolution in 1906, and the protests in the early 1960s where religious and secular forces worked together to oppose the Shah's suspension of parliament. In short, Iranians had no reason to think there might be anything to fear from a revolution led by the clergy since things had generally turned out fine in the past. Second, many of them had not read Khomeini's writings directly, and certainly not his work on the doctrine and practice of *vilayat-e faqih*. The speeches he made from abroad in the run-up to the revolution had not provided much detail about the specifics of the post-revolutionary order, and most people were happy to rally behind his Islamism as a surrogate form of anti-Pahlavi discourse. Khomeini's public relations handlers had also been careful to package the clerical agenda in a way that would appeal to mixed audiences. Finally, even those, such as the secular-nationalists, who were aware of Khomeini's intentions, were under the impression that they would be able to outflank him after the revolution and to co-opt the religious sector. Underestimating the organization and capacity of Khomeini's supporters, they were largely blindsided when, in the month following the revolution, he systematically cracked down on any and all groups within the revolutionary network who questioned his authority or seemed likely to do so in the future. This led to mass arrests, "disappearances," and many killings, particularly among communists, secular-nationalists, and Islamist elements not aligned with Khomeini. The Islamic left, best represented by the Mojahiden-i-Khalq movement, was outlawed and subsequently operated as an underground opposition group. The Ayatollah's loyalists usurped the *komiteh* worker's organizations that had been used to organize strikes and protests during the revolution, and through this network they enforced conformity with the new order. Not even the *ulama* escaped this purge. The majority of religious scholars—while certainly opposed to the Shah and only too happy to make common cause alongside one of their own—did not agree with Khomeini's doctrine on religious grounds, and even less with his political aspirations. Many of them simply chose to keep quiet, but those who did speak out—such as the senior Ayatollah Shariatmadari—were silenced, placed under house arrest, or worse. The dust had hardly settled from the revolution when, in September 1980, Iraq invaded Iran in the hope of catching the latter off guard and preoccupied with internal matters. Instead, the occasion of war with an Arab neighbor led by a highly secular regime provided Khomeini with a new source of national unity and a rallying cry to defend, and perhaps even to spread, the impulse of his recent revolution.

Khomeini held a national referendum in early 1979 asking the population to endorse the idea of an Islamic Republic, and based on this mandate he proceeded to draft a constitution. The first draft of this was rather more secular than he had hoped, and so it was handed over to an assembly of clerical experts for revision, resulting in the present version (subsequently amended in 1989). It is this document that defines the framework and institutions of Iran's new Islamic government—or the Islamic Republic of Iran as it was henceforth to be called. In addition to affirming the principle of divine sovereignty (Article 2), the "General Principles" section of the constitution also stipulates that all laws and regulations in the Islamic Republic are to conform to the *shari'ah* (Article 4). Khomeini's doctrine of *vilayat-e faqih* is also enshrined here (Article 5) through a statement confirming that, in the absence of the hidden Imam, leadership of the community falls to the Islamic legal specialist (*faqih*). It then goes on to link this specifically to the office of the Supreme Leader or Guide, described below.

In addition to the familiar tripartite division of executive, legislative, and judiciary branches of government, the Iranian constitution also provides for several unique institutions and organs that have a major impact on the distribution of political power within the system—most of which are staffed by, and under the control of, the clerics. The most important of these is the office of the Leader (*rahbar*), or Guardian-Jurist (*valiy-i faqih*)—commonly known as the Supreme Leader. In addition to setting national priorities and overseeing the "general policies of the Islamic Republic," the Supreme Leader also possesses a number of unique powers and competences that make his office far and away the most powerful within the political system. The armed forces (especially the elite Islamic Revolutionary Guards Corps, IRGC), police, and security apparatus of the Republic all answer directly to the Supreme Leader, and he also appoints the head of the Judiciary and regulates the country's media and information services. In short, all of the instruments associated with the exercise of power in a modern state are reserved for the Supreme Leader. While the country does have a separate President, many of the powers commonly associated with the executive branch of a government are reserved for the Supreme Leader in the Iranian system. The president of the republic has the power to appoint ministers, although two of these (defense and intelligence) are customarily agreed in consultation with the Supreme Leader.

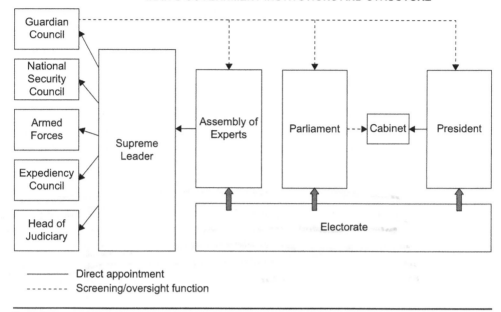

IRAN'S GOVERNMENT INSTITUTIONS AND STRUCTURE

Figure 5.4 Governmental structure of Iran

A further instrument of the Supreme Leader's control is to be found in the Guardianship Council. Its main task is to oversee legislation enacted by the country's parliament (the Islamic Consultative Assembly), ensuring that all laws passed are compatible with the *shari'ah*. The Guardianship Council also vets all candidates for the parliament, presidency, and the Assembly of Experts (see below). Of the Council's 12 members, half are appointed directly by the Supreme Leader and the other six proposed by the Judiciary and then approved by the parliament. Should an irreconcilable dispute arise between the parliament and the Guardianship Council, the matter is referred to the Expediency Council. Created by a 1989 constitutional amendment, this Council—all of whose members are appointed by the Supreme Leader—is charged with settling the aforementioned disputes and also with offering *ad hoc* advice to the Supreme Leader on matters of his choosing. The final body unique to the Islamic Republic is the Assembly of Experts, which in theory supervises the office of the Supreme Leader. The Assembly, whose 86 members are popularly elected every eight years, is charged with selecting the Supreme Leader (who serves for life) and also has the power to dismiss him, although the body has never publicly challenged its appointee. In Iran the president and members of parliament are all popularly elected, both serving terms of four years. While the system is clearly grossly stacked in favor of the Supreme Leader who, through his lifetime appointment, is not regularly accountable to the populace, it is worth noting that Iran's record of holding regular elections for both parliament and the presidency—and respecting their outcomes, even when they do not turn out to the Supreme Leader's liking—is one of the better in the Muslim world. Of course, the Supreme Leader possesses such a preponderance of power that he has nothing to fear in terms of day-to-day institutional politics should a president or parliament ever oppose him. It is also interesting to note that within the Iranian system, membership in one of the aforementioned bodies or councils does not preclude one from serving on another at the same time. For example, former president Ali Akbar Hashemi Rafsanjani has served simultaneously as chairman of the Expediency Council and deputy chair of the Assembly of Experts.

Iran became an increasingly closed society from 1980, as new regulations promulgated by conservative clerics began to affect various aspects of daily life. Women, in particular, bore the brunt of these changes. Veiling was made mandatory from 1983, and family laws were revised to permit polygamy, child and temporary marriages, and the progressive gender segregation of more and more public space. Politics in the country was dominated by a single party, the pro-Khomeini Islamic Republican Party, but even within this group a number of clear factions had started to emerge after a few years. Conservatives favored a privileged political role for the clergy, and strict adherence to traditional social norms. They were the inheritors of the *ulama*'s historical alliance with the *bazaari* merchants, and so their economic views tended to favor private enterprise and property. Indeed, much of their wealth was to be found in the *awqaf* ("pious endowments") system—technically a form of private asset. The hardline revolutionary faction, on the other hand, was not happy with this *status quo*. They sought a radical redistribution of wealth in the name of social justice and the nationalization of industry. This impasse made it particularly difficult for the much-needed land reform process to make significant headway during the 1980s. By 1984, with inflation high, money in short supply, and oil prices low, there arose from amongst the conservatives a sub-faction of "pragmatic realists", who realized that significant economic liberalization was the only way to ease Iran's fiscal pressures—a trend that was reinforced when Rafsanjani assumed the presidency. In terms of foreign policy, the hardliners were stridently anti-Western in their orientation (and anti-American in particular; this was the faction that had orchestrated the U.S. Embassy siege), and sought to export the revolution to other Muslim countries. The conservatives, on the other hand, emphasized relations with other Muslim countries, but—although certainly not pro-American—were less unequivocal in their condemnation of the West or the possibility of Iran normalizing its relations with the rest of the world.[46]

That rest of the world, and particularly Iran's neighbors, had certainly taken note of the 1979 upheaval in Tehran. Third World revolutionary movements were emboldened by Khomeini's success, and the regimes they opposed expressed new fears that the Iranian model might spread to other settings in the developing world. Closer to home, Arab countries with significant Shi'i populations—notably Saudi Arabia, Bahrain, and Kuwait—all experienced various levels of unrest in the wake of the revolution. Iran also reached out to their oppressed co-religionists in Lebanon, providing vital support for the founding and evolution of Hizbullah (see Chapter 6)—patronage that continues to this day. Likewise, Khomeini provided support for Shi'i opposition movements in neighboring Iraq, a factor that continues to be important today in post-Saddam Iraq (see Chapter 6). The Iran–Iraq War (1980–88) enacted an enormous toll on both countries, but Iran's use of "human wave" tactics—whereby members of the paramilitary Basij Corps would repeatedly throw themselves at enemy lines, or clear mine-fields with their bodies—created an entire generation of "martyrs" for the revolution and provided a sense of national unity that distracted from domestic political woes. Iran's hopes for the rehabilitation of its international image were not helped in 1989 when Khomeini issued a statement condemning the British novelist Salman Rushdie to death. In Khomeini's estimation, Rushdie's novel *The Satanic Verses* contained blasphemies that made its author an apostate from Islam, and hence subject to death.[47]

By the late 1980s, voices of dissent began to be heard from within the clerical establishment itself. Some, such as Khomeini's former right-hand man Hossein Ali Montazeri, found themselves subject to public rebuke after requesting that the government consider the consequences of some of its failures. Montazeri, who had been selected in 1985 by the Assembly of Experts to succeed Khomeini as the Supreme Leader, found himself stripped of this office-in-waiting and later placed under house arrest for six years. When Khomeini eventually died in 1989, the power struggle between conservatives and hardliners anticipated by some observers never materialized. The Supreme Leadership passed to the former president Ali Khameini, and parliamentary speaker Ali Akbar Hashemi Rafsanjani was elected president. A series of constitutional amendments in 1989 had abolished the position of prime minister and afforded the president new powers. The choice of Khameini as Supreme Leader, it should be noted, was somewhat controversial because, as a religious scholar, he was relatively junior. He was quickly given a "field promotion" from the rank of Hujjat al-Islam to Ayatollah, but even this could not smooth over the fact that his credentials were more political and administrative than religious. For some this marked something of a reconceptualization of the Supreme Leader's role after Khomeini's passing. The constitutional revisions had also defined the Guide's role more clearly, laying stronger emphasis on his political qualifications.

The period of Rafsanjani's presidency (1989–97) is generally identified with the rise of a third significant force in Iranian politics, that of the pragmatists. This group, who tended to draw from the ranks of the conservatives, sought cautiously to introduce certain liberalizing reforms. With Rafsanjani as their figurehead, the main task facing them was to put Iran's economic affairs in order and to reconstruct the country after the indecisive but costly war with Iraq. A number of five-year development plans were introduced, coupled with the introduction of economic policies that would make it easier for Iran to qualify for loans from international financial institutions (IMF, World Bank) that could permit the country's infrastructure to be rebuilt. This became all the more challenging when, in 1995, the United States introduced a comprehensive ban on business dealings with the Islamic Republic. Rafsanjani also permitted considerably more debate within both the media and parliament, and it became commonplace to hear executive policies and initiatives criticized openly. While this period saw a relative decline in the influence of the hardliners (particularly after the Iraq War), this did not mean that the pragmatists had a free hand. The 1992 parliamentary elections brought the assembly firmly into the hands of the conservatives, and this created certain constraints on Rafsanjani's latitude to maneuver and to pursue grand national developmental schemes—meaning that his efforts to reform the economy brought mixed results.

While Rafsanjani's rule was characterized by certain shifts of power within the existing order and a modicum of carefully controlled openness, it was not until the election of Mohammad Khatami as president in 1997 that the landscape of Iranian politics was significantly reconfigured. Khatami, a philosopher and former culture minister who had been somewhat sidelined by the establishment for his liberal views, was one of three figures going up against the clergy's "official" candidate, parliamentary speaker Ali Akbar Nateq Nuri. The latter had received Khameini's endorsement, and the commander of the Revolutionary Guard issued orders to vote for him—prompting many observers to assume that his victory was a foregone conclusion.[48] The pragmatists, for their part, quietly endorsed Khatami's candidacy. Against all expectations, Khatami won an overwhelming victory, taking 69 percent of the vote. He had campaigned on a platform of reform and openness, messages that resonated with Iran's younger voters—and particularly with women, whose support was shown by subsequent analysis to have been decisive in his victory. The conservative clergy were rather taken aback by the scale of Khatami's triumph, with some immediately posing questions as to his suitability to serve in the executive. He was likened by them to *ulama* involved in leading the 1906 Constitutional Revolution, and conservatives were reminded that this process had resulted in a secular constitution—implying, in effect, that Khatami was a threat to the post-revolutionary order. Seeking to stay above the factional fray, as had Khomeini before him, Khameini as Supreme Leader welcomed Khatami's victory and endorsed the idea of debating the values and meaning of the revolution. Daniel Brumberg, arguing that Khatami's thinking reveals him to be opposed to the very idea of clerical dominance, because "they lack adequate knowledge of matters extrinsic to Islam," noted that he was nevertheless "always careful to reach this conclusion through Khomeini"—and thereby to remain on side in the eyes of the conservatives.[49] Some had expressed surprise that, with his liberal record, Khatami had been permitted by the Guardianship Council even to stand as a candidate. It may have been that, having regarded Nateq Nuri as a sure thing for the presidency, Khatami was selected by the Council in order to give the impression of greater pluralism in terms of the range of views represented in the election. Khatami's new cabinet, once formed, certainly reflected his reformist orientation, but he was still constrained by the Supreme Leader in terms of his appointments to the key security posts. Significantly, he appointed a woman to serve as one of the Republic's vice presidents—the first time since the revolution that a woman had held a high executive office.

Khatami came to embody a generation's hopes for liberalization in Iran. In the months following his election, expectations for the enactment of meaningful reform by his government grew tremendously—but the political space afforded him to pursue this agenda certainly did not. Khatami also won great admiration overseas, where many saw him as the harbinger of a pro-Western counter-revolution. In this regard, there are certain parallels to be drawn between the rise to power of Mohammad Khatami in Iran and that of Mikhail Gorbachev in the Soviet Union. Gorbachev's *glasnost* and *perestroika* projects were seen by many observers outside the Soviet Union as an attempt by its premier to roll back communism altogether. In fact, Gorbachev was still firmly committed to the basic Soviet model and to socialism—he only wanted to reform them. Similarly, Khatami was perceived by some outside Iran as a force working to undo the Islamic Revolution and re-Westernize Iran. Khatami, however, remained committed to the ideals of the Islamic Revolution, and sought rather to make it more sustainable through reform and greater openness. Khatami will have been well aware, given the balance of power between the presidency and the various bodies controlled by the conservative clerics, that he would face an uphill battle all the way.

While Khatami's ability directly to enact significant reform was limited by restrictions incumbent upon his office, his election emboldened a nascent grassroots reform movement within Iran. Over the next few years, it grew rapidly to become the largest popular political faction within the country, culminating in a reformist sweep (71 percent of seats) in the 2000 parliamentary poll. Led by the Islamic Iran Participation Front, the reformists commanded strong support across the universities and the middle classes. Their emergence was associated with enormous growth in the number of nongovernmental organizations and civil society organizations—particularly newspapers and other media forums—with strong support for these initiatives coming from Khatami's office. Unsurprisingly, it was not long before tensions between the reformists and the conservative clergy came into the open. In 1998, legal action against Tehran's pro-reform mayor brought students onto the street, and soon the government began to close down reformist publishing houses on a regular basis. Most of these simply reopened immediately under a different name, but these actions demonstrated Khatami's inefficacy in the face of press and censorship laws shaped entirely by the Supreme Leader's judiciary. An even more oppressive press bill passed in 1999 prompted even wider demonstrations and a police crackdown. Khatami initially supported these protests, but he was later pressured by conservatives to denounce the students' defiance. The conservatives were also able to rely on at least two other forces within Iranian society to add to their own pressure on the reformists. The *bazaari* merchants, for example, were keen to continue the special economic favors they enjoyed under the *status quo,* and so worked where possible to undermine reformist influence. More worrying were various pro-clerical vigilante groups who showed up and attacked student protests. While it is not entirely clear whether these were actually controlled by the clerics, it is certain that, at the very least, little was done to curb their activities.

By 1999, however, the reformists were making considerable inroads into the political system. Local and municipal elections were held in Iran for the first time, and reformist groups scored a strong victory. Since these seats were not subject to review by the Guardianship Council, most councils ended up with at least one woman member. The height of the reformists' electoral success came during the 2000 national parliamentary elections, when almost three-quarters of the seats were won by Islamic Iran Participation Front-oriented candidates. By way of protest against conservative interference in reform efforts, Khatami prevaricated about whether to run for re-election in 2001. In the end he chose to stand and was returned with an even larger majority than in 1997. The reformist parliament mounted a legislative counter-attack on the conservatives the following year, seeking expanded powers for the president and a reduction in the purview of the Guardianship Council. Despite a few concessions on the part of the clerical establishment, such as Ayatollah's Montazeri's release from house arrest in 2003, the conservatives began a concerted and systematic crackdown on the reform movement. Press censorship increased dramatically, with a number of reformist outlets shut down permanently. In the run-up to the 2004 parliamentary elections, the Guardianship Council deemed a great many of the reformist candidates ineligible to stand, and conservatives ended up winning a little over half the seats. Without a viable candidate for the 2005 presidential elections (Khatami was ineligible to stand for a third consecutive term), the best the reformists could hope for was a strong showing by the conservative pragmatist Ali Akbar Rafsanjani. After two rounds of voting, however, Rafsanjani was defeated by his hardline opponent Mahmoud Ahmadinejad. This seemed to spell an end to the reform movement, as all political offices sympathetic to their position were now firmly back under clerical control.

It is difficult to make an evaluation of Khatami's presidency. Clearly he was not able to achieve much in the way of sustained liberalizing reform. Many observers concluded that he would not have been able to do this without forcing a direct and likely very violent confrontation with the forces of the regime—and clearly he was not prepared to go this far. While he may have disappointed many of those who put faith in him, Khatami opened sufficient space for the reformist aspirations of Iran's educated youth generation to be seen around the world. That said, this same generation still faces socioeconomic challenges in addition to a lack of political freedom. Of the 1.5 million applicants to Iranian universities in 2001, spaces were available for only 10 percent. Fewer than 1 percent of university graduates are able immediately to enter employment. Khatami's fortunes were also not helped when the United States, while recognizing the existence of strong reformist sentiment in Iran, named the Islamic Republic as part of an international "axis of evil" alongside Iraq and North Korea in the wake of the September 11, 2001 attacks. This action was all the more bewildering to the Iranians after the assistance they had provided in helping to stabilize Afghanistan in the wake of the fall of the Taliban. This new hostility from Washington allowed the conservatives to reclaim the mantle of anti-Americanism, and to portray the reformists as allies of U.S. imperial designs in the region. In the end, it became clear that the logical conclusions of Khatami's thinking simply could not be contemplated in the contemporary environment. He was not, however, the sole ideologue of the reformist movement. Figures such as the philosopher Abdolkarim Soroush, combining "neo-Marxist sociology and mystical individualism," emerged as a major critic of the clerical state after having initially served the revolution and helping to institutionalize it.[50] He argues, for example, that Islam and state need to be kept apart not because religion corrupts politics, but rather the converse—that politics, with its base and immoral pursuit of power, poses a threat to the purity of religion. His writings have earned a considerable following both in Iran and abroad, and he has tended to spend long periods outside Iran lecturing at Western universities. From within the clerical establishment itself, reformist voices have arisen, such as that of Mohsen Kadivar, whose reformist-oriented political theories earned him a prison sentence in the late 1990s.

The election of Mahmoud Ahmadinejad in 2005 marked the rise of a hardline neo-Khomeinism in Iranian politics. While highly conservative, his political base was not the religious scholars or their merchant allies. Ahmadinejad, a former mayor of Tehran, was above all a populist, and his rhetoric was aimed squarely at the socioeconomically dispossessed of Iran. Where Khatami had reached out to the educated young middle and lower-middle classes, Ahmadinejad packaged himself for the country's poor. The largely uneducated generation that had grown up with, and often fought in, the Iran–Iraq war formed the heart of his constituency. These former *basijis*, the volunteer martyrdom forces composed mainly of untrained teenagers who would throw themselves at Iraqi positions to clear the way for the regular army, took heart in Ahmadinejad's populist revolutionary nationalism and his promises to improve their standard of living. True to form, almost immediately upon taking office his rhetoric turned extremely hardline, calling for the eradication of Israel and questioning the truth of the Holocaust as a historical event. Anti-Americanism was also a strong component of his election platform, and in 2006 he raised tensions with the United States and the international community by reopening Iran's nuclear program.

Ahmadinejad's presidency was characterized by consistent and ever greater levels of conflict between his office and the Supreme Leader, the parliament, and the Islamic Revolutionary Guards Corps—the country's three major power centers. His personal style was not in keeping with Iran's political elites (something that endeared him to many of his grassroots supporters), he failed to tackle Iran's increasingly dire economic situation, and he was prone to making extreme statements that angered the Supreme Leader and reflected poorly on Iran in international circles. Already by 2006, Ahmadinejad saw his loyalists disqualified or defeated in elections to the Assembly of Experts. While the 2008 parliamentary elections spelled more doom and gloom for Iran's thoroughly decimated reform movement—most of whose candidates were once again disqualified—it also marked the onset of a period of particularly intense squabbling between the presidency and the leadership of the legislature. By the parliamentary elections, the office of the Supreme Leader effectively intervened on behalf of anti-Ahmadinejad forces in parliament by disqualifying (via its control of the Guardianship Council) any candidates from the president's camp who were critical of the clerics.

The 2009 presidential election marked an important turning point for Iranian politics. In the face of widespread popular discontent with his leadership, Ahmadinejad had to confront a strong challenge from two reformist candidates. Former Prime Minister Mir-Hossein Mousavi and Mehdi Karroubi (a reformist cleric) both enjoyed widespread popular support. Mousavi in particular was seen as having a strong chance of defeating Ahmadinejad in a second round run-off. A crisis erupted when, just two hours after polls closed, the country's election commission announced final results, with Ahmadinejad winning outright in the first round. After some hesitation, the Supreme Leader announced that the election results—broadly seen both inside and outside Iran as fraudulent—should be respected. Thousands of Iranians took to the streets in the following days, with a particularly strong showing by young people making extensive use of cell phones and social media to communicate and coordinate their demonstrations. This heralded the birth of what became known as the "Green Movement," a diffuse opposition network inspired, and nominally headed, by Mousavi and Karroubi. While many outside Iran, and particularly in the U.S.,

© Damir Sagolj / Reuters

Figure 5.5 Green Movement protestors in Iran's controversial 2009 election

perceived the protests as pro-democracy and pro-Western, the reformist credentials of Mousavi—himself a former Prime Minister (1981–89) of the Islamic Republic—need to be understood in the context of broad-based effort in recent years to eliminate genuine reformers from Iran's political system. Some observers hence made the point that Mousavi looked like a reformist only when measured against Ahmadinejad's extreme orientation.[51]

The 2009 street protests were regarded as sufficiently threatening to the regime to deploy force against demonstrators. Over several days, paramilitary Basiji forces joined regular police to break up protests with batons, tear gas, and in some cases firearms—resulting in dozens of casualties and a still unknown number of deaths. Once it was clear that the regime was willing to use intense and seemingly arbitrary violence against protestors, the demonstrations subsided and the Green Movement became a largely quiet, underground affair. From 2010–12 elements of the movement organized protests, but it never developed into a mass movement.

Perhaps the most significant political development surrounding the 2009 protests and their aftermath was what it revealed about factionalism and power struggles within senior clerical circles. When the protests broke out, Rafsanjani, who was then serving as chairman of the Assembly of Experts, refrained from endorsing the Supreme Leader's validation of the elections and instead issued a statement emphasizing the need for open discussion of Iran's problems. This move pointed to a growing rift within the highest levels of the clerical establishment, with Rafsanjani appearing to be openly challenging the Supreme Leader's authority. While efforts were made to cover up any appearance of a conflict between the two, tensions continued to simmer. These came to a head once again around the next presidential election in 2013, when Rafsanjani—the clear front-runner to succeed Ahmadinejad—had his candidacy denied by the Guardianship Council.

Ahmadinejad's second term as president was dominated by ongoing tensions with parliament and the Supreme Leader, as well as a growing distance between his office and the IRGC—which had previously provided one of his staunchest bases of popular support. Some wondered whether the IRGC, generally regarded as subordinate to the Supreme Leader, might be emerging as an autonomous political force in its own right, particularly given its enormous stakes in the country's economy.[52] Iran's international relations during this period were dominated by ongoing controversy over its atomic energy program, and accusations that it was seeking to develop nuclear weapons. During much of 2012 it seemed that a pre-emptive strike by Israel on Iran's nuclear facilities was a real possibility, although the imminent removal of Ahmadinejad from presidency (his second and final term was nearly up) served as a mitigating factor. Broader regional developments presented Iran with a combination of challenges and opportunities. While Ahmadinejad praised the Arab Uprisings of 2011 for toppling U.S.-backed authoritarian leaders such as Hosni Mubarak, his position appeared hypocritical to many Iranians in light of ongoing repression of reformist voices and other opposition elements at home. Shi'i protests in Bahrain, the sectarian nature of Syria's uprising, and the political success of Islamists after the Uprisings, however, also provided Iran with new opportunities to exert influence across the region. The 2013 presidential elections in the Islamic Republic brought a surprise victory by Hassan Rouhani—a long-time political insider and a relative moderate—and the possibility of a new direction for Iran.

Three aspects relating to the role of Islam in Iranian politics emerge from our survey as particularly noteworthy. First there is the fact that the religious scholars were no strangers to the political landscape, having played an important role in anti-monarchical politics several times throughout modern Iranian history. In this sense, they encountered very little in the way of social barriers when seeking to enter mass popular politics in the lead-up to the Islamic Revolution in the 1970s; indeed, it was the clerics who provided the only viable mobilizing framework. Second, and somewhat related, is the fact that while this was an Islamic revolution in name, it was actually a highly heterogeneous affair in terms of who actually took part. Without the support of a broad range of social classes, sectors, and political orientations, it is unlikely that the religious leaders would have had the human resources necessary successfully to mount such an upheaval in the social order. Finally, although the ruling religious regime is often thought of in monolithic terms, it becomes very easy to identify a broad spectrum of interests, policies, and political visions that define several clear factions within the clerical establishment itself.

As this chapter has shown, the "Islamic state" varies considerably from context to context depending on the circumstances of its establishment and the configuration of social and political forces within the various national settings in which such polities exist. "Islam as the system" does not necessarily tell us much about what kind of politics we are likely to find in such a state. In the case of Saudi Arabia, the royal family managed until fairly recently to keep a tight lid on political opposition of any sort, while in Pakistan—an Islamic state with a very different source of legitimacy—we find political history defined in terms of the ebbs and flows of different visions of Islamic polity. Iran, as a revolutionary state based on an innovative doctrine of direct clerical rule, seems to have gone furthest of all in terms of institutionalizing within the state social actors and discursive forms defined almost exclusively in religious terms. But as former Iranian president Mohammad Khatami once wrote:

> If we limit ourselves to the appearances of and have a narrow view of religion, then the concept of "Islamic Republic" itself will mean separation from Islam. Where did you ever have anything called a republic in Islam? Where in Islam—the beginnings of Islam—do you find anything called a parliament?[53]

His point here is that it is impossible to understand the meaning, nature, and form of the Islamic state today without reference to the discourse of political modernity that inevitably frames its very formation. For him, the religious nature of the state is not achieved by placing the word "Islamic" in front of the word "republic," but rather in assessing the normative implications inherent in various arrangements of power and social order. On this reading, certain institutions in avowedly non-Islamic settings could still qualify as "Islamic," and *vice versa.*

Common to all three cases we have examined in detail above is the idea of embracing an Islamic state as part of transition from one social order to another—but not generally in the context of a prior dissolution of order or an extended conflict that has tended to prevent the establishment of societal stability. In the next chapter we move on to examine several cases where Islam has sought to fill the vacuum of an absent state or social authority, or has emerged as a mobilizing (and sometimes competing) discourse in situations of protracted violent conflict—Islam, in other words, for lack of a system.

BOX 5.4 HASSAN AL-TURABI AND SUDAN'S "ISLAMIC EXPERIMENT"

In 1989, a military *coup d'état* brought General Omar al-Bashir to power in Sudan. It soon became clear, however, that the main beneficiary (and likely instigator) of this turn of events was the National Islamic Front (NIF), Sudan's Muslim Brotherhood affiliate. The NIF was led by Hassan al-Turabi, an inveterate Islamist politician and intellectual trained in Europe. Turabi's party presided over what he termed an "Islamic experiment," seeking to broaden and deepen existing *shari'ah* laws while consolidating their grip on power by filling key government posts. Political parties were outlawed and Islamic law declared throughout the country: Sudan had seemingly joined the ranks of the "Islamic states" alongside Pakistan, Iran, and Saudi Arabia. Over the course of the 1990s the situation evolved into a power struggle between Turabi and Bashir as the latter saw the military's influence eroded by various NIF (now renamed the National Congress) power plays. Turabi, who had since risen to become Speaker of the Parliament and leader of a National Congress splinter party called the Popular Congress Party (PCP), fell foul of Bashir by signing unauthorized agreements with separatist movements in the country's south and found himself jailed or under house arrest from 2001 to 2005. Turabi's alleged involvement with the Justice and Equality Movement, an Islamist militia opposed to Khartoum's policies in the Darfur conflict, found him once again at odds with the government. He was jailed for several months in 2009 after calling for Bashir to be tried for war crimes the International Criminal Court over Sudanese government conduct in the Darfur crisis. While still nominally head of the PCP, Turabi's advanced age has led him to take a back seat in terms of day-to-day politics.

Turabi's efforts to implement a model of the Islamic state in Sudan must be understood against the backdrop of that country's ethno-religious demographics, multiple ongoing conflicts, and Turabi's own unique approach to political pragmatism and public messaging. Sudanese politics have long been plagued by sectarian and tribal rivalries, overlaid by a major civil war pitting the Arab Muslim government of the north against the mostly sub-Saharan African population (mostly Christian or animist) of the south. Despite repeated assurances by Turabi to the effect that Islamic law would apply only to Muslims, the continued persecution of non-Muslim citizens throughout Sudan has left many suspicious of the "Islamic experiment." In 2005, a Comprehensive Peace Accord was signed between the southern Sudanese People's Liberation

Figure 5.6 Sudanese Islamist leader Hassan al-Turabi

© Mohamed Nureldin Abdallah / Reuters

Movement and Bashir's government. It created a largely autonomous region in the south that eventually became the new country of South Sudan following a 2011 referendum on full independence from Sudan.

Many observers have pointed to a certain ambiguity—some say duplicity—in Turabi's conduct as both ideologue and politician. While many of his writings, particularly those aimed at Western audiences, seem to advance relatively liberal and progressive interpretations of Islam (e.g. women are not required to wear veils, should be fully employed and can act as *imams;* alcohol should be tolerated in the privacy of the home), Turabi seems to have done little to bring about the implementation of these ideals in the context of the Islamic state in Sudan. His position on issues such as the proper means for transitioning to an Islamic political order also seems to have shifted and swayed over the years, depending on the state of Sudanese politics and the relative political fortunes of his party at any given time. While extolling the virtues of democracy and political pluralism in his writings, Turabi has played a key role in maintaining Sudan's authoritarian system after 1989. In the early 1990s, he served as coordinator-in-chief of a new international network of Islamist movements, hosting several conferences attended by leading MB parties and movements. Turabi also invited Usama Bin Laden to Sudan in 1991, providing him refuge and support after the latter had been forced out of his native Saudi Arabia.

NOTES

1 J. Piscatori, "Ideological Politics in Saudi Arabia," in J. Piscatori (ed.), *Islam in the Political Process,* Cambridge: Cambridge University Press, 1983, pp. 56–72.
2 G. Kepel, *The War for Muslim Minds,* Cambridge, MA: Harvard University Press, 2004, p. 164.
3 Kepel, op. cit., p. 175.
4 M. Al-Rasheed, *A History of Saudi Arabia,* Cambridge: Cambridge University Press, 2002, p. 167.
5 Al-Rasheed, op. cit., p. 171.
6 Al-Rasheed, op. cit., p. 183.
7 S. Lacroix, "Between Islamists and Liberals: Saudi Arabia's New 'Islamo-Liberal' Reformists," *Middle East Journal* 58, 2004, pp. 345–365.
8 O. Ashour, *The Deradicalization of Islamists: Transforming Armed Islamist Movements,* London: Routledge, 2009.
9 International Crisis Group, "Saudi Arabia Backgrounder: Who are the Islamists?," *ICG Middle East Report* 31, 2004, p. 8.
10 J. Esposito, *Islam and Politics,* 4th edn, Syracuse, NY: Syracuse University Press, 1984, p. 119.
11 Esposito, op. cit., p. 124.
12 Esposito, op. cit., p. 173.
13 H. Haqqani, *Pakistan: Between Mosque and Military,* Washington, DC: Carnegie Endowment for International Peace, 2005, p. 152.
14 Esposito, op. cit., p. 185.
15 Haqqani, op. cit., p. 138.
16 Haqqani, op. cit., p. 152.
17 S. V. R. Nasr, "Islamic Opposition in the Political Process: Lessons from Pakistan," in J. Esposito (ed.), *Political Islam: Revolution, Radicalism, or Reform?,* Boulder, CO: Lynne Rienner, 1997, pp. 148–149.
18 M. Ahmad, "Islamic Fundamentalism in South Asia: The Jamaat-i-Islami and the Tablighi Jamaat," in M. Marty, R. Appleby (eds), *Fundamentalisms Observed,* Chicago, IL: University of Chicago Press, 1991, p. 483.
19 Haqqani, op. cit., p. 139; Nasr, op. cit., p. 149.
20 Esposito, op. cit., p. 185.
21 Nasr, op. cit., p. 146.
22 Haqqani, op. cit., p. 113.

23 Haqqani, op. cit., p. 112.
24 V. Nasr, "The Rise of "Muslim Democracy," *Journal of Democracy* 16, 2005, 14.
25 S. V. R. Nasr, *Islamic Leviathan: Islam and the Making of State Power,* New York: Oxford University Press, 2001, p. 156.
26 "The Future Looks Bearded," *The Economist: Survey of Pakistan,* July 8 2006, p. 8.
27 Ahmad, op. cit., p. 485.
28 Ahmad, op. cit., p. 492.
29 Nasr, "Islamic Opposition in the Political Process," op. cit., p. 141.
30 Esposito, op. cit., p. 126.
31 H. Munson, *Islam and Revolution in the Middle East,* New Haven, CT: Yale University Press, 1988, p. 53.
32 B. Moin, "Khomeini's Search for Perfection: Theory and Reality," in A. Rahnema (ed.), *Pioneers of Islamic Revival,* London: Zed Books, 1994, p. 74.
33 Moin, op. cit., p. 81.
34 L. C. Brown, *Religion and State: The Muslim Approach to Politics,* New York: Columbia University Press, 2000, p. 165.
35 R. Khomeini, "The Form of Islamic Government," in H. Algar (trans.), *Islam and Revolution: Writings and Declarations of Imam Khomeini (1941–1980),* Berkeley, CA: Mizan Press, 1981, pp. 48–49
36 Moin, op. cit., p. 89.
37 V. Martin, *Creating an Islamic State: Khomeini and the Making of a New Iran,* New York: I.B. Tauris, 2000, p. 117.
38 Khomeini, op. cit., p. 55.
39 Khomeini, op. cit., p. 59.
40 Khomeini, op. cit., p. 60.
41 Brown, op. cit., p. 169.
42 Martin, op. cit., p. 93.
43 Munson, op. cit.
44 A. Sreberny-Mohammadi, A. Mohammadi, *Small Media, Big Revolution: Communication, Culture, and the Iranian Revolution,* Minneapolis, MN: University of Minnesota Press, 1994.
45 Munson, op. cit., p. 63.
46 Esposito, op. cit., pp. 222–223.
47 J. Piscatori, "The Rushdie Affair and the Politics of Ambiguity," *International Affairs* 66, 1990, pp. 767–789.
48 N. Keddie, *Modern Iran: Roots and Results of Revolution,* New Haven, CT: Yale University Press, 2003, p. 269.
49 D. Brumberg, *Reinventing Khomeini: The Struggle for Reform in Iran,* Chicago, IL: University of Chicago Press, 2001, p. 199.
50 Brumberg, op. cit., p. 207.
51 R. F. Worth, "As Iran Votes, Talk of a Sea Change," *New York Times,* June 12, 2009, p. A1.
52 A. Nader, "The Revolutionary Guards," United States Institute of Peace *Iran Primer,* http://iranprimer.usip.org/resource/revolutionary-guards
53 "Khatami on Religious Thought Renewal," *Iran Daily,* June 21, 1999, cited by B. Bakhtiari, "Dilemmas of Reform and Democracy in the Islamic Republic of Iran," in R. Hefner (ed.), *Remaking Muslim Politics: Pluralism, Contestation, Democratization,* Princeton, NJ: Princeton University Press, 2005, p. 118.

CHAPTER 6

Islam for lack of a system: Islamism in weak and failed states

This chapter represents the last in a series of three thematically organized accounts of contemporary Muslim politics under various political circumstances. We have looked already at the evolution of Islamism as a political strategy where groups and parties seek to enter the political system (Chapter 4). We then went on to examine how Muslim politics play out in three countries where the state is, to some degree, defined in terms of Islam. In this chapter we look at several cases of Islam and politics in settings where a state has collapsed or, due to ongoing military occupation and violent conflict, is functionally absent or, at best, very weak. As we will see, many of the same discursive and mobilizing mechanisms are at work in these situations. The political environment of a weak or absent state, however, often presents Muslim actors with a very different set of opportunity structures.

In the case of a failed state, Islamist actors generally do not need to worry about the problem of defining themselves *vis-à-vis* an existing (and potentially hostile) political authority, or about devising a strategy to challenge or confront the ruling state. But neither will they enjoy the relatively luxurious circumstances of political opposition, where one can sit back and cast barbs at the state without being required to implement alternatives, or being held to account. Once in power, on the other hand, any legitimacy or support they may derive from their religious identity will quickly be put to the test once faced with the realities of actually running a country. In cases of state failure, the relevant exigencies are much more demanding as it will often be necessary to recreate (or create anew, in some cases) the foundations of government and public administration. In a situation of military occupation, on the other hand, many of the same constraints associated with a hostile state may bear on the activities of Islamist groups. As we will see, however, under circumstances characterized by the presence of multiple currents of liberation discourse (nationalist, leftist, religious), Islamists and occupying authorities may find themselves entering into odd constellations of alliance or quietism in the pursuit of various short- and medium-term goals. In political climates defined primarily in terms of liberation from an external power, the repertoire of political symbols available to Islamic actors, and their articulation in terms of religion, will also differ from situations of straightforward opposition to an existing state. Finally, where state capacity is weak, Islamist actors who are well organized, well funded, and well managed may emerge as parallel service providers or, in some areas, may even begin to resemble "shadow governments" in terms of how deeply they become entrenched as legitimate guarantors of welfare and public order as well as promulgators of resistance to foreign enemies.

We should clarify how the cases examined in this chapter differ from certain others we have already looked at and which, at first glance, may represent political climates that seem to display many of the same features we have detailed above. In looking at Egypt, for example, we emphasized the "retreat of the state" as a provider of social welfare in the context of economic liberalization and public sector reform. As we saw, Islamist actors at the societal and even local neighborhood level worked to fill the void left by the absent state, and so built for themselves an enormous pool of social capital and popular legitimacy. While we also look in this chapter at situations where Islamists offer social services that a central state is unable or unwilling to provide, the crucial difference rests in the fact that in these cases the state is missing altogether, or is so weak as to be wholly absent from people's considerations regarding alternative sources of welfare or political identity. In other words, unlike in Egypt where the state, despite its "retreat" from the realm of the social, was still a dominant presence in terms of its public order and security capacities, we are dealing here with situations where it is dubious as to whether the existing political authorities would even meet the bare minimum requirements to qualify as a state—such as Max Weber's conception of the state as possessing a monopoly over the capacity to use violence. In short, in this chapter we are dealing with situations where Islamists operate in settings in which political sovereignty and national legitimacy are ambiguous at best, and potentially are up for grabs.

BOX 6.1 NIGERIA: *SHARI'AH* LAW AND THE POLITICS OF FEDERALISM

Between 1999 and 2003, 12 states in northern Nigeria passed legislation implementing varying degrees of *shari'ah* law. In the wake of this development, certain areas of the north have seen instances of violence associated with "vigilante justice" and several high-profile human rights cases—most notably that of Amina Lawal who, in 2002, was sentenced to death (eventually overturned on appeal) by a *shari'ah* court on charges of adultery. From 2009, a local movement for protecting Muslim rights, Boko Haram, turned militant and has since been implicated in several dozen bombings killing over a thousand people, including in the country's federal capital (see Box 6.4, "Boko Haram: the 'Nigerian Taliban'?"). The group claims that it is fighting to establish *shari'ah* law in Nigeria at the federal level.

What drove the enforcement of *shari'ah* in the north, and how can we understand it as an example of Muslim politics? Rather than representing an upswing in the fortunes of conservative Islamists, the emergence of the *shari'ah* legislation is, first and foremost, a regional response to Nigeria's return to civilian rule in 1998 after 15 years of martial law and several army coups. There were concerns in the north that a civilian government would be weak on law and order, promoting certain northern leaders to search for solutions couched in idioms—such as Islam—with local appeal. A second and related issue concerns the division of power between the central government and the various constituent states of the Nigerian federation. Here we see Islamic language and symbols being mobilized as part of a politics that asserts strong regional and cultural identities *vis-à-vis* a federal state still seeking to consolidate its position under civilian rule.

Nigeria's population of 132 million is believed to be 50 percent Muslim, with the majority of those professing Islam living in the north of the country. Various ethnic, linguistic, tribal, and sectarian cleavages and tensions have been endemic to Nigerian politics since independence from Britain in 1960.

We also looked at Iran, which, having experienced a revolution, may appear to be subject to some of the same considerations regarding the reconstruction of state institutions. Iran, however, was neither a classic failed state nor the victim of a protracted conflict or civil war. It was certainly a state that had lost popular legitimacy, but that is very different from a state that fails in the sense of comprehensive institutional decay. Its revolution was also a relatively short-lived affair, meaning that a new political authority was able to set about the business of governing relatively quickly, and was also able to tap into some level of continuity in terms of existing institutions and human resources—while, of course, adding some unique institutions of its own. The core point is that in setting up the Islamic Republic of Iran in the wake of the 1979 revolution, Khomeini faced a very different set of political and structural challenges than those confronting the Taliban in 1996 as they went about the business of converting their country into the Islamic Emirate of Afghanistan.

Our exploration of Muslim politics in weak, failed, and conflict states is carried out via three main case studies, with supplementary coverage of two further examples. First, we examine the rise of Hamas in the occupied territories of Palestine. After a brief overview of its origins and the basic course of its political career to date, the evolution of its political and military strategy in a complex and constantly changing political environment is analyzed. We have two main areas of focus with regard to Hamas. First we consider the enormous social base the movement developed for itself (particularly in Gaza) through a comprehensive network of social services. This is examined in terms of popular legitimacy and capacity to mobilize for political and military operations. Second, we consider its relations with the Palestine Liberation Organization (PLO) and, later, the PA in terms of competing for national legitimacy. How did Hamas adapt the Islamist project to a political setting defined in terms of resistance to occupation and national liberation? We then look at Hamas' decision to enter politics, which led to a surprise victory in the 2006 Palestinian legislative elections. Finally we assess the subsequent period of factionalism within Palestinian politics, episodes of renewed hostility with Israel, and more recent efforts to achieve reconciliation between key Palestinian groups.

A second case analysis focused on Hizbullah in Lebanon provides a useful comparative perspective on an Islamist movement originally founded in the context of violence—in this case the Lebanese Civil War (1975–90)—but which then sought to integrate itself into the mainstream political process while simultaneously preserving its armed capabilities and vast network of civil society and charitable services. Here our focus is on Hizbullah's political role after 1992, particularly in the aftermath of Syria's 2005 withdrawal from Lebanon. As will become clear, with significant turbulence in regional geopolitics in recent years, Hizbullah's role in Lebanese politics—and the Arab world more broadly—seems increasingly to be driven by imperatives relating to survival, power maximization, and the protection of foreign sponsors amidst renewed sectarian tensions across the region after the Arab Uprisings.

Our third case study is the Taliban of Afghanistan. We look at the circumstances that permitted them to come to power in the aftermath of the civil war that broke out in Afghanistan following the withdrawal of Soviet forces. Of particular interest is the interaction between the Taliban's form of austere public religious normativity and prevailing religious norms in Afghanistan. While it is clear that the people of Afghanistan welcomed the Taliban, not only because of their promise to restore order, but also because of their religious basis, it emerges that the popular Afghan conception of what a religious state means and looks like did not correspond to the literal Islamism of the Taliban *mullahs*. This fact, complicated by persistent ethno-sectarian rivalries and the new regime's utter lack of administrative experience, meant that the Islamic Emirate of Afghanistan was fatally crippled from the very outset. A failed state gave way to what was, at best, a "quasi-state."[1] We also look at how the Taliban has reconstituted itself, perhaps with a different strategic focus, in the aftermath of U.S. military intervention in Afghanistan in 2001, as well as more recent efforts to imagine what it might mean for the Talban to reach a negotiated political settlement with the Afghan state.

ISLAMISM IN PALESTINE: NATIONALISM, CHARITY, AND VIOLENCE

Hamas is a complex and controversial entity. It has been variously described as a political movement, a terrorist group, and a social welfare organization. The difficulty in analyzing Hamas arises from the fact that it is, in fact, all three—but not reducible to any one of them. The highly politicized and often polarized environment in which all of these manifestations of Hamas operate also poses significant challenges to the would-be analyst. To those focused primarily on the security of Israel, Hamas is clearly first and foremost a terrorist group. To those, on the other hand, who see Israel's occupation of Palestine as illegal and dehumanizing, Hamas represents a legitimate form of resistance. The account offered here does not try to make the case for one or the other of these two positions, but seeks instead to explore the circumstances under which the discourse and ideology of Hamas have evolved, and also how and why, at given times, it has made particular choices from among the various strategic and tactical options available to it. In a climate in which "terrorism" has become such a loaded term, its association with a particular group runs the risk of obscuring the fact that terrorism is a tactic rather than an ideology. To characterize (or dismiss) a movement solely in reference to its use of a particular tactic does not help us, as political analysts, to explain how it mobilizes people and symbols in the pursuit of its political goals. Glenn Robinson puts it well when he writes:

> [B]y labeling Hamas a terrorist group, [we] ignore most of what Hamas actually does. Hamas is a social movement with thousands of activists

and hundreds of thousands (perhaps millions) of Palestinian sympathizers, and it engages in extensive political and social activities far removed from suicide bombers. Second, it is always problematic to speak of terrorist groups (or states), as opposed to groups (or states) that periodically use acts of terror for tactical political reasons. By understanding terrorism in tactical terms rather than as a generic group attribute, rational responses become potentially more effective and less obviously politically hypocritical.[2]

Hamas is particularly difficult to assess in this regard since, while much of its charitable activity is indeed "far removed" from its suicide bombers, there is also significant evidence to suggest that some within the political bureau of Hamas have direct control over the activities of its military wing. And yet we cannot understand why the movement enjoys such widespread support among Palestinians, even those who eschew violence and/or have little interest in an Islamic state, unless we look at Hamas in its totality. Likewise, without a holistic analysis, we will achieve little understanding of the internal dynamics of the movement and hence be unable to identify where it may be headed in the future.

Our coverage of Hamas is divided into two main sections. In the first we examine the origins of the movement, and provide a brief overview of its activities from the time of the first *intifada* in 1987 up to the 2006 electoral victory that brought it to power in the PA. The second section provides an analytical focus on several major topics and themes relating to Hamas. We look at its social base, structure, and funding; its ambivalent and constantly changing relationship with the PLO, particularly the dominant Fatah faction); the evolution of Hamas' discourse, strategy, and topics from the time of its founding; and, finally, various aspects of the internal Hamas sociology (factions, generational differences, etc.) that may indicate the group's political future. We then analyze the circumstances that brought Hamas to power in 2006 and the various challenges posed by its control of the PA and the Palestinian Legislative Council (PLC). Finally, we look at the subsequent factionalism in Palestinian politics and the *de facto* division of the Occupied Territories, the impact of renewed hostilities with Israel, and the implications of recent efforts to achieve a reconciliation between Hamas and other Palestinian groups.

Hamas: Origins, evolution, and political career

Hamas as a distinct political movement was born in December 1987 at the inception of the first Palestinian *intifada* ("shaking off"), or uprising, against the Israeli occupation of the West Bank and Gaza. Hamas is an acronym for *Harakat al-Muqawama al-Islamiyya* ("Islamic Resistance

Movement"); the word *hamas* also means "enthusiasm" or "zeal" in Arabic. While formally constituted in the late 1980s, the social roots of Hamas go back much further and can be found in the Palestinian branch of the Muslim Brotherhood, which was established during Hasan al-Banna's lifetime. During much of the MB's history in Palestine, control of its operations was divided between Egypt and Jordan, with the Gaza region falling to the former and the West Bank to the latter—particularly after the West Bank was annexed to Jordan in 1950. After 1967, when Gaza and the West Bank both came under Israeli control, the Gaza branch in particular was increasingly isolated from both the central MB organization and its other Palestinian affiliates. Where before 1967 the MB had been politically active against Israel—even sending Brotherhood volunteers to fight in Palestine in the late 1940s and early 1950s—it confined itself almost exclusively to religious and social affairs for the next 20 years.[3]

In the late 1960s, the leadership of the MB in Gaza fell to a young activist, Ahmed al-Yassin. Sheikh Yassin, as he commonly came to be known, was a schoolteacher and *mufti* who had studied at Al-Azhar in Cairo, and also had undergone teacher training. Before taking over the reins of the MB, he had served as the *imam* in several mosques and also as a teacher in schools run by the United Nations Relief Works Agency (UNRWA).[4] From the 1970s, Yassin oversaw the creation of a rapidly expanding network of charities and social services in Gaza. The central institution in this endeavor was the Mujamma al-Islami ("Islamic Center"), founded by Yassin in 1973. This body became the core of the MB's activities in Gaza, and its influence grew rapidly as it came to encompass dozens and then hundreds of autonomous social organizations. Many religious institutions in Gaza also came under its control. An influx of funding from Saudi Arabia during the 1970s also allowed it to build more places of worship, and by 1986 40 percent of all mosques in the area were run by the MB.[5] Israel, seeking to curry favor with the Islamists as a check on the growing influence of the Palestinian left, also provided funds for the endowment of *awqaf*—a tactic they would try to use again at the founding of Hamas. In 1978, the Islamic University of Gaza was founded and also began to work closely with the Mujamma. Much of the Hamas intellectual leadership would eventually emerge from the faculty and administrative ranks of this institution. We should note that while the MB also established similar associations in the West Bank, they were not as closely integrated and many were still controlled from Jordan—unlike the Gaza institutions, which were almost entirely home-grown and -managed.[6]

The path leading to the formation of Hamas out of the MB begins in the 1980s, when certain tensions regarding the Brotherhood's overall sociopolitical strategy began to emerge. As the occupation wore on, a faction of MB radicals—dissatisfied with the organization's confinement to the religious and social spheres—broke away to form Islamic Jihad. This armed group, whose formation can in some regards be compared with the violent MB splinter groups that appeared in Egypt in the 1970s such as Takfir w'al Hijra and the Gemaa Islamiyya, proceeded to undertake various militant acts against the Israeli occupation forces. Their activities, while confined to a very small group, served to raise tensions considerably and to prime the Occupied Territories for a more active form of resistance.[7] In this climate, certain tensions brewing within the MB became more pronounced. Essentially this broke down as a division between a younger generation, unassociated with the MB before 1967, who wanted to take a more politically active stance towards the Occupation; and the older, Jordanian-linked faction that preferred to continue focusing on religious and social activity. The *intifada* became the wedge that separated the two.[8] For the younger generation, the idea of waiting until society has become properly Islamized before moving to political action—the classic Brotherhood gradualist approach—was not suited to conditions of direct military occupation by a foreign power, in this case Israel.[9] Turning to the notion of *jihad,* they sought to invest the Brotherhood in Palestine with a new "doctrinal conviction" and to find in Islam a theology of liberation.[10]

On December 8, 1987 an Israeli truck crashed into two Palestinian taxis, killing their occupants. Seeing this as a deliberate act of aggression, Palestinians took to the streets in several days of protests that were fanned and sustained by a number of preceding and subsequent acts of violence. The evening after the bus incident, Sheikh Yassin held a meeting with several other MB leaders in Gaza—most notably Abd al-Aziz al-Rantisi, who would later become a key figure in Hamas—at which they determined to establish a political movement to coordinate and lead an active resistance in the name of Islam. The formation of Hamas was formally announced in February as the level and intensity of protests and street violence grew, much of it organized out of Gaza by the new group. This uprising, which became known as the *intifada,* was a complex affair. It was led primarily by the Palestinian youths (*shabab*), but found active participation from all walks of life and political persuasions. Its coordination was by no means confined to the ranks of the Islamists. The PLO, the leading nationalist force, was another major player and this group—whose top-file leadership was living in exile in Tunisia at the time—formed a coordinating body of its own (the Unified National Leadership) to organize protests and general strikes. It both complemented and competed with Hamas in this regard (see below). Where the activities of Islamic Jihad served as the "accelerant" toward the *intifada*'s ignition during the 1980s, the uprising itself was conducted by ranks mobilized by both nationalists and Islamists.[11] The MB in Palestine initially kept some distance from Hamas in case it failed and prompted an Israeli crackdown on the Brotherhood's religious activities. However, several months into the *intifada,* when it was clear that Hamas had staying power (and, interestingly, once the MB saw merchants and *bazaari* joining in the uprising), they proudly declared Hamas to be their "strong arm."[12] Over the next few months, the Palestinian MB merged itself, and its institutions, completely into Hamas—becoming, effectively, the same organization.[13] Even Israel initially handled Hamas very gently, hoping that its presence would split the Palestinian population between Islamist and nationalists—leading to greater political disunity within the Occupied Territories.[14] As the frequency and intensity of the protests grew, so did Hamas' profile and popular reputation. When the foreign-based PLO leadership made a bid for political normalcy by recognizing Israel and renouncing violence, Hamas was well positioned to claim that it was now the only Palestinian force still willing and able to pursue active resistance in the name of national liberation.[15] Not only that, but, for the time being at least, its leadership was based in Palestine and actually living through the Occupation, unlike the PLO's seniors abroad.

In 1989, the *intifada*—which until this point had consisted almost exclusively of strikes, street protests, and low-level violence involving rock-throwing youths and burning tires—took a new turn. Hamas began for the first time to use firearms and explosives against Israeli forces, prompting a swift response by the Israeli Defense Force (IDF) who arrested and imprisoned Sheikh Yassin. In this power vacuum, control of Hamas for the next two years (until Yassin was released in a prisoner swap) shifted to the group's expatriate leadership—most notably Mousa Abu Marzuq in the United States.[16] In 1991, in order to protect its military forces from the IDF and clarify the group's command structure, Hamas formally established a separate military wing, the Izz al-Din al-Qassam Brigades—named after an MB resistance fighter from the 1930s who had led operations against the British and Zionist Jews.[17] Over the next decade, as Hamas began to make increasing use of violent tactics, the Brigades would become for much of the outside world the public face of Palestinian Islamism. During this same period, Hamas broke completely with the PLO in terms of cooperation due to the latter's willingness to participate in the U.S.-sponsored Madrid peace process. Even before the talks began, the Islamists dismissed this as a form of capitulation, in effect, to Israel's terms for resolving the conflict.

As Hamas attacks against the IDF expanded from 1991 and grew to encompass civilian targets inside Israel itself, the Israeli government attempted in late 1992 to undertake what it regarded as a comprehensive "house cleaning" of Palestinian religious radicalism by deporting over 400 Islamist intellectuals and leaders to a remote mountain-top village in southern Lebanon. The Islamists managed to convert this into a major public relations coup, however, when the world's media arriving to interview these exiles found a group of highly articulate intellectuals and professionals shivering in the cold, rather than cadre of crazed militants.[18] By this time the *intifada* had stalemated around a war of attrition that was highly costly to the Israelis in military and political terms, and to the Palestinians for both economic and political reasons. In 1993, after months of secret discussions—during which both Israelis and Palestinians swore publicly that they would never sit down together around a negotiating table—it was announced that Israel and the PLO had devised and were ready to sign a Declaration of Principles (DOP) providing for mutual recognition and security guarantees, as well as the first phase of a gradual handover of political autonomy to a new Palestinian Authority. Hopes for a rapid settlement, with significant political and economic dividends for the Palestinian population, increased exponentially in the aftermath of the signing of what became known as the "Oslo Agreement"—named for the Norwegian capital where most of the content had been negotiated. Oslo also permitted Yasser Arafat to stage a triumphant return from exile and to reclaim the mantle of Palestinian national leadership. For its part, Hamas found the Oslo agreement very worrying from both a normative and a political point of view. It regarded the piecemeal approach to Palestinian autonomy contained in the treaty to be highly problematic. It seemed to them, and to many other Palestinians, that Arafat had given away much in return for very little, in that the core issues of the conflict (final status, Jerusalem, Palestinian right of return) were all left untouched. They also feared the political boost this would give to the PLO and particularly Arafat's Fatah faction, which looked set to take over the newly established PA. Hamas joined the Palestinian Forces Alliance, an Oslo-rejectionist coalition comprised of various groups who feared the agreement would turn Palestine into a series of Arab "Bantustans" (as per the South African model)—that is, enclaves of Palestinians surrounded on all sides by Israel.[19] The Islamists demonstrated they still had some basis of popular support in late 1993 by winning the student council elections at Bir Zeit University, the first time in 20 years that Fatah had not been victorious there.[20]

As the first elections for the new PA approached, Hamas found itself considerably divided over how to respond. The rejectionists wanted nothing whatsoever to do with the PA, and the radicals wanted to combine this with renewed aggression against Israel to try and scuttle the agreement altogether. The pragmatists and moderates within Hamas felt the organization would be able to have more impact from within the PA and advocated full participation.[21] Sheikh Yassin, back in prison (under a life sentence) by this time, hesitantly endorsed the group's participation. In the end, the hardliners won out and the Islamists boycotted the elections. Even after the victory of the rejectionists, it was still unclear to them how best to proceed. While hoping to see the peace deal unravel over time, they were very aware that a hopeful Palestinian population still endorsed the terms of Oslo for the most part, and they were wary of damaging this support through a new campaign of violence aimed at destroying the fragile entente. When the peace process began to go awry after the assassination of Israeli Prime Minister Yitzhak Rabin by a Jewish militant in late 1995, Hamas escalated the pace of a series of post-Oslo attacks that had started the previous year. In the run-up to Israel's 1996 election, Hamas carried out numerous attacks on civilian targets in Israel, ensuring a victory for the right-wing candidate Benjamin Netanyahu. Over the next several years, Hamas suffered a range of setbacks. Arafat and the PA were strongly pressured by Israel to contain Hamas, and to this end the PA police forces rounded up and imprisoned a large number of the movement's operatives. Its latitude of maneuver on the home front was severely curtailed as the PA also took over control of a number of its institutions and mosques—regarded by Hamas, effectively, as a declaration of civil war. Indeed, clashes between forces loyal to Hamas and PA police occurred in the summer of 1996. In 1999 Jordan moved against the Palestinian Islamists' political bureau in Amman, forcing its leadership into exile in Syria.[22] One positive development for Hamas during this period was that Sheikh Yassin was released from prison in 1997 in another prisoner swap, this time with Jordan after the authorities in Amman captured two Israeli agents who had attempted to assassinate Khaled Meshal, the head of the Hamas political bureau.

By 2000, Hamas' political influence and operational space had been significantly curtailed as Arafat consolidated his increasingly autocratic rule over the Occupied Territories. As the Americans sponsored a last-ditch round of comprehensive peace negotiations between Arafat and Israel's Labor government that autumn, the far-right-wing Israeli opposition leader Ariel Sharon paid a provocative visit to the *Haram al-Sharif* in Jerusalem's Old City, the third holiest site in Islam. This was the catalyst for the release of a wide range of Palestinian frustrations and, as regular protests and clashes settled in over the next few months, a second *intifada* was declared. Arafat hoped to seize the new *intifada* as an opportunity to distract from the dismal state of his government and reunify the population around his leadership of a new resistance effort. However, he found the ranks of his own Fatah faction highly divided, with the younger generation of leaders who had been inside Palestine during the first *intifada* (rather than living relatively comfortably in exile abroad) fed up with Arafat's authoritarian system of cronyism and patronage that denied them any effective role in the PA. The second *intifada,* which saw the PA headquarters placed under Israeli quarantine, hence served only to emphasize Arafat's inefficacy and to increase the popularity of both the younger Fatah leaders and Hamas. Where stone-throwing youths had been the iconic image of the first *intifada,* Hamas raised the stakes considerably from 2001, with frequent suicide bombings causing large numbers of civilian and military casualties in Israel. Once Sharon came to power in Israel, the crackdown on all forms of Palestinian resistance, but Hamas in particular, kicked into high gear. In 2004, in a show of force and to emphasize a new zero-tolerance policy, the IDF assassinated Sheikh Yassin with a helicopter gunship, and several weeks later also killed his replacement, Abd al-Aziz al-Rantisi. While this "decapitation" attack certainly initially left Hamas in political disarray, the symbolism involved led to an enormous upswing in popular support for Hamas among Palestinians—even within the majority that did not share their Islamist vision. Yasser Arafat, seeking to stem the by now constant barrage of criticism aimed at him from all sides, reluctantly introduced a division of powers within the PA that created a new prime ministership. Behind the scenes, however, he worked to keep power concentrated in his own hands. When he died in late 2004, the PA—and the Fatah old guard in particular—were bitterly despised by the population of the Occupied Territories.

When the 2006 elections for the Palestine Legislative Council (the Palestinian parliament) came around, Hamas this time announced that it would participate. While opinion polls showed that Fatah was severely handicapped and everyone expected Hamas to do well, the result that finally transpired was not widely anticipated: the Islamists won a landslide, taking enough seats to allow them to form the PA government. While Fatah's Mahmoud Abbas had won the presidency after Arafat's death, ensuring that the PLO would still have a key role in government, the day-to-day administration of the Palestinian territories was to be in the hands of Hamas. With the world still shocked and wondering how this as-yet politically untested organization would reconcile its record of militancy with the responsibilities of holding official office, Hamas conferred within itself as to several political options—including setting up a government of national unity by inviting non-Hamas politicians into its cabinet. In the end it decided to go it alone and appointed Ismail Haniyeh, a relatively young moderate who had led the faction arguing for Hamas' participation in the first elections in 1996, as the new Prime Minister.

Explaining and understanding Hamas

Before looking at the experience of Hamas since its electoral victory in 2006, we need to gain a better understanding of the group as a social movement. To this end we will spend some time analyzing the group's social base, structure, and funding in an effort to explain the foundations of its popular legitimacy. Looking at how the relationship between Hamas and the PLO evolved over the years since the founding of the former will provide insight into how Hamas has responded to a shifting political field. Both of these will then allow us to consider the overall trajectory in the Islamists' discourse and tactics in recent years, before finally exploring the internal sociology of the movement for clues as to where Hamas may be going in the future.

As noted above, Hamas draws much of its popular support and legitimacy from the vast network of social services it has established over the years. This is not something that Hamas created from scratch when it was established in 1987; rather, these various social organizations were inherited from its parent organization, the Muslim Brotherhood, which had been cultivating them for two decades before Hamas even appeared on the scene.[23] In this connection, it is worth observing that the MB's recruitment patterns in Palestine during the 1980s shifted to include a much larger proportion of middle-class and well-educated supporters. Not only did they bring with them the technical skills and managerial know-how required to run a vast and closely integrated network of associations, but they also brought to the MB a political consciousness that was increasingly impatient with the Brotherhood's exclusive focus on religious and social activity. This was indeed important to them, but they were ready for more political activism alongside their social work.[24] The MB's only real Islamist competitor, Islamic Jihad, while more active in terms of armed resistance, was unable to establish itself as a mass movement at the social level in the way the MB had. Islamic Jihad hence had very little to draw upon in terms of social capital, and only a very narrow base of popular support.[25] In addition to the social welfare services provided by Sheikh Yassin's network, the Mujamma al-Islami gained further local legitimacy through the provision of various mediation and arbitration services.[26] By combining both social services *and* social authority in this way, we can see how, by the time Hamas was created, the foundations of its political legitimacy were already well established.

The structure of Hamas is complicated and intricate (see Figure 6.1). Its central decision-making body is the Political Bureau (*al-Maktab al-Siyasi*), currently based in Qatar after many years in Damascus, which is composed of the central leadership and various ministerial-like organs. The exact relationship of the military wing—the Izz al-Din al-Qassam Brigades—to the Political Bureau is the subject of considerable controversy (see below), but it seems to operate with some degree of autonomy (within broad parameters prescribed by the political office) while also sometimes acting on specific taskings from the political wing. Within the brigades are to be found a number of specialized units focusing on weapons development, internal security, and so forth. Hamas also runs a recruitment program within Israeli jails. In terms of the organization's social wing, we are talking about an enormous network of social organizations and services, many of which are formally autonomous but coordinated via the Mujamma al-Islami. They are not directly under the control of the Political Bureau, but maintain close affiliations with it, and some of their directors have a role in the political office, or have done in the past.

The sources of funding for Hamas' social services and military operations are many, diverse, and frequently overlapping. Ziad Abu-Amr has identified six major sources for the Hamas budget: direct donations from the Occupied Territories; support from sympathetic Islamist movements in other countries (particularly the MB, but some have also cited Al-Qaeda in

Figure 6.1 Hamas organizational diagram

Source: Adapted from Shaul Mishal and Avraham Sela, *The Palestinian Hamas,* New York: Columbia University Press, 2006

this regard); donations from Hamas-run foundations and private individuals abroad; foreign governments sympathetic to the movement's causes (particularly Iran, Qatar, and Saudi Arabia); relatively small amounts from the PLO; and, finally, various investment instruments established by Hamas.[27] To this list we can also add, somewhat ironically, the Israeli government, which during the 1980s, as we have noted, provided funding for some of the social organizations that eventually became the basis of Islamist popular support as a means to undermine the growth of leftist influences within the mainstream national resistance movement. It took a little bit of time for Hamas to gain the confidence of regional governments sympathetic to the Palestinian cause, since it was initially assumed that the movement was just a newly politicized wing of the MB—a group with which many of these states (Egypt and Syria in particular) had problems in the past. But this did not prove to be an impediment for long.[28] Since 2007, Hamas has also had access to another significant source of funding. Israel's closure of the Rafah crossing in the wake of the 2006 Gaza War and the 2007 Hamas takeover of Gaza led to the construction of some 1,000 tunnels for smuggling goods between Gaza and Egypt. Some estimates suggest that by 2009, Hamas was raising $150–200 million per year by regulating and taxing tunnel-based commerce, making these conduits by far the movement's most lucrative source of income.[29]

Next we will want to look more closely at the Hamas activists and supporters. The movement's leadership and its intelligentsia, much like other movements we have looked at, such as the MB and Jama'at-i Islami, is drawn primarily from members of the professional and technocratic class.[30] During the 1980s and 1990s, the MB and later Hamas made considerable inroads in terms of their representation within professional associations and syndicates. Before regular elections were held under the PA, university councils were often regarded as the best way to gauge the relative support for various Palestinian political factions. During the first *intifada*, Hamas made an impressive dent here, rivaling Fatah at many schools and gaining outright control of several student councils. The leadership of Hamas have often cited universities as more important to them as political spaces than mosques. The latter are often tied to *awqaf* controlled by Israel or Jordan, while the educational settings enjoy relative autonomy.[31]

The social base of Hamas support is generally highly conservative and skeptical of secularism, which it equates with the inefficacy and corruption of the PLO.[32] The rank-and-file supporters of Hamas tend to come from lower-middle and working-class backgrounds, and tend to be socialized into the movement's values through exposure to its social services network. To better understand the appeal and popularity of Hamas' welfare services, it will be useful to consider certain demographic aspects of the Occupied Territories. A full 70 percent of the Palestinian population are under the age of 30, and 40 percent are under 15. The availability of skilled and professional employment is scarce, with fewer than 20 percent of secondary school and university graduates finding regular work upon completing their education.[33] The overall unemployment rate in the Palestinian territories is very high, at around 23 percent—and when Israel closes its borders to Palestinian day laborers, this figure can surge significantly.[34] Given the corruption and inefficacy of the PLO and the PA, the Hamas welfare charities are sometimes the only option people have.

This network of organizations is so diverse as to cover almost every sphere of social activity. Just to provide a sense of the array of what Hamas has on offer, we might consider the following aggregate list, compiled from the various services cited by a selection of leading researchers:

- charitable societies
- hospitals
- dispensaries
- kindergartens and schools (religious and secular)
- sporting clubs
- elderly homes
- tithing (*zakat*) committees
- computing centers
- libraries
- scholarships
- legal aid

- summer camps
- recreation facilities.

Hamas does not require users of these services to join the movement, although there are certainly special benefits reserved for activists, as well as a "Martyr's Fund" that supports the families of those who die in the course of militant operations. It has been estimated that some 95 percent of the Hamas budget goes to support this network of services, and they are by far the best-known face of Islamism throughout the Occupied Territories.[35] Many, as has been pointed out, use them not because they identify with the religious basis (although for many this is indeed a factor), but because they are the only services available, or the only ones that can be trusted. For a long time, Hamas was the only organization the UNRWA in Palestine trusted to deliver and distribute food donations.[36] Some observers have noted that even Palestinian political opponents of Hamas who want to make humanitarian donations will do so via the Islamists' social organizations since they are the only ones they feel they can trust—unlike Fatah—not to embezzle the funds.[37] Quite simply, the Palestinian public has come to trust Hamas-provided social services, but not their PLO counterparts.[38] We should emphasize again that many, if not most, users of the Hamas services network are not active supporters of the Political Bureau, nor do they share the movement's vision for an Islamic state in Palestine. Some researchers have cited evidence, admittedly limited in scope, suggesting that many of those who make use of Mujamma al-Islami facilities and services do not participate in other Islamist activities—or that they are even aware of the Islamist linkages.[39] This latter claim is perhaps somewhat overstated, given that most of the Islamist facilities feature subtle (and sometimes quite overt) elements of evangelism such as posters and other media.

But just how much support does Hamas have among the Palestinian population? If we were to use the results of the most recent Palestine Legislative Council elections in 2006 as an indicator, we would be talking about somewhere in the neighborhood of 45 percent—which is in line with the figure that the Hamas leadership has traditionally claimed (40–50 percent). But there is reason to believe that this figure reflects a relatively large protest vote against Fatah at that time, rather than active endorsement of the Hamas vision. Various observers have tried to estimate the base level of active political support for Hamas among Palestinians, and have come up with widely varying figures. A polling agency in the Occupied Territories came up with the figure of 18 percent, although its methodology is disputed.[40] A study by a Hamas-affiliated academic of the professional syndicate elections in the West Bank suggested an aggregate tally for the Islamists of 45 percent and, for the PLO and its affiliates, 50 percent.[41] A 2013 poll by the Palestinian Center for Policy and Survey Research found that when Palestinians were asked to indicate whom they would vote for if new legislative elections were held immediately, 30 percent opted for Hamas—with a somewhat higher figure (38 percent) in Gaza.[42]

Participation in Islamist social activities or use of their facilities also should not be regarded as a zero-sum game in terms of representing a choice of Hamas at the expense of the PLO. As a member of an Islamist football club, quoted in Michael Jensen's research, put it:

> I liked the PLO very much; I liked [Yasser Arafat]. During the *Intifada* we suffered very much at the hands of the Israelis. They shot at us. They killed many of us. I wanted a change, I wanted to do something to redress this injustice and suffering. So then Hamas did something. During that time, when people were hurting daily, they sought comfort in religion. People went to religion to pray to God to help us during the *Intifada*.[43]

This statement provides us with some insight as to why Arafat's position on Hamas social services was a version of "can't live with them, can't live without them."[44] It is not that Palestinians choose Hamas to the exclusion of other political options, but rather that the Islamists have developed a reputation for themselves of "walking the talk." In addition to their armed resistance to Israeli occupation, they also provide the Palestinian people with services that help to alleviate the worst effects of the Occupation—and they do so far more effectively than any other social or political force in the territories. The Islamist welfare network is effective, dependable, and—particularly today, in comparison with Fatah—free of corruption. For many, it is worth reiterating, it has been the only available source of welfare under very difficult socioeconomic circumstances. It is therefore not surprising that people rally around Hamas when it is under threat or criticized. In some cases this may just be an instrumental "don't bite the hand that feeds you" response, but for the most part, the organization genuinely has the respect of the Palestinian people—respect, moreover, that the secular nationalist alternative in Fatah sorely lacks. In 2006, they were clearly able to turn this into an electoral advantage. By the same token, however, if the ability and willingness of Hamas to engage in active resistance is a source of their popularity, this means they require the ongoing presence of something to resist in order to keep that support and legitimize their continued existence. For this reason, along with the fact that it is ideologically opposed to peace with Israel, Hamas is less predisposed than other political forces to contemplate a negotiated settlement. This prompts some to point out that while Hamas may be skilled at alleviating the symptoms of Palestinian suffering, it is less apt directly and realistically to confront the political conflict at the root of that suffering. With the Gaza strip effectively run separately from the rest of the Palestinian territories since 2007, increasingly isolated in the international realm, and Hamas unable to solve day-to-day problems, it is not surprising that the Palestinian Islamists have seen a significant drop in political support.

© AP Photo/Muhammed Muheisen

Figure 6.2 Street art supporting Hamas

We can now move on to examine how the Hamas ideology, discourse, and political strategy has evolved since its founding. Crucial to this, of course, has been the issue of its relationship with the PLO. Despite the phenomenal support the Islamists garnered for themselves during the course of the *intifada,* we need to bear in mind that in absolute terms, their popularity never eclipsed that of Yasser Arafat and the PLO. Hamas was never in a position actually to challenge Fatah's leadership of the Palestinian cause—until, that is, the 2006 PLC elections. If we look at the text of the Hamas Charter, we find the Islamists going to great lengths to emphasize their efforts as a complement to those of the nationalists. The PLO is referred to as "closest to us" and as being "like a father or brother." That said, the Charter does go on to point out that the secular approach espoused by the PLO is not acceptable to Hamas.[45] In 1988, the Palestine National Council, along with its renunciation of violence and recognition of Israel, declared the existence of a Palestinian state. Interestingly, Hamas—still very young as an organization—begins here to display its independence from the main MB organization in terms of how it responds to this declaration. While the Cairo-based mother organization welcomed the newly declared Palestinian state, Sheikh Yassin—from within the Occupied

Territories—asked skeptically how it would be possible to have such a state when no Palestinian territory had yet been liberated.[46] Over the next few years, Hamas and the PLO—while in theory partners in the *intifada*—also competed with each other for control of the popular uprising. For example, the PLO's Unified National Leadership and Hamas maintained separate and uncoordinated calendars for calling general strikes.[47] They also differed in terms of their priorities. For example, on the days of general strikes, the PLO issued orders for schools under its control to be let out in order to maximize the size of the protests. Hamas, by contrast, kept students in the classroom on its strike days, arguing that their education would prove more important in the long run.[48] There are also, of course, any number of political, tactical, and security reasons why it would have made sense for the two organizations to institute various forms of "traffic control" around the protests.

Tensions between the two factions became more pronounced in 1992 when a new Labor government came to power in Israel promising—or, in the eyes of the Hamas rejectionists, threatening—to make peace with the Palestinians within a year.[49] The PLO's willingness to entertain concerted peacemaking, particularly in the wake of the Madrid process, which Hamas had bitterly opposed, led to open clashes between the Islamists and Fatah, an act which some observers have suggested led Hamas temporarily to "lose the streets," given the PLO's majority support and the gathering hopes around the possibility of a negotiated settlement.[50] But Hamas revealed itself to be highly attuned to the realities of this shifting political balance. At the very same time as the two sides were fighting it out on the streets of Gaza, there was an internal document circulating within the Hamas political bureau that outlined the pros and cons of a full range of possible approaches to the PLO, from a complete boycott to a demand for full participation in any political process.[51]

Hamas was just as taken aback as the rest of the world when the Oslo agreement was announced in September 1993. Indeed, it is also likely that the PLO leadership would have gone out of its way to deny the existence of the secret negotiation channel that produced it for fear of prompting a strong Hamas backlash. In the spring of 1994, the PLO and Hamas signed a political truce of sorts in an act that angered Israel. Yitzhak Rabin, the Israeli Prime Minister, clearly had been looking to Arafat to begin treating the Islamists as criminals, rather than to make new declarations of solidarity with them.[52] Hamas was soon caught in a bind since, as noted above, although it was strenuously opposed to the Oslo Accords and the peace process more generally, it did not want to risk alienating itself from a newly hopeful Palestinian population that had decided to put its faith in Arafat and the exchange of peace for land. Hence its offer of a "ceasefire" with the Occupation in early 1994 (see below) in order to demonstrate that even it was willing to consider a possible future alongside an Israel whose name it still would not utter publicly. Hamas decided to lay low for the time being and wait for the peace process to fall apart—even going so far as to enter into another rapprochement with Arafat in the run-up to the 1996 elections that the Islamists had decided to boycott.[53] When Rabin was assassinated in late 1995, throwing off a warming relationship between Israel and Syria (a peace agreement had already been signed with Jordan earlier that year), Hamas decided it was the right moment to go on the offensive against the peace process. There ensued over the next few months an acceleration of attacks on Israeli civilian targets, with the result that the right-wing Likud party in the form of Prime Minister Benjamin Netanyahu came to power in Israel. Relations with the PLO and the PA reached their nadir when Arafat sent his new police forces against the Islamists in the face of Israeli threats to withdraw from future peace talks unless the PA put an end to Islamist violence.

The political and popular fortunes of Hamas did not revive until the outbreak of the second *intifada,* when it once again found itself at the forefront of widespread discontent at not only continued Israeli occupation and oppression, but also the failure of the peace process to pay out any of the dividend that had been promised, and the growing authoritarianism within the PA. While Arafat had hoped to turn the new protests to his advantage, the only credible Fatah faces on the streets were figures themselves opposed to the PLO autocracy. These were generally younger Fatah activists such as Marwan Barghouti, who had entered politics during the first *intifada* while the PLO old guard was in Tunis. When Arafat set up his PA executive, these younger figures were all but shut out from any meaningful positions of political influence.[54]

Aside from the difficult "antagonistic cooperation" that generally defined the Hamas relationship with Fatah, how did the Islamist strategy evolve over the years in other respects?[55] Mishal and Sela have pointed out that in some respects the founding of Hamas was as much about ensuring the survival of the MB in Palestine as it was about seizing an opportune moment to "go political." As the scale of violence and general unrest in the Occupied Territories grew in the run-up to 1987, the MB's Mujamma al-Islami began to fear that either Islamic Jihad or the PLO would turn the new climate to its advantage.[56] Hamas did have an immediate and major impact on the ideological terrain of Palestinian resistance, however, because it developed a political discourse that permitted Islam and nationalism to become entwined in the popular imagination. And more than just Islam as religion, this was an approach that turned Islam into a discourse of active resistance, a *jihad* against the illegitimate occupation of Palestine—itself a divinely ordained endowment (*waqf*) to be protected by whatever means necessary. But they were also able to tap into and mobilize the existing MB social base, not only in terms of its network and facilities, but also in terms of its socializing and mobilizing capacity. In the vision of Sheikh Yassin and Hamas, only a "fortified society" (educated, employed, healthy) would be able to engage in the *jihad*. Therefore it was vitally important for social development work to occur alongside and in parallel with active, armed resistance.[57] Hamas political activism and the MB's socialization and welfare efforts were hence wholly symbiotic. In explaining its worldview and seeking to mobilize the Palestinian masses, Hamas relied on a series of cultural framings that combined elements of the classic MB program with a number of idioms specific to the Palestinian condition in order to create a "more authentic nationalism."[58] These included, in addition to the idea of Palestine as a sacred territory or *waqf*, the Islamist standard bearer, "Islam is the solution"; the notion of a larger Jewish conspiracy; and (especially after 1993) the virtue of patience on the part of the Palestinian people, who should not settle for a compromised peace agreement that was bound to fail.[59]

Sheikh Ahmed Yassin was himself notoriously ambiguous when it came to the idea of whether a negotiated settlement with Israel would ever be possible. We have already noted the Islamists' tendency to avoid taking completely obstructionist positions at times when it seemed a negotiated settlement might be possible—although they would always refrain from opening up an ideological can of worms for themselves by refusing to recognize the legitimacy of Israel outright. Consider the following excerpt from an interview with Sheikh Yassin, quoted by Ziad Abu-Amr:

> *Question:* Do you recognize Israel?
> *Answer:* If I recognized Israel, the problem would be finished, and we would have no right left as Palestinians.
> *Question:* But if Israel withdrew from the West Bank and the Gaza Strip, would you recognize it?
> *Answer:* When it withdraws, I will say.
> *Question:* But at that time, should it be recognized?
> *Answer:* I leave this matter to the representatives of the Palestinian people.
> *Question:* Who are they?
> *Answer:* Those whom the Palestinian people will elect.[60]

Yassin reveals here a distinctly pragmatic streak, one that—as in the case of the Hamas 1994 offer of a "ceasefire with the occupation"—implicitly recognizes not only the existence of Israel, but also the possibility of Palestinian coexistence with it, and the permissibility of the Palestinian people (rather than a *fatwa*) determining the nature of their future relations with Israel. On other occasions, when asked about the compatibility of Islamism with democracy in Palestine, Yassin had insisted that he would need to respect the will of the Palestinian people to choose their own political system, even if they opted for communism. While some have declared this to be nothing more than instrumentalism, others have cited consistent evidence that much of the Hamas leadership is wholly pragmatic when it comes to political issues.[61] The Islamists appeared to demonstrate an affinity for *realpolitik* in the wake of the Oslo Accords, seeking primarily to delay implementation of the agreement rather than to destroy it.[62] Some within Hamas even claimed that several of the bomb attacks committed in its name between 1994 and 1997 were not officially sanctioned by the movement.[63]

Indeed, the issue of the Hamas military wing and who controls it is a complex one. Some observers claim that it operates almost wholly autonomously of the Political Bureau, citing the authority of the latter over the brigades as "more symbolic than concrete."[64] Others argue strongly that there is persuasive evidence of a link between the external headquarters and the military wing—or even that military operations are carried out under the direct and unique orders of the political office.[65] What is most likely to be the case, however, is that the relationship has varied over the course of Hamas' political career. There have been periods when Izz al-Din al-Qassam has been left to operate autonomously, attacking at the time and with the means of its own choosing, so long as it does not stray outside certain broadly prescribed boundaries. At other times, however, it is likely that hardliners within the overseas Political Bureau have exercised direct planning and operational control over Hamas attacks. In this regard it would also be worthwhile to give some consideration to the decision by Hamas, in 1994, to extend its tactics to encompass attacks on Israeli civilian targets. Before this date, Hamas had targeted only elements of the Israeli security apparatus. Various spokesmen for Hamas have sought to justify this move in different ways. Some have argued that attacks on Israeli settlers in the West Bank and Gaza are justified because they are themselves armed and have attacked Palestinians in the past. Others have employed somewhat labored logic to point out that because Israel's army has a policy of universal conscription for the Israeli population, then all of its citizens are potential or former members of the IDF. The mainstream justification used by Hamas for attacking civilians, Khaled Hroub argues, is essentially the same as the one previously used by the PLO before its renunciation of violence.[66] Namely, that because the Palestinians do not have the power and military wherewithal to defend themselves in conventional warfare, they have no choice but to seek to create in the minds and national psyche of their occupiers, military and civilian alike, a sense of insecurity that will ultimately lead them to withdraw from the disputed territories—in other words, to induce fear as a political weapon. While Hamas has come under widespread criticism for its policy of targeting civilians, there is evidence of a debate within the organization as to whether such attacks are indeed justifiable—one that generally breaks down along the lines of a broader sociological divide, and this is what we will turn to now.

Since the time of the first *intifada,* there have been pronounced differences within Hamas between those—mostly of a longer MB pedigree—who have been cautious about the pace and extent of Islamist political activism; and those—many of whom joined Hamas directly without any prior MB experience—who viewed the movement as a vehicle for active and immediate radicalism.[67] This difference between the Hamas pragmatists or moderates and the Hamas radicals has often broken down along the lines of the distinction between the movement's external leadership abroad, and the leaders within the Occupied Territories. Jean-Francois Legrain, for example, points out that at the time of the 1991 Gulf War, the group's leaders in Amman sided with the Jordanian MB and supported Saddam Hussein, whereas Hamas leaders in Gaza mostly kept quiet.[68] We see this divide again in 1996 at the time of the first elections for the PA, where moderate "insiders" such as Ismail Haniyeh, the Palestinian Prime Minister after the 2006 elections, wanted to participate but were overruled by the external leadership. Indeed, there ensued a complicated debate during which a wide variety of political options were considered, ranging from a campaign of violence to undermine the peace agreement, to open participation in PA politics, to disbanding the movement and returning to exclusively religious and social activity.[69] Sheikh Yassin himself drifted back and forth between the pragmatist and radical camps, and his capacity to do so is part of what made him such an effective and popular leader. As regards the 1996 elections, for example, he offered in a letter from his jail cell a cautious recommendation for Hamas to participate:

> Holding elections is now an issue for the Palestinians; the Islamists are divided between supporting participation and those opposing it; as far as I am concerned, but only God knows, I consider it is better to participate than to abstain, providing that the Council be empowered with legislative privileges (*tashri*); as a matter of fact we are opposed to what is happening in the streets, so why not express our opposition within the legislative institution which will de jure become in the future the authority representing that Palestinian people? [This participation] will reassert the strength of the Islamic presence on the arena and will prevent it from losing ground because of its isolation.[70]

From the late 1990s, then, it became clear that the division between the Hamas internal and external leadership, which had been evolving since as early as Sheikh Yassin's arrest in 1989, has solidified along the lines of clear difference in strategic vision. The radicals within the external political bureau—young, skilled, adept at fundraising abroad—wanted to impose Islam from above, and sought to use their control of the group's military brigades to achieve this. The internal leaders, those based within the Occupied Territories, were mainly older MB stalwarts who preferred to Islamize from the societal level up.[71] But there is also some evidence that within the internal leadership are to be found younger pragmatists whose political vision shares something in common with the "new Islamists" we examined earlier (see Chapter 4)—insofar as they are at least convinced that political participation within a democratic framework is the way forward, even if, we should note, their vision of the politics that should flow from that participation is not entirely in keeping with liberal norms. Jeroen Gunning characterizes this rift as a cleavage between the "absolutists" of the group's external political bureau and the "pragmatists" based in Gaza itself.[72]

Hamas in power and the two Palestines

In the Palestine Legislative Council elections of January 2006, Hamas, campaigning under the name "Change and Reform," won 74 out of 132 seats, giving it a 56 percent controlling majority of the assembly and the opportunity to form the first non-Fatah-dominated PA government. The level of corruption and autocracy within Fatah had reached new heights and they were widely seen as a discredited political force. Nonetheless, it was assumed they would still win at least a plurality of seats and be forced into a coalition government. Hamas was expected to do well, but very few—perhaps not even Hamas itself—anticipated an outright majority victory. The Hamas victory can be explained in terms of three factors, as follows.

- A protest vote, at least in part, against Fatah's corruption and a swing towards Hamas as the only alternative political force with any credibility as a provider of effective governance and societal welfare.
- The superiority of the Hamas political mobilization machinery and its sheer ability to turn out voters through its vast infrastructure of organizations and informal networks.
- The fact that, in recent years, Hamas had shown itself to be the most consistent and committed advocate of active resistance against the ongoing Israeli occupation.

Western powers were shocked by the Islamist victory, and the United States found itself in a situation where it was forced quickly to cut off financial aid to the PA, since Hamas is on the U.S. State Department's list of designated terrorist organizations. The Hamas military wing declared a truce when the party was elected, but refused to disband as the U.S. and Europe insisted. The weeks following the election provided worrying images of Hamas' own security forces patrolling the streets and occasionally confronting regular PA police, most of whom were drawn from the ranks of Fatah.

Tensions between Hamas and Fatah escalated throughout the rest of 2006 and into the following year. Fatah politicians refused to participate in the PA government that Hamas formed, and PA security forces refused to take orders from the Islamists. With regard to the Middle East peace process, the so-called Quartet powers (U.S., UN, European Union, and Russia) demanded that Hamas accede to the terms of the 1993 Oslo Accords by recognizing Israel's legitimacy and renouncing violence—both of which it refused to do. Increasingly isolated on the international front, the Hamas–Fatah tensions soon broke into open conflict. The first half of 2007 saw persistent tit-for-tat acts of violence committed by both sides. Despite efforts by Saudi Arabia to broker an agreement between the two Palestinian sides, the situation had deteriorated significantly by June 2007. When Hamas discovered that Fatah was seeking to bring international shipments of armaments into the West Bank that could be used against Hamas, it effectively "seceded" from the PA and asserted direct and exclusive political control over the Gaza Strip—with the latter effectively cut off from the rest of Palestinian society in the West Bank.

Meanwhile, a low-intensity conflict between Hamas militants and Israeli forces had been ongoing since 2005, involving exchanges of rockets and artillery fire that killed dozens on both sides. In the summer of 2008, Egypt brokered a ceasefire between the two sides but it never fully took effect. Attacks by both sides escalated in November and December as the formal ceasefire period drew to a close. The two sides were unable to reach mutually acceptable terms for a renewal of the ceasefire and, as violence once again began to flare, Israel opted for what it hoped would be decisive action. On December 27, 2008 Israel launched a multi-phase military campaign against Hamas and Gaza that would last some three weeks and result in the deaths of over 1,000 Palestinians and a dozen Israelis. The 2008–09 Gaza War (or "Operation Cast Lead" as it was known in Israeli military parlance) involved Israeli air, naval, and ground units, including incursions by Israeli troops into Gaza itself. Israel targeted a wide range of Hamas military and training facilities, as well as individual Hamas political leaders and governmental offices. Hundreds of the Palestinians killed in the conflict were civilians, prompting international condemnation of what was perceived by many to be disproportionate use of force by the Israelis. For its part, Israel maintained that Hamas fighters were deliberately using Gaza's civilian population as "human shields." The international commission that eventually investigated the conflict found evidence of wrongdoing on both sides. The war left the Gaza Strip in ruins and, with Israel enforcing a complete blockade of the territory, a humanitarian crisis soon developed. Efforts by international activists to break Israel's blockade in order to deliver food and medical supplies to Gaza—such as the Turkish flotilla referenced in Chapter 4—created a public relations crisis for Israel and had a significant impact on its regional relations.

From 2011 there were significant efforts underway to achieve a reconciliation between the two estranged Palestinian factions, Hamas and Fatah. The Egyptian military brokered an agreement in principle to form a caretaker government of national unity, with legislative and presidential elections—both several years overdue by that point—in 2012. The deal quickly foundered, however, with Hamas unwilling to have the PA's incumbent prime minister, Salam Fayyad, continue in that role during the interregnum leading up to elections. A subsequent agreement made in Qatar the following year also produced little progress as both sides accused each other of wrangling over the details of elections and of harassing each other's security forces.

It is also clear that internal divisions within Hamas became even more pronounced after the 2007 split with Fatah and the West Bank, and in the aftermath of the 2011 Arab Uprisings. As Syria's uprising and eventual civil war gathered steam, Hamas relocated its external political bureau headquarters. Mousa Abu Marzuq took up residence in Egypt, while executive committee chairman Khaled Meshal decamped to Doha, Qatar. Ismail Haniyeh, the former Hamas prime minister in Gaza, sought but failed to gain control of the movement's political bureau in April 2013. As a new round of Middle East peace talks started in the summer of 2013—with the Palestinian side represented exclusively by Fatah leader and PA President Mahmoud Abbas—hardliners such as Meshal and Marzuk made clear their continued displeasure with Fatah. At the same time, however, the ousting of the MB-led government in Egypt represented a setback for the Hamas political leadership, who had been relying on Morsi's stature and prominence to advance their goals. Prospects for Palestinian reconciliation continued to look bleak while Hamas faced both internal factionalization as well as the near-impossibility of providing for effective governance in an increasingly isolated Gaza.

HIZBULLAH'S MULTIFACETED ISLAMISM: MILITIA, POLITICAL PARTY, SERVICE PROVIDER

We turn now to the case of an Islamist movement whose origins bear a striking resemblance to those of Hamas, even though its sectarian—and, arguably, theological—orientation is considerably different. While its origins lie in a loose alliance of Shi'i clerics in the early years of Lebanon's Civil War, Hizbullah's dramatic rise to prominence as a revolutionary militia is linked to Israel's invasion of Lebanon in the early 1980s. It emerged in the context of a broader social movement that sought to ground the political and economic disenfranchisement of Lebanon's Shi'a—a segment of society whose share of the country's wealth and political power fell far short of its large population size—in a distinctly Shi'i narrative of dispossession and popular mobilization (see Box 2.2, "The Sunni–Shi'i divide in Islam"). Lebanon's political context is also unique in terms of how it approaches the question of religious pluralism. Unlike secular systems that seek to make legal and political systems "blind" to the question of religious affiliation, Lebanon's so-called "Confessional System" features a power-sharing arrangement based on religion. The country's president is always a Maronite Christian and its prime minister a Sunni Muslim. While the speakership of the parliament is traditionally reserved for a Shi'i Muslim, the position wields little practical political power and the country's Shi'a have long decried their exclusion from meaningful political influence.

Hizbullah, established formally in 1985, first made a name for itself through a concerted campaign of suicide bombings and other attacks on Israeli forces and their proxies, emerging as a rival to Amal, Lebanon's other major Shi'i militia and political movement. During this time, Hizbullah's stated aims were the removal of Israeli and Western forces, and the achievement of a revolutionary Islamic state in Lebanon. Its chief ally and benefactor in this was Iran, still fresh from its own Islamic Revolution (1979) and seeking to export the model to other Shi'i settings. Much of Hizbullah's activism was directly bankrolled by Tehran, with crucial political support also coming from Syria.

Hizbullah reluctantly accommodated itself to the political realities of the 1989 Taif Agreement that effectively ended the Civil War. Unlike other militia groups, however, Hizbullah managed to keep hold of its weapons—arguing that so long as Israel continued to occupy southern Lebanon (which it did until 2000), its armed stance was required to guarantee the safety of Shi'a in the south and also the territorial integrity of Lebanon. For its part, the weak central government (under strong Syrian influence until 2005) was only too happy to "outsource" the defense of the country's southern flank to a much better-trained (thanks to Iran) and more experienced army. Throughout much of the 1990s, Hizbullah forces were engaged in exchanges with Israeli forces along the southern border.

In a major change of tactics associated with the advent of a new political reality in Lebanon, Hizbullah's new Secretary General—the young cleric Sayyid Hassan Nasrallah—decided to contest the 1992 parliamentary elections. It was helped along in this decision by its sponsor Iran, which by the early 1990s was ruled by a faction of conservative pragmatists (see Chapter 5) more concerned with Iran's economy than the export of revolution. Hizbullah won a clear majority of those seats reserved for Shi'i candidates and began the process of creating a full political party structure. Taking a cue from Hamas in the Palestinian territories, Nasrallah also oversaw the creation of a vast infrastructure for the provision of social services (some free, others for payment) in Shi'i areas, essentially filling gaps in, for example, education, healthcare, garbage collection, electricity, and water provision, where the state was absent. Since 1991, Hizbullah has run its own TV station, *Al-Manar* (*The Beacon*), which has a large following among Palestinians in addition to being highly popular with Lebanese Shi'a. While Hizbullah has become somewhat less financially dependent on Iran in recent years, a great deal of its social service work and military arsenal is still funded in whole or in part by Tehran and other Iranian-controlled foundations (generally estimated at $100 million per year).

Following the assassination of Lebanese Prime Minister Rafik Hariri in 2005, Hizbullah found itself leading a pro-Syrian bloc in Lebanese politics. The so-called "March 8" alliance takes its name from the date of a major pro-Syrian demonstration in downtown Beirut in 2005. The premise behind this mass gathering was to thank Syria for its role in ending the Lebanese Civil War, stabilizing Lebanon, and supporting Lebanese resistance to Israeli occupation. A week later, a massive counter-demonstration brought anti-Syrian political forces together in an alternative "March 14" alliance led by Saad Hariri, son of the slain former prime minister. Many of Lebanon's subsequent internal political conflicts revolved around disagreements between the Hizbullah-led pro-Syrian bloc and the anti-Syrian bloc over the scope and direction of the UN's Special Tribunal for Lebanon, which was convened to investigate Rafik Hariri's assassination and to indict conspirators.

Political violence in the north of Lebanon points to an exacerbation of sectarian divisions—with pro-Assad Alawite communities battling anti-Assad Sunni communities in Tripoli—reflecting sectarian cleavages within Syria itself. There is also evidence of a growing militarization of Lebanon's Sunni community, especially among economically disadvantaged communities in Tripoli and the rural north. In the northern Bekaa Valley, where the authority of the Lebanese state is weak, Sunni volunteers for the armed struggle against the Assad regime reportedly received basic weapons training at *ad hoc* locations. Some have also speculated that Saad Hariri has encouraged the formation of Salafi militias—with funding provided by Saudi Arabia—to provide a counterbalance to Hizbullah.

On July 12, 2006, Israel invaded Lebanon and launched a major military operation designed to inflict maximum damage on Hizbullah and its infrastructure. The conflict began when Hizbullah operatives attacked two armored Israeli Humvees patrolling the border fence. Israel seized the opportunity to attempt to destroy Hizbullah once and for all. Over the course of the 34-day war, a quarter of Lebanon's population was displaced and Lebanon's infrastructure was decimated. While Israel's primary goal was to "root out" Hizbullah fighters and facilities, the movement operations and infrastructure were so thoroughly woven into civilian settings that it became impossible for Israel to destroy Hizbullah without inflicting mass casualties on the Lebanese citizenry. Ultimately, the costs to Israel—both militarily and to its international standing—were too great to permit it to complete its objectives. A UN Security Council Resolution (UNSCR) detailed terms of a ceasefire in August 2006, including a withdrawal of all Israeli forces from Lebanon and the disarming of Hizbullah. The fact that the latter provision was never enacted—neither the Lebanese Army nor the UN's interim peacekeeping force was willing to confront Hizbullah over its weapons—combined with the fact that Hizbullah was able to out-perform the Lebanese government in efforts to rebuild after the war, meant that many regarded the 2006 conflict as a net gain politically for Hizbullah, even at enormous cost to Lebanon.

The political divisions in Lebanon were already apparent in the early days of the war when Prime Minister Fouad Siniora's March 14 alliance government issued a statement disavowing the war, censuring Hizbullah, and blaming it for triggering the Israeli response—a sentiment that was echoed in Riyadh, Amman, and Cairo. As the Israeli operation expanded and as the extent of the Israeli targeting of civilian areas and national infrastructure became clear, the Siniora administration changed its position, accusing Israel of waging an all-out war on Lebanon. As the war drew to a close, the government claimed that it had secured a negotiated end to the war, that UNSCR 1701 was in line with Lebanese interests, and that it had coordinated with Hizbullah throughout. Hizbullah's leaders, on the other hand, argued that members of the March 14 coalition had actually lobbied Israel and the United States to launch a war on Hizbullah and had given information to the enemy. They asserted that the government's position at the outset of the war gave political cover to Israel, that the government had tried to corner and weaken Hizbullah while the fighting was ongoing, and that the government wanted to use UNSCR 1701 to achieve American and Israeli goals of disarming Hizbullah—goals that they were not able to achieve through war.

The sharp differences between the Siniora government and Hizbullah were further exacerbated by continued political wrangling over the establishment and scope of an international tribunal to investigate the Hariri assassination. Much of the controversy over the text of the tribunal agreement revolved around how to define responsibility for the crimes. The March 14 alliance wanted a broad definition so that not only those who committed the crimes would be held responsible, but also any of their accomplices or superiors who had authority over them. Ultimately, in November 2006, Hizbullah and its political allies withdrew from Lebanon's cabinet shortly before the cabinet approved the draft UN plans for a tribunal. The departure of five pro-Syrian ministers loyal to Hizbullah and the Amal movement, after the collapse of talks on giving the March 8 alliance more say in government, stripped the cabinet of all Shi'ite representation. This marked the start of a series of political crises that effectively paralyzed the country in the interim. As the crisis unfolded, Hizbullah stepped up its pressure on the Siniora government, mobilizing its supporters, organizing demonstrations, and calling a general strike. The aim of the demonstrations was to force the Siniora government to resign and to bring Hizbullah into the political process through the establishment of a national unity government, in which it demanded more than one-third of the cabinet seats. This would effectively give Hizbullah and its allies veto power, as well as the ability to bring down the government. A period of grave political instability and sectarian violence ensued and a wave of political assassinations gripped the country.

In November 2007, President Emile Lahoud stepped down after the parliament failed to elect his successor. A boycott by the March 8 alliance effectively denied the Siniora government the necessary two-thirds quorum to elect a new President. General Michel Suleiman soon emerged as a consensus candidate (under Lebanon's confessional system, the President must be from the Maronite Christian community). However, Suleiman's election could not take place until a number of fundamental disagreements between the March 14 and March 8 camps were resolved—including whether a government of national unity should be formed, and how electoral laws should be amended in preparation for the forthcoming parliamentary elections in 2009.

As the political impasse dragged on, in May 2008 the Siniora government announced that it would act to close down a private telephone network operated by Hizbullah in south Lebanon and the southern suburbs of Beirut, and accused Hizbullah of placing surveillance cameras on a road outside the airport to monitor pro-government officials. The telephone network was used mainly for communication between Hizbullah members during the war with Israel in 2006—and Hizbullah claimed that it was a vital component of its military capacity to defend Lebanon from future Israeli incursions. The Siniora cabinet also dismissed the director of security of Beirut's international airport, a figure close to Hizbullah. On May 8, 2008, minutes after Nasrallah referred to the government's actions as "a declaration of open war," heavy street battles began between pro-Hizbullah and pro-government forces. By the end of the following day, government supporters in Beirut had surrendered their arms to the Hizbullah-led opposition, and Hizbullah effectively had seized more than half of the capital city. The Lebanese army declined to intervene—fearing a split in its ranks along sectarian lines, as had happened during the civil war. The crisis prompted a round of negotiations between the parties in Doha, Qatar. In the ensuing Doha Agreement, the Hizbullah-led March 8 alliance secured a veto over cabinet decisions and agreement was reached on the formation of a unity government. With a new president in place by the next year, Siniora formed a national unity government in the summer of 2008, giving effective veto power to Hizbullah, and ending the political stalemate and six weeks of arguments over the makeup of the 30-member cabinet.

In parliamentary elections held in June 2009, the March 14 alliance, led by Rafik Hariri's son Saad, won 71 of 128 seats, while Hizbollah's March 8 alliance secured 57 seats. Saad Hariri was nominated as prime minister-designate. The elections were a clear victory for the March 14 bloc—but shifting regional realities, local power struggles, and the imperative of a coalition government prevented the parties from agreeing on a cabinet until November 2009. Within weeks, the new government formally endorsed Hizbullah's right to keep its weapons. However, tensions over the scope and direction of the UN's Special Tribunal for Lebanon—charged with investigating the assassination of former Prime Minister Rafik Hariri—continued to simmer. In its early stages, the investigation implicated top-level Syrian security officials. However, the tribunal soon shifted its focus to Hizbullah. In July 2010, Hizbullah leader Hassan Nasrallah disclosed that Saad Hariri had informed him months previously that his party was likely to be implicated in Hariri's assassination—but that the plot would be attributed to "rogue" elements within Hizbullah.

In July 2010, Grand Ayatollah Mohammed Hussein Fadlallah died aged 74. Fadlallah was Lebanon's leading Shi'a cleric. Long before the Islamic Revolution in Iran in 1979, Fadlallah supported the establishment of an Islamic state in Lebanon, although he remained sensitive to the wishes of Lebanon's Christian, Sunni, and Druze populations. At times Fadlallah identified himself with Hizbullah, but at other times he opposed the movement's views. Officially, the movement follows Iran's Supreme Leader Ali Khameini, and Hizbullah's Secretary General serves as one of his official representatives in Lebanon. In contrast with Hizbullah, Fadlallah rejected Khomeini's concept of the *vilayat-e faqih*. He was, however, widely recognized by the Shi'a as a source of spiritual authority to whom the faithful should turn for guidance, and many Hizbullah supporters regarded him as a spiritual mentor.

In January 2011, 11 ministers from the March 8 alliance resigned from the cabinet, bringing down Hariri's short-lived government. Later that month, a Hizbullah-backed candidate, Najib Mikati, was appointed as the prime minister-designate, tilting the balance of power toward the March 8 alliance. Five months later, after much political wrangling, Mr Mikati unveiled a new cabinet. With the March 8 alliance awarded 16 out of 30 seats, critics dubbed the new administration a "Hizbullah government." In July 2011, the UN's Special Tribunal for Lebanon issued sealed arrest warrants—the details of which soon leaked—for four men in connection with the Hariri killing. All of them were members of Hizbullah. Nasrallah declared that his movement would not permit the men to be arrested and the cases against them proceeded *in absentia*.

Saad al-Hariri has been in self-imposed exile in Europe since 2011, citing security concerns. His absence—combined with a weakening of his financial patronage network—effectively has left a vacuum in moderate Sunni leadership in Lebanon. This leadership vacuum is being filled by new figures such as Sheikh Ahmad Assir, the Salafist *imam* of the Bilal bin

Rabah mosque in Sidon, who has become a national figure, delivering speeches in central Beirut and Tripoli, appearing on television interviews, and boldly criticizing Hizbullah and Amal. In an interview in June 2012, Assir accused Hizbullah of using its political power to dominate Lebanon and isolate the Sunni community, charging that the Shi'a party's arms were no longer intended for resistance against Israel, but to subjugate Lebanon to its will.

While recent unrest in Syria undoubtedly has had a spillover effect, it appears unlikely that the Arab Uprisings will be replicated in Lebanon. In the first place, both the March 14 and March 8 political coalitions are mass-based popular movements. Thus a large number of Lebanese citizens support one or other coalition. Secondly, Lebanon is not an authoritarian state but, rather, a parliamentary democracy structured according to the principle of power sharing between sects. It has a functional constitution, a system of checks and balances, and an active judiciary, and holds regular and competitive parliamentary elections. Finally, the Lebanese state does not enjoy a monopoly over the use of violence within its borders, and its coercive capacities are weak. In short, the force of the Lebanese army is not relied upon to prop up an authoritarian system.

However, it has become increasingly clear that the persistent anti-Assad insurgency has resulted in a further loss of Syrian influence in Lebanon, and Hizbullah is no longer seen to exercise the same level of control over state institutions as it once did. Arrests of Hizbullah opera-tives and confiscations of weapons in 2012 were considered politically significant in that the Lebanese Army previously had shied away from directly confronting Hizbullah. Thus it is clear that the conflict in Syria had eroded Hizbullah's power in Lebanon. While Hizbullah had stead-fastly denied that its members were in action alongside Syrian forces, the confirmation of the deaths of several of its senior operatives in Syria highlighted the extent of Hizbullah's role in attempting to shore-up the al-Assad regime. By 2013, there was increasing evidence that Hizbullah fighters were directly involved in fighting rebel forces in Syria seeking to topple the Assad regime. With Lebanon's political landscape increasingly polarized in relation to pro- and anti-Syrian alignments, Mikati resigned his prime ministership in the spring of 2013 amidst persistent fears that the Syrian crisis would spill over directly into Lebanon. The religious dimension of Hizbullah's identity also took on new salience in the after-math of the Arab Uprisings and in light of the Syrian conflict. With heightened sectarianism breaking out across the region, Hizbullah's Shi'i orientation began to have implications beyond the Lebanese domestic context. It seemed to be part of a broader dynamic in the Middle East whereby sectarian identities coincided with the contours of embattled minority groups fighting for political survival (Syria), or majorities seek-ing to claim rights against minority rulers (Bahrain) or to consolidate power after years of disenfranchisement (Iraq). And amidst these new sectarian dynamics, Hizbullah's chief sponsor, Iran, the region's major Shi'i power broker, sought to stoke these tensions to its advantage.

As an analyst of Muslim politics, trying to discern which of Hizbullah's many roles—militia, political party, or provider of social services—represents its true identity is not particularly helpful. Rather, it is important to recognize that Hizbullah is all of these things. Its leaders are able to spread their social and political capital across the full breadth of these activities, pragmatically emphasizing whatever role is most useful at a given political juncture. What we should be trying to figure out, however, is how the organization's political choices and responses to particular situations narrow or expand its range of options over time. In other words, even as Hizbullah tries to maintain all three modes of operation, might not political realities and changing circumstances on the ground force it to evolve in particular directions? Also worthy of note is the way that Hizbullah manages to combine a Shi'i identity with elements of Lebanese nationalism, enabling it to lay claim to constituencies beyond its sectarian base.

BOX 6.2 ISLAMISTS AND THE SYRIA CONFLICT

The Syrian branch of the Muslim Brotherhood was founded before World War II, but has been banned as a legal political group since the 1960s. Following a violent campaign by the state against the Brotherhood in 1982 in and around the city of Hama—in which the secular Ba'athist regime of Hafez al-Asad killed thousands of Islamists—the Syrian MB was driven completely underground as a movement. While the group was a signatory to the Damascus Declaration of 2005—a document designed to show unity of purpose among Syria's disparate and mostly exilic opposition groups—it did not have an appreciable political profile until after the Arab Uprisings.

As in Egypt, Tunisia, and Libya, Syria's Islamists were not at the forefront of the popular protests that swept the region in 2010–11. Most of the Syrian MB's key figures were living as exiles outside the country, and the group's ability to mobilize popular support within Syria was initially limited. The MB was allotted a handful of seats on the Syrian National Council, a body formed in 2011 to act as a coordinating forum for the opposition and to rally international support for rebels fighting Bashar al-Asad's regime. Over time, the MB's influence within this organization, and its successor, the Syrian National Coalition, grew to outweigh its relatively modest formal role. Within Syria itself, the MB grew in influence by helping to build ties between various armed resistance factions through creating the Commission for Civilian Protection. Armed members of the Syrian MB have joined militia groups loosely allied with the Free Syrian Army, such as the Syrian Islamic Liberation Front. Even as the group has exerted itself with some success in opposition and rebel circles, the level of popular political support that the MB enjoys in Syria has remained difficult to discern.

Other Islamist factions have played a key role in the Syrian uprisings, particularly in the realm of violent resistance to the Asad regime. In addition to the Syrian Islamic Liberation Front—an MB-led coalition of Islamist militias—Salafi fighters have been active on the ground under the auspices of their own Syrian Islamic Front. One of the most effective, but also controversial, rebel elements fighting the Syrian regime has been Jabhat al-Nusra ("The Defense Front"), a Salafi–jihadi organization formed in 2012 and aligned with the global

Figure 6.3 Supporters of Jabhat al-Nusra in Syria
Source: © Caroline Neil/NPR

jihadist movement. The group's leadership has denied any formal affiliation with other Al-Qaeda groups in the region (particularly its Iraqi branch), but acknowledges Al-Qaeda's chief, Ayman al-Zawahiri, as someone to whom the group owes allegiance. Al-Nusra's fighters, many of whom gained significant experience during the Iraqi insurgency against the U.S., have been among the more effective military units in defeating Syrian government forces and have frequently overshadowed their more secular counterparts in the Free Syrian Army (FSA), the "official" armed wing of the rebel movement. For its own part, the FSA has sought to distance itself from the Nusra Front, whose ideology it opposes. The Nusra Front is widely suspected of being supported by benefactors in the Arab Gulf region, particularly Qatar and Saudi Arabia.

THE TALIBAN IN AFGHANISTAN: DEOBANDISM, ETHNICITY AND GEOPOLITICS

Afghanistan offers us an example of "Islam for lack of a system" that differs in significant ways from the cases of Palestine and Lebanon above. The period of the Taliban's rule in Afghanistan (1996–2001) was characterized by the imposition, on a society ravaged by nearly two decades of continual warfare, of a highly austere and literal interpretation of Islam. Initially welcomed by the Afghan populace in the hope that they would be able to restore some semblance of peace and order, the Taliban's model of an Islamic political order soon revealed itself to be at sharp odds with many Afghan religious and social norms. In this section we provide a brief overview of the immediate domestic and geopolitical background that preceded the emergence of the Taliban as a political force in 1994. We then examine the major features and events of the Taliban's five years in power, including their approach to governance and relations with the outside world. Particular attention is given to the impact of the Taliban's rule on women in Afghanistan. In the analytical section that follows, we explore the political sociology of the Taliban as a movement. Who were they? What shaped and animated their religious and political consciousness? We also consider the various factors that led to their stunning success and rapid takeover of most of the country. This is followed by an examination of the Taliban's ideology and religio-political worldview, and we make a number of observations about Taliban-style Islam in the context of Afghanistan's prevailing religious norms. Finally, we consider some possible futures for the Taliban which, as a movement, has proven resilient and capable of reinventing and reasserting itself in recent years.

Background: Afghan resistance, civil war, and the geopolitics of energy

Essentially a valley between two formidable mountain ranges, Afghanistan has figured heavily in the geostrategic considerations of regional and world powers for many years. As an ethnolinguistically diverse society with strong regional and tribal traditions, Afghan national identity has been premised on the common religion, Islam, that unites these disparate groups, and also on a strong sense of commitment to Afghan territorial integrity. Afghanistan was the focus of a considerable strategic rivalry between Britain and Russia in the early twentieth century known as the "Great Game," or, to the Russians, "the Tournament of Shadows." A version of this same contest would repeat itself nearly 100 years later, when Afghanistan became the subject of Cold War contention between the United States and the Soviet Union.

In the early 1970s, Afghanistan was still under the rule of King Zahir Shah from an ethnically Pashtun family, the Durrani, that had figured prominently in Afghan history for centuries. Various political tensions were beginning to emerge at this time, with Zahir Shah's Prime Minister, Muhammad Daud Khan, looking to embark on an ambitious modernization plan. At Kabul University, however, Marxists opposed to both Daud Khan and the royalists were beginning to make their voices heard. In 1973 Daud Khan overthrew Zahir Shah and declared a new republic. Now president, Daud Khan faced continual pressure from leftist forces over the next five years. In 1978 he was himself toppled in a communist coup that brought the People's Democratic Party of Afghanistan (PDPA) to power.[73] The latter's socialist program did not prove particularly popular when they tried to export it beyond the comparatively cosmopolitan confines of Kabul, with the PDPA meeting significant resistance in the provinces of the country. Using the now endangered PDPA regime as pretense, the Soviet Union invaded Afghanistan in December 1979.

Over the next nine years, the Soviet forces fought a war of attrition against an Afghan resistance force commonly known as the mujahideen. Despite their superior armaments and military technology, the Soviets could not decisively win what quickly turned into a guerilla war in unfamiliar and highly inhospitable terrain. For their part, the mujahideen regarded the war as a *jihad,* and their religiously inspired persistence and superior knowledge of the land played major roles in allowing them to hold off their far better-armed foes. Several other factors were instrumental in the mujahideen's eventual victory. Paramount among these is the fact that they were receiving massive amounts of financial and military aid from the United States and Pakistan, mostly coordinated through the Inter-Services Intelligence directorate of the latter, but with considerable CIA involvement as well. This comprised the supply of money, training, and weapons to mujahideen forces, as well as logistical and medical support from just over the border. One particularly decisive element here was the U.S. decision to supply the mujahideen with shoulder-mounted Stinger missile systems that permitted them to "snipe" Soviet helicopter gunships. Although American military assistance officially started after the Soviet invasion, subsequent historical evidence suggests the United States was aiding the mujahideen a full half year before the USSR intervention in the hope of coaxing the latter into what U.S. National Security Advisor Zbigniew Brezinski was quite rightly convinced would become the Soviet "Vietnam."

Pakistan had many reasons to become an active supporter of the mujahideen. It had been wanting for some time to cultivate a strong strategic relationship with the United States, and the Soviet war in Afghanistan provided the perfect opportunity. By sponsoring the mujahideen, much of whose leadership drew from the ethnically dominant Pashtun areas of southern Afghanistan on the Pakistani border, Pakistan was also able to ensure its influence over those tribal elements that might try to make common cause with Pakistani Pashtuns inside its own rather tenuous northern border. Furthermore, it was distinctly in Pakistan's interest to maintain Afghanistan as a "buffer state" between itself and the Muslim regions of the USSR to the north. Another important aspect of the Soviet war was the presence in Afghanistan, from the early 1980s, of a relatively large number of foreign Muslim fighters who traveled to the region to fight in solidarity with the mujahideen. These "Arab Afghans," as they came to be known, are discussed in greater detail in Chapter 7. Among them was one Usama Bin Laden, who would later go on to found the Al-Qaeda global jihadi network, and to play a decisive role in the future of the Taliban.

In 1988 the Soviet Union decided to cut its losses and began to withdraw troops from Afghanistan, a process completed by 1989. Much to everyone's surprise, the communist government, led by Najibullah, managed to stay in power until 1992 by striking a number of deals with provincial power brokers. When the government did eventually fall, however, Afghanistan entered a dark period of civil war between rival mujahideen factions. Once their common enemy was gone from the scene, rivalries old and new emerged within the ranks of the mujahideen. These groups—which broke down largely along ethnic and regional lines—were well armed and still had access to considerable resources left over from the generous funding they received during the resistance. The key figures here were ethno-regional warlords, such as Hikmatyar and Rabbani, each of whom also headed a nominally Islamist political party. During the mujahideen period, all Pakistani financial aid was funneled through these party structures, so in some regards the "re-ethnicization" of Afghan politics in the wake of the Soviet withdrawal can be seen as a byproduct of the resource clusters associated with various mujahideen warlords.[74] In some regards, it was also just a scramble for power between heavily armed political rivals. As

Thomas Barfield puts it, "each faction leader realized that if he did not obtain power now, he never would."[75] For the next four years these clans fought it out, with the civilian population caught in between them and often bearing the brunt of the effects of this conflict. After nearly a decade of fighting a war forced on them by an external power, the people of Afghanistan were now suffering at the hands of their own leaders. Exchanges of rocket attacks, for example, killed hundreds, and many populated areas were cut off from basic resources. After a long war with the Soviets, things just seemed to get worse during what came to be known as *topakeyano daurai*, the "time of the gunmen."[76]

Before we go on to examine the direct circumstances leading to the formation of the Taliban, it would be helpful to say something briefly about the new geopolitical context in which the future of Afghanistan was playing out. The dissolution of the Soviet Union prompted various regional and world powers to reassess their strategic postures. The United States, in particular, was interested in the energy resources to be found around the basin of the Caspian Sea and began to assess various routes by which oil and gas might be transported to seaports for onward shipping. In the early 1990s, one possible route that would allow it to bypass Iran involved pipelines through Afghanistan and Pakistan. For this reason, Washington DC was keeping a careful eye on the situation in Afghanistan and continuing its cooperation with Pakistan (whose strategic calculus remained basically the same) with the aim of achieving stability in the latter's northern neighbor. Iran, for its part, would have preferred to cash in on pipelines flowing through its territory. When the Taliban emerged, then, seeming to promise a new sense of stability and order for Afghanistan, Iran found itself opposing the new movement both ideologically and strategically. Ideologically because it was led by radical Sunnis who were vehemently anti-Shi'i in their outlook, and strategically because the Taliban risked creating conditions that would allow precious energy supplies to bypass Iran altogether.[77]

The rise and political career of the Taliban, 1994–2001

The Taliban (meaning "students") emerged as an organized movement in the summer of 1994 out of the southwestern city of Qandahar. Its leader, Mullah Omar, had fought in the Afghan resistance against the Soviets, but was not considered a major (or even minor) figure in the Afghan political scene. More of a local notable, the popular story surrounding the Taliban's formation has it that Mullah Omar led a small group of young Qandahari men (most of whom had studied at *madrasas* in Pakistan—hence "Taliban") against a gang of local criminals who had been raping and pillaging in the area. From here the movement grew very quickly, spurred on, it would seem, from various forces on the other side of the Pakistani border. Over the next two years, the Taliban assumed control of more and more of the predominantly Pashtun areas of the south, earning a reputation among locals for putting an end to clan rivalries and petty crime, and enforcing public order and safety—the first time any social force had been able to do so for two decades. It is clear that, even from this early stage, the Taliban was receiving considerable support from Pakistani intelligence, and it appeared that it had been chosen by the latter to serve as Islamabad's new "client" up north, in replacement of Gulbuddin Hikmatyar's Hizb-i Islami faction which had proved ineffectual in implementing Pakistan's agenda.[78] As they grew in numbers and confidence and began to move into the north of the country, several of the rival warlord factions sought to establish a temporary alliance to counter the threat from this new and unexpected force.[79] This was to little avail, however, as the Taliban proceeded apace through the provinces, taking Qandahar in late 1994, the western city of Herat in the late summer of 1995, and, finally, the capital itself, Kabul, exactly a year later. Resistance to the Taliban was pushed further and further into the north of the country, and it was in this area, around cities such as Mazar-i-Sharif—which changed hands twice in 1997—that the Northern Alliance under Ahmed Shah Massoud would make its stand against Mullah Omar's forces.

Perceptions of the Taliban among Afghanis varied considerably. Some within the civilian population associated it with a return to royalism, since many of the Taliban leaders were from the same Pashtun Durrani tribe as the king. Among the various warlord clans, however—particularly the non-Pashtuns—they were seen as agents of Pakistan or Pashtun nationalists.[80] We have already mentioned Iran's fears that the rise of the Taliban represented a new source of American strategic influence, a concern shared by many within Afghanistan itself. It is indeed true that, during its early period, the United States essentially pursued a "hands-off" policy, generally trusting the Pakistanis to serve as stewards of their mutual interests in the region.[81] In some ways, the Taliban served to unite various forces in Pakistan usually at odds with each other but who had a common interest in seeing the Taliban succeed—although for very different reasons. The political party of the religious scholars, the JUI, supported them on religious grounds, whereas the secular government of Benazir Bhutto appreciated their strategic utility.

BOX 6.3 IRAQ AFTER SADDAM: SECTARIANISM AND MUSLIM POLITICS

Given the demographics of Iraq, it was inevitable that religion would emerge as a major political issue in the aftermath of the 2003 U.S.-led war that toppled the regime of Saddam Hussein. For the country's majority Shi'i population, in particular, an end to minority Sunni rule represented an unprecedented political opportunity. As the security situation remained fundamentally unstable over the next few years, however, and with foreign militant Islamists fanning the flames of sectarian dissent, religion became much more than just a form of symbolic currency in Iraq. Rather, the Shi'i–Sunni cleavage quickly emerged as the organizing principle of post-Saddam politics, with many Iraqis seeking refuge in sectarian formations that felt safer and more reliable than a weak central government still largely beholden to the United States and its ongoing military occupation. While national religious figures, such as the senior Shi'i cleric Grand Ayatullah Ali Sistani, urged moderation and refrained from direct involvement in politics, other sectarian leaders, such as the young activist Muqtada al-Sadr and his militia, positioned themselves as defenders of the Shi'a against Sunni attacks—emerging as major new players on the Iraqi political landscape.

Iraqi parliamentary politics is also dominated by religion, with both of the leading non-Kurdish coalitions organized along sectarian lines. Islamist parties play prominent roles in both, such as the Shi'i Islamic Dawa Party and Supreme Council for the Islamic Revolution in Iraq and the Sunni Iraqi Islamic Party—which represents the MB tendency in Iraq.

The issue of Islam's role in legislation proved divisive during early negotiations over the country's new constitution, and there have been persistent concerns raised about the extent to which the Iranian model of clerical rule might prove attractive to some of the more revolutionary Shi'i factions. In addition to concern about Iran's influence over the Shi'a and the possibility of region-wide ignition of sectarian tensions, some have wondered about neighboring Saudi Arabia's likely response to a major Shi'i power play in Iraq. While Prime Minister Nouri al-Maliki's Islamic Da'wa Party nominally supported Iran's Islamic Revolution in the 1980s, it rejects the idea of theocratic rule for Iraq. While his party is clearly based on a Shi'i Islamist platform, Al-Maliki's tenure as Prime Minister has been tempered by the need to focus on basic issues such as security, rule of law, and economic stability. From 2010, Al-Maliki faced a parliament in which his party's coalition sat alongside two others of roughly equal strength.

Once in power, the Taliban as a movement more or less ceased to exist, as Mullah Omar and his associates went about the business of trying to build a functioning government.[82] Much of this was pure trial and error, since many of the group's top leaders had very little experience in public administration. Furthermore, after almost 20 years of conflict and civil war, the country's existing governmental institutions were in tatters. Mullah Omar established a central consultative council, or *shura,* as the executive branch of government, and under it a number of regional *shuras* associated with the main provincial population centers. One of the early missteps they made was to appoint as the leaders of these provincial *shuras*—some of which were located in areas where the population still harbored considerable suspicion towards the Taliban—individuals with little or no ties to the local area.[83] In 1997 Mullah Omar announced to the world that the name of the country was being changed to the "Islamic Emirate of Afghanistan," its former identity as a republic having been deemed Western and un-Islamic. In terms of international recognition, the Taliban managed to gain official endorsement from only three countries: Pakistan (for obvious reasons), Saudi Arabia (which saw in its austere version of Islam the influences of Wahhabism), and the United Arab Emirates (which had considerable economic interests in the country).

Gilles Kepel characterizes Taliban governance as being confined to three core areas: morality, commerce, and war.[84] We will want to dwell more extensively on the question of public morality under the Taliban, but would also do well to consider briefly the second two aspects. With regard to war, Mullah Omar established a command hierarchy for the movement's forces, with the goal of continuing their efforts to bring more of the country under Taliban control. These forces fought throughout the entire period of the Taliban's tenure in government, and, by the time of their demise in the fall of 2001, had managed eventually to bring all but a pocket of far northeastern Afghanistan, which was being held by Ahmed Shah Massoud's forces, under their control. In terms of commerce, the Taliban did very little for the country's almost exclusively agricultural economy. With very little going on in the way of state regulation in many areas, Afghanistan soon became a throughput haven for smuggled and counterfeit goods, many of them emanating from new duty-free ports in the Gulf.[85] By taking a cut from this trafficking, the regime was able to establish a source of income to supplement the aid it was receiving, at least in the early days, from Pakistan and Saudi Arabia. Both of these countries came under considerable pressure from the United States to cut back on their support for the Taliban once it became clear that they were systematically abusing human rights and allowing elements of the global jihadi network (see Chapter 7) to operate with impunity in Afghanistan.

The Taliban was particularly notorious for the strict moral code it implemented and enforced on the population of Afghanistan. The sources of this are to be found in the particularly conservative variant of Islam that many of its leaders had been taught at *madrasas* in Pakistan. Most of these schools are affiliated with the Deobandi movement, named after a seminary established in India in the nineteenth century that became the center of a movement seeking to reform and purify Islam along lines that closely resembled the teachings of Muhammad Ibn Abdul Wahhab, founder of the austere Wahhabi school. The Wahhabi tendencies of the Taliban were most clearly on display in the form of the "vice and virtue squads" they established to roam around towns enforcing public morality—much like the *mutawwa* police in Saudi Arabia. Some of the policies they implemented included a total ban on music, movies, dancing, and television, a requirement that men grow beards, the enforcement of daily prayers, and the introduction of *hudud* justice—the Qur'anically prescribed penal code mandating capital punishment for murder and adultery, and limb amputation for theft.[86] Likewise, anyone converting to Christianity was threatened with a death sentence.[87]

Afghan women suffered particularly harshly under the Taliban, with the rigid Deobandi legal code serving to reinforce the highly conservative gender norms that already characterized Pashtun customary law. Women were forced to cover themselves from head to toe in a *burqa,* a practice that already existed in some parts of the country, but that had never been enforced. The structure of this garment was so comprehensively concealing as to leave only a small grill for air in front of the mouth. Women were also required to bring a male relative with them anytime they ventured out in public. For the most part, however, the Taliban's policies were actually designed to eliminate women from public space as much as possible. Girls were initially forbidden from attending schools since separate schools for them had not yet been established and the education of boys was considered more important (girls were later allowed to attend school). Women were also banned from the workplace, creating significant new economic hardships for already impoverished families. In many cases these were widows whose husbands had been killed during the Soviet war, and they were now forced to take desperate measures—begging, drug trafficking, prostitution—to provide for their families. Obviously, many of these measures opened them up to the risk of harsh punishment at the hands of the Taliban if caught. Perhaps most worrying is the fact that, for the first two years of Taliban rule, women had no practical access to healthcare. As women they could not be treated by male doctors, and since women doctors were banned from the workplace, there was nowhere for them to go. As in the case of their position on schooling for girls, the Taliban eventually amended this policy.

Governance under the Taliban was wholly ineffectual. By trying to implement directly what they had been taught out of dusty medieval tomes in *madrasas*—and, moreover, by implementing *only* what they had been taught, and not being willing to think or act outside those boundaries—the Taliban quickly brought an already decimated Afghan state closer to the brink of collapse. Most of its ministries were wholly inoperative, and the more effective of its civil servants turned out on the streets because their association with the bureaucracy rendered them "too modern." As Gilles Kepel put it:

> The summary exercise of [governmental] functions did not make the Islamic Emirate of Afghanistan anything like a modern state: in fact it was more a community organized according to Deobandi norms but merely "swollen" to the dimensions of a country subjected to moral coercion on the inside and *jihad* on the edges.[88]

As it became increasingly alienated from both Afghan society and the international community, the Taliban only seemed to become more radical. In 2001, for example, it used infantry units to destroy the famed statues of the Buddha at Bamyan, claiming their presence to be incompatible with the strictly monotheistic ethos of Islam. When a coalition of renowned Islamic scholars from the Middle East issued a *fatwa* indicating that such monuments should be left intact, it was summarily dismissed by Mullah Omar.[89] Coming under increased harassment from the Taliban, and accused of Christian proselytizing, many international NGOs withdrew their programs and services from Afghanistan at about this same time. As far as Mullah Omar was concerned, sovereignty and the capacity to legislate normativity were invested exclusively in God. If these values happened to conflict with international ethics, there was no contest: Islam overrules any human normative construct.[90] Several observers have noted that this further radicalization of the Taliban occurred in conjunction with, and can perhaps be partly explained by, two other developments. First, the last remaining senior moderate within the Taliban executive *shura*, Muhammad Rabbani, died in the spring of 2001. Second, Pakistan and Saudi Arabia had cut off much of their support for the Taliban in response both to international pressure (in the case of Pakistan) and, in the case of Saudi Arabia, extreme displeasure at the fact that the Taliban was providing sanctuary for Usama Bin Laden—a sworn enemy of the Kingdom.[91] The Taliban by this point was coming to rely increasingly on Bin Laden's financial largesse and was hence more susceptible to his influence. It was clear—and highly displeasing—to many Afghans that Arabs and other foreigners associated with Bin Laden were playing a large role in Mullah Omar's military operations against the Northern Alliance.[92] In October 2001, within weeks of an American assault in reprisal for the September 11, 2001 attacks on the United States, the Taliban government of Afghanistan fell swiftly from power. Many of its key leaders, including Mullah Omar, escaped and melted into the complex mountainous terrain along the Pakistani border. Most Afghans rejoiced at the downfall of the harsh regime and hardly blinked an eye as thousands of American troops poured into their country. After all, in their minds the Taliban had effectively just spent several years allowing Pakistanis and Arabs to run the country.

© Al-Manar

Figure 6.4 Taliban fighters in Afghanistan

Explaining and understanding the Taliban

Before moving on to examine the re-emergence and evolution of the Taliban since 2002, it will be helpful to spend some time looking at the nature and composition of the movement more generally. One thing that is particularly remarkable about the Taliban is that very few in Afghanistan had heard of it or its leaders before it took over the country. There seemed almost to be something spontaneous about its formation. The political mobilization of student movements was nothing new in Afghanistan, however, and neither was it surprising that the Taliban was able to generate human resources so quickly, once we understand how it recruited. In historical terms, there is a tradition of student-led political movements that dates back to the period of British rule in the nineteenth century.[93] More recently, *madrasas* in both Afghanistan and Pakistan had proven to be fertile recruiting grounds for the ranks of the mujahideen during the war with the Soviets.[94] In the case of the Taliban, Mullah Omar needed only to send word to some of the leading *madrasas* in the Northwest Frontier Province of Pakistan, such as the famed Dar ul-Uloom Haqqania, for them to shut down the schools and send the students north to fight. The Taliban also had Pakistani intelligence actively recruiting, training, and sending soldiers north.

So we can make the following observations about the social composition of the Taliban forces. In ethnic terms, they were overwhelmingly Pashtun—indeed, prompting many beyond the southern provinces to fear a "Pashtunization" of Afghanistan once they appeared. They are Sunni

313

Muslims with strong roots in the vast network of Deobandi *madrasas* that dot the landscape of southern Afghanistan and northern Pakistan.[95] We should also note that many within their ranks were refugees from Afghanistan who had fled to, or been born in, Pakistan during the Soviet occupation. Many of them had never even been to Afghanistan, or had only just returned during the civil war following the Soviet withdrawal. The Pakistani *madrasas* had played a vital role in the lives of refugees during the war. Where the modernist Islamist Jama'at-i Islami (JI) in Pakistan, associated with the thinking of Abu'l-A'la Mawdudi, had sought to cultivate mainly an educated, middle class following, the Deobandis fashioned themselves into the champions of the rural poor.[96] *Madrasas* such as Samiul Haq's Dar ul-Uloom Haqqania in northern Pakistan provided free education, food, and for orphans or those who had nowhere to live, free housing as well. These schools also held out the hope of some sort of social mobility.[97] The Northwest Frontier Province capital of Peshawar was essentially a "war economy" town during the conflict with the Soviets, with all manner of logistics, recruitment, and procurement being managed from its center. The *madrasas* became the conduits of choice for rapid movements into lucrative positions with the mujahideen organizations. Many of the Taliban leaders were exactly of this background, having been schooled in Pakistan and then joined the ranks of the mujahideen fighters. Also interspersed within the Taliban forces were a fairly large number of Pakistanis who had been recruited out of *madrasas* or trained directly by Pakistani military intelligence—leading some to label Taliban an Afghan–Pakistani "hybrid."[98] Many in Afghanistan and around the world marveled at the Taliban's rapid military success, wondering how a group of young, inexperienced students could prove so adept at defeating battle-hardened warlord forces. The answer, of course, lies in the fact that their leaders were all experienced mujahideen, and they were receiving all manner of assistance from Pakistan.

In order to understand the worldview of the Taliban rank and file, it is vital to understand the world of the Deobandi *madrasa*. Life in these institutions revolved around rote memorization of the Qur'an and other religious texts for hours on end, usually interspersed only with breaks for religious observance. They were very insular spaces—often in highly remote areas—and generally cut off from the world.[99] Students came to know and conceive of the world mainly through the teachings and texts they encountered between the walls of the classroom, and through the attitudes that prevailed among the teachers. The version of the Deobandi curriculum taught in these schools shared much in common with Salafi and Wahhabi doctrine. It was highly conservative, very literalist, and quite categorical in its moral logic. In short, these were not spaces to learn critical thinking skills; they were settings in which knowledge defining the boundaries of the permissible and the forbidden was imparted. In the *madrasa,* it was also quite easy to imagine the Islamic utopia—a textual polity—without ever having to consider how the exigencies and realities of human culture and society might disrupt its realization. In other words these were, in keeping with Olivier Roy's characterization of the "neo-fundamentalist" trend in Islam, "deculturing" spaces.[100] This was an Islam stripped of local cultural, ethnic, or tribal custom. The socialization of these students, religious and otherwise, was hence fundamentally different from what they would have experienced back home in Afghanistan, where ethnic and tribal identity is everything. These were somehow de-Pashtunized Pashtuns whose sole sense of public identity derived from a very puritanical breed of Islam.

The Taliban were able to use this worldview to their advantage in terms of recruiting from the ranks of ex-*madrasa* students. Many of these refugee students had returned home in the early 1990s and were shocked at what they encountered upon visiting their home country for the first time.[101] In their minds, a victory by the righteous mujahideen over the forces of atheism could only mean that Afghanistan would now be the model Islamic society—just as the mullahs taught back in the schools. What they found, however, was a country torn asunder by ethnic rivalry and greedy, power-grabbing warlords. Violence and crime ruled the streets. Thus when the call came for them to put the Islam they had learned into practice and join the ranks of a new mujahideen—one that would rid Afghanistan not of infidel communists, but of un-Islamic thought and practice—they responded enthusiastically.

We have already described the rapid success enjoyed by the Taliban, with most of Afghanistan falling under their control in a very short period—and all accomplished by a movement with no history and no formal social base to speak of. How can this be explained? One leading analyst of Afghanistan, Larry Goodson, attributes the Taliban's success to five factors, as follows.[102]

- Ethnicity—it was able to make quick progress and gather considerable momentum in the southern part of the country around Qandahar, where fellow Pashtuns were in the majority and readily accepted it.
- Religiosity—as an Islamist movement that "walked the talk" when it came to implementing *shari'ah* and enforcing public order, the Taliban's emphasis on piety and virtue won it many admirers. Its religious practice was also very close to the prevailing Pashtun tribal customs, which made its acceptance less of a reach in the south than in other, religiously heterogeneous parts of the country.
- Fatigue and attrition—after nearly 20 years of constant war, the populace was willing to accept anyone who held out the hope of restoring peace, order, and some semblance of normal life. "War weariness" had set in.[103] The various clans and factions that could have opposed the Taliban had spent the past few years wearing each other down, and were in no position to resist the sweeping rise of the new movement.

- Money—significant foreign assistance and various internal revenue streams allowed the Taliban to buy off the leadership of any would-be opponents.
- Pakistan—in addition to the recruitment, training, logistics, and weapons support provided from south of the border, various *madrasas* associated with the Deobandi network in Pakistan and its political party counterpart, the JUI, provided the Taliban with thousands of students.

The rise of the Taliban can be seen to represent a range of continuities and discontinuities in terms of local religious norms and the relationship of religion to politics. In terms of continuities, it represents, as Thomas Barfield has pointed out, the latest phase in a debate that has ensued for a century in Afghanistan between traditionalists and modernizers.[104] In the former camp we would find, for example, royalists and clerics, and in the latter faction republicans and communists. In this particular iteration, we find the Taliban trying to effect a moral "ruralization" of the comparatively modern, cosmopolitan (a dangerous quality in their minds), urban space of Kabul.[105] David Edwards sees this as a return to "village identity" through a rejection of the institutions of modernity (e.g. universities, government bureaucracy—hence the decline of the Afghan civil service under the Taliban).[106]

The discontinuities represented by the Taliban are, however, far more numerous. Barry Rubin notes that within the Taliban project are to be found both elements of regionalism and ideology.[107] While its ethnic composition certainly allowed the Taliban to benefit from the dominant Pashtun character of its southern stronghold around Qandahar, it was—by the very same token—perceived as a purveyor of "Pashtun extremism" by the inhabitants of disparate ethnosectarian regions in Afghanistan. Indeed, it is fair to say, as several observers have pointed out, that under the Taliban, sectarian polarization and the "ethnic stakes" both became considerably more pronounced in Afghanistan.[108] There was nothing in their religious ideology, however, that should, or did, predispose them to any particular systematic political strategy or agenda. As Barbara Metcalf puts it:

> None of the Deobandi movements has a theoretical stance in relation to political life. They either expediently embrace the political culture of their time and place, or withdraw from politics completely. For the Taliban, that meant engaging with the emerging ethnic polarities in the country and seeking allies wherever they could find them.[109]

And yet certain distinct attributes of the Taliban's political tactics can indeed be discerned—particularly during the early phase of its activity. For the most part these were correctives to recent trends in Afghan political life that they found distasteful. The emergence of strong cults of personality around particular warlords during the recent civil war, for example, led them to pursue an "anti-charismatic" approach that sought as much as possible to downplay the role and profile of individual leaders in favor of the morality embodied in the practices of their social movement.[110] Similarly they also worked to transcend the factional and political party lines that had taken root within the various mujahideen factions and the religious classes during the Soviet period. These parties represented modern forms of *bid'a* (innovation) that threatened the solidarity and unity of the *umma*. In a properly Islamic society, political parties would be superfluous and would only produce strife and the pursuit of narrow interests at the expense of piety.[111]

BOX 6.4 BOKO HARAM: THE "NIGERIAN TALIBAN"?

Afghanistan is not the only country that has witnessed the emergence of militant Islamic movements seeking to impose Islamic law in the context of eroded or uneven state capacity. Nigeria, a country whose population is approximately evenly divided between Muslims and Christians, has witnessed recent efforts to introduce *shari'ah* law in its northern, Muslim majority states (see Box 6.1 on Nigeria above). The ensuing conflicts reflect deeply seated disputes over federalism and ethnic politics in Nigeria. The Boko Haram movement, founded out of a group that sought in 2001 to detach from Nigerian society to form a pure Islamic community, has pursued an agenda that looks remarkably similar to that of the Taliban in many respects. Its name is usually and not incorrectly translated as "Western education is forbidden," but the term *boko* also refers to a particular class of Nigerian elites co-opted by British imperial control and viewed by the movement as culturally corrupt. Its name hence signifies the dual rejection of the dominant Nigerian political class as well as Western cultural influences. Its goal is to extend *shari'ah* law from the provincial/state level in the north to the federal level so that all of Nigeria becomes an Islamic state. While some have suggested that Boko Haram should be regarded as an affiliate of Al-Qaeda, its origins and activities—even where militant (including numerous bombings that have killed over 1,000 people since 2009)—suggest a political agenda focused firmly on Nigeria.

It has also been noted that, in some respects, the Taliban introduced innovations of their own in terms of reconfiguring the alignment of forces between religion, tribe, and the state in Afghanistan.[112] Where religion had previously played a mediating role between tribe and government—unifying the former where necessary, and likewise reining in the latter—the Taliban now sought to define and occupy the state. This represented a fundamental shift in the traditional role of religion. And the transformation was by no means confined to the functional dimensions of religion in Afghan society. The very form and content of the religion seemed alien to many outside the more conservative Pashtun areas in the south. Afghan Islam traditionally has been very flexible in terms of dealing with sectarian differences and multiple interpretations of Islam. Many Afghans, for example, were tolerant of, and embraced, Sufi teachings and practices. The Taliban, on the other hand, "instituted an uncompromising moral severity and inflexibility that . . . [did] not mesh well with Afghan sensibilities."[113] Islamic scholars viewing the Taliban from outside Afghanistan saw something that appeared as retrograde Pashtun tribal custom masquerading as religion. Even some radical Salafi sheikhs were led to characterize the Taliban's *ulama* as "half-scholars."[114] From within Afghanistan, however—particularly outside the south—the problem appeared to be just the reverse: the Taliban apparently had abandoned local traditions of religious tolerance for a strict and ruthless Islam, something quite foreign, imported from Saudi Arabia and Pakistan.[115]

What has become of the Taliban since they were removed from power by the United States, and Hamid Karzai's government installed in their place? We will recall that, back in October 2001, many of the key leaders in the movement, including Mullah Omar, escaped into the mountains bordering Pakistan. From as early as 2002 there were signs that elements of the Taliban were regrouping, although as a far less centralized entity. They engaged in a number of attacks on foreign aid workers in the south of the country, and seemed now to be touting themselves primarily as a Pashtun nationalist force to maintain pressure on Karzai's attempts at unifying the nation.[116] In addition to these militant activities, Taliban-connected forces continued to enforce Islamic justice and public virtue in pockets of southeastern Afghanistan.[117]

The Taliban that re-emerged over the next few years seemed different in many key respects from the group that had first taken over the country in 1996. This "neo-Taliban," as Antonio Giustozzi and others have termed it, seemed to have a more pragmatic orientation.[118] While still identified with Mullah Omar and other key figures of what came to be known as the "Quetta Shura" (named for the Pakistani city where the Afghan Taliban's key leaders are believed to have taken refuge after 2001), the movement's agenda and priorities seem to have shifted in response to new political realities. Placing less emphasis on an ambitious plan for the top-down enforcement of "pure" Islamic governance, the neo-Taliban has tended to focus more on the kinds of local law-and-order issues that proved to be a winning formula during their efforts in the late 1990s. While continuing to strongly criticize—and actively target—foreign forces in Afghanistan, much of their critique has been reserved for the government of Hamid Karzai.

They blame the Afghan president for the persistence of lawlessness, insecurity, and economic malaise in most regions beyond the capital and its immediate environs.

The new Taliban strategy also has entailed severing its ties, both rhetorically and, so far as can be observed, operationally, with Al-Qaeda and other foreign jihadist elements. The movement has instead been keen to emphasize its "Afghan" character and to portray itself as engaged in an effort to fuse Islam and Afghan nationalism in pursuit of political project that aspires to bring better governance to all Afghan ethnic groups and tribes. In practice, however, it has been difficult for the Taliban to gain broad buy-in from diverse groups in Afghan society, for two reasons. First, its active membership continues to be limited to Pashtuns from the south of the country and it has continued to find itself at odds—including instances of violent conflict—with other ethnic and sectarian groups. Second, based on its history and continued reliance on support from Islamabad, many in Afghanistan outside the movement's Pashtun base continue to regard the Taliban as a surrogate force working on behalf of the Pakistani intelligence services—despite recent efforts to play up its Afghan character.

The Taliban also has not lost any of its militancy. From 2006 there has been a concerted effort on the part of the movement—as well as various allied groups—to step up attacks on both foreign forces taking part in the International Security Assistance Force, and Afghanistan's own army and police loyal to Karzai and the central government. Over the course of a number of fighting seasons through 2008, the Taliban made considerable progress in reconsolidating its effective control over much of the south of the country and using tactical alliances with various warlords and other militant networks to make inroads elsewhere. Indeed, by this point the label "Taliban" had become somewhat indeterminate. It ceased to be used exclusively in reference to members of the movement controlled by the Quetta Shura, and took on a much broader remit. By 2009 the term was frequently invoked to refer to the loose alliance of the Quetta Shura, the network around militant Islamist and ex-mujahideen leader Jalauddin Haqqani, and Gulbuddin Hekmatyar's Hizb-e-Islami. Indeed, the label seemed to take on something of a "brand" quality and was used opportunistically by any number of militant elements who wanted to profit from the association.[119] The United States increasingly began to rely on unmanned aerial vehicles, or "drones," to target leaders and militants associated with these groups. In some cases, Taliban fighters managed to infiltrate the Afghan National Army only to desert and return to their local militias after drawing salary and weapons from the national military. The country's security situation became so precarious that in 2009 the newly inaugurated U.S. president Barack Obama announced that 17,000 additional American troops would be sent to Afghanistan to deal with the new Taliban insurgency.

Afghan president Hamid Karzai also came under considerable pressure during this period to improve security throughout the country and to lay the groundwork for sustainable economic progress. Unable to project the power and capacity of the state much beyond Kabul, he found himself increasingly reliant on alliances with various regional warlords. These relationships were both financially and politically costly to maintain, with Karzai constantly forced to compromise his own national development objectives in order to accommodate requests from provincial power brokers in order to keep them on side. In 2009, Karzai won a disputed presidential election that was surrounded by widespread accusations of fraud and vote rigging. By 2010, Karzai realized that in the longer term he would have to achieve a negotiated political settlement with the Taliban. That year saw the establishment of a new "High Peace Council," headed by former president Burhanuddin Rabbani, to serve as a forum for pursuing reconciliation between the central government and the various militant groups. The assassination of Rabbani in 2011 marked the nadir of efforts to achieve reconciliation with the Taliban.

The Taliban has also regularly signalled its willingness to enter into political talks with both the U.S. and the Afghan government, but finding a reliable interlocutor with appropriate Quetta Shura connections proved difficult. Assessments as to the Taliban's sincerity about reaching a political solution varied. Once the U.S. announced that it would have all its combat forces out of Afghanistan by 2014, many saw the Taliban as essentially engaged in a waiting game: talking about negotiations but actually planning for a time when it would be in a position to reassert military control throughout the country. Others believed that the Taliban saw advantages to reaching a settlement prior to 2014, since it had made a calculation that, with many well-resourced and armed regional warlords back in play, it would be much more difficult to assert widespread control than it had been in the 1990s. In 2012, the Taliban announced that it would be opening a political office in Doha, Qatar, which would serve as a hub for its negotiation efforts, but the opening of the office the following year was surrounded by significant controversy and ongoing wrangling between the U.S. and Hamid Karzai over who should be responsible for leading political negotiations with the Taliban.

The "post-2014" question hangs over all of the country's political future. Questions about Karzai's political future (he has vowed to step down in 2014), the nature of the ongoing international—and especially U.S.—military presence in the country, and economic viability all bear directly on what some have characterized as the "ungovernability" of Afghanistan.[120] Others, such as Barfield, have contended that the country is not so much ungovernable as it is unrealistic to expect that—given the nature of Afghan society—overreliance on centralized forms of government is the answer to the country's problems. He argues that historically most Afghans have accepted and respected the basic legitimacy of a centralized government—although the ability of the latter to extend its reach evenly across the country is an unrealistic expectation.[121] One possible interpretation of the Taliban's longer-term strategy, then, would be to see it as pursuing something akin to a "Hizbullah model" (see above), whereby it participates in mainstream politics while simultaneously running a shadow state in certain provinces and maintaining a militia as a hedge against threats from the state and foreign forces.

BOX 6.5 CENTRAL ASIA: "OFFICIAL ISLAM" AND ITS ALTERNATIVES

Since the early 1990s, Islam has emerged—however unevenly—as a potent political force in the Muslim-majority states of the former Soviet Union. During the decades of Soviet rule, it is important to note, Islam never disappeared completely, despite the Communist Party's strong aversion to religion. Rather, Moscow sought to reorganize and harness the power of Islam for its own geopolitical purposes—such as gaining Cold War support from other Muslim nations in the Middle East and elsewhere. Although most mosques were effectively closed down or diverted to other uses, many aspects of religion continued to be present in the rhythm and culture of everyday life in Central Asia. The social roots of the Sufi brotherhoods were particularly strong in the region, and not easily eradicated—even by the mighty Soviet state.

The post-Soviet period saw an inevitable renewal in Central Asian religious life, but this has assumed many forms. Many of the "official *muftis*" of the communist period sought similar accommodations with the post-independence political elites, serving as the new conduits of state-sanctioned Islam. Other groups sought a more ambitious social and political role for religion, advocating various forms of Islamism, and some settings—most notably Uzbekistan and Tajikistan—have seen radical Islamists engaged in violent attempts to overthrow regimes. Groups such as the Islamic Renaissance Party (Hizb ut-Tahrir; see Chapter 7), and the Islamic Movement of Uzbekistan—represent these various strategies.

Central Asia has also become the target of a wide range of Islamization efforts originating from outside the region. Significant amounts of Saudi money poured in to support mosque-building efforts after the Soviet Union fell in 1991, and various Turkish groups—including representatives of the state *Diyanet* (see Chapter 4)—have also sought influence among their linguistic kin in Central Asia. Most notably, the movement around the popular preacher–teacher Fethullah Gülen (see Chapter 8) has opened a number of schools throughout Central Asia and these enjoy considerable popularity—prompting some governments in the region to view them with suspicion despite the group's moderate orientation. This is part of a broader pattern whereby incumbent regimes have sought to justify efforts to oppress and marginalize Islamic groups—and particularly those with transnational ties—by portraying them as potential security risks.

As Central Asian societies and their Muslim populations become more aware of global Islamic trends going forward, it is likely that the "religious public sphere" in the region will diversify significantly—much to the chagrin of governments that would prefer to limit local consumption of Islam to its preferred "domesticated" variants. It is also possible that pressure for greater openness and democracy in these countries could prompt the emergence of opposition movements focused on ending corruption—and that some of these groups might embrace an Islamic platform to gain greater legitimacy. This region also remains a zone of interest for various militant groups, and ongoing instability in neighboring areas—particularly in the aftermath of the U.S. withdrawal from Afghanistan in 2014—could see heightened Islamic radicalism in Central Asia.

Further study

A. Khalid, *Islam After Communism: Religion and Politics in Central Asia*, Berkeley, CA: University of California Press, 2007.

E. McGlinchey, *Chaos, Violence, Dynasty: Politics and Islam in Central Asia*, Pittsburgh, PA: University of Pittsburgh Press, 2011.

ISLAM FOR LACK OF . . . OR INSTEAD OF A SYSTEM?

This chapter has surveyed several cases, two of them in considerable depth, where Muslim political actors have sought to fill public voids left by weak, failed, or failing states. As we have seen, this dynamic is particularly prevalent in conflict and post-conflict settings. Clear contrasts have emerged with the various other cases of Islamism and Islam–state relations that we have examined in earlier chapters. Unlike the "Islamic authoritarianism" of

Iran or Sudan, none of the Islamist forces examined above was able (or, in at least one case—that of Afghanistan—even had any desire) to rely on complex, modern bureaucracies to promulgate and enforce their vision of an Islamic political order. Similarly, and unlike Islamist movements and political parties in countries such as Egypt, Turkey, Jordan, and Pakistan, the efforts of groups examined above have not been based primarily around devising strategies to challenge a well-established, entrenched, and stable state, or to infiltrate a political sphere denied to them. Rather, the Islamists featured here have tended to develop capacities and competences that allow them to operate in situations of political uncertainty, instability, and unpredictability, and furthermore, those defined by an absence—or a newly emerging sense—of institutionalized political process.

Looking across the range of cases we have surveyed in this chapter, several common points or patterns present themselves.

- **Islamist and Muslim social movements as providers of services that weak, failed, or surrogate states lack the capacity to deliver on their own** (e.g. Hamas, Hizbullah, Deobandi *madrasas*). This represents a mode of Islamism defined not in terms of instituting a formal political order based on Islam, but rather Islam as a social consciousness seeking to "fortify society" to a point where it can itself become the source of a popular political impulse in search of Islamic public normativity. Indeed, in some cases this kind of arrangement may be viewed by Islamists as preferable to the actual exercise of state power, since the latter would force them to be accountable to a wider range of stakeholders and could entail considerable reputational risk if they fail in the exercise of formal governance.

- **Islamism that develops in the context, and at the vanguard, of a popular resistance movement against foreign occupation** (e.g. Hamas, Hizbullah, Afghan mujahideen, Iraq). Islam functions as a form of nationalist discourse that derives its legitimacy from religion, or competes with other forms of organized resistance for the nationalist mantle. Here we identified striking similarities between Hamas and Hizbullah, which both emerged as Islamist alternatives in the context of conflicts involving foreign occupation, and where each succeeded in out-performing secular rivals both in providing basic services to citizens and in offering what was perceived as effective resistance to Israeli occupation and invasionary forces. Thus the political and broader structural environments in which Hamas and Hizbullah found themselves seemed to be stronger determinants of the nature and form of their Muslim politics—both of which involved the combination of party politics, social services, and militancy—than their rather different theological and sectarian orientations.

- **In the absence of a state capable of articulating a viable or unified national project or imaginary, the conflation of Islamism with a**

variety of sub-national identity formations (ethnicity, sectarianism, etc.). Contrary to the Islamism as nationalism model described just above, this is a situation that can work against the consolidation of a stable, nationally unified state in the aftermath of conflict (e.g. Iraq, Lebanon, Afghanistan).

It should be emphasized again that "Islam for lack of a system" does not represent a rigid category of analysis with a thick set of structural determinants. Rather, much like the idea of "Islam as the system," it suggests in broad terms some of the characteristics that define certain contexts of Muslim politics. Just as the analyses offered in the previous chapter did not in any way suggest that the dynamics of Muslim politics in countries such as Saudi Arabia and Iran can be understood only by reference to the fact these are, nominally, Islamic states, neither has the present chapter sought to imply that Islamism in Palestine and Afghanistan is to be understood exclusively in relation to the relative absence of strong, centralized political authority. Rather, as in the earlier chapters, the goal here has been to help the reader understand the variety of political opportunity structures, mechanisms of social mobilization, and symbolic resources available to Muslim actors in those situations where a recent or ongoing conflict (or failed state) has opened spaces for Islam to reach into, renegotiate, and articulate anew the meaning and practice of public normativity.

Having now, over the course of six chapters, explored the historical evolution of Islam and politics, the theory and early development of Islamism as a political project, and numerous case studies illustrating various Islamist modes and strategies across a variety of national political environments, we now move on to examine the interaction of Muslim politics and globalization through two chapters focused on key contemporary issues. Chapter 7 addresses the origins and evolution of the modern jihadist movement, including significant coverage of Usama Bin Laden and Al-Qaeda. This is followed by a concluding chapter that considers the debate on "post-Islamism" and the question of whether the forces of globalization may be having a qualitative impact on the nature and forms of Islamic activism and Muslim politics found in contemporary national and transnational settings.

NOTES

1 R. Jackson, *Quasi-States: Sovereignty, International Relations and the Third World,* Cambridge: Cambridge University Press, 1990.
2 G. E. Robinson, "Hamas as Social Movement," in Q. Wiktorowicz (ed.), *Islamic Activism: A Social Movement Theory Approach,* Bloomington, IN: Indiana University Press, 2004, p. 112.
3 J. Esposito, *Islam and Politics,* 4th edn, Syracuse, NY: Syracuse University Press, 1984, p. 228.

4 M. Jensen, "Islamism and Civil Society in the Gaza Strip," in A. Moussalli (ed.), *Islamic Fundamentalism: Myths & Realities,* Reading: Ithaca Press, 1998, p. 200.

5 G. Usher, "What Kind of Nation? The Rise of Hamas in the Occupied Territories," in J. Beinin, J. Stork (eds), *Political Islam: Essays from Middle East Report,* New York: I.B. Tauris, 1997, p. 340.

6 J. Legrain, "Hamas: Legitimate Heir of Palestinian Nationalism?," in J. Esposito (ed.), *Political Islam: Revolution, Radicalism, or Reform?* Boulder, CO: Lynne Rienner, 1997, p. 163.

7 Esposito, op. cit., p. 229.

8 Z. Abu-Amr, *Islamic Fundamentalism in the West Bank and Gaza:* Muslim Brotherhood and Islamic Jihad, Bloomington, IN: Indiana University Press, 1994, p. 83.

9 M. Levitt, *Hamas: Politics, Charity, and Terrorism in the Service of Jihad,* New Haven, CT: Yale University Press, 2006, p. 30.

10 Abu-Amr, op. cit., p. 85.

11 Legrain, op. cit., p. 160.

12 G. Kepel, Jihad: *The Trail of Political Islam,* Cambridge, MA: Harvard University Press, 2002, p. 154.

13 Robinson, op. cit., p. 127.

14 Usher, op. cit., p. 341.

15 Legrain, op. cit., p. 165.

16 S. Mishal, A. Sela, *The Palestinian Hamas: Vision, Violence, and Coexistence,* New York: Columbia University Press, 2000, p. 58.

17 Mishal, Sela, op. cit., p. 64.

18 Kepel, op. cit., p. 327.

19 Legrain, op. cit., p. 167; Usher, op. cit., p. 344.

20 Usher, op. cit., p. 344.

21 Legrain, op. cit., p. 172.

22 Kepel, op. cit., p. 341.

23 Kepel, op. cit., p. 156.

24 Robinson, op. cit., p. 121.

25 Kepel, op. cit., p. 151.

26 Abu-Amr, op. cit., p. 70.

27 J. Burr, R. Collins, *Alms for Jihad: Charity and Terrorism in the Islamic World,* Cambridge: Cambridge University Press, 2006, pp. 216–221.

28 K. Hroub, *Hamas: Political Thought and Practice,* Washington, DC: Institute for Palestine Studies, 2000, p. 148.

29 N. Pelham, "Gaza's Tunnel Phenomenon: The Unintended Dynamics of Israel's Siege," Journal of Palestine Studies 41, 2012, pp. 6–31.

30 Esposito, op. cit., p. 229.

31 Robinson, op. cit., p. 128; Jensen, op. cit., p. 203.

32 Usher, op. cit., p. 347.

33 Kepel, op. cit., p. 152.

34 Palestinian Central Bureau of Statistics, "State of Palestine: 2013," www.pcbs.gov.ps

35 Robinson, op. cit., p. 127.

36 Esposito, op. cit., p. 230.

37 Hroub, op. cit., p. 236.

38 Hroub, op. cit., p. 235.

39 Jensen, op. cit., pp. 214, 210.

40 Hroub, op. cit., pp. 229–230.
41 Hroub, op. cit., p. 217.
42 Palestinian Center for Policy and Survey Research, "Palestinian Public Opinion Poll 48," June 2013, www.pcpsr.org/survey/polls/2013/p48e.html
43 Jensen, op. cit., pp. 213–214.
44 Robinson, op. cit., p. 127.
45 Abu-Amr, op. cit., p. 82.
46 Abu-Amr, op. cit., p. 72–73.
47 Kepel, op. cit., p. 153.
48 Hroub, op. cit., p. 238.
49 Mishal, Sela, op. cit., p. 121.
50 Usher, op. cit., pp. 346–347.
51 Mishal, Sela, op. cit., p. 121.
52 Usher, op. cit., pp. 346–347.
53 Kepel, op. cit., p. 330.
54 Kepel, op. cit., pp. 323–333; Legrain, op. cit., p. 169.
55 Mishal, Sela, op. cit., p. 96.
56 Mishal, Sela, op. cit., p. 35.
57 Hroub, op. cit., p. 234.
58 Robinson, op. cit., p. 134.
59 Robinson, op. cit., pp. 130–134.
60 Abu-Amr, op. cit., p. 32.
61 Hroub, op. cit., p. 210.
62 Usher, op. cit., p. 343.
63 Esposito, op. cit., p. 231.
64 Ibid.; Legrain, op. cit., p. 171.
65 Mishal, Sela, op. cit., p. 65; Levitt, op. cit., p. 241.
66 Hroub, op. cit., pp. 247–248.
67 Legrain, op. cit., p. 170.
68 Ibid.
69 Esposito, op. cit., p. 232.
70 Legrain, op. cit., p. 172.
71 Mishal, Sela, op. cit., pp. 161–162.
72 J. Gunning, *Hamas in Politics: Democracy, Religion, Violence,* London: Hurst, 2010, pp. 269–70.
73 T. Barfield, "An Islamic State Is a State Run by Good Muslims: Religion as a Way of Life and Not an Ideology in Afghanistan," in R. Hefner (ed.), *Remaking Muslim Politics: Pluralism, Contestation, Democratization,* Princeton, NJ: Princeton University Press, 2005, p. 221.
74 Barfield, op. cit., p. 223.
75 Barfield, op. cit., p. 225.
76 D. Edwards, *Before Taliban: Genealogies of the Afghan Jihad,* Los Angeles, CA: University of California Press, 2002, p. 288.
77 B. Rubin, "Afghanistan under the Taliban", Current History 98, 1999, p. 87.
78 Barfield, op. cit., p. 227.
79 Edwards, op. cit., p. 289.
80 L. Goodson, *Afghanistan's Endless War: State Failure, Regional Politics, and the Rise of the Taliban,* Seattle, WA: University of Washington Press, 2001, p. 108.
81 Rubin, op. cit., p. 88.
82 Rubin, op. cit., p. 81.

83   Ibid.
84   Kepel, op. cit., p. 229.
85   Kepel, op. cit., pp. 230–231.
86   Esposito, op. cit., p. 235.
87   Barfield, op. cit., p. 233.
88   Kepel, op. cit., p. 231.
89   Kepel, op. cit., pp. 233–234; Barfield, op. cit., p. 232.
90   Barfield, op. cit., p. 232.
91   Kepel, op. cit., p. 234.
92   Barfield, op. cit., p. 233.
93   Edwards, op. cit., p. 291.
94   Rubin, op. cit., p. 80.
95   Rubin, op. cit., p. 85.
96   Kepel, op. cit., p. 225.
97   Edwards, op. cit., p. 292.
98   Edwards, op. cit., p. 293.
99   Kepel, op. cit., p. 225.
100 O. Roy, *Globalized Islam: The Search for a New Ummah,* New York: Columbia University Press, 2004, p. 258–265.
101 Barfield, op. cit., p. 229.
102 Goodson, op. cit., pp. 109–110.
103 Edwards, op. cit., p. 295.
104 Barfield, op. cit., p. 230.
105 Kepel, op. cit., p. 229.
106 Edwards, op. cit., p. 294.
107 Rubin, op. cit., p. 80.
108 Goodson, op. cit., p. 132.
109 B. Metcalf, "'Traditionalist' Islamic Activism: Deoband, Tablighis, and Talibs," ISIM Papers 4, Leiden: Institute for the Study of Islam in the Modern World, 2002.
110 Edwards, op. cit., p. 294.
111 Edwards, op. cit., p. 298.
112 Edwards, op. cit., p. 296.
113 Edwards, op. cit., p. 300.
114 Sheikh Omar Bakri Muhammad, personal interview with author, London, July 2002.
115 Barfield, op. cit., p. 232.
116 S. Zunes, "Afghanistan: Five Years Later," Foreign Policy in Focus Report, October 2006.
117 E. Rubin, "In the Land of the Taliban," New York Times Magazine, October 22, 2006.
118 A. Giustozzi, *Koran, Kalashnikov, and Laptop: The Neo-Taliban Insurgency in Afghanistan,* New York: Columbia University Press, 2009.
119 A. Giustozzi, *Negotiating with the Taliban: Issues and Prospects,* New York and Washington, DC: Century Foundation, 2010, p. 3.
120 J. Singh, "Exit Afghanistan?," Project Syndicate, November 12, 2012, www.project-syndicate.org/commentary/turmoil-after-america-s-withdrawal-from-afghanistan-by-jaswant-singh
121 T. Barfield, *Afghanistan: A Cultural and Political History,* Princeton: Princeton University Press, 2012.

CHAPTER 7

Radical Islamism and *jihad* beyond the nation-state

> The life of the Muslim umma is solely dependent on the ink of its scholars and the blood of its martyrs. What is more beautiful than the writing of the umma's history with both the ink of a scholar and his blood, such that the map of Islamic history becomes colored with two lines: one of them black—that is, what the scholar wrote with the ink of his pen—and the other one red—what the martyr wrote with his blood.
>
> Abdullah Azzam

Since the early 1990s, numerous acts of violence around the world have been committed in the name of Islam—perhaps none so dramatic or far-reaching in its global effects as the September 11, 2001 attacks on New York and Washington DC by militants associated with Usama Bin Laden's Al-Qaeda network. This act led to a renewed debate about the meaning and place of violence and *jihad* in Islam. What does Islam say about violence and the conditions under which it is permissible? How widespread is support for this kind of violence among Muslims? What leads one to become a religious militant? What is Al-Qaeda and how did it come about? These are all questions that we explore in the present chapter, with a view to achieving a more nuanced understanding of contemporary Islamic radicalism. We first need to explain how the ideology and methods of radical Islamists differ from mainstream Islamism. While the point is often made—correctly—that violent Islamists represent a small fringe minority of Muslims, and even of Islamists, there are important points of connection and intersection to be drawn with other forms of politicized Islam, and also with various intellectual and theological debates that have been ongoing for some time within the Islamic tradition. We also need to explain the geopolitical circumstances that led to the genesis and evolution of the contemporary global jihadist movement. To this end we examine the phenomenon of the so-called "Afghan-Arabs"—citizens of Arab countries who traveled to Afghanistan during the Soviet occupation (1980–88) to fight with the mujahideen against the USSR (see Chapter 6). Simultaneous and subsequent developments in Egypt and Algeria will also turn out to be salient in terms of the emergence of a Jihadi movement global in scope.

One of the major themes that emerges over the course of this chapter is a shift in the nature of jihadi activity from an emphasis on the governments of Arab and Muslim countries to a new focus on targeting foreign forces that occupy Islamic lands or persecute Muslims—in other words, the United States and those allied with it. This development has produced a new kind of "transnational" or "nomadic" jihadi fighter whose senses of political identity and aspiration are not defined in terms of effecting change in the country whose citizenship he happens to hold. Unlike groups that we looked at in the previous chapter, such as Hamas and Hizbullah (whose goals are primarily if not exclusively national in orientation), for these new militants, the terrain of the *jihad* is truly global in scope—and likewise the geography of their activism. It is for this reason that this chapter is defined in terms of Islam and militancy "beyond the nation-state." Today, even several violent Islamist groups whose efforts are primarily local or regional in nature have become affiliates (some on a purely *ad hoc* basis, others more enduringly) of the global jihadi network. Thus for us to focus our analysis purely on Al-Qaeda as an organizational entity would be to miss the central impulse of the transnational *jihad* movement.

In terms of theology and ideology, we spend some time discussing the concept of *jihad* in terms of both its classical meaning in Islamic learning, and key debates among various doctrinal factions as to its contemporary relevance and permissibility. We then move on to look at the sociology and infrastructure of contemporary jihadi and radical Islamist groups through case studies of two groups: Al-Qaeda and Hizb ut-Tahrir (HT). Who joins these radical movements and for what reasons? What kinds of backgrounds and biographies predispose someone to membership in a jihadi group? Through what mechanisms are potential activists recruited, acculturated, and "radicalized" into the movement and its mindset? Why do these militants subscribe to the authority of religious leaders whose formal credentials are often dubious and whose views are so out of step with mainstream Muslim sentiment and scholarship? After considering these various issues, we address some of the logistical dimensions of radical networks, including their methods of organization, communication, and finance. In the case of both of these—sociology and infrastructure—it emerges that the jihadi movement not only takes advantage of various aspects of contemporary globalization, but, it will be argued, can be understood only by reference to globalizing processes and their social effects. Globalization, in other words, was a prerequisite condition for the emergence of this particular Islamic worldview. Al-Qaeda, as Peter Bergen puts it, "is as much a creation of globalization as a response to it."[1]

DEFINING AND CONCEPTUALIZING RADICAL ISLAMISM

This chapter is structured around an analysis of what we are calling "radical Islamism." What does this term connote, and how does it differ from other forms of Islamism that we looked at in earlier chapters? We will recall that Islamism was defined in terms of an aspiration to institute a political order that reflects the norms of Islam, and the *shari'ah* more specifically. For the most part the Islamist groups we have dealt with to this point—such as the MB in Egypt or the JI in Pakistan—have taken the form of political parties or social movements. In Chapter 6 we also looked at several movements emphasizing violent resistance in the name of Islam—the Afghan mujahideen, Hamas in Palestine, and Hizbullah in Lebanon. We also noted, however, that the militant agendas of these groups have been geared toward political goals defined in terms of national liberation and Islamism within a single state. Hamas and Hizbullah, as we saw, also have political wings and engage in broader social service and charity activities. The radical Islamists that constitute the focus of the present chapter are markedly different in terms of their goals and methods. Like the Islamists we studied in Chapters 4 and 5, they seek to implement an Islamic political order, and like the Islamic resistance movements of Chapter 6, they are willing to use violence to achieve these ends. Their understanding of these concepts and tactics is significantly different from mainstream Islamism, however. Radical Islamism, as defined here, is characterized by:

- a vision of Islamic political order that rejects the legitimacy of the modern sovereign nation-state and seeks to establish a pan-Islamic polity or renewed caliphate; and/or
- an emphasis on violent struggle (*jihad*) as the primary or even the exclusively legitimate method for the pursuit of political change.

This political orientation is hence radical in two senses—its politics and its methods. It is politically radical insofar as it rejects the contemporary system of territorially defined sovereign nation-states as illegitimate and seeks to replace it with a *shari'ah*-based, pan-national Muslim polity—usually defined in terms of a re-established caliphate (see Chapter 2). It is also radical in that most of the groups pursuing this political worldview advocate *jihad* as a legitimate—indeed, often a required—method for bringing about desired political change. Unlike the radicals, the Islamists we looked at in Chapters 4 and 5 generally have sought to make progress toward an Islamic political order via political (electoral, legislative, power-sharing) or social (civil society, informal networking) means. Those who have employed violence have done so only on a national scale and, according to their account, only after other means of achieving change had been exhausted.

Groups differ among themselves—often quite substantially—in terms of how much emphasis and priority they lend each of these two dimensions of radicalism. Usama Bin Laden's *jihad*, for example, focused more on the removal of foreign forces from Muslim territories than on the establishment of a new caliphate. The HT ("Party of Liberation") movement, on the other hand, puts much greater emphasis on the need for a caliphate, and prefers to pursue this as much as possible via nonviolent means. And even among those who focus primarily on *jihad*, as we will see, there is considerable debate as to timing, targets, and the legitimate boundaries of violent activism. In this regard it is important to note that an individual's participation in, or support for, Islamic radicalism should not be viewed as synonymous with their having abandoned all sense of morality or adopting an "any and all means are justified" approach to the conduct of political violence. Most decisions to use violence of this sort are made in the context of a complex normative matrix whose terms and boundaries are continually in dispute among the scholars and leaders of these movements.[2] Members of some jihadi groups have sometimes criticized and broken off connections with members of other movements whom they deem to have transgressed certain lines of legitimate conduct—such as, for example, targeting noncombatants ("innocents") or making disproportionate use of violence. Radicalism cannot therefore be conceived as a monolithic category. Rather, like all political orientations, it has within it a spectrum of thought and action, and debates and tensions are ongoing between the various points along that spectrum. The methods employed by some Islamic radicals are so extreme and shocking that many observers have difficulty differentiating between the disparate ideologies and worldviews that drive jihadi activists—tending to lump them all together into a single category. To do so is, however, an analytical mistake as it papers over important differences that would allow us to acquire a more thorough understanding of the forces that shape the political worldviews of these various groups.

We have already mentioned that the extreme politics and methods of these groups clearly distinguish them from mainstream Islamists, many of whom strongly and consistently condemn their activities. While it is certainly important to emphasize the extent to which the jihadis represent a clear break from the Islamist center, and to point out that they represent the extreme end of the spectrum of Muslim politics, it would also be a mistake to assume they emerged *sui generis* with no basis in pre-existing Islamic political ideologies. Important lines of connection and continuity with major Islamist thinkers and movements do exist, and are hence important to emphasize alongside the more innovative and aberrational aspects of the global jihadi movement. What is the nature of these linkages? The first thing to note is that they are not in any sense current lines of cooperation or coordination. As we have already noted, mainstream Islamists, for the most part, strongly repudiate the jihadis, and *vice versa*. In order to understand these relationships we need to go back to Egypt in the late 1960s and early 1970s, during the time when the MB had been driven underground and its key ideologues, such as Sayyid Qutb (see Chapter 3), had been captured, exiled, or killed. Qutb is in many respects the key figure here. His particular understanding of *jihad* and radical Islamic activism are central to the thinking of contemporary jihadi leaders and scholars. We will also recall from earlier discussions that when the MB was "rehabilitated" and co-opted by Anwar Sadat during the 1970s, its leadership renounced violence altogether. This prompted several more militant factions of the brotherhood to break away and form groups such as Takfir w'al-Hijra, Gemaa Islamiyya, and Islamic Jihad—the latter of which was responsible for Sadat's assassination in 1981. Mohammad Farag, a chief activist in the Jihad group, provided a manifesto—*The Neglected Duty,* a reference to *jihad*—that would become the standard reference point for a new generation of Egyptian jihadis. In it, he made the case that *jihad* should be carried out wherever Muslim lands were under the control of unbelievers (secularists, nationalists)—even if, crucially, these leaders claimed to be Muslim (the so-called "near enemy"). This view was echoed in scholarly discourse by a young, blind dissident *alim,* Sheikh Omar Abdel Rahman, who would later go on to serve as the spiritual guide to Gemaa Islamiyya and to be convicted in the planning of the first World Trade Center bombing in 1993.

This doctrine constituted not only a major departure from classic theories of *jihad* (see below), but also heralded a new era of Islamist violence committed against and within Muslim states. In the eyes of Farag, and many jihadis to follow, the MB's commitment to political quietism had betrayed the spirit of its greatest martyr, Sayyid Qutb. By abandoning active resistance to the Egyptian state, in their view, the Brotherhood was willfully neglecting an obligation that Qutb had come to discern through his own suffering and eventual death at the hands of Nasser's regime. The Egyptian jihadis of the 1970s and 1980s hence understood themselves to be the inheritors of Sayyid Qutb's legacy of active struggle. They also saw themselves as a righteous movement in contrast to the MB, which in their view effectively had thrown in its lot with that of the infidel regime. During the 1980s and 1990s, their trajectory would intersect in important ways with that of a group whose jihadi worldview was shaped by different, but not less influential, experiences.

GEOPOLITICS AND THE MAKING OF THE GLOBAL JIHADI MOVEMENT

The emergence of the contemporary global jihadi movement can be explained only within the context of late Cold War geopolitics. The watershed event here was undoubtedly the ten-year Soviet war in Afghanistan (1979–89). After Moscow seized Kabul—ostensibly to prop up a failing socialist regime, but primarily to secure a strategic foothold near South Asia and the Middle East—local mujahideen fighters (as the Afghan resistance, organized along tribal lines, was known) fought a decade-long guerilla war of attrition against Soviet troops. Hailed as a *jihad* against atheist forces, the persistence and commitment of the Afghan fighters earned them considerable attention from the rest of the Muslim world—and particularly within Islamist circles. Soon a number of radical Arab Islamists, whose efforts previously had been confined to resistance against states and occupiers in their home countries, began to find their way to Afghanistan to join the struggle. They formed the vanguard of a generation of "Arab Afghans" who, over the next decade, would find in Afghanistan the vision and human resources that would allow them to begin constituting a new pan-Islamic network of jihadi activism. These fighters—or, in most cases, would-be fighters (very few of them had any military experience)—came from all over the Muslim and Arab world. Estimates of their numbers vary from 5,000 to 50,000, but it is likely to have been in the tens of thousands.[3] Nearly every country in the Middle East was represented, but with particularly large contingents from Egypt, Algeria, and the Gulf. Volunteers from non-Arab countries could also be found. This diversity provided an *umma*-oriented *esprit de corps* among the itinerant militants, giving them a sense of being part of something much larger than the liberation of an occupied country. Indeed, for many of them, Afghanistan was a relatively foreign concept and not really one in which they had any personal investment. The symbolism of fighting for a "real" Muslim cause was what counted. Others came in search of training and recruits that could later be used against regimes at home. This was not quite yet a vision of global *jihad,* but it began to provide the raw ingredients for shaping just such a consciousness.[4] As David Cook puts it:

> For many, this equation of jihad with the war in Afghanistan was powerful and liberating. Although the largely Arab Muslim volunteers probably played only a small part in the eventual defeat of the Soviet forces in Afghanistan, the campaign was the first time in centuries that people

from all over the Muslim world had gathered together—irrespective of their ethnic and sometimes doctrinal differences—to fight exclusively *for the sake of Islam*. Thus, the battlefield of Afghanistan was the religious and social incubator for global radical Islam in that it established contacts among a wide variety of radicals from Muslim anti-governmental and resistance movements and fused them together.[5]

One of the most important founding figures within this movement was Abdullah Azzam, a Palestinian and a member of the MB who moved to Afghanistan shortly after the Soviet invasion. Azzam, who would later play a major role in cultivating the thinking of Usama Bin Laden, established the so-called Maktab al-Khadamat ("Services Bureau") as a way-station and guest-house for Arab fighters. One of his publications, *Ilhaq bi-l-qafila* (*Join the Caravan*) circulated in the Arab world and became an important early recruiting tool for the Afghan *jihad*. Azzam's thinking was along the same lines as that of Sayyid Qutb and Muhammad Farag, but he went even further in stressing the obligation of all Muslims to wage *jihad* in the occupied lands of Palestine and Afghanistan. We should note that, at this point, the focus of jihadi theory on the part of these ideologues was still very much on the liberation of Muslim territories rather than on the idea of a general global effort against the enemies of Islam.[6] Some saw Afghanistan as an opportunity to gain some *jihad* experience without having to worry about the repressive state security services found in most Arab countries. This was a relatively "open" environment where volunteers could receive training and gain some battlefield experience before heading back to tackle the "near enemy" at home. Some of the leaders also hoped that success in Afghanistan might serve as a "trophy Jihad" that would inspire a new generation of activists to take up arms against infidel regimes back home. Azzam played a major role in creating the culture and lore of the Arab Afghans. He authored, for example, numerous martyrologies—descriptions of the feats and miracles associated with jihadis who had made the ultimate sacrifice.[7] Through these, the Arab Afghan experience came to have an associated mythology that aided in both recruitment and the inculcation of discipline and commitment on the part of those already in the field. Abdullah Azzam played an instrumental role in shaping Usama Bin Laden's worldview and convincing him that in the Afghan war he had found his calling.[8] Had Azzam not been assassinated in 1989, some speculate, he rather than Bin Laden might have served as Al-Qaeda's chief, since the core concept for the organization was really Azzam's.[9]

Arab Afghans were not the only ones hoping to derive benefit from the Afghan situation. Three other external players exerted a particularly important influence over the course of the Afghan war of resistance, and—both directly and indirectly—over the efforts of the Arab jihadi forces. First, there was the United States, which saw in assistance to Afghanistan an opportunity not only to block communist expansion, but also to wear down Soviet forces in a manner similar to what had befallen its own military in Vietnam. To this end, they provided training and weaponry to the mujahideen forces, generally via the CIA or local proxies. While there is no evidence to suggest that the Arab Afghans were ever directly aided by the United States, it is certainly the case that the Americans were aware of their presence and saw no harm in it. Afghanistan's neighbor, Pakistan, seized the chance to strengthen its relationship with the United States by supporting anti-Soviet forces and simultaneously to boost its Muslim credentials. Not only were all manner of pro-mujahideen forces—including the Arab Afghans—permitted to use Pakistani territory as a staging ground, but additional direct assistance was provided by Pakistan's Inter-Services Intelligence. A post-Soviet, pro-Pakistan regime in Afghanistan also would have permitted Islamabad access to the Muslim states of the USSR, as well as "strategic depth" in terms of its ongoing rivalry with India.[10] Finally, Saudi Arabia, increasingly vying with Iran for leadership of the Muslim world in the wake of the latter's 1979 Islamic revolution (see Chapter 5), saw Afghanistan as an opportunity to demonstrate its commitment to a Muslim struggle while simultaneously pushing its Wahhabi variant of Sunni Islam. We should note that, while Al-Qaeda has claimed that it never accepted financial assistance from any of these three governments—claiming instead that its activities were bankrolled by donations from private charities and the Muslim masses, there is considerable evidence to suggest that cash from the Gulf did make up a sizeable proportion of their operating capital.[11]

Turning back to the Arab Afghans, it is important to note that very few of them stayed in Afghanistan for the full decade of the war with the Soviets. Many traveled just on short "tours" to get a taste of *jihad,* others rotated in and out, and many stayed for a few years before returning to their country of origin or proceeding elsewhere. Those who returned home often played important roles in terms of changing or challenging the course of Islamism in their countries. Returning Algerians, for example, became central players in Ali Belhadj's radical wing of the Front Islamique du Salut (FIS) and later in the Armed Islamic Group (see Box 3.2, "Algeria: Islamists *almost* in power). In Jordan, ex-Afghans formed the short-lived Muhammad's Army as a challenge to the political methods of the MB. And in Egypt, many of the militants in Gemaa Islamiyya and Islamic Jihad who took part in the 1990s campaign of violence in that country were alumni of the Afghan Jihad. Thousands of students from Pakistani *madrasas* on the Afghan border had played an active role, and many of these went on to join the insurgency in Kashmir. After the Soviet withdrawal and Afghanistan's descent into civil war (see Chapter 6), there was a general dispersion of the Arab Afghans, but some stayed in the country. Most notably, a small but loyal contingent developed around the person of Usama Bin Laden, a Saudi citizen who had come to Afghanistan and fallen under the tutelage of

Abdullah Azzam. Bin Laden, whose family was among the Kingdom's leading industrialists, quickly developed a reputation as a dedicated fighter and a superb logistician. He also had considerable monetary resources at his disposal, at least initially, although analysts differ as to how much of this he actually directed towards jihadi causes versus how much he raised through connections and networking. Also in Afghanistan from the very early days, and soon closely tied to Bin Laden, was Ayman al-Zawahiri, a medical doctor and the leader of Egypt's Islamic Jihad who would eventually fold his group into Bin Laden's network.

The founding of Al-Qaeda ("The Base") dates to this period around the end of the Afghan war, and can be associated with Bin Laden's efforts to constitute a network of jihadis prepared to continue the *jihad* in an itinerant, transnational mode. This move actually reflected a crucially important evolution in the contemporary doctrine and scope of *jihad* that we will discuss further below. Bin Laden spent a short period back in Saudi Arabia, but quickly fell foul of the authorities over his stringent critique of their willingness to permit U.S. forces, instead of his Muslim network, to defend the Kingdom against a possible attack by Saddam Hussein's forces. Bin Laden and his cadres relocated to Sudan in the early 1990s at the invitation of Islamist ideologue Hassan al-Turabi (see Box 5.4, "Hassan al-Turabi and Sudan's 'Islamic Experiment'"), and he was stripped of his Saudi citizenship shortly thereafter. In Sudan, Bin Laden set about developing a number of business interests connected to infrastructure development (presumably to raise capital for future *jihad* efforts), but as his rhetoric and politics turned increasingly anti-Western, Sudan came under increasing pressure from the West to kick him out. Bin Laden's forces, for example, had confronted and targeted American troops during the latter's intervention in Somalia in 1992, and he was a suspect in the 1995 bombing of U.S. troop barracks in the Eastern Province of Saudi Arabia. In 1996, Turabi finally capitulated and, with U.S. consent, Bin Laden returned to Afghanistan, where he took up residence under the protection of the newly established Taliban regime (see Chapter 6)—a development that had itself been facilitated by Pakistan, again with apparent U.S. compliance.[12] It was at this time that Bin Laden's Al-Qaeda network entered into the active phase that would soon earn it a worldwide reputation.

THE EVOLUTION OF MODERN JIHADI IDEOLOGY

Before we move on to look more closely at Al-Qaeda and the sociology of contemporary Islamic radicalism, it is important to gain a better understanding of a key Islamic concept that is often invoked today in connection with Islam and militancy. The notion of "*jihad*" is frequently used both to describe and to justify violence in the name of Islam. But what does *jihad* actually mean and how have debates about its purpose and permissibility evolved in the modern era?

The term *jihad* has various meanings in Islam and these are often a source of considerable confusion for the casual observer. Literally, the verbal root of the word in Arabic refers to notions of struggle or exertion. Classical Islamic scholars differentiated between two primary idioms of *jihad:* the Greater Jihad (*jihad al-akbar*) and the Lesser Jihad (*jihad al-asghar*). The Greater Jihad refers to one's spiritual or inner struggle to overcome the self (*nafs*) in the course of submitting fully to the path of God. It is about the effort one expends to live one's life in accordance with the *shari'ah* and to affirm the core tenants of faith. The Lesser Jihad—conceived as such because it is never an end in itself, but only a means towards achieving the Greater Jihad—refers to the outward struggle to implement or defend Islam, which can be physical or violent in nature. Over the centuries, religious scholars have sub-speciated these general categories in various ways, differentiating, for example, between *jihad al-qalb* ("struggle of the heart"), *jihad b'il-lisan* ("struggle by the tongue"), *jihad bil-qalam* ("struggle by the pen"), and *jihad bil-sayf* ("struggle by the sword"). It is not therefore a matter of trying to discern which is the "real" meaning of *jihad,* but rather understanding how and why different senses of the term have come into play. Sufis, for example, have tended to lay great emphasis on the notion of spiritual struggle. Islamists, on the other hand, have emphasized the outward dimension—but not necessarily always in reference to warfare. The idea of *jihad bil-yad* ("struggle by the hand"), for instance, can refer to nonviolent political activism or expending financial resources. While the inward and outward senses of *jihad* are both widely used in the classic literature of Islam, it should also be pointed out that occurrences of the term *jihad* in historical and political texts have generally carried a martial connotation. It is for this reason that the term "*jihad*" is frequently, but incorrectly, translated as "holy war."

To understand the discourse on *jihad* as a form of warfare, it is first important to gain some insight into classical Islamic conceptions of "moral geography" and just war theory. Classical scholars divided the world into two primary "zones": *dar al-islam* (the domain of Islam) and *dar al-harb* (the domain of war). The first of these refers to lands under the control of Muslim rulers and where the laws and regulations of Islam are implemented. It is permissible to use force to defend *dar al-islam* if it is attacked. *Dar al-harb,* on the other hand, refers to those lands ruled by non-Muslims and, more particularly, where Muslims are being prevented from living according to Islam. Classical doctrine held it permissible to wage offensive *jihad* against these territories. As the doctrine of *jihad* evolved, it came to emphasize an almost exclusively defensive concept of *jihad*—particularly once the various wars of conquest had achieved a considerable expansion of Muslim territorial holdings (see Chapter 2). During Ottoman times, a third zone, that of *dar al-ahd* (domain of treaty), was created to cover Christian territories in Southeastern Europe with whom the Ottomans had made tributary arrangements. Some recent theorists have also used this term to describe the arrangements by which Muslim and non-Muslims live together in non-Muslim states.[13] We can say then that the general consensus among scholars, prevalent until quite recently, was that *jihad* was permitted only in order to defend Muslim lands that come under attack from outside. Moreover, on this understanding, *jihad* could be declared only by the proper authorities. As an inherently political practice, it made no sense outside of the framework of the Islamic caliphate or a Muslim sultanate. To accompany the core principles, there was also developed a detailed *fiqh al-jihad* (jurisprudence of warfare) that detailed the regulations and norms pertaining to the use of force. This covered much the same ground as the rules relating to *jus in bello* in Western just war theory—for example, the doctrine of proportional force, distinctions between combatants and noncombatants, and so forth.

The modern transformation in *jihad* doctrine closely parallels the development of the Wahhabi and Salafi approaches discussed in Chapter 2. Again we begin with Muhammad Ibn Abdul Wahhab in the eighteenth century. We have already discussed the political alliance with Muhammad Ibn Saud that allowed him to propagate his zealously puritanical understanding of Islam (see Chapter 5). One of the obstacles to Wahhabism's expansion beyond the confines of central Arabia was the unwillingness of other Muslim tribes and clans—many of which subscribed to various forms of Sufi practice—to adopt its norms. Abdul Wahhab was hence led to reinterpret classical Islamic doctrines regarding the boundaries of belief such that these non-Wahhabi Muslims could be declared infidels—that is, subjected to *takfir*. The lands they occupied could therefore be regarded as *dar al-harb* and hence legitimately attacked. This piece of *ijtihad* represented a major revision to one of the most enduring principles of jurisprudential consensus, that Muslims do not wage war against other Muslims. Moreover, as the tribal leader of a desert province with highly porous frontiers, it was not at all clear that Muhammad Ibn Saud even possessed the necessary political authority to declare a legitimate *jihad*. Several generations later, as one might expect, the interpretation of *jihad* by those in the Reformist tradition (Afghani, Abduh, Rida, etc.) not only sought a return to the meaning found in the classical approach, but even introduced *ijtihad* that went in quite the opposite direction of Abdul Wahhab's—that is, taking Qur'anic verses that seemed quite unambiguously to enjoin violence against particular groups and reinterpreting them to de-emphasize the martial dimension or the necessity of using physical force.[14]

For the purposes of understanding contemporary Salafi–jihadi violence, however, we need to move forward another couple of generations to consider once again the contributions of Sayyid Qutb, ideologue of the MB during its radical phase. Qutb's conception of *jihad* needs to be understood within the framework of the other core concept that animates his thinking, namely the idea of the modern world as a world of *jahiliyya*, or pre-/un-Islamic ignorance (see Chapter 3). Qutb's overall worldview, of which his idiom of *jihad* forms an intrinsic part, is itself a comprehensive and revolutionary reinterpretation of the social and political implications of Qur'anic normativity. In a world dominated by secularism, capitalism, atheism, imperialism, and immorality—a world where even nominally Muslim rulers have abandoned Islam in pursuit of these vices—distinctions such as *dar al-islam* and *dar al-harb* no longer make sense. All the world is in need of repair, and there are no meaningful borders of *dar al-islam* to defend.[15] This does not mean, however, that *jihad* is forbidden; rather, these are the very conditions that instill it as a duty. The capacity of Muslims freely to choose and practice their religion is everywhere denied, and revolutionary *jihad* is required to remedy this state of affairs. Anyone who prevents the realization of Islam is therefore a legitimate target of *jihad*. *Jihad*, for Qutb, cannot be understood in relation to notions of "proper legal authority" or "offensive versus defensive war." *Jihad* is about reclaiming for God a sovereignty that has been usurped. It is about making space in the world for His order and making sure that no earthly power is in a position to block the choice by Muslims to live according to that order.[16] To be clear, though: the aim is not to compel people to accept Islam, for this must be an individual choice, freely made. Rather, it is about Qutb's reinterpretation of the conditions under which that choice can be made. Where *jahiliyya* reigns, no Muslim, or potential Muslim, is in a position truly to make that choice.[17] Who, then, are the agents of *jihad*? We have already noted that for Qutb, all Muslims must accept the obligation to struggle towards the realization of Islam. More particularly, however, he lays great emphasis on the hope that a "Qur'anic generation" will arise—one that will, to use a computing metaphor, hit the reset button or "reboot" Islam into a basic installation or safe mode. This "Qur'anic generation" will have no need for the apparatus of classical Islamic learning since its sources, like Qutb's, will be none other than, and exclusively, the literal word of God as found in the Qur'an.[18]

It is not surprising that Qutb's revolutionary worldview found considerable purchase among the radical breakaways from the Egyptian MB a decade after his death. His ideas confirmed their suspicion that the Brotherhood as a movement had effectively abandoned Islam to become part of the *jahiliyya* order. A number of subsequent thinkers and activists made contributions or added new areas of emphasis to Qutb's ideas on *jihad*. We may recall Muhammad Farag's notion of *jihad* against the "near enemy"—that is, the governments of states in the Muslim world that had adopted secularism and nationalism, and had circumscribed the practice of Islam—an idea that was already present in Qutb's work. In the mind of latter-day interpreters, to quote Wiktorowicz, "Western influence over Arab governments through foreign assistance, IMF loans, military connections and political alignments renders these governments 'puppets' of the West and its Zionist allies in the Middle East. Arab regimes are thus considered the functional equivalent of foreign occupiers."[19] This is a principle that Farag made operational via the assassination of Anwar Sadat in 1981. Later, Abdallah Azzam, whom we have mentioned above, channeled and inflected Qutb's thinking in the Afghan context by laying out an explanation as to why *jihad* was a duty impingent on all believers. Offensive *jihad* against unbelievers was indeed, as Qutb argued, a duty—but one that was to be regarded as *fard kifaya,* that is, as a collective obligation. This means that, so long as some group of Muslims is undertaking the effort (classically, an "official" Muslim army), then no individual action need be taken. If, however, a Muslim land comes under attack by infidels, then *jihad* becomes a matter of *fard ayn,* or individual obligation. Every Muslim is expected to join the fight to re-establish the integrity of Muslim borders, with the highest obligation falling on those closest to the incursion—hence Azzam's appeal to the "Arab Afghans."[20]

THE NEW GLOBAL *JIHAD* AND ITS DISCONTENTS: FROM "NEAR ENEMY" TO "FAR ENEMY"

In the decade following the conclusion of the Afghanistan war, the doctrine of *jihad* among radical Islamists underwent a significant evolution. To begin exploring this, we need to start with the immediate aftermath of the conflict. The vast majority of Arab Afghans at this point returned to their home countries and, as we have noted, many of them became involved in various forms of Islamic radicalism on the home front. Much of the intensity of the Islamic violence in countries such as Algeria and Egypt during the 1990s, for example, can be understood as a direct result of the injection into national settings of battle-hardened Arab Afghans keen to continue the fight. But, as Fawaz Gerges notes, most of these eventually "met their Waterloo on homefront battlefields."[21] Others preferred to continue operating in the expatriate mode and to look for other Muslim causes to defend. Thus, during the 1990s, we saw contingents of Arab Afghans fighting in settings such as Bosnia, Chechnya, and Kashmir. In many cases, their hardline and highly militant Islam did not mesh at all well with local religious norms, such as the strong Sufi tradition in the Balkans and the Caucasus. There to fight on behalf of Muslim populations, they were not necessarily regarded as a welcome addition by the forces they had supposedly come to defend. In both cases—homeland struggles and new Muslim defensive jihadi—the main point to make is that even when the Afghan war ended, radical Islamists found themselves with plenty of other opportunities to continue the fight.

We have already covered the movements of Usama Bin Laden's group during much of the 1990s, but have said less about how notions of *jihad* were evolving within his camp. Ayman al-Zawahiri, the leader of Egyptian Islamic Jihad, had been drawing closer and closer to Bin Laden. By the mid-1990s his authority in the circle was second only to the Saudis, and he soon folded the Islamic Jihad group into Bin Laden's—hoping, some have argued, to displace Bin Laden's leadership and gain control of what he hoped were considerable and much-needed funds for his own program. From the mid-1990s, Zawahiri developed an alternative vision for the jihadi movement. Having noted the failure of the homeland radicals to succeed in bringing about revolution, he began to argue that the movement's failure lay in its inability to mobilize the *umma* as a whole against a common enemy.[22] Emboldened by the fall of the Soviet Union, some within Bin Laden's circle were beginning to come around to the idea that Muslims should be taking the fight against *jahiliyya* directly to the source—namely, the Crusaders (the United States and its Western allies) and the Zionists (Israel, as backed by the United States). This new emphasis on the "far enemy" was a major departure for Zawahiri who, throughout most of his time in Afghanistan, had viewed the mujahideen's mountains as a training zone for later battles on the home front.[23] In some regards, the doctrine that Zawahiri now began to promulgate was Sayyid Qutb and Abdullah Azzam pushed to their logical extreme. If all the world is *jahiliyya* and Muslims are under duress or assault everywhere, then the *jihad* must be fought in all places by all Muslims—a violent reinterpretation, in some regards, of Jamal ad-Din al-Afghani's pan-Islamist ideology (see Chapter 2). We should also note that globalization is, in some respects, a crucial enabling dimension to this vision. Previously, on Azzam's account, one was relieved from the obligation of *jihad* if one was not near enough to, or could not travel to, the battlefield.[24] With a worldwide theater of operations, and given the relative ease of transnational travel and communication, the idea of "global *jihad*" began to take on real meaning.

The small movement soon began to adapt its organizational structure to the new vision. In the late 1980s, as the Afghan war wound down, Bin Laden had formed a loose organization called Qaedat al-Jihad ("The Jihad Base"), or Al-Qaeda for short. Its purpose was to allow for ongoing communication and coordination between a core grouping of Arab Afghans with shared views of the movement's priorities. Al-Qaeda now became Bin Laden's primary operational unit, with its ideology increasingly defined in terms of striking at the "far enemy" (the United States)—a new idiom, in other words, of global *jihad*. In 1998, the World Islamic Front for Jihad was formed as a loose coalition of radical groups (several of them splinter factions from radical groups with a more domestic orientation) willing to wage *jihad* on a global scale. Connections also began to be forged with various other local and regional groups with radical tendencies. Thus, from the very beginning, Al-Qaeda was as much a network or "umbrella organization" as it was a discrete entity unto itself.

Figure 7.1 Al-Qaeda leader Usama bin Laden

© Reuters

Al-Qaeda and its affiliates have carried out, or been involved in, numerous attacks against American interests since the mid-1990s. These include the Khobar Towers bombing of 1996, the bombing of the U.S. embassies in Kenya and Tanzania in 1998, the attack on the USS Cole in 2000, the September 11, 2001 attacks on the World Trade Center in New York City and the Pentagon in Washington DC, the Bali bombing of 2002, the assassination of U.S. foreign service personnel in Jordan in 2002, bombings in Morocco and Turkey in 2003, the Madrid bombings of 2004, and the July 7 bomb attacks in London. This track record would suggest that Al-Qaeda has been largely successful in redefining the doctrine and methodology of *jihad* in favor of its preferred focus on the "far enemy." In fact, there has been considerable infighting within the jihadi movement since the mid-1990s, and Al-Qaeda now finds itself in a rather embattled position on the fringes of this current rather than in a front-and-center, defining leadership role. The point here is that while the methods employed by Al-Qaeda and the spectacles they create have done much to define the jihadi movement, in the popular imagination, according to Bin Laden's vision, the global jihadists have actually come under considerable criticism in recent years from other jihadi leaders who see them as having over-stepped important boundaries.

Criticism of the new transnational *jihad* has come from a variety of sources and has been prompted by numerous factors. Some of the key figures here are former scholars and leaders associated with groups such as Egypt's Gemaa Islamiyya—such as Karam Zuhdi and Nageh Ibrahim—who appear to have changed their views after having been imprisoned.[25]

From 1997 they published a series of texts known as the *Tashih al-Mafahim* (*Corrections of Concepts*) arguing that jihadist ideals had been misapplied. A number of former Saudi dissident *ulama* such as Safir al-Hawali and Salman al-Awda (see Chapter 5) also seemed to reassess their positions. In 2007, for example, Al-Awdah wrote an open letter to Bin Laden in which he criticized the Al-Qaeda leader's excessive use of violence and questioned whether anything of value to Muslims had been achieved through the global *jihad.* Even more significantly, in that same year, one of the premier ideologues of Egypt's Islamic Jihad, Sayyid Imam al-Sharif, writing under the name "Dr. Fadl," published a critique of the jihadist movement entitled *Advice Regarding the Conduct of Jihadist Action in Egypt and the World.*

In some cases, the views now articulated by these figures—frequently referred to as jihadist "recantations"—have come under considerable suspicion since their circumstances give the appearance of them having been co-opted by the respective regimes. Some skeptics have also pointed out that most of these texts do not categorically reject the legitimacy of *jihad* as a method for achieving Islamist goals, and still feature highly intolerant and extremist views.[26] Aspects of their core critique, however, appear to be accepted by many jihadis still operating outside the reach of the authorities.[27] Jihadi intellectuals living in exile in Europe, such as Hani al-Sibai and Omar Rushdi, have also come out against Bin Laden and the global jihadis.[28] As Mohammed Derbala, a Gemaa Islamiyya strategician, has put it with regard to Bin Laden, "their hearts are with [him], but their swords are against [him]."[29] Needless to say, a great number of quietist Salafis, such as the late Muhammad Nasir al-Din al-Bani and Saudi figures such as Abdel Nasser al-Obeikan, who have been against *jihad* all along, have come out against Al-Qaeda, along with leading conservative *ulama* linked to the MB, and Azhari sheikhs such as Yusuf al-Qaradawi and Muhammad Hussein Tantawi.

We are of course most interested in the debate *within* the jihadi movement, since this offers us the clearest sense of how the internal debate among those who favor *jihad* is shaping up. While different critics of Al-Qaeda from within the jihadi camp have their own areas of primary complaint, we can summarize the range of issues generally regarded as problematic in the following way.

- The shift of emphasis from the "near enemy" to the "far enemy" was a strategic mistake, and, moreover, not sufficiently grounded in religious evidence. This shift suited Bin Laden's circumstances and was facilitated by his resources—but it did not represent the general will of the jihadi movement.
- Al-Qaeda's "successes" have led regimes to crack down on Islamist movements and particularly jihadis all over the Muslim world—making it increasingly difficult today for them to carry out operations against the near enemy.

- The act of *takfir*—that is, declaring Muslims to be infidels in order to justify one's disagreement with them, or in order to carry out operations against Muslim civilians—was being used far too freely and without regard or respect for proper authority in doing so.
- Disproportionate use of force, both in terms of the scale of killing and destruction and in terms of the targets selected. This had in fact been an ongoing issue within the broader jihadi movement since the intense GIA operations in Algeria during the 1990s, in which thousands of civilians were killed.

There are signs that these various lines of critique have been having an impact on Al-Qaeda's ability to find and retain quality recruits. The further critiques offered by mainstream scholars and intellectuals, to whom Muslims are far more likely to listen than the jihadis, severely discredited Bin Laden and his ilk—a fact borne out by recent opinion poll surveys in the Muslim world. In the Arab world in particular, the number of people expressing any degree of favor towards Al-Qaeda has fallen significantly in recent years.[30] This apparent trend against global jihadism will be taken up again in the conclusion to this chapter, when we look at how the movement has evolved in recent years.

AL-QAEDA: FRANCHISING GLOBAL *JIHAD*

What is Al-Qaeda and what are its aims? How is the group organized, where does its financing come from, and what does its membership look like? This section offers a description of Al-Qaeda and some of its basic features. We then proceed to look more specifically at the sociology of the movement. In particular, we look at the two distinct generations of Al-Qaeda activists who differ greatly in terms of both their origins and professional backgrounds, and in terms of how and why they are drawn into the network. Issues of mobilization and radicalization also receive some attention, and we return to the question of Salafi–jihadi ideas and their role in shaping the worldviews of radical activists. Finally, after looking at recent shifts in the global organization of jihadism and the implications of Usama Bin Laden's death, some aspects of Al-Qaeda as a social movement are examined.

Al-Qaeda ("the base") evolved in Afghanistan during the final years of the 1980s. The basic rubric for the group was devised by Abdullah Azzam, who had in mind to create a mobile fighting force that could be dispatched anywhere in the world to assist Muslim fighters—"an Islamic rapid reaction force," in the words of one observer.[31] After Azzam's death, Bin Laden took over the nascent organization, which at this point was more of a verbal memorandum of understanding between a small group of like-minded individuals, albeit one backed by an impressive network of logistics and transnational activist contacts. As Bin Laden and Zawahiri shaped their new jihadi vision over the next decade, Al-Qaeda's importance among the many nominal entities under their control rose significantly. By the late 1990s, Al-Qaeda was firmly established as Bin Laden's primary operational unit. It was to be the militant vanguard of a new jihadi vision aimed at combating the "far enemy." Bin Laden's main goal after the Gulf War of 1991 came to be the removal of American forces from Saudi Arabia—or as he, refusing to recognize the legitimacy of the Saudi royal family, preferred to refer to it, the "Land of the Two Holy Mosques." While he certainly paid lip service to other Muslim causes, particularly Palestine, where Israeli occupation in his mind was a function of American support for Zionism, it is clear from his statements at this time that Bin Laden's focus was on the United States. The general tenor of his vision can be gauged from two documents produced in 1996 and 1998, the *Declaration of Jihad* and the statement on the *World Islamic Front*.

Al-Qaeda's structure and organization also evolved exponentially during these same years. Bin Laden systematically built up a vast global network of political affiliations, financial interests, logistical handlers, and—of course— activist cells. All of these were tightly integrated, functionally differentiated, and organized into a clear division of labor, all designed to feed and sustain Al-Qaeda's capacity to wage *jihad*. This infrastructure was so complex and had so many layers—often with multiple "firewalls" between them—that many of the entities enmeshed within it were not even aware they were part of a giant jihadi operation. Rohan Gunaratna summarizes it thus:

> Al-Qaeda is . . . characterized by a broad-based ideology, a novel struc-
> ture, a robust capacity for regeneration and a very diverse membership
> that cuts across ethnic, class and national boundaries. It is neither a sin-
> gle group nor a coalition of groups: it comprises a core base or bases in
> Afghanistan, satellite terrorist cells worldwide, a conglomerate of Islamist
> political parties, and other largely independent terrorist groups that it
> draws on for offensive actions and other responsibilities. Leaders of all
> the above are co-opted as and when necessary to serve as an integral part
> of Al-Qaeda's high command, which is run via a vertical leadership struc-
> ture that provides strategic direction and tactical support to its horizontal
> network of compartmentalized cells and associate organizations.[32]

In many respects, then, at the height of its operations, Al-Qaeda was best characterized as a "holding company," which—in addition to its own cells— could tap directly into a wide range of otherwise autonomous organizations to leverage their particular skills and capabilities for a given operation.

Al-Qaeda's cell structure is particularly important in terms of understanding its ability to operate a vast network of activists and yet remain undetected. Composed generally of two to fifteen members, these cells—based mainly in

Western countries—operated via their leaders through an exclusively vertical chain of authority. The lack of horizontal ties between them meant that cells were never aware of each other's existence or whereabouts—and sometimes not even all the members of a given cell knew each other. This cell model has been widely used by clandestine activist groups of all sorts. Most widely associated with various Marxist–Leninist groups, it was also extensively employed by the MB in its early phases (see Chapter 3). Al-Qaeda's ability to forge *ad hoc* or affiliate relationships with other Islamist and radical entities was also key to its operational capacity. Sometimes these were regional or even local groups that had built up a strong presence in an area of interest to Al-Qaeda, but where the network had limited capacity. This is the best way to think of Al-Qaeda's relationship with the Jemah Islamiah group in Southeast Asia, a radical group seeking to establish a caliphate in that region. Although many of Jemah's key figures, such as Hambali, its chief tactician, have been described as members of Al-Qaeda, they are actually best thought of as local "subcontractors" to whom Bin Laden's network have outsourced a particular operation, such as the Bali bombing of 2002. Al-Qaeda seems to have been wholly pragmatic in forming these relationships. Network affiliates are not universally Salafi–jihadi in orientation. Some are Shi'i, and some—it appears—are not even Muslim. Rather, these are groups that share a desire to attack the United Sates and are happy to enter into cooperative relationships with capable partners. In return for rendering services to Al-Qaeda, its contractors could expect not only financial reward, but also to gain access to Bin Laden's networked resources (logistics, training) to aid in the pursuit of their own goals—not to mention the prestige that accrues in activist circles from working with Al-Qaeda.

Bin Laden, trained in economics and management rather than religion and Islamic jurisprudence, built a robust network of financial interests that permitted Al-Qaeda to sustain its operations and to bankroll allies and affiliates. While many popular accounts suggest that much of this work was funded directly by his own personal fortune, the reality is that Bin Laden was not sitting on billions that could simply be channeled into militant activities. Rather, most of the money he did have was used to create a system of investments and business interests that would provide a source of continual funding for Al-Qaeda's shadow empire of *jihad*. During the early Afghan period, Bin Laden could count on generous funding from Pakistan and various states in the Gulf (Saudi Arabia, Kuwait), but once the war was over, this mostly dried up in terms of direct government contributions. He had, however, managed to build up a significant base of contacts and relationships with private foundations, charities, and wealthy individuals who would prove to be a crucial source of funding as Al-Qaeda's operational portfolio developed. Bin Laden found it necessary to make cash payments to various groups and governments, not only directly to assist his operations, but also to buy him breathing space or connivance. His generous support of the Taliban government in Afghanistan is one clear example of this.[33] The finance network was funded through an array of investment schemes and small businesses, with all revenues to Al-Qaeda funneled through a careful money-laundering system involving hundreds if not thousands of bank accounts all over the world. The globalization of finance was hence key to the globalization of Al-Qaeda. The organization possessed a special council charged with ensuring that all of its financial operations were conducted in accordance with the *shari'ah*.[34] Bin Laden also made use of the informal *hawala* system to transfer money. This method, initially developed in South Asia, permits sums to be sent from one town—or even one country—to another based on relationships of trust that link the various parties involved in the process. There is no record of the transaction and no means by which to track it. Many of the same conduits and contacts were also part of Al-Qaeda's logistics capacity, which enabled the group to move personnel and materials around the world very quickly. Gunaratna suggests that Bin Laden devised "the most complex, robust and resilient money-generating and money-moving network yet seen" and one is indeed led to speculate as to whether Al-Qaeda might better be thought of as a finance and logistics operation first, and as a terrorist group second.[35]

Al-Qaeda made extensive use of communications, both strategically and tactically. On the strategic front, Bin Laden demonstrated a mastery of the modern global media through a series of high-profile statements and interviews released to major networks (CNN, Al-Jazeera). He could be assured—through careful timing, his choice of topic, and even language—of gathering an instant worldwide audience. His statements were usually passed to networks and websites through several orders of separation. Partly this was the operational security for which the group had become renowned, but it also helped to heighten the sense of mystery surrounding communications from Al-Qaeda. Western media and government analysts would spend subsequent days poring over, dissecting, and interpreting these messages. It is interesting to note, as some observers have, that Bin Laden's target audiences for these communications were chosen very strategically. In particular messages he employs symbology and message framings that are aimed at very particular, sometimes niche, audiences. Sometimes he is addressing the world as a whole, or the United States more specifically. Other times a message that gets a worldwide airing, however, was intended primarily for a very specific Islamist or jihadi group. On the tactical side, Al-Qaeda became well known for its extensive use of satellite telephones, information technology, encryption, and steganography. From the late 1990s, once it became clear to Bin Laden that he was being closely monitored by various intelligence agencies, he stopped making widespread use of electronic forms of communication and began to rely instead on direct person-to-person contacts.

Much has also been made of Al-Qaeda's network of training facilities, centered primarily in Afghanistan. Not only were the group's own operatives trained here, but Bin Laden would make it possible for other jihadi groups to send personnel to these camps. Many of the recruitment videos produced by Al-Qaeda feature the training sites, which Bin Laden was clearly keen to show off. They were also among the highest-priority targets of the U.S.'s counter-offensive against Al-Qaeda, beginning with the 1998 bombings of camps in Afghanistan and a suspected weapons production facility in Sudan. The group also produced training manuals and guidebooks that provided copious details about how to operate in a wide variety of environments and how to undertake various sorts of attacks, from manufacturing explosives to the use of various weapons systems. The most famous of these is probably the *Encyclopedia of the Afghan Jihad,* a book that compiled and synthesized thousands of accounts of mujahideen and Arab Afghan operations, serving as an invaluable "institutional memory" of the war that could be used by later jihadis.[36] There is also evidence that in its operations Al-Qaeda utilized aspects of modern management science, including post-attack assessment and evaluation reports to enable the improvement of future operations.[37]

Al-Qaeda's active membership was diverse, and varied considerably in terms of its size and composition over the years. Initially made up, as we will see below, almost exclusively of Arab Afghan alumni, it began from the 1990s to attract Muslim fighters from all over the world, including a number of converts from the West. The training camps, at any given time, would be populated by jihadis from the Philippines, Libya, Somalia, Bangladesh, and northern California. There is evidence to suggest that all positions of administrative consequence, and certainly those with any military command responsibility, were firmly in the hands of Arabs—with Arabic also serving as the movement's *lingua franca.*[38]

Perhaps one useful metaphor for thinking about Al-Qaeda, particularly in terms of its resilience and regenerative capacities, is to compare it to the internet. Like the internet, Al-Qaeda at its height was in many ways a

© AFP

Figure 7.2 Al-Qaeda leader Ayman al-Zawahiri

"network of networks." The technology behind the internet was designed in the late 1960s by researchers working for the U.S. Department of Defense, who sought to create a system for exchanging data that would be impervious to a nuclear strike by the Soviet Union. To this end, they created various forms of redundancy into the core data-transfer technology that would permit messages to continue to be sent across the network even if entire sections of it were destroyed. The internet is also decentralized in terms of its structure, meaning that there is no single choke point or control unit on which other operations depend. Al-Qaeda certainly possessed this redundant capacity insofar as its integrated network of operations was able to continue functioning even if part of it was closed down or destroyed. Al-Qaeda does, however, possess a more centralized control mechanism in the form of its top leadership—but even this had proven to be remarkably resilient and capable of becoming portable very quickly in the face of threats, as witnessed in Bin Laden's ability to evade capture when the United States invaded Afghanistan in 2001. Even if Al-Qaeda's ability to centrally command and control militant operations has been severely degraded—as both military and law enforcement operations against its finance network seem to have done—there is evidence, as we will see below, to suggest that its influence and capacities have been channeled into other manifestations and modes of operation, despite declining popular support.

THE SOCIOLOGY OF RADICAL ISLAM: MOBILIZATION, IDENTITY, AND AUTHORITY

Now that we have a basic understanding of Al-Qaeda's aims and structure, we can move on to look in greater depth at those who choose to associate with it and work on its behalf. This section investigates various dimensions of the sociology of radical Islam. We focus more specifically on shifting trends across two generations of jihadi activists, and also on the question of how Salafism as a form of religious discourse interacts with processes of identity formation to shape the worldviews of would-be activists in particular ways. How does radicalization occur, and what is it about particular forms of religious authority that attracts and holds the loyalty of followers? We will also discuss some of the ways in which radical Islamist groups can be thought of in terms of social movements more broadly conceptualized.

As Olivier Roy has noted in his book *Globalized Islam,* it is possible to identify two distinct generations of Al-Qaeda activists. The comparative sociology of these groups is telling in terms of what it allows us to discern about the evolving nature of the jihadi discourse and movement. The first generation of Al-Qaeda operatives, those who constituted the bulk of the organization in the late 1980s and very early 1990s, were generally citizens of Muslim countries and had direct prior experience of political or militant activism either in their home country, as Arab Afghans, or—most commonly—both. They generally had very little experience of the West, and their axis of movement was generally confined to Afghanistan, Muslim conflicts in neighboring countries, and their country of origin.[39] The second wave of Al-Qaeda personnel, from the 1990s, by contrast, tended to have strong connections to the West. Many were recruited in Europe (and to some extent North America) or were citizens of Muslim countries who had spent some time living, studying, or training in the West as expatriates. Important to note about this second generation, Roy tells us, is the "deterritorialized" nature of its Muslim identity. Where the original Al-Qaeda activists were firmly socialized in a nation-state environment and had developed their Islamist consciousness primarily in terms of its circumstances, this new generation of jihadis often had weak senses of national and religious identity. For many in the first wave, transnationalism was something of a reach, an idea they needed to get their heads around; for the second generation, however, it was a natural way of life—the "jihadi jet set."[40]

In order to better understand this new mode of malignant cosmopolitanism, we need to look more closely at how and why radical religious discourse resonated with these deterritorialized identities. We discuss these processes primarily in the context of the recruitment and socialization of young Muslims in Western contexts, since Al-Qaeda and other radical groups seem to have relied heavily on these settings to provide many of the foot soldiers for their second-generation operations. In terms of the first wave, the socialization into *jihad* occurred primarily through existing radical Islamist structures whose activities and leaderships became increasingly transnational from the 1980s. When looking at the second wave, however, we are confronted with a situation in which ideologues and recruiters are often handed a *tabula rasa* Muslim identity (in the form of a new convert or an immigrant Muslim experiencing new-found sense of religiosity) upon which they employ a range of discursive and disciplining techniques to inculcate certain worldviews and activist tendencies. This may sound like we are referring to something akin to brainwashing, but at work here is actually a much more sophisticated process of socialization that leverages existing cognitive, ideational, and identity formations to sculpt a very particular form of global Muslim subjectivity.

Several observers have already noted the "deculturing" or "universalizing" dimensions of Salafi Islam.[41] These two terms refer, respectively, to the analytical and normative aspects of a similar phenomenon. Salafism, with its hostility toward religious innovation (*bid'a*), aims to rid Islam of anything that has entered the faith through contact with various local, "cultural" beliefs and practices. Syncretism, in the Salafi view, is the enemy. Its anti-*madhhab* stance is further evidence of this. There are no schools of jurisprudence to debate between, Salafis insist—there is only Islam. In a normative sense this has proven very appealing to many young Muslims living in the West who feel alienated by their parents' understanding of Islam (see Chapter 8). Their parents seem trapped in an understanding of Islam as it was practiced in, for example, the village in Bangladesh from which they migrated 20 years ago. They seem obsessed with details relating to how one should hold one's hands while praying, saints' days, various festivals—but nothing to do with religion and modern life. Rejecting the "village Islam" of their parents, they go in search of a form of Islam that speaks to the issues and challenges of living as a Muslim in a global world—and, moreover, a Muslim caught between two senses of identity. The second and third immigrant generations have generally been born and raised in the West and are well versed (and often comfortable with) its cultural patterns and norms. At the same time, they are aware of belonging to a different and, at times, disparate identity formation, that of Islam. They search for a universal form of religion that will help them to reconcile what they are (Muslims) with where they are (the West), and that will also help to provide them with some sense of meaning and purpose.

This search for a universal idiom of Islam can lead in two general directions. In some cases it prompts young Muslims in the West to emphasize those aspects of their religion that reflect global human rights norms, democracy, and political and cultural pluralism: the *umma* as an integral part of a common global humanity. But this same search for universal Islam can also lead towards a universalism defined, religiously, in Salafi terms—and, politically, in terms of Muslim struggles the world over: the *umma* as a righteous community under assault. While there is no sure way of determining which of these two general currents will prevail when it comes to a given individual, it is possible to make observations about how and why the Salafi discourse in particular may seem appealing under certain circumstances. It is also important to note that only a very tiny minority of those drawn to Salafi Islamist circles in the West ever get anywhere near the battlefield of *jihad*. For many, political Salafism is a "phase" they go through before either slipping into a conservative but non-Islamist mode of religious practice or, in some cases, becoming so disillusioned with the movement that they begin to question the very basis of Salafism, or even Islam. We have already referred above to the deculturing nature of Salafi Islam. Several other aspects of the radical discourse merit our attention in terms of their interaction with identity and shifting religious norms in Western contexts.

Meaning-making and identity-constitutive worldviews

For those Western Muslims who experience their dual identity as confusing and destabilizing, radical Islamic discourses can provide a matrix of meaning that permits them to derive a clearer sense of purpose and worldview. By shifting the focus of their identity away from the apparent tension between being, for example, simultaneously British and South Asian, and orienting it instead toward a resolution of this tension in a universal, Salafi Islam and membership in the global *umma*, radical ideologues help culturally disoriented Muslims (or recent converts, as yet unsure of their way in Islam) to experience their lack of clear identity foothold not as a weakness or an absence, but rather as something empowering that invests them with the ability to be a "real" Muslim—and, moreover, to prove it by becoming politically engaged on behalf of the embattled *umma*. Describing the appeal of the radical Islamist group Hizb ut-Tahrir (HT; see below), one former member put it this way:

> They had a very profound analysis of why the Islamic world is in such an abysmal state, how it declined and most importantly how we can elevate ourselves from this position, and break free. The group was not allied to any political regime, it was not operating on the basis of personal or financial motivation, it didn't have a sectarian approach. As long as you are a Muslim and are committed to its beliefs and its causes, you are welcome to join the party.[42]

A previously liminal identity thus rediscovers itself as part of the vanguard of a new global movement. Radical Salafism accomplishes a gradual "desocietization" whereby adherents withdraw further and further from the ambient mainstream community, associating exclusively with other "real Muslims," and gradually detaching themselves from the national-societal contexts in which they live.

"Sheikhly" charisma and the ethics of care

Another dimension of Muslims' attraction to radical movements relates to the personal charisma associated with the scholars and leaders of these movements. Various observers have noted that, within Al-Qaeda's second wave, a great many of those recruited in the West have been living on the margins of society—often coming from broken homes and families, unemployed, involved in petty crime, and so forth. The leaders of the radical groups, as one analyst has documented, tend to display a genuine sense of care for those who come into their circle.[43] For many young Muslims living on the margins, frequently subject to racism and discrimination, this may represent the first time anyone has ever seemed to take a genuine interest in them and the direction of their life. The personal charisma of radical ideologues hence seems vitally important in terms of creating an emotional bond with members of the group.[44]

Salafism and techno-scientific cognitive style

Many drawn to the radical movements are not, by any means, marginalized members of society. Rather, they often have a very high level of education, are employed, and even have a family in some cases (compare with the demographics of mainstream Islamist groups such as the MB). Theirs is not a lack of social integration, but rather a seemingly successful (or at least partially successful) integration process that has gone awry. Elements of the identity and worldview crises alluded to above begin to enter the picture, and they come to the radical circles in search of a clearer sense of meaning. Well aware of the educational background of these potential recruits—many of whom will have graduated from top scientific and engineering schools—the religious scholars and intellectuals will often articulate radical Islamist ideology in a form that fits comfortably with the "cognitive style" and methods of analysis to which their students are accustomed. Salafi Islam is particularly conducive to this approach. The grammar of Salafism suits the structure of modern scientific knowledge production. When teaching Salafi Islam to such a group, for example, a *sheikh* can diagram it on a board such that it closely resembles problem-solving methods or engineering flowcharts. Given that much of the Salafi discourse can be explained in terms of discrete categories of analysis, it becomes a relatively straightforward matter to communicate its teachings in a way that allows a follower with a techno-scientific education to work methodically through a given situation (framed in terms of religiously given normative categories) and eventually to achieve—just as science does—a single, correct answer at the end of that process. This answer, it should be noted, is not subjective and nor is it open to interpretation. It is the end result, again, just like science, of an "objective" method whose infallibility is beyond reproach. Faith in science as a technical method becomes faith in Salafism as a religious method.

Activism, violence, and "instinctual" religious knowledge

Observers and analysts of radical Islam have speculated as to the process that leads an individual to become willing to engage in violence, or other forms of "high-risk" activism.[45] Is it the religion itself that "radicalizes" them? Is it the teachings of a senior religious scholar, who eventually convinces them that violence in the name of Islam is not only permitted, but required of them? Limited anecdotal evidence actually suggests that many individuals come into radical circles having already decided that they want to undertake violent *jihad*. Some, in fact, may only very recently have become Muslim, or "reactivated" a previously dormant sense of religiosity.[46]

Thus it is not Salafism itself or the authority of religious scholars that serves as the "radicalizing agent," but rather prior life experiences and worldviews that have culminated in a decision actively to seek participation in political violence. The religious authority of Salafi sheikhs, in any case, is anything but absolute. While those who engage in *jihad* do seek religious justification for their actions, they may sometimes do so after having already decided to act. In this regard, given the lack of religious hierarchy in Islam, it becomes easy for them to shop around—via the internet or personal connections—to find a *sheikh* who will authorize and, moreover, provide textually grounded (and hence irreproachable) evidence as to why violence is permitted or even required in a given situation. It is also worth recalling here Sayyid Qutb's teachings about how activist interpretations are privileged above those of religious scholars (see Chapter 3). For someone strongly molded in the "Qutbist" worldview, there is the potential that they may even untether themselves from formal sources of religious authority altogether. This phenomenon is illustrated in testimony given by the widow of a jihadi accused of planning the 2004 Madrid train bombings: "Sometime we received texts [by religious scholars] from the internet, but my husband did not read them, his relationship to *jihad* was instinctual."[47] Thus, while activists may operate in frameworks whose general normative parameters are defined by a given religious authority, their willingness to engage in violence is not necessarily a learned behavior accruing exclusively from their participation in this network. Moreover, it seems that under certain circumstances they may disconnect from, or simply ignore, those aspects and teachings emanating from formally trained religious scholars that are dissonant with the activist orientation to which they have committed.

HIZB UT-TAHRIR AND *KHILAFAH:* A NONVIOLENT RADICAL ISLAMISM?

Al-Qaeda understandably has been the focus of considerable attention and analysis in recent years, but are there not to be found today other radical Islamist movements, not already affiliated with Al-Qaeda, and which espouse a different approach to revolutionary politics? One such group that we will examine below is Hizb ut-Tahrir (HT). It is a radical group in that its primary goal is the re-establishment of a global caliphate. It prefers to do so on a gradual basis, however—one country at a time—and without the use of violence (despite claims by others to the contrary—see below). Where Al-Qaeda clearly can be labeled a jihadi organization, HT's emphasis on the caliphate leads us to regard it as a *khilafist* group.

Hizb ut-Tahrir al-Islami (the "Islamic Liberation Party") significantly predates Al-Qaeda. Founded in Jerusalem in 1952 by Taqi ud-Din al-Nabhani, HT emphasized from the beginning the importance of establishing a single party (*hizb*) through which Muslims could work for the re-establishment of the caliphate (*khilafah*). In the eyes of Nabhani and his followers, it was only through revolutionary action in concert that the world's Muslims could restore themselves to a position of global power. In this sense, the founding of Nabhani's movement marks a reincarnation of certain elements found in earlier discourses on pan-Islam, yet with a stronger emphasis on the importance of a single Muslim polity. Nabhani faced considerable opposition from the Jordanian state (which still controlled Jerusalem at that time), and also found it difficult to develop a mass following for his party. With Arab nationalism gathering strength as the dominant political ideology of the day, appeals for a new caliphate fell largely on deaf ears. Hizb ut-Tahrir found itself moving underground at the same time as it began to establish small footholds in other Arab countries. Noted to be particularly strong in Turkey, where memory of the Ottoman caliphate still endures to some extent, the group's activities in the Middle East and Asia (outside the reach of anti-HT propaganda in the Arab world) have been well documented during the first decades of its existence.[48]

The structure of HT, while highly fluid in practice, is organized around a series of hierarchical committees. The party maintains a worldwide central leadership committee headed by an *amir* (leader), currently Ata Abu Rashta. The group does not disclose the location of the central committee, but it is variously reported as being based in Lebanon, Jordan, or the Palestinian Territories. Each nation (or "province," since the party does not recognize the validity of the nation-state model) in which HT operates possesses a five- to ten-member committee headed by a *mu'tamad* (regional leader). These national leadership councils subdivide into smaller local (usually urban) committees under a *naqib* (local head) and neighborhood study circles guided by a *mushrif* (study circle guide). In countries where it has been subject to persecution by the authorities, HT has been known to adopt a rigorously enforced cell structure. Much of the activities—and even the identities—of the group's leadership are highly secretive. Sometimes even senior country leaders know very little about the opaque global leadership structure. It is reported that there are certain issues and topics on which country branches are required to consult the central leadership before speaking or acting, and some have noted the presence of central leadership representatives observing and advising "field" offices in other countries.

Sporadic references to crackdowns on HT branches in North Africa and Turkey can be found throughout the 1970s and 1980s, and the group resurfaced to a torrent of negative publicity in Britain in the early to mid-1990s. Having engaged in a heavy recruiting drive at UK universities, HT found itself banned from British higher education campuses by the National Union of Students following accusations of anti-semitic activities. The group's *mu'tamad* in the UK at the time, Sheikh Omar Bakri Muhammad, emerged during this time as a controversial public figure, challenging all

Muslims in the UK to adopt the pursuit of *khilafah* as the only possible course of Islamically authentic political action available to Muslims. Although its beliefs and program remained a minority tendency, the radical political position adopted by the group managed effectively to polarize the British Muslim community for a short period.[49] Seeking to label all who rejected the caliphate as Western collaborators—or, in Bakri's terms, "chocolate Muslims"—HT prompted a vigorous debate about the political imperatives of Islam as a minority community. In 1996, after significant disagreements arose within the UK leadership of HT as to the theological basis for the group's political activities and the scope of its work, Bakri left the group to found the al-Muhajiroun movement. This latter organization, which Bakri styled as Salafi (he sees HT as Ash'ari in its *aqeeda*) and closer in orientation to the jihadi worldview of Bin Laden, lasted until 2004 when it was abruptly closed down by its leader, who later fled the country when Islamists began attracting increased attention from British law enforcement in the wake of the July 7, 2005 bombings in London. Severely discredited in the eyes of Muslims and non-Muslims alike, HT retreated from the public eye for several years, leaving the limelight in the UK to groups such as al-Muhajiroun. Attention to HT's activities increased again in the summer of 2001, but this time centered on Central Asia, where reports had emerged of active cells organized out of Uzbekistan that authorities were trying to link with Al-Qaeda.[50] A vigorous debate ensued, particularly in Washington DC policy-making circles, as to whether HT members in Central Asia were involved in violence. Amongst sporadic but rarely corroborated reports to this effect, the International Crisis Group issued a report in 2003 indicating that there was no evidence to suggest that HT members had committed violent acts in the region. Although London remains an important site of fundraising, recruitment, and coordination for the group, HT's political activism seems increasingly to be focused elsewhere, with Pakistan, Indonesia, Jordan, and Palestine claimed as major areas of focus at the present time. The movement seems to be growing particularly quickly in Indonesia, where its leader, Ismail Yusanto, has been active in organizing rallies. Hizb ut-Tahrir was banned in Germany in 2003 on account of engaging in anti-semitic activities.

Sources of support for HT vary considerably from context to context, and in this sense it is difficult to produce something like a profile of a "typical" party member. It has proven itself skillful in adapting its discourse to local conditions and in appealing to a wide range of particular grievances. In the early 1990s, for example, it was successful in recruiting among second- and third-generation South Asian immigrants in the UK, many of whom had been raised with a form of Islam they regarded as disengaged from worldly issues and political imperatives. Alienated by their parents' "culturally distorted" Islam (see above) and socially adrift in a society into which mainstream integration proved difficult, the discourse of radical resistance offered by HT appeared highly attractive. By placing *khilafah*—a marginal ideal at best in mainstream Muslim political thought—firmly at the center of its religious discourse, HT was able to take advantage of a relative lack of religious knowledge on the part of its young recruits. When asked about the extent of desire in the *umma* for a new caliphate, group members often give a general answer about Muslims desiring greater unity. When it is put to them that such a desire does not necessarily translate into support for *khilafah,* and that those seeking a political order based on Islam might prefer groups such as the MB (the most popular Islamist tendency in the Arab world), HT supporters tend to explain that Muslims will eventually realize that the correct political implementation of Islam must necessarily lead to *khilafah.*

So how, in HT's view, will this new caliphate come about? The party's political discourse begins by recognizing the lack of any "executive structure" in the Muslim world as a major problem and one that must, according to a *shari'ah* obligation impingent upon all Muslims, be rectified. In terms of its methods, it seeks to style itself as nonderivative in the sense that it does not study and emulate the approaches taken by previous Islamist movements. Instead, it seeks to go back to the basic legislative sources of the religion—the Qur'an, *hadith,* and *usul al-fiqh.* The correct method for establishing *khilafah* is fixed and can, it claims, be found in the *shari'ah,* but this should be distinguished from "means and style," which is necessarily specific to place and time. Hizb ut-Tahrir, at least in the UK, explains that its work is intellectual and political, and in this regard it rejects militant methods. Realizing the close relationship between force and power, however, HT does speak of actively seeking *nussrah*—support from the armed forces or those responsible for security and public order—in countries where it operates, but claims that this is a form of activity controlled exclusively by the party's central leadership. While appealing to a young and generally well-educated audience, the group finds support for its program by simultaneously adopting a populist rhetoric designed to link socioeconomic disenfranchisement to religiosity. For example, HT's publicity literature in the UK defines capitalism as "the detachment of religion from life." Regarding the geographical scope of its activities, the group expresses a willingness to work anywhere and everywhere, but suggests that the caliphate has the best chance of being re-established in those lands where a precedent already exists (i.e. the Middle East and former Ottoman territories). While global *khilafah* remains the party's ultimate goal, it espouses a gradualist approach.

Hizb ut-Tahrir describes three general phases to its work. During the first of these, the "culturing" phase, the basic structure of the party is assembled and members are socialized into its beliefs, agenda, and worldview. Once it is on firm footing, the party can then move on to phase two, "interaction," which involves going out into society to explain the necessity of *khilafah* and to call Muslims to support or join the party. The third and final phase, "seeking power," is where the most concerted use of *nussrah* is made in order to actually establish *khilafah*. Hizb ut-Tahrir formally rejects violence as a means to achieve political change, and is committed—publicly at least—to pursue power exclusively through peaceful means. Privately, some members will indicate that at the very final stages of phase three, a "push" might be required to bring about an actual change in power, but they see this is something akin to a *coup d'état* (its impulse having arisen, presumably in the military via HT's *nussrah*) rather than any kind of *jihad*.

Widespread suspicion still obtains as to HT's involvement in, or willingness to use, violence, despite its claims to the contrary and the fact that no solid evidence exists to suggest that the party has ever employed militant tactics. There is, however, some evidence that points to former members of the party becoming involved in violence after leaving HT. For example, two former students of Omar Bakri Muhammad were recruited by Hamas to carry out suicide attacks in Israel in 2003. This has led some to claim that, regardless of whether HT itself espouses violence, its ideology and radical program constitute "waypoints" on the road to violence. Their fear is that members of the party more inclined toward immediate radical activism may become disillusioned with the party's "gradualist" approach and desert it in favor of the jihadi ranks.

Hizb ut-Tahrir's potential to evolve into a mass movement, which Al-Qaeda never did, is difficult to assess. There have been signs recently, however, that it is trying to broaden its appeal, particularly in the wake of 9/11 when it began to come back out into the open in the UK after a half-decade of relative quiet. There are signs that the movement has been on an active recruitment drive, trying to bring into its fold those Muslims who share Usama Bin Laden's critique of Western secular imperialism, but who reject his violent methods. Hizb ut-Tahrir, on this account, becomes the non-jihadi alternative route to world Islamic revolution. One of the obstacles to HT growing its membership beyond the young and overwhelmingly male "hotheads" who attended its angry rallies on British university campuses in the 1990s is the fact that, for most Muslims (and certainly those in Europe), the caliphate was simply an issue to which they could not relate. They wanted an Islamic movement that would address the issues and problems they faced in their day-to-day lives rather than one that seemed to be narrowly obsessed with a vision of Islamic political utopia. To this end, after 9/11, HT in the UK seemed to change its tune considerably, at least in terms of its public image. It began participating in meetings and forums with other Muslim groups, including ones that the HT of the 1990s, under Omar Bakri Muhammad, would never have considered communicating or collaborating with. There was also a short-lived effort to publish an Islamic lifestyle magazine, *Salam,* which folded after several issues. The name of the party never appeared on this publication and the caliphate was never covered in its pages. Rather, it was trying to find new markets for HT by addressing issues such as multicultural marriage. In the reasoning of the leadership, the party—still trapped somewhere between phases two and three of its work plan—needed to find a voice and vision that would get people listening. Once people saw that the party was addressing issues they cared about, it stood to reason, they might become more interested in its political priorities. Many observers of British Muslim politics have dismissed this facelift and the appearance of a "kindler, gentler" HT as pure instrumentalism, claiming that the same old radical ideas lurk just below the surface.[51] Like many of the more radical movements operating in the UK, HT reduced its public profile considerably after the July 2005 London bombings. The UK government has reviewed HT several times in the years following the attacks with a view to possibly proscribing the movement in Britain, but each time it has opted to take no action in the absence of evidence that the group is involved in illegal activities. 2008 and 2009 saw HT accused of involvement in efforts to infiltrate the Pakistani army and in connection with radical activities in Turkey. The Arab Uprisings have seen an upsurge in HT activities in the Middle East, particularly in Tunisia and in Syria, where HT members have been active in the rebel forces fighting Bashar al-Assad's regime.

How should we think about HT's breed of radicalism in comparison with that of Al-Qaeda? Bringing in a metaphor from the Bolshevik Revolution, we might think of HT as the advocates of "*khilafah* in one country," in contrast to the more "Trotskyite" Al-Qaeda, which favors continual worldwide *jihad.* Some among the leadership of these movements have also traveled ideologically over the course of their careers. Hizb ut-Tahrir's (and later al-Muhajiroun's) Omar Bakri Muhammad—a former member of the MB—has been fairly comfortably involved, it would seem, with a diverse range of political movements and doctrinal orientations. Looking at their overall political goals, however, certain common themes clearly arise. It can be said that both groups seek to render the worldviews of local Muslims more global, but not in a cosmopolitan, tolerant sense. Promulgating Islam as a higher-order identity, would-be supporters are asked to de-emphasize national affiliations in the name of the *umma* and to understand the suffering of Muslims in other lands as their own—and as circumstances into which they are obliged by their religion to intervene. In this sense, the khilafist–jihadi agenda might be said to hold the greatest appeal for those whose sense of belonging is already in flux—those disjunct from mainstream society and somehow adrift. Radical Islamist discourses structured around a strong antagonism to prevailing social orders hence serve to crystallize political identities and affiliations. The clarity of vision and moral certainty of Salafi Islam become more attractive to some than the indeterminacy and relativism of more moderate, pluralist approaches.

The political discourse of both groups also makes frequent use of the notion of *kuffar* ("unbelievers", infidels) as a technique of moral othering. This is where the obsession with normative categories begins to take on a social reality. Non-Muslim others are figured as those beyond the pale of social responsibility. Although, contrary to popular belief, Salafi discourse does not require Muslims to engage in armed conflict with *kuffar* wherever they may be found (unless they are themselves laying siege to Muslims— which, today, in the view of many Salafi groups they are); unbelievers are understood to be located outside the normative remit of social relations. By placing the unbeliever in a category of radical difference, the possibility of coexistence premised on cultural pluralism and political civility is precluded.

LOOKING AHEAD: FUTURE FORMATIONS OF RADICAL ISLAM

Examined from a sociological perspective, as this chapter shows, radical Islamist movements such as Al-Qaeda and HT do not appear to be so different from other organized social movements that participate in "contentious politics."[52] The same collectivization of discontent combined with processes of mobilization around opportunity structures and resource capabilities is clearly present here. The "micromobilization" of social capital as concentrated in small cells of like-minded individuals permits relationships of solidarity to be converted into mutually supporting activist units as "sentiment pools" coalesce around a more rigid and deployable political framework.[53] Some analysts have emphasized the sense in which Salafi jihadis display some of the same characteristics as "new social movements." This label refers to "post-materialist" groups organized primarily around a common set of values or normative commitment—that is, a particular sense of "the good."[54] As Quintan Wiktorowicz puts it:

> Similar to many new social movements, the Salafis are attempting to build new identities and alternative norms that challenge dominant cultural codes, and in so doing they create an "imagined community" and networks of activists determined to reproduce and expand a particular interpretation of Islam. Such networks ... bypass traditional rule-making institutions, such as tribes or states, by creating endogenously produced sets of understandings about individual behavior and social interactions.[55]

Thus the Islamist radicals can be thought of as one example of a much broader category of "anti-systemic" social movement seeking to challenge the normative premises of the current world system, a point also made by

Olivier Roy.[56] Where some groups focus on the socioeconomic dimensions of uneven resource distribution as a byproduct of the modern capitalist system, the radical Islamists associate the latter with an imperializing secularism that contravenes a social and political order they believe to be divinely sanctioned. This does not mean that Bin Laden and his ilk share the views or goals of, for example, various anti-globalization movements. Indeed, in many if not most regards their views on social norms, permissible forms of activism, and end goals are quite diametrically opposed. Rather, we want to make the point that Al-Qaeda represents a highly extreme form of the more generally recognizable phenomenon of contemporary anti-systemic social activism.

What directions might radical Islam take in the future? Is it possible to discern today any new patterns in its organization and methods? How will its fortunes fare? Beginning with the latter question, there are those such as Fawaz Gerges who argue, based on considerable research, that Al-Qaeda's fortunes as a social movement are on the decline. We have already discussed various negative reactions to Bin Laden's approach within the jihadi movement itself, and the precipitous decline in recent years in popular support being expressed for the Al-Qaeda leader. Gerges contends that due to a number of factors, the international campaign against terrorism not withstanding, Al-Qaeda's recruitment pool has dried up severely in recent years. He also senses an ongoing "general realignment within the jihadist current against, not in favor of, Al-Qaeda and global *jihad*."[57] It seems that Bin Laden has had to rely on jihadi recruits of increasingly inferior quality, as those with meaningful skills and experience trend away from the Al-Qaeda model. Some would cite the case of Abu Musab al-Zarqawi in evidence of this. Until killed by U.S. forces in 2006, Zarqawi had been the head of Al-Qaeda's operations in Iraq after the 2003 American invasion. Rather than having been handpicked for this task from among a pool of top candidates, Zarqawi more or less claimed the mantle of Al-Qaeda in Iraq for himself after operating independently for some time—with Bin Laden reluctantly acquiescing to the merger of Zarqawi's organization (al-Tawhid w'al-Jihad) into Al-Qaeda's overall structure. Zarqawi's reputation within jihadi circles was less that of a spiritual warrior and more a criminal thug prone to excessive violence. He became a figure of acclamation for the movement only after the United States cited his presence in Iraq as evidence of a nonexistent partnership between Saddam Hussein and Al-Qaeda. Even then, Zarqawi's cult of personality became a recruiting tool only among very young, mainly Western, "wanna-be" jihadis, rather than among the hardened activists, most of whom found him highly distasteful. Indeed, in 2005, Ayman Al-Zawahiri, then Al-Qaeda's deputy leader, wrote a letter to Zarqawi in which he appears to chastise the Al-Qaeda in Iraq leader for excessive use of violence against Muslim civilians. Was the fact that Bin Laden could do no better than Zarqawi to run Al-Qaeda's operations in Iraq evidence that most of the seasoned radical activists had by that point deserted him? Was Al-Qaeda becoming increasingly reliant on amateur jihadists outside its control?

It will take some time to discern how fatal the intra-jihadi debates, the U.S.-led war on terror, and the 2011 death of Bin Laden will prove to Al-Qaeda's fortunes. It is clear now, however, that the group has not been able to mobilize the Muslim masses around its message. There may be those in the slums of various cities in the global south who wear T-shirts declaring Bin Laden to be a new Ché Guevara, but, as Gilles Kepel puts it, "Bin Laden has been unable to unify poor urban youth, the Muslim middle classes, and the Islamist intelligentsia into a coalition capable of repeating the only triumphant Islamic revolution the world has ever seen: the one that took place in Iran in 1979."[58] But does Al-Qaeda really need to mobilize the masses in order for the global jihadi movement to be considered successful? In comparison with the MB, Fawaz Gerges points out that Al-Qaeda "has no parallel supporting social, political, or educational institutions." "In comparison with the Brotherhood," he continues, "Al-Qaeda is a skeleton of an organization. Now it has been reduced to an ideological label, a state of mind, and a mobilizational outreach program to incite attacks worldwide."[59]

But might we not by the very same token see this shift in Al-Qaeda's role as evidence of its durability, albeit in different forms? In 2008, two leading terrorism experts, Bruce Hoffman and Marc Sageman, debated the question of Al-Qaeda's continued relevance. Hoffman argued that Al-Qaeda "Central"—the entity then led by Bin Laden—continued to possess significant operational capacities and should continue to be regarded as a key player in the global jihadist movement going forward.[60] Sageman, by contrast, who had just published a book on what he termed "leaderless *jihad*," suggested that Al-Qaeda Central's time had passed and that it no longer represented the centre of gravity for global jihadi activity.[61] Instead, argued Sageman, the future of jihadism lay in the efforts of autonomous, self-radicalizing small groups or individuals with a desire to undertake violent acts, but with no formal training and little to no contact with Al-Qaeda itself. The two positions, of course, are not mutually exclusive, and there seemed to be evidence that both arguments had merit—including evidence found in the Pakistani compound where Bin Laden was killed in 2011 that indicated ongoing operational planning on the part of Al-Qaeda Central.

However, a good number of the attacks and attempted operations carried out in the years following the Hoffman–Sageman exchange seemed superficially to favor the latter's argument. The 2009 Fort Hood shooting, the attempted "underwear" bombing of an airliner later that same year, the failed Times Square bombing in 2010, and the Boston Marathon bombing of 2013 all seemed to fit the model of leaderless *jihad*. While several of the perpetrators of those acts had certainly encountered, and even communicated with, latter-day jihadi ideologues associated with some of Al-Qaeda's regional branches—such as Anwar al-Awlaki of Al-Qaeda in the Arabian Peninsula (see below)—they were neither trained nor formally tasked by the likes of Bin Laden or Zawahiri. In this respect, it might now be possible to ask whether this new breed of largely autonomous militant autodidacts might represent the advent of a "third generation" of jihadi activists.

There is also plenty of middle ground between the idea of Al-Qaeda Central as a key actor and the atomized activities of independent jihadi band-wagoners. In looking at global Islamic militancy today, Olivier Roy points to a trend that he terms "franchising." This involves regional or local groups with varying levels of connection to Al-Qaeda Central undertaking operations in the name of its general worldview and sometimes with a degree of consultation or strategic coordination.[62] Indeed, much of the current focus on Al-Qaeda operations concerns the activities of its various regional franchises. The most significant of these are as follows.

- **Al-Qaeda in Iraq** (or "Al-Qaeda in the Land of the Two Rivers")—established in 2003 in the immediate aftermath of the U.S. invasion of Iraq, this group was first operated independently by Abu Musab al-Zarqawi before joining forces with Al-Qaeda Central in 2004. Focused primarily on stirring up sectarian violence, Zarqawi's actions and extreme methods soon found him falling out of favor even with Iraqi Sunnis, as well as his benefactors in Al-Qaeda Central. Killed by the U.S. in 2006, Zarqawi was succeeded by Abu Ayyub al-Masri, but Al-Qaeda in Iraq found itself on the defensive in the wake of successful U.S. efforts to mobilize Sunni tribal leaders against the foreign jihadists. Al-Qaeda in Iraq remains active in Iraq, however, using suicide bombing operations to stoke sectarian sentiments amidst the country's ongoing political volatility.
- **Al-Qaeda in the Islamic Maghreb** (AQIM)—formed in 2006 through a merger between Al-Qaeda and what was previously the Salafist Group for Preaching and Combat (GSPC)—itself a splinter of the Algerian GIA (see Box 3.2, "Algeria: Islamists *almost* in power"). While levels of direct operational coordination with Al-Qaeda Central are unclear, AQIM has provided the global jihadist movement with renewed access to experienced Algerian fighters, as well as access to the North African diaspora in Europe. The group has engaged in suicide bombings in Algeria in 2007 and, more recently, has sought to take advantage of the security vacuum in the Saharan and Sahel that followed from the Arab Uprisings. This has allowed the group to mobilize local jihadist allies to seize territory in Mali in late 2012 and 2013, and likely to have a hand in the 2012 attack on the U.S. consulate in Benghazi. Splinter elements of AQIM also attacked an industrial facility in Algeria in 2013.

- **Al-Qaeda on the Arabian Peninsula** (AQAP)—initially assembled out of cadres of Saudi fighters returning from Iraq and other conflicts, the group that constituted itself as AQAP also attracted a number of Saudi ex-Arab Afghans. Its early militant operations (2003–05) prompted a heavy-handed response from Saudi security forces, which managed to kill many of the group's key leaders and capture many of its main operatives. Supporters of AQAP were the main target of Saudi Arabia's much-vaunted deradicalization efforts from 2005 (see Chapter 5). Thereafter, the group's center of gravity shifted to the south, where it was able to operate with relative impunity in Yemen's tribal areas. This next phase of AQAP operations saw the rise to global prominence of Anwar al-Awlaki, a Yemeni-American who had become radicalized and left the U.S. to serve as AQAP's chief ideologue. Awlaki's influence was frequently cited by some of the figures associated with efforts to attack the United States in the period 2009–11. Awlaki is also regarded as the mastermind of an Al-Qaeda English-language magazine, *Inspire,* specifically designed to appeal to would-be "casual" jihadists living in the West. This led the U.S., which had been making increased use of drone attacks on AQAP, to target Awlaki directly. He was killed by an unmanned aerial vehicle in 2011.
- **Al-Shabab**—originally a militia operating under the umbrella of the Islamic Courts Union in Somalia, a Taliban-like movement that sought to bring law and order to the chaos of the war-torn Horn of Africa. Al-Shabab gained notoriety in the early 2000s through a number of attacks on foreign aid workers and Somali clan leaders opposed to the Islamic Courts Union (ICU)'s *shari'ah*-oriented agenda. After helping the ICU to consolidate control of Mogadishu and various other expanses of territory across Somalia, Al-Shabab caught the attention of U.S. security officials when their adoption of suicide bombing tactics—not previously seen in the Horn of Africa—led to speculation that the group was adopting the tactics, and perhaps forming an alliance with, Al-Qaeda Central. An Ethiopian partial invasion of Somalia provided Al-Shabab with a new focus from 2006, and by 2010 the group formally announced an alliance with Al-Qaeda. There has been little evidence, however, that the group had widened its focus to a global agenda as a result, with subsequent attacks all focused on Somalia's internationally-recognized transitional government.

While these groups do not represent the sole organizational manifestations of Al-Qaeda today, they are the largest and most prominent regional networks. But, as evidence recovered from the compound where Bin Laden was killed in 2011 indicated, even Al-Qaeda Central continued to be actively involved in operational planning. From early 2012, the global *jihad* movement gained another franchise in the form of the Nusra Front, an

Al-Qaeda-oriented militia that emerged as a major player in the Syrian rebel forces seeking to bring down Bashar al-Assad.

Usama Bin Laden was killed in May 2011 by a U.S. special forces operation after extensive intelligence analysis had tracked him to a compound in the Pakistani garrison city of Abbottabad. In addition to killing Al-Qaeda's leader, the U.S. recovered a large trove of information—from documents and computer files—about Al-Qaeda activities and strategic planning. Shortly thereafter, Ayman al-Zawahiri was formally named as the new leader of Al-Qaeda Central. The direct impact of Bin Laden's death on Al-Qaeda and the global jihadist movement has been difficult to discern. Ayman Al-Zawahiri has faced the disadvantages of being neither a seasoned jihadi veteran with combat experience (and the credibility that comes with that status), nor particularly charismatic. His role in Al-Qaeda traditionally had been that of a master strategist and planner rather than someone who naturally leads. Many analysts had long contended that Bin Laden's death would be largely irrelevant for Al-Qaeda, since the group's added value to the jihadist cause lay primarily in its broad operational model and the worldview it espoused—both of which were now widely disseminated. With the primary focus of Al-Qaeda activity firmly located in the group's regional franchises—in addition to ongoing but isolated efforts by individuals or small groups in Europe and North America to undertake violent efforts in the name of its cause—it appears that Bin Laden's direct leadership had ceased to be a major factor in Al-Qaeda for some time.

In light of all this, there are perhaps three ways in which we might conceptualize the meaning and significance of the Al-Qaeda "brand" today.

- *Al-Qaeda as **ideology**:* a worldview or mindset consisting of a general critique of the prevailing world system shared by a wide range of radical Islamist groups (some affiliated with Al-Qaeda, some not), and also a desire to strike actively at the perceived sources of global injustice and enforced secularism—mainly the United States and its allies.
- *Al-Qaeda as **mythology**:* the worldview described above can also be marketed as a legendary status symbol well after Al-Qaeda's own active career (or, with Bin Laden's death in 2011, the life of its leaders) has come to an end. The Al-Qaeda "brand name" continues to inspire not only radical Islamists, but all manner of popular anti-systemic movements who now have evidence, based on Al-Qaeda's example, that it is possible to mount successful attacks on the sources of world hegemony.
- *Al-Qaeda as **technology**:* in this sense, the movement provides a basic model or template for networked organization and activism, aspects of which can be emulated by various "franchises" across various scales—local, national, regional, and global.

As ideology, mythology, and technology, then, it seems likely that some aspect of Al-Qaeda will continue to exert influence in radical Islamist circles, even if and when its operational capacity is destroyed or disappears altogether. The popular appeal of radical Islam, particularly in its activist variant, will continue to be limited to a very small and highly extreme minority of Muslims. Many of the symbols it champions and aspects of its overall critique, however, will still resonate more widely in the Muslim world. How will these views manifest themselves politically as we enter what some are calling a "post-Islamist" age, and just who in this complex environment speaks for Islam? These are questions that we take up in the final chapter.

NOTES

1 P. Bergen, *Holy War, Inc.: Inside the Secret World of Osama Bin Laden*, New York: Touchstone, 2001, p. 200.
2 F. Devji, *Landscapes of the Jihad: Militancy, Morality, Modernity*, Ithaca, NY: Cornell University Press, 2005; F. Devji, *The Terrorist in Search of Humanity: Militant Islam and Global Politics*, London: Hurst, 2009.
3 O. Roy, *Globalized Islam: The Search for a New Ummah*, New York: Columbia University Press, 2004, p. 297.
4 F. Gerges, *The Far Enemy: Why Jihad Went Global*, Cambridge: Cambridge University Press, 2005, p. 12.
5 D. Cook, *Understanding Jihad*, Berkeley, CA: University of California Press, 2005, p. 128.
6 Gerges, op. cit., pp. 12–13.
7 Cook, op. cit., p. 153.
8 Cook, op. cit., p. 131.
9 R. Gunaratna, *Inside Al Qaeda: Global Network of Terror*, New York: Columbia University Press, 2002, p. 86.
10 Roy, op. cit.; B. Rubin, "Afghanistan under the Taliban," *Current History* 98, 1999, p. 84.
11 Gerges, op. cit., p. 75.
12 G. Kepel, *The War for Muslim Minds*, Cambridge, MA: Harvard University Press, 2004, p. 121.
13 T. Ramadan, *To be a European Muslim*, Leicester: The Islamic Foundation, 1999.
14 Cook, op. cit., pp. 96–97.
15 Cook, op. cit., p. 105.
16 Gerges, op. cit., p. 5.
17 Cook, op. cit., p. 106.
18 Cook, op. cit., p. 108.
19 Q. Wiktorowicz, "The New Global Threat," *Middle East Policy* 8, 2001, p. 26.
20 Wiktorowicz, op. cit., p. 23.
21 Gerges, op. cit., p. 27.
22 Gerges, op. cit., p. 25.
23 Gerges, op. cit., p. 13.

24 Wiktorowicz, op. cit., p. 23.
25 Gerges, op. cit., p. 200.
26 M. Lynch, "Dr. Fadl's Review of Jihad," *Abu Ardvark*, November 27, 2007, http://abuaardvark.typepad.com/abuaardvark/2007/11/dr-fadls-review.html
27 L. Wright, "The Rebellion Within," *The New Yorker*, June 2, 2008, pp. 227–236.
28 Gerges, op. cit., pp. 200–228.
29 M. Derbala, quoted in Gerges, op. cit., p. 233.
30 Pew Research Global Attitudes Project, Survey Data 2002–13; http://pewglobal.org
31 Gunaratna, op. cit., p. 21.
32 Gunaratna, op. cit., p. 54.
33 Gunaratna, op. cit., p. 57.
34 Gunaratna, op. cit., p. 59.
35 Gunaratna, op. cit., p. 61.
36 Gunaratna, op. cit., p. 70.
37 Gunaratna, op. cit., p. 75.
38 Gunaratna, op. cit., p. 98.
39 Roy, op. cit., pp. 257–258.
40 Roy, op. cit., p. 302.
41 Roy, op. cit., p. 258; P. Mandaville, "Sufis and Salafis: The Political Discourse of Transnational Islam," in R. Hefner (ed.), *Remaking Muslim Politics: Pluralism, Contestation, Democratization*, Princeton, NJ: Princeton University Press, 2005, pp. 314–315.
42 M. Whine, "Hizb ut-Tahrir in Open Societies," in Z. Baran, *The Challenge of Hizb ut-Tahrir: Deciphering and Combating Radical Islamist Ideology*, Washington, DC: The Nixon Center, 2004.
43 Q. Wiktorowicz, *Radical Islam Rising: Muslim Extremism in the West*, Lanham, MD: Rowman & Littlefield, 2005.
44 Gerges, op. cit., p. 34.
45 Wiktorowicz, op. cit., p. 4.
46 M. Sageman, *Understanding Terror Networks*, Philadelphia, PA: University of Pennsylvania Press, 2004.
47 Gerges, op. cit., p. 8.
48 S. Taji-Farouki, *A Fundamental Quest: Hizb al-Tahrir and the Search for the Islamic Caliphate*, London: Grey Seal, 1996.
49 P. Mandaville, *Transnational Muslim Politics: Reimagining the Umma*, London: Routledge, 2001, p. 129.
50 A. Rashid, *Jihad: The Rise of Militant Islam in Central Asia*, New York: Penguin, 2002, p. 135.
51 Dilwar Hussain, personal interview with the author, London, June 2006.
52 C. Tilly, S. Tarrow, *Contentious Politics*, Boulder, CO: Paradigm Publishers, 2006.
53 Q. Wiktorowicz, "The Salafi Movement: Violence and Fragmentation of Community," in M. Cooke, B. Lawrence (eds), *Muslim Networks from Hajj to Hip Hop*, Chapel Hill, NC: University of North Carolina Press, 2005, p. 210; D. Snow, E. B. Rochford, Jr., S. K. Worden, R. D. Benford, "Frame Alignment Processes, Micromobilization, and Movement Participation," *American Sociological Review* 51, 1986, pp. 464–481.
54 R. Inglehart, *Culture Shift in Advanced Industrial Society*, Princeton, NJ: Princeton University Press, 1990.

55 Wiktorowicz, op. cit., p. 211.
56 Roy, op. cit., p. 317.
57 Gerges, op. cit., p. 229.
58 Kepel, op. cit., p. 151.
59 Gerges, op. cit., p. 40.
60 E. Sciolino, E. Schmitt, "A Not Very Private Feud Over Terrorism," *New York Times*, June 8, 2008. www.nytimes.com/2008/06/08/weekinreview/08sciolino.html
61 M. Sagemen, *Leaderless Jihad: Terror Networks in the 21st Century*, Philadelphia, PA: University of Pennsylvania Press, 2008.
62 Roy, op. cit., p. 323.

CHAPTER 8

Towards post-Islamism? Globalization and Muslim politics

The success of Islamists in the wake of the 2010–11 Arab Uprisings seemed to confirm the dominance of political Islam as a sociopolitical force in the Middle East. Combined with the rise of Turkey's AKP (see Chapter 4) and the routinized participation of Islamist parties in electoral politics across the Arab world, South Asia, and Southeast Asia, there seems to be strong evidence that religiously based parties have become a firm fixture in Muslim politics. Moreover, there seems to be a growing consensus that Islamists have reached an accommodation with at least the procedural aspects of democracy—that is, participating in and respecting the results of elections—and that political Islam would likely grow in significance as these groups find ever more opportunities to compete for political support.

But is there not perhaps also a very different story to tell about Islamism and future trajectories of Muslim politics? For some years now there have been a group of scholars wondering whether we might have entered the age of "post-Islamism." With political Islam so prominent in world news headlines, it would seem on the face of it that anyone talking about post-Islamism is out of touch with reality. When we look at their arguments as part of a broader analysis of how Muslim politics have evolved over the course of the past generation, however, the advocates of post-Islamism seem to be standing on firmer ground. This chapter reviews the debate on post-Islamism, and asks whether the analytic paradigm it provides might be a useful way of understanding the future of Muslim politics in a world defined largely by the impact of globalization. It begins with an overview of post-Islamism as a concept, examining the arguments of major proponents and critics alike. Since post-Islamism is associated with the idea of the individualization of religious experience and activism (versus e.g. membership in formal political organizations), we then move on to an analysis of the politics surrounding changes in the nature of how Muslims around the world are thinking about the question of religious authority in Islam. This is approached primarily through an analysis of the discourse of prominent contemporary Islamic voices and thought leaders based in the realm of satellite television and other forms of new media. The chapter concludes with some thoughts on how these media-based networks of new Islamic voices and their followers might be thought of as a form of "new social movement" that has the potential to reshape the nature—and future—of Islamic activism and Muslim politics.

POST-ISLAMISM: A CONCEPT AND ITS CRITICS

The concept of post-Islamism is most commonly associated with the "French School" of Islamist analysis—namely Olivier Roy and Gilles Kepel. Roy initiated the debate in 1992—without yet, however, using the term "post-Islamist"—with his book *The Failure of Political Islam*.[1] In this work he claimed that the failure of Islamists to advance their agenda through successfully obtaining state power was evidence that the movement had failed. Furthermore, the fact that some of them had begun to participate within pluralistic political systems as if their candidacy represented just another option among many (rather than God-given, indisputable normativity) was also seen as evidence that Islamism had become "domesticated" and had moved so far away from its initial formulations as to have become irreparably diluted. Even after Islamist parties triumphed in elections and assumed state power in the aftermath of the 2011 Arab Uprisings, Roy argues that his post-Islamism thesis continues to hold true since, as he sees it, the Islamists in Tunisia and Egypt have failed to offer a distinctive ideological vision.[2]

In a subsequent 2004 book-length elaboration, this time framed explicitly in terms of "post-Islamism," Roy provides a more thorough sociological account of how and why Islamism is changing.[3] In addition to the failure of Islamists to gain state power and their willingness to participate in political processes, Roy sees evidence of our entry into the era of post-Islamism in the following factors.

- Islamist movements are now almost universally **nationalist in orientation**, and have mostly dropped the rhetoric of pan-Islamic solidarity and *umma*-based identity. In other words, the world system of nation-states is no longer contested.

- There is *no geostrategic value* to accrue from pursuing an Islamist path, in the sense that the global system as it is currently configured rewards those who conform to the norms of free markets and democracy rather than the requirements of *shari'ah*.
- Even where they do contest elections, there is *no "Muslim vote"* on which Islamists can reliably depend; Muslims at the polls tend to vote their interests rather than their religious identities.
- By emphasizing democracy and civil society while trying to enter the political field, Islamists have contributed to the *inadvertent modernization and secularization* of their societies.
- Contemporary *"re-Islamization" is about the privatization of religion* and the triumph of individualistic conceptions of piety and the sacred over collective and socially mobilized Islamist projects. Religion and politics are here redefined as autonomous spheres.

For Roy, then, the utopian vision of the original Islamists has slowly dissolved over the years such that today, Islamism represents little more than a group of socially conservative political parties that are qualitatively indiscernible from any other political current.[4] He sees Islamist parties as having been worn down and more or less oppressed into political integration—to a point that they have actually, in some cases, become more open to democratic ideals than the authoritarian states that seek to control them.[5] The revolutionary edge of Islamism, in his analysis, has given way to accommodation within the existing system and—likewise—the rhetoric of social justice has disappeared from Islamist discourse.[6] Even quasi-revolutionary Islamists have turned on their own project when it appeared to interfere with national interests. Roy sees Sudanese President Bashir's jailing of Islamist ideologue Hassan al-Turabi and his subsequent initiation of peace talks with leaders of the Southern Sudanese People's Liberation Army as evidence of this.[7] Even the Taliban in Afghanistan, he points out, did not bother to create a strong, centralized Islamic state even though it had free reign to do so.[8] And in recent years, even some of the former jihadi groups have displayed a willingness to form political parties and contest democratic elections (see Chapter 4). With regard to the heightened public religiosity visible in many Muslim countries, Roy sees nothing to favor the fortunes of Islamism. He sees this phenomenon—"re-Islamization," in his terms—primarily as the triumph of privatized, individualistic religion over socially mobilized, political struggle. It is worth quoting him at length on this since we will want to return to some of his specific language when we later move on to a critical discussion of the post-Islamist argument:

> Contemporary re-Islamization is a cluster of individual practices that are used as a means of finding jobs, money, respect, and self-esteem, and bargaining with a marginalized state that has played on conservative

re-Islamization but been unable to control it. The reference to Islam is everywhere and nowhere; it is diluted, pragmatically put forward for any purpose, ostensibly expressed in dress and speech, and instrumentalized in courts. In this sense . . . re-Islamization has nothing to do with state power and could not be labeled "totalitarian" . . . The aim [of re-Islamization] is to reconstruct a true Muslim community by starting from the individual. It is based on an individual reappropriation of Islamic symbols, arguments, rhetoric and norms.[9]

Gilles Kepel, arguing essentially along the same lines in an essay entitled "Islamism Reconsidered," points out that Islamists today will frequently deploy the language of universal human rights rather than advancing Islamic alternatives.[10] He points also to the lack of a clear and cohesive program on the part of Islamists, citing the fact that their discourse appears variously and simultaneously to contain elements of both a reactionary rightist politics (moral structures, *shari'ah,* veiling) and an emancipatory progressive agenda (social justice, anti-hegemony).[11] He also echoes Roy's point to the effect that the paths followed by some Islamists appear to have led toward greater secularization. "Paradoxically," Kepel argues, "the Islamist movement may have generated the conditions for its own obsolescence."[12]

There are a range of comments and objections that might be offered in response to Roy's (and, by extension, Kepel's) characterization of the post-Islamist condition. We should begin, however, by asking what their understanding of post-Islamism tells us about how they view Islamism, politics, and religion more generally. It is clear that for Roy, Islamism refers only to projects that seek to achieve an Islamization of the social order by capturing state power. In this regard, and bearing in mind what we learned in Chapter 3, it is tempting to wonder if this is too narrow a conceptualization of Islamism. Certainly there have been in the past, and, indeed, continue to exist today, Islamists who understand their goals primarily in terms of achieving state power. In the early days of the Muslim Brotherhood and Jama'at-i Islami, however, both of these movements saw themselves as seeking first and foremost the Islamization of society. It is only when, in their view, the state began to interfere with this process and to suppress their activities that some Islamists movements shifted toward a more conventionally political stance. In short, Islamism has always had within it multiple and sometimes contradictory strands of thought and action. Thus we are led to agree with Salwa Ismail when she suggests that "before declaring the advent of post-Islamism, we should question the assumption that Islamism was ever coherent and homogenous."[13]

Roy is correct to point out that many Islamists have dropped their rhetoric to the effect that it is not possible to compromise with Islam when it comes to participation in the political sphere, and are now happy to take what they can get when it comes to finding support from electorates or would-be political partners.[14] Islamists now make a case for their agenda based on the interests of voters rather than simply, as they often did in the past, stating the inherent superiority of their approach because of its basis in Islam. But does this necessarily mean we have entered a post-Islamist phase? Many of these groups continue to call for laws to be made compatible with the *shari'ah*. Is this still not a gradualist manifestation of an Islamism that ultimately aspires to control the institutions of government? Roy continues to get hung up on the idea that an Islamic order can only come to pass by Islamist movements holding state power. In this regard he misses both "nonpolitical" paths to the Islamization of the social order and also the possibility that in some Islamist visions, the modern state may be viewed not as a goal to capture, but as an obstacle to true Islamization. This is why we must question his depiction of the Taliban's lack of enthusiasm for establishing a strong central state as evidence of their post-Islamist character. Could it not be that in the Taliban version of Islamism, modern centralized political power was viewed as un-Islamic? That they fired half of the country's civil servants and bureaucrats upon taking power would suggest that they harbored considerable contempt for the instruments of modern political power.

Some observers have suggested that Roy stops short of recognizing the presence of Islamism when actors and movements stop short of centralized power, because his understanding of Islamism is calibrated in terms of a homology with revolutionary movements of the left.[15] What Kepel sees as a lack of clear program within the Islamist movement should not be seen as indicative of its having lost its way, but rather of the fact that Islamism has always been somewhat ambiguous when placed on a traditional spectrum of politics understood in terms of right and left. As we pointed out earlier in this volume, it is the fact that elements of both rightist and leftist thought have always sat comfortably within Islamism that, in many ways, permitted it to survive in political landscapes subject to strongly shifting winds. As to Roy's claim that "social justice" has disappeared from the rhetoric of Islamism, one need only to think of those Islamists—such as Tariq Ramadan—who have joined the anti-globalization movement in the name of Islamic social justice, or of the popularity of political parties that emphasize social justice as a form of anti-corruption discourse (e.g. AKP in Turkey and JPD in Morocco). Certainly some of the meanings have changed with the withering of traditional leftist politics, but this does not mean that the symbols have lost their potency. Likewise, simply because an Islamist movement endorses the values contained within "non-Islamic" normative discourses—e.g. human rights or freedom of expression—this does not mean that they have abandoned Islamism. To suggest that this is the case, as Kepel does, would imply the impossibility of any kind of "overlapping consensus" between Islamic values and the morality of other systems.[16] Similarly, when Islamists criticize the positions and policies of other Islamists, they are not necessarily undermining the integrity of Islamism as a whole. Indeed, some have interpreted this ability to engage in "auto-critique" or "auto-reform" to represent a further maturing of the Islamist project, rather than its demise.[17]

Salwa Ismail points out that Roy's conceptualization of post-Islamism reveals considerable poverty in his understanding of the political.[18] His dismissal of "morality-based activism," as represented by the re-Islamization trend (private/individualist), suggests that he relies on an overly materialist conception of politics in which political efficacy is understood to equate exclusively with participation in formal, institutionalized structures (legislatures, elections, etc.).[19] Ismail urges us instead to interpret the entry of symbolic and normative contestation into the social realm as the opening of new spaces for the conduct of politics, rather than as the abandonment of the political.[20] The Islamist socialization of the civil societal realm in countries such as Egypt, for example, has certainly given rise to the dissemination of normative codes and practices that would not gain the official approval of the state and hence take on a distinctly political character.[21] What we are dealing with, then, is not an absence of the political, but rather a situation of comparative hegemony—with the state totalizing the space of the political, and Islamism reigning in the societal realm.

Ismail's critique of post-Islamism à la Roy also gets us some of the way toward a better understanding of the point made above about how we can read, in globalization and everyday practice within Muslim society, the creation of new spaces of the political. Islamism, on this interpretation, does not abandon politics, but rather pursues the political through functionally differentiated spaces, taking advantage of existing and new social practices—often, as we have seen, far more effectively than the state is able to. As Ismail puts it:

> The fundamental argument here is that the strategies used by Islamists intertwine with existing forms of social organization. The modalities of constituting power and authority are articulated internally, out of the structural arrangements and the strategic choices of actors. Inasmuch as they are part of the fabric, it is natural that many of the Islamists have adapted strategies that are the same as those pursued by the communities in which they have been active.[22]

Therefore we should not regard the movement of symbols and signs related to Islam into the realm of the social as, in Roy's terms, the "banalization" of Islam. He seems to view the association of religious symbols with everyday practices as representing a movement away from "real" religion—suggesting, as Ismail claims, that he has very particular ideas about what counts as Islamic and un-Islamic practices—or "real Islam."[23] She would rather we view this process not as one where religion becomes subjugated to the logic of the social, or its normative priority de-emphasized in favor of other codes. Rather, "this process must be understood in terms of the interaction of religion with the social as entailed in the mobilization of particular religious traditions and their reworking and re-insertion into new domains."[24]

Other writers respond to Roy from a different angle. Francois Burgat, for example, suggests that the movement of Islam from the political into the social sphere is hardly a "new" finding indicating the advent of a new phase beyond Islamism. He points out that much of the literature on Islamism for the past several decades has been emphasizing the Islamist occupation of the social sphere as a constitutive feature of Islamist practice and a vital aspect of their political strength.[25] Through their domination of society, Burgat argues, "Islamists implacably continue to be both advance guard and main body of mobilized activity."[26] He also argues that it is not possible to say that Islamism has been defeated until we can identify an alternative political ideology and social force possessed of the same mobilizing potential.[27] This latter point is perhaps somewhat weaker in that we might counter to the effect that if "liberal autocratic" states such as Egypt have succeeded in thoroughly regulating the practice of democratic politics (and democratic language games in the public sphere), and if the Islamists are now operating primarily in a democratic mode, then the state is, in effect, controlling the Islamists.

Another observer of post-Islamism, Asef Bayat—who was actually the first to coin and use the term—argues that we need to differentiate between two versions of this concept.[28] The first of these sees post-Islamism as a condition whereby Islamists come to question the efficacy and legitimacy of their own ideology, and thus begin hemorrhaging support from their core constituency.[29] This is very much the sense in which Roy and Kepel use the term. However, Bayat also sees in post-Islamism the name of a normative project: "a conscious attempt to conceptualize and strategize the rationale and modalities of transcending Islamism in social, political, and intellectual domains. Yet post-Islamism is neither anti-Islamic, un-Islamic, nor is it secular."[30] Bayat first used the term in relation to post-revolutionary Iran during the period of Hashemi Rafsanjani's rule, whereby the latter sought to work through some of the apparent contradictions between Islam as implemented in the system of the Islamic Republic and that country's ability to pursue national development (see Chapter 5). In contemporary usage, however, Bayat seems to associate the term more closely with forms of political discourse that look like what some have termed "progressive Islam."[31] We see this when Bayat tells us that post-Islamist movements are now about "emphasizing rights instead of duties, plurality in place of a single authoritative voice, historicity rather than fixed scriptures . . . [they] acknowledge, in other words, ambiguity, multiplicity, inclusion, and compromise in principles and practice."[32] He also makes the important point that Islamism and post-Islamism are not zero-sum conditions. It is quite possible, he asserts, for Muslims to partake simultaneously in aspects of both practices.

Another way to think about post-Islamism is to equate this trend with a transformation in how Muslims think about religiously inspired social activism, and shifts in how and where they undertake such activity. The post-Islamism we have in mind here, then, is not one that describes the demise of efforts to establish an Islamic social order. It is most definitely not, as Roy and Kepel seem to see it, the acceptance by Islamists of Francis Fukuyama's thesis regarding the "end of history"—whereby all competitors of capitalism and liberal democracy (including Islamism) have been vanquished.[33] Rather, this approach to moving beyond Islamism is about the transformation of the Islamist project into a strategy whereby the pursuit of Muslim politics occurs across a wide variety of spheres and domains. Post-Islamism, that is, not as the abandonment of Muslim politics, but rather as their reconstitution in forms more suited to a globalized world—a world in which, we might want to suggest, the state is only one among many sites of the political.

GLOBALIZATION AND MUSLIM POLITICS

How has globalization affected the nature of Muslim politics? The preceding chapters have certainly drawn attention, where relevant, to how changing political economies—a common component of the globalization narrative—have interacted with the evolution of political Islam in particular national settings. In the context of post-Islamism, however, we will want to link globalization to a different set of explanatory factors. Insofar as globalization is associated with a decline in state capacity and the emergence of alternative forms of polity and social formation, it helps us to focus on the ways in which post-Islamism is associated with networked forms of social movement that accumulate and exert social power outside the realm of the state. But the globalization story becomes most relevant in connection with a different aspect of post-Islamism. Olivier Roy's emphasis on the individualization of religiosity under conditions of post-Islamism leads us to ask questions about how individual Muslims source and consume religious knowledge and the communicative processes through which they make it relevant to their daily lives. For this reason, our discussion below focuses primarily on the question of how globalization shapes Islamic authority and the production of religious knowledge.

In this section we examine various dimensions of religious authority in the contemporary Muslim world in relation to processes of globalization. This includes looking at the rise of new voices and claims to Islamic authority, and how they relate to the persistence and transformation of traditional sources of religious knowledge. Particular attention is paid to the emergence of networked models of religious authority and the increasingly transnational relationships upon which they are premised. The role of new media and ICTs is also examined, and this leads on to a discussion of how we might be seeing today not only a shift in the location and nature of Islamic authority, but also a transformation in how and why Muslims seek and make use of religious knowledge.

We should begin by briefly reviewing what we mean when talking about globalization as a set of transformational processes. In Chapter 1 we touched on various sociological and economic accounts of globalization, and outlined some of the concrete manifestations of globalization in the world. We associated globalization primarily with the increased interconnectedness and extension of social relations over world-space, and the rise of a world economy premised on neoliberal norms. In terms of how globalization manifests itself in the world, there are three dimensions in particular to be mentioned as a preface to our discussion of Islamic authority.

- *Structural interdependence*—the interpenetration of markets, economies, and policy spheres has meant that national and local settings are increasingly implicated in decision-making processes (political, fiscal, etc.) that occur elsewhere. At the individual level, this entails a greater level of "exposure" to external risks and outcomes, and a higher level of awareness and sensitivity to the world as a single social, political, and economic space.[34] In the developing world, in particular, this has focused attention on global structures of socioeconomic inequality and power asymmetries.
- *Transnational "people flows"*—under globalizing conditions there has been a distinct increase in the number and frequency of peoples moving across borders. This is primarily for purposes of labor migration, and can involve both guest-worker schemes and semi-permanent or permanent settlement. Temporary professional and educational travel is more common today, alongside leisure travel and tourism. The prevalence of civil wars in weak and failing states has also meant an enormous increase in the number of refugees and asylum seekers moving over frontiers and seeking refuge abroad.
- *New media and information technologies*—with the advent of long-distance and wireless telephony, satellite television, and the internet, it has become progressively easier and less expensive for greater numbers of people to communicate across borders. Furthermore, a number of these technologies also reduce the barriers associated with reaching mass audiences, such that individuals can more easily "broadcast" and groups with shared interests can create and sustain networks even when geographically dispersed.

It is also important to situate these phenomena within the wider context of global political and economic modernization in order to understand their implications in terms of how people understand their political identities and interests. Particularly in the developing world, where most of the world's Muslims live, modernizing processes and the mixed experience that many populations have had with them have been at the root of much of the politics we looked at in Chapters 4 and 5. As socioeconomic expectations rose within an emerging and newly enfranchised (in educational and economic, if not necessarily political, terms) middle class, a growing sense of frustration at the reproduction of global structures of inequality within their own domestic spheres has been, in many cases, the hallmark experience of modernization in the developing world. The persistence of relatively high levels of authoritarianism (often operated through traditional and informal structures of social power—e.g. tribes, clans, ruling families) has led to a sense of political inefficacy among populations unable to hold their leadership accountable for failed policies. This is the backdrop against which we have to consider the three manifestations of globalization outlined above and what they might mean in terms of new opportunities for political activities and a new role for religious authority within these politics.

BOX 8.1 THE DANISH CARTOON AFFAIR

In September 2005, the Danish newspaper *Jyllands Posten* published a series of cartoon depictions of Muhammad, the Prophet of Islam. Most famous among them was an image depicting the turban on Muhammad's head as a bomb. Several months after the publication of the cartoons, protests broke out in a number of Muslim countries almost simultaneously (an interesting globalization story in itself, involving the internet, satellite TV, and transnational activist networks). Angered by what they perceived as an attack on the Prophet and an insult to Islam at a time when global tensions were high in the aftermath of the 9/11 attacks and the U.S. invasion of Iraq, rioters attacked Danish embassies, and several countries initiated an embargo on Danish goods. In Europe, the "Danish cartoon affair" prompted a debate about how to strike a balance between freedom of speech and respect for cultural difference. It also fuelled an ongoing debate about whether the values of Europe's rapidly growing Muslim community were compatible with Western norms.

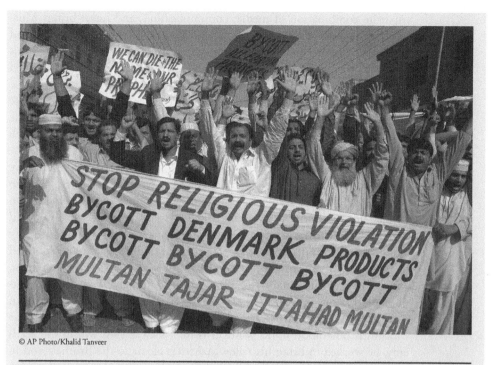

© AP Photo/Khalid Tanveer

Figure 8.1 Pakistani protesters rally against Denmark to show their anger against the reproduction of cartoons depicting the Prophet Muhammad in Danish newspapers, March 7, 2008, in Multan, Pakistan

Authorities old and new: Global *ulama* and new religious intellectuals

Let us turn more specifically to the question of Islamic religious authority in the context of globalization, considering some of the ways transnational people flows, new media, and greater structural interdependence in the world might be having an impact within various spheres of Muslim politics. In the first instance there are a number of fairly straightforward points to be made about a greater sense of awareness amongst Muslims of the issues and challenges facing their co-religionists, and of the multiple interpretations and understandings of their religion. Through media, communication, and travel, a greater consciousness of "Muslim issues" can develop, and this potentially has a tremendous impact on the sorts of politics people take an interest in, and where they turn to for guidance and leadership in address-ing these issues—a question we looked at in Chapter 7 with regard to radical movements, and one we return to again below. Second, the same tripartite combination of media, communication, and travel brings Muslims into contact with an increasingly diverse range of interpretations and practices of Islam, and the voices of authority that represent them. This makes it possible for a Muslim living in a particular setting to be exposed simultaneously to certain messages circulating in his or her local mosque community, and a quite different—perhaps even contradictory—discourse emanating from the *ulama* of a religious show on satellite TV, or an online religious chat room. Moreover, the new ideas encountered may very well come from outside the *ulama* or the religious establishment.

In discussing the *ulama* in Chapters 2 and 3, we indicated both a relative decline in their social influence since the early twentieth century, and also the phenomenon of secular national states intruding on, and seeking to co-opt, their authority to speak on behalf of Islam. But we have also noted that religious scholars remain a vitally important source of Islamic authority alongside new competing voices. How have the traditional *ulama* responded to globalization and the rise of new transnational voices—many of them, such as Usama Bin Laden—highly radical and militant? Perhaps the paradigmatic case is to be found in that of Sheikh Yusuf al-Qaradawi. An Egyptian trained at Al-Azhar, Qaradawi was closely associated with the Muslim Brotherhood in his younger years. As an activist within the academy, he worked to bring his fellow Azharites closer to the Brotherhood in terms of their thinking and goals. Jailed as part of the government's crackdown on the Islamists in 1954, he left Egypt soon after and has since made his career abroad. Based for many years now in the Gulf Sheikhdom of Qatar (where he serves as Dean of the Shari'ah Faculty at Qatar University), Qaradawi has developed a reputation as an independent scholar untainted by association with state power. Although he is no longer formally associated with the MB, many MB members still regard his thinking as the pre-eminent scholarly manifestation of the Brotherhood tradition today.[35]

Qaradawi rose to regional fame among a mainstream audience in the late 1990s through his program on the Al-Jazeera satellite program, *Shari'ah w'al-Hayat* (*Shariah and Life*). We describe the show in greater detail below, but the important thing to note for now is Qaradawi's ability to discuss, and offer opinions on, a wide range of contemporary and "modern" issues (science and technology, globalization, health, etc.) while still remaining firmly anchored within the classical traditions of Islamic learning. Qaradawi's appeal, however, is not limited to the Arab world—indeed, in many regards he represents the best example today of a thoroughly global *alim*. His works have been translated into dozens of languages and can be found on the bestseller shelves of Islamic bookstores from Los Angeles to Cape Town to Jakarta. He has developed a particular following among Muslim communities in the West, especially in Europe. Muslims living in the West, where Islam is a minority religion and reliable sources of religious knowledge can be hard to find, have often sought ways to find Islamically

Figure 8.2 Yusuf al-Qaradawi speaks on Al-Jazeera satellite television

© Esam Al-Fetori / Reuters

"authentic" solutions to the unique issues and problems they face as religious minorities. Qaradawi's aforementioned ability to bridge these two worlds explains in great measure his appeal to European Muslims.

Interestingly, Qaradawi has actively sought to cater for this and others among his various global publics. Over the past decade he has worked to establish something like a global infrastructure for the dissemination of his particular religious worldview. Actively embracing technologies that would have made Jamal al-Din al-Afghani, his pan-Islamist forebear, green with envy, Qaradawi has established institutions and research centers such as the European Council for Fatwa and Research in Ireland, designed expressly to provide religiously sanctioned advice on a wide range of matters to Muslims living in Europe. A popular bilingual website, *Islamonline.net*, also operates under his general guidance. In the early 2000s he led efforts to establish an International Union of Muslim Scholars that seeks to unite *ulama* from a wide range of sectarian backgrounds—Sunni, Shi'i, *Ibadi, Yazidi*, etc.—in the name of global Islamic ecumenism. He also played a prominent role in the 2005 International Islamic Conference held in Amman, Jordan. At this event, a multi-sectarian gathering of religious scholars issued a joint statement that sought to reassert the authority of the *ulama* to pronounce on matters of religion. More specifically, it emphasized the un-Islamic character of the practice of *takfir*, that is, excommunication or the declaration of other Muslims as infidels. This latter piece was clearly an effort by mainstream *ulama* to counter the radical discourse of Salafi–jihadi voices that seek to apostatize any Muslim who disagrees with their views. It also provides us with a way of reading the overall trajectory of Qaradawi's discourse and worldview. In the wake of Egypt's 2011 revolution, Qaradawi returned triumphantly to Cairo to lead prayers in Tahrir Square but did not play an active role in that country's turbulent transitional politics.

We can perhaps best think of Qaradawi's overall enterprise as an attempt to "re-center" Islam for a global audience.[36] This is an approach that seeks to pull Muslims back from both of the extremes mentioned at the opening of this chapter, radical militancy and progressive liberalism alike. Qaradawi exhorts Muslims toward moderation, reminding them that the Qur'an figures Muslims as a "community of the middle." Qaradawi is both popular and controversial because he straddles the line between different camps. Salafis and ultra-conservative literalists find him "too modern" and overly willing to engage extensively and borrow ideas from non-Muslims, while liberals find many of his views far too conservative and "traditional." Some of his views have also been politically controversial. While his has been one of the loudest and most consistent voices condemning acts of terrorism such as the 9/11 attacks, he has also stated in the past that Palestinian suicide attacks on Israeli civilians are legitimate—prompting some Western governments, including the United States, to place him beyond the pale. It is undoubtedly the case, however, that figures such as Qaradawi are working to put the likes of Al-Qaeda out of business. For most Muslims his is a voice of authentic moderation and centrism, and yet it still advocates an Islam (and, moreover, an Islam*ism*) that most secular liberals find repugnant. This has placed many advocates of political liberalism in a significant conundrum when trying to figure out how, and whether to, engage with Qaradawi. As a figure of undisputed authority representing the views of a great many moderate (in the sense of rejecting violence) Muslims, he would appear to be a prime interlocutor. Many of his more controversial and conservative views, however, make some (in the West, at least) hesitant to do so.

But perhaps it does not make sense to place so much emphasis or importance on a single individual. Indeed, in some ways Qaradawi's greatest influence lies in the political potential inherent within the generation of young Muslims—many of them living in the West—who have internalized his core ideas, but who reject certain of his views. Many of them have read Qaradawi primarily as someone who shows them the possibility of being modern and authentically Islamic at the same time. Their politics are premised primarily on active participation as citizens of particular nation-states, rather than an Islamist project seeking to overturn the political order.

Qaradawi's "engaged *alim*" approach is not the only form of Islamic authority that has been making waves among modern, educated Muslims.

Authors such as Olivier Roy have spoken about the rise of what he calls "new Islamist intellectuals."[37] These are individuals who are often highly educated, but not trained as religious scholars in the traditional sense. Indeed, they may often be specialists in fields such as science and engineering, and capable of formulating a religious discourse that appeals to others who share their background far more effectively than the traditional approach of classically trained *ulama*. Many of these new religious intellectuals are largely self-taught in terms of their religious knowledge, but manage to find supporters by articulating religion in a vernacular that resonates with the times. Roy distinguishes these figures both from *ulama*—whose authority is premised on the systematic and methodical exegesis of texts, but rejected by the new religious intellectuals as either too obscure or allied with the state—and from Westernized Muslim intellectuals who appear to have abandoned the sacredness of the text, treating it as an object readily open to critical inquiry as if it had the same status as any other text. It is worth quoting Roy at length to better understand the political implications of this mode of knowledge production:

> The state has no means by which it can control the new Islamist intellectual in his social function. His thought does not correspond to his social position, he does not live from his profession, the networks of his activities are on the fringe of institutions, when they are not entirely clandestine. He operates in remote places (meeting houses, sites of worship, educational centers) and in spaces outside of the traditional society that the state has not resocialized (the new suburbs).
>
> The new intellectual has an autodidactic relationship to knowledge. Knowledge is acquired in a fragmented (manuals, excerpts, popular brochures), encyclopedic, and immediate manner: everything is discussed without the mediation of an apprenticeship, a method, or a professor . . . The new media, such as radio, television, cassettes, and inexpensive offset brochures, make snatches of this content available. The new intellectual is a tinkerer; he creates a montage, as his personal itinerary guides him, of segments of knowledge, using methods that come from a different conceptual universe than the segments he recombines, creating a totality that is more imaginary than theoretical.[38]

Who, then, are these new Islamist intellectuals? We have already seen many of them in earlier chapters. Hassan al-Banna and, to some extent, Sayyid Qutb (see Chapter 3) from the MB were key progenitors of this mode. Ali Shariati (see Chapter 5), ideologue of Iran's Islamic revolution, is also a prime example here—cobbling together elements of Marxism and Islam across a matrix of modernity's *mustadafin* ("dispossessed"). We might even regard Usama Bin Laden (Chapter 7) as new Islamic intellectualism taken to its most radical extreme.

Where Roy has focused on the role that new Islamist intellectuals have played in building the social base of conventional Islamist movements such as the MB, others have drawn our attention to the role played by a different kind of intellectual in fostering reformist and progressive approaches to Islam.[39] These are the various "reformist" scholars of contemporary Islam, figures who would usually fall into Roy's category of Westernized intellectual—although such categorizations in this case cannot always be made so quickly or easily, particularly if they are understood to entail an abandonment of faith. A great many of the reformist Muslim scholars working today—figures such as Abdolkarim Soroush in Iran (see Chapter 5), Fatima Mernissi in Morocco, Muhammad Shahrur in Syria, the late Nurcholish Madjid in Indonesia, and Amina Wadud or Ebrahim Moosa in the United States—have developed highly innovative and pluralistic interpretations of Islam that combine a variety of Islamic and Western sources and methods. While many of them have considerable followings in the Western academy (and, sometimes much to their chagrin, Western capitals), the highly intellectualized and theoretically complex style of their academic discourse renders their work largely inaccessible to most Muslims.[40]

Not all of these new religious intellectuals can be defined as clearly "Islamist" or "liberal-modernist" in orientation. Some of them advance a religious discourse that bridges aspects of both approaches. One such "hybrid" figure of particular importance is the Turkish populist preacher and religious entrepreneur, Fethullah Gülen (see Box 8.2, "The Gülen 'movement': A product of globalization?"). The vast social movement structured around Gülen embodies elements of Sufi personal renewal and orthodox pietism combined with an emphasis on modern education, wealth generation, and Turkish nationalism. Drawing on the teachings of the early twentieth-century reformer Bediüzzaman Said Nursi (d. 1960) and the subsequent Nurçu movement, Gülen has sought to combine Islamic ethics with modern (secular) education. His works consist of a number of books that are closely read by his followers and disciples and, more concretely, an attempt to export his distinctive model of the Muslim society via a vast network of schools concentrated in Turkey, Central and Southeastern Europe, and Central Asia—but also found today all over the world including in Europe and North America. These schools are based on a secular curriculum of arts, sciences, and foreign languages, but the teachers in the schools are all generally members of the Gülen movement. While the Gülen movement is not itself directly involved in politics, there are at least two important political dimensions to its work. The first of these relates to linkages between the ruling AKP party in Turkey (see Chapter 4) and the Nurçu movement from which it, like the Gülen group, draws its base. The second aspect relates to a possible interpretation of the Gülen movement's longer-term goals. It has been noted by some observers that Gülen's religious thinking and normative practice is, at root, quite orthodox.[41] In other words, he is not interested in new, liberal interpretations of Islam. There are some who see in his schools and his targeting of possible future elites an attempt to "de-Kemalize" the Turkish establishment by creating a generation of public administrators and business leaders willing to allow more space for public religiosity. By emphasizing secular education, nationalism, and modernity in his schools, he operates in ways the Kemalist state must respect—while still remaining grounded in, and offering supplementary education in, religion.

BOX 8.2 THE GÜLEN "MOVEMENT": A PRODUCT OF GLOBALIZATION?

© Reuters

Figure 8.3 Fetullah Gülen

Many followers of the Turkish religious leader Fethullah Gülen reject the idea that there is any such thing as a Gülen movement, preferring to view themselves as part of a religious community (*cemaat*) inspired by his teachings. Gülen's closest deputies insist that there is no "command-and-control" relationship between the man himself—resident since the 1990s in the United States—and the hundreds of schools inspired by his teachings and located around the globe. Regardless of how it is described, however, it is clear that the followers of Gülen have built a global infrastructure to advance their goals. Funded by significant donations of personal income from the Anatolian business figures who comprise some of Gülen's closest followers, the *cemaat's* network includes media outlets (newspapers and television), a university, a philanthropic wing, and many civil society organizations (research centers, professional syndicates, etc.) in addition to the schools for which it is best known.

Further study

J. Hendrick, *Gülen: The Ambiguous Politics of Market Islam in Turkey and the World*, New York: New York University Press, 2013.

H. Yavuz, *Toward an Islamic Enlightenment*, Oxford: Oxford University Press, 2013.

H. Yavuz, J.L. Esposito (eds), *Turkish Islam and the Secular State: The Global Impact of the Fethullah Gülen Nur Movement*, Syracuse, NY: Syracuse University Press, 2003.

Another important figure of this sort is Tariq Ramadan. Born in Switzerland, Ramadan is the grandson of MB founder Hassan al-Banna. Trained in both Western philosophy and traditional Islamic sciences, Ramadan emerged in the mid-1990s as a leading voice among young European Muslims. His core message was one of civic and social engagement, encouraging young Muslims in the West to participate in the mainstream life of their host societies rather than to "ghettoize" themselves, as had their parents during the first generations of Muslim immigration to Europe. While insisting that one's commitments as a Muslim and one's obligations as a citizen of, say, France were not mutually incompatible, Ramadan's work reveals an inevitable debt to his family's MB affiliations when he cites the importance of religion as a normative compass for public life—a position that put him at odds with the intellectual and policy-making establishments in France, and apparently also the United States when, in 2004, Washington DC denied him a work visa to take up a university professorship in the U.S. Ramadan has also emphasized the idea that Muslims living in the West are in a position to define the future of Islam by virtue of the freedoms that they enjoy. As a social activist, Ramadan has sought to draw connections between the Islamic emphasis on social justice and the general goals of the anti-globalization/global justice movement. Like Qaradawi, he is viewed by a growing constituency of admirers around the world as a Muslim intellectual who addresses the contemporary, lived experience of Islam in a globalizing world, while remaining "authentically Islamic" by virtue of his family's heritage and his emphasis on the continued importance of tradition and jurisprudence.

But whose religious discourse reigns supreme today—the *ulama* or the new religious intellectual? Of course there is no single answer here. What we have tried to draw attention to above is the changing nature of the relationship that modern individuals have with religious knowledge—not necessarily abandoning it, but producing and consuming it in new ways (more on this below). *Ulama* such as Yusuf al-Qaradawi have sought to adapt their discourse to these changing circumstances, actively incorporating modern questions and concerns into their scholarly deliberations. Indeed, Qaradawi has even warned in his work against the possible excesses of the new Islamist intellectuals when it comes to politics. While endorsing the idea of an Islamic "awakening" (*sahwa*—his term for the much-needed revival in public religious consciousness), he cautions that unless religious scholars play a role as partners or guides, those working with improvised religious knowledge are likely to get some things wrong at best, and even perhaps to turn violently radical.[42] While this is clearly a warning about "Bin Ladenism," we can also see *ulama* today seeking to reclaim a role for themselves in mainstream Islamism of the MB variety. Qaradawi, for example, has been working on a book project that takes Hassan al-Banna's teachings and expounds on them from the point of view of Islamic jurisprudence.

But how, we still want to ask, does an individual make sense of these multiple viewpoints and reconcile them with his or her self-understanding of Islam and experience of daily life? How are choices made about which of these several and quite discrepant paths, all of which are apparently prescribed and mandated by Islam, an individual Muslim will follow? These are questions that can be explored more fully by examining various aspects of contemporary Islam's listening publics and the distinct forms of post-Islamist politics in which they are implicated.

THE ROLE OF NEW MEDIA AND POPULAR ISLAM: A VIRTUAL UMMAH?

Much has been written about the impact of new media on Islam and politics in recent years, with various observers emphasizing very different aspects of this phenomenon. Some scholarly accounts have emphasized the pluralizing effects of new Muslim media spheres, while popular media coverage tends toward a focus on the internet as a space of radical Islamist networking, or satellite television as a conduit for Islamic terrorism.[43] Our purpose in what follows, however, is not to come to definitive conclusion about whether new media have a pluralizing or radicalizing effect on Muslim politics. Instead, we provide an analysis of how new communications technologies have had an impact not only on how and where Muslims seek religious authority, but also on how the communicative practice associated with new media correlate with the emergence of innovative forms of Islamic activism and social movement.

As Charles Hirschkind has argued, the scholarly debate about the impact of modernity and new media on religious practice has generally been framed in terms of two seemingly exclusive processes: media as permitting the extension of religion's disciplining and authoritative properties so as to facilitate conformity with a particular moral order; or media as opening new spaces of deliberation and a concomitant democratization of authority in the religious sphere.[44] While new arenas of religious discourse have certainly been created, this does not necessarily mean that the messages, values, and norms communicated within these spaces are also new. It can be argued that in many cases traditional forms of authority and articulation work very well in new media spaces, and indeed have used these spaces to reach out to an expanded audience base. In other cases, however, we find that new Muslim public spheres do allow for some level of pluralization in religious discourse, lowering the barriers to participation and permitting new figures to lay claim to Islamic authority. In the end, though, we cannot truly understand the impact of new media on Islamic authority without placing it in the context of changing patterns in terms of how Muslims understand and consume religion, and also the control and ownership of information sources.

Our account of new media and Islam picks up where we left off above when discussing the impact of mass education on the authority of the *ulama*. The central dynamic here is the same, but potentially even more radical: not just more and more Muslims having direct access to the primary sources of religious authority, but also the possibility that more and more Muslims can now put forward their own views on Islam before a mass audience. But first, a few words of clarification regarding what is meant here by "new media." While new technologies are certainly heavily implicated in the two main forms of new media we will be examining below—namely satellite television and the internet—the impact on religious authority has more to do with changing patterns of access to, and ownership of, the media than with the technologies themselves. Thus the "newness" of these media lies not just in the fact that they are often enabled by technological advancements, but also in the nature and structure of their social impact. Several dimensions or "effects" of this phenomenon are of particular significance, as follows.

- *The rise of mass audiences*—a phenomenon that begins with the printing press and the first wide-circulation newspapers, the ability of a particular message to reach mass audiences (in the hundreds of thousands if not millions) is today primarily associated with broadcast media such as television and satellite television, but also with new information technologies such as the internet.
- *Reduced production barriers*—not only are ever-larger audiences able to receive messages, but new media such as the internet also make it relatively easy for almost anyone to produce and disseminate information.
- *Proliferating spheres of participation*—the combination of the previous two effects makes for considerably increased conversation and deliberation across a multitude of communicative spheres. While not necessarily always democratizing or pluralizing in the sense of making space for disparate views to be heard and considered equally, scales of participation are markedly augmented. The advent of social media and various social network platforms—such as *Facebook* and *Twitter*—have served as significant force multipliers for this effect.
- *Changing patterns of ownership and control*—some new media forms make it possible to challenge or transcend prior forms of regulating access to information. Satellite television, for example, provides an alternative to state-owned channels—yet its content still remains subject to certain market considerations. The relatively low cost of setting up a presence on the internet and the ability to host it beyond the reach of state authorities make it possible for individuals and groups to have a political voice far less susceptible to official censorship.

In several places this book has already mentioned various examples of media becoming an integral part of Muslim politics. In Chapter 2, for example, we saw Jamal al-Din al-Afghani make extensive use of late-nineteenth-century "new media" to publish the journal *Al-Urwat al-Wuthqa* (*The Firmest Bond*) and circulate it to a transnational Muslim audience out of an office in Paris, France. Later we saw the important role that smuggled audio cassettes of Ayatollah Khomeini's sermons played in preparing the way for the 1979 Islamic Revolution in Iran, and also the "denial of service" tactics employed against Saudi government fax machines by the Islamist opposition in London. Lebanon's Hizbullah has its own satellite TV station, *Al-Manar*, and we have talked about the important role of Salafi–jihadi websites in sustaining the transnational radical movement.

Looking at more mainstream internet use among Muslims, there are a number of key points to make. The first of these is that, until relatively recently, it was possible to talk about the internet having an impact on Muslims only in the West. This is due to the fact that in most Muslim-majority countries, internet penetration rates are still very low (see Table 8.1). It was primarily in diasporic contexts that we began to see "Islamic" websites

Table 8.1 Internet penetration rates for select Muslim countries (% individuals using the Internet per country)

Afghanistan	5.5
Algeria	15.23
Bangladesh	6.3
Egypt	44.1
Indonesia	15.4
Iran	26
Iraq	7.1
Jordan	41
Kuwait	79.2
Kyrgyzstan	21.7
Lebanon	61.3
Libya	19.9
Malaysia	65.8
Morocco	55
Nigeria	32.8
Pakistan	10
Qatar	88
Saudi Arabia	54
Senegal	19.2
Sudan	21
Syria	24.3
Tunisia	41.4
Turkey	45.1
UAE	85
Uzbekistan	36.5
Yemen	17.5

Source: International Telecommunications Union (2012)

during the second half of the 1990s. These chat rooms, discussion boards, and portals emerged as alternative spaces for the discussion of religion and Muslim identity and as sources of information about the availability of religious services in contexts where access to such resources was often scarce. On the discussion boards associated with these sites could often be found various conversations and debates about the merits and defects of various schools of thought in Islam and their representative scholars. But Muslims would also put forward their own understandings and interpretation of various matters relating to religious practice, and also jurisprudence. In short, some of these forums became new spaces of *ijtihad,* no doubt greatly assisted by the fact that by the late 1990s it was possible to use a search engine to comb vast online databases of *hadith* and other key textual sources. Sites sprang up where users could submit by e-mail or online form a request for a *fatwa,* and a response would be received, also electronically, from a "scholar" of Islam. Given the anonymous nature of internet communications, however, it was often difficult to discern anything about the credentials of the *ulama* on the other side of these web portals. In at least one case it turned out that the scholar in question was an enterprising graduate student in engineering at a university in the southern United States who moonlighted as an *alim*.[45] The important point to be made here is that, in formal terms, the juridical opinions dispensed on these sites often looked very similar to those produced by scholars with formal training. These lay "experts" had learned to mimic the grammar and forms of juridical discourse and, with a thousand miles between them and their audience, were able to masquerade as bona fide *ulama*. Certainly there was a market waiting to be tapped: immigrant Muslims generally have less easy access to religious expertise, so it is not surprising that even once online *fatwa* services and satellite TV call-in shows were established in the Middle East, most of the queries came from Muslims living in the West.

This does not mean, however, that the traditional *ulama* ignored the advent of information technology. A great many Islamic universities quickly recognized the values of computerized storage as an archival medium, and began scanning many of the classical works of Islamic learning. Soon a number of websites associated with prominent *ulama* came online and it became possible to access a select range of their works and scholarly opinions online. One particularly important development in this area was the establishment of islamonline.net, a site associated with, and under the general guidance of, Sheikh Yusuf al-Qaradawi. Qaradawi's site, in both English and Arabic, has become very popular with Muslims in the West, since they perceive it as affiliated with a renowned figure of indisputable authority. Today, many of the major religious scholars from various sects and schools of thought have a presence on the web, with a particularly strong showing by major Shi'i figures such as the late Grand Ayatollah Ali Montazeri (www.amontazeri.com); Muhammad Hussein Fadlallah, regarded by many as the spiritual leader of Hizbullah (www.bayynat.org.lb); and Grand Ayatollah Ali Sistani in Iraq (www.sistani.org).

The form of new media that has had the most significance in the wider Muslim world, however, is undoubtedly satellite television. The Qatari-based Pan-Arab channel Al-Jazeera emerged in the late 1990s as the first of several satellite-based news channels (which now include Dubai's Al-Arabiya and Saudi Arabia's al-Ekhbariya) seeking to break the mold of standard state-controlled media in the Arab world. Al-Jazeera sought to define itself as an open, pluralistic, and uncensored forum through its slogan "*al-ra'i w'al-ra'i al-akhr*" ("one view, another view"). In addition to its continual news coverage, groundbreaking shows such as "*al-ittija al-muwakis*" ("the opposite direction") quickly won a mass following through their hard-hitting, critical discussion of current affairs. Arab audiences watched while, for the first time, government figures and other public authorities were subjected to no-holds-barred questioning regarding their policies and were forced to defend themselves. Unsurprisingly, the station ruffled some feathers among those governments targeted by its programming, prompting complaints to the Qatari authorities. To Arab audiences, however, this simply proved that a media outlet in their region was finally playing the critical and investigative role they had long hoped for.

It was also Al-Jazeera that first catapulted Sheikh Yusuf al-Qaradawi to widespread regional prominence. On the show *Shari'ah w'al-Hayat* (*Shari'ah and Life*), where he has been a mainstay, Qaradawi discusses all manner of topics, many of which—such as matters relating to medical technology and sex—are not the standard fare of religious television programming in the Arab world. Callers are invited to phone in with questions, and Qaradawi dispenses wisdom and guidance live on air for all to see. This program helped him to develop a unique reputation as a classical scholar of impeccable pedigree (he is a graduate of Al-Azhar University) and undisputed authority, but one who was willing to discuss and deliberate on "modern" subject matter and to help Muslims to see Islam as relevant to specific issues of the day. We should note that, despite the "interactive" phone-in component of Shari'ah w'al-Hayat, the show is still rather traditional in that it is structured around a revered religious authority dispensing knowledge; it is not a forum for the discussion of different interpretations of religion. As Jakob Skovgaard-Petersen puts it, "Yusuf al-Qaradawi represents the Shari'ah, and everybody else represents life."[46] In more recent years, satellite channels devoted exclusively to religious programming, such as Saudi Arabia's *Iqra*, have been established and launched the careers of a new generation of popular religious figures—not least of all the Islamic "televangelist" Amr Khaled (see below)—who serve up a rather different sort of religious television.

"Popular Islam": Piety, consumption, and public religion

The point above about websites as arenas for the discussion of competing interpretations of religion and scriptural sources helps us toward recognizing another important phenomenon associated with the migration of religious discourse and symbolic capital into spaces not formally constituted as "religious." Some scholars have noted how the introduction of religious commodities—posters, games, models, key chains, various talismans—into local economies of meaning have led to novel interpolations of "Muslimness" and modern life.[47] Others have looked more specifically at how the mass circulation and incorporation of certain media forms into everyday life have opened new spaces of public religion. Hirschkind, for example, has studied the impact of audio cassette recordings of sermons in Cairo, pointing out that, in many cases, the conveyance of authoritative speech from the mosque to the car or into the home does not represent simply a new extension of religion's disciplining power. He argues instead that these cassettes and the conversations they provoke often occasion considerable deliberation and debate regarding the boundaries of religious normativity. In this sense they create new Muslim public "counterpublics," in which listeners turn into active agents for the social production of religious knowledge and public religiosity.[48] Similar to what can be seen on the aforementioned website discussion boards, "reference to authoritative Islamic sources does not close debate. Instead, the lines of argument pivot precisely on the proper interpretation of those sources."[49]

Other examples allow us to take this insight further and—in keeping with the insights of the post-Islamism thesis—to ask questions about how the commodification and repackaging of religiosity may in fact also indicate a shift in how Muslims in certain settings understand and pursue political or socially transformative action in the name of Islam. Among Muslim communities in the West, for example, the commodified commingling of religious symbols and the aesthetics of youth culture have seen the emergence of product lines that might be associated with something like "cool Islam"—hip-hop music, clothes, comedy, etc. The American Muslim hip-hop act Native Deen and the British *nashid* (religious chant or song) singer Sami Yusuf represent this trend, as do various clothing lines such as Muslim Gear.[50] Beyond allowing one to be cool while being Muslim, some of these products also incorporate elements of religiously prescribed normativity, in effect subsuming the fulfillment of religious obligations within practices of consumption. We can cite the rise of "*hijab* fashion" as an example of this, and also the advent of retail schemes that permit Muslims to pay their *zakat* tithe by purchasing certain products that generate a percentage of their value in charitable donations. Jenny White, writing about Turkey, talks about what she terms the rise of a "Muslimhood" model that involves the use and consumption of objects imbued with religion (books, games, TV shows) in all aspects of everyday life.[51]

Some observers have seen in this a shift in the way Muslims understand the location and nature of doing politics. As Amel Boubekeur has noted:

> [T]he Islamic identity need no longer be represented as political, ideological, and institutional, but as the choice of an individual consumer . . . Where the traditional Islamist militancy was heavy, expensive, and very framed, the Islamic identity suggested by this new culture sets up mobilizations, identifications, modes of actions, and participation that is less expensive, less stigmatizing. The classical notions of Islamism, such as the sacrifice for the cause and the suffering, weak, and dominated disappear. What is proposed is the revalorization of the personal pleasure of consumption, success, and competitiveness.[52]

This trend is not confined to Muslims in the West. In the Arab world it can be seen, for example, in the meteoric rise of the television preacher Amr Khaled. With a purely secular educational background, Khaled's programs on the Saudi-owned Iqra religious channel owe a considerable debt to the style and discourse of American televangelists such as Billy Graham and Joel Osteen, and talk-show hosts such as Oprah Winfrey. We can best understand the phenomenon by contrasting Amr Khaled with previous idioms of religious television. Egypt's most popular TV *sheikh* through much of the 1990s had been the venerable Muhammad al-Sha'arawi. Broadcasting from a mosque in the traditional attire of a religious scholar, the aesthetics of his show were austere, sober, reverent—that is, *religious* according to the conventional style. Sha'arawi's discourse represented, for the most part, the Islam of the Egyptian state. This was an Islam of worship, piety, and morality—an Islam that belonged in the home, in the mosque, and in one's commitment to education, work, and family; politics, much less *jihad,* never entered the picture. With the rise of Al-Jazeera, this mold was broken by Yusuf al-Qaradawi, the former Muslim Brother broadcasting from beyond the reach of the Egyptian state. It is not so much that Qaradawi's discourse represented a direct and overt politicization of religion, but that he would pronounce on any and all topics that happen to be raised. Arab publics, unsurprisingly, had a lot of questions about the political implications of their religion and issues such as democracy, the legitimacy of various regimes, relations with the West, and the meaning and role of *jihad.*

© Dana Smillie/Bloomberg via Getty Images

Figure 8.4 Popular Egyptian television preacher Amr Khaled

If Sha'arawi was state Islam, and Qaradawi a voice of mainstream Islamism operating beyond the effective reach of state authority, Amr Khaled represents a third approach.[53] Gone are the turban and cloak of the *alim*, replaced instead by a young, clean-shaven man attired in a designer Western suit. His set is modern, ergonomic; it looks like *Oprah Winfrey*. The content and style of the program is very different from either of the *sheikhs*. Khaled does not preach, lecture, or offer religious opinions according to the norms of Islamic scholarly discourse. His speech is not characterized by pronouncements about whether various practices or behaviors are *halal* ("permissible") or *haram* ("forbidden") by the *shari'ah*. Amr Khaled's Islam is one of hope, prosperity, and the possibility of gaining God's love, favor, and forgiveness. It emphasizes piety, not simply as a matter of ritual obligation, but as a way in the world that complements the pursuit of personal success and affluence. As Tammam and Haenni argue:

> The secret of his success [is] that he position[s] himself outside the rivalry between political and official Islam, by offering a religious product compatible with the modern expectations of the urban middle classes: a worldly religion that talks about inner peace and spiritual well-being, and rejects religious observance in which rite is an end in itself. It refuses to see Allah as a God of retribution.[54]

Amr Khaled is not, however, a purveyor of liberal or progressive Islam; this is most certainly not an "Islam is whatever you make of it" approach. He emphasizes, for example, the importance of many traditional social norms associated with religion, such as the headscarf. But such observances need not involve renouncing the pleasures of life. Indeed, a good Muslim, on Khaled's account, should seek to acquire wealth and to make others want to emulate their success. This approach has earned Amr Khaled a tremendous following among the young, educated, socially mobile middle classes of Egypt and other Arab countries—particularly among women, who find in his gentleness and openness a refreshing contrast to the dour disposition of traditional *ulama*. Perhaps not surprisingly, Khaled has come in for considerable criticism from a variety of more traditionally religious camps. *Ulama* question his credentials and his authority to speak about matters of religion at all. For example, when Amr Khaled enjoined Muslims to enter into cultural dialogue with the West in the aftermath of the 2005–06 Danish Cartoon Crisis (see Box 8.1, "The Danish cartoon affair"), none other a personage than Yusuf al-Qaradawi questioned whether he possessed the qualifications to pronounce on what Muslims should do. The MB and figures associated with it—perhaps alarmed at the prospect of losing an entire generation to this new trend—have dismissed Amr Khaled as a representative of "air-conditioned Islam."[55] Tariq Ramadan, for instance, castigated him for avoiding difficult social and political issues, claiming that once viewers realize the superficiality of his religious discourse, they will abandon him in favor of a more socially engaged, activist Islam.

As regards the Egyptian state's attitude toward Amr Khaled, it would appear on the surface that his approach to religion is right in line with their desire to push a modernized and personalized form of Islam compatible with capitalism and economic growth. But the relationship is considerably more complicated than that, as evidenced by the fact that, several years after he began broadcasting, the Egyptian government told him to stop working or leave Egypt—leading Amr Khaled to move his headquarters to the United Kingdom for some years. What appears to have worried the Egyptian state is not so much the content of his programming, which—as we have seen—would be regarded as wholly innocuous, but rather the fact that his enormous following represents a base of potential social mobilization on a national scale. Some have expressed fears that he was actually working in conjunction with the MB—a wolf in sheep's clothing, so to speak—and that once the moment turned ripe, he would turn his followers to the cause of Islamism. Others, taking a warning from Tariq Ramadan's critique of Khaled, feared that a large segment of the latter's supporters would, once they had developed a taste for a more activist stance, desert Amr Khaled in favor of the Brotherhood. Whatever his larger intentions, if any, it is clear that Amr Khaled's project evolved in directions that took on more activist undertones. In his later program, *Suna'a al-Hayah* (*Lifemakers*), Khaled urged his viewers to channel their piety into social welfare and community development projects, and to send in accounts and video footage of their efforts so that they could be broadcast for all to see. It also provided an opportunity for networking between these "lifemakers" so as to enable them to leverage and scale up the impacts of each other's projects. This "taking Islam into the streets" was, of course, viewed as rather problematic by the state, and, in the case of Egypt looked remarkably similar to some of the activities of the early MB under Hassan al-Banna. While Amr Khaled was not directly involved in the street politics that produced the 2011 Egyptian revolution, he can perhaps be credited with a contributing role by helping to inculcate a sense of the possibility for change amongst Egyptian youth.

All these concerns about the potential Islamism lurking in Amr Khaled's project, however, miss the essentially post-Islamist character of his approach. While transformation and social change have clearly been part of his agenda, they were pursued in a manner that neither asked fundamental questions about the prevailing political order, nor sought directly to advise or influence the keepers of that order—as the MB did and still does. This is a rather different kind of collective action. Boubekeur puts it thus:

> The traditional intra-Islamic modes of action and mobilization, such as aggressive street demonstrations and political militancy, make less sense. The new Islamic elites reinterpret their relations . . . in terms of networks

and partnerships. Notions of partnership will develop according to standards of competence and competitiveness.[56]

Or, in other words, according to free market norms. When translated into politics, this approach would likely lead Egyptian voters toward the centrist blend of religion and modern political economy represented by the Hizb ul-Wasat or other "Muslim democratic" parties (see Chapter 4) rather than toward the MB. This orientation is part of a wider trend found in other parts of the Muslim world. In Indonesia, for example, the popular preacher Abdullah Gymnastiar, who at the height of his popularity commanded audiences of up to 80 million, incorporates elements of modern motivational speaking and management strategy into his religious discourse.[57] The Turkish religious entrepreneur Fetullah Gülen (see above) is another figure who emphasizes the Islamic injunction to pursue personal wealth, creating—in Boubekeur's words—a form of "Islamic ethic allied with cultural globalization."[58]

This chapter has explored the prospects of post-Islamism through an examination of the rapidly shifting landscape of contemporary Islamic authority in the context of globalization and the changing nature of public religiosity. We have surveyed both the major actors involved in advancing claims to religious authority, and the diverse range of audiences to which they appeal. Various forms of new media and patterns of consumption emerged as particularly important in the context of a new post-Islamist approach to Muslim politics and Islamic social movements.

What are the prospects for these new Muslim movements, and what can they tell us about the future of Muslim politics more generally? Activism of this sort is significant because it challenges us to reconsider our assumptions about what counts as a social movement and how we go about identifying them. The information and communications technologies widely available today not only allow traditional social movements to broaden the scope of their outreach, but also serve as vehicles and vessels through which a new type of movement can be constituted. While the understanding of politics, and the methods through which these groups work, are rather different from the approaches found in political party-based organizations or revolutionary movements, these new religious movements are important to keep in the analytical frame. They can appear and grow in popularity very rapidly, introducing new dynamics into what are often already quite volatile political environments in the Middle East and elsewhere. Finally, there is also the possibility of eventual cross-fertilization between these new religious movements and the traditional spaces and institutions of political Islam. In the case of Gülen and the AKP in Turkey, this already seems to be happening to some degree. Down the line, might some within the Egyptian *Wasatiyya* movement, perhaps, find a partnership with someone like Amr Khaled to be similarly attractive? Above all, such new movements need to be on the radar because of the ways in which they have reconfigured the ecology of Islamic activism, carving out a distinctive and rapidly evolving space in which social mobilization in the name of Islam assumes a diverse range of forms embedded in everyday life.

NOTES

1 O. Roy, *The Failure of Political Islam*, London: I.B. Tauris, 1994.
2 O. Roy, "Islam: The Democracy Dilemma," in R. Wright (ed.), *The Islamists Are Coming: Who They Really Are*, Washington, DC: Woodrow Wilson International Center for Scholars, 2012, pp. 13–20.
3 O. Roy, *Globalized Islam: The Search for a New Ummah*, New York: Columbia University Press, 2004, pp. 58–99.
4 Roy, op. cit., p. 75.
5 Roy, op. cit., p. 74–75.
6 Roy, op. cit., p. 77.
7 Roy, op. cit., p. 74.
8 Roy, op. cit., p. 98.
9 Roy, op. cit., p. 99.
10 G. Kepel, "Islamism Reconsidered," *Harvard International Review* 22, 2000, 26.
11 Kepel, op. cit., p. 22.
12 Kepel, op. cit., p. 26.
13 S. Ismail, *Rethinking Islamist Politics: Culture, the State, and Islamism*, London: I.B. Tauris, 2003, p. 175.
14 Roy, op. cit., pp. 72–75.
15 Ismail, op. cit., p. 169.
16 J. Rawls, "The Idea of an Overlapping Consensus," *Oxford Journal for Legal Studies* 7, 1987, pp. 1–25.
17 Ismail, op. cit., p. 163; C. Wickham, "The Causes and Dynamics of Islamist Auto-Reform," *ICIS International* 6, 2006, pp. 6–7.
18 Ismail, op. cit., p. 168.
19 Ismail, op. cit., p. 160.
20 Ismail, op. cit., p. 167.
21 Ismail, op. cit., p. 168.
22 Ismail, op. cit., p. 171.
23 Ismail, op. cit., p. 170.
24 Ismail, op. cit., p. 173.
25 F. Burgat, *Face to Face with Political Islam*, New York: I.B. Tauris, 2003, p. 180.
26 F. Burgat, op. cit., p. 182.
27 Ibid.
28 A. Bayat, "The Coming of a Post-Islamist Society," *Critique: Critical Middle East Studies* 9, 1996, pp. 43–52; A. Bayat, "What is Post-Islamism?," *ISIM Review* 16, 2005, p. 5.
29 Bayat, ibid.
30 Ibid.
31 O. Safi (ed.), *Progressive Muslims: On Justice, Gender, and Pluralism*, Oxford: Oneworld, 2003.

32 Ibid.
33 F. Fukuyama, *The End of History and the Last Man,* New York: Harper, 1993.
34 U. Beck, *Risk Society: Towards a New Modernity,* London: Sage, 1992.
35 Azzam Tamimi, interview with the author, London, June 2006.
36 J. Skovgaard-Petersen, B. Graf (eds), *The Global Mufti: The Phenomenon of Yusuf al-Qaradawi,* London: Hurst, 2009.
37 O. Roy, *The Failure of Political Islam,* London: I.B. Tauris, 1994, pp. 89–106.
38 Roy, op. cit., pp. 95–97.
39 C. Kurzman (ed.), *Liberal Islam: A Sourcebook,* Oxford: Oxford University Press, 1998.
40 P. Mandaville, "What Does Progressive Islam Look Like?" *ISIM Newsletter,* June 2003.
41 B. Agai, *Zwischen Netzwerk und Diskurs: Das Bildungsnetzwerk um Fethullah Güülen,* Schenefeld: EB-Verlag, 2004.
42 J. Skovgaard-Petersen, "The Global Mufti," in B. Schaebler, L. Stenberg (eds), *Globalization and the Muslim World: Culture, Religion, and Modernity,* Syracuse, NY: Syracuse University Press, 2004, pp. 153–165.
43 D. Eickelman, J. Anderson (eds), *New Media in the Muslim World: The Emerging Public Sphere,* Bloomington, IN: Indiana University Press, 2003; Mandaville, op. cit.; S. Glasser, S. Coll, "The Web as a Weapon," *The Washington Post,* August 9 2005, A01.
44 C. Hirschkind, "The Ethics of Listening: Cassette-Sermon Audition in Contemporary Egypt," *American Ethnologist* 28, 2002, 623–649; C. Hirschkind, "Civic Virtue and Religious Reason: An Islamic Counterpublic," *Cultural Anthropology* 16, 2001, pp. 3–34.
45 Mandaville, op. cit.
46 Skovgaard-Petersen, op. cit., p. 158.
47 G. Starrett, "The Political Economy of Religious Commodities in Cairo," *American Anthropologist* 97, 1995, pp. 51–68.
48 Hirschkind, "Civic Virtue and Religious Reason," op. cit.
49 Hirschkind, "Civic Virtue and Religious Reason," op. cit., p. 9.
50 See www.muslimgear.com
51 J. White, "The End of Islamism? Turkey"s Muslimhood Model," in R. Hefner (ed.), *Remaking Muslim Politics: Pluralism, Contestation, Democratization,* Princeton, NJ: Princeton University Press, 2005, pp. 87–111.
52 A. Boubekeur, "Cool and Competitive: Muslim Culture in the West," *ISIM Review* 16, 2005, p. 13.
53 L. Wise, "'Words from the Heart': New Forms of Islamic Preaching in Egypt," M.Phil. thesis, St. Antony's College, Oxford University, 2003.
54 P. Haenni, H. Tammam, "Egypt's air-conditioned Islam," *Le Monde Diplomatique,* September 2003.
55 Ibid.
56 Boubekeur, op. cit., p. 12.
57 C. Watson, "A Popular Indonesian Preacher: The Significance of AA Gymnastiar," *Journal of the Royal Anthropological Institute* 11, 2005, pp. 773–792.
58 Boubekeur, op. cit., p. 12.

CHAPTER 9

Conclusion: The Arab Uprisings and beyond

This book has covered considerable ground in seeking to understand the nature of contemporary Muslim politics. We began by tracing the intellectual and political roots of modern Islamism in the context of state formation in the Muslim world. We then examined various explanatory accounts of Islamism, before moving on to the first of several case studies. After working through multiple examples of Islam and politics in the system, as the system, and in the absence of a system, we moved on to analyze the nature of today's transnational Islamic radicalism. An examination of several other major spaces and institutions through which Muslim politics occur today brought us, in the previous chapter, to examine the arguments of those who argue that we have entered the age of "post-Islamism." It has become clear, through our wanderings across the many terrains of Muslim politics, that we are not dealing with a monolithic phenomenon. Islam and politics commingle in almost infinite variety across a vast range of settings, issues, actors, and levels of analysis.

In seeking to highlight these many, and often quite disparate, trajectories of contemporary Muslim politics, we find ourselves faced with a considerable challenge in concluding this volume. Ours has been primarily a survey effort, an attempt to reveal to the reader the myriad shapes and forms of Muslim politics across the *umma,* and less an attempt to assert a discrete thesis or argument. While certainly structured in our approach, we have not sought to impose a single organizing principle on our coverage of Islam and politics. Therefore, to try in this final chapter to force artificial convergence on so diverse a phenomenon in the hope of pithy summary would be to defeat the basic premise of our approach. So, rather than seeking to draw together and reconcile the divergent strands of Muslim politics running through this book, we will leave them to run their many and as yet indeterminate courses. Our efforts here focus instead on three tasks. First we delve back into the morass of empirical material thus far presented, and from it pick out several key themes and cleavages that might be identified as among the drivers of Muslim political futures. These are presented across three principal domains: Islamist politics, religious knowledge, and Muslim identity. The final section of this conclusion then offers some reflections on various aspects of globalization and globalizing processes in terms of how they may inflect the many futures of Muslim politics.

KEY THEMES AND TENSIONS: ISLAMIST POLITICS, RELIGIOUS KNOWLEDGE, MUSLIM IDENTITY

The wealth of empirical and case-study material we have explored over the course of this volume suggest that there are three "meta-issues" around which we might build a discussion of the major themes and tensions present in today's Muslim politics. These are the changing nature of Islamist politics; the politics of religious knowledge; and then, finally, several issues relating to how Muslims understand their identity—and, in particular, their political identity—in the context of globalization. We consider each of these in turn.

Islamist politics

As has become clear, particularly through our analysis of Islam "in the system" in Chapter 4, the standard model of Islamist politics seems to be undergoing considerable transformation today in many contexts. We presented this as a shift to a "new Islamism," and located it in the activities of various parties and groups that have sought to build a Muslim politics around themes such as justice and development (including e.g. Turkey's AKP, the PJD in Morocco, PKS in Indonesia) and the Islamic "centrist" movement elsewhere in the Arab world. Read by some as the harbingers of a new era of "Muslim democracy," this shift certainly merits some careful consideration in terms of what it reveals about the fault lines present within the Islamist project, and the hints it provides as to where it might be going. The first point to be made here relates to the shifting sociology of Islamism. In the cases of AKP and the internal politics of the Muslim Brotherhood, we saw breakaway factions from within traditional Islamist movements splitting off to pursue a different course. For the most part, these were younger activists who had concerns about a lack of meaningful participation on two fronts. First, internally, they felt as if the stewardship of their "mother" parties, the Egyptian MB and Refah/Virtue, respectively, was in the hands of an "old guard" who were behind the times in terms of their strategic vision, and also unwilling to allow the younger generation any meaningful say in the making of party policy. On the external front, and related to the first point, this new generation felt as if the reactionary policies and practices of the old guard prevented the party from evolving to a point where it would have the opportunity to participate in the discussion and resolution in the political sphere of crucial questions now facing their respective societies. While the AKP rode to power on a powerful wave of popular dissatisfaction with Turkey's corrupt political system, their futures—and that of centrist Islamism more generally—will depend on how the strategic vision of these movements fits in with prevailing public sentiments. An important point here, and one made by several observers such as Ray Baker and Graham Fuller, is that, in many respects, the discourse of traditional Islamism is an "Islam of fear" or "the Islam that says no."[1] In other words, it is a breed of politics more concerned with delineating between right and wrong, imposing moral strictures, and telling people what they can and cannot do, rather than offering positive and distinctive solutions to pressing problems. The "new Islamists," with their emphasis on pragmatism and policy rather than public virtue, are seeking to redress this by figuring Islam as a discourse of progress and social justice. So we see here a distinct generational divide over vision and strategy. But that may itself be too simple an analysis. As the work of scholars such as Carrie Wickham shows, this is not simply a divide between young and old, with the young Islamists preferring pragmatism and the old Islamists mired in ideological dogma. Rather, she suggests, there has been a far more complicated process of Islamist self-learning at work, one that pervades the Islamist movement as a whole.[2] Indeed, it is possible to identify older "new Islamists" and also younger activists who have elected to remain with the Brotherhood—both of who believe that the MB is perfectly capable of accommodating, indeed becoming the vanguard of, a new Islamist pragmatism.

But the future of Islamism is not only about internal upheavals. Much of it will depend on the wider political and societal environments in which Islamist actors operate. It is likely that, in the future, the AKP—regardless of its decade of dominance in Turkish politics—will have to contend with a political environment that no longer views it as an innovation. As with all political discourses and programs, contradictions and mixed track records emerge. In many ways this will be "Muslim democracy's" first real test— that is, having its vision and implementation assessed in terms of the value they add to a political marketplace characterized by what Brumberg calls "dissonance" (meaning a multiplicity of distinct and competing political agendas).[3] The AKP has, for the most part, stayed away from "religious" issues, and yet it has a party base that is looking for it to address these—and, all the while, the Turkish army (guardians of the Kemalist legacy) and increasingly skeptical segments of the Turkish population watch carefully over its shoulders. In Egypt, too, much hinges on whether, in the aftermath of the July 3, 2013 coup that removed Mohammed Morsi, Islamists can rebuild a working accommodation with the military and other forces in society that will permit them to become a normalized facet of the political landscape. The volatility and mistrust that characterized the immediate post-Mubarak period, much of it generated by the Islamists themselves, suggest that this will not be an easy task.

Much of this comes down to the question of whether traditional Islamists will be able to summon the imagination required to accommodate their conception of an Islamic political order with the concept of power sharing. This is particularly relevant with respect to the issue of how Islamists understand the meaning of *shari'ah,* and the practical implications of building a legal system on Islamic law in societies where multiple conceptions of *shari'ah*—even among Muslims—are to be found.

The pursuit of a *shari'ah*-based political order has long been a hallmark—perhaps even the defining or constitutive—feature of Islamism. Within Islamist circles, and amongst interested outside observers, there has always been considerable speculation as to just what exactly this would entail. Practices have also varied. There are a number of countries in the Muslim world today, for example, where otherwise secular states are happy to allow issues of personal status (marriage, inheritance, etc.) to be regulated by *shari'ah* while reserving for themselves the conduct of other areas of the law (e.g. criminal justice, civil matters). Some aspects of the *shari'ah* seem rather clear-cut if imported wholesale from scriptural and jurisprudential sources (e.g. personal status, *hudud* punishments). But we can also identify issue areas where the traditional sources have very little to say (e.g. medical ethics, regulatory policy) beyond general principles. And it is on this very question that the debate turns: to what extent does the "*shari'ah*-ization" of policy and law mean the direct and literal application of prescriptions found in classical Islamic jurisprudence, or to what extent does it mean creating a legal code infused with the moral principles found within the teachings of religion (see Box 2.1, "What is *shari'ah?*")? For those within the literalist camp, the issue has been one of legislative authority. If sovereignty is God's alone, the authority to legislate rests similarly within the realm of the divine. The idea of the people as legislators is rejected; hence, also, the rejection by early Islamists of legislative democracy (see Chapter 3). The other camp argues that the *shari'ah* in its ostensible form is already the product of centuries of human interpretation and deliberation by religious scholars. Since revelation proceeds via language, and language always involves human interpretation, "the people" are already intrinsically involved in its legal codification. The safest thing would therefore be to identify the general moral standards expressed by these teachings (as found in the Qur'an and *sunna*) and to allow these to act as the guiding principles, rather than the direct content, of legislation.

There certainly exist today Islamists who firmly espouse each of these two positions. Most, however, combine elements of both. To provide just a sample of some views expressed by Islamist intellectuals and leaders who have sought to find a middle approach:

> Shari'ah can only ever apply in a direct and literal form to Muslim citizens. Non-Muslims can have their affairs regulated by their own personal status tradition, or be subject to a state civil code that might be informed by the "spirit" and "principles" of shari'ah.[4]
>
> The specific implementation of a given point of shari'ah should be left up to the ijma (consensus) of those governed by it. Therefore the citizens should choose from among a range of possible interpretations of a given legal point.[5]

So here are two positions—ranging from instrumentalism to pragmatism—that illustrate for us the diversity of views on this issue to be found amongst contemporary Islamists. Pushing the defenders of Islamism as *shari'ah* to substantiate their claims, Graham Fuller asserts that "there is no visible correlation between application of Shari'ah law and the attainment of a better society and governance in today's Muslim world."[6] Declaring himself more a fan of the idea that "Islam is the solution" (in the sense of religion as a source of moral guidelines and spiritual resources for the conduct of everyday life) than of the claim that "*shari'ah* is the solution," Fuller goes on to advocate the need continually to reinterpret Islamic principles in order to make them relevant to contemporary conditions and predicaments.[7] There are certainly Islamists who would agree with Fuller, but others who would offer a variety of retorts. Some would claim that the reason *shari'ah* has not appeared to better society is because there is nowhere today where it is being properly applied. The examples of Saudi Arabia and Afghanistan under the Taliban would likely be dismissed by many contemporary Islamists as too extreme; likewise, in Iran, the idea of clerical rule is still seen as too much of an innovation. Some, of course, would take issue with the way in which Fuller is likely defining "better society and governance"—but others, particularly among the new Islamists, would likely agree with him.

The question of *shari'ah* becomes particularly important when we come to consider questions relating to the role and rights of women. A political party holding conservative views regarding gender roles is not, in and of itself, a barrier to democratic participation, since such groups are to be found in all societies. The problem here is more one of a potential conflict between the principle of the equality of all citizens, regardless of gender, and legislation that would seek to enshrine the differentiated rights of men and women (as found in the Qur'an and *sunna*) within a political framework. Again, the positions here vary considerably from context to context. There are conservative Islamists, particularly in countries in which tribal norms run strong, who would prefer a literalist application of Qur'anic strictures with regard to gender. Others argue that those aspects of the Qur'an and *sunna* should be read as products of their time that were articulated to match with prevailing norms. Rather, what should be extracted from this, in their view, is the idea that men and women have differentiated social roles, but that in legal terms they should be regarded as equals.

This debate is also one that seems, in practice, to break down along the lines of the old and new Islamists mentioned above. The advocates of Muslim democracy, such as the AKP in Turkey, have not included *shari'ah* in their legislative agenda. Indeed, their core support comes from a movement that understands religion largely in privatized and individualized terms (see Chapter 4). Islam for them is a source of morality, and, moreover, a morality that should guide their conduct within all spheres of life. But this is very different from saying that Islam's morality should be enshrined in law. For many of the "new Islamists," then, Islam is about turning religion into an agenda for anti-corruption, economic justice, and the pursuit of personal prosperity and happiness—hence, in Ray Baker's terms, an "Islam without fear." The divide between old and new Islamists, as we have mentioned, is useful in terms of reading developments within the sociology of the movement. The evolving position of Islamism on the question of *shari'ah*, however, will serve as an important indicator of where the movement is going in terms of its normative discourse.

The final issue to be considered under Islamist politics is the question of pluralism and political inclusiveness. For many skeptical about Islamism, this has long been the crux of the issue—hence the enduring power of the Islamism as "one man, one vote, one time" discourse; that is, the fear that, once Islamists are in power, they would modify the political system to make sure they could never be voted out. It appears that Islamists gave up long ago on the idea of a totalist politics. As we will recall from Chapter 3, early Islamism eschewed the idea of party politics along the lines that it would likely lead to strife and *fitna* (disorder) within society. In their view, once an Islamic political order had been achieved, there would be no need for party politics. For some years now, Islamist parties in countries such as Jordan, Malaysia, Morocco, and Pakistan have been contesting and respecting the results of elections alongside parties representing a wide range of political orientations. It seems that, for the most part, Islamists today have achieved a firm accommodation with the procedural aspects of democracy (e.g. running in, and respecting the results of, elections) even as they may find it difficult to embrace a more robust conception and practice of political pluralism. As banned opposition movements, their internal politics tended to be rather nontransparent and—with a few exceptions (such as some experimental alliances with non-Islamists mentioned below)—and rather exclusivist *vis-à-vis* outside actors. No doubt this partly explains some of the difficulty that Egypt's MB faced when it won Egypt's presidency in 2012. Democratic transition seemed to demand a greater and more rapid comfort with pluralism than the Islamists were able to muster.

The politics of religious knowledge and authority

It is often remarked that today we are witnessing a struggle within Islam, a battle for Muslim "hearts and minds" contested among different claimants to true and authentic Islam. We examined many of these dynamics with regard to religious authority in Chapter 8. As became clear to us through that discussion, the crux of the issue is less about who speaks for Islam, and more about the Muslims who are listening. Claims to religious authority are never absolute. Neither religious scholars, nor "new Islamist intellectuals," nor populist media preachers possess undisputed authority to define and mandate the meaning and social requirements of religion. The important point to bear in mind is that the Muslims who constitute the target audience for these claims are not listening solely "as Muslims." Muslims are also students, mothers, voters, shoppers, sports fans, agricultural laborers, and software developers. As such, they pursue multiple lines of social affiliation and understand their public identities in pluralistic terms. Their understandings of, and orientations toward, religion and its relevance to these various spheres of everyday life vary tremendously. Does this mean that Islam is just one of many prisms through which they engage the world? Yes, but this does not mean that it necessarily has a special or privileged role to play in how those who consider themselves believers engage the issues and problems in their lives. It does mean, however, that it becomes impossible to assume that the content and prescriptions of successful claims to Islamic religious authority articulated before Muslim audiences will determine the political behavior of the latter. Nodding to oneself while the *imam* rails against the immorality of modern society does necessarily mean joining an Islamist party the very next day.

Many observers of the Muslim world have asked why the reformist, modernist, or liberal variants of contemporary Islamic thought do not seem to have a strong following among Muslims today. Some have taken this to be evidence of Islam's anti-liberal or undemocratic character. But here we need to ask the same questions about who is listening. Generally, we might postulate, it is not that Muslims outright "reject" the ideas of reformist Islam (see Chapter 8), but more that they have difficulty relating them to the circumstances of their social reality. We have already mentioned in Chapter 8 that there is a formal barrier to the wider reception of these ideas in the very language employed for their articulation. But beyond that, there is also the question of the extent to which these reformist ideas correspond to the lived experience and needs of most Muslims. Let us consider an example. Many of the reformists emphasize the compatibility of Islam and democracy, showing very elegantly that, at its roots, the *shari'ah* is primarily a discourse of equality and participatory governance. It is also the case, however, that many citizens of Muslim-majority countries have lost all faith in the idea that their ruling regimes will ever make space for real democracy. Indeed, many have become jaded regarding the whole notion of politics. "Politics" for them is simply a space in which traditional patterns of elite influence and client–patron relationships play out. It has nothing to do with stakeholder citizens deciding collectively on their societies' futures. They have little interest in politics, because "being political," or acting politically in the conventional sense of that term, does not seem to have any bearing on their lives. Discourses on the democratic essence of Islam, therefore, elicit little more than shrugged shoulders in the lower middle-class suburbs of Cairo and Karachi.

Hardline and radical discourses, on the other hand, at least seem to capture something of the reality of existence in these settings. When Usama Bin Laden railed against the West and new forms of imperialism, it was at least possible for Muslims to see themselves as part of the reality he described. The vast majority of them found his solutions and methods to be ridiculous and immoral, but he did address issues to which they were able to relate. So, while this certainly does not make for, as Al-Qaeda's leaders would wish, a mass mobilization of Muslims in support of the global jihadist movement, it does mean that many Muslims see little reason to invest in counter-discourses of supposed democracy and prosperity. The purveyors of the latter are seen, and are easily portrayed, as agents of Westernization. Not only are their ideas seen as largely irrelevant to the circumstances of most Muslims, but their legitimacy is in question. Under conditions where many Muslims see themselves as subject to the continuing influence of colonialism and imperialism (albeit in new forms), it becomes difficult for promises of socioeconomic and political deliverance to be taken seriously.

Clearly, then, making room for reformist and liberalizing Islamic discourses is much more than making people comfortable with the idea of multiple interpretations of religion (although this is a piece of it). Rather, it is more a case of attending to the geopolitical, domestic political, and socio-economic realities that make it difficult for people to see anything of relevance to their lives in such ideas. Muslims will not invest in reformist Islam unless they have reasons to buy into the idea that the political and economic realities of their lives can also be reformed. Until then, reformist Islam will still read to many Muslims as an invitation to buy into the very system that maintains the hegemonies they see all around them. Under these circumstances, where no-one else appears to be offering realistic alternative solutions, people will continue to be drawn to political discourses that at least narrate to them, and reflect, the conditions of their disenfranchisement—even as they reject *en masse* the sometimes radical and militant prescriptions that accompany these claims. Radicals and ultra-conservatives pursue a "politics of authenticity" by questioning whether reformist discourses represent anything more than the corruption of Muslim minds with Western values and ideas. Clearly, as Graham Fuller argues, it makes little sense to speak about the "authenticity" of either Western or Islamic ideas, since both bear the traces of so many historical, cultural, and political encounters.[8] Islamism is hardly a rejection of modernity—rather, it affirms the idea of individual political subjectivity and the possibility to achieve positive, progressive change through human agency. These are ideas clearly present in both the Western liberal and Islamic traditions. It is, therefore, not a matter of making better claims to "true" Islam by reformists, or of finding comprehensive evidence to the effect that reformist values are consonant with the jurisprudential sources of Islam. To play this game is to remain trapped within a discourse of authenticity. Rather, this debate should be reconstituted as a "politics of relevancy" and played out within the realm of the political. Muslims will respond pragmatically to solutions that actually affect their lives much more than they will to assurances that the ideas behind those solutions are Islamic.

Muslim political identity in the shadow of the *umma*

Olivier Roy has written about the "deterritorialization" of Muslim political identity, while other writers have spoken of "transnational political Islam" or "reimagining the *umma*."[9] All of these authors are trying to capture the sense today in which Muslims sometimes appear to be caught between the universalizing and particularistic aspects of their identity. Accompanying this is further deliberation and debate as to what holding a Muslim identity means in political terms. As the various case studies we examined have shown us, it is evident that the solution to this question plays out rather differently across disparate contexts. In Western countries, for example, where Muslims (some of them "deterritorialized" in Roy's sense of the term) live as religious minorities under political systems controlled by non-Muslims, this has sometimes produced debates about whether it is permissible for Muslims to participate politically in such systems. How, in other words, should they regard issues related to the rights and duties associated with citizenship in states ruled by non-Muslims? In countries where Muslims are in the majority, the question of Muslim political identity has been engaged rather differently. It is less a question here of whether it is legitimate to participate in governments run by non-Muslims, and more a question of whether Muslims have a religiously prescribed duty to pursue the establishment of an Islamic political order through politics. In these contexts, as we have seen, it is the very fact that Muslims hold a wide range of views about what their religion says about politics and public life that accounts for the multiplicity and diversity of Muslim politics that we have seen over the course of this volume.

BOX 9.1 POLITICAL ISLAM IN EUROPE AND NORTH AMERICA: ISLAMISTS IN MUSLIM-MINORITY SETTINGS

What does it mean to be an Islamist in a context where Muslims represent a distinct religious minority, and where legal arrangements explicitly mandate a separation between religion and the functions of state? While many of the Islamist groups—and particularly the Muslim Brotherhood—have had a presence in Europe and North America for several decades now, they have had to adjust the purposes and goals of their movement to suit very different conditions. Where it might have made sense to work towards establishing an Islamic state in countries where the vast majority of the population is Muslim and where *shari'ah* law already has some official standing, such an agenda makes little sense where Muslims represent fewer than 5 percent of the population, as is the case in most Muslim-minority settings in the West.

In the United States, for example, Muslim Students Associations were established on a number of university campuses from the 1960s by members of the MB who had come to the West for higher education. No doubt some of these figures, who planned one day to return to their home countries, welcomed the opportunity to meet and work in open societies where Islamists were not subject to the same kinds of oppression as they were in many countries in the Arab world ruled by secular regimes, such as Egypt and Iraq. As the Muslim American population grew and diversified, however, it outgrew the rather narrow project of Islamism (many of whose priorities were out of touch with the needs of this community). Those Islamists who chose to remain in the U.S.— including figures who went on to form other organizations, such as the Islamic Society of North America, the Council on American Islamic Relations, and the Muslim American Society—found themselves focusing more broadly on issues of civil rights, the specific religious needs of Muslim communities, and, especially after the attacks of 9/11, a growing wave of Islamophobia in the U.S.

In Western Europe, the MB influence was present in organizations such as the Union des Organisations Islamique de France, the Islamische Gemeinschaft in Deutschland, and the Muslim Association of Britain. Among the mainly South Asian Muslim population of the United Kingdom were affiliates of the Jama'at-i Islami party such as the Islamic Foundation in Leicester, the UK Islamic Mission, and the Islamic Forum Europe. While some of these groups undoubtedly worked—and to some extent continue to work—on behalf of their parent organizations in the Middle East and South Asia by engaging in diasporic fundraising and publicity work, many younger Muslims today find their agenda and goals to be largely irrelevant to their day-to-day lives. Some members of these organizations subsequently have gone on to establish successor organizations focused on transforming formerly Islamist programs into agendas that facilitate compatibility between Islamic beliefs and living as a British or French citizen.

While certain radical groups such as Hizb ut-Tahrir (HT) and some elements of the global jihadi movement (such as Al-Shabaab) have sought to find a following among young Muslims living in the West (see Chapter 7), Muslims for the most part have not tried to form Islamic political parties in the West. Among the first generation of Muslim immigrants in Europe, political participation was very low, illustrative of a wider tendency among this cohort to remain largely separate from mainstream society. Younger Muslims have been more politically active, however, but generally opting to vote for whichever of the major political parties best represents their interests and values. In the UK, for example, this has translated into widespread Muslim support for the Labour Party, generally regarded as more attuned to the plight of immigrants and more comfortable with multiculturalism. The political fallout from 9/11 and subsequent terrorist attacks in Europe—such as the July 2005 London Tube bombings—prompted widespread Islamophobia in both the United States and Europe. Certain extremist groups, such as HT (see Chapter 7), that had been arguing for Muslims to stay out of politics, sought—but largely failed—to create a wedge issue around the permissibility of Muslims voting in the democratic elections of non-Islamic governments. In the U.S., growing Islamophobia—coupled with a widespread lack of knowledge about Islamic culture and beliefs—saw some groups on the political right mobilizing around what they portrayed as an effort by American Muslim organizations to bring *shari'ah* law to the United States. In both the U.S. and Europe, however, the vast majority of Muslims have no ties to formal Muslim organizations and do not organize politically around their religious beliefs.

Further study

J. Laurence, *The Emancipation of Europe's Muslims: The State's Role in Minority Integration*, Princeton, NJ: Princeton University Press, 2012.

R. Meijer, E. Bakker (eds), *The Muslim Brotherhood in Europe*, New York: Columbia University Press, 2013.

J. S. Nielsen (ed.), *Muslim Political Participation in Europe*, Edinburgh: Edinburgh University Press, 2013.

Pew Forum on Religion, *Muslim Networks and Movements in Western Europe*, Washington, DC: Pew Research Center, 2010.

While some Muslim political actors, particularly those working in the vein of transnational radicalism (see Chapter 7), have sought to mobilize Muslim hearts and minds around global, pan-Islamic agendas, most evidence today suggests that Muslim political identities are oriented primarily towards national or even local concerns. The ideal of the *umma* is simply far too abstract for most Muslims to relate to their daily lives. This does not mean, however, that globalization is irrelevant in terms of its effects on Muslim political considerations. In addition to Muslim attitudes toward the various political–economic effects commonly associated with globalization (see below), it is also the case that the increased senses of interconnectedness and communication associated with globalization have led to much higher levels of informed awareness about events going on in the world—a phenomenon that is, of course, hardly confined to Muslim settings. This means that geopolitical events and factors have come to play a larger role in Muslim political considerations. Even if Muslim identities remain primarily nationalized, this does not mean that it is not possible for them to make common cause with co-religionists elsewhere, or to sympathize with "Muslim" issues. This relates to the sense in which religion constitutes today an important sense of post-materialist identity and the basis for transnational social movements. In the same way that American and German environmental activists can jointly advocate for curbs on greenhouse gases without German and American political identity becoming one and the same, so can Senegalese and Malaysian Muslims advocate for an end to Israel's occupation of Palestine without this implying anything in particular about the existence of a new, global Muslim identity.

But there is another important point to be made about globalization and Muslim political identity, one that brings us firmly into the territory of the debate on post-Islamism (see Chapter 8). This relates to the idea, advanced by various writers, that globalization may be having an impact on the modalities and locations through which politics occur. If globalization is understood to mean the hegemony and pervasive penetration of a particular mode of neoliberal economy, then it would stand to reason that globalization also has some effect on the reconfiguration of subjectivity and personhood. We see this particularly in the idea that globalization gives rise to forms of subjectivity defined and premised primarily in terms of practices relating to consumption. As the expression of particular values and moral systems in the public sphere increasingly comes to be intertwined with forms of consumption, these same lifestyle practices begin to take on political connotations. Likewise, as states become primarily the guardians of the neoliberal order in a globally interdependent system of markets, rather than politically "neutral" spaces in which competing visions of the good life vie for power, we are witnessing a retreat of the political into the social sphere—where, as we have just pointed out, social identities are increasingly structured by practices of consumption. This is much more complicated than simply a claim to the effect that "we are what we buy." Rather, we are trying to indicate here a sense in which consumptive practices come to assume politically normative connotations at the same time as public identities find themselves increasingly figured in terms of consumptive practice. In many of the societies we examined in our case studies, the point was made that Islamist politics have been confined to, and have thoroughly socialized, many aspects of the social sphere. This would suggest that there is considerable potential for unique and innovative idioms of Muslim politics to occur in those settings where religiosity, consumption, and social identity find themselves occupying the same space. It is here that the notion of post-Islamism becomes relevant, since some observers have seen in it signs of the privatization or individualization of religious practice. Rather than viewing this simply as evidence of the growing secularization (in the Western sense) of Muslim society under globalization—and hence the end of Islamism as a meaningful political project—we might also want to entertain the possibility that post-Islamism refers to a relocation and transformation of the political in terms of its interaction with Muslim subjectivity.

For our purposes in this volume, the notion of post-Islamism is best understood in reference to the combination of the shift from "old" to "new" Islamism, the bottom-up approach to Islamization, and—particularly—the rise of new forms of religious authority outside the framework of either traditional religious scholarship or conventional Islamist politics. Amr Khaled would be a good example of this (see Chapter 8), as would some of the new discourses of Muslim identity to be found in the West. Where some might be tempted to dismiss the emergence of Muslim hip-hop bands and clothing lines as purely apolitical symptoms of consumer culture, others will see in them new forms of identity politics and new spaces for the contestation of normatively laden signs and symbols. On the fringes of Islamism, then, might we not be seeing the rise of a very different kind of "radical" Islamist politics? Hints of it are to be found in the "punk Islam" novel by Muhammad Michael McKnight, *The Taqwacores;* or in the emergent networks of Sufi–anarchist movements—themselves closely allied with anti-globalization and global justice causes (see below). In this sense, post-Islamism is best understood not as the abandonment of Muslim politics, but rather as their reconstitution in forms more suited to a globalized world—a world in which, we might want to suggest, the state is only one among many sites of the political.

GLOBALIZATION AND THE FUTURE OF MUSLIM POLITICS

By way of concluding this volume, it might be interesting to think a little about some of the various social, economic, and political—including geopolitical—trends associated with globalization and how they might play out in terms of their effects on Islamism and Muslim politics. We have suggested above that we are already seeing important effects in this regard in terms of the evolving strategy of traditional Islamist movements as they simultaneously engage democratic politics while continuing to exert influence within the spheres of the social and—increasingly—the individual. What broader transformations might globalization bring to the landscapes of Muslim politics as macro forces—primarily economic ones—play out in the context of specific localities and societies? Moreover, are these trends that favor the growth and consolidation of Islamism in their present forms?

For many analysts, globalization has been associated with a steep rise in urban poverty.[10] On the peripheries of many global cities in the Muslim world—Cairo, Istanbul, etc.—we find enormous slum areas inhabited by millions of people who, by and large, tend not to be integrated into existing social welfare arrangements as provided by the state. In these areas, we find vast informal sectors for the conduct of commerce, governance, and justice—forms of social and political life that do not appear on official radar. As we have seen above, particularly in the case of Egypt, these are the environments in which Islamist movements such as the MB have tended to thrive. Their charity services and voluntary associations, many of which operate through informal networks well suited to the social climate of urban peripheries, permit them to build considerable mass constituencies and to accumulate social capital through the provision of services beyond the capacity of the state. In this regard, then, we might want to wonder about correlations between increased urban poverty in Muslim-majority countries and the strength of Islamist social influence and mobilizing potential.

What about globalization's economic effects more generally and their impact on Muslim society? Henry and Springborg make the interesting point that some of the best-developed infrastructures for the support of global banking and financial systems are to be found in some of the most "traditional" and conservative Muslim nations today—such as Saudi Arabia.[11] This has much to do with the way the political economies of some of these countries, through energy production, have come to play a crucial and privileged role within the global economy, to the exclusion of other Muslim nations lacking hydrocarbon resources. This "semi-peripheral" status, in the terms of world-systems theorists, has permitted them to build strong strategic relationships with powerful client states in the West, and often to avoid the worst effects of global structural adjustment efforts.[12] Some of the smaller states, particularly in the Arab gulf region, have clearly decided to play the globalization game. One can think, in particular, of a country such as the UAE. The emirates of Dubai and Abu Dhabi have sought in recent years to establish themselves as key nodes of globalization in the region, providing duty-free logistics, import–export, forwarding services, and quality-of-life residential and leisure facilities. They seek similarly to participate in the culture of global elites through the hosting of major golf and tennis tournaments, and for mass audiences by establishing themselves as major tourism and shopping destinations.

Most of the Muslim world, however, has missed out on globalization, and would seriously question whether the seeds of Muslim prosperity are contained within it. For many Muslims, globalization is still associated with Westernization and new forms of hegemony. Some see in this fact the potential for hardline Islamists to benefit. As Brumberg puts it:

> Globalization has reinforced such paranoia [of the West] by expanding the gap between the haves and have-nots. Globalization's losers fill the urban slums of Rabat, Algiers, Cairo, and Amman, creating an enormous pool of potential recruits for illiberal Islamism, whereas the winners are found among the Westernized intelligentsia and small business community.[13]

While globalization certainly could lead many Muslims toward reactionary forms of Islamism, this does not by any means represent the only political trajectory open to them. In countries where anti-globalization movements and networks are well-organized, we could well find Muslims joining forces with a wide spectrum of political opinion—green, leftist, luddite—all united by virtue of their opposition to neoliberal economics. The well-known European Muslim intellectual and activist Tariq Ramadan is to be found today as much in global justice circles as he is to be found in front of exclusively Muslim audiences. There is room here, also, for traditional Islamism. Some scholars have pointed to efforts by some Islamists to make common cause with forces of the political left.[14] The British branch of the MB, for example, has sent delegations to the various meetings of the World Social Forum in Venezuela and elsewhere. Global Muslim activism should hence not be thought of exclusively in terms of illiberal Islamism or radical jihadism. There is plenty of scope for Muslims dissatisfied with the global systemic *status quo* to make common cause with a much broader coalition of social and political movements organized around what they perceive as the alienating and disenfranchising effects of neoliberal globalization.

For most Muslims, however, politics will continue to be understood primarily in local and national terms. But this does not mean we should discount globalization or, more particularly, geopolitics, from our analytical consideration. Muslim activists and voters, well-networked and connected, as we have seen, are highly informed and have strong opinions with regard to issues such as state cooperation with international financial institutions. Geopolitics is also vital here. Quite aside from concerns about invasive neoliberalism, most Muslims have serious concerns about a wide range of world issues, from U.S. policy in the Middle East, to Turkish membership in the European Union, to tensions between Pakistan and India, to a post-9/11 American-led "War on Terror" that often appears to Muslims to have strong undertones of Islamophobia—and that seems to continue in other forms, even as the U.S. wars in Afghanistan and Iraq have concluded. While Islamist parties reflect these concerns in their platforms and public messaging, they are by no means exclusively Islamist issues. Such concerns tend also to be adopted by almost all segments of the political spectrum. Where these matters have an impact on the Islamist political field, however, is where it comes to political pluralism and the acceptance by Muslims of approaches and ideas strongly identified with the West. This insight would suggest that the pluralization of the Muslim political field is something that needs to be pursued, not exclusively in terms of promoting openness and democracy within Muslim countries, but also by addressing democratic deficits attendant in the conduct of world politics more generally.

The challenge of moving beyond Islamism, as we have tried to suggest throughout this book, is about widening the boundaries of what counts as Muslim politics. Islamism, in both its "old" and "new" variants, will no doubt continue to be an important feature on the Muslim political landscape for the foreseeable future. As we have seen in recent years, Islamists will continue to be popular political actors and capable of winning elections—even as they will likely continue to struggle in meeting the practical challenges of governance in Egypt, Tunisia, and elsewhere.

In the aftermath of the 2011 Arab Uprisings, Islamist parties clearly have managed to capitalize on their enormous competitive advantage *vis-à-vis* other political forces in terms of political organization, their ability successfully to represent themselves as consistent (and often oppressed) critics of the previous *status quo,* and their claim—by virtue of proximity to religious values—to be free of corruption and unethical politics. However, in the coming months and years, they will need to contend with a number of broader trends and political realities.

- The intense pluralization of Islamic space in recent years has meant that traditional "incumbents" such as the MB have lost a monopoly on the claim to represent the sole articulators of a social and political project premised on Islam. This observation speaks to the ongoing relevance of one particular school of thought in the study of contemporary Muslim politics—the post-Islamism thesis (see Chapter 8). We need to remember that, in its more refined forms, this approach argues not that Islamist parties *per se* will disappear, but rather that political Islam as an ideological project will become increasingly diffuse in the face of forces pushing these groups to the political center, and the arrival of rival claimants to religious virtue across a range of sectors beyond the realm of formal politics.

- Once we have moved beyond a point where "Islam" functions as a political currency whose legitimacy derives in large part from its opposition to the previous *status quo* in new post-authoritarian contexts such as Egypt and Tunisia (rather than from specific ideological content), political actors will be judged primarily by the outcomes of their actions and policies—and less by the symbols and rhetoric they embrace. Will seasoned oppositionists, used to relying on relatively vague slogans and amorphous formulations ("Islam is the solution"; "civil state with an Islamic reference"), be able to reinvent themselves as problem-solvers and purveyors of effective governance? And, in the face of a political environment in which non-Islamic political forces represent perhaps only a small minority in key institutions, who will they be able to blame if and when their solutions do not deliver? The spectacular fall of Egypt's MB president, Mohammed Morsi, in 2011 suggests that there is little patience for gradualism and little interest in ideological rigidity in the face of very real socioeconomic and political challenges.

- As indicated by the Egyptian military coup of July 3, 2013 that removed MB president Mohammed Morsi, Islamists operate in environments characterized by the presence of influential political elements—militaries, security services, remnants of prior regimes—that possess the capacity to disrupt, sabotage, or put an end to Islamist government altogether. Far from being isolated "spoilers" residing within an invisible "deep state," these opponents of Islamism have demonstrated that they are capable of mobilizing influential segments of society in support of their cause.

We also need to ask a different—and in some ways more fundamental—set of questions about the changing nature of social and political movements more broadly. Theorists of so-called "new social movements" have been arguing since the late 1980s about the existence of movements that aspire and work towards the achievement of particular goals, but not necessarily with the same concept of "politics" or political change as conventional political groups. A hallmark feature of these new movements—and one that was certainly on display in 2011—relates to the fact that the very nature of this kind of solidarity ("weak ties") means that, in organizational terms, new social movements look rather different from conventional political groupings. They are less rigid and hierarchical, and rely more on diffuse, horizontal networks. To be sure, we are not dealing with a zero-sum game here. Old and new social movements can, and will, continue to coexist. The rise of the latter, however, has important implications for the former, and will likely force it to make changes to accommodate new dynamics of communication, connectivity, and social organizing empowered by, for example, the rise of social media and spaces of everyday life outside the control of more formal movements.

It is clear that conventional, mainstream Islamist movements are facing an unprecedented opportunity to demonstrate that they can deliver in terms of solving practical problems. But, at the end of the day, they will have to work with non-Islamic parties and social forces to address the deep-seated problems that plague the region, and it is likely that over time it will become increasingly clear that there is nothing uniquely "Islamic" about the solutions that work. So their political fate will begin to depend more on the claim that their proximity to Islam makes them harder-working and more ethical—all of which will be more difficult to sustain over time as other political forces close the gap between the current comparative advantage of the Islamists. So, going forward, the question may become whether there is still even a recognizably distinct object called "political Islam." Indeed, it seems to be increasingly difficult today to provide an easy answer to the question "what is Islamism?" It is clear that, going forward, we will need to treat Islamists such as the MB as part of a wider Islamic ecology of actors, movements, and voices—at the same time as their own agenda and objectives become a function of their fortunes *vis-à-vis*, and relations with, other actors in the formal political realm.

In the future, Islamist actors increasingly will find themselves contending not only with various secular political currents, but also with new forms of Muslim politics that contest their vision of an Islamic social order, and that seek to propose alternative idioms of Islamization and public religiosity. But we should not view this, as some proponents of the post-Islamism thesis have suggested, as an unbundling of religion and politics—that is, as a shift toward unconscious secularism. Nor should we impart any particular sense of directionality to the politics entailed in this shift. Post-Islamist forms of Muslim politics are not necessarily reformist or progressive by nature—indeed, many Muslims today find in the security and authenticity of ultraconservative Salafism a paradigm of religiosity eminently suited for global life. Rather, moving beyond Islamism—like moving beyond the state—means the erasure of the boundaries that supposedly constitute "religion" and "politics" as separate domains in the first place. Only through making this move, we might contend, does it become possible to fully appreciate the impact of globalization on the Muslim world, and to understand the complex array of forces and relations that enact—and through which are enacted—all manner of Muslim politics.

NOTES

1 R. Baker, *Islam Without Fear: Egypt and the New Islamists,* Cambridge, MA: Harvard University Press, 2003; G. Fuller, *The Future of Political Islam,* New York: Palgrave Macmillan, 2004.
2 C. Wickham, "The Causes and Dynamics of Islamist Auto-Reform," *ICIS International* 6, 2006, pp. 6–7.
3 D. Brumberg, "Islamists and the Politics of Consensus," *Journal of Democracy* 13, 2002, p. 112.
4 H. al-Turabi, "The Islamic State," in J. Esposito (ed.), *Voices of Resurgent Islam,* New York: Oxford University Press, 1983, pp. 241–251.
5 R. Ghannouchi, "The Participation of Islamists in a non-Islamic Government," in A. Tamimi (ed.), *Power Sharing Islam?,* London: Liberty, 1993, pp. 51–63.
6 Fuller, op. cit., p. 198.
7 Fuller, op. cit., pp. 200–201.
8 Fuller, op. cit., p. 201.
9 O. Roy, *Globalized Islam: The Search for a New Ummah,* New York: Columbia University Press, 2004; P. Mandaville, *Transnational Muslim Politics: Reimagining the Umma,* London: Routledge, 2001.
10 M. Davis, *Planet of Slums,* London: Verson, 2006; R. Neuwirth, *Shadow Cities: A Billion Squatters, A New Urban World,* New York: Routledge, 2005.
11 C. Henry, R. Springborg, *Globalization and the Politics of Development in the Middle East,* Cambridge: Cambridge University Press, 2001, p. 225.
12 G. Arrighi (ed.), *Semiperipheral Development,* Beverly Hills, CA: Sage, 1985.
13 Brumberg, op. cit., p. 102.
14 J. Schwedler, J. A. Clark., "Islamist–Leftist Cooperation in the Arab World," *ISIM Review* 18, 2006, pp. 10–11.

APPENDIX

Key economic and political indicators for selected Muslim countries

Country	Total Population	% Muslim	HDI Rank	GDP (Billions of USD)	GDP Growth	Freedom House	Transparency International Ranking (higher = more corrupt)
Afghanistan	31,108,077	99.8	175	18	7	NF	174
Algeria	38,087,812	98.2	93	208	2.5	NF	105
Bangladesh	163,654,860	90.4	146	115.6	6.3	PF	144
Egypt	85,294,388	94.7	112	257	2.2	PF	118
Indonesia	251,160,124	88.1	121	878	6.2	F	118
Iran	79,853,900	99.7	76	514.1	1.8	NF	133
Iraq	31,858,481	98.9	131	210.3	8.4	NF	169
Jordan	6,482,081	98.8	100	31.2	2.8	NF	58
Kuwait	2,695,316	86.4	54	176.6	8.2	PF	66
Lebanon	4,131,583	59.7	72	42.9	1.4	PF	128
Libya	6,002,347	96.6	64	–	2.1	PF	160
Malaysia	29,628,392	61.4	64	303.5	5.6	PF	54
Morocco	32,649,130	99.9	130	96.7	2.7	PF	88
Nigeria	174,507,539	47.9	153	262.6	6.6	PF	139
Pakistan	193,238,868	96.4	146	231.2	4.2	PF	139
Palestine	4,440,127	97.5	110	–	–	–	–
Saudi Arabia	26,939,583	97.1	57	576.8	6.8	NF	66
Senegal	13,300,410	95.9	154	14.2	3.7	F	94
Somalia	10,251,568	98.6	–	–	–	NF	174
Sudan	34,847,910	71.4	171	58.8	–10.1	NF	173
Syria	22,457,336	92.8	116	73.7	3.2	NF	144
Tajikistan	7,910,041	99.0	125	7	8.0	NF	157
Tunisia	10,835,873	99.8	94	45.7	3.6	PF	75
Turkey	80,694,485	98.6	90	789.3	2.2	PF	54
UAE	5,473,972	76.0	41	360.2	4.9	NF	27
Uzbekistan	28,661,637	96.5	114	51.1	8.2	NF	170
Yemen	25,408,288	99.0	160	35.6	.1	NF	156

Notes: The Human Development Index (HDI) is a UNDP statistical indicator that assigns country rankings on the basis of several quality-of-life factors, with higher rankings corresponding to higher standards of living; GDP growth is annual year-on-year growth (latest available figure); the Freedom House rankings designate countries as Free (F), Partially Free (PF) or Not Free (NF) based on an analysis of political rights and civil liberties; the Transparency International rankings measure perceptions of national corruption, with more corrupt countries at the higher end of the scale.

Sources: CIA World Factbook (Population data); Pew Research Center (Muslim demography); World Bank World Development Indicators (GDP, GDP growth); UNDP, *Human Development Report 2013* (HDI); Freedom House, *Freedom in the World Report 2013*; Transparency International, *Corruption Perceptions Index 2012*.

SUGGESTIONS FOR FURTHER READING

Readers who would like to explore topics and themes covered in this book beyond the references cited within are advised to consult the following works.

POLITICAL ISLAM (GENERAL, COMPARATIVE AND THEORETICAL)

M. Ayoob, *The Many Faces of Political Islam,* Ann Arbor, MI: University of Michigan Press, 2007.

A. Bayat, *Making Islam Democratic: Social Movements and the Post-Islamist Turn,* Palo Alto, CA: Stanford University Press, 2007.

———, *Post-Islamism: The Changing Faces of Political Islam,* Oxford: Oxford University Press, 2013.

J. Beinin, J. Stork (eds), *Political Islam,* London: I.B. Tauris, 1997.

A. Boubekeur, O. Roy (eds), *Whatever Happened to the Islamists? Salafis, Heavy Metal Muslims, and the Lure of Consumerist Islam,* London: Hurst, 2012.

N. Brown, *When Victory Is Not An Option: Islamist Movements in Arab Politics,* Ithaca, NY: Cornell University Press, 2012.

F. Burgat, *Face to Face with Political Islam,* New York: I.B. Tauris, 2003.

J. Clark, *Islam, Charity and Activism: Middle-Class Networks and Social Welfare in Egypt, Jordan, and Yemen,* Bloomington, IN: Indiana University Press, 2004.

D. Eickelman, J. Piscatori, *Muslim Politics,* revised edn, Princeton, NJ: Princeton University Press, 2004.

J. Esposito, *Islam and Politics,* 4th edn, Syracuse, NY: Syracuse University Press, 1998.

G. Fuller, *The Future of Political Islam,* New York: Palgrave, 2003.

R. Hefner (ed.), *Remaking Muslim Politics: Pluralism, Contestation, Democratization,* Princeton, NJ: Princeton University Press, 2005.

S. Ismail, *Rethinking Islamist Politics: Culture, the State, and Islamism,* London: I.B. Tauris, 2003.

A. Karam (ed.), *Transnational Political Islam: Religion, Ideology, and Power,* London: Pluto Press, 2004.

G. Kepel, *Jihad: The Trail of Political Islam,* Cambridge, MA: Harvard University Press, 2002.

P. Mandaville, *Transnational Muslim Politics: Reimagining the Umma,* London: Routledge, 2003.

R. Martin, A. Barzegar (eds), *Islamism: Contested Perspectives on Political Islam,* Palo Alto, CA: Stanford University Press, 2009.

R. Meijer (ed.), *Global Salafism: Islam's New Religious Movement,* New York: Columbia University Press, 2009.

B. Milton-Edwards, *Islamic Fundamentalism Since 1945,* London: Routledge, 2005.

M. Moaddel, *Islamic Modernism, Nationalism, and Fundamentalism: Episode and Discourse,* Chicago, IL: University of Chicago Press, 2005.

J. Piscatori, *Islam in a World of Nation-States,* Cambridge: Cambridge University Press, 1986.

O. Roy, *The Failure of Political Islam,* London: I.B. Tauris, 1994.

———, *Globalized Islam: The Search for a New Ummah,* New York: Columbia University Press, 2004.

J. Schwedler, *Faith in Moderation: Islamist Parties in Jordan and Yemen,* New York: Cambridge University Press, 2006.

F. Volpi, *Political Islam Observed,* London: Hurst, 2010.

——— (ed.), *Political Islam: A Critical Reader,* London: Routledge, 2010.

C. Wickham, *The Muslim Brotherhood: Evolution of an Islamist Movement,* Princeton, NJ: Princeton University Press, 2013.

Q. Wiktorowicz (ed.), *Islamic Activism: A Social Movement Theory Approach,* Bloomington, IN: Indiana University Press, 2004.

S. Zubaida, *Islam, the People and the State: Political Ideas and Movements in the Middle East,* London: I.B. Tauris, 1993.

———, *Law and Power in the Islamic World,* London: I.B. Tauris, 2005.

MUSLIM POLITICS IN SPECIFIC COUNTRIES AND REGIONS

M. Al-Rasheed, *Contesting the Saudi State: Islamic Voices from a New Generation,* Cambridge: Cambridge University Press, 2006.

J. Alagha, *Hizbullah's Identity Construction,* Amsterdam: Amsterdam University Press, 2011.

M. Alshamsi, *Islam and Political Reform in Saudi Arabia: The Quest for Political Change and Reform,* London: Routledge, 2010.

S. Arjomand, *After Khomeini: Iran Under His Successors,* Oxford: Oxford University Press, 2009.

D. Avon, A. Khatchadourian, *Hezbollah: A History of the Party of God,* Cambridge, MA: Harvard University Press, 2012.

M. Ayoob, H. Kosebalaban (eds), *Religion and Politics in Saudi Arabia: Wahhabism and the State,* Boulder, CO: Lynne Rienner, 2008.

T. Barfield, *Afghanistan: A Cultural and Political History,* Princeton, NJ: Princeton University Press, 2012.

Ü. Cizre, *Secular and Islamic Politics in Turkey: The Making of the Justice and Development Party,* London: Routledge, 2007.

R. Crews, A. Tarzi (eds), *The Taliban and the Crisis of Afghanistan,* Cambridge, MA: Harvard University Press, 2009.

L. Deeb, *An Enchanted Modern: Gender and Public Piety in Shi'i Lebanon,* Princeton, NJ: Princeton University Press, 2006.

F. Devji, *Muslim Zion: Pakistan as a Political Idea,* Cambridge, MA: Harvard University Press, 2013.

B. Eligür, *The Mobilization of Political Islam in Turkey,* Cambridge: Cambridge University Press, 2010.

A. Giustozzi, *Koran, Kalashnikov, and Laptop: The Neo-Taliban Insurgency in Afghanistan,* New York: Columbia University Press, 2009.

———, *Decoding the New Taliban: Insights from the Afghan Field,* New York: Columbia University Press, 2012.

J. Gunning, *Hamas in Politics: Democracy, Religion, Violence,* London: Hurst, 2010.

T. Hegghammer, *Jihad in Saudi Arabia: Violence and Pan-Islamism Since 1979,* Cambridge: Cambridge University Press, 2010.

H. Iqtidar, *Secularizing Islamists? Jama'at-e-Islami and Jama'at-ud-Da'wa in Urban Pakistan,* Chicago, IL: University of Chicago Press, 2011.

S. Lacroix, *Awakening Islam: The Politics of Religion Dissent in Contemporary Saudi Arabia,* Cambridge, MA: Harvard University Press, 2011.

L. Lybarger, *Identity and Religion in Palestine: The Struggle Between Islamism and Secularism in the Occupied Territories,* Princeton, NJ: Princeton University Press, 2007.

B. Milton-Edwards, S. Farrell, *Hamas: The Islamic Resistance Movement,* Cambridge: Polity Press, 2010.

M. Nelson, *In the Shadow of Shari'ah: Islam, Islamic Law, and Democracy in Pakistan,* New York: Columbia University Press, 2007.

A. R. Norton, *Hezbollah: A Short History,* Princeton, NJ: Princeton University Press, 2009.

R. Rabil, *Religion, National Identity, and Confessional Politics in Lebanon: The Challenge of Islamism,* New York: Palgrave Macmillan, 2011.

B. Rougier, *Everyday Jihad: The Rise of Militant Islam among Palestinians in Lebanon,* Cambridge, MA: Harvard University Press, 2007.

S. Roy, *Hamas and Civil Society in Gaza: Engaging the Islamist Social Sector,* Princeton, NJ: Princeton University Press.

B. Rutherford, *Egypt After Mubarak: Liberalism, Islam, and Democracy in the Arab World,* Princeton, NJ: Princeton University Press, reprint edn, 2013.

R. Scott, *The Challenge of Political Islam: Non-Muslims and the Egyptian State,* Palo Alto, CA: Stanford University Press, 2010.

R. Shaery-Eisenlohr, *Shi'ite Lebanon: Transnational Religion and the Making of National Identities,* New York: Columbia University Press, 2008.

G. Starrett, *Putting Islam to Work: Education, Politics, and Religious Transformation in Egypt,* Berkeley, CA: University of California Press, 1998.

S. Toor, *State of Islam: Culture and Cold War Politics in Pakistan,* London: Pluto, 2011.

B. Turam, *Between Islam and the State: The Politics of Engagement,* Palo Alto, CA: Stanford University Press, 2006.

R. Varzi, *Warring Souls: Youth, Media, and Martyrdom in Post-Revolution Iran,* Durham, NC: Duke University Press, 2006.

J. White, *Islamist Mobilization in Turkey: A Study in Vernacular Politics,* Seattle, WA: University of Washington Press, 2002.

——, *Muslim Nationalism and the New Turks,* Princeton, NJ: Princeton University Press, 2012.

C. Wickham, *Mobilizing Islam: Religion, Activism, and Political Change in Egypt,* New York: Columbia University Press, 2002.

Q. Wiktorowicz, *The Management of Islamic Activism: Salafis, the Muslim Brotherhood, and State Power in Jordan,* Albany, NY: State University of New York Press, 2001.

M. H. Yavuz, *Secularism and Muslim Democracy in Turkey,* Cambridge: Cambridge University Press, 2009.

M. Zeghal, *Islamism in Morocco,* Princeton, NJ: Markus Wiener, 2008.

▌ PRIMARY SOURCE READERS ON ISLAM AND POLITICS

J. Donohue, J. Esposito (eds), *Islam in Transition: Muslim Perspectives,* 2nd edn, New York: Oxford University Press, 2006.

R. Euben, M. Qasim Zaman (eds), *Princeton Readings in Islamist Thought,* Princeton, NJ: Princeton University Press, 2009.

C. Kurzman (ed.), *Liberal Islam: A Sourcebook,* Oxford: Oxford University Press, 1998.

——, *Modernist Islam, 1840–1940: A Sourcebook,* Oxford: Oxford University Press, 2002.

M. Moaddel, K. Talattof (eds), *Modernist and Fundamentalist Debates in Islam,* New York: Palgrave, 2002.

ISLAMIC HISTORY

J. Berkey, *The Formation of Islam: Religion and Society in the Near East, 600–1800,* Cambridge: Cambridge University Press, 2003.

M. Hodgson, *The Venture of Islam: Conscience and History in a World Civilization,* 3 vols, Chicago, IL: University of Chicago Press, 1974.

I. Lapidus, *A History of Islamic Societies,* 2nd edn, Cambridge: Cambridge University Press, 2002.

———, *Islamic Societies to the Nineteenth Century: A Global History,* Cambridge: Cambridge University Press, 2013.

R. Schulze, *A Modern History of the Islamic World,* London: I.B. Tauris, 2002.

ISLAMIC POLITICAL THOUGHT AND THINKERS

K. Abou el-Fadl, *And God Knows the Soldiers: The Authoritative and Authoritarian in Islamic Discourses,* Lanham, MD: University Press of America, 2001.

I. Abu-Rabi, *Intellectual Origins of Islamic Resurgence in the Modern Arab World,* New York: SUNY Press, 1995.

A. An-Naim, *Toward an Islamic Reformation: Civil Liberties, Human Rights, and International Law,* Syracuse, NY: Syracuse University Press, 1996.

R. Baker, *Islam Without Fear: Egypt and the New Islamists,* Cambridge, MA: Harvard University Press, 2003.

G. Bowering (ed.), *The Princeton Encyclopedia of Islamic Political Thought,* Princeton, NJ: Princeton University Press, 2012.

L. Carl Brown, *Religion and State: The Muslim Approach to Politics,* New York: Columbia University Press, 2000.

H. Enayat, *Modern Islamic Political Thought: The Response of the Shi'a and Sunni Muslims to the Twentieth Century,* London: I.B. Tauris, 2005.

S. Khatab, *The Political Thought of Sayyid Qutb: The Theory of Jahiliyya,* London: Routledge, 2006.

N. Lahoud, *Political Thought in Islam: A Study in Intellectual Boundaries,* London: Routledge, 2011.

J. Landau, *The Politics of Pan-Islam: Ideology and Organization,* Oxford: Clarendon Press, 1990.

V. Nasr, *Mawdudi and the Making of Islamic Revivalism,* New York: Oxford University Press, 2002.

F. Rahman, *Islam & Modernity: The Transformation of an Intellectual Tradition,* Chicago, IL: University of Chicago Press, 1984.

A. Rahnema (ed.), *Pioneers of Islamic Revival,* 2nd edn, London: Zed Books, 2006.

———, *An Islamic Utopian: A Political Biography of Ali Shari'ati,* London: I.B. Tauris, 2000.

A. Sachedina, *The Islamic Roots of Democratic Pluralism,* New York: Oxford University Press, 2001.

M.Q. Zaman, *Modern Islamic Thought in a Radical Age: Religious Authority and Internal Criticism,* Cambridge: Cambridge University Press, 2012.

THE ISLAMIC STATE

A. Afsaruddin, *Islam, the State, and Political Authority: Medieval Issues and Modern Concerns,* New York: Palgrave, 2011.

M. Al-Rasheed, C. Kersten (eds), *Demystifying the Caliphate,* London: Hurst, 2013.

A. Ali Engineer, *The Islamic State,* New Delhi: Vikas Publishing House, 1994.

A. Belkeziz, *The State in Contemporary Islamic Thought,* London: I.B. Tauris, 2009.

A. El-Affendi, *Who Needs an Islamic State?*, London: Grey Seal, 1991.

N. Feldman, *The Rise and Fall of the Islamic State*, Princeton, NJ: Princeton University Press, 2010.

W. Hallaq, *The Impossible State: Islam, Politics, and Modernity's Moral Predicament*, New York: Columbia University Press, 2012.

S. V. R. Nasr, *Islamic Leviathan: Islam and the Making of State Power*, New York: Oxford University Press, 2001.

SHI'ISM

H. Dabashi, *Shi'ism: A Religion of Protest*, Boston, MA: Belknap, 2011.

L. Louër, *Shi'ism and Politics in the Middle East*, New York: Columbia University Press, 2012.

———, *Transnational Shia Politics: Religious and Political Networks in the Gulf*, New York: Columbia University Press, 2008.

M. Momen, *An Introduction to Shi'i Islam*, New Haven, CT: Yale University Press, 1985.

Y. Nakash, *Reaching for Power: The Shi'a in the Modern Arab World*, Princeton, NJ: Princeton University Press, 2006.

V. Nasr, *The Shi'a Revival: How Conflicts Within Islam Will Shape the Future*, New York: Norton, 2006.

Y. Richard, *Shi'ite Islam: Polity Ideology and Creed*, Oxford: Blackwell, 1995.

JIHAD AND RADICALISM

A. Afsaruddin, *Striving in the Path of God: Jihad and Martyrdom in Islamic Thought*, Oxford: Oxford University Press 2013.

M. Bonner, *Jihad in Islamic History: Doctrines and Practice*, Princeton, NJ: Princeton University Press, 2008.

J. Brachman, *Global Jihadism: Theory and Practice*, London: Routledge, 2008.

J. Burr, R. Collins, *Alms for Jihad: Charity and Terrorism in the Islamic World*, Cambridge: Cambridge University Press, 2006.

J. Calvert, *Sayyid Qutb and the Origins of Radicalism*, New York: Columbia University Press, 2010.

D. Cook, *Understanding Jihad*, Berkeley, CA: University of California Press, 2005.

F. Devji, *Landscapes of the Jihad: Militancy, Morality, Modernity*, Ithaca, NY: Cornell University Press, 2005.

———, *The Terrorist in Search of Humanity: Militant Islam and Global Politics*, London: Hurst, 2009.

F. Gerges, *The Rise and Fall of Al-Qaeda*, Oxford: Oxford University Press, 2011.

M. Hafez, *Why Muslims Rebel: Repression and Resistance in the Islamic World*, Boulder, CO: Lynne Rienner, 2003.

N. Lahoud, *The Jihadis' Path to Self-Destruction*, New York: Columbia University Press, 2010.

B. Lia, *Architect of Global Jihad: The Life of Al-Qaeda Strategist Abu Mus'ab Al-Suri*, Oxford: Oxford University Press, 2008.

R. Peters, *Jihad in Classical and Modern Islam: A Reader*, Princeton, NJ: Markus Wiener, 1996.

M. Sageman, *Understanding Terror Networks*, Philadelphia, PA: University of Pennsylvania Press, 2004.

———, *Leaderless Jihad: Terror Networks in the 21st Century*, Philadelphia, PA: University of Pennsylvania Press, 2008.

Q. Wiktorowicz, *Radical Islam Rising: Muslim Extremism in the West*, Lanham, MD: Rowman & Littlefield, 2005.

ISLAM AND NEW MEDIA

L. Abu-Lughod, *Local Contexts of Islamism in Popular Media,* Amsterdam: Amsterdam University Press, 2006.

G. Bunt, *Virtually Islamic: Computer-Mediated Communication and Cyber Islamic Environments,* Cardiff: University of Wales Press, 2000.

———, *Islam in the Digital Age: E-Jihad, Online Fatwas, and Cyber-Islamic Environments,* London: Pluto Press, 2003.

———, *iMuslims: Rewiring the House of Islam,* Chapel Hill, NC: University of North Carolina Press, 2009.

D. Eickelman, J. Anderson (eds), *New Media in the Muslim World: The Emerging Public Sphere,* Bloomington, IN: Indiana University Press, 2003.

M. El-Nawawy, S. Khamis, *Islam Dot Com: Contemporary Islamic Discourses in Cyberspace,* New York: Palgrave Macmillan, 2011.

P. Howard, *The Digital Origins of Dictatorship and Democracy: Information Technology and Political Islam,* Oxford: Oxford University Press, 2010.

N. Sakr, *Satellite Realms: Transnational Television, Globalization and the Middle East,* London: I.B. Tauris, 2001.

A. Sreberny, G. Khiabany, *Blogistan: the Internet and Politics in Iran,* London: I.B. Tauris, 2010.

A. Sreberny-Mohammadi, A. Mohammadi, *Small Media, Big Revolution: Communication, Culture, and the Iranian Revolution,* Minneapolis, MN: University of Minnesota Press, 1994.

ISLAM AND WOMEN

L. Ahmed, *Women and Gender in Islam: Historical Roots of a Modern Debate,* New Haven, CT: Yale University Press, 1992.

———, *A Quiet Revolution: The Veil's Resurgence, from the Middle East to America,* New Haven: Yale University Press, 2012.

A. Barlas, *"Believing Women" in Islam: Unreading Patriarchal Interpretations of the Qur'an,* Austin, TX: University of Texas, 2002.

L. Deeb, *An Enchanted Modern: Gender and Public Piety in Shi'i Lebanon,* Princeton, NJ: Princeton University Press, 2006.

P. van Doorn-Harder, *Women Shaping Islam: Reading the Qur'an in Indonesia,* Champaign, IL: University of Illinois Press, 2006.

D. Kandiyoti (ed.), *Women, Islam and the State,* Philadelphia, PA: Temple University Press, 1991.

S. Mahmood, *Politics of Piety: The Islamic Revival and the Feminist Subject,* Princeton, NJ: Princeton University Press, 2005.

Z. Mir-Hosseini, *Islam and Gender: The Religious Debate in Contemporary Iran,* Princeton, NJ: Princeton University Press, 1999.

Z. Mir-Hosseini et al., *Gender and Equality in Muslim Family Law: Justice and Ethics in the Islamic Legal Process,* London: I.B. Tauris, 2013.

Z. Salime, *Between Feminism and Islam: Human Rights and Sharia Law in Morocco,* Minneapolis: University of Minnesota Press, 2011.

J. Tucker, *Women, Family, and Gender in Islamic Law,* Cambridge: Cambridge University Press, 2008.

GLOSSARY

alim	Religious scholar (singular of *ulama*)
aqeeda	Creed, or tenets of belief
Ayatollah	Literally, "Sign of God;" high-ranking Shi'a cleric
bid'a	Innovation
dar al-ahd	"Land of Treaty"
dar al-harb	"Land of War"
dar al-islam	"Land of Islam"
da'if	A weak *hadith*
da'wa	Propagation of the religion; "calling" to Islam
din wa dawla	"Religion and state"
faqih	Legal scholar or jurist
fatwa	Opinion or edict of a legal scholar (plural: *fatawa*)
fiqh	Islamic legal science
fitna	Social discord
hadith	Report about the Prophet Muhammad
hajj	Pilgrimage to Mecca
halal	Permissible
haram	Forbidden
hijra	Migration
hizb	Party or group
hudud	Prescribed punishments in Islamic law
Hujjat al-Islam	Literally, "Proof of Islam;" middle-ranking Shi'a cleric

ijma	Consensus
ijtihad	Independent reasoning or judgment
intifada	"Shaking off;" mass uprising
islah	Reform
isnad	Chain of transmission in reference to *hadith*
hawala	Pre-modern monetary transfer system
jahiliyya	Pre- or non-Islamic ignorance
jihad	Religious struggle; of a spiritual and/or worldly nature
kalam	Scholastic theology
khilafa	The institution of rule by the caliph
madhhab	School of Islamic law (plural: *madhahib*)
madrasa	Religious school
majlis al-shura	Consultative council
mufti	Scholar who issues a *fatwa*
mutawwa	Religious police
mujahideen	Those who perform *jihad*
nasiha	Advice or counsel, as given to a figure in authority
qadi	Judge
qanun	Non-religious law
qiyas	Legal methodology based on analogical deduction
sahih	Sound *hadith*
salaf	Pious ancestors; the first three generations of Muslims
Salafism	Movement seeking return to the practices of the *salaf*
Shi'a	Partisans (of Ali); the largest minority sect in Islam
shari'ah	Religious law
shura	Consultation
sira	Biographical literature about the Prophet
sunna	"Orthodox" traditions of the Prophet
Sunni	The people of tradition or orthodoxy; vast majority of Muslims
Sufism	Islamic mysticism

tafsir	Qur'anic exegesis
tahdith	Modernization
tajdid	Renewal
tarbiya	Education/human development
tariqa	Sufi order
tawhid	Divine unity
ulama	Religious scholars (singular: *alim*)
umma	The community of Muslims, potentially global in scope
usul al-fiqh	Principles of legal science
vilayat-e faqih	Guardianship of the legal scholar (Persian)
waqf	Charitable endowment (plural: *awqaf*)
zakat	tithe

INDEX

Page references for figures are in *italics* and tables are shown in **bold**.

Abbas, Mahmoud 281, 295
Abbasid dynasty 38–39, 40
Abd al-Raziq, Ali 14–15, 67–68
Abd al-Wahhab, Muhammad Ibn 208–209
Abduh, Muhammad 48–49, 61–62, 67, 68,
  144
Abdul Aziz, King of Saudi Arabia 109,
  211–212, 214, 215, 217–218, 222
Abdullah, King of Saudi Arabia 227–228
Abdullah I, King of Jordan 178
Abdullah II, King of Jordan 182
Abu Bakr (first caliph) 33
Abu Dhabi 414
Afghan-Arabs *see* Arab Afghans
al-Afghani, Jamal ad-Din 48, 58–61, *61*, 62, 67
Afghanistan: Arab Afghans 306, 333–334,
  335–336, 340; Deobandi *madrasas*
  314–315; future role of the Taliban
  320–321; geopolitical influences 307;
  history 305–307; mujahideen, Pakistani
  support for 237, 305–306; Soviet war
  113, 305, 333; *see also* Taliban
Ahmad, Mirza Ghulam 231
Ahmadinejad, Mahmoud 261–264
Ahmadis 231
AKP (Justice and Development Party): as
  Islamist party 173–174, 404–405; in
  legislative elections **129**; as Muslim
  democratic party 132, 133; in power
  170–173, 402–403; as role model 177,
  186; support base 168–170
al-Afghani, Jamal ad-Din 341
Alawis 52–53
Al-Azhar University, Cairo 67, 76, 156, 197

Al-Gammaa al-Islamiyya 152
Algeria: Al-Qaeda in 363; Arab Afghans 335;
  Armed Islamic Group (GIA) 117–118;
  elections 114, 115–118, *117*, 126, *186*,
  194
Ali (fourth caliph) 34–35, 37
alim (religious scholar) 13, 40, 43, 391
al-islam din wa dawla ("Islam is [both]
  religion and state") 14
*Al-Islam wa usual al-hukm (Islam and the
  Principles of Governance)* (al-Raziq) 67–68
Al-Jazeera 391–392
Al-Nahda 126
Al-Qaeda: communications strategy 347;
  comparison with Hizb ut-Tahrir
  359–360; formation of 336, 344–345;
  funding 335, 345–346; global jihadi
  movement 341–344, 345; *jihad,*
  concept of 340–341; membership 348;
  operatives 348, 349–350; organizational
  structure 345–346, 348–349; Qutb's
  influence on 104–105; regional
  franchises 363–364; symbolism of
  365–366; ties with Jabhat al-Nusra 304;
  training facilities 348; waning influence
  of 360–363; *see also* Bin Laden, Usama
Al-Qaeda in the Islamic Maghreb (AQIM)
  363
Al-Qaeda on the Arabian Peninsula (AQAP)
  225, 364
Al-Qiyam Society 116
Al-Shabab 364
AMAL (Afwaj al-Muqawama al-Lunaniyya)
  113, **128–129**, 296, 298, 301

Anwar Ibrahim 238, 239
Arab Afghans 306, 333–334, 335–336, 340, 348
Arab Uprisings 2011: rise in sectarianism 53; Saudi Arabia and 223–224; Syria and 302; Tunisia and 150, 159; *see also* Egypt
Arabia, history of 30–32
Arab-Israeli wars 93, 111, 124, 216
Arafat, Yasser 279, 280, 281, 288
al-Asad, Bashar 302
Asharism 38, 47
Atatuk, Mustapha Kemal 65, 69–72, 162, 163
auto-reform 190, 194
al-Awdah, Salman 221, 223–224, 343
al-Awlaki, Anwar 225
awqaf (charitable endowment) 94, 163, 247, 256, 276, 284
Ayub Khan, Muhammad 232–233
Azzam, Abdullah 328, 334, 336, 340, 344
Azzam, M. 138

Ba'ath Party 72–73
Baker, R. 142, 144
Bakri, Sheikh Muhammad Omar 358–359
Bali bombing 3.42, 176, 346
Bangladesh 233–234
al-Bani, Muhammad Nasir al-Din 343
al-Banna, Hassan: assassination of 79, 93; contrasted with Mawdudi 82, 84, 85; early life 75–76; founding of Muslim Brotherhood 76–77; image of *79*; Islamism of 76–79; as new Islamist intellectual 383; role of the state 77–78; Sufism of 76, 91
Bayat, Asef 375
Belhadj, Ali 116, *117*
Bhutto, Benazir 240, 241, 308
Bhutto, Zulfikar Ali 233–234
bid'a (innovation) 47, 48, 58, 101, 209, 317, 350
Bin Baz, Sheikh 217, 221
Bin Laden, Usama: in Afghanistan 306; Al-Qaeda funding structure 346–347; Arab Afghan supporters 335–336; Azzam's influence 334; concept of jihad 331; death of 365; evolution of Al-Qaeda 344–345; image of *342*; and Islamic revivalism 58; as new Islamist intellectual 383; in Saudi Arabia 221–222; in Sudan 336; USA

as far enemy 44, 341–342, 345; *see also* Al-Qaeda
Boko Haram 272, 317
Bosnia 21, 340
Bouazizi, Muhammad 150
Boubekeur, A. 393, 396–397
Bourdieu, Pierre 125
Bouteflika, Abdelaziz 118
Brumberg, D. 127, 133, 194–195, 258–259
Burgat, F. 375

caliphate (*khilafah*): abolition of 62–63; al-Banna on 77; democratic (Mawdudi) 82; legal authority 15, 44–45; post-caliphate theories 65–69; and radical Islamism 330–331; rashidun caliphs 33–36; re-establishment of 354–355, 357
The Caliphate, or the Supreme Imamate 67
Catholic Church 10
Central Asia 321–322
centrist Islamism 144–148, 152
Christian church: formal hierarchy 13; and the state, historical 9–10
Cold War: Afghanistan, impact on 305–307; global jihadi movement 333–336; Islamist politics beyond 112–115; US relations during 72, 110, 236
colonialism: anti-colonialism and Islamic reformism 58–63; anti-colonialism and Islamism 76, 80, 81–82; decolonialization and nationalism 62, 65, 69; dual legal systems 16; European colonies in the Muslim world (1914) *66*
Committee for the Defense of Legitimate Rights (CDLR) 222–223
Committee of Union and Progress 69–70
Cook, D. 333–334

Damascus 37, 38
Danish Cartoon Affair 378–379, 395
dar al-ahd ("Land of Treaty") 337, 338
dar al-harb ("Land of War") 338, 339
dar al-islam ("Land of Islam") 339
Daud Khan, Muhammad 305
da'wa (propagation of the religion) 76, 102, 126, 138, 178, 186
Day of Ashura 51
deduction, analogical (*qiyas*) 42
democracy: and Islamist parties 114–115, 126–127, 188–190, 193–196, 405–406;

Islamists in legislative elections **128–129**; and new Islamism 130; *see also* Muslim Democracy
Demokrat Party 164
Deobandi movement: *madrasas* 242–243, 314–315, 316; Taliban and 310–311
ad-Din, Jamal 48
Diyanet 70, 72, 163, 322
Druze 52–53
Dubai 414

effendiyya (middle classes) 93–94
Egypt: and Amr Khaled 396; April 6 movement 149; Christian population 232; constitution, post-revolution 155–156; economy 93–94, 136; *effendiyya* (middle classes) 93–94; Free Officers Revolution, 1952 96; Hizb al-Wasat 131; Islamism, compared to Turkey 168; January 25 Revolution 150–151; Kifaya movement 146, 150; militant groups 105–106, 158; as Muslim Democracy 133–134; nationalism movement 62; post-revolutionary politics 151–159, *196*; retreat of the state 136–138, 271; Salafi political parties 50, 152–155, *154*, 158; Saudi-Egyptian rivalry 216; state formation 72–73, 93–94; Tahrir Square, Cairo 150, *151*; Tamarod 157; *see also* al-Banna, Hassan; Muslim Brotherhood (MB) Egyptian branch; new Islamism
Enlightenment, the 9–10
En-Nahda 159–161
Epistle of Light (Nursi) 164
Erbakan, Necmettin 166, 167, 168, 169–170
Erdoğan, Recep Tayyip 169–174, *171*
Esposito, J. and Voll, J. 138
Europe: adoption of sovereign state model 9; European colonies in the Muslim world (1914) *66*; imperialism 56–57; liberalism and secularism 13–14; Muslim political activity 410; new Islamist intellectuals 380–381; political liberalism 10–11; religion and social activity 11–12; *see also* West, the

Faisal, King of Saudi Arabia 214, 216, 217, 218
faqih (legal specialist) 13, 40, 43, 206; *see also* jurisprudence (*fiqh*)

Farag, Mohammad 332, 339–340
fatwa (legal opinions): on the internet 390–391; *mufti* 40, 43; overview of 43–44
fiqh (jurisprudence) 40; *see also* jurisprudence (*fiqh*)
fiqh al-jihad (jurisprudence of warfare) 338
FIS (Islamic Salvation Front) 114, 115–118, *117*, 126, **128**, *186*, 335
Five Pillars of Islam 31, 235
FJP (Freedom and Justice Party) **128**, 151–152, 192
France: imperialism 62, 72, 115–116; *laïcisme* 11
Free Officers Revolution 96
Front de la Liberation national (FLN) 116, 117, 118

Gaza 275–276, 283, 286, 294, 295
Gemaa Islamiyya 104, 106, 277, 332, 335, 342–343
geopolitical influences: Afghanistan 307; global jihadi movement 333–336; Islamism 112–115, 123; Muslim politics in the future 415
Gerges, F. 361
Ghannouchi, Rachid 159, 160, *160*, 161
GIA (Armed Islamic Group) 117–118
global jihadi movement 333–336, 341–344, 345; *see also* Al-Qaeda
globalization: Al-Qaeda 347; global Muslim activism 414–415; the global *ulama* 379–382; impact on Muslim politics 24–26, 143–148, 376–377; and the Muslim identity 411–412; and religious consumption 392–393, 412–413; resurgence of Salafism 50–51
Great Britain: Hizb ut-Tahrir (HT) in 355–356, 358–359; interests in Middle East 62; religious pluralism 12
Guardianship Council 255, 260
Gül, Abdullah 171
Gülen, Fethullah 166, 384–386, 397
Gulf War, 1991 219–220
Gunaratna, R. 345
gunpowder empires 53–56, *55*

hadith (reports about the Prophet Muhammad): *isnad* 40; origins of 31; in Salafism 47; verification of 40
hajj (pilgrimage) 31

Hamas: active resistance tactics 278, 280; attacks against Israel 278, 279–280, 289, 290, 294; election of 114, 281, 293; funding 282–283; ideology 274–275, 289–291; Israeli crackdowns against 278, 280–281; in legislative elections **129**; and the MB 277–278, 287–288; militant wing (Izz al-Din al-Qassam Brigades) 278, 282, 291; organizational structure 282, 283–284, *283*; origins of 113, 275–277; and the Oslo Agreement 279–280, 289; the PLO and 278, 280, 287–289, 294, 295; political factionalism 292, 295; social services provision 281–282, 284–285; support base 282, 284, 285–286, *287*
Hanafi rite 56
Hanbali school 46, 209
Haniyeh, Ismail 281, 292, 295
Hashemite dynasty 177
al-Hawali, Safar 221, 223, 343
hijra (migration) 32, 211
Hizb al-Wasat 131, 143, 145, 148, 152
Hizb ut-Tahrir (HT): caliphate, re-establishment of 331, 354–355, 357; compared to Al-Qaeda 359–360; ideology 357–358; support base 352, 356–357; in the UK 355–356, 358–359
Hizbullah: clerical support for 300; formation of 113, 296; internal political conflict (March 14 alliance) 297–302; Iranian support 296–297; in legislative elections **128**; overview of 295–296; and sectarian conflicts 297, 299, 301–302; social services provision 296–297; *see also* Lebanon
al-Hudaybi, Hasan 95–96
hudud (prescribed punishment) 41, 85, 140, 235, 311
Hukumat-i Islami (Islamic Government) 248–250
human rights: and Islamism 372, 373; in Morocco 183; new Islamism 127, 130; in Nigeria 272; in Saudi Arabia 109–110; in Turkey 170; and the *umma* 351; within the Wasatiyya 143–144; *see also* women
Husayn 37
al-Husir, Sati 69

al-Husri, Sati 69
Hussein, Saddam 203, 211, 220, 292, 336

IAF (Islamic Action Front) **128**, 131–132, 180–183, *180*, 189–190
Ibn Abd al-Wahhab, Muhammad 210–211, 338
Ibn Saud, Abdul Aziz 62, 211–212, 217
Ibn Saud, Muhammad 210–211, 338
Ibn Taymiyya 46, 48, 209
identity, Muslim: and globalization 411–412; as a minority population 409–410; and the political order 408–413; and radical Islamism 350–351, 408
ijma (consensus) 41, 42, 404
ijtihad (independent judgement): on the internet 390; and *jihad* 338; in jurisprudence 43–44; Mawdudi on 83–84; in Salafism 47
Ikatan Cendekiawan Muslim Se-Indonesia (ICMI) 175
Ikhwan 211–212
India 73–74, 80–82, 229–230, 242
Indonesia: Islam and politics in 174–177; pancasila 175; PKS (Prosperous Justice Party) *176*, 177; popular Islam 397; religous leaders, political role of 20
International Crisis Group 356
International Islamic Conference (2005) 381–382
internet *see* new media
Iran: anti-Americanism 261; clerical/political tensions 256, 257, 262, 263–264; constitution 254; distrust of the Taliban 307, 308; governmental structure 254–256, *255*; "Green Movement" 262–263, *263*; history 245–247; invasion by Iraq 254; Islam and politics in 264–265; Islamic revolution 111–112, 113, 251–252, 272–273; as Islamic state 206; liberalizing reforms 258–261; neo-Khomeinism 261–264; political pragmatism 257–258; post-revolutionary politics 252–254; Qajar dynasty 112, 245–246; role of women 256; support for Hizbullah 296–297; Supreme Leader's role 254–255; *ulama*, political role of 246, 247, 253; *vilayat-e faqih* ("guardianship of the jurist") 248, 250, 253, 254

Iran-Iraq war (1980–88) 254, 257
Iraq: Al-Qaeda in 363; invasion of Iran 254, 257; sectarianism 53, 308–309
Islam: authority figures 13; global Muslim population 4–5, *6–7*, **8**; knowledge production and religion 12–13; origins of 28–31; regional/cultural factors 21–22, 31, 34; relationship of politics and religion 12–17, 19–20, **20**; social value 16–17; submission to the divine 30–31; territorial expansion, historical 33–34, *35*, 37–38
Islam is the solution (MB slogan) 125, 143, 197, 404, 416
Islamic, term 23
Islamic Action Front (IAF) 131–132, 180–183, *180*, 189–190
Islamic Jihad: assassination of Sadat 105, 106, 111; formation of 276–277; links with Al-Qaeda 336, 341; militancy of 332; Qutb's influence on 104–105, 332; support base 282, 335
Islamic Reformation 13
Islamic reformism 58–63, 405–408
Islamic revivalism 57–58, 74–75, 111
Islamic Salvation Front (FIS) 114, 115–118, *117*, 126, *186*, 335
Islamic states: Nigeria as 114; overview of 203–207, 265; role of women 226–227; Sudan as 113–114; *see also* Iran; Pakistan; Saudi Arabia
Islamic Tendency Movement (MTI) 126, 159
Islamism: academic debates on 86–87; auto-reform 190, 194; concepts of 86–87, 372–374; electoral successes, post Arab uprising 192–193; emergence of 74–75, 125; in failed states 270–271, 322–324; geopolitical influences 112–115, 123; modernism of 107–108; political aims 193–194; as political opposition 191–193; and political pluralism 196–198, 405–406; shift to new Islamism 130–131, 401–405; social profile 123–127, 402–403; and social spaces 374–375; term 22; urban nature of 108, 124, 169; *see also* democracy; new Islamism; radical Islamism
Islamist intellectuals, new 382–384
Ismail, S. 374–375
Ismailis ("Seveners") 52–53

isnad (chain of transmission) 40
Israel: anti-Hamas crackdowns 278, 280–281; assassination of Sheikh Yassin 280–281; funding of Hamas 276, 283; Gaza War (2008–9) 294; Hamas attacks against 278, 279–280, 289, 290, 294; invasion of Lebanon 297–298; Oslo Agreement 279, 288–289; *see also* Hamas
Izz al-Din al-Qassam Brigades 278, 282, 291

Ja'fari legal school 52
jahiliyya (pre/non-Islamic ignorance) 101–103, 219, 339, 341
Jemah Islamiah 346
JI (Jama'at-i Islami) 81, 230, 235, 236, 237, 240, 243
jihad: concepts of (violence v. struggle) 103–104, 331, 336–338; Egyptian MB offshoots and 332–333; global jihadi movement 329, 333–336, 341–344, 345; jihadist recantations 342–343; just war theories 338; liberation of Muslim lands 334; links with Islamism 332; Mawdudi on 84; Palestinian suicide bombers 21; Qutb on 97, 102–105, 332, 338–339; Salafi jihadis 50, 338–340; *see also* radical Islamism
Jinnah, Muhammad Ali 73, 229–230, 231
Jordan: Arab Afghans in 335; elections 178–179, 180–181, 182; Hizb al-Wasat 182; IAF and democratic politics 131–132, 188–190; IAF/regime relations 180–183, *180*, 190–191; MB political involvement 187–188; MB support base 186–187, 188–189; MB/regime relations 177–180; and Palestine 189; political reforms 178, 181
JUI (Jamaat Ulama-i-Islam) **129**, 242, 243, 308, 316
jurisprudence (*fiqh*): authoritative sources 42; and caliph's authority 44–45; Egypt, post-revolution 156; emergence of 40; *fatwa* 43–44; Hanbali school 46, 209; *ijtihad* 43–44; of the Muslim Brotherhood 91
Justice and Development Party (AKP, Turkey) *see* AKP (Justice and Development Party)

Justice and Development Party (PDJ, Morocco) 131, 133, 183–184, *184*

Ka'aba 29
Karzai, Hamid 318, 319, 320
Kemalism 70–72, 162, 163, 174; *see also* Turkey
Kepel, G. 218, 312, 372, 373
Khadija 30
Khaled, Amr 393–397, *394*
Khameini, Ali 257–258
Khatami, Mohammad 258–261, 265
Khawarij 36, 38
khilafah see caliphate (*khilafah*)
Khomeini, Ayatollah 111–112, 247–251, *250*, 273
Kifaya movement 146, 150
Kitab al-Tawhid (The Book of Divine Unity) 58, 209
knowledge production: in Islam 12–13; and Islamic reformism 59–60; new Islamist intellectuals 382–384; and religious faith 10–11, 12
Kotku, Mehmed Zahid (Zahid Efendi) 165

Lebanon: Civil War 113; Doha agreement 299; elections 296, 299–300; Hariri, Rafik assassination of 297, 298, 300; internal political conflict 297–302; Israeli invasion of 297–298; overview 295–296; relations with Syria 297, 301; *see also* Hizbullah
liberalism: in Europe 10–11; and national self-determination 62; and secularism 13–14

Madani, Abbasi 116, *117*
madrasas (religious schools): Deobandi 314–315; Pakistani 243, 313–314, 335
Madrid peace process 179, 278, 288
Mahathir Mohamed 238–239
Malaysia: parallel legal system 41; state-led Islamization 238–239
al-Maliki, Nouri 309
Mardin, S. 165
Martin, V. 251
Mawdudi, Abu Ala 49
Mawdudi, Sayyid Abu'l-A'la: anti-colonialism of 80, 81–82; contrasted with al-Banna 82, 84, 85; on democracy 82, 83–84; early life 80–81; formation of JI 81; on *ijtihad* 83–84; image of *79*; influence on Qutb 101; on Islamic revolution 84–85; jailing of 231; non-nationalism of 81, 82, 230; sovereignty of God 82–83

Mecca: the Grand Mosque 218; *hajj* (pilgrimage) 31; history 29–30, 32; under Ibn Saud 211; polytheism of 30
Medina 32, 211
Mehmet II 54
Mehmet VI 56
Metcalf, B. 316
military, the: in Pakistan 230, 234, 240, 244–245; political role of 133; in Turkey 172
Mitchell, R. 92
Moaddel, M. 94
modernism, of Islamism 91, 94, 107–108, 125
Montazeri, Hossein Ali 257
morality: Five Pillars of Islam 31; Islamic and political systems 5–9, 14–15; just war theories 337–338; under the MB 125; *mutawwa* (Saudi Arabia) 213–214; new Islamism 405; and reason, Muslim context 12–13; and Shari'ah 38, 41–42, 59–60; under the Taliban 310–312, 318; through Islamism 125
Morocco: constitutional reforms 183, *186*; Islamist political participation 183–186; Justice and Charity (Al-Adl w'al-Ihsan) 185; PJD (Parti de la Justice et du Dévelopment) **129**, 131, 133, 183–184
Morsi, Mohammed 153, 155–157, *157*
Mosaddeq, Mohammed 247
MTI (Mouvement de la Tendance Islamique) 126, 159
Mu'awiya 34, 36, 37
Mubarak, Hosni 105, 106, 135, 139–141, 149, 150
Mughal Empire 54
al-Muhajiroun movement 234
Muhammad, Prophet: death of and succession to 32–33; as embodiment of Qur'anic teaching 29, 31; migration to Yathrib (Medina) 32; prophethood of 29–30
Muhammad's Army (Jaysh Muhammad) 179, 335
Muhammad's Youth 105–106

mujahideen forces 237, 305–306, 314, 334–335
Mujamma al-Islami 276, 282, *283*, 285
al-Mulk, Nizam 15
Musharraf, Pervez 240–242
Muslim, term 5, 23
Muslim Brotherhood (MB) **128**
Muslim Brotherhood (MB) Egyptian branch: anti-government/British stance 93–95; compared to Salafis 154–155; early political role 78–79; evolution and expansion 76–77, 89–91, 95; factionalism 90–91, 96, 131, 144–145, 147–148, 152, 402; FJP party 151; and the Free Officers 96, 99; and Hizb al-Wasat 145; international MB-inspired groups 89, 106–107, 108; leadership of al-Hudaybi 95–96; as modernist 91, 94, 107–108; under Mubarak's regime 105–107, 135, 139–141, 149–150; organizational structure 91–92; political strategies 105–107, 138, 139, 146–147, 149; as post-revolutionary political force 152–159, 194, 195, 403; as proto-Islamist movement 107–108; role in popular uprising 150–151; under Sadat 105–107, 135; and Salafi Islamists 50; as social movement 136–139, 413; sociopolitical stance 93–95, 106, 133–139; support base 90, 93–95, 123, 125–126, 135; as underground opposition movement 96–97
Muslim Brotherhood (MB) Jordanian branch: factionalism within 188–189; IAF/regime relations 177–183; political involvement 187–188; support base 186–187
Muslim Brotherhood (MB), Palestinian branch 276–278, 287–288
Muslim Congresses (1924–31) 68–69
Muslim Democracy: AKP as (Turkey) 132, 133, 173–174; Egypt as 133–134; Indonesia as 174–177; overview of 132–134, 402–403; and political pluralism 195, 405–406; *see also* democracy
Muslim League 73–74, 81, 229–230, 240, 241
Muslim politics: emergence of 39–40; and globalization 24–26; political strategies

158–159; term 22–24; twentieth century 108–109
Muslim world, the 18–19
Mutahhari, Murtaza 251
Mutahida Majlis Amal (MMA) 240–241, 242
mutawwa (religious police) 213–214
Mu'tazili school of thought 38, 47
muwahhidun (monotheists) 210

al-Nabhani, Taqi ud-Din 354–355
Naqshbandiyya 45, 164
Nasr, V. 132, 133, 134, 170, 244
Nasrallah, Sayyid Hassan 296, 299 300
Nasser, Gamal Abdel 72–73, 96, 99, 216
Nateq Nuri, Ali Akbar 258, 259
National Democratic Party (NDP) 135, 140, 147, 162
National Salvation Party (NSP) 166–167
nationalism movement: and colonial independence 62, 65, 69; and foreign occupation 323; and state formation 69–74
nation-state: and Islamism 74–85, 207; modern 65; post-caliphate theories 65–69; and radical Islamism 330–331, 350; and secularism 9, 11–12, 13–14; state formation and nationalism 69–74
new Islamism: academic debates on 88; contrasted with Islamism 130–131, 401–405; as democratic 130; electoral successes 131–132; emergence of 127–128; in the future 148; Hizb al-Wasat 131, 143, 145, 148; Wasatiyya movement 142–144, 145–146, 148
new media: internet use 389–391, **390**; Islamic authority and 388–389; Muslim globality 24, 26, 376–377; and religious practices 387–388; *see also* technology
new social movements (NSMs): globalized Muslim interests 415; Wasatiyya movement as 143–144
Nigeria 20, 114, 272, 317
9/11 attacks: Saudi Arabia and 224; US reprisals, Afghanistan 312; USA/Pakistan relations 240
Nurçu movement 164–166, 168, 169, 384
Nursi, Said 164

Omar, Mullah 307, 318
Oslo Agreement 279–280, 289

Ottoman Empire 15–16, 54–56
Ozal, Turgut 167, 170

Pahlavi dynasty 112, 246–247, 252
Pakistan: constitution 230, 231; formation
    of 73–74, 229; Islamic modernization
    232–233; as Islamic state 110, 206,
    230–231, 233, 234–237, 242–245;
    madrasas 313–314, 335; under Musharraf
    240–242; partition 233–234; political
    instability 239–240, 241–242; protesters
    rally against Denmark *379*; relations
    with the USA 236–237, 240; role of
    the military 230, 234, 240, 244–245;
    support for Afghani *mujahideen* 237,
    305–306, 335; and the Taliban 241–242,
    308, 312, 319; *see also* Mawdudi, Sayyid
    Abu'l-A'la
Pakistan Muslim League (PML) 240, 241
Pakistan National Alliance (PNA) 234–235
Pakistan Peoples Party (PPP) 233–234, 240,
    241, 242
Palestine: elections 279, 281, 292, 293; *intifada*,
    first 113, 275, 277–279, 286; *intifada*,
    second 280–281; Oslo Agreement
    279, 288; Palestinian Authority 279;
    population demographic 284; suicide
    bombers 21; *see also* Hamas; PLO
    (Palestine Liberation Organization)
Pan-Arabism movement 72–73, 113, 216
Pan-Islam 60, 62, 216, 330, 333, 370, 411
Partai Persatuan Pembangunan (PPP) **128**,
    175
Parti Islam Se-Malaysia (PAS) **129**, 238–239
PDJ (Justice and Development Party,
    Morocco) 131, 133, 183–184, *184*
People's Democratic Party of Afghanistan
    (PDPA) 305
PKS (Prosperous Justice Party) **128**, *176*, 177
PLO (Palestine Liberation Organization):
    exiled leadership 277, 278; Fatah 280,
    281, 285, 289; relations with Hamas
    287–289, 294, 295
political Islam: emergence of 86; relious
    minorities and 231–232; role of women
    226–227; term 22–23
politics: definition of 5–8; and Islam 14,
    19–20, **20**; lack of in Qur'an 14; and
    religion, relationship 8–9; and social
    spaces 374–375

popular Islam: consumption of 392–393;
    and new media 387–392; and public
    religion 393–394
post-Islamism: academic debates on 88–89;
    Amr Khaled as voice of 396–397;
    concepts of 370–376, 412–413; and
    globalization 376–377; new Islamist
    intellectuals 382–384
PPP (Pakistan People's Party) 233–234, 240,
    241, 242

Qadiriyya 45
Qajar dynasty 112, 245–246
al-Qaradawi, Yusuf 142, 144, 380–382, *381*,
    387, 391, 392, 394, 395
Qatar 391–392
qiyas (analogical deduction) 42
Qur'an: as authoritative source, jurisprudence
    42; lack of political detail/guidance 14;
    revelation of to Muhammad 29–30
Qutb, Muhammad 218
Qutb, Sayyid: anti-Government stance 99–100;
    influence of 49, 89, 104–105; influence
    of Mawudi on 101; Islamism of 100–105;
    on *jahiliyya* 101–103; on *jihad* 97,
    102–105, 332, 338–339; life of 97–99,
    98, 100; as new Islamist intellectual 383;
    Signposts on the Road (Ma'alim fi al-Tariq)
    99–100, 103; Sufism of 100
Qutbism 104–105, 106

Rabin, Yitzhak 288, 289
radical Islamism: as anti-systemic social
    movement 360–361; charisma of scholars/
    leaders 352; commitment to activism
    353–354; concepts of 330–331; and
    deterritorialized identities 350–351,
    408; and Salafism 350–354; *see also*
    Al-Qaeda; Hizb ut-Tahrir (HT); *jihad*
Rafsanjani, Ali Akbar Hashemi 257–258,
    263–264
Ramadan, Tariq 386–387, 395, 414
rashidun caliphs 33–36
Refah Party 166–167
Reformation, the 10, 11
re-Islamization 371–372
religion, politics and 8–9, 19–20, **20**
religious authority and knowledge 406–408
religious scholarship see *ulama* (religious
    scholars)

Renaissance, the 9–10
repression leads to radicalization argument
114–115, 194
Republican People's Party (RPP) 163
Revolutionary Command Council (RCC)
96, 99
Rida, Rashid 14, 48, 49, 67
Robinson, G. 274–275
Roy, O. 370–373, 374, 382–384
Rushdie, Salman 21, *21*, 43, 257

al-Sadat, Anwar 105, 123, 124, 135
Safavid Empire 54
Sahwa movement 219, 221, 224
Salafism: compared to Wahhabism 48, 58; in
Egypt 50, 152–155, *154*, 158; identity
and radical Islamism 350–352; overview
of 45–47, 50–51; Salafi Islamists 50;
Salafi jihadis 50, 338–340; salafi method
46–47; Salafi quietists 49; techno-
scientific style 353; as transnational 155;
see also Wahhabism
Salafist Group for Preaching and Combat
(GSPC) 118, 363
Salafiyya movement 61–62, 67, 76, 101
salat (prayer) 31
satellite television 51, 380, 391–392
Saudi Arabia: anti-Shi'i stance 210, 232;
Arab Uprisings, impact of 223–224;
Committee for the Defense of
Legitimate Rights (CDLR) 222–223;
Consultative Council (Majlis) 220,
222, 226; foreign policy 211–212,
215–217; foundation of 62; future
reforms 226–228; human rights in
109–110; Ikhwan revolt 211–212;
involvement in Afghanistan 335; as
Islamic state 109–110, 205; Islamist
political opposition 217–225; kingdom's
history 210–212; "Memorandum of
Advice" 221; *mutawwa* 213–214; oil
reserves/revenues 212, 215, 216, 219;
palace/*ulama* relations 207–208, 212,
213–215, 221; palace/wider society
relations 212–213, 215; relations with
the USA 110, 212, 215–216, *215*, 220,
224; Sahwa ("awakening") movement
219, 221, 224; Salafism in 50; Saudi-
Egyptian rivalry 216; siege of the Grand
Mosque 217; Wahhabism 48, 58, 207,

208–210; women's rights 213, 220,
222, 225–226
sawm (fasting) 31
Schwedler, J. 88, 190
science: and Islamic reformism 59–60; and
reason, Muslim context 12–13
sectarianism: rise, post-Arab Uprisings 53;
Sunni-Shi'i divide 51–53
secularism: advent, the Renaissance 9–10;
and liberalism 13–14; in Muslim legal
systems 15–16; secular nationalism
(Turkey) 65, 69–72, 162, 163, 174;
and the sovereign state 9, 11–12, 13–14
al-Shaab 142
al-Sha'arawi, Muhammad 394
shahada (bearing witness) 31
shari'ah (religious law): criticism of ruler's
implementation 102; *hudud* (prescribed
punishment) 41, 85, 140, 235, 311; in
the legal system 15–16, 38; in Nigeria
272; overview of 41–42; in political
systems 14, 403–405; *see also* Islamic
states
Shari'ah w' al-Hayat (Shariah and Life)
(TV program) 380, 392
Shariati, Ali 251, 383
Sharif, Nawaz 240
al-Sharif, Sayyid Imam 343
Shi'i Islam: emergence of 37; *imamate* 52;
origins of 33; and Sunni divide 51–53,
309; *see also* Hizbullah; Lebanon
shirk (idolatry) 30
al-Shubailat, Laith 179
Signposts on the Road (Ma'alim fi al-Tariq)
99–100, 103
social capital: Egypt and the MB 136–138,
271, 413; Hamas 281–282; of Islamism
92, 125–126, 165, 191, 193, 195,
374–375; MB, Jordan 186–187
Social Justice in Islam (Qutb) 98, 100
social movement theory 86–87
Somalia 364
Soroush, Abdolkarim 15, 384
sovereign state model 9, 10, 11–12, 13–14,
65; *see also* nationalism movement
state, the: and the church, historical 9–10;
deep state 127, 172; as instrument of
reform (Mawdudi) 84; and Islam 13;
social institutions and religious values
11–12, 16–17; social service provision

271, 323; state failure and Islamism 270–271, 322–324

Sudan: Bin Laden in 336; as an Islamic state 113–114, 266–268, 371

Sufism: al-Banna, Hassan 76; Naqshbandi Sufism 164; overview of 45–46

Suharto, Thojib 175

suicide bombers 21, 275, 280, 296, 358, 363, 364, 382

sunna ('Orthodox' traditions of the Prophet) 31, 42, 47, 405

Sunni Islam: four schools of jurisprudence 38; *imamate* 52; and Shi'ia divide 51–53, 309

Syria: Islamists and the conflict 302–304; Jabhat al-Nusra 303–304, *303*; Mu'awiya, governorship 34, 36; relations with Lebanon 297, 301; sectarianism 53

Tablighi Jamaat 109, 236

takfir (excommunication) 102, 209–210, 338, 344, 381–382

Takfir w'al-Hijra 105–106, 125, 332

Taliban: Deobandi movement 310–311, 314; formation of 307–308; governance of 309–310, 311–312; moral code 310–311; neo-Taliban strategies 318–321; Pakistani support for 241–242, 308, 312, 319; Pashtun identity and 308, 313, 315, 316, 318, 319; political and religious tactics 316–318; rapid success of 308, 315–316; Taliban fighters 313–314, *313*; women's rights under 311; *see also* Afghanistan

Tammam, H. and Haenni, P. 395

tawhid (oneness) 14, 30–31, 46, 58, 209

taxation systems 34, 37, 39

technology: and Islamic reformism 59–60; and reason, Muslim context 12–13; *see also* new media

television, satellite 51, 391–392

terrorism, tactics 274–275

Towards a Contemporary Islamic Vision 142

transnationalism *see* Al-Qaeda; globalization; *jihad*

tribalism 31, 34

Tripp, C. 99, 100, 101, 103

Tunisia: Al-Nahda 126; En-Nahda 159–161; MTI 126; popular uprising 150, 159; Salafi politics 155; Salafism 161

al-Turabi, Hassan 266–268, *267*, 336, 371

Turkey: AKP (Justice and Development Party) **129**, 132, 133, 168–174; Diyanet 70, 72, 163, 322; Gülen Fethullah 384–386, 397; Islamism, compared to Egypt 168; Islamist political parties 114, 166–168; military involvement in politics 162, 172, 244; National Salvation Party (NSP) 166–167; Nurçu movement 164–166, 168, 169, 384; Refah Party 166–167; Republican People's Party (RPP) 163; social Islam 164–166; state ideology/secular nationalism (Kemalism) 65, 69–72, 162, 163, 174; Sufism 164; Taksim square protests 173; Turkish in the Latin alphabet 70, *71*

Two Nations theory 73, 229–230

ulama (religious scholars): adaption to new technology 390–391; changing role of 379–383; *fatwa*, issuing 43; globalization and communication 51, 379–380; on *jihad* 104; and new Islamist intellectuals 383–387; role in political society 39–40, 44; under Umayyad dynasty 38

Umar (second caliph) 34–35

Umayyad dynasty 37–38

umma (global community): globalization and 26, 54, 408–409, 411; *jihad* and 333, 341; over the nation-state 359, 370; and universal idiom of Islam 351–352

Union of Soviet Socialist Republics (USSR) 113, 305, 333

United States of America (USA): Afghanistan and 305–306, 319, 320, 334–335; as the "far enemy" (global jihad) 341–342; Muslim population 409; Pakistan and 236–237; religion and social activity 11–12; Saudi Arabia and 110, 212, 215–216, *215*, 220, 224

urbanization, and Islamism 124, 169

Uthman (third caliph) 34

Wahhab, Muhammad Ibn Abdul 57–58

Wahhabism: compared to Salafism 48; in Saudi Arabia 48, 58, 207, 208–210; *takfir*, concept of 209–210, 338; and the Taliban 311

Wahid, Abdurrahman 175

Wasatiyya movement 142–144, 145–146, 148; *see also* Hizb al-Wasat
West, the: Muslim population in 410; Muslims and new Islamist intellectuals 386–387, 391; Muslims and religious consumption 393; and al-Qaradawi, Yusuf 382; secularism in 9–12; *see also* Europe
Wiktorowicz, Q. 187, 339–340, 360
Wiktorowicz, Q. and Farouki, S.T. 187, 193
women: in Iran 256; in Islamic states 226–227; in Pakistan 235; in Saudi Arabia 213, 220, 222, 225–226; under the Taliban 311
World Islamic Front for Jihad 341

al-Yassin, Ahmed (Sheikh Yassin) 276, 277, 278, 279, 280, 287–288, 289–290, 292
Yathrib (Medina) 32
Yavuz, H. 169
Yemen 50, 193, 216, 364
Yemeni Reformist Union 132
Young Men's Muslim Association (YMMA) 90
Young Turks 62, 69–70, 163

Zaidis ("Fiver") 52–53
zakat (tithe) 31, 78, 235
al-Zarqawi, Abu Musab 361–362
al-Zawahiri, Ayman 58, 336, 341, 345, *348*, 361, 365
Zia ul-Haq, Muhammad 234–237, 244
Zubaida, S. 108

CPSIA information can be obtained at www.ICGtesting.com
Printed in the USA
BVOW09s1146240914

368095BV00003B/13/P